TEACHER'S EDITION

MOSAIK 1

German Language and Culture

VISTA®
HIGHER LEARNING

Boston, Massachusetts

On the cover: Traditional frame houses, Freudenberg, Germany

Publisher: José A. Blanco
Professional Development Director: Norah Lulich Jones
Editorial Development: Brian Contreras, Sharla Zwirek
Project Management: Sally Giangrande
Rights Management: Ashley Dos Santos, Annie Pickert Fuller
Technology Production: Fabián Montoya, Paola Ríos Schaaf, Erica Solari
Design: Radoslav Mateev, Gabriel Noreña, Andrés Vanegas
Production: Manuela Arango, Oscar Díez, Adriana Jaramillo Ch.

Student Text ISBN: 978-1-68005-053-0
Teacher's Edition ISBN: 978-1-68005-073-8
Library of Congress Control Number: 2016947899

1 2 3 4 5 6 7 8 9   WC   21 20 19 18 17 16

Contents

	KONTEXT	FOTOROMAN	KULTUR	STRUKTUREN	WEITER GEHT'S
KAPITEL 1	**LEKTION 1A Hallo! Wie geht's?**				
	Kontext: Wie geht's? **Aussprache und Rechtschreibung:** The German alphabet	**Folge 1:** Willkommen in Berlin!	**Im Fokus:** Hallo, Deutschland! **Porträt:** Das Brandenburger Tor	**1A.1** Gender, articles, and nouns **1A.2** Plurals **1A.3** Subject pronouns, **sein**, and the nominative case **Wiederholung** **Zapping:** *Deutsche Bahn*	**Panorama:** Die deutschsprachige Welt **Lesen:** Adressbuch **Hören** **Schreiben** **Wortschatz**
	LEKTION 1B				
	Kontext: In der Schule **Aussprache und Rechtschreibung:** The vowels **a, e, i, o,** and **u**	**Folge 2:** Oh, George!	**Im Fokus:** Die Schulzeit **Porträt:** Der Schultag	**1B.1 Haben** and the accusative case **1B.2** Word order **1B.3** Numbers **Wiederholung**	
KAPITEL 2	**LEKTION 2A Schule und Studium**				
	Kontext: An der Universität **Aussprache und Rechtschreibung:** Consonant sounds	**Folge 3:** Checkpoint Charlie	**Im Fokus:** Uni-Zeit, Büffel-Zeit **Porträt:** Uni Basel	**2A.1** Regular verbs **2A.2** Interrogative words **2A.3** Talking about time and dates **Wiederholung** **Zapping:** *TU Berlin*	**Panorama:** Berlin **Lesen:** Karlswald-Universität **Hören** **Schreiben** **Wortschatz**
	LEKTION 2B				
	Kontext: Sport und Freizeit **Aussprache und Rechtschreibung:** Diphthongs: **au, ei/ai,** and **eu/äu**	**Folge 4:** Ein Picknick im Park	**Im Fokus:** Skifahren im Blut **Porträt:** Mesut Özil	**2B.1** Stem-changing verbs **2B.2** Present tense used as future **2B.3** Negation **Wiederholung**	
KAPITEL 3	**LEKTION 3A Familie und Freunde**				
	Kontext: Johanna Schmidts Familie **Aussprache und Rechtschreibung:** Final consonants	**Folge 5:** Ein Abend mit der Familie	**Im Fokus:** Eine deutsche Familie **Porträt:** Angela Merkel	**3A.1** Possessive adjectives **3A.2** Descriptive adjectives and adjective agreement **Wiederholung** **Zapping:** *Bauer Joghurt*	**Panorama:** Die Vereinigten Staaten und Kanada **Lesen:** Hunde und Katzen **Hören** **Schreiben** **Wortschatz**
	LEKTION 3B				
	Kontext: Wie sind sie? **Aussprache und Rechtschreibung:** Consonant clusters	**Folge 6:** Unsere Mitbewohner	**Im Fokus:** Auf unsere Freunde! **Porträt:** Tokio Hotel	**3B.1** Modals **3B.2** Prepositions with the accusative **3B.3** The imperative **Wiederholung**	
KAPITEL 4	**LEKTION 4A Essen**				
	Kontext: Lebensmittel **Aussprache und Rechtschreibung:** The German **s, z,** and **c**	**Folge 7:** Börek für alle	**Im Fokus:** Der Wiener Naschmarkt **Porträt:** Wolfgang Puck	**4A.1** Adverbs **4A.2** The modal **mögen** **4A.3** Separable and inseparable prefix verbs **Wiederholung** **Zapping:** *Yello Strom*	**Panorama:** Österreich **Lesen:** Die ersten Monate in Graz **Hören** **Schreiben** **Wortschatz**
	LEKTION 4B				
	Kontext: Im Restaurant **Aussprache und Rechtschreibung:** The German **s** in combination with other letters	**Folge 8:** Die Rechnung, bitte!	**Im Fokus:** Wiener Kaffeehäuser **Porträt:** Figlmüller	**4B.1** The dative **4B.2** Prepositions with the dative **Wiederholung**	

	KONTEXT	FOTOROMAN	KULTUR	STRUKTUREN	WEITER GEHT'S
ÜBERBLICK Reviews material from MOSAIK 1					
KAPITEL 1	**LEKTION 1A Feiern**				
	Kontext: Feste feiern **Aussprache und Rechtschreibung:** The consonantal **r**	**Folge 1:** Frohes neues Jahr!	**Im Fokus:** Das Oktoberfest **Porträt:** Die Sternsinger	**1A.1** The **Perfekt** (Part 1) **1A.2** Accusative pronouns **1A.3** Dative pronouns **Wiederholung** **Zapping:** *Penny*	**Panorama:** Bayern **Lesen:** Deutschland heute **Hören** **Schreiben** **Wortschatz**
	LEKTION 1B				
	Kontext: Kleidung **Aussprache und Rechtschreibung:** The letter combination **ch** (Part 1)	**Folge 2:** Sehr attraktiv, George!	**Im Fokus:** Deutsche Modewelt **Porträt:** Rudolf Moshammer	**1B.1** The **Perfekt** (Part 2) **1B.2 Wissen** and **kennen** **1B.3** Two-way prepositions **Wiederholung**	
KAPITEL 2	**LEKTION 2A Trautes Heim**				
	Kontext: Zu Hause **Aussprache und Rechtschreibung:** The letter combination **ch** (Part 2)	**Folge 3:** Besuch von Max	**Im Fokus:** Fribourg **Porträt:** César Ritz	**2A.1** The **Präteritum** **2A.2 Da-, wo-, hin-,** and **her-** compounds **2A.3** Coordinating conjunctions **Wiederholung** **Zapping:** *Hausarbeit*	**Panorama:** Die Schweiz und Liechtenstein **Lesen:** Schweizer Immobilien **Hören** **Schreiben** **Wortschatz**
	LEKTION 2B				
	Kontext: Hausarbeit **Aussprache und Rechtschreibung:** The German **k** sound	**Folge 4:** Ich putze gern!	**Im Fokus:** Haushaltsgeräte **Porträt:** Johanna Spyri	**2B.1 Perfekt** versus **Präteritum** **2B.2** Separable and inseparable prefix verbs in the **Perfekt** **Wiederholung**	
KAPITEL 3	**LEKTION 3A Urlaub und Ferien**				
	Kontext: Jahreszeiten **Aussprache und Rechtschreibung:** Long and short vowels	**Folge 5:** Berlin von oben	**Im Fokus:** Windenergie **Porträt:** Klima in Deutschland	**3A.1** Separable and inseparable prefix verbs (**Präteritum**) **3A.2** Prepositions of location; Prepositions in set phrases **Wiederholung** **Zapping:** *Urlaub im grünen Binnenland*	**Panorama:** Schleswig-Holstein, Hamburg und Bremen **Lesen:** Die Nordseeküste Schleswig-Holsteins in 6 Tagen **Hören** **Schreiben** **Wortschatz**
	LEKTION 3B				
	Kontext: Reisen **Aussprache und Rechtschreibung:** Pure vowels versus diphthongs	**Folge 6:** Ein Sommer in der Türkei?	**Im Fokus:** Flughafen Frankfurt **Porträt:** Der ICE	**3B.1** Infinitive expressions and clauses **3B.2** Time expressions **3B.3** Indefinite pronouns **Wiederholung**	
KAPITEL 4	**LEKTION 4A Verkehrsmittel und Technologie**				
	Kontext: Auto und Rad fahren **Aussprache und Rechtschreibung:** Long and short vowels with an **Umlaut**	**Folge 7:** Ein Ende mit Schrecken	**Im Fokus:** Die deutsche Autobahn **Porträt:** Clärenore Stinnes	**4A.1** Das **Plusquamperfekt** **4A.2** Comparatives and superlatives **Wiederholung** **Zapping:** *Mercedes Benz*	**Panorama:** Hessen und Thüringen **Lesen:** Vierfarbdrucker Installationsanleitung **Hören** **Schreiben** **Wortschatz**
	LEKTION 4B				
	Kontext: Technik und Medien **Aussprache und Rechtschreibung:** The German **l**	**Folge 8:** Ein Spaziergang durch Spandau	**Im Fokus:** Max-Planck-Gesellschaft **Porträt:** Darmstadt	**4B.1** The genitive case **4B.2** Demonstratives **Wiederholung**	

KONTEXT	FOTOROMAN	KULTUR	STRUKTUREN	WEITER GEHT'S
ÜBERBLICK Reviews material from MOSAIK 2				

KAPITEL 1

LEKTION 1A Gesundheit

| **Kontext:** Die Alltagsroutine
Aussprache und Rechtschreibung: Vocalic **r** | **Folge 1:** Guten Morgen, Herr Professor! | **Im Fokus:** Die Kur
Porträt: Nivea | **1A.1** Reflexive verbs with accusative reflexive pronouns
1A.2 Reflexive verbs with dative reflexive pronouns
1A.3 Reciprocal verbs and reflexives used with prepositions
Wiederholung
Zapping: *Central Krankenversicherung* | **Panorama:** Mecklenburg-Vorpommern und Brandenburg
Lesen: Andis Blog / Fit in 10 Minuten!
Hören
Schreiben
Wortschatz |

LEKTION 1B

| **Kontext:** Beim Arzt
Aussprache und Rechtschreibung: Syllabic stress | **Folge 2:** Im Krankenhaus | **Im Fokus:** Apotheken
Porträt: Röntgen | **1B.1** Der Konjunktiv II
1B.2 **Würden** with the infinitive
Wiederholung | |

KAPITEL 2

LEKTION 2A Stadtleben

| **Kontext:** Besorgungen
Aussprache und Rechtschreibung: The glottal stop | **Folge 3:** Gute Neuigkeiten | **Im Fokus:** Fußgängerzonen
Porträt: Die Deutsche Post | **2A.1** Subordinating conjunctions
2A.2 Adjectives used as nouns
2A.3 Das Futur I
Kurzfilm: *Fanny* | **Panorama:** Niedersachsen und Nordrhein-Westfalen
Lesen: Hermann Hesse, *Allein*; Paul Celan, *Todesfuge*
Hören
Schreiben
Wortschatz |

LEKTION 2B

| **Kontext:** In der Stadt
Aussprache und Rechtschreibung: Loan words (Part 1) | **Folge 4:** Sabites Nacht | **Im Fokus:** Kabarett
Porträt: Pina Bausch | **2B.1** Prepositions of direction
2B.2 Talking about nationality
Wiederholung | |

KAPITEL 3

LEKTION 3A Beruf und Karriere

| **Kontext:** Im Büro
Aussprache und Rechtschreibung: Loan words (Part 2) | **Folge 5:** Sag niemals nie | **Im Fokus:** Familienunternehmen
Porträt: Robert Bosch | **3A.1** Relative pronouns
3A.2 The past tenses (review)
Wiederholung
Kurzfilm: *Die Berliner Mauer* | **Panorama:** Baden-Württemberg, das Saarland und Rheinland-Pfalz
Lesen: Peter Bichsel, *Der Erfinder*
Hören
Schreiben
Wortschatz |

LEKTION 3B

| **Kontext:** Berufe
Aussprache und Rechtschreibung: Recognizing near-cognates | **Folge 6:** Schlechte Nachrichten | **Im Fokus:** Sozialversicherungen
Porträt: Der Marshallplan | **3B.1** Das Futur II
3B.2 Adjective endings (review)
Wiederholung | |

KAPITEL 4

LEKTION 4A Natur

| **Kontext:** In der Natur
Aussprache und Rechtschreibung: Intonation | **Folge 7:** In der Kunstgalerie | **Im Fokus:** Landschaften Deutschlands
Porträt: Alexander von Humboldt | **4A.1** Der Konjunktiv der Vergangenheit
4A.2 Das Partizip Präsens
Wiederholung
Kurzfilm: *Bienenstich ist aus* | **Panorama:** Sachsen-Anhalt und Sachsen
Lesen: Rose Ausländer, *Meine Nachtigall*; Rainer Maria Rilke, *Der Panther*
Hören
Schreiben
Wortschatz |

LEKTION 4B

| **Kontext:** Die Umwelt
Aussprache und Rechtschreibung: Tongue twisters | **Folge 8:** Auf Wiedersehen, Berlin! | **Im Fokus:** Grüne Berufe in Sachsen
Porträt: Michael Braungart | **4B.1** Der Konjunktiv I and indirect speech
4B.2 The passive voice
Wiederholung | |

There's more to **Mosaik** than meets the page

The **Mosaik** Supersite provides a learning environment designed especially for world language instruction. Password-protected and program-specific, this website provides seamless textbook-technology integration that helps build students' love for language learning.

For students:

- engaging media
- motivating user experience
- superior performance
- helpful resources
- plenty of practice

For educators:

- proven instructional design
- powerful course management
- time-saving tools
- enhanced support

Integrated content means a more powerful student experience

- Streaming videos—episodic dramatic series, authentic TV clips, and authentic short films
- All program audio in downloadable MP3 format
- Textbook activities and additional online-only practice—most with automatic feedback
- Video Chat and Partner Chat activities for conversational skills practice
- My Vocabulary for personalized language study
- Audio-sync readings for all **Lesen** selections
- Cultural readings in all levels and literary selections in **Mosaik 3**
- Online Student Activities Manual fully integrated with the Supersite gradebook

Specialized resources ensure a successful implementation

- Online assessments and Testing Program files in an editable format
- Audioscripts and videoscripts with English translations
- Grammar presentation slides
- Editable block and standard lesson plans
- IPAs with grading rubrics
- Digital Image Bank
- Answer keys
- "I Can" worksheets

Educator tools facilitate instruction and save time

Virtual Chat

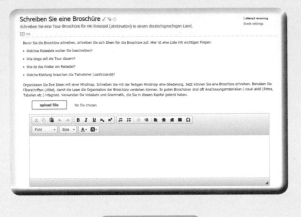

In-line editing

Easy course management

A powerful setup wizard lets you customize your class settings, copy previous courses to save time, and create your all-in-one gradebook. Grades for teacher-created assignments (e.g., pop quizzes, class participation) can be incorporated for a true, up-to-date cumulative grade.

Customized content

Tailor the Supersite to fit your needs. Create your own open-ended or video Partner Chat activities, add video or outside resources, and modify existing content with your own personalized notes.

Grading tools

Grade efficiently via spot-checking, student-by-student, and question-by-question options. Use in-line editing tools to give targeted feedback and voice comments—it's the perfect tool for busy language educators!

Assessment solutions

Administer online quizzes and tests. Use any pre-built assessment "as is" or customize them to meet your specific needs, including: adding or removing questions from a section, reordering sections or questions, and changing point values for questions.

Plus!

- A communication center for announcements, notifications, and student help requests
- Voiceboards for oral assignments, group discussions, homework, and more
- Reporting tools for summarizing student data

- Single sign-on for easy integration with your school's Learning Management System*
- Live Chat for video chat, audio chat, and instant messaging with students

* available for select LMSs

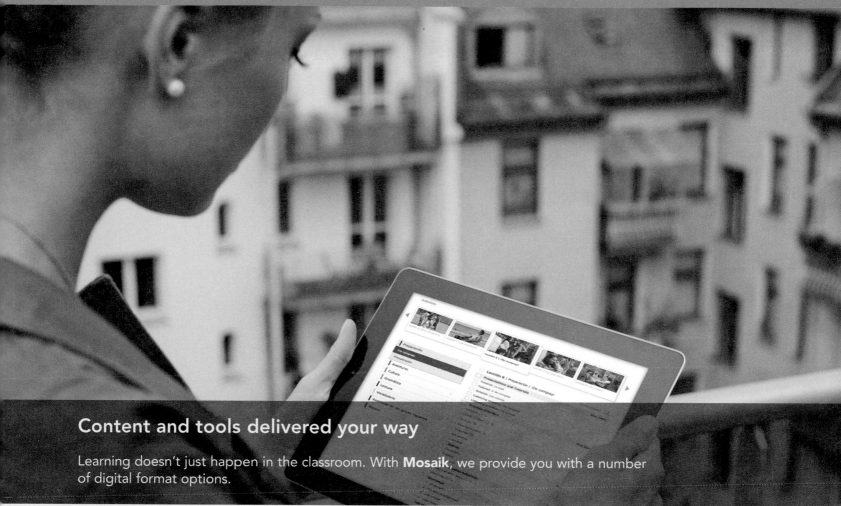

Content and tools delivered your way

Learning doesn't just happen in the classroom. With **Mosaik**, we provide you with a number of digital format options.

vText (Online)

- Browser-based electronic text for online viewing
- Links to all mouse-icon textbook activities*, audio, and video
- Access to all Supersite resources
- Highlighting and note taking
- Easy navigation with searchable table of contents
- iPad®-friendly*
- Single- and double-page view and zooming
- Automatically adds auto-graded activities to the gradebook

Available on any PC or device that has Internet connectivity.

eBook (Downloadable)

- Downloadable electronic text for offline viewing
- Embedded audio for anytime listening
- Easy navigation with searchable table of contents
- Highlighting and note taking
- Single-page view and zooming

When student is connected online:

- Links to all mouse-icon textbook activities*, audio, and video
- Access to all Supersite resources
- Automatically adds auto-graded activities in teacher gradebook

Available for a maximum of 2 computers and 2 mobile devices.

 Visit **vistahigherlearning.com/interactive-texts** to learn more.

*Students must use a computer for audio-recording.

For the **Teacher**: Plan

COMPONENT TITLE	WHAT IS IT?	📖	Ⓢ	💿
Teacher's Edition	Teacher support for core instruction	•	•	
Audioscripts	Scripts for all audio selections: • Textbook audioscripts • Testing audioscripts • Lab audioscripts • Virtual Chat audioscripts		•	•
Essential Questions	Chapter-level Essential Questions to guide instruction		•	•
Index of AP® Themes & Contexts	Listing of where the German AP® Themes and Contexts are addressed in each chapter	•	•	•
Lesson Plans	Editable block and standard schedules for every lesson		•	•
Pacing Guides	Guidelines for how to cover the instructional material for a variety of scenarios (standard and block schedules)	•	•	•
Scope & Sequence	Suggested sequence of study broken out by chapters and sections	•	•	•
Videoscripts and Translations	Scripts and translations for all videos: • *Fotoroman* • *Zapping*		•	•

For the **Teacher**: Teach

COMPONENT TITLE	WHAT IS IT?	📖	Ⓢ	💿
Digital Image Bank	Images and maps from the text to use for presentation in class, plus a bank of illustrations to use with teacher-generated content		•	•
Grammar Presentation Slides	Textbook grammar presentation in an editable PowerPoint format		•	•
Info Gap Activities with Answer Key	Info Gap activity worksheets and answer key		•	•
Program Audio	• Textbook Audio • Lab Program Audio		•	•
Student Activities Manual Answer Key	Answers to all activities in the Student Activities Manual (Workbook/Lab Manual/Video Manual)		•	•
Textbook Activity Worksheets	Supplemental spoken and written activities in an editable format		•	•
Video Collection	Program video, including: • *Fotoroman* • *Zapping*		•	•

For the **Teacher**: Assess

COMPONENT TITLE	WHAT IS IT?	📖	Ⓢ	💿
"I Can" Worksheets	Lesson objectives broken down by chapter section and written in a student-friendly "I Can" statement format		•	•
Integrated Performance Assessments	IPA tasks with grading rubrics		•	•
Testing Program with Answer Key	Lesson quizzes, chapter tests, and cumulative exam		•	•
Testing Program Audio	Audio to accompany all assessments		•	•

For the **Student**

COMPONENT TITLE	WHAT IS IT?	▮	Ⓢ	⦿ DVD
Student Edition	Core instruction for students	●	●	
Audio-synced Readings	Audio to accompany all *Lesen* sections		●	
Dictionary	Easy digital access to a dictionary		●	
eBook	Downloadable Student Edition		●	
End-of-lesson Vocabulary Lists	Core vocabulary for each lesson, with linked audio online		●	
Flashcards	Provide an easy way to study vocabulary (available as part of My Vocabulary)		●	
Fotoroman Video	Engaging storyline video		●	●
Lab Manual Activities Audio	Audio to accompany the Lab Manual portion of the Student Activities Manual		●	●
My Vocabulary	A variety of tools to practice vocabulary		●	
Partner Chats	Work with a partner online to record a conversation via video or audio and submit for grading		●	
Student Activities Manual	Combined Workbook/Lab Manual/Video Manual aligned to each lesson	●	●	
Textbook Audio	Audio to accompany all textbook listening activities		●	
Textbook Mouse Activities	Textbook activities that can also be completed digitally; many provide immediate feedback		●	
Virtual Chats	Record and submit a simulated video or audio conversation with a native speaker for online grading		●	
Vocabulary Hot Spots	Vocabulary presentations with embedded audio		●	
Voiceboards	Collaborative spaces for oral assignments, group discussions, homework, and projects		●	
vText	Virtual interactive textbook for browser-based exploration • Links to all mouse-icon activities, audio, and video • Note-taking capabilities		●	
WebSAM	Online version of the Student Activities Manual, embedded in the online gradebook, with many auto-graded options		●	
Web-only Activities	Additional online practice for students		●	
Zapping Video	Authentic TV clips from across the German-speaking world		●	

▮ Print   Ⓢ Supersite   ⦿ DVD Teacher's DVD Set

Beginning with the
student in mind

Familie und Freunde

KAPITEL
3

LEKTION 3A	LEKTION 3B	WEITER GEHT'S
Kontext Seite 96–99	**Kontext** Seite 114–117	Seite 134–140
• Johanna Schmidts Familie	• Wie sind sie?	**Panorama: Die Vereinigten Staaten**
• Final consonants	• Consonant clusters	**und Kanada**
		Lesen: Read an article about pets.
Fotoroman Seite 100–101	**Fotoroman** Seite 118–119	**Hören:** Listen to a conversation
• Ein Abend mit der Familie	• Unsere Mitbewohner	between two friends.
		Schreiben: Write a letter to a friend.
Kultur Seite 102–103	**Kultur** Seite 120–121	Kapitel 3 Wortschatz
• Eine deutsche Familie	• Auf unsere Freunde!	
Strukturen Seite 104–113	**Strukturen** Seite 122–133	
• **3A.1** Possessive adjectives	• **3B.1** Modals	
• **3A.2** Descriptive adjectives and	• **3B.2** Prepositions with the accusative	
adjective agreement	• **3B.3** The imperative	
• Wiederholung	• Wiederholung	
• Zapping		

Chapter opener photos highlight scenes from the **Fotoroman** that illustrate the chapter theme. They are snapshots of the characters that students will come to know throughout the program.

Content lists break down each chapter into its two lessons and one **Weiter Geht's** section, giving an at-a-glance summary of the vocabulary, grammar, cultural topics, and language skills covered.

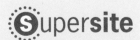

upersite

Supersite resources are available for every section of each chapter at **vhlcentral.com**. Icons show you which textbook activities are also available online, and where additional practice activities are available. The description next to the ⓢ icon indicates what additional resources are available for each section: videos, audio recordings, readings, presentations, and more!

Setting the stage
for communication

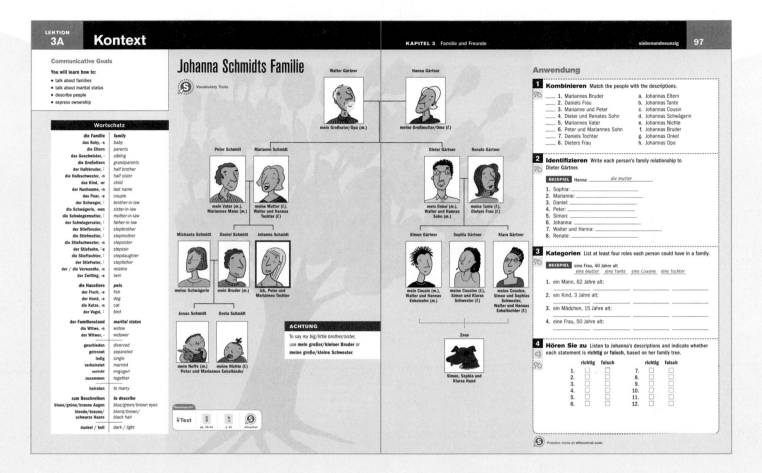

Communicative goals highlight the real-life tasks students will be able to carry out in German by the end of each lesson.

Illustrations introduce high-frequency vocabulary through expansive, full-color images.

Wortschatz sidebars call out important theme-related vocabulary in easy-to-reference German-English lists.

Ressourcen boxes indicate what print and technology ancillaries reinforce and expand on every section of every lesson.

Achtung boxes provide additional information about how and when to use certain vocabulary words or grammar structures.

Kontext always contains an audio activity that accompanies either the **Anwendung** or the **Kommunikation** practice activities. **Anwendung** follows a pedagogical sequence that starts with simpler, shorter, discrete recognition activities and builds toward longer, more complex production activities.

⟨S⟩upersite

- Audio recordings of all vocabulary items
- Audio for **Kontext** listening activity
- Image-based vocabulary activity with audio

- Textbook activities
- Additional online-only practice activities

Engaging students in
active communication

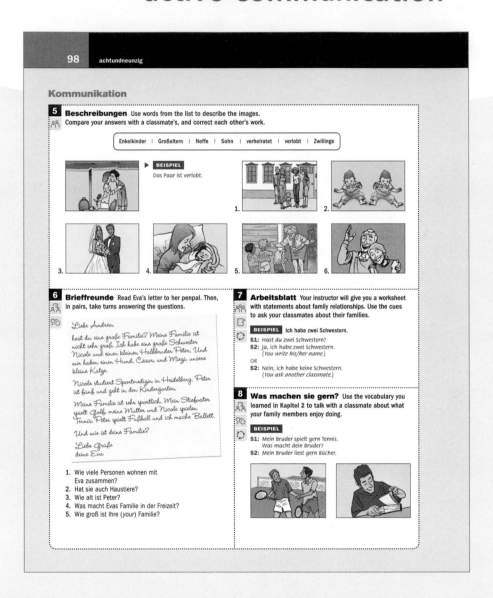

98   achtundneunzig

Kommunikation

5 Beschreibungen Use words from the list to describe the images. Compare your answers with a classmate's, and correct each other's work.

Enkelkinder | Großeltern | Neffe | Sohn | verheiratet | verlobt | Zwillinge

▶ BEISPIEL
Das Paar ist verlobt.

1.   2.

3.   4.   5.   6.

6 Brieffreunde Read Eva's letter to her penpal. Then, in pairs, take turns answering the questions.

Liebe Andrea,

hast du eine große Familie? Meine Familie ist nicht sehr groß. Ich habe eine große Schwester Nicole und einen kleinen Halbbruder Peter. Und wir haben einen Hund, Cäsar, und Miezi, unsere kleine Katze.

Nicole studiert Sportmedizin in Heidelberg. Peter ist fünf und geht in den Kindergarten.

Meine Familie ist sehr sportlich. Mein Stiefvater spielt Golf, meine Mutter und Nicole spielen Tennis, Peter spielt Fußball und ich mache Ballett.

Und wie ist deine Familie?

Liebe Grüße
deine Eva

1. Wie viele Personen wohnen mit Eva zusammen?
2. Hat sie auch Haustiere?
3. Wie alt ist Peter?
4. Was macht Evas Familie in der Freizeit?
5. Wie groß ist Ihre (your) Familie?

7 Arbeitsblatt Your instructor will give you a worksheet with statements about family relationships. Use the cues to ask your classmates about their families.

BEISPIEL Ich habe zwei Schwestern.

S1: Hast du zwei Schwestern?
S2: Ja, ich habe zwei Schwestern.
    (You write his/her name.)
OR
S2: Nein, ich habe keine Schwestern.
    (You ask another classmate.)

8 Was machen sie gern? Use the vocabulary you learned in Kapitel 2 to talk with a classmate about what your family members enjoy doing.

BEISPIEL

S1: Mein Bruder spielt gern Tennis. Was macht dein Bruder?
S2: Mein Bruder liest gern Bücher.

Kommunikation activities make use of discourse-level prompts, encouraging the creative use of vocabulary in interactions with a partner, a small group, or the entire class.

Pair and group icons indicate communicative activities—such as role play, games, personal questions, interviews, and surveys—for interpersonal and presentational practice.

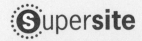upersite

• Chat activities for conversational skill-building and oral practice

Authenticity
in pronunciation and spelling

Explanations of German pronunciation and spelling are presented clearly, with abundant model words and phrases. The red highlighting feature focuses students' attention on the target structure.

Practice pronunciation and spelling at the word- and sentence-levels. The final activity features illustrated sayings and proverbs that present the target structures in an entertaining cultural context.

The audio icon at the top of the page indicates that the explanation and activities are recorded for convenient use in or outside of class.

Supersite

- Audio recording of the **Aussprache und Rechtschreibung** presentation
- Record-and-compare activities

Fotoroman
bridges language and culture

Fotoroman is a versatile episodic video that can be assigned as homework, presented in class, or used as review.

Conversations reinforce vocabulary from **Kontext**. They also preview structures from the upcoming **Strukturen** section in context.

Personen features the cast of recurring **Fotoroman** characters, including four students living in Berlin: George, Sabite, Meline, and Hans.

Nützliche Ausdrücke calls out the most important words and expressions from the **Fotoroman** episode that have not been formally presented. This vocabulary is not tested. The blue numbers refer to the grammar structures presented in the lesson.

Übungen activities include comprehension questions, a communicative task, and a research-based task.

Supersite

- Streaming video for all episodes of the **Fotoroman**
- End-of-video **Zusammenfassung** section where key vocabulary and grammar from the episode are called out
- Textbook activities

Culture
presented in context

Im Fokus presents an in-depth reading about the lesson's cultural theme. Full-color photos bring to life important aspects of the topic, while charts support the main text with statistics and additional information.

Tipp boxes provide helpful tips for reading and understanding German.

Porträt spotlights notable people, places, events, and products from the German-speaking world. This article is thematically linked to the lesson.

Deutsch im Alltag presents additional vocabulary related to the lesson theme, showcasing words and phrases used in everyday spoken German. This vocabulary is not tested.

Die deutschsprachige Welt focuses on the people, places, dialects, and traditions in regions where German is spoken. This short article is thematically linked to the lesson.

Im Internet boxes, with provocative questions and photos, feature additional cultural explorations online.

Ⓢupersite

- **Kultur** reading
- **Im Internet** research activity expands on the chapter theme
- Textbook activities
- Chat activities for conversational skill-building and oral practice

Grammar
as a tool not a topic

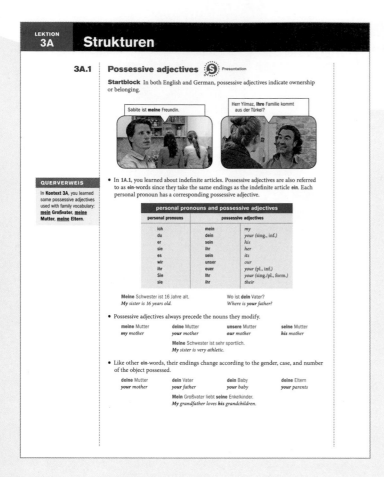

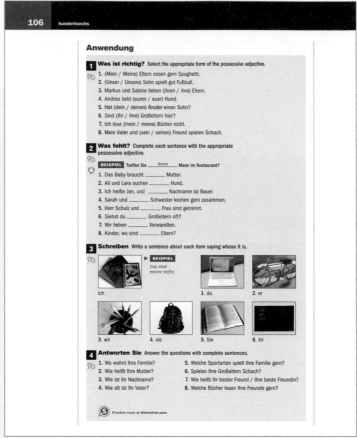

Startblock eases into each grammar explanation, with definitions of grammatical terms and reminders about grammar concepts which are already familiar.

Querverweis boxes call out information covered in earlier lessons or provide cross-references to related topics that will be covered in future lessons.

Achtung boxes clarify potential sources of confusion and provide supplementary information.

Jetzt sind Sie dran! is the first opportunity to practice the new grammar point.

Anwendung offers a wide range of guided activities that combine lesson vocabulary and previously learned material with the new grammar point.

Kommunikation activities provide opportunities for self-expression using the lesson grammar and vocabulary. These activities feature interaction with a partner, in small groups, or with the whole class.

Supersite

- Grammar presentations
- Textbook activities
- Additional online-only practice activities
- Chat activities for conversational skill-building and oral practice

Carefully scaffolded
lesson review

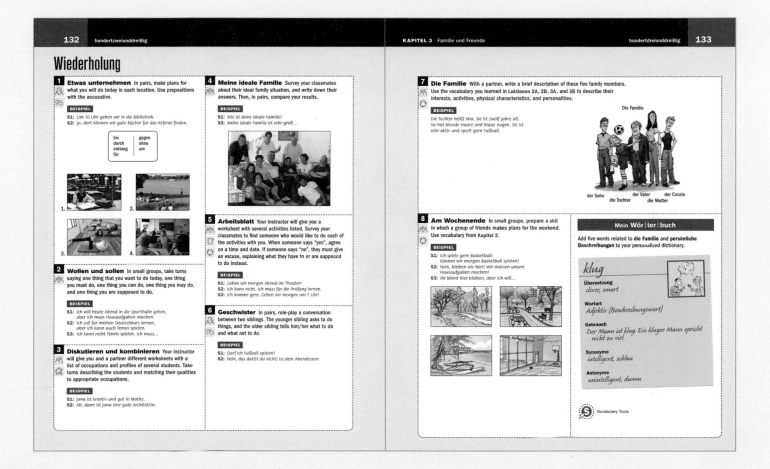

Wiederholung activities integrate the lesson's grammar points and vocabulary with previously learned vocabulary and structures, providing consistent, built-in review.

Pair and group icons indicate communicative activities—such as role play, games, personal questions, interviews, and surveys for interpersonal and presentational practice.

Information gap activities, identified by interlocking puzzle pieces, engage partners in problem-solving situations.

Recycling icons call out activities that practice the lesson's grammar and vocabulary along with previously learned material.

Mein Wörterbuch in the B lesson of each chapter offers the opportunity to increase vocabulary comprehension and the contextualization of new words.

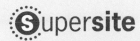

Supersite

• Chat activities for conversational skill-building and oral practice

Authentic cultural media
for interpretive communication

Zapping presents TV commercials from the German-speaking world. Post-viewing activities check comprehension.

Summary provides context for each video clip.

Photos and captions provide key information to facilitate comprehension.

Analyse post-viewing activities encourage exploration of the broader idea presented in each video clip.

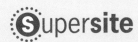

- Streaming video of the TV clip with teacher-controlled subtitle options

- Textbook activities

Perspective
through geography

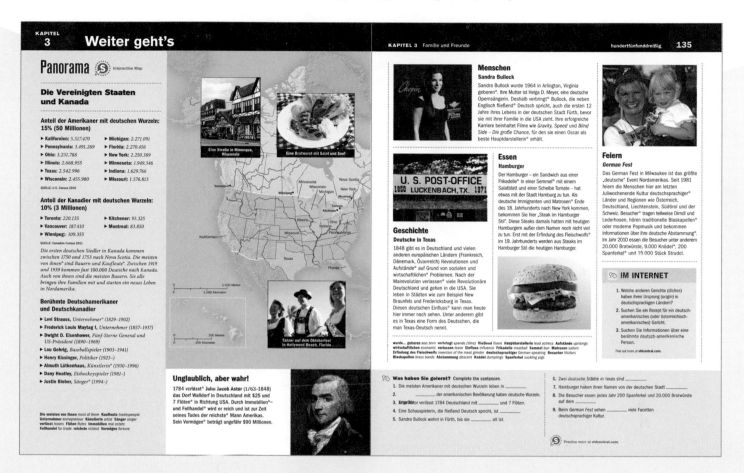

Panorama offers interesting facts about the featured city, region, or country.

Maps point out major geographical features and situate the featured region in the context of its immediate surroundings.

Readings explore different aspects of the featured region's culture, such as history, landmarks, fine art, literature, and insight into everyday life.

Unglaublich, aber wahr! highlights an intriguing fact about the featured region.

Comprehension questions check understanding of key ideas.

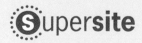

Supersite

- Map with statistics and cultural notes
- **Im Internet** research activity
- Textbook activities

Reading skills
developed in context

Vor dem Lesen presents useful strategies and activities that help develop stronger reading abilities.

Readings are tied to the chapter theme. The selections recycle vocabulary and grammar learned.

Nach dem Lesen consists of post-reading activities that check comprehension.

Supersite

- Audio-sync reading that highlights text as it is being read
- Textbook activities
- Chat activities for conversational skill-building and oral practice

Listening and writing skills
developed in context

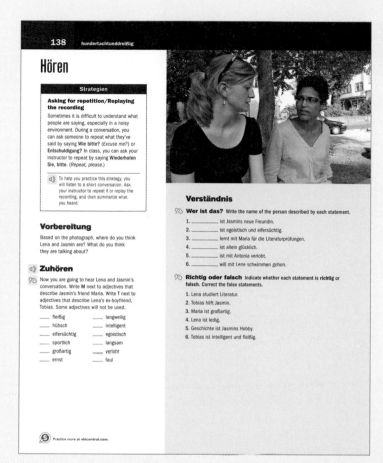

Hören

Strategien

Asking for repetition/Replaying the recording

Sometimes it is difficult to understand what people are saying, especially in a noisy environment. During a conversation, you can ask someone to repeat what they've said by saying **Wie bitte!** (*Excuse me?*) or **Entschuldigung?** In class, you can ask your instructor to repeat by saying **Wiederholen Sie, bitte.** (*Repeat, please.*)

To help you practice this strategy, you will listen to a short conversation. Ask your instructor to repeat it or replay the recording, and then summarize what you heard.

Vorbereitung

Based on the photograph, where do you think Lena and Jasmin are? What do you think they are talking about?

Zuhören

Now you are going to hear Lena and Jasmin's conversation. Write **M** next to adjectives that describe Jasmin's friend Maria. Write **T** next to adjectives that describe Lena's ex-boyfriend, Tobias. Some adjectives will not be used.

____ fleißig   ____ langweilig
____ hübsch   ____ intelligent
____ eifersüchtig   ____ egoistisch
____ sportlich   ____ langsam
____ großartig   ____ verlobt
____ ernst   ____ faul

Verständnis

Wer ist das? Write the name of the person described by each statement.

1. _____ ist Jasmins neue Freundin.
2. _____ ist egoistisch und eifersüchtig.
3. _____ lernt mit Maria für die Literaturprüfungen.
4. _____ ist allein glücklich.
5. _____ ist mit Antonia verlobt.
6. _____ will mit Lena schwimmen gehen.

Richtig oder falsch Indicate whether each statement is **richtig** or **falsch**. Correct the false statements.

1. Lena studiert Literatur.
2. Tobias hilft Jasmin.
3. Maria ist großartig.
4. Lena ist ledig.
5. Geschichte ist Jasmins Hobby.
6. Tobias ist intelligent und fleißig.

Practice more at vhlcentral.com.

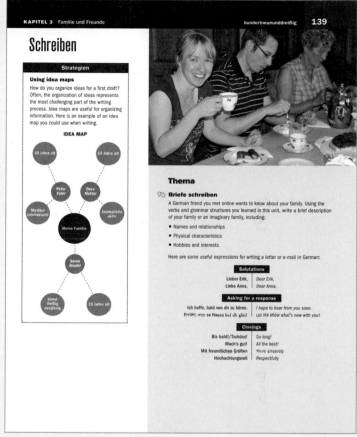

Schreiben

Strategien

Using idea maps

How do you organize ideas for a first draft? Often, the organization of ideas represents the most challenging part of the writing process. Idea maps are useful for organizing information. Here is an example of an idea map you could use when writing.

IDEA MAP

- 45 Jahre alt
- 43 Jahre alt
- Peter *Vater*
- Dora *Mutter*
- Mutter *Intellektuell*
- Journalistin *aktiv*
- Meine Familie
- Sören *Bruder*
- blond fleißig ausgiebig
- 15 Jahre alt

Thema

Briefe schreiben

A German friend you met online wants to know about your family. Using the verbs and grammar structures you learned in this unit, write a brief description of your family or an imaginary family, including:

- Names and relationships
- Physical characteristics
- Hobbies and interests

Here are some useful expressions for writing a letter or e-mail in German:

Salutations	
Lieber Erik,	*Dear Erik,*
Liebe Anna,	*Dear Anna,*

Asking for a response	
Ich hoffe, bald von dir zu hören.	*I hope to hear from you soon.*
Erzähl, was es Neues bei dir gibt!	*Let me know what's new with you!*

Closings	
Bis bald!/Tschüss!	*So long!*
Mach's gut!	*All the best!*
Mit freundlichen Grüßen	*Yours sincerely*
Hochachtungsvoll	*Respectfully*

Hören uses a recorded conversation or narration to develop listening skills in German, while **Strategien** and **Vorbereitung** are preparation for an audio listening activity.

Zuhören serves as a guide to the recorded segment, and **Verständnis** checks comprehension.

In the **Schreiben** section, **Strategien** provides useful preparation for the writing task presented in **Thema.**

Thema presents a writing topic and includes suggestions for approaching it. It also provides words and phrases that may be useful in writing about the topic.

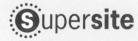

- Audio for **Hören** activities
- Textbook activities
- Additional online-only practice activity

- Composition writing activity for **Schreiben**
- Chat activities for conversational skill-building and oral practice

Vocabulary

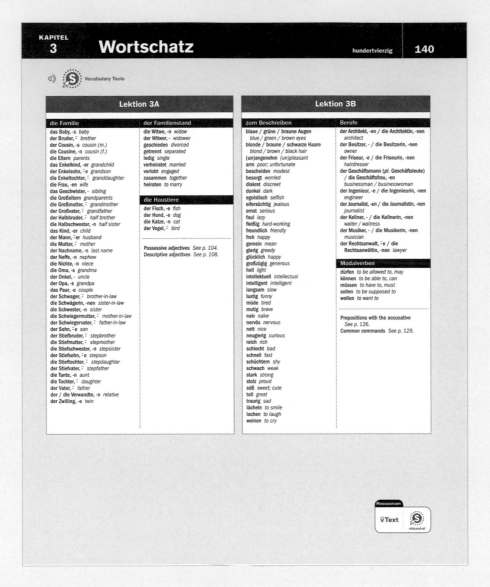

| KAPITEL 3 | **Wortschatz** | hundertvierzig | 140 |

🔊 **Vocabulary Tools**

Lektion 3A

die Familie

das Baby, -s *baby*
der Bruder, - *brother*
der Cousin, -s *cousin (m.)*
die Cousine, -n *cousin (f.)*
die Eltern *parents*
das Enkelkind, -er *grandchild*
der Enkelsohn, -e *grandson*
die Enkeltochter, - *granddaughter*
die Frau, -en *wife*
das Geschwister, - *sibling*
die Großeltern *grandparents*
die Großmutter, - *grandmother*
der Großvater, - *grandfather*
der Halbbruder, - *half brother*
die Halbschwester, -n *half sister*
das Kind, -er *child*
der Mann, -er *husband*
die Mutter, - *mother*
der Nachname, -n *last name*
der Neffe, -n *nephew*
die Nichte, -n *niece*
die Oma, -s *grandma*
der Onkel, - *uncle*
der Opa, -s *grandpa*
das Paar, -e *couple*
der Schwager, - *brother-in-law*
die Schwägerin, -nen *sister-in-law*
die Schwester, -n *sister*
die Schwiegermutter, - *mother-in-law*
der Schwiegervater, - *father-in-law*
der Sohn, -e *son*
der Stiefbruder, - *stepbrother*
die Stiefmutter, - *stepmother*
die Stiefschwester, -n *stepsister*
der Stiefsohn, -e *stepson*
die Stieftochter, - *stepdaughter*
der Stiefvater, - *stepfather*
die Tante, -n *aunt*
die Tochter, - *daughter*
der Vater, - *father*
der / die Verwandte, -n *relative*
der Zwilling, -e *twin*

der Familienstand

die Witwe, -n *widow*
der Witwer, - *widower*
geschieden *divorced*
getrennt *separated*
ledig *single*
verheiratet *married*
verlobt *engaged*
zusammen *together*
heiraten *to marry*

die Haustiere

der Fisch, -e *fish*
der Hund, -e *dog*
die Katze, -n *cat*
der Vogel, - *bird*

Possessive adjectives See p. 104.
Descriptive adjectives See p. 108.

Lektion 3B

zum Beschreiben

blaue / grüne / braune Augen
 blue / green / brown eyes
blonde / braune / schwarze Haare
 blond / brown / black hair
(un)angenehm *(un)pleasant*
arm *poor; unfortunate*
bescheiden *modest*
besorgt *worried*
diskret *discreet*
dunkel *dark*
egoistisch *selfish*
eifersüchtig *jealous*
ernst *serious*
faul *lazy*
fleißig *hard-working*
freundlich *friendly*
froh *happy*
gemein *mean*
gierig *greedy*
glücklich *happy*
großzügig *generous*
hell *light*
intellektuell *intellectual*
intelligent *intelligent*
langsam *slow*
lustig *funny*
müde *tired*
mutig *brave*
naiv *naïve*
nervös *nervous*
nett *nice*
neugierig *curious*
reich *rich*
schlecht *bad*
schnell *fast*
schüchtern *shy*
schwach *weak*
stark *strong*
stolz *proud*
süß *sweet; cute*
toll *great*
traurig *sad*
lächeln *to smile*
lachen *to laugh*
weinen *to cry*

Berufe

der Architekt, -en / die Architektin, -nen
 architect
der Besitzer, - / die Besitzerin, -nen
 owner
der Friseur, -e / die Friseurin, -nen
 hairdresser
der Geschäftsmann (pl. Geschäftsleute)
 / die Geschäftsfrau, -en
 businessman / businesswoman
der Ingenieur, -e / die Ingenieurin, -nen
 engineer
der Journalist, -en / die Journalistin, -nen
 journalist
der Kellner, - / die Kellnerin, -nen
 waiter / waitress
der Musiker, - / die Musikerin, -nen
 musician
der Rechtsanwalt, -e / die
 Rechtsanwältin, -nen *lawyer*

Modalverben

dürfen *to be allowed to, may*
können *to be able to, can*
müssen *to have to, must*
sollen *to be supposed to*
wollen *to want to*

Prepositions with the accusative
 See p. 126.
Common commands See p. 129.

Ressourcen vText | vhlcentral

Wortschatz presents the chapter's active vocabulary in logical groupings, including notation of plural forms. Words are separated by corresponding A and B lessons.

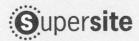

Supersite

- Audio recordings of all vocabulary items
- My Vocabulary

World-Readiness Standards
for Learning Languages

Mosaik blends the underlying principles of ACTFL's World-Readiness Standards with features and strategies tailored specifically to build students' language and cultural competencies.

THE FIVE C'S OF FOREIGN LANGUAGE LEARNING	
Communication	**Students:** 1. Interact and negotiate meaning in spoken, signed, or written conversations to share information, reactions, feelings, and opinions. (Interpersonal mode) 2. Understand, interpret, and analyze what is heard, read, or viewed on a variety of topics. (Interpretive mode) 3. Present information, concepts, and ideas to inform, explain, persuade, and narrate on a variety of topics using appropriate media and adapting to various audiences of listeners, readers, or viewers. (Presentational mode)
Cultures	**Students use German to investigate, explain, and reflect on:** 1. The relationship of the practices and perspectives of the culture studied. 2. The relationship of the products and perspectives of the culture studied.
Connections	**Students:** 1. Build, reinforce, and expand their knowledge of other disciplines while using German to develop critical thinking and to solve problems creatively. 2. Access and evaluate information and diverse perspectives that are available through German and its cultures.
Comparisons	**Students use German to investigate, explain, and reflect on:** 1. The nature of language through comparisons of the German language and their own. 2. The concept of culture through comparisons of the cultures studied and their own.
Communities	**Students:** 1. Use German both within and beyond the school to interact and collaborate in their community and the globalized world. 2. Set goals and reflect on their progress in using languages for enjoyment, enrichment, and advancement.

Adapted from ACTFL's Standards for Foreign Language Learning in the 21st Century

Six-step instructional design

Take advantage of the unique, powerful six-step instructional design in **Mosaik**. With a focus on personalization, authenticity, cultural immersion, and the seamless integration of text and technology, language learning comes to life in ways that are meaningful to each and every student.

STEP 1

Context

Begin each lesson by asking students to provide from their own experience words, concepts, categories, and opinions related to the theme. Spend quality time evoking words, images, ideas, phrases, and sentences; group and classify concepts. You are giving students the "hook" for their learning, focusing them on their most interesting topic—themselves—and encouraging them to invest personally in their learning.

STEP 2

Vocabulary

Now turn to the vocabulary section, inviting students to experience it as a new linguistic code to express what they already know and experience in the context of the lesson theme. Vocabulary concepts are presented in context, carefully organized, and frequently reviewed to reinforce student understanding. Involve students in brainstorming, classifying and grouping words and thoughts, and personalizing phrases and sentences. In this way, you will help students see German as a new tool for self-expression.

STEP 3

Media

Once students see that German is a tool for expressing their own ideas, bridge their experiences to those of German speakers through the **Fotoroman** section. The **Fotoroman** storyline video presents and reviews vocabulary and structure in accurate cultural contexts for effective training in both comprehension and personal communication.

STEP 4

Culture

Now bring students into the experience of culture as seen from the perspective of those living in it. Here we share German-speaking cultures' unique geography, history, products, perspectives, and practices. Through **Zapping** students experience and reflect on cultural experiences beyond their own.

STEP 5

Structure

Through context, media and culture, students have incorporated both previously learned and new grammatical structures into their personalized communication. Now a formal presentation of relevant grammar demonstrates that grammar is a tool for clearer and more effective communication. Clear presentations and invitations to compare German to English build confidence, fluency, and accuracy.

STEP 6

Skill synthesis

Pulling all their learning together, students now integrate context, personal experience, communication tools, and cultural products, perspectives, and practices. Through extended reading, writing, listening, speaking, and cultural exploration in scaffolded progression, students apply all their skills for a rich, personalized experience of German.

Learning to Use Your **Teacher's Edition**

Mosaik offers you a comprehensive, thoroughly developed Teacher's Edition (TE). It features student text pages overprinted with answers to all activities with discrete responses. Each page also contains annotations for a few selected activities that were written to complement and support varied teaching styles, to extend the already rich contents of the student textbook, and to save you time in class preparation and course management.

Because the **Mosaik** TE is different from teacher's editions available with other German programs, this section is designed as a quick orientation to the principal types of teacher annotations it contains. As you familiarize yourself with them, it is important to know that the annotations are suggestions only. Any German question, sentence, model, or simulated teacher-student exchange is not meant to be prescriptive or limiting. You are encouraged to view these suggested "scripts" as flexible points of departure that will help you achieve your instructional goals.

For the Chapter Opening Page

- **Suggestion** A discussion topic idea, based on the Chapter Opener photo

For the Lessons

- **Suggestion** Teaching suggestions for working with on-page materials, carrying out specific activities, and presenting new vocabulary or grammar

- **Expansion** Expansions and variations on activities

- **Vorbereitung** Suggestions for talking about the **Fotoroman** pages before students have watched the video or studied the pages

- **Nützliche Ausdrücke** A list of expressions taken from the **Fotoroman** that students may need to study before watching the episode

- **Partner and Virtual Chats** Assignments that develop students' communication skills with the convenience of the Supersite

- **Communication Icons** are tagged to activities that engage students in one of the three different modes of communication:

- **Interpretive communication** Exercises that target students' reading or listening skills and assess their comprehension

- **Presentational communication** Ideas and contexts that require students to produce a written or verbal presentation in the target language

- **Interpersonal communication** Activities that provide students with opportunities to carry out language functions in simulated real-life contexts or engage in personalized communication with others

Please check the **Mosaik** Supersite at **vhlcentral.com** for additional teaching support.

Differentiation

Knowing how to appeal to learners of different abilities and learning styles will allow you to foster a positive teaching environment and motivate all your students. Here are some strategies for creating inclusive learning environments. Extension and expansion activities are also suggested.

Learners with Special Needs

Learners with special needs include students with attention priority disorders or learning disabilities, slower-paced learners, at-risk learners, and English language learners. Some inclusion strategies that work well with such students are:

Clear Structure By teaching concepts in a predictable order, you can help students organize their learning. Encourage students to keep outlines of materials they read, classify words into categories such as colors, or follow prewriting steps.

Frequent Review and Repetition Preview material to be taught and review material covered at the end of each lesson. Pair proficient learners with less proficient ones to practice and reinforce concepts. Help students retain concepts through continuous practice and review.

Multi-sensory Input and Output Use visual, auditory, and kinesthetic tasks to add interest and motivation, and to achieve long-term retention. For example, vary input with the use of audio recordings, video, guided visualization, rhymes, and mnemonics.

Additional Time Consider how physical limitations may affect participation in special projects or daily routines. Provide additional time and recommended accommodations.

Different Learning Styles

Visual Learners learn best by seeing, so engage them in activities and projects that are visually creative. Encourage them to write down information and to think in pictures as a long-term retention strategy. Reinforce their learning through visual displays such as diagrams, videos, and handouts.

Auditory Learners best retain information by listening. Engage them in discussions, debates, and role-playing. Reinforce their learning by playing audio versions of texts or reading aloud passages and stories. Encourage them to pay attention to voice, tone, and pitch to infer meaning.

Kinesthetic Learners learn best through moving, touching, and doing hands-on activities. Involve such students in skits and dramatizations; to infer or convey meaning, have them observe or model gestures such as those used for greeting someone or getting someone's attention.

Advanced Learners

Advanced Learners have the potential to learn language concepts and complete assignments at an accelerated pace. They may benefit from assignments that are more challenging than the ones given to their peers. The key to differentiating for advanced learners is adding a degree of rigor to a given task. Examples include sharing perspectives on texts they have read with the class, retelling detailed stories, preparing analyses of texts, or adding to discussions. Here are some other strategies for engaging advanced learners:

Timed Answers Have students answer questions within a specified time limit.

Persuading Adapt activities so students have to write or present their points of view in order to persuade an audience. Pair or group advanced learners to form debating teams.

Best Practices

The creators of **Mosaik** understand that there are many different approaches to successful language teaching and that no one method works perfectly for all teachers or all learners. These strategies and tips may be applied to any language-teaching method.

Maintain the Target Language

As much as possible, create an immersion environment by using German to *teach* German. Encourage the exclusive use of the target language in your classroom, employing visual aids, mnemonics, circumlocution, or gestures to complement what you say. Encourage students to perceive meaning directly through careful listening and observation, and by using cognates and familiar structures and patterns to deduce meaning.

Cultivate Critical Thinking

Prompt students to reflect, observe, reason, and form judgments in German. Engaging students in activities that require them to compare, contrast, predict, criticize, and estimate will help them to internalize the language structures they have learned.

Encourage Use of Circumlocution

Prompt students to discover various ways of expressing ideas and of overcoming potential blocks to communication through the use of circumlocution and paraphrasing.

Assessment

As you use the **Mosaik** program, you can employ a variety of assessments to evaluate progress. The program provides comprehensive, discrete answer assessments as well as more communicative assessments that elicit open-ended, personalized responses.

Diagnostic Testing

The **Wiederholung** section in each lesson provides you with an informal opportunity to assess students' readiness for the listening, reading, and writing activities in the **Weiter geht's** section. If some students need additional practice or instruction in a particular area, you can identify this before students move on.

Writing Assessment

At the end of each chapter, the **Weiter geht's** section includes a **Schreiben** page that introduces a writing strategy, which students apply as they complete the writing activity. These activities include suggestions that will focus students' attention on what is important for attaining clarity in written communication.

Testing Program

The **Mosaik** Testing Program offers two quizzes for each **Lektion**, one test per chapter, one cumulative exam per level, IPAs with rubrics for every chapter, oral testing suggestions with grading rubrics, audioscripts for listening comprehension activities, and all answer keys. The quizzes, tests, and exams may administered online, and may be customized by adding, eliminating, or moving items according to your classroom and student needs. Editable RTFs are also available in the Resources area of the Supersite and on the Teacher Resources DVD.

Portfolio Assessment

Portfolios can provide further valuable evidence of your students' learning. They are useful tools for evaluating students' progress in German and also suggest to students how they are likely to be assessed in the real world. Since portfolio activities often comprise classroom tasks that you would assign as part of a lesson or as homework, you should think of the planning, selecting, recording, and interpreting of information about individual performance as a way of blending assessment with instruction.

You may find it helpful to refer to portfolio contents, such as drafts, essays, and samples of presentations when writing student reports and conveying the status of a student's progress to his or her parents.

Ask students regularly to consider which pieces of their own work they would like to share with family and friends, and help them develop criteria for selecting representative samples of essays, stories, poems, recordings of plays or interviews, mock documentaries, and so on. Prompt students to choose a variety of media in their activities wherever possible to demonstrate development in all four language skills. Encourage them to seek peer and parental input as they generate and refine criteria to help them organize and reflect on their own work.

Strategies for Differentiating Assessment

Here are some strategies for modifying tests and other forms of assessment according to your students' needs and your own purposes for administering the assessment.

Adjust Questions Direct complex or higher-level questions to students who are equipped to answer them adequately and modify questions for students with greater needs. Always ask questions that elicit thinking, but keep in mind the students' abilities.

Provide Tiered Assignments Assign tasks of varying complexity depending on individual student needs.

Promote Flexible Grouping Encourage movement among groups of students so that all learners are appropriately challenged. Group students according to interest, oral proficiency levels, or learning styles.

Adjust Pacing Pace the sequence and speed of assessments to suit your students' learning needs. Time advanced learners to challenge them and allow slower-paced learners more time to complete tasks or answer questions.

Integrated
Performance Assessment

Integrated Performance Assessments (IPA) begin with a real-life task that engages students' interest. To complete the task, students progress through the three modes of communication: they read, view, and listen for information (interpretive mode); they talk and write with classmates about what they have experienced (interpersonal mode); and they share formally what they have learned (presentational mode).

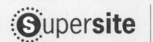 **S**upersite | Editable worksheets in the **Content > Resources** area of the Supersite

---

Integrated Performance Activity   **Kapitel 3**

Context

A student exchange program is looking for families to host students from German-speaking countries over the summer, and your family wants to participate. Write a profile of your family to help the exchange coordinators select a student to stay with you.

Interpretive Task

While you are thinking of ways to describe your family, you overhear two of the current exchange students talking about their friends. Listen to the conversation between Lena and Jasmin on page 138 of your textbook. Write down any descriptive words that apply to someone in your family.

Interpersonal Task

Compare your list with a partner's and discuss the similarities and differences you find between your descriptions. Make suggestions for additional details that would improve your partner's family profile.

Presentational Task

Write a profile of your family, using your original ideas and those suggested by your partner. Include as much detail as you can.

	5 points	3 points	1 point
Interpretive	The student provides a rich description of his or her family.	The student provides only some descriptive words in the profile of his or her family.	The student has difficulty identifying descriptive words to use in a profile of his or her family.
Interpersonal	The student can complete a basic conversation demonstrating mutual understanding. The result of the conversation is an improved description of his or her family.	The student can complete a basic conversation with only some difficulty in mutual understanding. The result of the conversation is a slightly improved description of his or her family.	The student can complete a basic conversation but does not reach mutual understanding. The student is not able to improve the description of his or her family.
Presentational	The student can provide a clear description with sufficient details.	Some details are missing from the student's description.	The description is unclear and lacks sufficient detail.

"I Can" Statements

Students can assess their own progress by using "I Can" (or "Can-Do") Statements. Use customizable "I Can" Worksheets provided for each chapter of **Mosaik** to guide student learning, and to train students to assess their progress.

Supersite | Editable worksheets in the **Content > Resources** area of the Supersite

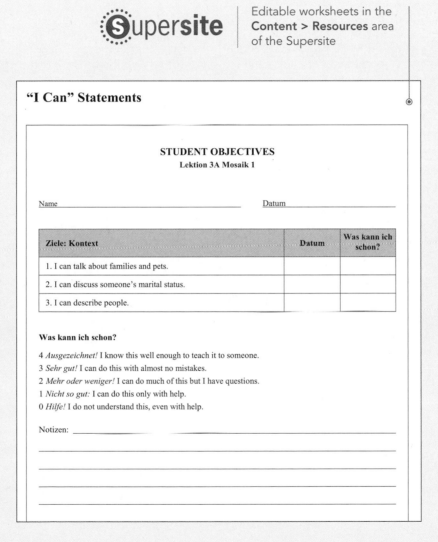

"I Can" Statements

STUDENT OBJECTIVES
Lektion 3A Mosaik 1

Name _____   Datum _____

Ziele: Kontext	Datum	Was kann ich schon?
1. I can talk about families and pets.		
2. I can discuss someone's marital status.		
3. I can describe people.		

Was kann ich schon?

4 *Ausgezeichnet!* I know this well enough to teach it to someone.
3 *Sehr gut!* I can do this with almost no mistakes.
2 *Mehr oder weniger!* I can do much of this but I have questions.
1 *Nicht so gut:* I can do this only with help.
0 *Hilfe!* I do not understand this, even with help.

Notizen: _____ _____

_____

_____

_____

_____

Engage all students

Learning German isn't all about grammar and memorization. **Mosaik** provides multiple ways to get students excited about the language and culture of German-speaking people.

Make It Personal

- Find out why students decided to learn German. Is it to speak to relatives? To interact with German-speaking friends on social media? To learn more about a particular element of German culture, film, or literature? Keep students motivated by helping them see how individual tasks lead to the larger goal of communicating with German-speaking people. Take the time to explore (and expand on) the **Kultur** and **Panorama** sections to engage students with daily life and geography, as well as fine and performing arts.

- Have students talk about themselves! The Teacher's Edition interpersonal communication annotations point out activities where students ask each other questions about their own lives. Personalizing the discussion helps keep students engaged with the material they are practicing in German.

Get Students Talking

Look for icons calling out pair and group work. Some great speaking activities include:

Supersite Virtual and Partner Chat activities:

- Offer opportunities for spoken production beyond the face-to-face classroom

- Help reduce students' affective filter and build confidence

- Provide a recorded portfolio of students' spoken work that can be easily graded

Info Gap activities: Give students these worksheets either electronically or in print, and have them work to get information from a partner.

Textbook Activity Worksheets: Get the whole class on their feet to participate in activities, such as surveys, using the language they have just been learning.

Take Advantage of Multimedia

For students:

- Are your students on YouTube every minute of their free time? Engage them with the TV advertisements in **Zapping**.

- Do your students want to study abroad in a German-speaking area of Europe? Get them engaged with the **Fotoroman** series featuring George, an American studying abroad in Berlin. Younger students are fascinated by what older students are doing, so the situations with university students should hold their interest.

- Make learning vocabulary engaging and effective for students with the My Vocabulary on the Supersite. They can focus on the vocabulary for each lesson or customize flashcard banks to study only those words they need to learn for an upcoming quiz. The flashcard tool is ideal for student self-study of vocabulary.

For teachers:

- Assign or use the audio-enabled Vocabulary Presentations on the Supersite to give students an interactive experience while they hear the new terms spoken by a native speaker of German.

- Use the Digital Image Bank to enliven your own digital or print activities.

- Have students follow along in their text as the selections in **Lesen** are read aloud by a native German speaker.

- Keep grammar instruction focused by using the Grammar Slides. Breaking up the instructional points into slides helps make the lesson more digestible.

- Don't forget to use the summaries of the **Fotoroman** to reinforce grammar instruction.

Addressing the Modes of Communication

Interpretive Skills

One of **Mosaik**'s greatest strengths is in fostering students' interpretive communication skills. The **Lesen** sections provide various types of authentic written texts and the **Zapping** and **Kurzfilm** videos feature German spoken at a natural pace. Encourage students to interact with as much authentic language as possible, as this will lead to long-term success.

- Audio activities

- **Fotoroman**

- **Kultur**

- **Zapping**

- **Panorama**

- **Lesen**

- **Hören**

Presentational Skills

Scaffolded writing tasks help students build solid writing skills in German. Many activities can be turned into either spoken or written presentations to create additional opportunities for students to practice in this mode.

- **Schreiben**

- **Wiederholung**

Interpersonal Skills

With the inclusion of abundant activities for classroom interaction as well as Partner and Virtual Chats online, students can practice their speaking skills by sharing personal information throughout each lesson.

- Pair and group activities

- Partner and Virtual Chats

General Suggestions for Using the *Fotoroman* Video Episodes

The **Fotoroman** section in each lesson and the **Fotoroman** video were created as interlocking pieces. All photos in **Fotoroman** are actual video stills from the corresponding video episode, while the printed conversations are abbreviated versions of the dramatic segment. Both the **Fotoroman** conversations and their expanded video versions represent comprehensible input at the discourse level; they were purposely written to use language from the corresponding lesson's **Kontext** and **Strukturen** sections. Thus, they recycle known language, preview grammar points students will study later in the lesson, and, in keeping with Krashen's concept of "i + 1," contain some amount of unknown language.

Because the **Fotoroman** textbook sections and the dramatic episodes of the **Fotoroman** video are so closely connected, you may use them in many different ways. For instance, you can use **Fotoroman** as a preview, presenting it before showing the video episode. You can also show the video episode first and follow up with **Fotoroman**. You can even use **Fotoroman** as a stand-alone, video-independent section.

Depending on your teaching preferences and school facilities, you might decide to show all video episodes in class or to assign them solely for viewing outside the classroom. You could begin by showing the first one or two episodes in class to familiarize yourself and students with the characters, storyline, style, and **Summary** sections. After that, you could work in class only with **Fotoroman** and have students view the remaining video episodes outside of class. No matter which approach you choose, students have ample materials to support viewing the video independently and processing it in a meaningful way. For each video episode, there are activities in the **Fotoroman** section of the corresponding textbook lesson, as well as additional activities in the **Mosaik** Video Manual section of the Student Activities Manual.

You might also want to use the **Fotoroman** video in class when working with the **Strukturen** sections. You could play the parts of the dramatic episode that correspond to the video stills in the grammar explanations or show selected scenes and ask students to identify certain grammar points.

You could also focus on the **Zusammenfassung** sections that appear at the end of each episode to summarize the key language functions and grammar points used. In class, you could play the parts of the **Zusammenfassung** section that exemplify individual grammar points as you progress through each **Strukturen** section. You could also wait until you complete a **Strukturen** section and review it and the lesson's **Kontext** section by showing the corresponding **Summary** section in its entirety.

On the **Mosaik** Supersite, teachers can control what, if any, subtitles students can see. They are available in German or in English, and in transcript format.

About **Zapping TV Clips** and Short Films

A TV clip or a short film from the German-speaking world appears in the first **Lektion** of each **Kapitel**. The purpose of this feature is to expose students to the language and culture contained in authentic media pieces. The following list of the television commercials and short films is organized by **Kapitel**.

MOSAIK 1

Kapitel 1
Deutsche Bahn
(29 seconds)

Kapitel 2
TU Berlin
(1 minute, 15 seconds)

Kapitel 3
Bauer Joghurt
(33 seconds)

Kapitel 4
Yello Strom
(39 seconds)

MOSAIK 2

Kapitel 1
Penny
(35 seconds)

Kapitel 2
Hausarbeit
(1 minute, 13 seconds)

Kapitel 3
Urlaub im grünen Binnenland
(3 minutes, 41 seconds)

Kapitel 4
Mercedes Benz
(35 seconds)

MOSAIK 3

Kapitel 1
Central Krankenversicherung
(23 seconds)

Kurzfilm

Kapitel 2
Fanny
(13 minutes, 45 seconds)

Kapitel 3
Die Berliner Mauer
(15 minutes)

Kapitel 4
Bienenstich ist aus
(15 minutes)

DAY		WARM-UP / ACTIVATE	PRESENT / PRACTICE / COMMUNICATE	REFLECT / CONCLUDE / CONNECT
1	Context for Communication	• Evoke student experiences and vocabulary for context; orient to **Kontext** **5 minutes**	• Present vocabulary through illustrations, Digital Image Bank (**Supersite**), phrases, categories, association [15] • Student pairs begin **Anwendung** [15] **30 minutes**	• Students restate context for vocabulary [5] • Introduce homework: select **Anwendung** (text/**Supersite**) [5] **10 minutes**
2	Vocabulary as a Tool	• Student groups review **Anwendung** from previous day and homework **5 minutes**	• Students complete **Anwendung** [15] • Students begin **Kommunikation** [15] **30 minutes**	• Introduce homework: **Supersite** flashcards, context illustrations and audio; end-of-chapter list with audio; remaining **Supersite** activities (as applicable) [5] • Students do select **Kommunikation** activities [5] **10 minutes**
3	Vocabulary as a Tool	• Student groups review **Anwendung** and **Kommunikation** activities **5 minutes**	• Students complete **Kommunikation** activities and/or do select **Info Gap** activities (**Supersite: Resources**) [15] • Present **Aussprache und Rechtschreibung** (**Supersite**) [15] **30 minutes**	• Students review vocabulary for assessment preparation [5] • Introduce homework: select **Aussprache und Rechtschreibung** (**Supersite**) activities [5] **10 minutes**
4	Media as a Bridge	• Reflection and preparation: **Kontext** assessment **5 minutes**	• Assessment: **Kontext** [20] • Clarity check on **Aussprache und Rechtschreibung** [5] • Orient students to **Fotoroman** through video stills [10] **35 minutes**	• Introduce homework: review stills for **Fotoroman** (text/**Supersite**) **5 minutes**
5	Media as a Bridge	• Review results of Assessment: **Kontext** **10 minutes**	• Orient students to **Nützliche Ausdrücke** [10] • View and discuss **Fotoroman** [20] **30 minutes**	• Introduce homework: select **Fotoroman** (text/**Supersite**) **Übungen** **5 minutes**
6	Media as a Bridge	• Review **Fotoroman Übungen**, as applicable **10 minutes**	• Use **Fotoroman** and **Nützliche Ausdrücke** for communication practice [20] • Pair/group work with **Fotoroman Übungen** [10] **30 minutes**	• Introduce homework: complete **Fotoroman** (text/**Supersite**) **Übungen** **5 minutes**
7	Culture for Communication	• Review **Fotoroman Übungen**, as applicable **5 minutes**	• Present select **Kultur** features in whole class or small groups, jigsaw, numbered heads together, etc. **35 minutes**	• Introduce homework: select **Kultur** (text/**Supersite**) **Übungen** **5 minutes**
8	Culture for Communication	• Student pairs/groups review **Kultur Übungen** **5 minutes**	• Focus on select **Kultur** items to confirm understanding [10] • Class, group, pair or individual research using **Im Internet** (**Supersite**) [25] **35 minutes**	• Introduce homework: complete **Im Internet** (**Supersite**) **5 minutes**
9	Structure as a Tool	• Whole class review of **Im Internet** research **10 minutes**	• Present grammar point A.1 using text, **Supersite** (presentations, grammar slides in **Resources**), and corresponding **Fotoroman** segments [15] • Student pairs/groups do A.1 **Jetzt sind Sie dran**, begin **Anwendung** [15] **30 minutes**	• Introduce homework: select **Anwendung** (text/**Supersite**) **5 minutes**
10	Structure as a Tool	• Student pairs share results of completed items in **Anwendung** **5 minutes**	• Students complete and/or review **Anwendung** [15] • Students begin A.1 **Kommunikation** [20] **35 minutes**	• Introduce homework: complete and/or review **Kommunikation** (text/**Supersite**) **5 minutes**

DAY	WARM-UP / ACTIVATE	PRESENT / PRACTICE / COMMUNICATE	REFLECT / CONCLUDE / CONNECT
11 Structure as a Tool	• Student pairs/groups review and/or present select **Kommunikation** **10 minutes**	• Lead discussion, review, or practice of grammar point A.1 [5] • Present grammar point A.2 using text, **Supersite** (presentations, grammar slides in **Resources**), and corresponding **Fotoroman** segments [15] • Student pairs/groups do A.2 **Jetzt sind Sie dran**, begin **Anwendung** [10] **30 minutes**	• Introduce homework: select **Anwendung** (text/**Supersite**) **5 minutes**
12 Structure as a Tool	• Student pairs share results of completed items in **Anwendung** **5 minutes**	• Students complete and/or review **Anwendung** [15] • Students begin A.2 **Kommunikation** [20] **35 minutes**	• Introduce homework: complete and/or review **Kommunikation** (text/**Supersite**) **5 minutes**
13 Structure as a Tool	• Student pairs/groups review and/or present select **Kommunikation** **10 minutes**	• Lead discussion, review, or practice of grammar point A.2 [5] • Present grammar point A.3 using text, **Supersite** (presentations, grammar slides in **Resources**), and corresponding **Fotoroman** segments [15] • Student pairs/groups do A.3 **Jetzt sind Sie dran**, begin **Anwendung** [10] **30 minutes**	• Introduce homework: select **Anwendung** (text/**Supersite**) **5 minutes**
14 Structure as a Tool	• Student pairs share results of completed items in **Anwendung** **5 minutes**	• Students complete and/or review **Anwendung** [15] • Students begin A.3 **Kommunikation** [20] **35 minutes**	• Introduce homework: complete and/or review **Kommunikation** (text/**Supersite**) **5 minutes**
15 Structure as a Tool	• Student pairs/groups review and/or present select **Kommunikation** **10 minutes**	• Student pairs/groups do **Wiederholung** **30 minutes**	• Introduce homework: prepare for assessment on **Strukturen** **5 minutes**
16 Authentic Media	• Students reflect in preparation for assessment on **Strukturen** **5 minutes**	• Assessment on grammar points [20] • Introduce and guide discussion of **Zapping**; show clip via **Supersite**; do **Verständnis** as a class [15] **35 minutes**	• Introduce homework: prepare for **Diskussion** from **Zapping** **5 minutes**
17 Context for Communication	• Class/groups/pairs engage in **Diskussion** from **Zapping** **5 minutes**	• Present vocabulary through illustrations, Digital Image Bank (**Supersite**), phrases, categories, association [15] • Student pairs begin **Anwendung** [15] **30 minutes**	• Students restate context of vocabulary [5] • Introduce homework: select **Anwendung** (text/**Supersite**) [5] **10 minutes**
18 Vocabulary as a Tool	• Student groups review **Anwendung** from previous day and homework **5 minutes**	• Students complete **Anwendung** **30 minutes**	• Students review and personalize key vocabulary in context [5] • Introduce homework: **Supersite** flashcards, context illustrations and audio; end-of-chapter list with audio; remaining **Supersite** activities (as applicable) [5] **10 minutes**
19 Vocabulary as a Tool	• Student groups review **Anwendung** from previous day and homework **5 minutes**	• Students do select **Kommunikation** activities [20] • Students do select **Info Gap** activities (**Supersite: Resources**) [10] **30 minutes**	• Students review and personalize key vocabulary in context [5] • Introduce homework: **Supersite** flashcards, context illustrations and audio; end-of-chapter list with audio; select **Kommunikation** activities (as applicable) [5] **10 minutes**

DAY	WARM-UP / ACTIVATE	PRESENT / PRACTICE / COMMUNICATE	REFLECT / CONCLUDE / CONNECT
20 Vocabulary as a Tool	• Student groups review **Kommunikation** from previous day and homework **5 minutes**	• Present **Aussprache und Rechtschreibung (Supersite)** [10] • Invite students to reflect on their pronunciation accuracy in preceding activities [15] **25 minutes**	• Students review vocabulary for assessment preparation [10] • Introduce homework: select **Aussprache und Rechtschreibung (Supersite)** activities [5] **15 minutes**
21 Media as a Bridge	• Reflection and preparation: **Kontext** assessment **5 minutes**	• Assessment: **Kontext** [20] • Clarity check on **Aussprache und Rechtschreibung** [5] • Orient students to **Fotoroman** through video stills [10] **35 minutes**	• Introduce homework: review stills for **Fotoroman** (text/**Supersite**) **5 minutes**
22 Media as a Bridge	• Review results of Assessment: **Kontext** **10 minutes**	• Orient students to **Nützliche Ausdrücke** [10] • View and discuss **Fotoroman** [20] **30 minutes**	• Introduce homework: select **Fotoroman** (text/**Supersite**) **Übungen** **5 minutes**
23 Media as a Bridge	• Review **Fotoroman Übungen**, as applicable **10 minutes**	• Use **Fotoroman** and **Nützliche Ausdrücke** for communication practice [20] • Pair/group work with **Fotoroman Übungen** [10] **30 minutes**	• Introduce homework: complete **Fotoroman** (text/**Supersite**) **Übungen** **5 minutes**
24 Culture for Communication	• Review **Fotoroman Übungen**, as applicable **5 minutes**	• Present select **Kultur** features in whole class or small groups, jigsaw, numbered heads together, etc. **35 minutes**	• Introduce homework: select **Kultur** (text/**Supersite**) **Übungen** **5 minutes**
25 Culture for Communication	• Student pairs/groups review **Kultur Übungen** **5 minutes**	• Focus on select **Kultur** items to confirm understanding [10] • Class, group, pair or individual research using **Im Internet (Supersite)** [25] **35 minutes**	• Introduce homework: complete **Im Internet (Supersite)** **5 minutes**
26 Structure as a Tool	• Whole class review of **Im Internet** research **10 minutes**	• Present grammar point B.1 using text, **Supersite** (presentations, grammar slides in **Resources**), and corresponding **Fotoroman** segments [15] • Student pairs/groups do B.1 **Jetzt sind Sie dran**, begin **Anwendung** [15] **30 minutes**	• Introduce homework: select **Anwendung** (text/**Supersite**) **5 minutes**
27 Structure as a Tool	• Student pairs share results of completed items in **Anwendung** **5 minutes**	• Students complete and/or review **Anwendung** [15] • Students begin B.1 **Kommunikation** [20] **35 minutes**	• Introduce homework: complete and/or review **Kommunikation** (text/**Supersite**) **5 minutes**
28 Structure as a Tool	• Student pairs/groups review and/or present select **Kommunikation** **10 minutes**	• Lead discussion, review, or practice of grammar point B.1 [5] • Present grammar point B.2 using text, **Supersite** (presentations, grammar slides in **Resources**), and corresponding **Fotoroman** segments [15] • Student pairs/groups do B.2 **Jetzt sind Sie dran**, begin **Anwendung** [10] **30 minutes**	• Introduce homework: select **Anwendung** (text/**Supersite**) **5 minutes**
29 Structure as a Tool	• Student pairs share results of completed items in **Anwendung** **5 minutes**	• Students complete and/or review **Anwendung** [15] • Students begin B.2 **Kommunikation** [20] **35 minutes**	• Introduce homework: complete and/or review **Kommunikation** (text/**Supersite**) **5 minutes**

DAY	WARM-UP / ACTIVATE	PRESENT / PRACTICE / COMMUNICATE	REFLECT / CONCLUDE / CONNECT
30 Structure as a Tool	• Student pairs/groups review and/or present select **Kommunikation** **10 minutes**	• Lead discussion, review, or practice of grammar point B.2 [5] • Present grammar point B.3 using text, **Supersite** (presentations, grammar slides in **Resources**), and corresponding **Fotoroman** segments [15] • Student pairs/groups do B.3 **Jetzt sind Sie dran**, begin **Anwendung** [10] **30 minutes**	• Introduce homework: select **Anwendung** (text/**Supersite**) **5 minutes**
31 Structure as a Tool	• Student pairs share results of completed items in **Anwendung** **5 minutes**	• Students complete and/or review **Anwendung** [15] • Students begin B.3 **Kommunikation** [20] **35 minutes**	• Introduce homework: complete and/or review **Kommunikation** (text/**Supersite**) **5 minutes**
32 Structure as a Tool	• Student pairs/groups review and/or present select **Kommunikation** **10 minutes**	• Student pairs/groups do **Wiederholung** **30 minutes**	• Introduce homework: prepare for assessment on **Strukturen** **5 minutes**
33 Skill Synthesis: Culture and Geography	• Students reflect in preparation for assessment on **Strukturen** **5 minutes**	• Assessment on **Strukturen** [20] • Present select **Weiter geht's - Panorama** features in whole class or small groups, jigsaw, numbered heads together, etc. [15] **35 minutes**	• Introduce homework: **Panorama - Was haben Sie gelernt?** activity/activities and/or initial research using **Im Internet** **5 minutes**
34 Skill Synthesis: Interpretive (Reading)	• Student pairs review homework from **Panorama** **10 minutes**	• Class review and discussion from **Panorama** [15] • Guide students through **Vor dem Lesen**, including **Strategien** [15] **30 minutes**	• Introduce homework: select **Vor dem Lesen** activities (text/**Supersite**) **5 minutes**
35 Skill Synthesis: Interpretive (Reading)	• Student pairs review homework from **Vor dem Lesen** **5 minutes**	• Students read **Lesen** (whole class or small groups) [25] • Students begin **Nach dem Lesen** [10] **35 minutes**	• Introduce homework: complete **Nach dem Lesen** activities (text/**Supersite**) **5 minutes**
36 Skill Synthesis: Interpretive (Listening)	• Share and discuss results from **Nach dem Lesen** **10 minutes**	• Guide students through **Strategien** and **Vorbereitung** in **Hören**; present selection [20] • Students (individuals, pairs, or small groups) do select **Verständnis** activities [10] **30 minutes**	• Introduce homework: complete **Verständnis** from **Hören** (text or **Supersite**) **5 minutes**
37 Skill Synthesis: Presentational (Writing)	• Student pairs check results from **Verständnis** **10 minutes**	• Guide students through **Schreiben**, including **Strategien** and **Thema** [15] • Review and preparation through use of communication activities, additional Partner Chat or Virtual Chat activities (**Supersite**) and **Wortschatz** (text/**Supersite**) [10] **25 minutes**	• Introduce homework: first draft of **Schreiben - Thema** • Review content and concepts for chapter assessment **10 minutes**
38 Skill Synthesis and Review	• Student pairs/groups do initial peer review of drafts of **Schreiben - Thema** **15 minutes**	• Review and preparation through use of communication activities, additional Partner Chat or Virtual Chat activities (**Supersite**) and **Wortschatz** (text/**Supersite**) and/or begin IPA (**Supersite: Resources**) **25 minutes**	• Confirm understanding of assessment content (and/or grading rubric if using IPA) • **Schreiben - Thema** due **5 minutes**
39 Assessment	• Confirm all students submitted **Schreiben - Thema** (text/**Supersite**) **5 minutes**	• Written or digital chapter assessment (from **Resources** section or **Assessment** section of **Supersite**, respectively) and/or complete IPA **40 minutes**	

DAY	WARM-UP / ACTIVATE	PRESENT / PRACTICE / COMMUNICATE
1 Context for Communication	• Present and practice first half of review section 1 (of 4) **25 minutes**	• Evoke student experiences and vocabulary for context; orient to **Kontext** [10] • Present vocabulary through illustrations, Digital Image Bank (**Supersite**), phrases, categories, association [15] **25 minutes**
2 Vocabulary as a Tool	• Present and practice second half of review section 1 (of 4) **15 minutes**	• Student pairs/groups review **Anwendung** from previous day and homework [10] • Students do **Kommunikation** activities [10] **20 minutes**
3 Media as a Bridge	• Present and practice first half of review section 2 (of 4) **20 minutes**	• Reflection and preparation: **Kontext** assessment [5] • Assessment: **Kontext** [20] **25 minutes**
4 Media as a Bridge	• Present and practice second half of review section 2 (of 4) **15 minutes**	• Review **Fotoroman** [5] • Second viewing and discussion/communication using **Fotoroman** [10] • Student pairs/groups complete **Fotoroman Übungen** [10] **25 minutes**
5 Culture for Communication	• Present and practice first half of review section 3 (of 4) **20 minutes**	• Student pairs/groups review **Kultur Übungen** [5] • Class, group, pair or individual research using **Im Internet** (**Supersite**) [20] **25 minutes**
6 Structure as a Tool	• Present and practice second half of review section 3 (of 4) **15 minutes**	• Student pairs share results of completed items in A.1 **Anwendung** [5] • Students complete A.1 **Anwendung** and **Kommunikation** [20] **25 minutes**
7 Structure as a Tool	• Present and practice first half of review section 4 (of 4) **20 minutes**	• Student pairs share results of completed items in A.2 **Anwendung** [5] • Students complete A.2 **Anwendung** and **Kommunikation** [15] **20 minutes**
8 Structure as a Tool	• Present and practice second half of review section 4 (of 4) **15 minutes**	• Student pairs share results of completed items in A.3 **Anwendung** [5] • Students complete A.3 **Anwendung** and **Kommunikation** [20] **25 minutes**
9 Authentic Media	• Students reflect in preparation for assessment on **Strukturen** **10 minutes**	• Assessment on **Strukturen** **35 minutes**
10 Context for Communication	• Evoke student experiences and vocabulary for context **5 minutes**	• Present vocabulary through illustrations, Digital Image Bank (**Supersite**), phrases, categories, association **35 minutes**

REFLECT	PRESENT / PRACTICE / COMMUNICATE	REFLECT / CONCLUDE / CONNECT
• Student pairs restate context of vocabulary **5 minutes**	• Students do **Anwendung** (individual, pairs, small groups) **25 minutes**	• Introduce homework: **Supersite** flashcards, context illustrations and audio; end-of-chapter list with audio; remaining **Supersite** activities (as applicable) **5 minutes**
• Students reflect on and take note of personal areas of strength and challenge **5 minutes**	• Students do select **Info Gap** activities (**Supersite**: **Resources**) [25] • Present **Aussprache und Rechtschreibung** (**Supersite**) [15] **40 minutes**	• Students review vocabulary for assessment preparation • Introduce homework: select **Aussprache und Rechtschreibung** (**Supersite**) activities **5 minutes**
• Students individually review points in **Aussprache und Rechtschreibung** **5 minutes**	• Orient students to **Fotoroman** through video stills [5] • Orient students to **Nützliche Ausdrücke** [15] • First viewing of **Fotoroman** [10] **30 minutes**	• Introduce homework: select **Fotoroman** (text/**Supersite**) **Übungen** **5 minutes**
• Students individually review and consolidate **Nützliche Ausdrücke** **5 minutes**	• Present select **Kultur** features in whole class or small groups, jigsaw, numbered heads together, etc. **35 minutes**	• Introduce homework: select **Kultur** (text/**Supersite**) **Übungen** **5 minutes**
• Students individually review and consolidate understanding of cultural information **5 minutes**	• Present grammar point A.1 using text, **Supersite** (presentations, grammar slides in **Resources**), and corresponding **Fotoroman** segments [15] • Student pairs/groups do A.1 **Jetzt sind Sie dran**, begin **Anwendung** [15] **30 minutes**	• Introduce homework: select A.1 **Anwendung** (text/**Supersite**) **5 minutes**
• Students individually reflect on and take note of personal areas of strength and challenge with regard to the grammar point and its use **5 minutes**	• Present grammar point A.2 using text, **Supersite** (presentations, grammar slides in **Resources**), and corresponding **Fotoroman** segments [25] • Student pairs/groups do A.2 **Jetzt sind Sie dran**, begin **Anwendung** [10] **35 minutes**	• Introduce homework: select A.2 **Anwendung** (text/**Supersite**) **5 minutes**
• Students individually reflect on and take note of personal areas of strength and challenge with regard to the grammar point and its use **5 minutes**	• Present grammar point A.3 using text, **Supersite** (presentations, grammar slides in **Resources**), and corresponding **Fotoroman** segments [25] • Student pairs/groups do A.3 **Jetzt sind Sie dran**, begin **Anwendung** [10] **35 minutes**	• Introduce homework: select A.3 **Anwendung** (text/**Supersite**) **5 minutes**
• Students individually reflect on and take note of personal areas of strength and challenge with regard to the grammar point and its use **5 minutes**	• Student pairs/groups do **Wiederholung** **35 minutes**	• Introduce homework: prepare for assessment on **Strukturen** **5 minutes**
	• Introduce and guide discussion of **Zapping**; show clip via **Supersite**; do **Verständnis** and **Diskussion** as a class **35 minutes**	• Introduce homework: preview **Kontext B** through pictures and word lists (text/**Supersite**) **5 minutes**
• Student pairs restate context of vocabulary **5 minutes**	• Students do **Anwendung** (individual, pairs, small groups) **35 minutes**	• Introduce homework: **Supersite** flashcards, context illustrations and audio; end-of-chapter list with audio; remaining **Supersite** activities (as applicable) **5 minutes**

DAY	WARM-UP / ACTIVATE	PRESENT / PRACTICE / COMMUNICATE
11 Vocabulary as a Tool	• Student pairs/groups review **Anwendung** from previous day and homework 5 minutes	• Students do **Kommunikation** activities 30 minutes
12 Media as a Bridge	• Reflection and preparation: **Kontext** assessment 5 minutes	• Assessment: **Kontext** 35 minutes
13 Media as a Bridge	• Review **Fotoroman Übungen** 10 minutes	• Second viewing and discussion/communication using **Fotoroman** [15] • Student pairs/groups complete **Fotoroman Übungen** [15] 30 minutes
14 Culture for Communication	• Student pairs/groups review **Kultur Übungen** 10 minutes	• Focus on select **Kultur** items to confirm understanding [10] • Class, group, pair or individual research using **Im Internet** (**Supersite**) [25] 35 minutes
15 Structure as a Tool	• Student pairs share results of completed items in B.1 **Anwendung** 5 minutes	• Students complete B.1 **Anwendung** and **Kommunikation** 35 minutes
16 Structure as a Tool	• Student pairs share results of completed items in B.2 **Anwendung** 5 minutes	• Students complete B.2 **Anwendung** and **Kommunikation** 35 minutes
17 Structure as a Tool	• Student pairs share results of completed items in B.3 **Anwendung** 5 minutes	• Students complete B.3 **Anwendung** and **Kommunikation** 35 minutes
18 Skill Synthesis: Culture and Geography	• Assessment on **Strukturen** 25 minutes	• Present select **Weiter geht's - Panorama** features in whole class or small groups, jigsaw, numbered heads together, etc. [25] • Class review and discussion from **Panorama** [10] 35 minutes
19 Skill Synthesis: Interpretive (Reading and Listening)	• Student pairs review homework from **Vor dem Lesen** 5 minutes	• Students read **Lesen** (whole class or small groups) [25] • Students do **Nach dem Lesen** [15] 40 minutes
20 Skill Synthesis: Presentational (Writing)	• Student pairs check results from **Verständnis** 10 minutes	• Guide students through **Schreiben**, including **Strategien** and **Thema**, and connect to chapter context [10] • Students prepare writing plan in discussion with partner [15] 25 minutes
21 Assessment	• Peer review of **Schreiben - Thema** 5 minutes	

REFLECT	PRESENT / PRACTICE / COMMUNICATE	REFLECT / CONCLUDE / CONNECT
• Students reflect on and take note of personal areas of strength and challenge	• Students do select **Info Gap** activities (**Supersite: Resources**) [25] • Present **Aussprache und Rechtschreibung** (**Supersite**) [15]	• Students review vocabulary for assessment preparation • Introduce homework: select **Aussprache und Rechtschreibung** (**Supersite**) activities
5 minutes	**40 minutes**	**5 minutes**
• Students individually review points in **Aussprache und Rechtschreibung**	• Orient students to **Fotoroman** through video stills [10] • Orient students to **Nützliche Ausdrücke** [15] • First viewing of **Fotoroman** [10]	• Introduce homework: select **Fotoroman** (text/**Supersite**) **Übungen**
5 minutes	**35 minutes**	**5 minutes**
• Students individually review and consolidate **Nützliche Ausdrücke**	• Present select **Kultur** features in whole class or small groups, jigsaw, numbered heads together, etc.	• Introduce homework: select **Kultur** (text/**Supersite**) **Übungen**
5 minutes	**35 minutes**	**5 minutes**
• Students individually review and consolidate understanding of cultural information	• Present grammar point B.1 using text, **Supersite** (presentations, grammar slides in **Resources**), and corresponding **Fotoroman** segments [15] • Student pairs/groups do B.1 **Jetzt sind Sie dran**, begin **Anwendung** [15]	• Introduce homework: select **Anwendung** (text/**Supersite**)
5 minutes	**30 minutes**	**5 minutes**
• Students individually reflect on and take note of personal areas of strength and challenge with regard to the grammar point and its use	• Present grammar point B.2 using text, **Supersite** (presentations, grammar slides in **Resources**), and corresponding **Fotoroman** segments [25] • Student pairs/groups do B.2 **Jetzt sind Sie dran**, begin **Anwendung** [10]	• Introduce homework: select **Anwendung** activities
5 minutes	**35 minutes**	**5 minutes**
• Students individually reflect on and take note of personal areas of strength and challenge with regard to the grammar point and its use	• Present grammar point B.3 using text, **Supersite** (presentations, grammar slides in **Resources**), and corresponding **Fotoroman** segments [25] • Student pairs/groups do B.3 **Jetzt sind Sie dran**, begin **Anwendung** [10]	• Introduce homework: select **Anwendung** (text/**Supersite**)
5 minutes	**35 minutes**	**5 minutes**
• Students individually reflect on and take note of personal areas of strength and challenge with regard to the grammar point and its use	• Student pairs/groups do **Wiederholung**	• Introduce homework: prepare for assessment on **Strukturen**
5 minutes	**35 minutes**	**5 minutes**
• Each student reviews what has just been presented from **Panorama**	• Guide students through **Vor dem Lesen**, including **Strategien**	• Introduce homework: **Panorama - Was haben Sie gelernt** activity/activities and/or initial research using **Im Internet**; and/or **Vor dem Lesen** activities (text/**Supersite**)
5 minutes	**15 minutes**	**5 minutes**
• Students individually reflect on understanding of **Lesen**	• Guide students through **Strategien** and **Vorbereitung** in **Hören**; present selection [20] • Students (individuals, pairs, or small groups) do **Verständnis** activities [10]	• Introduce homework: complete **Verständnis** from **Hören** (text/**Supersite**)
5 minutes	**30 minutes**	**5 minutes**
• Confirm understanding of assessment content and/or grading rubric if using **IPA** (**Supersite: Resources**) [5]	• Students work on **Schreiben - Thema** and/or review chapter content	• Introduce homework: prepare for chapter assessment and/or complete **Thema** (text/**Supersite**)
10 minutes	**35 minutes**	**5 minutes**

• Written or digital chapter assessment (from **Resources** section or **Assessment** section of **Supersite**, respectively) and/or complete **IPA**

40 minutes

AP® German Themes & Contexts

Long-term success in language learning starts in the first year of instruction. **Mosaik** incorporates AP® themes and contexts into all **Kultur**, **Zapping**, **Kurzfilm**, and **Weiter geht's** sections. **Mosaik** exposes students to the themes early in their language learning career. This will allow them to build the broad background they need to succeed on the AP® German Language and Culture Exam.

The numbers following each entry can be understood as follows:

(2)115 = **(Volume)** page
As shown, the entry above would be found in Volume 2, page 115.

MOSAIK 1

German Language and Culture

VISTA®
HIGHER LEARNING

Boston, Massachusetts

On the cover: Traditional frame houses, Freudenberg, Germany

Publisher: José A. Blanco
Professional Development Director: Norah Lulich Jones
Editorial Development: Brian Contreras, Sharla Zwirek
Project Management: Sally Giangrande
Rights Management: Ashley Dos Santos, Annie Pickert Fuller
Technology Production: Fabián Montoya, Paola Ríos Schaaf, Erica Solari
Design: Radoslav Mateev, Gabriel Noreña, Andrés Vanegas
Production: Manuela Arango, Oscar Díez, Adriana Jaramillo Ch.

Student Text ISBN: 978-1-68005-053-0
Library of Congress Control Number: 2016947899

1 2 3 4 5 6 7 8 9   WC   21 20 19 18 17 16

MOSAIK 1

German Language and Culture

		KONTEXT	FOTOROMAN

KULTUR

STRUKTUREN

WEITER GEHT'S

		KONTEXT	**FOTOROMAN**

KULTUR	STRUKTUREN	WEITER GEHT'S

The *Fotoroman* Episodes

Fully integrated with your textbook, the **Mosaik Fotoroman** contains 8 dramatic episodes—one for each lesson of the text. The episodes relate the adventures of four students who are studying in Berlin.

The **Fotoroman** dialogues in the printed textbook lesson are an abbreviated version of the dramatic episode featured in the video. Therefore, each **Fotoroman** section can be used as preparation before you view the corresponding video episode, as post-viewing reinforcement, or as a stand-alone section.

As you watch the video, you will see the characters interact using the vocabulary and grammar you are studying. Their conversations incorporate new vocabulary and grammar with previously taught language. At the conclusion of each episode, the **Zusammenfassung** segment summarizes the key language functions and grammar points used in the episode.

The Cast

Learn more about each of the characters you'll meet in **Mosaik Fotoroman**:

George
is from Milwaukee, Wisconsin.
He is studying Architecture.

Meline
is from Vienna.
She is studying Business.

Hans
is from Straubing, in Bavaria.
He studies Political Science and History.

Sabite
is from Berlin.
She studies Art.

About **Zapping TV Clips**

A TV clip from the German-speaking world appears in the first **Lektion** of each **Kapitel**. The purpose of this feature is to expose students to the language and culture contained in authentic media pieces. The following list of the television commercials is organized by **Kapitel.**

Kapitel 1

Deutsche Bahn

(29 seconds)

Kapitel 2

TU Berlin

(1 minute, 15 seconds)

Kapitel 3

Bauer Joghurt

(33 seconds)

Kapitel 4

Yello Strom

(39 seconds)

Ancillaries

- **Student Activities Manual (SAM)**

  The Student Activities Manual consists of three sections: the Workbook, the Video Manual, and the Lab Manual. The Workbook activities provide additional practice of the vocabulary and grammar for each textbook lesson. The Video Manual section includes activities for the **Mosaik Fotoroman**, and the Lab Manual activities focus on building your listening comprehension, speaking, and pronunciation skills in German.

- **Lab Audio MP3s**

  The Lab Audio MP3 files on the Supersite contain the recordings needed to complete the Lab Manual activities in the Student Activities Manual.

- **Textbook Audio MP3s**

  The Textbook Audio MP3 files contain the recordings needed to complete the listening activities in **Kontext**, **Aussprache und Rechtschreibung**, **Hören**, and **Wortschatz** sections. The files are available on the **Mosaik** Supersite.

- **Fotoroman Video**

  All episodes of the **Fotoroman** are available for streaming on the **Mosaik** Supersite.

- **Online Student Activities Manual (WebSAM)**

  Completely integrated with the **Mosaik** Supersite, the WebSAM provides online access to the SAM activities with instant feedback and grading. The complete audio program is online and features record-submit functionality for select activities.

- **Mosaik Supersite**

  The Supersite (**vhlcentral.com**) gives you access to a wide variety of interactive activities for each section of every lesson of the student text, including: auto-graded activities for extra practice with vocabulary, grammar, video, and cultural content; teacher-graded Partner Chat, Virtual Chat, and composition activities; reference tools; the **Zapping** TV commercials; the **Fotoroman** episodic videos; the Textbook Audio MP3 files, the Lab Program MP3 files, and more.

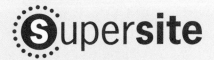

Each section of your textbook comes with activities on the **Mosaik** Supersite, many of which are auto-graded with immediate feedback. Plus, the Supersite is iPad®-friendly*, so it can be accessed on the go! Visit **vhlcentral.com** to explore the wealth of exciting resources.

KONTEXT	• Image-based vocabulary activities with audio • Additional activities for extra practice • **Aussprache und Rechtschreibung** presentation followed by record-compare activities	• Textbook activities • Chat activities for conversational skill-building and oral practice
FOTOROMAN	• Streaming video for all episodes of the **Fotoroman** with teacher-controlled options for subtitles • Textbook activities	• **Zusammenfassung** section with key vocabulary and grammar from the episode • Additional activities for extra practice
KULTUR	• Culture reading • Internet search activity	• Textbook activities • Additional activities for extra practice
STRUKTUREN	• Grammar presentations • Chat activities for conversational skill-building and oral practice • Streaming video of **Zapping** TV clip	• Textbook activities • Additional activities for extra practice
WEITER GEHT'S	**Panorama** • Interactive map with statistics and cultural notes • Additional activity for extra practice **Im Internet** • Internet search activity • Textbook activity with auto-grading **Lesen** • Audio-sync reading • Additional activities for extra practice • Textbook activities	**Hören** • Textbook activities • Additional activities for extra practice **Schreiben** • Submit your writing assignment online
WORTSCHATZ	• Audio recordings of all vocabulary items	• My Vocabulary to create lists and flashcards

Plus! Also found on the Supersite:

- All textbook and lab audio MP3 files
- Communication center for teacher notifications and feedback
- A single gradebook for all Supersite activities

- WebSAM online Workbook/Video Manual and Lab Manual
- vText online, interactive student edition with access to Supersite activities, audio, and video

*Students must use a computer for audio-recording.

Icons

Familiarize yourself with these icons that appear throughout **Mosaik**.

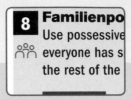

Online Activities

The mouse icon indicates when an activity is also available on the Supersite.

Pair Activities

Two heads indicate a pair activity.

Group Activities

Three heads indicate a group activity.

Recycle

The recycling icon indicates that you will need to use vocabulary and grammar learned in previous lessons.

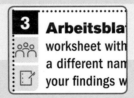

Partner and Virtual Chat Activities

Two heads with a speech bubble indicate that the activity may be assigned as a Partner Chat or a Virtual Chat activity on the Supersite.

Listening

The listening icon indicates that audio is available on the Supersite.

Worksheets

The activities marked with these icons require worksheets that your teacher will provide for you to complete the activity in a group.

Info Gap Activities

Two heads with a puzzle piece indicate an activity which will be done with a partner using a handout your teacher will provide.

Ressourcen

Ressourcen boxes tell you exactly what print and digital resources you can use to reinforce and expand on every section of the textbook lesson with page numbers where applicable.

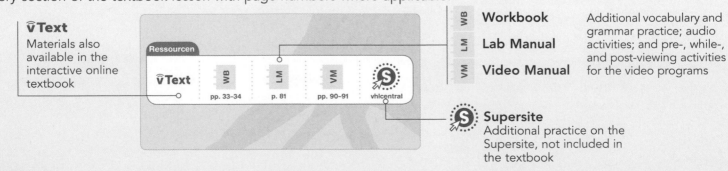

v̂Text
Materials also available in the interactive online textbook

Workbook
Lab Manual
Video Manual

Additional vocabulary and grammar practice; audio activities; and pre-, while-, and post-viewing activities for the video programs

Supersite
Additional practice on the Supersite, not included in the textbook

Why Learn German?

Explore Your Future

Are you already planning your future career? Employers in today's global economy look for workers who know different languages and understand other cultures. Your knowledge of German will make you a valuable job candidate, especially if you want to work abroad in the European Union.

In addition, studying a foreign language can improve your ability to analyze and interpret information and help you succeed in many other subject areas. When you first begin learning German, your studies will focus mainly on reading, writing, grammar, listening, and speaking skills. Many people who study a foreign language claim that they gained a better understanding of English. German can even help you understand the origins of many English words and expand your own vocabulary in English. Then, when you travel to a German-speaking country, you'll be able to converse freely with the people you meet. You'll find that speaking to people in their native language is the best way to bridge any culture gap.

The German-Speaking World

The German language is spoken primarily in Germany, Austria, and Switzerland and holds official status in Belgium, Liechtenstein, Luxembourg, and the European Union. The United States has the largest German-speaking population outside of Europe. After English and Spanish, German is the third most commonly spoken language in over a dozen states in the nation. After Hispanics, German descendants are the largest ethnic group in the U.S., making up about one third of the German diaspora worldwide.

German culture has a broad historical past dating back more than two thousand years. From Goethe to Mozart and from Gutenberg to Einstein, German language and culture has influenced the spheres of arts and sciences. Today, the German-speaking population has major economic and political importance in the European Union and beyond.

How to Learn German

Start with the Basics

As with anything you want to learn, start with the basics and remember that learning takes time! The basics are vocabulary, grammar, and culture.

Vocabulary | Every new word you learn in German will expand your vocabulary and ability to communicate. The more words you know, the better you can express yourself. Focus on sounds and think about ways to remember words. Use your knowledge of English and other languages to figure out the meaning of and memorize words like **Wasser, Apfel, Buch, Karte,** and **Fisch.**

Grammar | Grammar helps you put your new vocabulary together. By learning the rules of grammar, you can use new words correctly and speak in complete sentences. As you learn verbs and tenses, you will be able to speak about the past, present, or future, express yourself with clarity, and be able to persuade others with your opinions. Pay attention to structures and use your knowledge of English grammar to make connections with German grammar.

Culture | Culture provides you with a framework for what you may say or do. As you learn about the culture of German-speaking communities, you'll improve your knowledge of German. Think about a word like **Kindergarten**, and how it relates to the level of education and who attends it. Think about and explore customs like **die Sternsinger** ("Star Singers" who dress up in costume on Epiphany) and how they are similar to celebrations with which you're familiar. Observe customs—watch people greet each other or say good-bye. Listen for idioms and sayings that capture the spirit of what you want to communicate.

Die Sternsinger in traditional costumes.

Listen, Speak, Read, and Write

Listening | Listen for sounds and for words you can recognize. Listen for inflections and watch for key words that signal a question such as **wie** (*how*), **wo** (*where*), or **was** (*what*). Get used to the sound of German. Play German pop songs or watch German movies. Borrow audiobooks from your local library. Don't worry if you don't understand every single word. If you focus on key words and phrases, you'll get the main idea. The more you listen, the more you'll understand!

Speaking | Practice speaking German as often as you can. As you talk, work on your pronunciation, and read aloud texts so that words and sentences flow more easily. Don't worry if you don't sound like a native speaker, or if you make some mistakes. Time and practice will help you get there. Participate actively in German class. Try to speak German with classmates, especially native speakers (if you know any), as often as you can.

Reading | Read the lyrics of a song as you listen to it, or read books you've already read in English translated into German. Use reading strategies that you know to understand the meaning of a text that looks unfamiliar. Look for cognates, or words that are related in English and German, to guess the meaning of some words. Read as often as you can, and remember to read for fun.

Writing | German has standardized and largely phonetic rules for spelling. You'll need to learn how to interpret the sounds of the German language, but once you do, you can become a proficient speller. Write for fun—make up poems or songs, write e-mails or instant messages to friends, or start a journal or blog in German.

Tips for Learning German

- Listen to German radio shows. Write down words that you can't recognize or don't know and look up the meaning.

- Watch German TV shows or movies. Read subtitles to help you grasp the content.

- Read German-language newspapers, magazines, or blogs.

- Listen to German songs that you like —anything from contemporary pop music to traditional **Volksmusik**. Sing along and concentrate on your pronunciation.

Practice, practice, practice!

Seize every opportunity you find to listen, speak, read, or write German. Think of it like a sport or learning a musical instrument—the more you practice, the more you will become comfortable with the language and how it works. You'll marvel at how quickly you can begin speaking German and how the world that it transports you to can change your life forever.

Beatrice Egli, Swiss pop singer

- Seek out German speakers. Look for cultural centers where German might be spoken in your community. Order from a menu at a Viennese restaurant in German.

- Pursue language exchange opportunities (**Schüleraustausch**) in your school or community. Join language clubs or cultural societies, and explore opportunities for studying abroad or hosting a student from a German-speaking country in your home or school.

- Connect your learning to everyday experiences. Research naming the ingredients of your favorite dish in German. Research the origins of German place names in the U.S., like Anaheim, California and Bismarck, North Dakota, or of common English words like *pretzel, hamster, pumpernickel, rucksack, waltz, dachshund, glitz,* and *strudel*.

- Use mnemonics, or a memorizing device, to help you remember words. Make up a saying in English to remember the order of the days of the week in German by using their abbreviations (Mo, Di, Mi, Do, Fr, Sa, So).

- Visualize words. Try to associate words with images to help you remember meanings. For example, think of different sorts of **Wurst** as you learn the names of different types of meat. Visualize a national park and create mental pictures of the landscape as you learn names of animals, plants, and habitats.

- Enjoy yourself! Try to have as much fun as you can learning German. Take your knowledge beyond the classroom and find ways to make the learning experience your own.

Hallo! Wie geht's?

Suggestion Ask students what the people in the photo are doing and what they might be saying to each other. Ask if students know any German greetings.

Teaching Tip Look for icons indicating activities that address the modes of communication. Follow this key:

→ representative←	**Interpretive communication**
←representative→	**Presentational communication**
representative↔representative	**Interpersonal communication**

Communicative Goals

You will learn how to:

- greet people and say good-bye
- make introductions
- use polite expressions

Active vocabulary Point out that all expressions used in the illustration are glossed in the **Wortschatz** on p.46. Tell students that they are responsible for learning all terms listed in the **Wortschatz**, as well as vocabulary introduced on the **Strukturen** pages. This is the content they will be expected to know for tests and quizzes.

AP* Theme: Contemporary Life
Context: Social Customs & Values

Wie geht's?

S Vocabulary Tools

Wortschatz

Begrüßung und Abschied	hellos and good-byes
Guten Morgen.	Good morning.
Guten Abend.	Good evening.
Gute Nacht.	Good night.
Bis dann.	See you later.
Bis gleich.	See you soon.
Bis morgen.	See you tomorrow.
Auf Wiedersehen.	Good-bye.
Schönen Tag noch!	Have a nice day!
Prima.	Great.
Es geht.	So-so.
(Nicht) schlecht.	(Not) bad.
Mir geht's nicht (so) gut.	I'm not (so) well.

Suggestion Point out that **Morgen** with a capital *M* means *morning*, as in **Guten Morgen**, while **morgen** with a lowercase *m* means *tomorrow*, as in **bis morgen**.

Höflichkeiten	polite expressions
Gern geschehen.	My pleasure.
Entschuldigung.	Excuse me.
Entschuldigen Sie.	Excuse me. (form.)
Es tut mir leid.	I'm sorry.

Suggestion Point out that the informal question **Wie heißt du?** is used in the dialogue between Markus and Anna on p.3.

ja	yes
nein	no
sich vorstellen	**introducing oneself**
Wie heißen Sie?	What is your name? (form.)
Schön dich/Sie kennen zu lernen.	Nice to meet you. (inf./form.)

Personen	people
die Frau	woman
der Freund / die Freundin	friend (m./f.)
der Junge	boy
das Mädchen	girl
der Mann	man

Suggestion Point out that **Frau** is used to address a woman regardless of her marital status.

Herr	Mr.
Frau	Mrs.; Ms.
wo?	where?
hier	here
da/dort	there

Suggestion Explain that German speakers often end a phone conversation with **Auf Wiederhören** (*Until we hear each other again*) instead of **Auf Wiedersehen** (*Until we see each other again*).

MICHAEL Guten Tag, Herr Brenner, wie geht es Ihnen?
HERR BRENNER Hallo, Michael! Es geht mir ziemlich gut. Und dir?
MICHAEL Mir auch, danke.

Suggestion Point out that **Gut(en)** means *good* and **Tag** means *day*. Tell students that this greeting can be used from morning to afternoon.

PAUL Vielen Dank!
JOHANNES Bitte!

MARIA Bis später, Lukas!
LUKAS Tschüss, Maria. Bis bald!

Suggestion Explain to students the differences between **bis bald**, **bis gleich**, **bis dann**, and **bis später**.

CHRISTOPH Guten Tag, Herr Arnold. Das ist Christina Schöller.
HERR ARNOLD Guten Tag, Frau Schöller!
CHRISTINA Freut mich.

Ressourcen

 v Text

 WB pp. 1–2

L M p. 61

 vhlcentral

ACHTUNG

There are formal and informal ways of saying *you* in German. Use **du** and its plural, **ihr**, in informal address; use **Sie** in formal situations.

MARKUS Guten Tag, ich heiße Markus. Und du? Wie heißt du?
ANNA Ich heiße Anna.
MARKUS Angenehm, Anna.

Suggestion Have students take turns greeting each other and introducing themselves using vocabulary from this section.

SOFIA Guten Tag, Katrin!
KATRIN Hallo, Sofia!
SOFIA Wie geht's?
KATRIN Mir geht's gut, danke! Und wie geht es dir? Alles klar?
SOFIA Sehr gut, danke!

Anwendung

1 Was passt? Put these expressions into the correct categories.

Bitte!	die Frau	der Mann
Danke.	der Freund	Tschüss!
Entschuldigung.	Guten Tag!	Wie geht's?

1 Suggestion Ask students to suggest additional items from this section that could be listed in each category.

Polite expressions	People	Hellos and good-byes
Danke.	die Frau	Wie geht's?
Entschuldigung.	der Mann	Guten Tag!
Bitte!	der Freund	Tschüss!

2 Was fehlt? Complete each conversation with the appropriate word.

1. —_____Vielen_____ Dank!
   —_____Gern_____ geschehen!
2. —Guten Morgen. Ich _____heiße_____ Daniel.
   —Guten _____Morgen_____, Daniel.
3. —Hallo, Lina! _____Wie_____ geht's?
   —_____Ziemlich/Sehr_____ gut.
4. —Auf _____Wiedersehen_____, Frau Stein. Schönen Tag noch!
   —_____Danke/Vielen Dank_____.
5. —Hallo, David! Das _____ist_____ Lara.
   —Hallo, Lara! Schön, dich _____kennen_____ zu lernen!
6. —Guten Abend, Herr Klein. Wie geht es _____Ihnen_____?
   —Hallo, Tom. Es geht _____mir_____ gut, danke. Und dir?

2 Expansion Have students write two more lines of dialogue for each conversation. Remind them to pay careful attention to the use of **du** and **Sie**.

3 Kurze Gespräche Listen to the conversations and decide whether each conversation is **höflich** (*formal*) or **vertraulich** (*informal*).

	höflich	vertraulich
1.	☐	☑
2.	☑	☐
3.	☐	☑
4.	☐	☑
5.	☑	☐
6.	☐	☑

3 Suggestion Before playing the audio recording, ask students to brainstorm ways of indicating formal and informal speech, such as the use of titles and last names versus first names.

4 Antworten Sie Provide an appropriate response to each question or statement you hear.

1. Ich heiße [name]. _____
2. Gut, danke. _____
3. Freut mich. _____
4. Gern geschehen. _____
5. Tschüss. _____
6. Danke. _____

4 Suggestion Have students listen to the recording and respond out loud to each prompt. Then, have them listen again and write down their answers.

 Practice more at **vhlcentral.com**.

Kommunikation

5 Minidialoge With a partner, select the response that best completes each conversation, then role-play the mini-dialogues.

5 Suggestion Before playing the audio recording, ask students to brainstorm ways of indicating formal and informal speech, such as the use of titles and last names versus first names.

1. —Guten Tag, Frau Meier!
   (a.)—Hallo, Frau Schneider!   b. —Nicht schlecht.
2. —Danke, Sabine.
   (a.)—Bitte.   b. —Bis bald!
3. —Auf Wiedersehen!
   a. —Prima.   (b.)—Tschüss!
4. —Wie heißen Sie?
   (a.)—Ich heiße Paul.   b. —Vielen Dank.
5. —Wie geht es Ihnen, Herr Huber?
   a. —Bis dann.   (b.)—Danke, gut.
6. —Ich heiße Anka.
   (a.)—Freut mich.   b. —Entschuldigung.
7. —Gute Nacht, Lara. Bis morgen.
   (a.)—Ja, bis dann.   b. —Freut mich.
8. —Guten Tag, Herr Melchior. Das ist mein Freund.
   a. —Gern geschehen.   (b.)—Angenehm.

5 Virtual Chat You can also assign activity 5 on the Supersite. Students record individual responses that appear in your gradebook.

6 Begrüßungen In small groups, look at the illustrations, then act out a short dialogue in which the people greet each other, ask each other's names, and ask each other how they are. Pay attention to the use of **du** and **Sie**. Answers will vary.

1. Professor Fink

2. Frau Sperber

3. Anja

4. Franz

6 Suggestion Have students act out their conversations in front of the class.

7 Diskutieren und kombinieren Your instructor will give you and a partner worksheets with descriptions of five people. Use the information from your worksheet to introduce yourself and talk about how you are. Role-play each of the five people on your worksheet. Answers will vary.

BEISPIEL

S1: Hallo, ich heiße Martin. Und du?
S2: Hallo, ich heiße Sandra. Wie geht's?
S1: Ziemlich gut. Und dir?

8 Kennen lernen In groups of three, introduce yourself and ask your partners how they are. Then introduce your partners to the members of another group. Answers will vary.

BEISPIEL

S1: Hallo, ich heiße Sina. Und wie heißt du?
S2: Ich heiße Katja. Hallo, Sina.
S1: Und wie geht's dir?
S2: Prima, danke. Und wie geht's dir?
S1: Ziemlich gut. Katja, das hier ist Thomas.
S3: Hallo, Katja. Schön dich kennen zu lernen.

Aussprache und Rechtschreibung  Audio

The German alphabet

The German alphabet is made up of the same 26 letters as the English alphabet. Although the alphabet is the same, many of the letters (**Buchstaben**) are pronounced differently.

Buchstabe		Beispiel	Buchstabe		Beispiel	Buchstabe		Beispiel
a	(ah)	Abend	i	(ih)	Idee	r	(err)	Regen
b	(beh)	Butter	j	(yot)	ja	s	(ess)	singen
c	(tseh)	Celsius, Café	k	(kah)	Katze	t	(teh)	tanzen
			l	(ell)	lesen	u	(ooh)	Universität
d	(deh)	danke	m	(emm)	Mutter	v	(fau)	Vogel, Vase
e	(eh)	Elefant	n	(enn)	Nase	w	(veh)	Wasser
f	(eff)	finden	o	(oh)	Oper	x	(iks)	Xylophon
g	(geh)	gut	p	(peh)	Papier	y	(üpsilon)	Yacht, Typ
h	(hah)	hallo	q	(koo)	Quatsch	z	(tset)	Zelt

The symbol **ß** (**Eszett** or **scharfes s**) is used instead of a double **s** in certain words. **Eszett** is never used at the beginning of a word. It is capitalized as **SS**.

ß (Eszett, scharfes S)   **Straße** (*street*)

An **Umlaut** (¨) can be added to the vowels **a**, **o**, and **u**, changing their pronunciation.

a	Apfel		ä	(a-Umlaut)	Äpfel
o	Ofen		ö	(o-Umlaut)	Öfen
u	Mutter		ü	(u-Umlaut)	Mütter

In German, all nouns are capitalized, no matter where they appear in a sentence. When spelling aloud, say **großes a** for *capital a*, or **kleines a** for *lowercase a*. To ask how a word is spelled, say: **Wie schreibt man das?** (lit. *How does one write this?*)

1 **Aussprechen** Practice saying the German alphabet and sample words aloud.

2 **Buchstabieren** Spell these words aloud in German.

1. hallo
2. Morgen
3. studieren
4. Explosion
5. typisch
6. Universität
7. Bäcker
8. Straße
9. Juwelen
10. Frühling
11. tanzen
12. Querflöte

3 **Sprichwörter** Practice reading these sayings aloud.

Wer A sagt, muss auch B sagen.[1]

Übung macht den Meister.[2]

Willkommen in Berlin! Video

Meline und George kommen nach Berlin. Hier treffen sie Sabite und Hans.
Ist es eine freundliche Begrüßung (*friendly welcome*)?

NATIONAL
communication
cultures
STANDARDS

MELINE (*am Telefon*) Lukas... ah, Kreuzberg, okay. Lukas...

SABITE Hallo?
GEORGE Hallo. Ich bin George. Wie heißt du?
SABITE Ich heiße Sabite. Nett dich kennen zu lernen.
GEORGE Nett dich kennen zu lernen, Sabite.

HANS Entschuldigung. Was für ein Chaos! Hier ist die Bürste... und der Lippenstift. Und hier ist das Handy.
MELINE (*am Telefon*) Tschüss, Lukas.

SABITE Alles in Ordnung?
GEORGE Hier sind die Schlüssel. Danke, vielen Dank.
SABITE Gern geschehen. Keine Ursache. Bis später.

HANS Ich heiße Hans. Schönen Tag!

GEORGE *Talk to you later.* Auf Wiederhören.

---

1 **Richtig oder falsch?** Choose whether each statement is **richtig** (*true*) or **falsch** (*false*).

1. Sabite hilft (*helps*) Hans. Falsch.

2. Meline ist am Flughafen (*airport*). Falsch.
3. George hat (*has*) die Schlüssel. Richtig.
4. Meline telefoniert mit (*calls*) Lukas. Richtig.
5. George trifft (*meets*) Sabite. Richtig.

6. Hans geht es ganz okay. Falsch.
7. Meline geht nach (*is going to*) Kreuzberg. Richtig.
8. Meline hat eine Bürste, einen Lippenstift und ein Handy. Richtig.
9. Sabite geht es gut. Richtig.
10. Hans sagt: „Willkommen in München." Falsch.

PERSONEN George Hans Meline Sabite

MELINE Ich bin's, Meline.
SABITE Meline, hallo. Nett dich kennen zu lernen.
MELINE Freut mich. Wie geht es dir?
SABITE Mir geht es gut.

SABITE Oh, das ist George. Hallo, George. Das ist Meline. Meline, George.
GEORGE Hallo.
MELINE Nett dich kennen zu lernen.
GEORGE Freut mich.

HANS George?
GEORGE Ja!
HANS Hallo! Ich bin Hans. Willkommen in Deutschland. Nett dich kennen zu lernen. Wie geht's?
GEORGE Ganz okay.

GEORGE Das ist Sabite.
SABITE Hallo.
HANS Hi.

Nützliche Ausdrücke

- **Wie heißt du?**
  What's your name?
- **Nett dich kennen zu lernen.**
  Nice to meet you.
- **Ist jemand da?**
  Anyone there?
- **Keine Ursache.**
  Don't mention it.
- **Auf Wiederhören.**
  Talk to you later.
- **Was für ein Chaos!**
  What a mess!
- **der Lippenstift**
  lipstick
- **das Handy**
  cell phone
- **Freut mich.**
  It's a pleasure.
- **Willkommen in Deutschland.**
  Welcome to Germany.

1A.1
- **Hier ist die Bürste.**
  Here's the brush.

1A.2
- **Hier sind die Schlüssel.**
  Here are the keys.

1A.3
- **Ich bin George.**
  I'm George.

Suggestion Tell students that they will learn more about the grammar structures previewed in each episode in the lesson's **Strukturen** section.

---

2 **Zum Besprechen** Imagine that you and your partner are exchange students meeting for the first time. Greet each other, give your names, and be sure to include an appropriate goodbye. Be prepared to present your conversation to the class. Answers will vary.

2 Partner Chat You can also assign activity 2 on the Supersite. Students work in pairs to record the activity online. The pair's recorded conversation will appear in your gradebook.

2 Suggestion This activity can also be done with groups of three or more.

3 **Vertiefung** Germany's tallest structure is the television tower (Fernsehturm) in Berlin. Use the Internet to find its nicknames in German. Answers include: Telespargel, St. Walter

IM FOKUS

AP* **Theme:** Contemporary Life
Context: Social Customs & Values

Hallo, Deutschland!

 Reading

Im Fokus Tell students that deciding whether to use **du** or **Sie** can be complex, even for native speakers.

SAYING "HELLO" CAN BE A COMPLEX social interaction. Should you shake hands? Kiss cheeks? Keep your distance? The answers depend on where you are, who you are, and who you're talking to.

In general, Germans shake hands more than Americans do, and eye contact is an important feature of this gesture. If you've just been introduced to someone, shake hands, look them in the eye, and say **Freut mich**. In a business setting, a handshake is more or less obligatory, but friends may or may not shake hands when greeting. As in North America, friends in Germany, Austria, and Switzerland can often be seen greeting each other with a hug or a kiss on the cheek.

Greetings vary depending on time of day, level of formality, and region. In formal situations, you can say **Guten Morgen** in the morning, **Guten Tag** from morning to late afternoon, and **Guten Abend** in the evening. In Bavaria or Austria, you are likely to hear **Grüß Gott°** at any time of day. **Hallo**, **Tag**, and **Grüß dich°** are all common informal greetings. In Bavaria, use **Servus°** to say hello or goodbye to friends.

Deciding between informal and polite forms of address requires some judgment. In general, use the familiar forms **du** and **ihr** with children, teenagers, family members, and fellow

TIPP

When entering or leaving a shop or small business, it is polite to say hello and goodbye to the sales clerk.

students. Use the polite form **Sie** with anyone else until they invite you to call them **du**. Always use **Sie** with people with whom you are not on a first-name basis. Address men as **Herr** and women as **Frau**, regardless of their marital status.

Im Fokus Tell students that **Fräulein**, equivalent to the English title *Miss*, is no longer used by most German speakers, but they may encounter it in older texts or films, or hear it used by older speakers.

Grüß Gott *Hello. (lit. Greet God)* **Grüß dich** *Hello. (lit. Greet you (inf.))* **Servus** *Hello; Good-bye (inf.)*

---

1 **Richtig oder falsch?** Indicate whether each statement is **richtig** (*true*) or **falsch** (*false*). Correct any false statements.

1. **Hallo** is an appropriate greeting to use with friends. **Richtig.**

2. When meeting someone new, shake hands and say **Freut mich**. **Richtig.**

3. You should always use **Sie** with other students.
   Falsch. You should use **du** with other students.

4. You should shake hands to greet business partners. **Richtig.**

5. German friends often greet each other with a hug. **Richtig.**

6. **Guten Abend** is an appropriate way to greet your boss in the morning.
   Falsch. Guten Morgen is an appropriate greeting in the morning.

7. You are more likely to hear **Grüß Gott** in Austria than in Berlin. **Richtig.**

8. **Du** is used to address adults you don't know.
   Falsch. Du is used with friends and family, not with strangers.

9. It is appropriate to address children with **du**. **Richtig.**

10. When you are not sure whether to use **Sie** or **du**, you should follow the lead of the other person. **Richtig.**

 Practice more at **vhlcentral.com**.

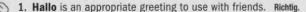

Deutsch im Alltag Have students take turns practicing the greetings from the list. Remind them that these items are not active vocabulary.

DEUTSCH IM ALLTAG

Wie geht's?

Geht's dir gut?	Are you all right? (inf.)
Und dir?	And you? (inf.)
Geht es Ihnen gut?	Are you all right? (form.)
Und Ihnen?	And you? (form.)
So weit, so gut.	So far, so good.
Spitze!	Great!
Schön dich zu sehen.	Nice to see you. (inf.)
Schön Sie zu sehen.	Nice to see you. (form.)
Herzlich willkommen.	Welcome.
Was geht?	What's up?

DIE DEUTSCHSPRACHIGE WELT

AP* Theme: Global Challenges **Context:** Communication

Auf Wiedersehen, Goodbye

One characteristic feature of the German language is its wealth of regional differences. Many dialects have their own greetings, from **Moin Moin** along the North Sea Coast to Switzerland's **Grüezi mitenand**. But how do German speakers say good-bye?

- **Auf Wiedersehen** and **tschüss** are the most standard good-byes.
- The formal Swiss counterpart is **Uf Widerluege.**
- The informal **Mach's gut** is similar in meaning to *Take care*.
- In Baden-Württemberg and the Saarland, **Ade** is common.
- In Austria, **Pfiati** is often used among friends.

Die deutschsprachige Welt Have students locate the countries and regions mentioned here in the map on p. 40 of their textbooks.

PORTRAT

Das Brandenburger Tor°
AP* Theme: Global Challenges
Context: Political Issues

On December 22, 1989, thousands cheered as West German Chancellor Helmut Kohl walked through the Brandenburg Gate to shake hands with East German Prime Minister Hans Modrow. It was the first time since the construction of the **Berliner Mauer°** in 1961 that East and West Germans had been permitted to pass through the gate.

Built in 1791, the **Brandenburger Tor** was one of fourteen toll gates that encircled the city. Over the next two centuries, the **Tor** withstood an invasion by Napoleon's soldiers, falling bombs in World War II, and the Cold War partition of East and West Germany. Today, the **Tor** is one of Berlin's most popular attractions, a symbol of German unity, and a monument to Berlin's tumultuous past.

Tor *Gate* **Berliner Mauer** *Berlin Wall*

Suggestion Tell students the origin and meaning of some regional greetings: **Moin Moin** derives from a Dutch word meaning *good* or *beautiful*. **Grüezi mitenand** means *Hello everyone* and is used to greet multiple people. **Pfiati** is derived from **Pfüat di**, meaning *(May God) protect you*. **Tschüss** is derived from *ciao*, and **Ade** from *adieu*.

🔗 IM INTERNET

Fashionably late isn't always fashionable. How do German and American manners differ when it comes to punctuality, greetings, and formality?

Find out more at **vhlcentral.com**.

3 Expansion Show students pictures of various people (an elderly person, a child, a teacher, etc.) and ask how they would greet each person.

---

2 **Was haben Sie gelernt?** Answer the questions. Answers may vary.

1. How would you say good-bye to a friend or fellow student in a German-speaking country? List three options.
   Tschüss, Ade, Pfiati, Mach's gut.
2. What did Germans celebrate at the Brandenburg Gate in 1989?
   They celebrated the opening of the border crossing and the fall of the Berlin Wall.
3. Name some historical events that occurred near the Brandenburg Gate.
   The invasion of Berlin by Napoleon, WWII, the building of the Wall, the fall of the Wall.
4. What does the Brandenburg Gate now symbolize?
   It symbolizes German unity.

3 **Sie sind dran** In pairs, practice meeting and greeting people in these situations. Answers will vary.

1. It's 10 a.m. and you run into your German professor at the grocery store. What do you say?
2. Now you're purchasing your groceries. How do you say "hello" and "good-bye" to the cashier?
3. Just as you're leaving the store, you run into an old friend. Say "hi" and ask how your friend is doing.

3 Partner Chat You can also assign activity 3 on the Supersite.

Ressourcen

v̂Text

vhlcentral

1A.1 Gender, articles, and nouns  Presentation

Startblock Like English nouns, German nouns can be either singular or plural and may be preceded by a definite or indefinite article. Unlike English nouns, all German nouns have a gender. German nouns are always capitalized, regardless of where they appear in a sentence.

Was für **ein Chaos**!

Hier ist **die Bürste**. Hier ist **das Handy**.

Gender

Suggestion Point out that nouns taught in this text are listed with their corresponding singular definite articles. Encourage students to memorize the article along with each noun, in order to remember its gender.

- All German nouns have a gender: masculine, feminine, or neuter. While most nouns referring to males are masculine and most nouns referring to females are feminine, the genders of nouns representing objects and ideas need to be memorized.

MASCULINE	FEMININE	NEUTER
der **Mann**	die **Frau**	das **Buch**
*the **man***	*the **woman***	*the **book***
der **Junge**	die **Blume**	das **Mädchen**
*the **boy***	*the **flower***	*the **girl***

ACHTUNG

Nouns ending with **-chen** are always neuter.

- Nouns ending with -**in** that refer to people are always feminine.

die Freund**in**	die Schüler**in**	die Professor**in**
*the (**female**) friend*	*the (**female**) student*	*the (**female**) professor*

Suggestion Give students examples of nouns with the feminine endings -**heit** and -**ung**. Ex: **die Freiheit, die Wohnung**.

- Other feminine noun endings include -**ei**, -**heit**, -**schaft**, -**ung**, and -**tät**.

die **Bäckerei**	die **Freundschaft**	die **Universität**
*the **bakery***	*the **friendship***	*the **university***

Definite and indefinite articles

- The definite article, equivalent to *the* in English, precedes a noun and indicates its gender. The masculine article is **der**, the feminine article is **die**, and the neuter article is **das**.

MASCULINE	FEMININE	NEUTER
der Tisch	**die Tür**	**das Fenster**
the table	*the door*	*the window*

- The definite article **die** is used with all plural nouns, regardless of gender.

QUERVERWEIS

You will learn more about forming plurals in **1A.2**.

	SINGULAR	PLURAL	
MASCULINE	**der** Tisch	**die** Tische	*the tables*
FEMININE	**die** Tür	**die** Türen	*the doors*
NEUTER	**das** Fenster	**die** Fenster	*the windows*

- The indefinite article **ein(e)** corresponds to *a* or *an* in English. It precedes the noun and matches its gender. Note that both masculine and neuter nouns take the form **ein**, while feminine nouns take **eine**.

MASCULINE	FEMININE	NEUTER
ein Tisch	**eine** Tür	**ein** Fenster
a table	*a door*	*a window*
ein Mann	**eine** Frau	**ein** Mädchen
a man	*a woman*	*a girl*

- There is no plural form of the indefinite article.

Er ist **ein Mann**. ▶ Sie sind **Männer**.
*He is **a man**.*   *They are **men**.*

Compound nouns

- Compound words are very common in German. As in English, two or more simple nouns can be combined to form a compound noun.

die Nacht + das Hemd = **das Nachthemd**
night   *shirt*   *nightshirt*

Hier ist **der Lippenstift**.

Expansion Give students additional examples of nouns that can combine to form compounds. Have them figure out the appropriate articles for the compound forms. Ex.: **das Land** (*the country*) **+ die Karte** (*the map*) **= die Landkarte** (*the (country) map*); **der Arm** (*the arm*) **+ das Band** (*the strap*) **+ die Uhr** (*the clock*) **= die Armbanduhr** (*the watch*).

- The gender and number of a compound noun is determined by the last noun in the compound.

das Haus + **die** Aufgabe = **die Hausaufgabe**
house   *assignment*   *homework*

die Nacht + **der** Tisch = **der Nachttisch**
night   *table*   *night table*

Jetzt sind Sie dran! Tell students that all the nouns listed are singular.

Ressourcen

v̂ Text

WB
pp. 3–4

LM
p. 63

S
vhlcentral

Jetzt sind Sie dran! Indicate the gender of each noun: **Maskulinum, Femininum,** or **Neutrum.**

	Maskulinum	Femininum	Neutrum			Maskulinum	Femininum	Neutrum
1. der Mann	✓	☐	☐	7. eine Frau	☐	✓	☐
2. die Freundin	☐	✓	☐	8. ein Mädchen	☐	☐	✓
3. der Junge	✓	☐	☐	9. ein Tisch	✓	☐	☐
4. das Hemd	☐	☐	✓	10. eine Nacht	☐	✓	☐
5. die Aufgabe	☐	✓	☐	11. die Universität	☐	✓	☐
6. ein Freund	✓	☐	☐	12. ein Buch	☐	☐	✓

Anwendung

1 Was fehlt? Write the appropriate article.

der, die, das

1. __das__ Fenster
2. __der__ Tisch
3. __der__ Student
4. __die__ Freundschaft

ein, eine

5. __eine__ Frau
6. __eine__ Tür
7. __ein__ Mann
8. __ein__ Mädchen

2 Ergänzen Sie Write each noun in the appropriate column. Include the definite and indefinite article.

Bäckerei	Haus
Buch	Hemd
Freund	Junge
Freundin	Schülerin

Maskulinum	Femininum	Neutrum
der Mann; ein Mann	die Bäckerei; eine Bäckerei	das Buch; ein Buch
der Freund; ein Freund	die Freundin; eine Freundin	das Haus; ein Haus
der Junge; ein Junge	die Schülerin; eine Schülerin	das Hemd; ein Hemd

3 Sätze Complete each sentence with the appropriate definite or indefinite article.

1. __Der__ Junge heißt Paul.
2. Wie heißt __die__ Lehrerin?
3. Jasmin ist __ein__ Mädchen.
4. __Das__ Buch ist prima!
5. __Die__ Türen sind hier.
6. Lara ist __eine__ gute Studentin.

4 Bilden Sie Wörter Write the compound word with the appropriate definite article.

▶ **BEISPIEL**

das Haus + die Aufgabe =
die Hausaufgabe

1. die Kinder + der Garten
= __der Kindergarten__

2. der Schlaf (*sleep*) +
das Zimmer (*room*) =
das Schlafzimmer

3. das Telefon +
die Nummer =
die Telefonnummer

4. der Computer +
das Spiel (*game*) =
das Computerspiel

 Practice more at **vhlcentral.com**.

Kommunikation

5 **Was ist das?** In pairs, take turns identifying each person or object. Provide both the definite and indefinite articles.

▶ **BEISPIEL**
S1: *der Junge*
S2: *ein Junge*

1. das Buch, ein Buch

2. die Frau, eine Frau

3. der Mann, ein Mann

4. die Tür, eine Tür

5. das Fenster, ein Fenster

6. das Mädchen, ein Mädchen

5 **Virtual Chat** You can also assign activity 5 on the Supersite. Students record individual responses that appear in your gradebook.

6 **Was passt zusammen?** In pairs, take turns creating compound nouns using words from the list. Write down each compound noun with the appropriate article. Sample answers are provided.

▶ **BEISPIEL**
S1: *der Schlüssel / der Ring*
S2: *der Schlüsselring*

der Handschuh, die Hauskatze, der Nachtbus, der Eisbär

der Schlüssel   **der Ring**

die Hand   **der Schuh**   **die Nacht**   **der Bus**

das Haus   **die Katze**   **das Eis**   **der Bär**

6 **Suggestion** Tell students the compounds they come up with don't have to be real words in German. Have them read out loud the compound words they created. Then, share with them the actual compounds (provided as sample answers) that can be made from combining the words listed, and have students guess their meanings.

7 **Was zeichne ich?** In small groups, take turns drawing pictures of nouns you've learned so far, for your partners to guess. The person who guesses correctly is the next to draw. Don't forget the article! Answers will vary.

8 **Gedächtnisspiel** Play a memory game. The first player says a noun with the appropriate definite or indefinite article, and the next player repeats the previous noun and says his or her own. Go around the class until someone forgets an item or uses the wrong article. That player starts the next round.

1A.2 **Plurals**  Presentation

Startblock Plurals in German follow several patterns. These patterns can help you remember the plural form of each noun you learn.

ACHTUNG

The best way to be sure of a noun's plural form is to memorize it when you learn the singular form. Being familiar with the patterns of plural formation can make this process easier.

Suggestion Point out that irregular plural forms exist in English as well as German. Ask students to brainstorm examples. Ex.: *child, children*; *mouse, mice*; *woman, women*; *deer, deer*.

ACHTUNG

Two plurals that do not follow the standard pattern for feminine nouns are **die Mütter**, plural of **Mutter**, and **die Töchter** (*daughters*), plural of **Tochter**.

Ressourcen

v̂ Text

WB
pp. 5–6

LM
p. 64

vhlcentral

- In German dictionaries and vocabulary lists, singular nouns are listed along with a notation that indicates how to form the plural. There are five main patterns for forming plural nouns.

notation	singular	plural
- ::	das Fenster ⟶ die Fenster die Mutter (*mother*) ⟶ die Mütter	
-e ::e	der Freund ⟶ die Freunde der Stuhl (*chair*) ⟶ die Stühle	
-er ::er	das Kind (*child*) ⟶ die Kinder der Mann ⟶ die Männer	
-n -en -nen	der Junge ⟶ die Jungen die Frau ⟶ die Frauen die Freundin ⟶ die Freundinnen	
-s	der Park ⟶ die Parks	

- Most masculine and neuter nouns form the plural by adding -**e** or -**er**. Plurals with the -**er** ending always add an **Umlaut** when the vowel in the singular form is **a**, **o**, or **u**.

  der Tag (*day*) ⟶ die Tag**e**   das Buch ⟶ die B**ü**ch**er**

- If the singular form of a noun ends in -**el**, -**en**, or -**er**, there is no additional plural ending, but an **Umlaut** is added to the stem vowel **a**, **o**, or **u**.

  der Apf**el** (*apple*) ⟶ die **Ä**pf**el**   das Zimm**er** (*room*) ⟶ die Zimm**er**

- For feminine nouns ending with -**in**, add -**nen** to form the plural.

  die Freund**in** ⟶ die Freund**innen**   die Schüler**in** ⟶ die Schüler**innen**

- For most other feminine nouns, add -**n** if the singular form ends in -**e**, -**el**, or -**er**. Add -**en** if it does not. Note that feminine plurals with these endings never add an **Umlaut**.

  die Blum**e** (*flower*) ⟶ die Blum**en**   die Frau ⟶ die Frau**en**

- The -**s** ending is added to most words borrowed from other languages and to most nouns ending with vowels other than **e**.

  das Sofa ⟶ die Sofa**s**   das Auto ⟶ die Auto**s**

 Jetzt sind Sie dran! Write the plural form of each singular noun and vice versa.

Singular

1. das Café ___die Cafés___
2. die Schülerin ___die Schülerinnen___
3. der Stuhl ___die Stühle___
4. die Tochter ___die Töchter___

Plural

5. die Zimmer ___das Zimmer___
6. die Universitäten ___die Universität___
7. die Äpfel ___der Apfel___
8. die Schüler ___der Schüler___

Anwendung und Kommunikation

1 **Schreiben** Write the plural form.

1. das Buch _____die Bücher_____
2. der Mann _____die Männer_____
3. der Tag _____die Tage_____
4. die Blume _____die Blumen_____
5. die Mutter _____die Mütter_____

6. das Auto _____die Autos_____
7. der Junge _____die Jungen_____
8. die Tür _____die Türen_____
9. das Kind _____die Kinder_____
10. der Park _____die Parks_____

2 **Plural** Complete each sentence with the plural form of the appropriate word.

BEISPIEL   Holiday Inn und Marriott sind _____Hotels_____.

Apfel	Buch	Freundin
Auto	Computer	Hotel
Blume	Freund	Tag

1. BMW und Volkswagen sind _____Autos_____.
2. Rosen und Tulpen (*tulips*) sind _____Blumen_____.
3. Dell, HP und Acer sind _____Computer_____.
4. Granny Smith und Macintosh sind _____Äpfel_____.
5. Eine Woche (*week*) hat sieben (*seven*) _____Tage_____.
6. Anna, Monika und Emma sind _____Freundinnen_____.
7. *Harry Potter* und *Sag mal* sind _____Bücher_____.
8. Lukas und Felix sind _____Freunde_____.

3 **Was ist das?** In pairs, take turns identifying each object, place, or person. Give both singular and plural forms. Sample answers are provided.

BEISPIEL
S1: *die Blume*
S2: *die Blumen*

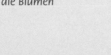

1.
das Mädchen, die Mädchen/ das Kind, die Kinder

2.
der Park, die Parks

3.
der Junge, die Jungen/ das Kind, die Kinder

4.
das Auto, die Autos

5.
das Fenster, die Fenster

6.
die Tür, die Türen

7.
der Stuhl, die Stühle

 Practice more at **vhlcentral.com**.

1A.3

Subject pronouns, *sein*, and the nominative case

 Presentation

Subject pronouns

QUERVERWEIS

German speakers often use the third-person singular pronoun **man** where English speakers would say *one* or *you*.

Students will learn more about the use of **man** in **Vol. 2, 3B.3**.

Suggestion Tell students that **ich** is capitalized only when it begins a sentence, unlike the pronoun *I* in English. Remind them that the formal **Sie** is always capitalized.

- In German, as in English, any noun can be replaced with an equivalent pronoun. A subject pronoun replaces a noun that functions as the subject of a sentence.

Maria ist nett. **Sie** ist nett. **Der Junge** ist groß. **Er** ist groß.
Maria is nice. *She is nice.* *The boy is tall.* *He is tall.*

subject pronouns		
	singular	plural
1st person	ich *I*	wir *we*
2nd person	du *you* (inf.) Sie *you* (form.)	ihr *you* (inf.) Sie *you* (form.)
3rd person	er *he/it* sie *she/it* es *it*	sie *they*

- The gender of a noun determines the gender of the pronoun that replaces it. German uses **er** for all masculine nouns, **sie** for all feminine nouns, and **es** for all neuter nouns.

Der Tisch ist klein. ▶ **Er** ist klein. **Das Buch** ist neu. ▶ **Es** ist neu.
The table is small. *It's small.* *The book is new.* *It's new.*

Suggestion Give students additional examples using **sie** and **Sie** and have them figure out which meaning is intended, based on context.

- The pronoun **Sie/sie** can mean *you*, *she*, *it*, or *they*, depending on context. Write **Sie** with a capital **S** to mean *you* in a formal context, and **sie** with a lowercase **s** to mean *she*, *it*, or *they*.

Das ist Frau Hansen.
   Sie ist Lehrerin.
*That's Mrs. Hansen. **She** is a teacher.*

Das sind Lara und Jonas.
   Sie sind Schüler.
*That's Lara and Jonas. **They**'re students.*

Woher kommen **Sie**?
*Where are **you** from?*

The verb *sein*

- Sein (*To be*) is an irregular verb: its conjugation does not follow a predictable pattern.

sein (*to be*)			
singular		**plural**	
ich **bin**	*I am*	wir **sind**	*we are*
du **bist**	*you are* (inf.)	ihr **seid**	*you are* (inf.)
Sie **sind**	*you are* (form.)	Sie **sind**	*you are* (form.)
er/sie/es **ist**	*he/she/it is*	sie **sind**	*they are*

Ich bin Amerikaner.   **Sie ist** Deutsche.   **Wir sind** Freunde.
I'm American.   *She's German.*   *We are friends.*

The nominative case

- German has four *cases* that indicate the function of each noun in a sentence. The case of a noun determines the form of the definite or indefinite article that precedes the noun, the form of any adjectives that modify the noun, and the form of the pronoun that can replace the noun.

German cases		
Nominativ	Der Mann ist alt.	*The man is old.*
Akkusativ	Ich verstehe **den** Mann.	*I understand the man.*
Dativ	Der Assistent zeigt **dem** Mann den neuen Computer.	*The assistant is showing the man the new computer.*
Genitiv	Das ist der Assistent **des** Manns.	*This is the man's assistant.*

- The grammatical subject of a sentence is always in the nominative case (**der Nominativ**). Subject pronouns are, by definition, nominative pronouns. The nominative case is also used for nouns that follow a form of **sein**, **werden** (*to become*), or **bleiben** (*to stay, to remain*).

Das ist **eine gute Idee**.   Wir bleiben **Freunde**.
*That's **a good idea**.*   *We're still **friends**.*

- The definite and indefinite articles you learned in **1A.1** are the forms used with nouns in the nominative case.

nominative articles				
	masculine	**feminine**	**neuter**	**plural**
definite	der Junge	die Frau	das Mädchen	die Jungen
indefinite	ein Junge	eine Frau	ein Mädchen	- Jungen

QUERVERWEIS

You will learn more about cases in **1B.1**, **3B.2**, **4B.1**, and **4B.2**.

Jetzt sind Sie dran!   For each noun, write the correct subject pronoun. For each pronoun, write the appropriate form of sein.

1. der Apfel ___er___
2. das Haus ___es___
3. die Jungen ___sie___
4. die Hausaufgabe ___sie___
5. Brigitte und ich ___wir___
6. die Schülerin und du ___ihr___
7. wir ___sind___
8. ihr ___seid___
9. du ___bist___
10. Sie ___sind___
11. ich ___bin___
12. er ___ist___

Anwendung

1 Was ist richtig? Select the appropriate subject pronoun.

1. (**Ihr**/ Wir) seid in Deutschland.
2. (**Er**)/ Ich) ist Katjas Freund.
3. (Du / **Sie**) sind nett!
4. (**Ihr**/ Ich) seid Amerikaner.

5. (**Wir** / Ich) sind Deutsche.
6. (**Ich**/ Du) bin Schülerin.
7. (Es / **Du**) bist prima!
8. (Ihr / **Sie**) ist intelligent.

2 Expansion Have students transform the subjects of items 1, 4, 6, and 8 into subject pronouns.

2 Was fehlt? Write the correct form of sein.

1. Herr und Frau Schlüter ___sind___ dort.
2. Lena und ich ___sind___ hier.
3. Ich ___bin___ Anna.
4. Du ___bist___ Schüler.
5. Herr Doktor, Sie ___sind___ Experte.
6. Das Buch ___ist___ sehr interessant.
7. Ihr ___seid___ Kinder.
8. Das Fenster und die Tür ___sind___ offen (*open*).

3 Sätze ergänzen Write the pronoun and the appropriate form of sein.

> **BEISPIEL**
> ___Sie sind___ im (*at the*)
> Restaurant.

1. ___Sie sind___
Freundinnen.

2. ___Er ist___
Deutschlehrer.

3. Mia, Tim und ich,
___wir sind___ Schüler.

4. Sara, ___du bist___
allein (*alone*).

5. ___Sie ist___
müde (*tired*).

6. Jan und du,
___ihr seid___ Freunde.

4 Bilden Sie Sätze Write complete sentences using sein. Then, replace the subjects with subject pronouns, where possible.

BEISPIEL Samuel / intelligent
Samuel ist intelligent. Er ist intelligent.

1. Lukas und ich / Schüler
Lukas und ich sind Schüler. Wir sind Schüler.
2. du / nett
Du bist nett.
3. es / ein gutes (*good*) Buch
Es ist ein gutes Buch.
4. Michael und du / in Deutschland
Michael und du seid in Deutschland. Ihr seid in Deutschland.

5. Danielle und Johanna / Deutsche
Danielle und Donna sind Deutsche. Sie sind Deutsche.
6. ich / Amerikaner
Ich bin Amerikaner.
7. Sie / unfair, Frau Henke
Sie sind unfair, Frau Henke.
8. das Haus / gigantisch
Das Haus ist gigantisch. Es ist gigantisch.

 Practice more at **vhlcentral.com**.

Kommunikation

5 **Was sehen Sie?** These pictures have been mislabeled. In pairs, take turns reading and correcting the labels. *Answers will vary.*

▶ **BEISPIEL** Kinder

S1: *Das sind Kinder.*
S2: *Nein, das sind Lehrerinnen.*

1. Stühle

2. ein Tisch

3. ein Lehrer

4. Autos

5. Männer

6. ein Fenster

6 **Beschreibungen** Tell your partner that you are like each of the people listed. *Answers will vary.*

 BEISPIEL Paul / in Amerika (du)
  Jan und Sara / tolerant (ihr)

S1: *Paul ist in Amerika, und du?*
S2: *Ich bin auch in Amerika. Jan und Sara sind tolerant, und ihr?*
S1: *Wir sind auch tolerant.*

1. die Lehrerin / intelligent (du)
2. Klara und Tim / Freunde (ihr)

3. Felix / romantisch (du)
4. Max und Lisa / Studenten (ihr)

7 **Freut mich!** In groups of three, role-play these situations. Each person should say something about him-/herself using a form of **sein.**

 BEISPIEL

S1: *Hallo, ich bin Max.*
S2: *Hallo, Max! Schön dich kennen zu lernen.*
  Ich bin Sara und das ist Julia. Wir sind Studentinnen.

1. You are meeting your classmates for the first time. Introduce yourself and ask how each person is doing.

2. You and your friend are invited to a birthday party. Exchange greetings and introduce yourselves to other guests.

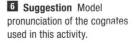

5 Virtual Chat You can also assign activity 5 on the Supersite. Students record individual responses that appear in your gradebook.

6 Suggestion Model pronunciation of the cognates used in this activity.

6 Partner Chat You can also assign activity 6 on the Supersite. Students work in pairs to record the activity online. The pair's recorded conversation will appear in your gradebook.

7 Expansion Have group members introduce themselves to the rest of the class.

Wiederholung

NATIONAL communication STANDARDS

4 Expansions
- Repeat this activity using the cards students created for **Memory-Spiel**.
- Divide the class into teams and play Pictionary using the lesson vocabulary.

1 Memory-Spiel

Memory-Spiel With a partner, create a set of cards to play Memory, featuring ten nouns you learned in this lesson. For each noun you draw, create a matching card showing the word with the definite article. Shuffle the cards and place them face down. Take turns matching pictures and words. Answers will vary.

der Apfel

2 Freut mich!

Freut mich! In pairs, practice introducing yourselves in formal and informal situations. Answers will vary.

2 Partner Chat You can also assign activity 2 on the Supersite.

3 Schatzsuche

Schatzsuche With a partner, find one word or phrase from this lesson that corresponds to each description. Compete against other pairs to see which team can complete their list first. Remember: all words must be spelled correctly, nouns must be preceded by the appropriate definite article, and no word or phrase can be used more than once. Answers will vary.

1. a feminine plural noun
2. a formal greeting
3. an informal way to say goodbye
4. a neuter noun that refers to a person
5. a response to the question "**Wie geht's**?"
6. a plural noun ending in -**s**
7. a sentence using a subject pronoun with **sein**
8. a noun that has identical singular and plural forms

4 Was ist das?

Was ist das? In pairs, take turns identifying the objects and people.

4 Partner Chat You can also assign activity 4 on the Supersite.

▶ **BEISPIEL**
S1: Was ist das?
S2: Das ist ein Auto.

1. Das ist ein Buch. ___ 2. Das ist eine Blume./Das sind Blumen. ___

3. Das ist ein Fenster. ___ 4. Das ist ein Sofa. ___

5. Das ist ein Park. ___ 6. Das sind Kinder. ___

5 Diskutieren und kombinieren

Diskutieren und kombinieren Your instructor will give you and a partner two worksheets with different images and labels. Work together to form the compound words.

6 Arbeitsblatt

Arbeitsblatt Your instructor will give you a worksheet (**das Arbeitsblatt**). Ask your classmates to say their names and spell them for you. Don't forget to greet them, ask how they are, and say thank you! Answers will vary.

BEISPIEL
S1: Guten Morgen!
S2: Hallo!
S1: Wie geht's?
S2: Es geht mir gut.
S1: Wie heißt du?
S2: Ich heiße Nadia.
S1: Wie schreibt man das?
S2: N-A-D-I-A.
S1: Wie ist dein Nachname (last name)?
S2: Mueller. M-U-E-L-L-E-R.
S1: Danke!

S Video

AP* Theme: Contemporary Life
Context: Entertainment, Travel, & Leisure

Suggestion After showing students the video, ask questions to facilitate comprehension. Ex: In the first scene, why do some of the people in the child's drawing have blank faces? In the second scene, why are the children happier?

Familien fahren° besser mit der Bahn

Deutsche Bahn (**DB**) is the German railway company, based in Berlin. The **Deutsche Bahn** offers a **Sparpreis** (*discount price*) for families. Children under age 15 ride free when accompanied by an adult and pay half-price fares when traveling alone. This advertisement presents the **Deutsche Bahn** as a convenient and comfortable transportation option for families, allowing parents and children to interact and enjoy themselves on the way to their destination.

Die Bahn macht mobil: www.bahn.de

Sag mal°, weißt du noch, wie die Beiden von vorne aussehen?°

Warum fragst du mich?° Du kennst die länger als ich.°

Jetzt mit Gratiseis° für Kinder.

fahren *ride* **Sag mal** *Say...* **weißt du..., wie die Beiden von vorne aussehen?** *do you know what those two look like from the front?* **Warum fragst du mich?** *Why are you asking me?*
Du kennst die länger als ich. *You've known them longer than me.* **Gratiseis** *free popsicle*

  Verständnis Circle the correct answers.

1. How much does the **DB** family package cost?
   (a. 49 euro)   b. 60 euro   c. 39 euro   d. 55 euro
2. What do children riding the train receive?
   a. Bücher   b. Äpfel   (c. Eis)   d. Blumen

Diskussion Discuss the following questions with a partner. Answers will vary.

1. What is train service like in your country? How do you think it compares with the services offered by the **Deutsche Bahn**?
2. Does this commercial make you want to travel by train in Germany? Why or why not?

Communicative Goals

You will learn how to:

- talk about classes
- talk about schedules

Suggestion Point out that many of these vocabulary items are compound nouns. Ask students to identify the compound nouns, then help them to figure out the meaning of the component words.

Wortschatz

im Unterricht	*in class*
der Computer, -	computer
das Ergebnis, -se	result; score
das Foto, -s	photo
die Frage, -n	question
die Hausaufgabe, -n	homework
der Kalender, -	calendar
die Klasse, -n	class
der Kuli, -s	ball-point pen
das Lehrbuch, ⁻er	(university) textbook
die Note, -n	grade (on an assignment)
die Notiz, -en	note
das Problem, -e	problem
die Prüfung, -en	test; exam
der Radiergummi, -s	eraser
die Sache, -n	thing
das Schulbuch, ⁻er	(K–12) textbook
die Stunde, -n	lesson
der Taschenrechner, -	calculator
der Tisch, -e	table; desk
die Tür, -en	door
das Zeugnis, -se	report card; grade report
Da ist/sind...	*There is/are...*
Ist/Sind hier...?	*Is/Are there... here?*
Hier ist/sind...	*Here is/are...*
Was ist das?	*What is that?*
Orte	*places*
das Klassenzimmer, -	classroom
die Schule, -n	school
die Universität, -en	university, college
die Bibliothek, -en	library
die Mensa, Mensen	(university) cafeteria
Personen	*people*
Wer ist das?	*Who is it?*
der Klassenkamerad, -en / die Klassenkameradin, -nen	(K-12) classmate
der Kommilitone, -n / die Kommilitonin, -nen	(university) classmate
der Professor, -en / die Professorin, -nen	professor
der Student, -en / die Studentin, -nen	(university) student

In der Schule — Vocabulary Tools

AP* Theme: Contemporary Life
Context: Education & Career

der Rucksack, ⁻e
der Bleistift, -e
die Uhr, -en
das Fenster, -
der Schüler, -
das Buch, ⁻er
die Schülerin, -nen
das Heft, -e
das Wörterbuch, ⁻er
der Stift, -e
der Papierkorb, ⁻e
das Blatt Papier, (*pl.* Blätter Papier)

Suggestion Tell students that **Schüler(in)** refers to a student in elementary school through high school, while **Student(in)** refers to a college or university student.

ACHTUNG

Don't confuse **Da ist...** (*There is...*) with **Das ist...** (*This is...*).

Ressourcen

vText — pp. 9–10

WB

LM — p. 66

vhlcentral

die Tafel, -n

DEUTSCHLAND

LIECHTENSTEIN

DIE SCHWEIZ   ÖSTERREICH

die Karte, -n

der Lehrer, -
(die Lehrerin, -nen f.)

der Schreibtisch, -e

der Stuhl, ⁻e

Anwendung

1 Expansion Ask students what other words from the lesson vocabulary could be included in each group.

1 Was passt nicht? Select the word that doesn't belong.

1. der Professor / das Problem / die Universität / die Studentin
2. das Fenster / das Schulbuch / die Notizen / das Heft
3. der Stift / der Bleistift / der Papierkorb / der Kuli
4. die Tafel / der Schreibtisch / der Stuhl / die Prüfung
5. die Tür / das Ergebnis / der Tisch / die Uhr
6. das Problem / der Radiergummi / die Frage / das Ergebnis

2 Ergänzen Sie Select the words that best complete each sentence.

1. Annika ist...
   a. der Stuhl.   b. die Schülerin.   c. die Stunde.
2. Wer ist das? Das ist...
   a. der Bleistift.   b. der Taschenrechner.   c. der Professor.
3. Wo sind die Bücher? Sie sind...
   a. in der Bibliothek. b. im Ergebnis.   c. im Papierkorb.
4. Frau Meier ist...
   a. die Lehrerin.   b. die Schülerin.   c. die Schule.
5. Im Klassenzimmer sind...
   a. Tische.   b. Noten.   c. Universitäten.
6. Das Quiz und der Test sind...
   a. Hausaufgaben.   b. Prüfungen.   c. Ergebnisse.

3 Was ist das? Label each item.

3 Suggestion Have students identify items in your own classroom. Ask students: **Ist hier eine Uhr? Wo ist die Tür?**, etc.

 **BEISPIEL** *der Bleistift*

1. ____der Stift/ der Kuli____
2. ____das Buch/das Schulbuch/das Lehrbuch/das Wörterbuch____
3. ____der Stuhl____

4. ____der Rucksack____
5. ____die Uhr____
6. ____die Tür____

4 Zuordnungen Write each word you hear in the correct category.

Orte		Personen	
1. die Schule		5. die Freundin	
2. die Mensa		6. der Lehrer	
3. das Klassenzimmer		7. die Professorin	
4. die Universität		8. der Schüler	

4 Expansion Have students give the plural form of each word.

 Practice more at **vhlcentral.com**.

Kommunikation

5 Was ist das?

In pairs, take turns pointing at items and people in your classroom and asking each other to identify them. Answers will vary.

BEISPIEL

S1: Was ist das?
S2: Das ist ein Bleistift. Wer ist das?
S1: Das ist der Lehrer.

5 Expansion Repeat the activity as a class, having students ask and answer questions about items in the classroom.

6 Im Rucksack

List six items that are in your backpack. Then, work with a partner and compare lists. Answers will vary.

In meinem (my) Rucksack ist/sind...

1. _____
2. _____
3. _____
4. _____
5. _____
6. _____

In _____s Rucksack ist/sind...

1. _____
2. _____
3. _____
4. _____
5. _____
6. _____

WERKZEUG

To say that something belongs to someone, add an **-s** to the person's name (**Marias Heft**; **Julians Buch**). Add an apostrophe if the name already ends in **-s** (**Niklas' Heft**; **Tobias' Buch**).

6 Expansion Bring in a bag filled with items such as pens, a calendar, a calculator, and so on. Pull them out one by one and ask students: **Ist das ein Bleistift oder ein Kuli? Ist das eine Uhr oder ein Taschenrechner? Ein Schulbuch oder ein Wörterbuch?** etc.

7 Ist da...?

In pairs, take turns asking each other questions about what you see in the illustration. Answers will vary.

BEISPIEL

S1: Ist da ein Papierkorb?
S2: Nein. Da ist ein Bleistift. Ist da...?

7 Partner Chat You can also assign activity 7 on the Supersite. Students work in pairs to record the activity online. The pair's recorded conversation will appear in your gradebook.

8 Ratespiel

Play Pictionary as a class. Answers will vary.

- Take turns going to the board and drawing images representing words from the lesson vocabulary.
- The person drawing may not write any letters or numbers.
- The person who correctly identifies the drawing in German gets to go next.

Aussprache und Rechtschreibung  Audio

The vowels *a*, *e*, *i*, *o*, and *u*

Each German vowel may be pronounced with either a long or a short sound. A vowel followed by **h** is always long. A double **oo**, **aa**, or **ee** also indicates a long vowel sound. In some words, long **i** is spelled **ie**.

| Fahne | wen | ihn | doof | Mut | diese |

A vowel followed by two or more consonant sounds is usually short.

| Pfanne | wenn | in | Sonne | Mutter | singst |

When the German letter **e** appears in the unstressed syllable at the end of a word, it is pronounced like the *e* in the English word *the*.

| danke | Schule | Frage | Klasse | Dinge | Vase |

In certain words, an **Umlaut** (¨) is added to the vowel **a**, **o**, or **u**, changing the pronunciation of the vowel.

| Bank | Bänke | schon | schön | Bruder | Brüder |

Suggestion To produce the **ü** sound, tell students to round their lips as if to pronounce the letter **u**, but then make the long **i** sound.

1 **Aussprechen** Practice saying these words aloud.

1. Kahn / kann
2. beten / Betten
3. Robe / Robbe
4. Buch / Butter
5. den / denn
6. Saat / satt
7. Rogen / Roggen
8. Sack / Säcke
9. Wort / Wörter
10. Stuhl / Stühle
11. Hefte
12. Tage

1 **Expansion** Tell students the meanings of any unfamiliar words.

2 **Nachsprechen** Practice saying these sentences aloud.

1. Der Mann kam ohne Kamm.
2. Wir essen Bienenstich und trinken Kaffee.
3. Am Sonntag und am Montag scheint die Sonne.
4. Das U-Boot ist unter Wasser.
5. Ich habe viele Freunde in der Schule.
6. Der Mantel mit den fünf Knöpfen ist schöner als die Mäntel mit einem Knopf.

3 **Sprichwörter** Practice reading these sayings aloud.

Sag mir, mit wem du gehst, und ich sage dir, wer du bist.[1]

Der frühe Vogel fängt den Wurm.[2]

[1] Tell me who your friends are, and I will tell you who you are.
[2] The early bird catches the worm.

Ressourcen

v Text   LM   vhlcentral
          p. 67

Fotoroman

Oh, George!  Video

George und Hans treffen (*meet*) Meline und Sabite im Biergarten.
Melines Handy klingelt...

Vorbereitung Have students review the **Nützliche Ausdrücke** before watching the video, in order to preview the episode content.

communication
cultures

NATIONAL STANDARDS

1

SABITE Wer ist es?
MELINE Lukas.
SABITE Oh, dein Freund?
MELINE Ja. Nein. Ja.

5

2

MELINE Wir haben Probleme.

KELLNERIN Bitte schön?
HANS Ein Wasser, bitte.
GEORGE Einen Kaffee und ein Stück Strudel.

3

MELINE Ich habe keinen Freund mehr.
SABITE Wie geht's dir?
MELINE Mir geht es sehr gut.

MELINE Hast du einen Freund?
SABITE Ja. Torsten. Er ist Student.
MELINE Hast du ein Bild?

6

GEORGE Sabite? Sabite, hallo.
SABITE Hallo.
HANS Hallo.
SABITE Was ist da drin?
GEORGE Lehrbücher! Wörterbuch... Hefte... Stifte... Kalender.
HANS Hast du auch einen Computer?

4

1 **Richtig oder falsch?** Indicate whether each statement is richtig or falsch.

1. George hat ein Wörterbuch. Richtig.
2. Sabite hat ein Bild von (*of*) Torsten. Richtig.
3. George will (*wants*) das Brandenburger Tor sehen (*to see*). Richtig.
4. Im Bauhaus-Museum gibt es viele Bücher. Falsch.
5. Meline telefoniert mit Lukas. Richtig.

6. Die Kellnerin hat einen Freund. Richtig.
7. Torsten ist Student. Richtig.
8. Hans hat einen Stadtplan. Richtig.
9. Die Kellnerin heißt Laura. Falsch.
10. George bestellt (*orders*) Kaffee und Steak. Falsch.

PERSONEN

 George   Hans   Meline   Sabite   Kellnerin

7

GEORGE Ich habe eine Idee. Hast du einen Stadtplan?
HANS Ja!
GEORGE Was muss ich in Berlin sehen? Das Brandenburger Tor!
HANS Checkpoint Charlie!

8

SABITE Potsdamer Platz!
GEORGE Marlene-Dietrich-Platz!
KELLNERIN Das Bode-Museum. Und das Jüdische Museum!

9

HANS Wie viele Kurse hast du belegt?
SABITE Ah, vier.
MELINE Bauhaus-Museum.
HANS Ja!
MELINE Im Bauhaus-Museum gibt es viele...
SABITE Stühle! Viele Stühle. Und Tische.

10

GEORGE Wie heißt sie?
SABITE Ähm, Leyna? Oh, George.
HANS Sie hat einen Freund?
GEORGE Ja.

Nützliche Ausdrücke

- **Prost!**
  Cheers!
- **Wer ist es?**
  Who is it?
- **Hast du ein Bild?**
  Do you have a picture?
- **Was ist da drin?**
  What's in there?
- **Hast du auch einen Computer?**
  Do you have a computer, too?
- **die Kellnerin**
  waitress
- **Bitte schön?**
  May I take your order?; May I help you?
- **das Wasser**
  water
- **der Kaffee**
  coffee
- **das Stück Strudel**
  a piece of strudel
- **Ich habe keinen Freund mehr.**
  I don't have a boyfriend anymore.
- **die Idee**
  idea
- **der Stadtplan**
  city map
- **Was muss ich in Berlin sehen?**
  What do I have to see in Berlin?
- **Ist alles in Ordnung?**
  Is everything alright?
- **Wie heißt sie?**
  What's her name?

1B.1
- **Wir haben Probleme.**
  We have problems.

1B.2
- **Hast du einen Stadtplan?**
  Do you have a city map?

1B.3
- **—Wie viele Kurse hast du?**
  —How many classes are you taking?
- **—Vier.**
  —Four.

2 **Zum Besprechen** With a partner, role-play a scene where one of you plays the waiter (**Kellner**) or waitress at a **Biergarten** and the other plays a customer ordering food. Here are some common items to order. Answers will vary.

eine Cola	ein Stück Strudel
einen Kaffee	einen Tee
einen Saft (*juice*)	ein Wasser

2 **Suggestion** This activity can also be done with groups of three or more. Have students take turns playing the roles of server and customers.

2 **Partner Chat** You can also assign activity 2 on the Supersite.

3 **Vertiefung** The characters mention several important sites and museums in Berlin. Research these and other monuments and plan a day of sightseeing in Berlin to present to the class. Mention at least three sites that interest you and include their names in German. Answers will vary.

3 **Suggestion** Preview the expression **es gibt** and encourage students to list some of the things they can see at each site.

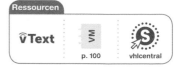

AP* **Theme:** Contemporary Life
Context: Education & Career

Die Schulzeit Reading

ALTHOUGH THE WORD AND THE concept were invented by **Friedrich Fröbel**, a teacher in 19th-century Germany, **Kindergarten** is called **Vorschule** in Germany. There are many privately-run **Kindergärten**, an equivalent of preschool.

Public school for German children starts at age six, with **Grundschule°**. For the first four years, all **Grundschüler** attend school together. But after age ten, students are streamed into three different kinds of schools, usually as recommended by their teacher.

The most academically rigorous option is **Gymnasium**. **Gymnasium** lasts eight years, and graduates need to pass difficult exit exams to earn their **Abitur°**. The "Abi" gives students access to competitive internships and a university education.

A more vocationally-oriented option is **Hauptschule**. Students typically finish **Hauptschule** at age 15 or 16. They may then attend **Berufsfachschule°**, where they can train for a variety of professions, from mechanics to physical therapy.

The third option is **Realschule**, which has stricter academic requirements than **Hauptschule**. After graduation, students may seek further schooling that will lead them into careers like banking, IT, or social work.

This three-track system has been in use for decades, but in recent years it has come under serious criticism. The **Abitur** is associated with higher social status, and more and more families push to have their children admitted into **Gymnasium**. **Realschule** still generally leads to solid employment opportunities, but there is now a stigma attached to **Hauptschule**, which makes the job search more difficult for its graduates.

In some states, there is a fourth option for secondary school students: the **Gesamtschule°**. These comprehensive schools have no entrance requirements. They offer college preparatory classes for students who perform well, general education classes for students with average performance, and remedial courses for those who need additional support. **Gesamtschulen** were introduced in 1969 with the hope of eliminating inequalities associated with the three-track system, but they have been slow to take root.

Grundschule *elementary school* **Abitur** *high school diploma* **Berufsfachschule** *vocational school* **Gesamtschule** *comprehensive school*

1 **Was fehlt?** Complete the statements.

1. ___Kindergarten___ is not part of the German public school system.
2. ___Friedrich Fröbel___ invented the word **Kindergarten**.
3. German elementary school is called ___Grundschule___.
4. Children normally begin school at age ___six___.
5. **Grundschule** lasts ___four___ years.

6. After age ten, students are streamed into three kinds of schools: **Gymnasium**, **Hauptschule**, and ___Realschule___.
7. **Gymnasium** graduates receive a diploma called the ___Abitur___.
8. Students who have earned their **Abitur** can attend ___university___.
9. After finishing ___Hauptschule___, students may attend **Berufsfachschule**.
10. The ___Gesamtschule___ offers an alternative to the three-track system.

DEUTSCH IM ALLTAG

Die Schule

die Abschlussfeier, -n	*graduation*
die Pause, -n	*recess*
der Schulleiter, -	*(male) principal*
die Schulleiterin, -nen	*(female) principal*
bestehen	*to pass a test*
durchfallen	*to flunk; to fail*
schwänzen	*to cut class*
langweilig	*boring*

DIE DEUTSCHSPRACHIGE WELT

AP* Theme: Contemporary Life   **Context:** Youth Culture

Ein süßer° Beginn

In German-speaking countries, the first day of school is a festive occasion. Excited **Erstklässler°** are presented with **Schultüten** by their parents on the morning of their first day of school. The **Schultüte** is a decorated paper cone, filled with candies, chocolates, school supplies, and other treats. With their unopened **Tüten** in hand, the **Erstklässler** set off for **Grundschule. Alles Gute für den ersten Schultag!°**

süßer *sweet* **Erstklässler** *first-graders* **Alles Gute für den ersten Schultag!** *Best wishes on your first day of school!*

Noten in Deutschland

Deutsche Noten:	1	2	3	4	5/6
US-Äquivalente:	A/A+	A-/B+	B/B-	C/D	D-/F

Suggestion Tell students that the grading systems are different in other German-speaking countries. In Switzerland 5 is the best grade.

PORTRÄT

Der Schultag
AP* Theme: Contemporary Life
Context: Education & Career

The school day in Germany typically lasts from 7:30 or 8:00 in the morning until 1:00 in the afternoon, with a 15-20 minute mid-morning break, called the **Große Pause**. Many schools do not have cafeterias, since students go home at lunch time. They then have the afternoon to do homework and participate in extracurricular activities. Students have only 6 weeks of summer vacation, but they get longer breaks during the school year, with 2 weeks off in the fall, 2 weeks for Christmas, and 2 weeks in the spring.

Die Deutschsprachige Welt Tell students that children often craft their own **Schultüten** in **Kindergarten**. Their parents then fill the **Tüten** before the first day of **Grundschule**.

TIPP

The German word for *one* is **eins**. A straight-A student is called **ein(e) Einserschüler(in)**.

🔗 IM INTERNET

Subjects: What subjects do students study at **Gymnasium**? What are **Pflichtfächer**? What are **Wahlfächer**?

Find out more at **vhlcentral.com**.

---

2 **Richtig oder falsch?** Indicate whether each statement is **richtig** or **falsch**. Correct the false statements.

1. Most German students eat lunch in their school cafeterias.
   Falsch. Many schools do not have cafeterias, since students go home at lunch time.
2. Students get a midmorning break called the **Große Pause**. **Richtig.**
3. Students get 12 weeks of vacation every summer.
   Falsch. Students have only 6 weeks of summer vacation.
4. Children in their first year of school are called **Kindergärtner**.
   Falsch. They are called **Erstklässler**.
5. The **Schultüte** is a test that elementary school students take on the first day. **Falsch.** The **Schultüte** is a cone full of treats.

3 **Die Schule: anders in Deutschland** In pairs, discuss the similarities and differences between school life in Germany or other German-speaking countries and in your country. What do you like best about each system? Why?

Suggestion Tell students that many changes to the German educational system have been proposed and/or implemented over the last decade. **Gymnasium** originally lasted nine years, but was shortened to eight, and the government is considering extending the number of years spent in elementary school and lengthening the school day.

Ressourcen

vText
vhlcentral

Strukturen

1B.1 *Haben* and the accusative case  Presentation

Startblock To describe what someone or something has, use the irregular verb **haben** with the accusative case.

Haben

haben (*to have*)			
ich **habe**	*I have*	wir **haben**	*we have*
du **hast**	*you have* (inf.)	ihr **habt**	*you have* (inf.)
Sie **haben**	*you have* (form.)	Sie **haben**	*you have* (form.)
er/sie/es **hat**	*he/she/it has*	sie **haben**	*they have*

Ich **habe** ein Buch.   Greta **hat** eine Karte.   Wir **haben** eine Frage.
*I **have** a book.*   *Greta **has** a map.*   *We **have** a question.*

The accusative case

- In **1A.3**, you learned that the function of a noun in a sentence determines its case, as well as the case of any article or adjective that modifies it. A noun that functions as a direct object is in the accusative case (**der Akkusativ**).

definite articles				
	masculine	**feminine**	**neuter**	**plural**
nominative	**der** Stuhl	**die** Tür	**das** Fenster	**die** Notizen
accusative	**den** Stuhl	**die** Tür	**das** Fenster	**die** Notizen

indefinite articles				
	masculine	**feminine**	**neuter**	**plural**
nominative	**ein** Stuhl	**eine** Tür	**ein** Fenster	**–** Notizen
accusative	**einen** Stuhl	**eine** Tür	**ein** Fenster	**–** Notizen

Der Lehrer hat **den Stift**.   Sie öffnet **die Tür**.
*The teacher has **the pen**.*   *She's opening **the door**.*

Ich kaufe **ein Bleistift**.   Wir haben hier **ein Problem**.
*I'm buying **a pencil**.*   *We have **a problem** here.*

Suggestion Give students additional examples to illustrate the use of the accusative with direct objects and the nominative with predicate nouns. Ex.: **Markus ist ein guter Freund. Sabine hat einen guten Freund**.

Suggestion Point out that in everyday speech, the final **e** is frequently dropped from the **ich** form. Ex.: **Ich hab' ein Buch.**

ACHTUNG

A direct object receives the action of a verb directly and answers the question *what?* or *whom?*

QUERVERWEIS

The accusative case is also used following certain prepositions. You will learn more about this usage in **3B.2**.

Ressourcen

v̂ Text

WB
pp. 11–12

LM
p. 68

S
vhlcentral

Jetzt sind Sie dran! **In the first column, complete the sentences using haben. In the second column, indicate whether each underlined phrase is in the Nominativ (N) or Akkusativ (A) case.**

1. Wir ___*haben*___ die Bücher.
2. Ich ___*habe*___ Fotos.
3. Herr Müller ___*hat*___ ein Haus.
4. Ihr ___*habt*___ morgen Schule.
5. Max und Julia ___*haben*___ viele Hausaufgaben.
6. Lena ___*hat*___ eine Theorie.

___N___ 7. Sie ist <u>eine gute Schülerin</u>.
___A___ 8. David hat <u>eine Frage</u>.
___A___ 9. Ich habe <u>ein Problem</u>.
___A___ 10. Du hast <u>einen Stuhl</u>.
___N___ 11. Ihr seid <u>Schüler</u>.
___A___ 12. Herr Meier trinkt <u>ein Glas Wasser</u>.

Anwendung und Kommunikation

1 Bilden Sie Sätze Write complete sentences.

 BEISPIEL   ich / haben / ein Radiergummi

Ich habe einen Radiergummi.

1. du / haben / ein Computer   Du hast einen Computer.
2. ihr / haben / ein Taschenrechner   Ihr habt einen Taschenrechner.
3. der Lehrer / haben / ein Buch   Der Lehrer hat ein Buch.
4. wir / haben / ein Problem   Wir haben ein Problem.
5. ich / haben / eine Frage   Ich habe eine Frage.
6. das Mädchen / haben / ein Freund   Das Mädchen hat einen Freund.

2 Was haben wir? Rewrite each sentence using **haben** with the subject provided.

 BEISPIEL   Das ist ein Computer. (Inge)

Inge hat einen Computer.

1. Das ist ein Rucksack. (Peter)   Peter hat einen Rucksack.
2. Das ist ein Kuli. (ich)   Ich habe einen Kuli.
3. Das ist ein Schulbuch. (ihr)   Ihr habt ein Schulbuch.
4. Das sind Fotos. (du)   Du hast Fotos.
5. Das ist ein Wörterbuch. (Erik und Nina)   Erik und Nina haben ein Wörterbuch.
6. Das ist eine Karte. (wir)   Wir haben eine Karte.

3 Was haben sie? With a partner, take turns saying what each person has.

▶ **BEISPIEL**

Patrick hat Fotos.

Patrick

1. du

Du hast Bücher.

2. die Schüler

Die Schüler/Sie haben Hefte.

3. Bettina

Bettina/Sie hat eine Uhr.

4. ich

Ich habe einen Taschenrechner.

5. du und Abdel

Du und Abdel/Ihr habt einen Rucksack.

6. wir

Wir haben einen Computer.

> **3 Virtual Chat** You can also assign activity 3 on the Supersite. Students record individual responses that appear in your gradebook.

4 Im Klassenzimmer In groups, take turns discussing what items are in your classroom and what each of you has brought to class. Answers will vary.

BEISPIEL

S1: *Was haben wir hier?*
S2: *Wir haben Stühle und Bänke.*

S1: *Was hast du?*
S2: *Ich habe ein Heft.*

> **4 Expansion** Call on individual students and have them describe what they and their group members have brought to class. Ex.: **Er hat ein Heft und einen Bleistift. Ich habe auch ein Heft und sie hat einen Kuli.**

 Practice more at **vhlcentral.com.**

1B.2

Word order  Presentation

QUERVERWEIS

You will learn how to form negative statements in **2B.3**.

Ressourcen

v̂ Text

WB
pp. 13–14

LM
p. 69

vhlcentral

Startblock By changing the order of words in a sentence, you can shift emphasis or turn a statement into a yes-or-no question.

Statements

- In German, the verb is always the second element in a statement. The first element is often the subject, but it can also be a time expression or a prepositional phrase.

1ST	2ND	3RD
Ich	**habe**	heute Abend viele Hausaufgaben.

*I **have** a lot of homework tonight.*

Heute Abend	**habe**	ich viele Hausaufgaben.

*Tonight I **have** a lot of homework.*

- A direct or indirect object may be placed in first position, but this is a less common phrasing, used to place emphasis on the object. When the subject is not the first element in the sentence, it immediately follows the verb.

1ST	2ND	3RD
Viele Hausaufgaben	**habe**	ich heute Abend.

*I **have** a lot of homework tonight.*

- You can use the conjunctions **und** (*and*), **aber** (*but*), and **oder** (*or*) to combine two statements into one sentence, without affecting the word order of either statement.

Heute Abend haben wir viele
Hausaufgaben **und** morgen haben wir Unterricht.
*Tonight we have a lot of homework **and** tomorrow we have class.*

Yes-or-no questions

- To turn a statement into a yes-or-no question, move the verb to the first position. Move the subject to the second position, since it must immediately follow the verb. Use **ja** or **nein** to respond to this type of question.

STATEMENT	QUESTION
Die Lehrerin ist nett.	▶ **Ist die Lehrerin** nett?
The teacher is nice.	*Is the teacher nice?*
Jetzt habt ihr einen Computer.	▶ **Habt ihr jetzt** einen Computer?
Now you have a computer.	*Do you have a computer now?*

Jetzt sind Sie dran! Turn each statement into a yes-or-no question.

1. Ich habe ein Buch.
   Habe ich ein Buch?/Hast du ein Buch? /Haben Sie ein Buch?

2. Ich bin Schülerin.
   Bin ich Studentin?/Bist du Studentin?/Sind Sie Studentin?

3. Das sind Mitschüler.
   Sind das Kommilitonen?

4. Der Apfel ist gut.
   Ist der Apfel gut?

5. Wir haben viele Fotos.
   Haben wir viele Fotos?/Habt ihr viele Fotos?/Haben Sie viele Fotos?

6. Tobias und Jasmin haben Rucksäcke.
   Haben Tobias und Jasmin Rucksäcke?

7. Lukas hat einen Taschenrechner.
   Hat Lukas einen Taschenrechner?

8. Ich habe ein Problem.
   Habe ich ein Problem?/Hast du ein Problem? /Haben Sie ein Problem?

Anwendung und Kommunikation

1 **Sätze** Combine each pair of sentences using **oder**, **aber**, or **und**, as indicated.

BEISPIEL Ben hat gute Noten. David hat schlechte Noten. (aber)

Ben hat gute Noten, aber David hat schlechte Noten.

1. Du hast ein Blatt Papier. Ich habe einen Bleistift. (und) Du hast ein Blatt Papier und ich habe einen Bleistift.
2. Ist das Buch gut? Ist es schlecht? (oder) Ist das Buch gut oder ist es schlecht?
3. Es geht mir ziemlich gut. Ich habe ein Problem. (aber) Es geht mir ziemlich gut, aber ich habe ein Problem.
4. Ist Ela da? Ist sie im Unterricht? (oder) Ist Ela da oder ist sie im Unterricht?
5. Wir haben heute viele Hausaufgaben. Morgen haben wir eine Prüfung. (und) Wir haben heute viele Hausaufgaben und morgen haben wir eine Prüfung
6. Ich heiße Sophia. Das ist Mia. (und) Ich heiße Sophia und das ist Mia.

2 **Noch einmal** Rewrite each sentence twice, changing the order of the underlined elements.

BEISPIEL Ich habe heute (*today*) eine Prüfung.

Heute habe ich eine Prüfung.
Eine Prüfung habe ich heute.

1. Tim hat heute Abend Deutschhausaufgaben. Heute Abend hat Tim Deutschhausaufgaben. Deutschhausaufgaben hat Tim heute Abend.
2. Max und Lisa haben ein Haus in Berlin. Ein Haus haben Max und Lisa in Berlin. In Berlin haben Max und Lisa ein Haus. Max und Lisa haben in Berlin ein Haus.
3. Wir sind jetzt im Unterricht. Jetzt sind wir im Unterricht. Im Unterricht sind wir jetzt.
4. Ich bin jetzt in Berlin. Jetzt bin ich in Berlin. In Berlin bin ich jetzt.

3 **Wer hat was?** In pairs, take turns asking and answering questions.

BEISPIEL Junge / Problem (nein / Frage)

S1: *Hat der Professor ein Problem?*
S2: *Nein, er hat eine Frage.*

1. Frau / Blatt Papier (nein / Foto) Hat die Frau ein Blatt Papier? Nein, sie hat ein Foto.
2. Emil und ich / Bleistifte (ja) Haben Emil und ich Bleistifte? Ja, ihr habt Bleistifte.
3. Lehrerin / Kalender (ja) Hat die Lehrerin (einen) Kalender? Ja, sie hat (einen) Kalender.
4. Schüler / Buch (nein / Heft) Hat der Schüler/Haben die Schüler ein Buch? Nein, er hat/sie haben ein Heft.

3 Partner Chat You can also assign activity 3 on the Supersite. Students work in pairs to record the activity online. The pair's recorded conversation will appear in your gradebook.

4 **Was ist los?** In groups, take turns asking and answering yes-or-no questions about the image. Answers will vary.

BEISPIEL

S1: *Haben die Schüler Bücher?*
S2: *Ja, sie haben Bücher.*

 Practice more at **vhlcentral.com**.

1B.3

Numbers  Presentation

Startblock As in English, numbers in German follow patterns. Memorizing the numbers from **1** to **20** will help you learn numbers **21** and above.

Sabite hat **vier** Kurse.

George ist **21** Jahre alt.

Suggestion Point out that in spoken German, **zwei** may be pronounced as **zwo** to avoid confusion with **drei**, especially in phone conversations.

Suggestion Write the telephone numbers of local businesses on the board and have students read the numbers aloud in German, first as individual digits, then as a series of two-digit numbers.

- Every number up to one million is written as a single word. Numbers from **13** to **19** follow a pattern similar to English, adding the ending **-zehn** to each single-digit number. Numbers from **21** to **99** repeat this pattern, adding **und** plus the number in the tens place to each single-digit number: [ones] + **und** + [tens].

25 = **fünf** + **und** + zwanzig ▶ **fünfund**zwanzig

ACHTUNG

Ask **Wie alt bist du?** when you want to know someone's age. Answer: **Ich bin [number]. / Ich bin [number] Jahre alt.**

numbers 0–99							
0	null	10	zehn	20	zwanzig	30	dreißig
1	eins	11	elf	21	einundzwanzig	31	einunddreißig
2	zwei	12	zwölf	22	zweiundzwanzig	40	vierzig
3	drei	13	dreizehn	23	dreiundzwanzig	45	fünfundvierzig
4	vier	14	vierzehn	24	vierundzwanzig	50	fünfzig
5	fünf	15	fünfzehn	25	fünfundzwanzig	60	sechzig
6	sechs	16	sechzehn	26	sechsundzwanzig	70	siebzig
7	sieben	17	siebzehn	27	siebenundzwanzig	80	achtzig
8	acht	18	achtzehn	28	achtundzwanzig	90	neunzig
9	neun	19	neunzehn	29	neunundzwanzig	99	neunundneunzig

Suggestion Model the German method of counting off on one's fingers, starting with the thumb and ending with the little finger.

- Note that the **s** in **eins** is dropped at the beginning of a compound word.

  41 = eins + vierzig ▶ **ein**undvierzig   **81** = eins + achtzig ▶ **ein**undachtzig

- Likewise, **sechs** and **sieben** are shortened when they precede the letter **z**.

  16 = **sech**zehn   **66** = sechsund**sech**zig
  17 = **sieb**zehn   **77** = siebenund**sieb**zig

Suggestion Tell students that in colloquial speech, the unit of currency is often omitted when stating a price. Ex.: **vier neunundneunzig**.

- In German, decimals are indicated by a comma (**Komma**), not a period (**Punkt**). When giving a unit of measurement (length, currency, etc.), say the unit instead of **Komma**. Note that units of currency are usually written after the number.

  25,4 = fünfundzwanzig **Komma** vier   **0,5** = null **Komma** fünf
  4,99 € = vier **Euro** neunundneunzig   **10,18 m** = zehn **Meter** achtzehn

QUERVERWEIS

You will learn more about interrogative words in **2A.2**.

- Use **Wie viel?** to ask *How much?* and **Wie viele?** to ask *How many?*

  Wie viel kostet das Buch?   **Wie viele** Blätter Papier habt ihr?
  How much does the book cost?   *How many pieces of paper do you have?*

numbers 100 and higher			
100	(ein)hundert	1.000	(ein)tausend
101	hunderteins	1.300	tausenddreihundert
128	hundertachtundzwanzig	5.000	fünftausend
200	zweihundert	10.000	zehntausend
300	dreihundert	50.000	fünfzigtausend
400	vierhundert	100.000	hunderttausend
500	fünfhundert	460.000	vierhundertsechzigtausend
600	sechshundert	1.000.000	eine Million
700	siebenhundert	1.050.000	eine Million fünfzigtausend
800	achthundert	7.000.000	sieben Millionen
900	neunhundert	1.000.000.000	eine Milliarde

- Note that German uses a period where English typically uses a comma to separate thousands, millions, etc.

2.320.000	1.999,99 €	5.225,00 $
2,320,000	*€1,999.99*	*$5,225.00*

- Numbers in the millions and higher are written as separate words.

2.016.000
zwei Millionen sechzehntausend

1.000.050.000
eine Milliarde fünfzigtausend

Mathematical expressions

- Use these expressions to talk about math.

mathematical expressions					
+	plus	×	mal	=	ist (gleich)
–	minus	÷	geteilt durch	%	Prozent

6 + 7 = 13
Sechs plus sieben ist dreizehn.
Six plus seven is thirteen.

8 – 2 = 6
Acht minus zwei ist gleich sechs.
Eight minus two equals six.

3 · 3 = 9
Drei mal drei ist gleich neun.
Three times three equals nine.

20 : 5 = 4
Zwanzig geteilt durch fünf ist vier.
Twenty divided by five is four.

Suggestion Have students practice reading these numbers aloud.

ACHTUNG

Note that German speakers typically use the symbol · to indicate multiplication and the symbol : to indicate division.

Jetzt sind Sie dran!   Write each number or equation in words.

1. 37
siebenunddreißig

2. 212
zweihundertzwölf

3. 49
neunundvierzig

4. 368
dreihundertachtundsechzig

5. 24
vierundzwanzig

6. 75
fünfundsiebzig

7. 1991
eintausendneunhunderteinundneunzig

8. 587
fünfhundertsiebenundachtzig

9. 16 + 15 = 31
Sechzehn plus fünfzehn ist (gleich) einunddreißig.

10. 97 – 17 = 80
Siebenundneunzig minus siebzehn ist achtzig.

11. 18 : 9 = 2
Achtzehn geteilt durch neun ist zwei.

12. 12 · 3 = 36
Zwölf mal drei ist sechsunddreißig.

Anwendung

1 **Eins, zwei, drei...** Fill in the missing number, then write the number in words.

BEISPIEL 0, 5, 10, ___15___ , 20; ___fünfzehn___

1. 2, 4, ___6___, 8, 10; ___sechs___
2. 0, 10, 20, ___30___, 40; ___dreißig___
3. 670, 671, 672, 673, ___674___; ___sechshundertvierundsiebzig___
4. 3.456, 3.457, 3.458, ___3.459___, 3.460; ___dreitausendvierhundertneunundfünfzig___
5. 35, 40, 45, 50, ___55___; ___fünfundfünfzig___
6. 1.899.996, 1.899.997, 1.899.998, 1.899.999, ___1.900.000___; ___eine Million neunhunderttausend___

2 **Wie alt bist du?** With a partner, take turns asking and saying how old each person is.

BEISPIEL Anna: 16

S1: Wie alt ist Anna?
S2: Sie ist sechzehn Jahre alt.

1. Tim: 19 Er ist neunzehn Jahre alt.
2. Sara: 11 Sie ist elf Jahre alt.
3. Herr Wolf: 73 Er ist dreiundsiebzig Jahre alt.
4. Frau Öztürk: 101 Sie ist hundertundein Jahre alt.

5. Niklas: 5 Er ist fünf Jahre alt.
6. Herr Braun: 42 Er ist zweiundvierzig Jahre alt.
7. Jasmin: 21 Sie ist einundzwanzig Jahre alt.
8. Frau Schröder: 67 Sie ist siebenundsechzig Jahre alt.

3 **Was sehen Sie?** Write how many there are of each item.

BEISPIEL

(860) Student
Da sind achthundertsechzig Studenten.

(5.937) Buch
1. ___Da sind fünftausendneunhundertsiebenunddreißig Bücher.___

(16) Mädchen
2. ___Da sind sechzehn Mädchen.___

(217) Tisch
3. Da sind zweihundertsiebzehn Tische.

(54) Auto
4. Da sind vierundfünfzig Autos.

(12) Stuhl
5. Da sind zwölf Stühle.

(4) Studentin
6. Da sind vier Studentinnen.

4 **Matheprofi** In pairs, take turns reading the equations out loud.

1. $67 + 4 = 71$
2. $16 + 28 = 44$
3. $91 - 6 = 85$
4. $45 - 7 = 38$

5. $24 : 4 = 6$
6. $989 : 43 = 23$
7. $58 \cdot 2 = 116$
8. $213 \cdot 3 = 639$

1. Siebenundsechzig plus vier ist (gleich) einundsiebzig.
2. Sechzehn plus achtundzwanzig ist (gleich) vierundvierzig.
3. Einundneunzig minus sechs ist (gleich) fünfundachtzig.
4. Fünfundvierzig minus sieben ist (gleich) achtunddreißig.
5. Vierundzwanzig geteilt durch vier ist (gleich) sechs.
6. Neunhundertneunundachtzig geteilt durch dreiundvierzig ist (gleich) dreiundzwanzig.
7. Achtundfünfzig mal zwei ist (gleich) (ein) hundertsechzehn.
8. Zweihundertdreizehn mal drei ist (gleich) sechshundertneununddreißig.

 Practice more at **vhlcentral.com**.

Kommunikatlon

5 Wie viele Einwohner hat...? In pairs, discuss the population of each city.

> **BEISPIEL** München: 1.330.440
>
> **S1:** Wie viele Einwohner (*inhabitants*) hat München?
> **S2:** München hat eine Million dreihundertdreißigtausendvierhundertvierzig Einwohner.

1. Berlin: 3.450.889   Berlin hat drei Millionen vierhundertfünfzigtausendachthundertneunundachtzig Einwohner.

2. Gelsenkirchen: 259.744   Gelsenkirchen hat zweihundertneunundfünfzigtausendsiebenhundertvierundvierzig Einwohner.

3. Hamburg: 1.783.975   Hamburg hat eine Million siebenhundertdreiundachtzigtausendneunhundertfünfundsiebzig Einwohner.

4. Dresden: 532.058   Dresden hat fünfhundertzweiunddreißigtausendachtundfünfzig Einwohner.

5. Stuttgart: 601.646   Stuttgart hat sechshunderteintausendsechshundertsechsundvierzig Einwohner.

6 Wie viel kostet...? In pairs, take turns asking about and saying the cost of each item. Answers will vary.

> **BEISPIEL**
>
> **S1:** Wie viel kostet ein Computer?
> **S2:** Er kostet eintausenddreihundertvierundzwanzig Euro siebzehn.

Auto	Apfel
Haus	Blume
Tisch	Heft
Computer	stuhl

7 Wie viel sind...? In pairs, discuss these exchange rates.

> **BEISPIEL** $120 = 83,44 €
>
> **S1:** Wie viel sind hundertzwanzig Dollar in Euro?
> **S2:** Das sind dreiundachtzig Euro vierundvierzig.

1. $450 = 312,70 €
2. $573 = 452,08 CHF (Schweizer Franken)
3. 781,45 € = 86.074,17 ¥ (Yen)
4. $1.628,50 = £985,88 (Pfund Sterling)

5. 3.816 € = £3.321,67
6. 6.487,15 CHF = $8.222,89
7. $14.005,90 = 9.733,30 €
8. £251.029 = $414.884,04

8 Ich habe mehr! In small groups, take turns exaggerating the number of items you have at home.

> **BEISPIEL**
>
> **S1:** Ich habe sieben Kulis.
> **S2:** Ich habe dreihundertfünfundneunzig Taschenrechner!
> **S3:** Und ich habe neuntausendvierundzwanzig Stifte!

1.253.687

6 Suggestion Bring in price listings from German-language web sites and have students read the prices aloud.

6 Virtual Chat You can also assign activity 6 on the Supersite.

7 Answers
1. vierhundertfünfzig Dollar/ dreihundertzwölf Euro siebzig.
2. fünfhundertdreiundsiebzig Dollar/ vierhundertzweiundfünfzig Schweizer Franken acht.
3. siebenhunderteinundachtzig Euro fünfundvierzig/sechsundachtzigtausendvierundsiebzig Yen siebzehn.
4. eintausendsechshundertachtundzwanzig Dollar fünfzig/neunhundertfünfundachtzig Pfund Sterling achtundachtzig.
5. dreitausendachthundertsechzehn Euro/dreitausenddreihunderteinundzwanzig Pfund Sterling siebenundsechzig.
6. sechstausendvierhundertsiebenundachtzig Schweizer Franken fünfzehn/achttausendzweihundertzweiundzwanzig Dollar neunundachtzig.
7. vierzehntausendfünf Dollar neunzig/neuntausendsiebenhundertdreiunddreißig Euro drcißig.
8. zweihunderteinundfünfzigtausendneunundzwanzig Pfund Sterling/vierhundertvierzehntausendachthundertvierundachtzig Dollar vier.

7 Virtual Chat You can also assign activity 7 on the Supersite.

8 Expansion Ask each student to make a list of items and quantities before beginning this activity. (Ex: **7 Kulis, 86 Rucksäcke, 98 Taschenrechner**....) As they do the activity, have students write down the numbers they hear and then compare with what their partner actually said.

Wiederholung

1 Fragespiel

Fragespiel In pairs, play a question game (**Fragespiel**) using the lesson vocabulary. Choose a person or object in the classroom. Your partner will ask yes-or-no questions to figure out the word you've chosen. Answers will vary.

BEISPIEL

S1: Bist du eine Sache?
S2: Nein.
S1: Bist du eine Person?
S2: Ja.
S1: Hast du einen Schreibtisch?
S2: Ja.
S1: Bist du ein Lehrer?
S2: Genau (*Exactly*)!

1 Suggestion Help students to select vocabulary that they can ask questions about. Circulate around the room to ensure that everyone is forming appropriate questions.

1 Partner Chat You can also assign activity 1 on the Supersite. Students work in pairs to record the activity online. The pair's recorded conversation will appear in your gradebook.

2 Mathe

Mathe Write two numbers between 1 and 100 on separate index cards. Then, in small groups, make a pile of everyone's cards, shuffle, and take turns drawing two cards from the pile. The person who draws must create a math problem using the numbers. The first person to answer the math problem correctly draws next. Answers will vary.

2 Expansion Have the whole class play this game, as a group or in teams.

BEISPIEL

S1: (*draws 55 and 5*) Fünfundfünfzig geteilt durch fünf.
S2: Fünfundfünfzig geteilt durch fünf ist elf.

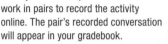

$$55 : 5 =$$

3 Ratespiel

Ratespiel In small groups, collect the items listed. One student leaves the group while the others distribute the items among themselves. The student then returns and tries to guess who has each item. Answers will vary.

BEISPIEL

S1: Hast du den Radiergummi?
S2: Nein.
S1: Hat Megan den Radiergummi?
S2: Nein, Simon hat den Radiergummi.

3 Suggestion Remind students to pay attention to articles when using nouns in the accusative case.

der Bleistift	der Radiergummi
das Buch	der Rucksack
das Heft	der Taschenrechner
der Kuli	die Uhr

4 Im Schreibwarenladen

Im Schreibwarenladen In groups of three, make a shopping list of school supplies. Then, role-play a trip to the store to buy the items you need. Present your scene to the class. Answers will vary.

BEISPIEL

S1: Guten Tag.
S2: Guten Tag. Haben Sie hier Hefte und Bleistifte?
S1: Ja, wir haben hier Hefte und Bleistifte.
S3: Wie viel kosten die Hefte?
S1: Sie kosten fünf Euro neunzig.

5 Diskutieren und kombinieren

Diskutieren und kombinieren Your instructor will give you and your partner worksheets with different pictures of a classroom. Do not look at each other's pictures. Ask and answer questions to identify seven differences (**Unterschiede**) between the two pictures. Answers will vary.

BEISPIEL

S1: Ich habe zwei Türen. Hast du auch zwei Türen?
S2: Nein. Ich habe eine Tür. Hast du einen Lehrer?
S1: Ja, ich habe auch einen Lehrer. Hast du...?

6 Arbeitsblatt

Arbeitsblatt Your instructor will give you a game board. Play the game with your partners. Count the spaces aloud in German as you play.

7 Interview

Interview Interview as many classmates as possible to find out if these statements (**Behauptungen**) apply to them. Write down their names.

BEISPIEL

S1: Hallo! Hast du einen Bleistift?
S2: Ja, ich habe einen Bleistift./
Nein, aber ich habe einen Kuli.

Behauptung	Name
1. Ich habe einen Bleistift.	Alexia
2. Ich bin 21 Jahre alt.	Markus
3. Ich habe ein Wörterbuch.	
4. Es geht mir gut.	
5. Ich bin Amerikaner(in).	
6. Ich bin Student(in).	
7. Ich habe ein Heft.	
8. Ich habe viele Hausaufgaben.	

8 Galgenmännchen

Galgenmännchen In small groups, play Hangman using the vocabulary you learned in **Lektion 1A** and **Lektion 1B**. For nouns, include the definite article. Give your partners a hint about each word. Answers will vary.

BEISPIEL

S1: Es ist eine Personeine Sache / ein Ort / ein Ausdruck (*expression*).
S2: Hat das Wort ein S?
S1: Nein. / Ja, das Wort hat zwei S.

8 **Suggestion** Tell students that letters of the alphabet are neuter.

Mein Wör | ter | buch

Throughout this book, you will be encouraged to keep a personalized dictionary. By associating words with images, examples of usage (**Gebrauch**), synonyms, and antonyms, you will create entries that are relevant to you, and you will be better able to retain these new words.

Add five words to your personalized dictionary related to the themes **Begrüßung und Abschied** and **In der Schule**.

Sehr erfreut.

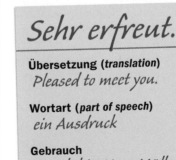

Übersetzung (*translation*)
Pleased to meet you.

Wortart (*part of speech*)
ein Ausdruck

Gebrauch
—Ich bin Herr Müller.
—Sehr erfreut.

Synonyme
Freut mich. / Angenehm. / Schön dich/Sie kennen zu lernen.

Antonyme
—

 Vocabulary Tools

AP* Theme: Global Challenges
Context: Geography

Panorama

Interactive Map

Die deutschsprachige Welt°

Länder° mit Deutsch als Amtssprache°

▶ Belgien

▶ Deutschland

▶ Italien (Region: Südtirol)

▶ Liechtenstein

▶ Luxemburg

▶ Österreich

▶ die Schweiz

Bevölkerung°

▶ **Belgien:** *10,4 Millionen Einwohner° (77.000 deutsche Muttersprachler°)*

▶ **Deutschland:** *81,1 Millionen Einwohner*

▶ **Italien:** *61,7 Millionen Einwohner (336.000 deutsche Muttersprachler)*

▶ **Liechtenstein:** *37.313 Einwohner*

▶ **Luxemburg:** *520.672 Einwohner (474.000 deutsche Muttersprachler)*

▶ **Österreich:** *8,2 Millionen Einwohner*

▶ **die Schweiz:** *8,1 Millionen Einwohner (4,8 Millionen deutsche Muttersprachler)*

QUELLE: das Haus der deutschen Sprache

Hauptstädte°

▶ **Belgien:** *Brüssel*

▶ **Deutschland:** *Berlin*

▶ **Liechtenstein:** *Vaduz*

▶ **Luxemburg:** *Luxemburg*

▶ **Österreich:** *Wien*

▶ **die Schweiz:** *Bern*

Wien, Österreichs Hauptstadt

Bern, Hauptstadt der Schweiz

Legend:
— Landesgrenzen
● Stadt
◉ Landeshauptstadt
✱ Hauptstadt

Unglaublich, aber wahr!

Belgien hat drei offizielle Sprachen°: Französisch, Niederländisch und Deutsch. Die deutschsprachige Region ist im Osten Belgiens. Circa° 76.000 Menschen leben° hier. Viele Belgier sprechen mindestens° zwei Sprachen.

AP* Theme: Families & Communities
Context: Diversity

---

deutschsprachige Welt *German-speaking world* Länder *countries*
Amtssprache *official language* Bevölkerung *population*
Einwohner *inhabitants* Muttersprachler *native speakers*
Hauptstädte *capitals* Sprachen *languages* Circa *Approximately*
leben *live* mindestens *at least*

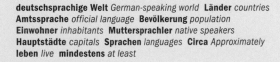

Suggestion Have students read the articles aloud.

Österreich

Die Alpen AP* Theme: Global Challenges
Context: Geography

Die Alpen sind das höchste Gebirge°
in Europa. Es ist circa 1.200 Kilometer
lang, und 29% sind in Österreich.
Deshalb heißt Österreich auch die
„Alpenrepublik". In Österreich leben
circa 4 Millionen Menschen° in den
Alpen. Das sind 50% aller Österreicher.
Der höchste Berg° in Österreich
ist der Großglockner. Er ist 3.798
Meter hoch.

Die Schweiz

Schokolade AP* Theme: Beauty & Aesthetics
Context: Cultural Perspectives

Die Schweiz ist bekannt für Banken, Uhren,
Messer° und natürlich° Schokolade. Die
bekanntesten Schokoladenfirmen sind Lindt,
Tobler, Sprüngli und Suchard. Suchard
produziert Milka Schokolade. Vor allem
die Schweizer essen Schokolade gern°.
Pro Jahr isst° jeder Schweizer 11,7
Kilogramm Schokolade. Niemand° auf
der Welt isst mehr Schokolade als° die
Schweizer. In Deutschland isst man 11,4
Kilogramm Schokolade pro Person,
in Österreich 7,9, und in den USA nur
5,2 Kilogramm.

Geschichte

Die Hanse

Die Hanse Point out that the
Hanse was the precursor to the
European Union and one of the
first international trade unions.

Die Deutsche Hanse ist eine Union
von Kaufleuten°. Sie existiert zwischen Mitte
des 12. Jahrhunderts° und Mitte des 17.
Jahrhunderts. Bis zu 200 Städte im
nördlichen Europa sind in der Union, wie
zum Beispiel Zuidersee (heutiges° Holland),
Hamburg, Bremen und Lübeck (heutiges
Deutschland), Stockholm (heutiges
Schweden), Danzig (heutiges Polen) und Riga
(heutiges Lettland°). Diese Städte liegen°
vor allem an der Nordsee und der Ostsee°.
AP* Theme: Global Challenges
Context: Economic Issues

Die Berliner Mauer

Deutschland

Die Berliner Mauer°

Die Berliner Mauer
Tell students that 3,40
Meter is read out loud
as **drei Meter vierzig**.

Vom 13. August 1961 bis 9. November
1989 ist die Berliner Mauer eine Grenze°
zwischen° Ost- und Westberlin. Die
Mauer umgibt° ganz Westberlin und
kreiert eine Insel°. Sie ist das Symbol des
Kalten Krieges°. Die Mauer ist 156,4
Kilometer lang. Sie ist zwischen 3,40 Meter
und 4,20 Meter hoch. Rund um Westberlin
stehen 302 Beobachtungstürme°.
AP* Theme: Global Challenges
Context: Political Issues

höchste Gebirge highest mountain range **Menschen** people **Berg** mountain **Mauer** Wall **Grenze** border
zwischen between **umgibt** surrounds **kreiert eine Insel** creates an island **des Kalten Krieges** of the Cold War
Beobachtungstürme watchtowers **Messer** knives **natürlich** of course **essen... gern** like to eat **isst** eats
Niemand Nobody **mehr... als** more... than **von Kaufleuten** of merchants **des 12. Jahrhunderts** of the 12th century
heutiges present-day **Lettland** Latvia **liegen** are located **Ostsee** Baltic Sea
Die Berliner Mauer Tell students that the dates **13. August** and **9. November** are read out loud as **der dreizehnte**
August and **der neunte November**. Explain that students will learn more about reading and writing dates in **2A.3**.

IM INTERNET

1. Machen Sie eine Liste mit den
   wichtigsten (*most important*)
   Städten in Deutschland, Österreich
   und der Schweiz.

2. Der 9. November 1989 ist das Ende
   der Berliner Mauer. Suchen Sie (*Look
   for*) Informationen über diesen Tag.

Find out more at **vhlcentral.com**.

Was haben Sie gelernt? Complete the statements.

1. Belgien hat ____drei____ offizielle Sprachen.

2. Die deutschsprachige Region ist im ____Osten____ Belgiens.

3. Ein anderer (*other*) Name für Österreich ist die ____Alpenrepublik____

4. Der ____Großglockner____ ist der höchste Berg in Österreich.

5. Die Berliner Mauer existiert von 1961 bis ____1989____ .

6. Die Berliner Mauer ist 156,4 ____Kilometer____ lang.

7. Die Schweizer Firma Suchard produziert ____Milka____ Schokolade.

8. Jeder ____Schweizer____ isst 11,7 Kilogramm Schokolade pro Jahr.

9. Die Hanse existiert im ____nördlichen____ Europa.

10. Bis zu ____200____ Städte sind in der Hanse.

 Practice more at **vhlcentral.com**.

Lesen  Audio: Reading

Vor dem Lesen
AP* Theme: Science & Technology
Context: Personal Technologies

Strategien

Recognizing cognates

Cognates are words in two or more languages that are similar in meaning and in spelling. Look for cognates to increase your comprehension when you read in German. However, watch out for false cognates. For example, you've already learned that in German, **Note** means *grade*, not *note*. Likewise, **bald** means *soon*, not *bald*, and **fast** means *almost*, not *fast*. Can you guess the meaning of these German words?

das Café	das Programm
der Doktor	das Restaurant
das Hotel	der Sommer
der Juli	das Telefon
das Museum	das Theater

Untersuchen Sie den Text

Look at this text. What kind of information does it present? Where do you usually find such information? Can you guess what this is?

Suchen Sie verwandte Wörter

Read the list of cognates in **Strategien** again. How many of them can you find in the reading? Do you see any additional cognates? Can you guess their English equivalents?

Raten Sie die Bedeutung

Besides using cognates and words you already know, you can also use context to guess the meaning of unfamiliar words. Find the following words in the reading and try to figure out what they mean. Compare your answers with a classmate's.

ägyptisch	Platz
Abakus	Straße

Suggestion
Point out that in German, the digits in phone numbers are listed in pairs. Have students practice reading the phone numbers for these listings out loud.

Adressbuch

Ägyptisches Museum

✉ **Residenzstraße 1**　📱 (089) 29 85 46
80333 München

Christian Hunner

✉ **Pfarrstraße 16**　📱 (089) 2 10 28 84
80667 München

Sparda-Bank

✉ **Arnulfstraße 15**　📱 (089) 5 51 42 – 4 00
80335 München

Heideck Apotheke°

✉ **Heideckstraße 31**　📱 (089) 1 57 52 52
80637 München

Il Galeone Ristorante Pizzeria

✉ **Hornsteinstraße 18**　📱 (089) 94 46 47 03
81679 München

Andreas Spitzauer

✉ **Appenzeller Straße 95**　📱 (089) 75 67 19
81475 München

Suggestion Point out to students that in German addresses, the house number follows the street name. Also, the state, or **Land**, is not included, and the postal code precedes the city.

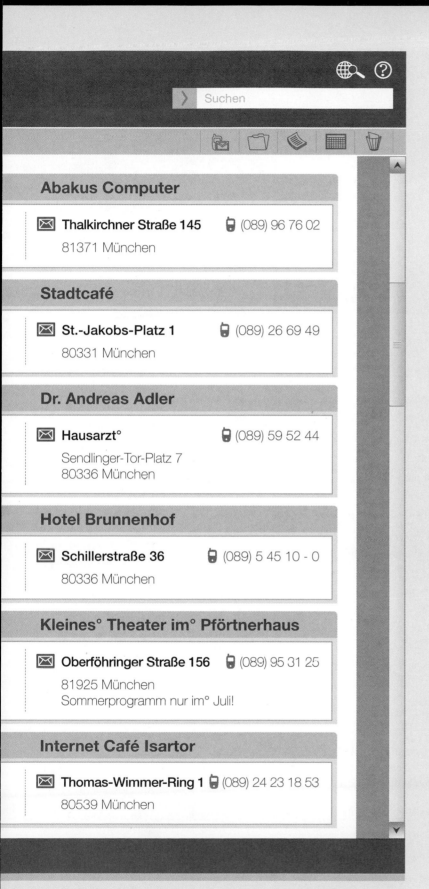

Abakus Computer

📧 Thalkirchner Straße 145   📱 (089) 96 76 02
81371 München

Stadtcafé

📧 St.-Jakobs-Platz 1   📱 (089) 26 69 49
80331 München

Dr. Andreas Adler

📧 Hausarzt°   📱 (089) 59 52 44
Sendlinger-Tor-Platz 7
80336 München

Hotel Brunnenhof

📧 Schillerstraße 36   📱 (089) 5 45 10 - 0
80336 München

Kleines° Theater im° Pförtnerhaus

📧 Oberföhringer Straße 156   📱 (089) 95 31 25
81925 München
Sommerprogramm nur im° Juli!

Internet Café Isartor

📧 Thomas-Wimmer-Ring 1   📱 (089) 24 23 18 53
80539 München

Nach dem Lesen

Wohin gehen sie? Say where each of these people should go, based on the clues.

BEISPIEL Lena loves to eat pasta but hates to cook.
Il Galeone Ristorante Pizzeria

1. Frau Scholz needs to reserve some hotel rooms.
   Hotel Brunnenhof

2. Christiane's computer is broken.
   Abakus Computer

3. Herr Meier thinks he has the flu.
   Dr. Adler/Heideck Apotheke/Hausarzt

4. Nina would like to see some ancient Egyptian art.
   Ägyptisches Museum

5. Herr and Frau Hansel want to go somewhere for coffee or tea.
   Stadtcafé/Internet Café Isartor

6. Andrea is meeting some friends for Italian food.
   Il Galeone Ristorante Pizzeria

7. Frau Müller needs to buy some aspirin for her daughter.
   Heideck Apotheke

8. Thomas wants to take his girlfriend to a play.
   Kleines Theater im Pförtnerhaus

9. Herr Trüb needs to deposit his paycheck.
   Sparda-Bank

10. Sebastian's computer is broken, but he needs to send an e-mail.
    Internet Café Isartor/Abakus Computer

Unsere Einträge Select three listings from the reading and use them as models to create similar listings in German that advertise places or services in your area.

BEISPIEL

*Stonydale Bank
Hunter Straße 206
50555 Stonydale
Tel. (555) 337-0665*

Suggestion You may want to have students complete this activity in pairs.

Apotheke *pharmacy* Hausarzt *family physician* Kleines *Small* im *in (the)* nur im *only in (the)*

Hören

Strategien

Listening for words you know

You can get the gist of a conversation by listening for words and phrases you already know.

 To help you practice this strategy, listen to these statements and make a list of the words you have already learned.

_____   _____

_____   _____

Vorbereitung

Where are the people in the photograph? What are they doing? Do you think they know each other? Why or why not? What do you think they are talking about?

 ## Zuhören

 As you listen, check the words you associate with Tanja and those you associate with Rainer.

Tanja	Rainer
✓ der Taschenrechner	___ der Radiergummi
___ der Computer	✓ die Hausaufgaben
✓ das Blatt Papier	___ das Heft
✓ zwei Bleistifte	✓ das Problem
___ die Prüfung	___ die Karte

Verständnis

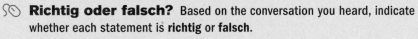 **Richtig oder falsch?** Based on the conversation you heard, indicate whether each statement is **richtig** or **falsch**.

1. Rainer ist Deutschlehrer.
   Falsch.
   _____

2. Tanja geht es gut.
   Richtig.
   _____

3. Rainer braucht (*needs*) einen Taschenrechner.
   Richtig.
   _____

4. Tanja hat ein Problem mit den Hausaufgaben.
   Falsch.
   _____

5. Rainer hat einen Bleistift für Tanja.
   Falsch.
   _____

6. Tanja hat ein Blatt Papier für Rainer.
   Richtig.
   _____

7. Tanja hat zwei Bleistifte.
   Richtig.
   _____

8. Rainer hilft (*helps*) Tanja bei den Hausaufgaben.
   Falsch.
   _____

 Stellen Sie sich vor! Introduce yourself in German to a classmate you do not know well.

- Greet your partner.
- Ask his or her name.
- Ask how he or she is doing.
- Introduce your partner to another student.
- Say good-bye.

Suggestion Students often gravitate towards other students they already know. Make sure to direct students to new partners.

Partner Chat You can also assign this activity on the Supersite. Students work in pairs to record the activity online. The pair's recorded conversation will appear in your gradebook.

Schreiben

Strategien

Writing in German

Writing can take many forms and serve many functions. You might write an e-mail to get in touch with someone, a blog entry to share your feelings or opinions, or an essay to persuade others to accept a point of view. Good writing requires time, thought, effort, and a lot of practice. Here are some tips to help you write more effectively in German.

DO

- Try to write your ideas in German.
- Decide what the purpose of your writing will be.
- Make an outline of your ideas.
- Use the grammar and vocabulary that you know.
- Use your textbook for examples of punctuation, style conventions, and expressions in German.
- Use your imagination and creativity to make your writing interesting.
- Put yourself in your reader's place to determine if your writing is interesting.

DON'T

- Don't translate your ideas from English to German.
- Don't simply repeat what is in the textbook or on a Web page.
- Don't use an online translator.
- Don't use a bilingual dictionary until you have learned how to use it effectively.

Strategien Emphasize the importance of outlining ideas in German, instead of translating from English. Encourage students to use the vocabulary and grammar they already know to complete this **Thema**.

Thema

✍ Machen Sie eine Liste

A group of German-speaking students will be spending a year at your school. Put together a list of people and places that might be useful or interesting to them. Your list should include:

- Your name, address, phone number(s), and e-mail address
- The names of two or three other students in your German class, their addresses, phone numbers, and e-mail addresses
- Your German instructor's name, office phone number, and e-mail address
- The names, addresses, and phone numbers of three places near your school where students like to go (a bookstore, a café or restaurant, a movie theater, etc.)

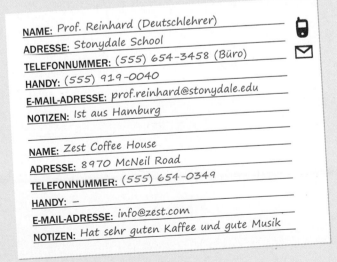

NAME: Prof. Reinhard (Deutschlehrer)
ADRESSE: Stonydale School
TELEFONNUMMER: (555) 654-3458 (Büro)
HANDY: (555) 919-0040
E-MAIL-ADRESSE: prof.reinhard@stonydale.edu
NOTIZEN: Ist aus Hamburg

NAME: Zest Coffee House
ADRESSE: 8970 McNeil Road
TELEFONNUMMER: (555) 654-0349
HANDY: —
E-MAIL-ADRESSE: info@zest.com
NOTIZEN: Hat sehr guten Kaffee und gute Musik

 Vocabulary Tools

Lektion 1A

Begrüßung und Abschied

Hallo./Guten Tag. *Hello.*
Guten Morgen. *Good morning.*
Guten Abend. *Good evening.*
Gute Nacht. *Good night.*
Bis bald./Bis gleich. *See you soon.*
Bis dann./Bis später. *See you later.*
Bis morgen. *See you tomorrow.*
Auf Wiedersehen. *Good-bye.*
Schönen Tag noch! *Have a nice day!*
Tschüss. *Bye.*
Alles klar? *Is everything OK?*
Wie geht's (dir)? *How are you? (inf.)*
Wie geht es Ihnen? *How are you? (form.)*
Prima. *Great.*
Sehr gut. *Very well.*
Ziemlich gut. *Fine.*
Und dir/Ihnen? *And you?*
Mir auch. *Me, too.*
Es geht. *So-so.*
(Nicht) schlecht. *(Not) bad.*
Mir geht's (sehr) gut. *I'm (very) well.*
Mir geht's nicht (so) gut. *I'm not
    (so) well.*

sich vorstellen

Wie heißt du? *What is your name?
    (inf.)*
Wie heißen Sie? *What is your name?
    (form.)*
Und du/Sie? *And you? (inf./form.)*
Das ist.../Das sind... *This is.../These
    are...*
Ich heiße... *My name is...*
Freut mich./Angenehm. *Pleased to
    meet you.*
Schön dich/Sie kennen zu
    lernen. *Nice to meet you. (inf./form.)*

Personen

die Frau, -en *woman*
der Freund, -e / die Freundin,
    -nen *friend*
der Junge, -n *boy*
das Mädchen, - *girl*
der Mann, ⁼er *man*
Herr *Mr.*
Frau *Mrs.; Ms.*

Höflichkeiten

Danke. *Thank you.*
Vielen Dank. *Thank you very much.*
Bitte. *Please./You're welcome.*
Gern geschehen. *My pleasure.*
Entschuldigung. *Excuse me.*
Entschuldigen Sie. *Excuse me. (form.)*
Es tut mir leid. *I'm sorry.*
ja *yes*
nein *no*

Orte

wo? *where?*
hier *here*
da / dort *there*

Nouns and articles *See pp. 10–11.*
Compound nouns *See p. 11.*
Plurals *See p. 14.*
Subject pronouns *See p. 16.*
sein *See p. 17.*
Nominative articles *See p. 17.*

Lektion 1B

im Unterricht

das Blatt Papier, (*pl.* Blätter
    Papier) *sheet of paper*
der Bleistift, -e *pencil*
das Buch, ⁼er *book*
der Computer, - *computer*
das Ergebnis, -se *result; score*
das Fenster, - *window*
das Foto, -s *photo*
die Frage, -n *question*
die Hausaufgabe, -n *homework*
das Heft, -e *notebook*
der Kalender, - *calendar*
die Karte, -n *map*
die Klasse, -n *class*
das Klassenzimmer, - *classroom*
der Kuli, -s *ball-point pen*
das Lehrbuch, ⁼er *(university) textbook*
die Note, -n *grade (on an assignment)*
die Notiz, -en *note*
der Papierkorb, ⁼e *wastebasket*
das Problem, -e *problem*
die Prüfung, -en *test; exam*
der Radiergummi, -s *eraser*
der Rucksack, ⁼e *backpack*
der Schreibtisch, -e *desk*
die Sache, -n *thing*
das Schulbuch, ⁼er *(K–12) textbook*
der Stift, -e *pen*
der Stuhl, ⁼e *chair*
die Stunde, -n *lesson*
die Tafel, -n *(black/white) board*
der Taschenrechner, - *calculator*
der Tisch, -e *table; desk*
die Tür, -en *door*
die Uhr, -en *clock*
das Wörterbuch, ⁼er *dictionary*
das Zeugnis, -se *report card;
    grade report*
Da ist/sind... *There is/are...*
Ist/Sind...hier? *Is/Are there... here?*
Hier ist/sind... *Here is/are...*
Was ist das? *What is that?*

Orte

die Schule, -n *school*
die Universität, -en *university, college*
die Bibliothek, -en *library*
die Mensa, Mensen *(university)
    cafeteria*

Personen

der Klassenkamerad, -en /die
    Klassenkameradin, -nen *(K–12)
    classmate*
der Kommilitone, -n / die
    Kommilitonin, -nen *(university)
    classmate*
der Lehrer, - / die Lehrerin,
    -nen *teacher*
der Professor, -en / die Professorin,
    -nen *professor*
der Schüler, - / die Schülerin,
    -nen *(K–12) student*
der Student, -en / die Studentin,
    -nen *(university) student*
Wer ist das? *Who is it?*

---

haben *See p. 30.*
Accusative articles *See p. 30.*
Yes-or-no questions *See p. 32.*
Numbers and math expressions
    See pp. 34–35

Schule und Studium

LEKTION 2A

Kontext Seite 48-51
- An der Universität
- Consonant sounds

Fotoroman Seite 52-53
- Checkpoint Charlie

Kultur Seite 54-55
- Uni-Zeit, Büffel-Zeit

Strukturen Seite 56-67
- **2A.1** Regular verbs
- **2A.2** Interrogative words
- **2A.3** Talking about time and dates
- Wiederholung
- Zapping

LEKTION 2B

Kontext Seite 68-71
- Sport und Freizeit
- Diphthongs: **au**, **ei/ai**, **eu/äu**

Fotoroman Seite 72-73
- Ein Picknick im Park

Kultur Seite 74-75
- Skifahren im Blut

Strukturen Seite 76-87
- **2B.1** Stem-changing verbs
- **2B.2** Present tense used as future
- **2B.3** Negation
- Wiederholung

WEITER GEHT'S

Seite 88-94
Panorama: Berlin
Lesen: Read a brochure for a university program.
Hören: Listen to a conversation about schedules.
Schreiben: Write a description of yourself.
Kapitel 2 Wortschatz

Suggestion Ask students who the people in the photo are, where they are, and what they are doing.

Teaching Tip Look for icons indicating activities that address the modes of communication. Follow this key:

→♙←	Interpretive communication
←♙→	Presentational communication
♙↔♙	Interpersonal communication

Communicative Goals

You will learn how to:

- talk about classes
- ask questions
- tell time

Tell students that **an der Universität** means *at the university*. Point out that **der** is a feminine article in the dative case, and that the dative is used in certain phrases describing locations, including the expressions **in der Schule** (*at school*) and **im Unterricht** (*in class*) from **1B Kontext**. They will learn more about the dative case in **Lektion 4B**.

An der Universität

Vocabulary Tools

AP* Theme: Contemporary Life
Context: Education & Career

Suggestion Explain to students that the **Abschlusszeugnis** is a document similar to a transcript, itemizing the course credits required to obtain a degree, including grades and GPA.

(die) Biologie

(die) Architektur

Ich studiere Physik (*f.*) und Chemie (*f.*).

Was studierst du?

(die) Kunst

(die) Mathematik

(die) Informatik

Wortschatz

das Studium	*studies*
der Abschluss, ⁻e/ das Diplom, -e	*degree*
das Abschlusszeugnis, -se/ das Diplom, -e	*diploma*
der Dozent, -en / die Dozentin, -nen	*college/university instructor*
das Fach, ⁻er	*subject*
das Seminar, -e	*seminar*
das Stipendium, -en	*scholarship*
die Veranstaltung, -en	*class; course*
die Vorlesung, -en	*lecture*
belegen	*to take (a class)*
gehen	*to go*
lernen	*to study; to learn*
studieren	*to study; to major in*
Orte	***places***
das Café, -s	*café*
der Hörsaal, Hörsäle	*lecture hall*
der Seminarraum, -räume	*college classroom*
die Sporthalle, -n	*gym*
zum Beschreiben	***to describe***
einfach	*easy*
interessant	*interesting*
langweilig	*boring*
nützlich / nutzlos	*useful / useless*
schwierig	*difficult*
der Stundenplan	***schedule***
der Montag, -e	*Monday*
der Dienstag, -e	*Tuesday*
der Mittwoch, -e	*Wednesday*
der Donnerstag, -e	*Thursday*
der Freitag, -e	*Friday*
der Samstag, -e	*Saturday*
der Sonntag, -e	*Sunday*
die Stunde, -n	*hour*
die Woche, -n	*week*
das Wochenende, -n	*weekend*
die Zeit, -en	*time*
montags/dienstags/ mittwochs	*on Mondays/Tuesdays/ Wednesdays*
morgens	*in the morning*
nachmittags	*in the afternoon*
abends	*in the evening*

Suggestion Explain that a **Diplom** is one of the degrees awarded by universities, in addition to others such as the **Magister** and the **Staatsexamen**.

ACHTUNG

Don't use an article when talking about a school subject or sport, or identifying someone's profession.

Julian studiert Psychologie.
Julian is studying psychology.

Anna spielt Basketball.
Anna plays basketball.

Herr Fischer ist Pilot.
Mr. Fischer is a pilot.

Ressourcen

v̂Text   WB pp. 17–18   LM p. 71   vhlcentral

(die) Psychologie

(die) Fremdsprachen (f., pl.)

(die) Wirtschaft

(die) Geschichte

(die) Naturwissenschaften (f., pl.)

Anwendung

1 **Was passt zusammen?** Match related words in the two columns.

_f_ 1. der Computer	a. die Fremdsprache
_c_ 2. die Vorlesung	b. die Sporthalle
_d_ 3. die Biologie	c. der Hörsaal
_e_ 4. das Diplom	d. die Naturwissenschaft
_h_ 5. Montag, Dienstag, Mittwoch...	e. der Abschluss
_a_ 6. Deutsch	f. die Informatik
_g_ 7. Sigmund Freud	g. die Psychologie
_b_ 8. der Basketball	h. die Woche

2 **Das Unileben** Listen to the conversation between Hannah and Mehmet and indicate which classes each of them is taking this semester.

Veranstaltungen	Mehmet	Hannah
Mathematik	X	
Physik	X	
Chemie		
Geschichte	X	X
Literatur	X	X
Kunst	X	
Psychologie		X
Medizin		X
Informatik		

3 **Was fehlt?** Complete the sentences. Use each word once.

abends	Naturwissenschaften
Dozentin	Seminarraum
Fremdsprachen	Stipendium
Hörsaal	Wirtschaft

1. Die Vorlesung von Professor Huber ist im _____Hörsaal_____ C.
2. Chemie, Physik und Biologie sind _____Naturwissenschaften_____.
3. Frau Klein ist _____Dozentin_____ an der Uni.
4. Für ein Studium in _____Wirtschaft/Naturwissenschaften_____ ist Mathematik nützlich.
5. Spanisch, Italienisch und Chinesisch sind _____Fremdsprachen_____.
6. Wir haben eine Veranstaltung in diesem (*this*) _____Seminarraum_____.
7. Eva hat ein _____Stipendium_____ und studiert in England.
8. Morgens und nachmittags gehen die Studenten in Seminare und Vorlesungen, und _____abends_____ gehen sie in die Bibliothek.

Kommunikation

NATIONAL communication STANDARDS

4 **Auf dem Campus** Write a caption for each picture. Complete the sentences to say what each person is studying and add one sentence giving your opinion of each course. In pairs, take turns reading your sentences out of order. Your partner must decide which picture each sentence refers to. Sample answers are provided.

4 **Suggestion** Before students do this activity, you may want to have them preview the conjugation of **studieren**, taught in **2A.1**. Call on individual students and ask: **Was studierst du?**

▶ **BEISPIEL**

Max studiert _Informatik_.
Informatik ist schwierig.

1. Daniela studiert _Spanisch_.
Spanisch ist nützlich.

Freud, österreichischer Psychologe...

2. Björn studiert _Psychologie_.
Psychologie ist einfach.

3. Anna studiert _Chemie_.
Chemie ist nutzlos.

4. Mia und ich studieren _Architektur_.
Architektur ist interessant.

---

5 **Ihr Studium** Indicate whether each statement is **richtig** or **falsch**, in your opinion. Then, compare your answers with a classmate's. Answers will vary.

5 **Virtual Chat** You can also assign activity 5 on the Supersite.

BEISPIEL

S1: Chemie ist nützlich. Richtig oder falsch?
S2: Falsch. Chemie ist nutzlos.

	richtig	falsch
1. Mathematik ist schwierig.	☐	☐
2. Fremdsprachen sind nützlich.	☐	☐
3. Literatur ist interessant.	☐	☐
4. Ein Abschluss in Psychologie ist nutzlos.	☐	☐
5. Prüfungen in Geschichte sind einfach.	☐	☐
6. Ein Wirtschaftsstudium ist langweilig.	☐	☐

---

6 **Arbeitsblatt** Your instructor will give you a worksheet. Keep a record of your classmates' answers to share with the class.

BEISPIEL

S1: Ist Mathematik einfach oder schwierig?
S2: Mathematik ist schwierig, aber nützlich.

7 **Diskutieren und kombinieren** Your instructor will give you and a partner different worksheets. Each worksheet includes part of Sarah's weekly schedule. In pairs, take turns asking each other questions to fill in the missing information and complete the schedule.

BEISPIEL

S1: Hat Sarah montags Chemie?
S2: Nein, sie hat mittwochs Chemie.
S1: Hat sie montags Geschichte?
S2: Ja, sie hat montagnachmittags Geschichte.
S1: Hat sie...?

5 **Expansion** Read the statements out loud and have students vote on whether each is **richtig** or **falsch**. Then have a class discussion about the results of the poll.

Aussprache und Rechtschreibung

 Audio

Consonant sounds

The German letter **g** has three different pronunciations. At the end of a syllable or before a **t**, it is pronounced like the *k* in the English word *keep*. In the suffix **-ig**, the **g** is pronounced like the German **ch**. Otherwise, **g** is pronounced like the *g* in the English word *garden*.

Tag	belegt	schwierig	gehen	fragen

The German letter **j** is pronounced very similarly to the letter *y* in the English word *young*. However, in a small number of loanwords from other languages, **j** may be pronounced like the *j* in *job* or the *g* in *mirage*.

jung	Januar	ja	jobben	Journal

The German letter **v** is pronounced like the *f* in the English word *fable*. In a few loanwords from other languages, **v** is pronounced like the *v* in the English word *vase*.

vier	Vorlesung	Vase	Universität	Volleyball

The German letter **w** is pronounced like the *v* in the English word *vote*.

wissen	Mittwoch	Wirtschaft	Wort	Schwester

Although most German consonants sound very similar to their English counterparts, there are five letters that represent different sounds than they do in English: **g, j, v, w,** and initial **c,** which will be discussed in **Vol. 2, 2B.**

Suggestion Tell students that the pronunciation of the final **-ig** sound has several regional variations.

Suggestion Have students look at the sample words and sentences on this page to identify cognates and words they already know. Tell students the meanings of any unfamiliar words or phrases.

1 **Aussprechen** Practice saying these words aloud.

1. Garten
2. Essig
3. Weg
4. Jahr
5. Journalist
6. joggen
7. Vater
8. verstehen
9. Violine
10. Wasser
11. zwischen
12. weil

2 **Nachsprechen** Practice saying these sentences aloud.

1. Wir wollen wissen, wie wir das wissen sollen.
2. In vier Wochen wird Veronikas Vater wieder in seiner Villa wohnen.
3. Gestern war Gregors zwanzigster Geburtstag.
4. Jeden Tag soll ich Gemüse und Grünzeug wie Salat essen.
5. Meine Schwester studiert Jura an der Universität Jena.
6. Viele Studenten jobben, um das Studium zu finanzieren.

3 **Sprichwörter** Practice reading these sayings aloud.

Was ich nicht weiß, macht mich nicht heiß.[2]

Es ist nicht alles Gold, was glänzt.[1]

[1] All that glitters is not gold.

[2] Ignorance is bliss. (lit. *What I don't know, doesn't bother me.*)

Ressourcen

v̂Text · LM p. 72 · vhlcentral

Checkpoint Charlie Video

George und Hans reden über (*talk about*) das Studium und über
Meline und Sabite. Ist Hans in Sabite verliebt (*in love*)?

Vorbereitung Have students look at scene 7 and try
to guess what Hans is reacting to. After they have
watched the video, have them review their predictions.

GEORGE Woher kommst du?
HANS Ich komme aus Straubing. Das ist
in Bayern.
GEORGE Wie viele Menschen leben dort?
HANS Hmm... etwa 100.000.

HANS Woher kommst du?
GEORGE Milwaukee, Wisconsin.
HANS Wie viel Uhr ist es dort?
GEORGE Wie viel Uhr ist es hier?
HANS Es ist Viertel vor zwei.
GEORGE Der Zeitunterschied ist sieben
Stunden. Also Viertel vor sieben morgens.

HANS Alles in Ordnung?
GEORGE Ich studiere Architektur, belege
Kurse in Städtebau, Physik, Mathematik
und Philosophie!

HANS Und du belegst einen Deutschkurs,
nicht wahr? Studieren ist nicht leicht.
George, du bist ein Mitbewohner und Freund.
Ich helfe dir.
GEORGE Wann?
HANS Morgens. Um 5.00 Uhr!

GEORGE Hey! Wir sind da!
HANS Check...
GEORGE ...point Charlie.

GEORGE Sabite kommt aus Prenzlauer
Berg. Und Meline?
HANS Was ist mit Meline?
GEORGE Woher kommt sie?
HANS Wien.

1 **Wer ist das?** Which character does each statement describe: George,
Meline, Sabite, or Hans?

1. _George_ hält ein Referat über Architektur und Kunst.
2. _Meline_ kommt aus Wien.
3. _George_ belegt einen Deutschkurs.
4. _Hans_ kommt aus Straubing.
5. _George_ studiert Architektur.

6. _George_ ist Hans' Mitbewohner und Freund.
7. _Sabite_ liest Bücher über Kunst und Mode.
8. _Sabite_ kommt aus Prenzlauer Berg.
9. _George_ kommt aus Milwaukee.
10. _Hans_ hilft (*helps*) George morgens um 5.00 Uhr.

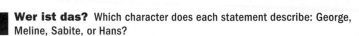

PERSONEN

George   Hans

HANS Sabite ist ganz anders. Sie liest Bücher über Kunst und Mode.
GEORGE Mode ist nutzlos. Ich halte am 20. Oktober ein Referat über Architektur und Kunst in Berlin. Sabite hilft mir.
HANS Was?
GEORGE Sabite studiert Kunst. Ich halte bald das Referat. Sie hilft mir.

GEORGE Alles in Ordnung, Hans?
HANS Ja, alles klar. Lernst du Philosophie mit Meline?
GEORGE Wo liegt das Problem?
HANS Was?
GEORGE Hans, findest du Sabite...

HANS Sabite ist nur eine Freundin.
GEORGE Okay.
HANS Also, ähm... hat Sabite einen Freund? Nein?
GEORGE Ich glaube nicht, dass sie einen hat.

HANS Du und Sabite, ihr seid nicht...?
GEORGE Nein!
HANS Okay.
GEORGE Okay.

Nützliche Ausdrücke

- **etwa**
  about
- **Wie viel Uhr ist es dort?**
  What time is it there?
- **der Zeitunterschied**
  time difference
- **Und du belegst einen Deutschkurs, nicht wahr?**
  And you're taking a German class, aren't you?
- **Ich helfe dir.**
  I'll help you.
- **Was ist mit Meline?**
  What's with Meline?
- **ein Referat halten**
  to give a presentation
- **Alles klar!**
  All right!
- **Wo liegt das Problem?**
  Where's the problem?
- **Sabite ist nur eine Freundin.**
  Sabite's just a friend.
- **Ich glaube nicht, dass sie einen hat.**
  I don't think she has one.

2A.1
- **Sabite studiert Kunst.**
  Sabite is studying art.

2A.2
- **Woher kommst du?**
  Where are you from?

2A.3
- **Es ist Viertel vor zwei.**
  It's a quarter to two.

Zum Besprechen In this episode, the characters talk about their classes. With a partner, discuss your classes and schedule. Mention what you are studying, how many courses you are taking, and which courses you have in the morning, afternoon, or evenings.
Answers will vary.

BEISPIEL

S1: *Welche Faecher hast du?*
S2: *Ich habe Fremdsprachen und Geschichte. Und du?*

3 **Vertiefung** George and Hans visit Checkpoint Charlie on their walk in Berlin. Find out more about this well-known landmark. What is its significance? What streets are nearby? What does "Charlie" refer to?
Sample answers: It was the main crossing point of the Berlin Wall; it is located at the junction of Friedrichstraße, Zimmerstraße, and Mauerstraße; "Charlie" comes from the letter C in the NATO phonetic alphabet.

2 **Partner Chat** You can also assign activity 2 on the Supersite.

Ressourcen

 v̂Text   VM p. 101   vhlcentral

AP* **Theme:** Contemporary Life
Context: Education & Career

NATIONAL
connections
cultures
STANDARDS

Uni-Zeit, Büffel-Zeit° Ⓢ Reading

HISTORICALLY, UNIVERSITY EDUCATION in Germany has been government-funded and free for all students. In the past few decades, some states introduced modest tuition fees—usually 500 Euros per semester. However, the fees proved so unpopular that they have since been abolished. As of October 2014, all public universities are again tuition-free, even for foreign students.

Apart from cost, there are other significant differences between German and American university life. German universities typically offer only a limited amount of dormitory housing. Most students live off campus, either commuting from home or renting an apartment shared with other students. Unlike in most American Universities, students must decide on a major before they begin their studies, and there is little flexibility in the choice of courses.

In the past few decades, there has been an initiative to standardize degree requirements between countries. Part of this restructuring has included a push to transition from 4- to 6-year **Diplom** and **Magister°** degrees to 3-year **Bachelor** degrees. This change has met with resistance from students, including complaints that it simply compresses the original curriculum into a shorter time frame. Many students also object to the shift toward a heavier workload with more frequent testing.

The percentage of students studying at private universities remains very small, but it is gradually increasing. Whereas public universities have had problems with over-crowding, private institutions can offer smaller class sizes, giving students more contact with professors.

Statistische Informationen zum Thema Studium	
Neue Studenten pro Jahr°	ca. 1.000.000
Studenten, die nach dem° Bachelor weiter studieren°	78%
Bachelor-Studenten, die zum Studieren ins Ausland gehen°	15%
Bachelor-Absolventen°, die 1,5 Jahre nach dem Abschluss Arbeit° haben	ca. 97%

QUELLE: Der Tagesspiegel

Büffel-Zeit *cramming time* **Diplom, Magister** *degrees available before the education reform* **pro Jahr** *per year* **die nach dem** *who after the* **weiter studieren** *continue their studies* **ins Ausland gehen** *go abroad* **Absolventen** *graduates* **Arbeit** *work*

---

1 **Richtig oder falsch?** Indicate whether each statement is **richtig** or **falsch**. Correct the false statements.

1. The majority of universities in Germany are public. **Richtig.**

2. German universities have always charged tuition fees.
   Falsch. Historically, German universities have not charged tuition fees.

3. Students in Germany have accepted reforms in education wholeheartedly.
   Falsch. There has been resistance from some students.

4. It takes more time to earn a **Bachelor**'s degree than it did to earn the **Magister** or the **Diplom**. **Falsch.** It takes less time.

5. Students now have a lighter workload with fewer tests.
   Falsch. There has been a shift toward a heavier workload with more frequent tests.

6. A small percentage of students study at private universities. **Richtig.**

7. Private and public universities charge the same tuition fees.
   Falsch. Private universities charge tuition, but public universities are free.

8. The majority of German students leave school after completing their Bachelor degree. **Falsch.** The majority of students continue their studies.

9. Most German students study abroad. **Falsch.** 15% go abroad.

10. In Germany, most students live in dormitories. **Falsch.** Most students live off campus.

 Practice more at **vhlcentral.com.**

DEUTSCH IM ALLTAG

Die Uni

der Besserwisser, -	know-it-all
der Mitbewohner, - / die Mitbewohnerin, -nen	roommate
das Referat, -e	presentation
das Schwarze Brett	bulletin board
das Studentenwohnheim, -e	dormitory
die Studiengebühr, -en	tuition fee
büffeln	to cram (for a test)

DIE DEUTSCHSPRACHIGE WELT

Der Bologna-Prozess

Die Bildungsminister° der Europäischen Union treffen sich erstmals° 1999 in Bologna in Italien. Das Ziel°: international einheitliche° Universitäts-Abschlüsse in ganz Europa und hohe° Mobilität für Studenten. In Europa müssen° Universitäten die Hochschulbildung° standardisieren. Bis zum° Jahre 2010 will man einen gemeinsamen° europäischen Hochschulraum° entwickeln°. Er wird im März 2010 in Budapest und Wien offiziell eröffnet°. 47 Mitgliedsländer° nehmen daran teil°. **AP* Theme:** Global Challenges **Context:** Political Issues

Bildungsminister secretaries of education **treffen... erstmals** meet for the first time **Ziel** goal **einheitliche** standardized **hohe** high **müssen** must **Hochschulbildung** higher education **Bis zum** Until **gemeinsam** common **Hochschulraum** Higher Education Area **entwickeln** develop **eröffnet** opened **Mitgliedsländer** member countries **nehmen... teil** participate

PORTRÄT

Uni Basel **Suggestion** Tell students that Paracelsus is famous for his statement: "**Alle Ding' sind Gift, und nichts ohn' Gift; allein die Dosis macht, daß ein Ding kein Gift ist.**" This is often paraphrased in English as "The dose makes the poison", a central principle of toxicology.

Universität Basel (gegründet° 1460): Viele brillante Wissenschaftler° belegen hier Vorlesungen und machen ihren° Abschluss in Medizin, Philosophie oder Psychologie. Der exzentrische Paracelsus (1493–1541) ist hier Professor für Medizin. Auch Holbein (1497–1543), Jung (1875–1961) und Hesse (1877–1962) leben° in Basel. Aber der berühmteste° Professor hier ist der Philosoph Friedrich Nietzsche (1844–1900).

Heute ist die Universität in Basel voller Leben° und sehr modern. Mehr als 13.000 Studenten sind hier. Viele studieren Biowissenschaften°. Andere° lernen Literatur, Wirtschaft oder Mathematik – für 850 Schweizer Franken pro Semester.
AP* Theme: Science & Technology **Context:** Social Impacts
gegründet founded **Wissenschaftler** scientists **machen ihren** make their **leben** live **berühmteste** most famous **voller Leben** full of life **Biowissenschaften** life sciences **Andere** Others

∞ IM INTERNET

Österreichische Universitäten. Wie ist das Studium in Österreich? Ist es mit dem (*with the*) deutschen System vergleichbar (*comparable*)?

Find out more at **vhlcentral.com**.

Expansion Have students search online for more information about the people mentioned in this article, as well as other famous intellectuals from Basel. Have them share their findings with the class.

---

2 **Was fehlt?** Complete the sentences.

 1. Nach der Bologna-Erklärung müssen viele Länder in Europa die Hochschulbildung ___standardisieren___.

 2. Der Bologna-Prozess hat als Ziel international einheitliche (Universitäts-)Abschlüsse.

3. Heute lernen Studenten in Basel Biowissenschaften, Literatur, Wirtschaft oder Mathematik.

4. Der berühmteste Professor der Universität Basel ist (Friedrich) Nietzsche.

3 **Studentenleben** In pairs, discuss the similarities and differences between student life in German-speaking countries and in the United States. Would you like to study in a German-speaking country? Which system do you think is best? Give reasons for your answers.
Answers will vary.

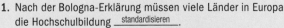 **3 Suggestion** Ask students what they like and dislike about their school experience. Is the workload too heavy?

Ressourcen

v̂ Text **S** vhlcentral

2A.1

Regular verbs  Presentation

Startblock Most German verbs follow predictable conjugation patterns in which a set of endings is added to the verb stem.

Ich **studiere** Architektur.

Lernst du Philosophie mit Meline?

QUERVERWEIS

In **Kapitel 1**, you learned the irregular verbs **sein** and **haben**. You will learn more about irregular verbs in **2B.1**.

ACHTUNG

Depending on the context, **sie lernt** can be translated as *she studies, she is studying,* or *she does study.*

- To form the present tense of a regular verb, drop the **-en** or **-n** ending from the infinitive and add **-e**, **-st**, **-t**, or **-en/-n** to the stem.

	lernen (*to study*)		wandern (*to hike*)	
ich	**lerne**	*I study*	**wandere**	*I hike*
du	**lernst**	*you study*	**wanderst**	*you hike*
Sie	**lernen**	*you study*	**wandern**	*you hike*
er/sie/es	**lernt**	*he/she studies*	**wandert**	*he/she hikes*
wir	**lernen**	*we study*	**wandern**	*we hike*
ihr	**lernt**	*you study*	**wandert**	*you hike*
Sie	**lernen**	*you study*	**wandern**	*you hike*
sie	**lernen**	*they study*	**wandern**	*they hike*

Lernst du Physik?
Are you studying physics?

Sie wandern im Sommer.
They go hiking in the summer.

- Regular verbs whose stems end in **-d** or **-t** add an **e** before the endings **-st** or **-t** for ease of pronunciation.

arbeiten (*to work*)			
ich **arbeite**	*I work*	wir **arbeiten**	*we work*
du **arbeitest**	*you work*	ihr **arbeitet**	*you work*
Sie **arbeiten**	*you work*	Sie **arbeiten**	*you work*
er/sie/es **arbeitet**	*he/she/it works*	sie **arbeiten**	*they work*

Suggestion Tell students that infinitives consist of a stem and an ending. Reinforce this idea by writing infinitives on the board and modeling the conjugation patterns. Ask students to identify the stem of each verb.

QUERVERWEIS

As in English, the simple present can sometimes be used to talk about a future action. You will learn more about this usage in **2B.2**.

Lena **arbeitet** in München.
Lena works in Munich.

Findest du Mathematik interessant?
Do you find math interesting?

Wartet ihr auf eure Freunde?
Are you waiting for your friends?

Die Hefte **kosten** zu viel.
The notebooks cost too much.

- Verbs whose stems end in **-gn** or **-fn** also add an **-e** before the endings **-st** and **-t**.

Es regnet morgen.
It's going to rain tomorrow.

Öffnest du das Fenster?
Are you opening the window?

- If a verb stem ends in **-s**, **-ß**, **-x**, or **-z**, the **-s** is dropped from the second person singular ending.

heißen *(to be named)*				
ich heiße	*I am named*	wir heißen	*we are named*
du heißt	*you are named*	ihr heißt	*you are named*
Sie heißen	*you are named*	Sie heißen	*you are named*
er/sie/es heißt	*he/she/it is named*	sie heißen	*they are named*

Du heißt Jonas, nicht wahr?
Your name is Jonas, right?

Mein Hund **heißt** Fritz.
My dog's name is Fritz.

Martin **reist** oft in die Schweiz.
Martin often travels to Switzerland.

Ihr **grüßt** den Lehrer nicht?
You're not going to greet the teacher?

common regular verbs (present tense)			
antworten	*to answer*	leben	*to live*
bauen	*to build*	lernen	*to learn; to study*
bedeuten	*to mean*	lieben	*to love*
begrüßen	*to greet*	machen	*to do; to make*
belegen	*to take (a class)*	öffnen	*to open*
brauchen	*to need*	regnen	*to rain*
bringen	*to bring*	reisen	*to travel*
finden	*to find*	sagen	*to say*
fragen	*to ask*	schreiben	*to write*
gehen	*to go*	spielen	*to play*
hören	*to hear; to listen to*	suchen	*to look for*
kaufen	*to buy*	verstehen	*to understand*
kommen	*to come*	warten	*to wait*
korrigieren	*to correct*	wiederholen	*to repeat*
kosten	*to cost*	wohnen	*to live (somewhere)*

Kaufst du Kaffee im Supermarkt?
Do you buy coffee at the supermarket?

Was **bedeutet** das auf Englisch?
What does that mean in English?

Ich **lerne** Deutsch.
I'm learning German.

Wir **belegen** Biologie.
We're taking Biology.

ACHTUNG

Note that the **du**, **er/sie/es**, and **ihr** forms of **heißen** are identical.

Suggestion Remind students that new verbs are also vocabulary items. Tell students that they should be able to recognize these verbs in all of their present-tense forms, but they will learn more about how to use them in later units.

QUERVERWEIS

Some verbs, including **bringen**, **finden**, **gehen**, and **schreiben** are regular in the present tense and irregular in the past tense.

Students will learn more about the past tense forms in **Vol. 2: 1A.1**, **1B.1**, and **2A.1**.

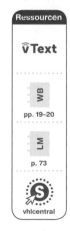

Ressourcen

v̂Text

WB
pp. 19–20

LM
p. 73

S
vhlcentral

Jetzt sind Sie dran! Write the appropriate form of the verb.

1. Wir ____lernen____ (lernen) Deutsch.
2. Der Student ____wiederholt____ (wiederholen) den Satz (*sentence*).
3. Ich ____warte____ (warten) auf den Bus.
4. Die Lehrerin ____korrigiert____ (korrigieren) die Prüfungen.
5. Du ____belegst____ (belegen) fünf Veranstaltungen.
6. Das Universitätsstudium ____kostet____ (kosten) sehr viel.
7. Ihr ____versteht____ (verstehen) Mathematik.
8. Wir ____brauchen____ (brauchen) viel Papier und viele Bleistifte für den Unterricht.
9. Anja und Thomas ____begrüßen____ (begrüßen) den Dozenten.
10. Ich ____kaufe____ (kaufen) eine Tasse Kaffee in der Mensa.
11. Wir ____machen____ (machen) nachmittags Hausaufgaben.
12. Du ____öffnest____ (öffnen) die Tür.

Anwendung

1 **Was ist richtig?** Select the verb that best completes each sentence.

1. Astrid und Jonas (wohnen / bedeuten) in Berlin.
2. Michaela (sucht / korrigiert) den Seminarraum.
3. Ich (baue / studiere) Informatik und Mathematik.
4. Wir (belegen / grüßen) sehr viele Vorlesungen.
5. (Belegst / Lebst) du in Deutschland oder in Österreich?
6. Ihr (macht / kauft) nachmittags Hausaufgaben.
7. (Warten / Kosten) Sie auf (*for*) den Bus, Professor Meier?
8. Du (sagst / reist) im Sommer nach (*to*) Spanien und Italien.

2 Expansion Have students write their own dialogues about the courses they are taking.

2 **Was fehlt?** Maria and Tim are meeting for lunch. Complete their conversation with the correct verb forms.

MARIA Hallo, Tim! Wie (1) __geht__ (gehen) es dir? Wie ist das Deutschseminar?

TIM Ach, es geht mir ziemlich gut. Im Seminar (2) __schreibt__ (schreiben) der Dozent viel an die Tafel, aber ich (3) __verstehe__ (verstehen) es gut. Und du? Wie (4) __findest__ (finden) du das Informatikseminar?

MARIA Ich (5) __liebe__ (lieben) Informatik! Wir (6) __bauen__ (bauen) heute einen Computer.

TIM Vielleicht (*Maybe*) (7) __belege__ (belegen) ich nächstes Semester auch Informatik. (8) __Machst__ (Machen) du viele Hausaufgaben?

MARIA Ja! Samstags und sonntags (9) __lerne__ (lernen) ich immer (*always*).

TIM Oje. Samstags und sonntags (10) __spielen__ (spielen) Max und ich Computer.

3 **Schreiben** Write complete sentences using the cues.

1. ich / kaufen / einen Apfel   Ich kaufe einen Apfel.
2. David / brauchen / das Wörterbuch   David braucht das Wörterbuch.
3. du / arbeiten / freitags und samstags   Du arbeitest freitags und samstags.
4. Lara / suchen / das Deutschbuch   Lara sucht das Deutschbuch.
5. Josef und ich / spielen / Basketball   Josef und ich spielen Basketball.
6. lernen / ihr / Spanisch / ?   Lernt ihr Spanisch?
7. der Dozent / wiederholen / das Experiment   Der Dozent wiederholt das Experiment.
8. Hans und Jana / leben / in Irland   Hans und Jana leben in Irland.
9. regnen / es / ?   Regnet es?
10. öffnen / du / das Fenster / ?   Öffnest du das Fenster?

 Practice more at **vhlcentral.com**.

Kommunikation

4 **Was fehlt?** Complete the sentences, and then, with a partner, take turns asking and explaining what each person is doing.

▶ **BEISPIEL**

Du ___hörst___ Musik.
S1: *Was mache ich?*
S2: *Du hörst Musik.*

1. Herr Becker ___arbeitet___.   2. Wir ___spielen___ Tennis.

3. Ihr ___lernt___ viel.   4. Ich ___kaufe___ ein neues Fahrrad.   5. Heinrich ___begrüßt___ den Mann.   6. Hans ___liebt___ Emma.

5 **Bilden Sie Sätze** In pairs, use items from each column to create six sentences. You may use some items more than once. Answers will vary.

BEISPIEL *Ich höre Musik.*

A	B	C
Ich	hören	Deutsch
du	lernen	Hausaufgaben
Alena	lieben	Kunst
Anna und ich	machen	Musik
ihr	spielen	Naturwissenschaft
die Studenten	verstehen	Tennis

6 **Persönliche Fragen** In pairs, take turns asking and answering the questions. Answers will vary.

1. Wie viele Kurse belegst du?
2. Lernst du Fremdsprachen?
3. Gehst du oft in die Sporthalle?

4. Was machst du morgens?
5. Was machst du nachmittags?
6. Was machst du abends?

7 **Gespräch** In pairs, fill in Student 2's half of the dialogue, then continue the conversation with your partner using at least four more regular verbs. Answers will vary.

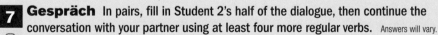

S1: Hallo! Studierst du hier an der Uni?
S2: …
S1: Ich auch! Was studierst du?
S2: …
S1: Ist Wirtschaft schwierig?
S2: …
S1: Montags und mittwochs habe ich Geschichte. Und du?
S2: …

6 Expansion Have students write a paragraph about themselves, including their name, age, major, and class schedule.

6 Virtual Chat You can also assign activity 6 on the Supersite. Students record individual responses that appear in your gradebook.

7 Virtual Chat You can also assign activity 7 on the Supersite.

2A.2

Interrogative words  Presentation

Startblock Use interrogative words to ask for information.

Wie viele Menschen leben dort?

Was ist mit Meline?

Suggestion Ask students additional questions using interrogatives from the list, and have students answer. Ex.: **Was ist das? Wer ist sie?**, etc.

interrogatives			
wann?	*when?*	wie?	*how?*
warum?	*why?*	wie viel(e)?	*how much/many?*
was?	*what?*	wo?	*where?*
welcher/welche/welches?	*which?*	woher?	*where (from)?*
wer/wen?	*who/whom?*	wohin?	*where (to)?*

- To ask an information question (one that cannot be answered with **ja** or **nein**), begin the question with an interrogative word.

  Wann beginnen wir?　　**Warum** machst du das?　　**Wo** ist Frau Schultz?
  ***When** do we start?*　　***Why** are you doing that?*　　***Where** is Mrs. Schultz?*

- Use **wer** when the person you're asking about is the grammatical subject of the verb and **wen** when the person is the direct object of the verb.

  Wer begrüßt den Professor?　　　**Wen** begrüßt der Professor?
  ***Who** is greeting the professor?*　　***Who(m)** is the professor greeting?*

- The form of **welcher** depends on the gender and number of the noun it modifies. Its three forms (**welcher/welche/welches**) have the same endings as the masculine, feminine/plural, and neuter forms of the definite article (**der/die/das**).

  Welche Professorin lehrt Mathematik?　　**Welcher Student** belegt Mathematik?
  ***Which professor** teaches mathematics?*　　***Which student** is taking math?*

- Use **woher** to ask people where they are from and **wohin** to ask where they are going.

  —**Woher** kommen Sie?　　　　—**Wohin** geht ihr?
  —Ich komme **aus Wien**.　　　　—Wir gehen **in die Bibliothek**.
  —*Where* are you *from?*　　　　—*Where* are you going?
  —*I'm from Vienna.*　　　　　　—*We're going to the library.*

Jetzt sind Sie dran! **Select the appropriate interrogative for each question.** **Expansion** Have students take turns asking each other the questions and giving logical answers, where possible.

1. (Woher / Wer) kommst du?
2. (Wohin / Wann) haben wir Deutsch?
3. (Was / Wohin) reisen wir?
4. (Wer / Wo) braucht ein Blatt Papier?
5. (Welche / Woher) Seminare sind einfach?
6. (Wer / Wen) liebst du?

Anwendung und Kommunikation

1 **Was fehlt?** Complete each sentence with an appropriate interrogative word.

1. _____Wann/Wo_____ spielen wir Tennis?
2. _____Wann/Woher_____ kommt die Dozentin?
3. _____Was_____ kaufst du für das Studium?
4. _____Warum/Wann_____ brauchst du einen Computer?
5. _Wo/Wann/Wie viel/Was_ lernst du?
6. _____Wie_____ alt bist du?
7. _Welche/Wie viele_ Kurse belegst du?
8. _____Wie viel_____ Zeit haben wir abends?

2 **Schreiben** Write questions using the cues. Pay attention to word order.

BEISPIEL Marie und Alex / woher / kommen
Woher kommen Marie und Alex?

1. der Hörsaal / wo / ist   Wo ist der Hörsaal?
2. wie / die Deutschvorlesung / ist   Wie ist die Deutschvorlesung?
3. gehen / wann / wir / in die Bibliothek   Wann gehen wir in die Bibliothek?
4. einen Kuli / wer / braucht   Wer braucht einen Kuli?
5. machst / was / du / samstags   Was machst du samstags?
6. wohin / gehen / nachmittags / die Studenten   Wohin gehen die Studenten nachmittags?
7. welches / belegt / Seminar / ihr   Welches Seminar belegt ihr?
8. lernt / warum / Paul / so viel   Warum lernt Paul so viel?

3 **Fragen** In pairs, write a question for each response.   Sample answers are provided.

BEISPIEL Ich komme <u>aus Wien</u>.
Woher kommst du?

1. Karl hat <u>montags, mittwochs und freitags</u> Vorlesungen.   Wann hat Karl Vorlesungen?
2. Die Bibliothek hat <u>3.726</u> Bücher.   Wie viele Bücher hat die Bibliothek?
3. <u>Das Seminar</u> ist langweilig.   Was ist langweilig?/Welches Seminar ist langweilig?
4. Das Heft kostet <u>3,50 €</u>.   Wie viel kostet das Heft?
5. Ich brauche das Buch <u>Siddhartha</u> für die Literaturvorlesung.   Welches Buch brauchst du für die Literaturvorlesung?
6. Ich wohne <u>in Berlin</u>.   Wo wohnst du?
7. <u>Der Dozent</u> wiederholt die Frage.   Wer wiederholt die Frage?
8. Anna liebt <u>Paul</u>.   Wen liebt Anna?

4 **Interview** Prepare six questions about school life using interrogative words. Then, survey your classmates.   Answers will vary.

 Practice more at **vhlcentral.com**.

3 **Virtual Chat** You can also assign activity 3 on the Supersite. Students record individual responses that appear in your gradebook.

4 **Expansion** Have each group of students make a set of flashcards with interrogative pronouns. One student chooses a card and asks a question with the selected word to someone in the group. That person must answer the question and select the next card.

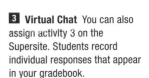

2A.3

Talking about time and dates  Presentation

Startblock Like English, German uses cardinal numbers (*one*, *two*, *three*) to tell time and ordinal numbers (*first*, *second*, *third*) to give dates.

Telling time

- To ask *What time is it?*, say **Wie spät ist es?** or **Wie viel Uhr ist es?**. To answer, say **Es ist** + [*hour*] + **Uhr** + [*minutes*].

Es ist ein Uhr./   **Es ist zwei Uhr./**   **Es ist zwölf Uhr./**
Es ist eins.   **Es ist zwei.**   **Es ist Mittag/Mitternacht.**

- Use **vor** and **nach** to indicate minutes before and after the hour. Use **Viertel vor** for *quarter to* and **Viertel nach** for *quarter past*. In these constructions, omit the word **Uhr**.

Es ist Viertel vor elf./   **Es ist zwanzig nach** vier./
Es ist zehn Uhr fünfundvierzig.   Es ist vier Uhr zwanzig.

- Use **halb** to mean *half an hour before*. Note that it is not equivalent to the English phrase *half past*.

Es ist halb zehn.   **Es ist halb sieben.**
Es ist neun Uhr dreißig.   Es ist sechs Uhr dreißig.

- Use the 24-hour clock when talking about train schedules, movie listings, and official timetables. Do not use the expressions **Viertel vor**, **Viertel nach**, or **halb** with the 24-hour clock.

    20.30 Uhr = zwanzig Uhr dreißig   **18.45 Uhr = achtzehn Uhr fünfundvierzig**
    8:30 p.m.   *6:45 p.m.*

- To specify the time at which an event or activity will take place, use **um** + [*time*].

    —**Um wie viel Uhr** beginnt der Film?   —**Um** sechzehn Uhr zehn.
    —***What time*** *does the movie start?*   —**At** *four-ten p.m.*

Ordinal numbers

- The ordinal numbers (**die Ordinalzahlen**) from 1ˢᵗ to 19ᵗʰ are formed, with a few exceptions, by adding **-te** to the corresponding cardinal numbers. To form all other ordinals, add **-ste** to the cardinal forms. Use a period to indicate the abbreviated form of an ordinal number.

ordinal numbers

1.	erste	*first*	7.	siebte	*seventh*	19.	neunzehnte	*nineteenth*
2.	zweite	*second*	8.	achte	*eighth*	20.	zwanzigste	*twentieth*
3.	dritte	*third*	9.	neunte	*ninth*	31.	einunddreißigste	*thirty-first*
4.	vierte	*fourth*	10.	zehnte	*tenth*	55.	fünfundfünfzigste	*fifty-fifth*
5.	fünfte	*fifth*	11.	elfte	*eleventh*	100.	hundertste	*hundredth*
6.	sechste	*sixth*	12.	zwölfte	*twelfth*	1000.	tausendste	*thousandth*

der **erste** Lehrer
*the **first** instructor*

die **zweite** Stunde
*the **second** lecture*

das **dritte** Fach
*the **third** subject*

Dates

die Monate (*months*)

Januar	April	Juli	Oktober
Februar	Mai	August	November
März	Juni	September	Dezember

Januar ist der erste Monat.
***January** is the first month.*

Dezember ist der zwölfte Monat.
***December** is the twelfth month.*

- Answer the question **Der Wievielte ist heute?** (*What is the date today?*) with **Heute ist der** + [*ordinal number* (+ *month*)].

  Heute ist **der erste Mai**.
  *Today is **May first**.*

  Heute ist **der einunddreißigste**.
  *Today is **the thirty-first**.*

  23. März 2010 ⟶ **23.3.2010**
  March 23rd, 2010 ⟶ *3/23/2010*

  7. Oktober 2014 ⟶ **7.10.2014**
  October 7th, 2014 ⟶ *10/7/2014*

- To specify the day on which an event or activity takes place, use **am** before the date, and add **-n** to the ordinal number. Use the question **Wann hast du Geburtstag?** to ask someone when their birthday is.

  Ich habe **am 7. (siebten) Juli** Geburtstag.
  *My birthday is **on July 7th**.*

  Am 1. (ersten) Januar beginnt das neue Jahr.
  *The new year begins **on January 1st**.*

- The pattern **am** + [*time expression*] is also used with days of the week.

  am Montag
  on Monday

  am Dienstag
  on Tuesday

  am Wochenende
  on the weekend

- Like English, German uses cardinal numbers to refer to a particular year.

  1895 = achtzehnhundertfünfundneunzig   **2016 = zweitausendsechzehn**

QUERVERWEIS

To form the accusative of ordinal numbers, add **-n** before masculine nouns. The feminine and neuter forms do not change.

Du trinkst deinen zweiten Kaffee.
You're having your second coffee.

Ich antworte auf die dritte Frage.
I'm answering the third question.

You will learn more about nominative and accusative adjective endings in **3A.2**

ACHTUNG

In writing, the day also comes before the month. Remember that an ordinal number is indicated by putting a period after the number.

Ressourcen

v̂ Text

WB
pp. 23–24

LM
p. 75

vhlcentral

Jetzt sind Sie dran!

Expansion Write some additional times and dates on the board and have students read them aloud.

Suggestion Show students this alternative question/answer pattern for recognition purposes only: **Den Wievielten haben wir heute? Heute haben wir den zweiundzwanzigsten Juni.** Point out the use of the accusative article and the **-n** added to the ordinal number.

A. Select the correct time.

1. **7:15 a.m.** Es ist (Viertel nach / Viertel vor) sieben.
2. **2:00 p.m.** Es ist zwei Uhr (morgens / nachmittags).
3. **10:30 a.m.** Es ist (halb zehn / halb elf) vormittags.
4. **12:00 p.m.** Es ist (Mittag / Mitternacht).
5. **7:55 a.m.** Es ist (acht / sieben) Uhr fünfundfünfzig.
6. **8:37 p.m.** Es ist (zwanzig Uhr / achtzehn Uhr) siebenunddreißig.

B. Write the correct date.

7. **14. Februar** Heute ist der ___vierzehnte___ Februar.
8. **28. Dezember** Heute ist der ___achtundzwanzigste___ Dezember.
9. **3. Juli** Heute ist der ___dritte___ Juli.
10. **30. Mai** Heute ist der ___dreißigste___ Mai.
11. **11. Oktober** Heute ist der ___elfte___ Oktober.
12. **7. August** Heute ist der ___siebte___ August.

Anwendung

1 Was ist richtig? Select the sentence that refers to the time shown.

1. (Es ist zwei Uhr.)/
   Es ist drei Uhr.

2. (Es ist Viertel
   vor eins.)/
   Es ist zwölf
   Uhr vierzig.

3. Es ist fünf
   Uhr zwanzig. /
   (Es ist zehn
   vor drei.)

4. (Es ist zwei Uhr)
   (fünfundvierzig.)/
   Es ist Viertel
   vor zwei.

2 Wie spät ist es? Write a sentence indicating the time shown on each clock or watch.

▶ **BEISPIEL**

Es ist Viertel nach vier.

p.m.

1. Es ist halb eins. / Es ist zwölf Uhr dreißig.

2. Es ist ein Uhr. / Es ist eins.

p.m.   p.m.   a.m.   a.m.

3. Es ist Viertel nach fünf. / Es ist siebzehn Uhr fünfzehn.

4. Es ist zehn nach acht. / Es ist zwanzig Uhr zehn.

5. Es ist halb sechs. / Es ist fünf Uhr dreißig.

6. Es ist Viertel vor elf. / Es ist zehn Uhr fünfundvierzig.

a.m.   p.m.

7. Es ist zwölf nach zwei. / Es ist vierzehn Uhr zwölf.

8. Es ist fünf nach sieben. / Es ist sieben Uhr fünf.

9. Es ist fünf vor vier. / Es ist drei Uhr fünfundfünfzig.

10. Es ist fünfundzwanzig vor Mittag. / Es ist fünfundzwanzig vor zwölf. / Es ist elf Uhr fünfunddreißig.

3 Suggestion Reinforce the difference between **am elften Oktober** and **der elfte Oktober**. Ex.: **Am elften Oktober haben Sie eine Prüfung. Der elfte Oktober ist ein Samstag.**

3 Wer hat Geburtstag? Write out the date indicated to say when each person's birthday is.

BEISPIEL Angela Merkel hat am (17.) _siebzehnten_ Juli Geburtstag.

1. Arnold Schwarzenegger hat am (30.) _dreißigsten_ Juli Geburtstag.

2. Heidi Klum hat am (1.) _ersten_ Juni Geburtstag.

3. Karl Lagerfeld hat am (10.) _zehnten_ September Geburtstag.

4. Michael Fassbender hat am (2.) _zweiten_ April Geburtstag.

5. Die Tennisspielerin Steffi Graf hat am (14.) _vierzehnten_ Juni Geburtstag.

6. Der Fußballspieler Mesut Özil hat am (15.) _fünfzehnten_ Oktober Geburtstag.

7. Die Musikerin Nena hat am (24.) _vierundzwanzigsten_ März Geburtstag.

8. Der Musiker Herbert Grönemeyer hat am (12.) _zwölften_ April Geburtstag.

9. Der Schauspieler (*actor*) Christoph Waltz hat am (4.) _vierten_ Oktober Geburtstag.

10. Die Schauspielerin Sibel Kekilli hat am (16.) _sechzehnten_ Juni Geburtstag.

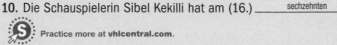
Practice more at **vhlcentral.com**.

Kommunikation

4 **Um wie viel Uhr...?** In pairs, look at the class schedule. Take turns asking and answering questions about the start times of classes. Answers will vary.

BEISPIEL

S1: Wann und um wie viel Uhr ist Literatur?
S2: Literatur ist dienstags und donnerstags um halb neun.

	Montag	Dienstag	Mittwoch	Donnerstag	Freitag
8.30		Literatur		Literatur	Chemie
9.25	Biologie	Biologie	Biologie		Chemie
10.20		Kunst		Kunst	
11.15	Informatik		Informatik		Informatik
12.10	Mathematik	Deutsch	Deutsch	Deutsch	Mathematik

5 **Der Wievielte ist heute?** In pairs, take turns pointing at different dates on the calendar and having your partner tell you the date. Answers will vary.

BEISPIEL

S1: Der Wievielte ist heute?
S2: Heute ist der dritte Oktober.

Oktober

Montag	Dienstag	Mittwoch	Donnerstag	Freitag	Samstag	Sonntag
		1	2	3	4	5
6	7	8	9	10	11	12
13	14	15	16	17	18	19
20	21	22	23	24	25	26
27	28	29	30	31		

6 **Geburtstage** Ask your classmates when their birthdays are. Find out whose birthday is closest to yours. Answers will vary.

BEISPIEL

S1: Wann hast du Geburtstag?
S2: Ich habe am siebten Dezember Geburtstag. Und wann hast du Geburtstag?
S1: Ich habe am neunten Oktober Geburtstag.

7 **Interview** In pairs, take turns asking and answering the questions. Answers will vary.

BEISPIEL

S1: Wann hast du Geschichte?
S2: Montags, mittwochs und freitags um Viertel nach elf. Und du?

1. Welcher Tag ist heute?
2. Wann hast du Geburtstag?
3. Wann gehst du in die Sporthalle?
4. Wie spät ist es?
5. Um wie viel Uhr gehst du in die Mensa?
6. Wann hast du Unterricht?

4 **Expansion** Ask students to describe their own schedules. In pairs, have them take turns asking and answering questions about their own classes and activities.

4 **Partner Chat** You can also assign activity 4 on the Supersite. Students work in pairs to record the activity online. The pair's recorded conversation will appear in your gradebook.

5 **Expansion** Bring an example of movie listings, TV schedules, or course schedules from a German school. In pairs, have students ask and answer questions about the schedules.

5 **Suggestion** Point out that on German calendars and schedules, **Montag** is listed as the first day of the week and **Sonntag** as the last.

7 **Virtual Chat** You can also assign activity 7 on the Supersite. Students record individual responses that appear in your gradebook.

Wiederholung

4 **Expansion** Show a time zone map and ask what time it is in a given place. Ex.: **Wie viel Uhr ist es in Bangkok?**

1 Graffiti In small groups, take turns drawing items from the lesson vocabulary and guessing what they are.
Answers will vary.

BEISPIEL

S1: Ist das ein Diplom?
S2: Nein!
S3: Ist das ein Stipendium?
S2: Ja, richtig!

2 Verabredungen Take turns asking and answering questions using the cues and the images. Answers will vary.

reisen

▶ **BEISPIEL**

S1: Wohin reist du im Sommer?
S2: Ich reise nach Spanien.

2 **Partner Chat** You can also assign activity 2 on the Supersite.

1. gehen

2. lernen

3. kosten

4. kaufen

5. hören

6. begrüßen

3 Feste Ask your classmates on what day these holidays fall. Add three additional holidays. Answers will vary.

BEISPIEL Weihnachten (*Christmas*)

S1: Wann ist Weihnachten?
S2: Weihnachten ist am 25. Dezember.

3 **Suggestion** Provide students with a calendar to consult for this activity.

- Silvester (*New Year's Eve*)
- Neujahrstag (*New Year's Day*)
- Columbus-Tag
- Halloween
- Veteranentag
- Heiligabend (*Christmas Eve*)

3 **Suggestion** Tell students about the German celebrations of **Aprilscherz, der Tag der Arbeit, and Erntedankfest** and explain how they differ from their American equivalents.

4 Zeitzonen In pairs, take turns telling your partner what time it is in each North American city and asking what time it is in a German-speaking country. Answers will vary.

4 **Partner Chat** You can also assign activity 4 on the Supersite.

BEISPIEL

S1: In Pittsburgh ist es fünfzehn Uhr zwölf. Wie viel Uhr ist es in Österreich?
S2: In Österreich ist es einundzwanzig Uhr zwölf. In Calgary ist es halb vier. Wie viel Uhr ist es in Deutschland?

Uhrzeit in...	Uhrzeit in Deutschland / in Österreich / in der Schweiz
Pittsburgh, PA: 15.12	+ 6 Stunden
Calgary, AB: 3.30	+ 8 Stunden
Fairbanks, AK: 22.54	+ 11 Stunden
Ft. Stockton, TX: 11.45	+ 7 Stunden
Hope, BC: 15.28	+ 9 Stunden
London, ON: 3.09	+ 6 Stunden
Needles, CA: 12.30	+ 9 Stunden
Tifton, FL: 21.36	+ 6 Stunden
Winnipeg, MB: 20.15	+ 7 Stunden

5 Arbeitsblatt Your instructor will give you a worksheet. Talk with your classmates to figure out the starting lineup of a race.

5 **Suggestion** Make sure students understand that **der Wievielte** is the masculine form and **die Wievielte** is the feminine form.

BEISPIEL

S1: Der Wievielte bist du?
S2: Ich bin der vierzehnte. Die wievielte bist du?
S1: Ich bin die achte.
S1 schreibt: Ben ist der vierzehnte.
S2 schreibt: Sarah ist die achte.

6 Diskutieren und kombinieren You and your partner each have two schedules. One shows your activities. The other shows a partial list of your partner's activities, with one activity missing each day. Ask and answer questions to complete both schedules.

BEISPIEL

S1: Was machst du am Sonntag um neun Uhr morgens?
S2: Ich mache Hausaufgaben. Und was machst du am Freitag um vier Uhr nachmittags?
S1: Ich habe Yoga.

S Video

AP* Theme: Contemporary Life
Context: Education & Career

Suggestion After showing students the video, ask questions to facilitate comprehension. Ex.: What types of subjects do students study at the TU? What degrees are offered at the TU?

TU Berlin

The **Technische Universität Berlin**, or **TU Berlin**, is a modern-looking institution with a long and impressive history. Founded in 1879, the **TU** is one of the biggest technical universities in Germany, and the only one in Berlin to offer an engineering degree (**Ingenieur-Abschluss**). The TU also has a larger percentage of international students (**Studenten aus dem Ausland**) than any other German university.

Vier Unis hat die Stadt zu bieten°. Die TU ist die zweitälteste°.

Nach vorn° präsentiert sie sich modern und sachlich°.

„Wir haben die Ideen° für die Zukunft°" heißt der Leitspruch°.

zu bieten *to offer* **zweitälteste** *second oldest* **Nach vorn** *From the front* **sachlich** *functional* **Ideen** *ideas* **Zukunft** *future* **Leitspruch** *motto*

Verständnis Circle the correct answers.

1. What percentage of **TU** students come from abroad?
   a. 5   b. 10   c. 20   d. 30
2. Which of the following is *not* one of the key subjects (**Schwerpunkte**) offered by the **TU**?
   a. Mathematik   b. Architektur   c. Physik   d. Chemie

Diskussion Discuss the following questions with a partner. Answers will vary.

1. In what ways is the **TU Berlin** similar to your school? How is it different?
2. Would you like to study at the **TU Berlin**? Why or why not?

Communicative Goals

You will learn how to:

- talk about sports
- talk about leisure activities

Remind students to omit the article when talking about a sport: **Stefan spielt Basketball.** Point out that **der Basketball** refers to the actual ball: **Julia kauft einen Basketball.**

Sport und Freizeit 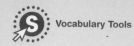 Vocabulary Tools

AP* Theme: Contemporary Life
Context: Entertainment, Travel, & Leisure

Wortschatz

Sportarten	*sports*
(der) (American) Football	*football*
(das) Golf	*golf*
(das) Hockey	*hockey*
(der) Volleyball	*volleyball*
das Schwimmbad, ⸚er	*swimming pool*
das Spiel, -e	*game*
der Sport	*sports*
das Stadion, Stadien	*stadium*
Fahrrad fahren (fährt)	*to ride a bicycle*
Ski fahren	*to ski*
schwimmen	*to swim*
trainieren	*to practice*
Freizeitaktivitäten	*leisure activities*
der Berg, -e	*mountain*
das Fahrrad, ⸚er	*bicycle*
die Freizeit	*free time*
das Hobby, -s	*hobby*
der Park, -s	*park*
der Strand, ⸚e	*beach*
der Wald, ⸚er	*forest*
angeln gehen	*to go fishing*
campen gehen	*to go camping*
essen gehen	*to eat out*
spazieren gehen	*to go for a walk*
klettern	*to (rock) climb*
kochen	*to cook*
(ein Pferd) reiten	*to ride (a horse)*
schreiben	*to write*
Spaß haben/machen	*to have fun / to be fun*
singen	*to sing*
tanzen	*to dance*
wandern	*to hike*

Suggestion Have students preview the conjugation of **fahren**, which will be covered in **2B.1**. Explain that **fahren** is listed with its third-person singular form because it has a stem change in the present tense.

ACHTUNG

Infinitives can be used as nouns in German. **Freitags habe ich Schwimmen. Samstags habe ich Reiten.** Infinitives used as nouns are neuter.

die Spielerinnen (*sing.* die Spielerin)

Sie spielen Tennis (*n.*).

das Spielfeld, -er/ der Platz, ⸚e

der Ball, ⸚e

die Mannschaft, -en

der Spieler, -

Er spielt Fußball. (spielen)

Sie verliert nicht gern. (verlieren)

die Karten (*sing.* die Karte)

Er gewinnt. (gewinnen)

Basketball (*m.*)

der Basketball

Sie spielen gern Schach (*n.*).

Baseball (*m.*)

Leichtathletik (*f.*)

Anwendung

1 Expansion Have students list additional words that could belong to each grouping.

1 Was passt nicht? Indicate the word that doesn't belong.

1. a. Basketball
   b. Schach
   c. Golf
   d. Tennis

2. a. der Strand
   b. der Spieler
   c. das Stadion
   d. der Platz

3. a. reiten
   b. schwimmen
   c. singen
   d. klettern

4. a. der Rucksack
   b. das Camping
   c. der Berg
   d. das Spielfeld

5. a. spazieren gehen
   b. kochen
   c. wandern
   d. reiten

6. a. die Freizeit
   b. die Schule
   c. die Aktivität
   d. das Hobby

2 Was fehlt? Complete the sentences with words from the list.

| Fußball | Schwimmbad | Spaß | spazieren | Tennisspielerinnen |

1. Serena und Venus Williams sind ___Tennisspielerinnen___.
2. Ski fahren macht im Winter viel ___Spaß___.
3. Wir schwimmen im ___Schwimmbad___.
4. Auf dem Spielfeld spielen wir ___Fußball___.
5. Im Park gehen wir ___spazieren___.

3 Zuordnen Write the activity that describes each picture.

Sample answers are provided.

▶ **BEISPIEL**

Leichtathletik trainieren

3 Expansion Ask students what they do in their free time. Ex.: **Spielen Sie Baseball oder Basketball? Fahren Sie Ski? Gehen Sie im Park spazieren?**

1. Ski fahren

2. campen gehen

3. Fahrrad fahren

4. Basketball spielen

4 Das Wochenende Listen to the conversation between Lukas, Max, and Michaela, and indicate who will be doing each activity.

	Lukas	Max	Michaela
1. Tennis spielen		✓	
2. kochen			✓
3. lernen		✓	✓
4. tanzen		✓	✓
5. klettern	✓		
6. Videospiele spielen	✓		

 Practice more at **vhlcentral.com.**

Kommunikation

5 **Berühmte Sportler** In pairs, match the athletes with the descriptions.

BEISPIEL

S1: Er spielt Fußball und kommt aus England.
S2: Es ist David Beckham.

___c___ 1. Er kommt aus der Schweiz und spielt Tennis.
___f___ 2. Er spielt Basketball.
___b___ 3. Sie ist eine Tennisspielerin aus Deutschland.
___d___ 4. Er schwimmt und hat viele olympische Medaillen (*medals*).
___a___ 5. Sie ist eine Skifahrerin aus Amerika.
___e___ 6. Er kommt aus Kalifornien und spielt Golf.

a. Lindsay Vonn
b. Steffi Graf
c. Roger Federer
d. Michael Phelps
e. Tiger Woods
f. LeBron James

5 **Expansion** Have students come up with their own prompts, real or fictitious. Ex.: **Sie ist groß und blond und sie spielt Gitarre und singt.** (Taylor Swift) **Er ist Hogwarts-Schüler.** (Harry Potter) **Sein Alter ego heißt „Slim Shady".** (Eminem)

---

6 **Machst du das gern?** In pairs, take turns telling each other whether you like or dislike each activity. Sample answers are provided.

BEISPIEL

S1: Ich schwimme gern. Und du?
S2: Ich schwimme auch gern. /
Ich schwimme nicht gern.

6 **Virtual Chat** You can also assign activity 6 on the Supersite. Students record individual responses that appear in your gradebook.

1.
Ich spiele (nicht) gern Schach.

2.
Ich tanze (nicht) gern.

3.
Ich spiele (nicht) gern Fußball.

4.
Ich reite (nicht) gern.

---

7 **Arbeitsblatt** Your instructor will give you a worksheet with information about activities. Ask your classmates what they like to do in their free time.

BEISPIEL Volleyball spielen

S1: Spielst du gern Volleyball?
S2: Ja. Ich spiele gern Volleyball./Nein. Ich spiele nicht gern Volleyball.

7 **Suggestion** Tell students to find at least one person for each activity.

angeln gehen	reiten	Fußball spielen
campen gehen	schwimmen	Schach spielen
kochen	singen	tanzen
spazieren gehen	Baseball spielen	Tennis trainieren
klettern	Basketball spielen	wandern

8 **Pantomime** Play charades in groups of four. Take turns acting out activities from the lesson vocabulary. The person who guesses the activity goes next. Answers will vary.

BEISPIEL

S1: Ist es Baseball?
S2: Nein.
S3: Ist es Tennis?
S2: Ja, es ist Tennis!

Aussprache und Rechtschreibung  Audio

Diphthongs: *au, ei/ai, eu/äu*

When one vowel sound glides into another vowel sound in the same syllable, the complex sound produced is called a diphthong. In German, this complex sound is said quickly and is not drawn out as it is in English. There are three diphthongs in German: **au**, **ei/ai**, and **eu/äu**.

faul	aus	Leine	Mais	neun	täuschen

The German diphthong written **au** begins with the vowel sound of the *o* in the English word *pod* and ends with a sound similar to the *oo* in the English word *loose*.

auf	Frau	Bauch	Haus	auch

The German diphthong written as **ei** or **ai** is pronounced very similarly to the *i* in the English word *time*. Remember that the German **ie** is not a diphthong, but simply a way of writing the long **i** sound, as in the word **sieben**.

Freitag	Zeit	Mai	Eis	schreiben

The German diphthong written as **eu** or **äu** is pronounced very similarly to the *oi* in the English word *coin*.

Zeugnis	Freund	Häuser	Europa	Deutsch

---

1 **Aussprechen** Practice saying these words aloud.

1. laufen
2. Kaufhaus
3. Rauch
4. Maus
5. mein
6. Wein
7. Mainz
8. reiten
9. treu
10. freuen
11. Leute
12. läuft

Suggestion Have students look at the sample words and sentences on this page to identify cognates and words they already know. Tell students the meanings of any unfamiliar words or phrases.

2 **Nachsprechen** Practice saying these sentences aloud.

1. Die Mäuse laufen einfach im Zimmer herum.
2. Tausende Leute gehen an uns vorbei.
3. Am Freitag habe ich leider keine Zeit.
4. Paul macht eine Europareise mit Freunden.
5. Meine Frau kauft ein neues Haus außerhalb von Mainz.
6. Für den Sauerbraten brauchen wir Rotweinessig.

3 **Sprichwörter** Practice reading these sayings aloud.

Schuster, bleib bei deinen Leisten.[1]

Einem geschenkten Gaul schaut man nicht ins Maul.[2]

[1] Stick with what you know. (lit. *Cobbler, stick with your shoe stretchers.*)

[2] Don't look a gift horse in the mouth.

Ressourcen

v̂Text | LM p. 77 | vhlcentral

Ein Picknick im Park Video

George und Meline treffen Sabite und Torsten im Park. Sie sprechen über Sport und ihre Hobbys. Kommt Meline Torsten zu nahe (*too close*)?

Vorbereitung Have students preview the images and write down three questions they want to have answered when they watch the video.

1

TORSTEN Das Fußballspiel beginnt um halb acht.
SABITE Es ist Viertel nach sechs. Niemand ist hier. George kommt von der Uni.

2

TORSTEN Spielt er Fußball?
SABITE Er spielt Baseball in der Freizeit. Er ist in einer Uni-Mannschaft.
TORSTEN Hat Meline Hobbys?
SABITE Sie fährt Ski und spielt Tennis. Sie gewinnt alles.

3

GEORGE Oh, vielen Dank! Wo sind Hans und Meline?
SABITE Meline kommt aus der Bibliothek. Hans hat eine Vorlesung.
GEORGE Studierst du auch, Torsten?
TORSTEN Ja. Ich studiere Chemie und Biologie.

4

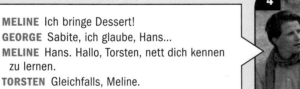

MELINE Ich bringe Dessert!
GEORGE Sabite, ich glaube, Hans...
MELINE Hans. Hallo, Torsten, nett dich kennen zu lernen.
TORSTEN Gleichfalls, Meline.

5

MELINE Du studierst Medizin?
TORSTEN Biologie.
MELINE Fährst du Ski?
TORSTEN Nee, meine Familie fährt nicht Ski. Aber ich wandere und klettere.

MELINE Ich komme aus Wien. Alle fahren Ski in den österreichischen Alpen. Wir haben viele Sportarten: Skifahren, Klettern, Fahrradfahren, Golf und Tennis. Spielst du auch Tennis?
SABITE Äh, Meline?
MELINE Hmmm?
SABITE Gehen wir spazieren.

6

1 **Was ist richtig?** Choose the words that best complete the sentences.

1. Torsten und Sabite sind (im Park)/ im Café).
2. George kommt (aus dem Stadion / von der Uni).
3. Meline fährt Ski und spielt (Golf / Tennis).
4. Torsten studiert Chemie und (Biologie / Physik).
5. Meline bringt (Kaffee / Dessert).

6. Alle fahren (Ski / Bob) in den österreichischen Alpen.
7. Sabite ist eifersüchtig auf (*jealous of*) (Meline / Torsten).
8. Meline trennt keine (Klassenkameraden / Paare).
9. (Frau Yilmaz / Herr Yilmaz) macht morgen Sauerbraten.
10. Hans weiß nicht, dass Sabite einen (Mitbewohner / Freund) hat.

Expansion Have students write simple sentences with the words that were not chosen.

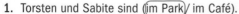
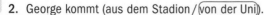
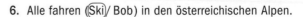

PERSONEN

 Torsten
 Sabite
 George
 Meline

7

SABITE Meline. Wir sind Mitbewohnerinnen. Freundinnen.
MELINE Und?
SABITE „Spielst du auch Tennis?"

8

MELINE Sabite. Keine Sorge. Ich trenne keine Paare.
SABITE Es ist okay, ich verstehe.

9

SABITE George, Meline, meine Mutter macht morgen Sauerbraten. Kommt ihr zum Abendessen?
MELINE Oh, danke, Sabite. Wir kommen.
TORSTEN Frau Yilmaz ist eine gute Köchin.
GEORGE Wow, vielen Dank. Und Hans?
SABITE Ich frage ihn.

10

MELINE Hans weiß nicht, dass Sabite einen Freund hat, oder?
GEORGE Er hat keine Ahnung.

Nützliche Ausdrücke

- **Niemand ist hier.**
  Nobody's here.

- **die Uni-Mannschaft**
  varsity team

- **Sie gewinnt alles.**
  She wins at everything.

- **glauben**
  to believe

- **aber**
  but

- **Alle fahren Ski in den österreichischen Alpen.**
  Everyone in the Austrian Alps skis.

- **Gehen wir spazieren.**
  Let's go for a walk.

- **Keine Sorge.**
  Don't worry.

- **das Abendessen**
  dinner

- **der Koch / die Köchin**
  cook

- **Hans weiß nicht, dass Sabite einen Freund hat, oder?**
  Hans doesn't know Sabite has a boyfriend, does he?

- **Er hat keine Ahnung.**
  He doesn't have a clue.

2B.1
- **Meine Familie fährt nicht Ski.**
  My family doesn't ski.

2B.2
- **Meine Mutter macht morgen Sauerbraten.**
  My mother is making sauerbraten tomorrow.

2B.3
- **Ich trenne keine Paare.**
  I wouldn't break up a couple.

---

2 **Zum Besprechen** In this episode, the characters talk about their favorite sports and pastimes. Interview your classmates to find out who shares your interests. Who likes the same sports? Who has the same hobbies? Answers will vary.

2 Suggestion Refer students to the script for scenes 3, 5, and 6 for model questions they can use to interview their classmates.

3 Suggestion Point out that the United States national soccer team has a German coach, Jürgen Klinsmann. Ask if any students saw the 2014 World Cup games, including the championship match between Germany and Argentina.

3 **Vertiefung** Fußball is one of the most popular sports in Germany. What is the name of the German national soccer league? Find the names of four prominent German soccer teams. Which team won last year's championship? (Fußball-)Bundesliga; Sample answers: FC Bayern München, VfL Wolfsburg, Bayer Leverkusen, Borussia Mönchengladbach; Answers will vary.

3 Expansion Have students research popular soccer players from Germany, Austria, and Switzerland and share their names with the class.

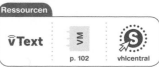

IM FOKUS

Skifahren im Blut

 Reading

AP* Theme: Contemporary Life
Context: Entertainment, Travel, & Leisure

IN ALPINE VILLAGES, LEARNING TO SKI is like learning to walk. Almost everyone does it, starting at a very young age. The beginner slopes are full of pre-school-aged children taking their first lessons. Skiing courses were required in Austrian schools until 1995, and many schools in Bavaria and Austria still offer **Skiwoche°**, a chaperoned week-long ski trip, as part of their curriculum.

Many of the world's best skiers come from German-speaking countries. Carina Vogt is a German **Skisprung-Weltmeisterin°** and **Olympiasiegerin°**.

Vogt won the first gold medal ever awarded for women's ski jumping at the 2014 Sochi Winter Olympic games, and in 2015 she won two World Cup gold medals for ski jumping, coming in third overall in women's events. In honor of her achievements, there is now a street named after her in her home town of Degenfeld in Baden-Württemberg.

Austrian Marcel Hirscher specializes in slalom and giant slalom. The son of two ski instructors, Hirscher has been skiing since age 2. In 2015, at the age of 26, he became the first **Weltmeister** ever to win the overall World Cup title for men's ski events four times in a row.

While the Alpine skiing tradition remains strong, environmental and economic sustainability have become major concerns. Ski tourism has had a serious impact on the ecology of the Alpine regions. With rising temperatures due to climate change, lack of snow is also becoming an issue. Snowmaking is expensive and uses vast amounts of water. And, while large ski resorts continue to draw visitors from all over the world, skiing is becoming less affordable for locals, with some smaller ski areas struggling to remain in business.

Österreich: Ski-Paradies	
Jährliche Anzahl an° Skitouristen	mehr als° 15,4 Millionen
Jährliche Einnahmen° durch Skifahren	mehr als 11 Milliarden Euro
Arbeitsplätze° im Skitourismus	312.625
Pistenfläche°	25.400 Hektar (254 km²)
Alpine Skiweltmeisterschaft 2015: Medaillen für Österreich	9 (5 Gold, 3 Silber, 1 Bronze)

QUELLE: Trend Wirtschaftsmagazin

Blut *blood* **Skiwoche** *ski week* **Skisprung-Weltmeisterin** *ski jump world champion* **Olympiasiegerin** *Olympic gold medalist* **Jährliche Anzahl an** *Annual number of* **mehr als** *more than* **Einnahmen** *revenue* **Arbeitsplätze** *jobs* **Pistenfläche** *skiable area*

---

1 **Was fehlt?** Complete the statements.

1. Austrian schools had mandatory ski classes until ____1995____.

2. In Bavaria and Austria, many school classes travel to the mountains for ____Skiwoche____.

3. ____Carina Vogt____ won the first ever Olympic gold medal for women's ski jumping.

4. Vogt won two ____World Cup____ gold medals in 2015.

5. There is a street named after Vogt in the town of ____Degenfeld____.

6. ____Marcel Hirscher____ started skiing at age 2.

7. Hirscher was the first ever four-time ____Weltmeister____ in men's ski events.

8. ____Snowmaking____ uses excessive quantities of water.

9. Ski tourism accounts for ____312,625____ jobs in Austria.

10. Austria won ____9____ medals in the 2015 Alpine Skiing World Championships.

 Practice more at **vhlcentral.com**.

Mehr Freizeit

der Fan, -s	fan
die Meisterschaft, -en	championship
der Spielstand, ⁻e	score
das Tor, -e	goal (in soccer, etc.)
faulenzen	to relax; to be lazy
joggen	to jog
fit	in good shape
sportlich	athletic
Los!	Start!; Go!

Die Deutschen und das Fahrrad

In Deutschland hat man im Schnitt° 6 Stunden und 34 Minuten Freizeit am Tag. Populäre Hobbys der Deutschen sind Videospiele, Lesen und natürlich° Sport. Die Deutschen sind leidenschaftliche° Fahrradfahrer. Kilometerlange Radwege° durchkreuzen° das Land, wie etwa° die Romantische Straße° in Bayern: sie führt an Schlössern° und vielseitigen Landschaften° vorbei°.

AP* Theme: Contemporary Life

Context: Entertainment, Travel, & Leisure

im Schnitt on average **natürlich** of course
leidenschaftliche passionate **Radwege** bike trails
durchkreuzen cross **wie etwa** such as **Straße** road
Schlössern castles **vielseitigen Landschaften** varied
landscapes **führt an... vorbei** leads past

Suggestion Tell students that **die Romantische Straße** is a road with an adjacent bike path that runs 350 km from Würzburg to Füssen.

Tooooooor!

Der talentierte und populäre Fußballer **Mesut Özil** spielt international für Deutschland. 2014 ist die deutsche Fußballnationalmannschaft in Brasilien bei der Weltmeisterschaft°. In allen sieben Spielen steht Mesut Özil in der Startelf°. Er erzielt° drei Tore und wird° mit der deutschen Nationalmannschaft Weltmeister. Özil ist Deutscher mit türkischer Abstammung° und kommt aus Gelsenkirchen. Er ist Moslem und betet vor jedem° Spiel. Man sagt, die Familie Özil ist ein gutes Beispiel für erfolgreiche° Integration von Ausländern° in Deutschland. Aber Özil spielt nicht nur° für deutsche Mannschaften. Seit° 2013 spielt er in England, für *Arsenal London*.

AP* Theme: Personal & Public Identities
Context: Alienation & Integration

Weltmeisterschaft World Cup **Startelf** starting line-up
erzielt scores **wird** becomes **mit türkischer Abstammung**
of Turkish descent **betet vor jedem** prays before every
erfolgreiche successful **Ausländern** foreigners
nicht nur not only **Seit** Since

IM INTERNET

Wandern: Was sind beliebte Wanderwege° in der Schweiz?

beliebte Wanderwege popular hiking trails

Find out more at **vhlcentral.com**.

---

2 **Richtig oder falsch?** In pairs, correct the false statements.

	richtig	falsch
1. On average, Germans have more than six hours of leisure time per day.	☑	☐
2. Biking is a popular sport in Germany.	☑	☐
3. Mesut Özil played in six games in the 2014 World Cup. Özil played in seven games.	☐	☑
4. Mesut Özil grew up in Turkey. He grew up in the German town of Gelsenkirchen.	☐	☑

3 **Bekannte Sportler** In pairs, take turns role-playing famous athletes who play each of the sports listed. Your partner must guess who you are.
Answers will vary.

BEISPIEL **3** **Partner Chat** You can also assign activity 3 on the Supersite.

S1: *Ich spiele Fußball und komme aus Deutschland.*
S2: *Bist du Mesut Özil?*

1. Golf
2. Baseball
3. Schwimmen
4. Tennis
5. Basketball
6. Fußball

QUERVERWEIS

See **2A.1** to review the present-tense conjugations of regular verbs.

2B.1

Stem-changing verbs  Presentation

Startblock Certain irregular verbs follow predictable patterns of spelling changes in their present-tense conjugations. These verbs use the regular endings, but have changes to their stem vowels in the **du** and **er/sie/es** forms. Most stem-changing verbs follow one of four patterns in the present tense.

ACHTUNG

The formal **Sie** forms are the same as the plural **sie** forms for all verbs. Starting in this lesson, **Sie** and **sie** (*pl.*) forms will be listed together in verb tables.

- a ⟶ ä

schlafen (*to sleep*)			
ich schlafe	*I sleep*	wir schlafen	*we sleep*
du schläfst	*you sleep*	ihr schlaft	*you sleep*
er/sie/es schläft	*he/she/it sleeps*	Sie/sie schlafen	*you/they sleep*

Schläfst du jede Nacht acht Stunden?
*Do you **sleep** eight hours every night?*

Sie **schlafen** im Studentenwohnheim.
*They **sleep** in the dormitory.*

- au ⟶ äu

laufen (*to run*)			
ich laufe	*I run*	wir laufen	*we run*
du läufst	*you run*	ihr lauft	*you run*
er/sie/es läuft	*he/she/it runs*	Sie/sie laufen	*you/they run*

Mehmet **läuft** am Strand.
*Mehmet **runs** on the beach.*

Sie **laufen** über das Spielfeld.
*They're **running** across the field.*

- e ⟶ i

	essen (*to eat*)			sprechen (*to speak*)	
ich	esse	*I eat*		spreche	*I speak*
du	isst	*you eat*		sprichst	*you speak*
er/sie/es	isst	*he/she/it eats*		spricht	*he/she/it speaks*
wir	essen	*we eat*		sprechen	*we speak*
ihr	esst	*you eat*		sprecht	*you speak*
Sie/sie	essen	*you/they eat*		sprechen	*you/they speak*

Wir **essen** in der Mensa.
*We're **eating** in the cafeteria.*

Sprichst du Englisch?
*Do you **speak** English?*

- Besides an e ⟶ i vowel change, **nehmen** (*to take*) and **werden** (*to become*) have additional changes in the **du** and **er/sie/es** forms.

ACHTUNG

Remember: when the verb stem ends in -**s**, drop the -**s** from the second-person singular ending.

	nehmen (*to take*)			werden (*to become*)	
ich	nehme	*I take*		werde	*I become*
du	nimmst	*you take*		wirst	*you become*
er/sie/es	nimmt	*he/she/it takes*		wird	*he/she/it becomes*
wir	nehmen	*we take*		werden	*we become*
ihr	nehmt	*you take*		werdet	*you become*
Sie/sie	nehmen	*you/they take*		werden	*you/they become*

Du **nimmst** jeden Tag den Bus.
*You **take** the bus every day.*

Ein Anfänger **wird** mit der Zeit Experte.
*A beginner **becomes** an expert over time.*

- e ⟶ ie

	lesen (*to read*)		sehen (*to see*)	
ich	lese	*I read*	sehe	*I see*
du	liest	*you read*	siehst	*you see*
er/sie/es	liest	*he/she/it reads*	sieht	*he/she/it sees*
wir	lesen	*we read*	sehen	*we see*
ihr	lest	*you read*	seht	*you see*
Sie/sie	lesen	*you/they read*	sehen	*you/they see*

Du **liest** viele Bücher.
*You **read** a lot of books.*

Seht ihr die Spieler?
*Do you **see** the players?*

- This table summarizes some common verbs with stem changes in the present tense. When a verb with a present-tense stem change is presented in this text, it will be listed with its third-person singular form: **lesen (liest)**.

common stem-changing verbs (present tense)			
a ⟶ ä		**e ⟶ i**	
braten	*to fry*	brechen	*to break*
fahren	*to go*	essen	*to eat*
fallen	*to fall*	geben	*to give*
fangen	*to catch*	helfen	*to help*
lassen	*to let, to allow*	nehmen	*to take*
schlafen	*to sleep*	sprechen	*to speak*
tragen	*to carry; to wear*	treffen	*to hit; to meet*
waschen	*to wash*	vergessen	*to forget*
		werden	*to become*
		werfen	*to throw*
au ⟶ äu		**e ⟶ ie**	
laufen	*to run*	empfehlen	*to recommend*
		lesen	*to read*
		sehen	*to see*
		stehlen	*to steal*

Fährst du nach Berlin?
*Are you **going** to Berlin?*

Es **gibt** dort ein sehr gutes Café.
*There **is** a very good café there.*

ACHTUNG

The verb **geben** is used in certain idiomatic expressions, such as **Es gibt** (*There is/There are*). Idiomatic expressions do not translate literally to English.

Ressourcen

v̂Text

WB
pp. 27–28

LM
p. 78

vhlcentral

Jetzt sind Sie dran!   Write the appropriate form of the verb.

1. Ich ___esse___ (essen) viele Äpfel.
2. Du ___hilfst___ (helfen) Sophie.
3. Ich ___gebe___ (geben) Tobias ein Buch.
4. Peter ___nimmt___ (nehmen) ein Taxi.
5. Ihr ___fahrt___ (fahren) gern Fahrrad.
6. Wir ___tragen___ (tragen) Rucksäcke.
7. Anna ___wird___ (werden) Informatikprofessorin.
8. Du ___liest___ (lesen) viele Bücher.
9. Er ___schläft___ (schlafen) bis 8 Uhr morgens.
10. Ihr ___sprecht___ (sprechen) Deutsch.
11. Die Schüler ___sehen___ (sehen) einen Film.
12. Du ___vergisst___ (vergessen) die Hausaufgaben.

Anwendung

1 **Was ist richtig?** Select the verb that best completes each sentence.

1. Hannah (schläft / isst) viele Äpfel.
2. Ich (lese / brate) ein Schnitzel.
3. Du (fährst / triffst) einen Porsche.
4. Wir (helfen / waschen) den Hund.
5. Alena und Daniel (treffen / sprechen) Deutsch, Englisch und Polnisch.
6. Ihr (lauft / fangt) 8 Kilometer.
7. Du (liest / wird) viele Bücher.
8. Du (gibst / triffst) Jasmin im Café.

2 **Schreiben** Write complete sentences using the cues.

1. Herr Schmidt / empfehlen / das Schnitzel
   Herr Schmidt empfiehlt das Schnitzel.
2. ich / wissen / die Antwort
   Ich weiß die Antwort.
3. du / fahren / das Auto
   Du fährst das Auto.
4. wir / treffen / Katrina und Paul
   Wir treffen Katrina und Paul.
5. Angela / lesen / gern
   Angela liest gern.
6. du / sprechen / Deutsch
   Du sprichst Deutsch.
7. ich / werden / Architekt
   Ich werde Architekt.
8. Peter / stehlen / einen Apfel
   Peter stiehlt einen Apfel.

3 **Was sehen Sie?** Complete the sentences. Sample answers are provided.

▶ **BEISPIEL**

Peter ___läuft___ gern im Park.

1. Sie ___schlafen___ in der Hängematte.

2. Tobi ___wäscht___ das Auto.

3. Der Footballspieler ___fängt___ den Ball.

4. Hans ___liest___ das Buch.

5. Er ___isst___ eine Bratwurst.

6. Ingrid ___trifft___ Rolf im Museum.

 Practice more at **vhlcentral.com**.

Kommunikation

4 **Bilden Sie Sätze** In pairs, create six logical sentences with items from each column. Some items may be used more than once. Answers will vary.

> **BEISPIEL** *Du empfiehlst die Torte.*

A	B	C
ich	empfehlen	Fußball im Stadion
du	lesen	Goethes *Faust*
Nina	sehen	die Torte
Elsa und ich	spielen	23 Jahre alt
Bianca und du	sprechen	viele Fremdsprachen
Olivia und Markus	werden	einen Film

5 **Wie bitte?** Adele is talking to her mother on the phone. You hear only Adele's side of the conversation. In pairs, reconstruct her mother's questions. Sample answers are provided.

> **BEISPIEL** *Ich fahre am Wochenende nach Hause (home).*
>
> *Wann fährst du nach Hause?*

1. Ja, ich schlafe gut.
   Schläfst du gut?
2. Ich esse um 7 Uhr abends.
   Wann isst du?
3. Ja, ich lese viel.
   Liest du viel?
4. Ich sehe Matthias im Unterricht.
   Wo siehst du Matthias? / Wen siehst du im Unterricht?

5. Ja, wir sprechen im Unterricht Deutsch.
   Sprecht ihr im Unterricht Deutsch?
6. Ja, Matthias und ich nehmen zusammen (*together*) den Bus.
   Nehmt ihr zusammen den Bus?
7. Ich treffe Matthias nachmittags im Café.
   Wo/Wann triffst du Matthias?
8. Ja, ich fahre oft Fahrrad.
   Fährst du oft Fahrrad?

6 **Wer macht was?** Use the cues to ask your classmates whether they participate in these activities. Answers will vary.

> **BEISPIEL**
>
> **S1:** *Spielst du Fußball im Stadion?*
> **S2:** *Nein, aber ich laufe im Park. Läufst du auch im Park?*

Fahrrad fahren	im Park laufen	im Stadion Fußball spielen
Ski fahren	im Schwimmbad schwimmen	Bälle werfen und fangen
viele Bücher lesen	den Bus nehmen	Freunde im Café treffen

7 **Im Park** In pairs, write a paragraph that describes the activities of the people shown. Use each of the verbs from the list at least once. Answers will vary.

> **BEISPIEL**
>
> **S1:** *Die Frauen gehen im Park spazieren.*
> **S2:** *Die Kinder reiten im Park.*

fahren	sehen
laufen	gehen
reiten	spielen
schlafen	treffen

5 **Virtual Chat** You can also assign activity 5 on the Supersite. Students record individual responses that appear in your gradebook.

6 **Expansion** Have students take notes on their classmates' answers and report their findings to the class. Ex.: **Michael spielt Baseball im Stadion. Anna fährt Fahrrad im Park.**

2B.2

Present tense used as future  Presentation

Startblock In German, as in English, you can use the present tense with certain time expressions to talk about the future.

> Heute Abend spielen wir Fußball.

> Morgen macht meine Mutter Sauerbraten.

ACHTUNG

To talk about *this morning*, you can say either **heute Morgen** or **heute früh**. Use **früh** (*early; in the morning*) instead of **Morgen** with the adverbs **morgen** and **übermorgen**.

Heute Morgen habe ich Biologie.
This morning I have biology.

Morgen früh habe ich Chemie.
Tomorrow morning I have chemistry.

QUERVERWEIS

You will learn more about adjectives and adverbs in **3A.2** and **4A.1**.

Students will learn more vocabulary related to the seasons in **Vol. 2, 3A**.

- The adverbs **heute** (*today*), **morgen** (*tomorrow*), and **übermorgen** (*the day after tomorrow*) are commonly used with the present tense to express future ideas. Use them with these time expressions to specify the time of day at which a future action will occur.

common time expressions			
Morgen	*morning*	Nachmittag	*afternoon*
Vormittag	*midmorning*	Abend	*evening*
Mittag	*noon*	Nacht	*night*

Morgen gehen wir einkaufen.
Tomorrow we're going shopping.

Heute Nachmittag gehe ich schwimmen.
This afternoon I'm going swimming.

- In **2A.3**, you learned to use **am** before dates and days of the week. Also use **am** with **Morgen, Vormittag, Mittag, Nachmittag, Abend,** or **Wochenende** to specify when something will occur. When both the day of the week and the time of day are specified, they form a compound noun: **Dienstagmittag, Mittwochabend.**

Am Wochenende gehen wir angeln.
*We're going fishing **this weekend**.*

Am Freitagnachmittag gehe ich zum Arzt.
*I'm going to the doctor's **Friday afternoon**.*

- Use **im** with months and seasons (**Frühling, Sommer, Herbst, Winter**).

Im Februar fahre ich Ski.
*I'm going skiing **in February**.*

Im Frühling gehe ich wandern.
*I'm going hiking **this spring**.*

- The adjective **nächste** (*next*) can be used with time-related nouns such as days of the week, seasons, and months. In this usage, it takes accusative endings.

nächsten Sommer
next summer

nächste Woche
next week

nächstes Jahr
next year

Jetzt sind Sie dran!   Select the appropriate word or phrase.

1. Wir fahren (nächstes / (nächste)) Woche nach Polen.
2. ((Am) / Im) Montagvormittag gehe ich spazieren.
3. ((Heute Abend) / Abend) spielt ihr Karten.
4. Ursula fährt (am / (im)) Februar Ski.
5. Wir wandern ((nächsten) / nächstes) Freitag im Wald.
6. ((Morgen Nachmittag) / Nachmittag) fahre ich Fahrrad.
7. Wir gehen (Nacht / (übermorgen)) klettern.
8. (Nächsten / (Nächstes)) Wochenende spielst du Tennis.

Ressourcen

v̂Text

WB
pp. 29–30

LM
p. 79

S
vhlcentral

Anwendung und Kommunikation

1 **Was passt?** Select the appropriate time expression.

1. Die nächste Prüfung ist (Nachmittag / (übermorgen)).
2. Ich fahre ((im) / am) März in Urlaub.
3. Spielst du ((am) / im) Abend Hockey?
4. Peter und Bettina fahren ((nächstes) / nächste) Wochenende in die Berge.
5. Gehst du (Nachmittag / (heute Nachmittag)) klettern?
6. (Nächstes / (Nächsten)) Sommer fahren wir an den Strand.

2 **Bilden Sie Sätze** Write sentences using the cues.

1. ich / gehen / heute Nachmittag / angeln Ich gehe heute Nachmittag angeln.
2. übermorgen / spielen / Roland / Baseball Übermorgen spielt Roland Baseball.
3. nächstes Jahr / fahren / Anja / an den Strand Nächstes Jahr fährt Anja an den Strand.
4. Patrick / treffen / Bianca / am Abend Patrick trifft Bianca am Abend.
5. am Sonntagabend / kochen / wir Am Sonntagabend kochen wir.
6. du / fahren / im Winter / Ski Du fährst im Winter Ski.

3 **Sätze** In pairs, use items from each column to make up sentences describing what each person is going to do. Answers will vary.

BEISPIEL

Wir sehen heute Abend einen Film.

A	B	C	D
ich	Fahrrad fahren	am Freitag	für einen Marathonlauf
du	gehen	heute Nacht	im Park
Angelika	spazieren gehen	Im Dezember	nach Österreich
wir	reisen	im Frühling	Freunde im Restaurant
ihr	trainieren	morgen Nachmittag	in die Disko
Otto und Gabi	treffen	nächstes Jahr	in den Bergen

3 **Expansion** Have students ask each other about their own plans for each of the times listed in column C. Ex.: **Was macht du am Freitag?**

4 **Fernsehen** In pairs, decide which TV programs you want to watch, and take turns asking each other when they will be on. Answers will vary.

BEISPIEL

S1: *Wann kommt TV total?*
S2: *TV total kommt morgen Abend / Mittwochabend.*

	Dienstag (heute)	Mittwoch	Donnerstag
10.00 Uhr	Reisen für Genießer	Lindenstraße	Türkisch für Anfänger
15.00 Uhr	Sport Aktuell	Das Supertalent	Die Sendung mit der Maus
19.00 Uhr	Formel 1	Hallo Deutschland	Deutschland sucht den Superstar
23.00 Uhr	Bauer sucht Frau	TV total	Familien im Brennpunkt

4 **Partner Chat** You can also assign activity 4 on the Supersite. Students work in pairs to record the activity online. The pair's recorded conversation will appear in your gradebook.

  Practice more at **vhlcentral.com**.

2B.3

Negation  Presentation

Startblock In **1B.2**, you learned to make affirmative statements and ask yes-or-no questions. To negate a statement or ask a negative question, use **nicht** or **kein**.

Nein, meine Familie fährt **nicht** Ski.

Ich trenne **keine** Paare.

Nicht

QUERVERWEIS

You have already learned to use **nicht** in the expressions **nicht schlecht** and **nicht (so) gut** (in **1A Kontext**) and **nicht gern** (in **2B Kontext**)

ACHTUNG

Ich spiele kein Tennis means *I don't play tennis (at all)*. **Ich spiele nicht Tennis** means *I'm not playing tennis (at the moment)*.

- In negative statements or questions, place **nicht** after the subject, conjugated verb, direct object, and definite time expressions, but before other sentence elements.

Ich gehe heute in die Sporthalle.
I'm going to the gym today.
▶ Ich gehe heute **nicht** in die Sporthalle.
*I'm **not** going to the gym today.*

Brauchst du den Fußball?
Do you need the soccer ball?
▶ Brauchst du den Fußball **nicht**?
Don't you need the soccer ball?

Die Spieler sind hier.
The players are here.
▶ Die Spieler sind **nicht** hier.
*The players are **not** here.*

Mathematik ist einfach
Math is easy.
▶ Mathematik ist **nicht** einfach.
*Math is **not** easy.*

- In some cases, the placement of **nicht** depends on which element of a statement the speaker wants to emphasize.

Ich spiele **nicht** Golf mit Tobias.
  Ich spiele mit Tobias Tennis.
*I'm **not** playing golf with Tobias.*
  I'm playing tennis with Tobias.

Ich spiele **nicht** mit Tobias Golf.
  Ich spiele mit Moritz Golf.
*I'm **not** playing golf with Tobias.*
  I'm playing golf with Moritz.

Wir sehen den Film heute **nicht**.
*We're **not** seeing the film today.*

Wir sehen den Film morgen, **nicht** heute.
*We're seeing the film tomorrow, **not** today.*

Die Studenten essen **nicht** in der Mensa.
*The students are**n't** eating in the dining hall.*

Die Studenten essen in der Mensa **nicht** gern.
*The students do**n't** like to eat in the dining hall.*

Hans weiß es **nicht**?

Er hat **keine** Ahnung.

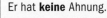

Kein

- **Kein** is the negative form of the indefinite article **ein**. Use **kein** to negate a noun preceded by an indefinite article or by no article.

—Haben Sie Zeit?
—*Do you have time?*

▶ —Nein, wir haben **keine** Zeit.
—*No, we don't have time.*

—Hat er ein Hobby?
—*Does he have a hobby?*

▶ —Nein, er hat **keine** Hobbys.
—*No, he has **no** hobbies.*

- **Kein** follows the same patterns of gender and case endings as **ein**. Note that, unlike **ein**, **kein** has a plural form.

kein				
	masculine	**feminine**	**neuter**	**plural**
nominative	kein Ball	keine Freizeit	kein Spiel	keine Karten
accusative	keinen Ball	keine Freizeit	kein Spiel	keine Karten

—Hast du **einen** Fußball?
—*Do you have **a** soccer ball?*

▶ —Nein, ich habe **keinen** Fußball.
—*No, I don't have **a** soccer ball.*

—Ist das **ein** Stadion?
—*Is that **a** stadium?*

▶ —Nein, das ist **kein** Stadion.
—*No, that's **not a** stadium.*

—Sind das Basketballspieler?
—*Are those guys basketball players?*

▶ —Nein, das sind **keine** Basketballspieler.
—*No, those aren't basketball players.*

Doch

- The word **doch** has no exact equivalent in English. Use it to contradict a negative question or statement.

—Ich habe **keine** Freunde.
—*I don't have **any** friends.*

▶ —**Doch**, du hast viele Freunde!
—*No, you have lots of friends!*

—Gehst du **nicht** zum Strand?
—*Aren't you going to the beach?*

▶ —**Doch**, ich gehe zum Strand.
—*Yes, I'm going to the beach.*

QUERVERWEIS

Words that have the same endings as **ein** are often called **ein**-words. You will learn about other **ein**-words in **3A.1**.

Suggestion Point out that the responses **Ja**, **Nein**, and **Doch** at the beginning of a sentence do not affect subject-verb word order.

Ressourcen

v̂ Text

WB
pp. 31–32

LM
p. 80

S
vhlcentral

Jetzt sind Sie dran! Complete the sentences with the appropriate form of **nicht** or **kein**.

1. Der Volleyballspieler ist ___*nicht*___ so fit.
2. Stefan hat ___keinen___ Fußball.
3. Wir machen die Hausaufgaben ___nicht___.
4. Übermorgen habe ich ___keine___ Vorlesung.
5. Uwe trainiert ___nicht___ und verliert das Spiel.
6. Ich habe ___kein___ Foto.

7. Bernhard spielt viel Fußball, aber er gewinnt ___keine___ Spiele.
8. Du schwimmst ___nicht___ im Schwimmbad.
9. Wir sehen den Film ___nicht___.
10. Ihr habt ___keine___ Freizeit.
11. Am Donnerstag fahren wir ___nicht___ in die Berge.
12. Es gibt hier ___kein___ Stadion.

Anwendung

1 Verneinen Sie Negate the sentences using nicht.

1. Wir haben die Karten.
Wir haben die Karten nicht.
2. Ich vergesse die Hausaufgaben.
Ich vergesse die Hausaufgaben nicht.
3. Wir reiten am Wochenende.
Wir reiten am Wochenende nicht.
4. Simon und Katrina sind hier.
Simon und Katrina sind nicht hier.
5. Du gehst in die Bibliothek.
Du gehst nicht in die Bibliothek.

6. Ihr verliert das Volleyballspiel.
Ihr verliert das Volleyballspiel nicht.
7. Thomas und Brigitte schwimmen am Nachmittag.
Thomas und Brigitte schwimmen am Nachmittag nicht.
8. Am Sonntag gehen wir angeln.
Am Sonntag gehen wir nicht angeln.

2 Antworten Sie Answer the questions using kein.

> **BEISPIEL**
>
> **S1:** Hast du Hobbys?
> **S2:** Nein, ich habe keine Hobbys.

1. Hat Peter ein Fahrrad?
Nein, Peter hat kein Fahrrad.
2. Habt ihr Freizeit?
Nein, wir haben keine Freizeit.
3. Sind das Spielerinnen?
Nein, das sind keine Spielerinnen.
4. Ist Berlin ein Land (country)?
Nein, Berlin ist kein Land.
5. Ist Alexandra eine Hockeyspielerin?
Nein, Alexandra ist keine Hockeyspielerin.

6. Hast du einen Basketball?
Nein, ich habe keinen Basketball.
7. Gibt es dort ein Stadion?
Nein, es gibt dort kein Stadion.
8. Spielst du Volleyball?
Nein, ich spiele keinen Volleyball.
9. Ist Salzburg ein Berg?
Nein, Salzburg ist kein Berg.
10. Haben Sie Karten?
Nein, ich habe keine Karten.

3 Was fehlt? Complete the conversation with nicht, kein, or doch.

KARIN Hallo, Alina! Geht's dir gut? Kommst du (1) __nicht__ heute Abend zum Training?

ALINA Heute Abend? (2) __Doch__! Aber morgen komme ich (3) __nicht__.

KARIN Warum (4) __nicht__?

ALINA Ich habe (5) __keine__ Zeit! Wir haben sehr viele Biologiehausaufgaben und übermorgen habe ich auch eine Chemieprüfung!

KARIN Hast du nicht vier Klassen?

ALINA (6) __Doch__, ich habe Biologie, Chemie, Physik und auch Mathematik.

Kommunikation

4 **Partnerinterview** In pairs, take turns asking each other questions.
Contradict your partner's questions using **nicht**, **kein**, or **doch**. Sample answers are provided.

BEISPIEL

S1: Hast du einen Basketball?
S2: Nein, ich habe keinen Basketball.
S1: Tanzt du nicht am Wochenende?
S2: Doch, ich tanze am Wochenende.

1. Spielst du Hockey?
   Nein, ich spiele kein Hockey.
2. Wanderst du im Wald?
   Nein, ich wandere nicht im Wald.
3. Fährst du im Dezember Fahrrad?
   Nein, im Dezember fahre ich nicht Fahrrad.
4. Hast du keine Hobbys?
   Doch, ich habe viele Hobbys.

5. Trainierst du für einen Marathonlauf?
   Nein, ich trainiere für keinen Marathonlauf.
6. Hast du nicht viele Hausaufgaben?
   Doch, ich habe viele Hausaufgaben.
7. Schwimmst du im Schwimmbad?
   Nein, ich schwimme nicht im Schwimmbad.
8. Bist du Tennisspieler(in)?
   Nein, ich bin kein Tennisspieler / keine Tennisspielerin.

4 **Expansion** Have students create their own questions to ask their partners.

4 **Virtual Chat** You can also assign activity 4 on the Supersite. Students record individual responses that appear in your gradebook.

5 **Das stimmt nicht!** In pairs, take turns making false statements about the photos. Correct your partner's false statements by negating them, then supply the correct answer. Answers will vary.

BEISPIEL

S1: Die Frau fährt Auto.
S2: Nein, sie fährt nicht Auto. Sie fährt Fahrrad.

1.

2.

3.

4.

5.

6.

5 **Partner Chat** You can also assign activity 5 on the Supersite. Students work in pairs to record the activity online. The pair's recorded conversation will appear in your gradebook.

6 **Ich habe es schlecht** In pairs, take turns coming up with exaggerations using **nicht** and **kein**. Contradict your partner's exaggerations using **doch**. Answers will vary.

BEISPIEL

S1: Wir haben keine Freizeit!
S2: Doch, wir haben viel Freizeit!

6 **Partner Chat** You can also assign activity 6 on the Supersite. Students work in pairs to record the activity online. The pair's recorded conversation will appear in your gradebook.

7 **Trauriger Jörn** In small groups, explain why Jörn is sad, using negative statements. Answers will vary.

BEISPIEL

S1: Jörn hat keine Freunde.
S2: Er lernt nicht und hat keine guten Noten.

Wiederholung

1 **Expansion** Have students add their partner's name to the list and ask questions in order to fill out their partner's row in the chart.

1 Gute Freunde
In pairs, look at the information provided about each person. Decide which of them are friends, based on their interests. Answers will vary.

BEISPIEL
Heidi fährt Ski und Florian fährt auch Ski.
Heidi und Florian sind Freunde.

	Tennis spielen	Musik hören	Bücher lesen	Ski fahren	Fahrrad fahren	Fremdsprachen sprechen
Heidi	✓	✓	✓	✓		✓
Daniela	✓	✓	✓	✓		✓
Magda	✓	✓	✓	✓		✓
Klaus		✓		✓		✓
Florian	✓	✓	✓	✓		
Oliver		✓			✓	✓

2 Begriffe raten
In small groups, take turns drawing pictures based on words or phrases you learned in **Lektionen 2A** and **2B**. The first person to guess the word or phrase draws next. Answers will vary.

BEISPIEL
S1: Spielt er Schach?
S2: Nein. Er spielt nicht Schach.
S3: Spielt er Karten?
S2: Ja, richtig!

3 Viele Fragen
Start a conversation with a classmate using the questions as prompts. Ask follow-up questions using time expressions. Answers will vary.

BEISPIEL
S1: Machst du viele Hausaufgaben?
S2: Ja, ich mache viele Hausaufgaben.
S1: Hast du heute Hausaufgaben in Geschichte?
S2: Nein, ich habe heute keine Hausaufgaben in Geschichte.

1. Liest du viele Bücher?
2. Reist du im Winter nach Kanada?
3. Sprichst du Deutsch?
4. Verstehst du Mathematik?
5. Machst du viel Sport?
6. Spielst du Schach?
7. Isst du viel Pizza?
8. Fährst du viel Fahrrad?

3 **Virtual Chat** You can also assign activity 3 on the Supersite. Students record individual responses that appear in your gradebook.

4 Diskutieren und kombinieren
Your instructor will give you and your partner different worksheets showing two schedules. Take turns asking and answering questions to find out the missing information from your partner's schedule.

BEISPIEL
S1: Wann gehst du ins Stadion?
S2: Nächsten Montag um halb fünf nachmittags.

5 Vermischtes
Use the cues to form questions. Then, in pairs, take turns asking and answering the questions. Answers will vary.

BEISPIEL
S1: Hast du heute Abend Freizeit?
S2: Nein, ich habe heute Abend keine Freizeit.

1. angeln gehen / du / am Sonntag
2. Tennis spielen / du / samstags
3. gehen / du / oft / in die Sporthalle
4. Tennisschuhe / haben / keine / du
5. du / reiten / am Wochenende
6. du / schlafen / viel / sonntags
7. für die Prüfung / lernen / nicht / du
8. du / nicht / aus Berlin / kommen

5 **Partner Chat** You can also assign activity 5 on the Supersite. Students work in pairs to record the activity online. The pair's recorded conversation will appear in your gradebook.

6 Arbeitsblatt
Your instructor will give you and your partner each a worksheet. Take turns asking questions to find each other's battleships.

BEISPIEL
S1: Liest Otto ein Buch?
S2: Treffer (Hit)! Er liest ein Buch./
Nein, kein Treffer. Er liest nicht.

	lesen	arbeiten
Otto		
Lukas und Maria		🚢

7 Marias Leben
In pairs, take turns asking and answering questions about Maria's activities. Sample answers are provided.

7 Partner Chat You can also assign activity 7 on the Supersite.

▶ **BEISPIEL**

Dienstag, 9.15

S1: *Was macht Maria am Dienstag um Viertel nach neun morgens?*

S2: *Am Dienstag um Viertel nach neun morgens macht Maria Hausaufgaben.*

1. morgen, 10.30
Was macht Maria vormittags um halb elf? Vormittags um halb elf lernt Maria Deutsch.

2. heute, 12.00
Was macht Maria heute Mittag? Heute Mittag spielt Maria Tennis.

3. Samstag, 14.00
Was macht Maria am Samstag um zwei Uhr nachmittags? Am Samstag um zwei Uhr nachmittags liest Maria ein Buch.

4. heute Nachmittag, 14.25
Was macht Maria heute Nachmittag um fünf vor halb drei? Heute Nachmittag um fünf vor halb drei trinkt Maria einen Kaffee.

5. nächsten Montag, 17.45
Was macht Maria nächsten Montag um Viertel vor sechs nachmittags? Nächsten Montag um Viertel vor sechs nachmittags trifft Maria eine Freundin.

6. Freitag, 23.15
Was macht Maria am Freitag um Viertel nach elf abends? Am Freitag um Viertel nach elf abends schläft Maria.

8 Minigeschichte
In small groups, make up a story about the people in the picture. Be as detailed as possible. You may want to give the people names.
Answers will vary.

BEISPIEL

S1: *Es ist Samstag und viele Studenten trainieren im Stadion.*
S2: *Niklas und David sind Basketballspieler, aber sie trainieren nicht...*

fangen	trainieren
gewinnen	treffen
laufen	verlieren
spielen	werfen

Mein Wör|ter|buch

Add five words related to the themes **an der Universität** and **Sport und Freizeit** to your personalized dictionary.

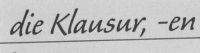

die Klausur, -en

Übersetzung
exam

Wortart
das Substantiv

Gebrauch
Ich lerne viel für die Klausur.

Synonyme
die Prüfung, das Examen, der Test

Antonyme
—

Vocabulary Tools

Weiter geht's

Panorama   Interactive Map

AP* Theme: Global Challenges
Context: Geography

Berlin

NATIONAL connections cultures STANDARDS

Die Stadt in Zahlen

▶ **Fläche:** *892 km² (Quadratkilometer)*

▶ **Einwohner° der Stadt Berlin:** *3.443.570*

▶ **Ausländer° in Berlin:** *503.945 (aus 186 Ländern)*

▶ **Touristen (2013):** *11.324.947*

▶ **Fastfood:** *Döner Kebap, erfunden° 1971 von Mehmet Aygün in Berlin; etwa 1.600 Verkaufsstellen° Currywurst (70 Millionen pro Jahr), erfunden 1949 von Herta Heuwer in Berlin; etwa 200 Verkaufsstellen*

▶ **Touristenattraktionen:** *das Brandenburger Tor, der Reichstag, die Gedächtniskirche, der Gendarmenmarkt, der Alexanderplatz, das Holocaust-Mahnmal, die Museumsinsel, der Potsdamer Platz, das Nikolaiviertel.*

QUELLE: Berlin - offizielles Hauptstadtportal

Berühmte Berliner

▶ **Friedrich II. (Friedrich der Große),** *König von Preußen° (1712–1786)*

▶ **Alexander von Humboldt,** *Naturforscher° (1769–1859)*

▶ **Gustav Langenscheidt,** *Deutschlehrer und Verlagsbuchhändler° (1832–1895)*

▶ **Berthold Brecht,** *Dramatiker° (1898–1956)*

▶ **Marlene Dietrich,** *Schauspielerin° und Sängerin° (1901–1992)*

▶ **Thomas „Icke" Häßler,** *Fußballspieler (1966–)*

▶ **Franziska van Almsick,** *Schwimmerin (1978–)*

Suggestion Tell students that Berlin has a Currywurst Museum. You may want to play Herbert Grönemeyer's song *Currywurst* for the class.

Expansion Ask students questions to review numbers. Ex.: **Wie viele Touristen besuchen Berlin 2013? Wie alt ist Franziska von Almsick?**

Expansion Ask students to plan a trip to Berlin for next year. Ask them what sites they will visit and what they will do on their trip.

Einwohner *inhabitants* **Ausländer** *foreigners* **erfunden** *invented*
Verkaufsstellen *points of sale* **König von Preußen** *King of Prussia*
Naturforscher *naturalist* **Verlagsbuchhändler** *publisher*
Dramatiker *playwright* **Schauspielerin** *actress* **Sängerin** *singer*
Weltkrieg *World War* **in Trümmern** *in ruins* **Gebäude zerstört** *buildings destroyed* **Wohnungen** *apartments* **Krankenhäuser** *hospitals*
beschädigt *damaged*

das Brandenburger Tor

der Alexanderplatz

die Museumsinsel

die Gedächtniskirche

Unglaublich aber wahr!

Am 2. Mai 1945 endet der 2. Weltkrieg° in Berlin. 28.5 km² der Stadt liegen in Trümmern°. Im Zentrum sind etwa 50% der Gebäude zerstört°. Etwa 600.000 Wohnungen° sind komplett zerstört. Die Infrastruktur der Stadt, Straßen, Schulen und Krankenhäuser° sind schwer beschädigt°. In Berlin leben noch 2,8 Millionen Menschen, vor dem Krieg sind es 4,3 Millionen.
AP* Theme: Global Challenges
Context: Political Issues

Geschichte
AP* Theme: Global Challenges
Context: Political Issues

Das DDR Museum

Seit 1989 sind Berlin und ganz Deutschland nicht mehr geteilt°. Das DDR Museum beleuchtet° das Leben in der ehemaligen° DDR: die Mauer, die Stasi° und den Alltag°. Die Ausstellung ist interaktiv. Man kann sich in einen echten° Trabant° oder ein authentisches DDR-Wohnzimmer° setzen. Geschichte zum Anfassen°!

Sport
AP* Theme: Contemporary Life
Context: Entertainment, Travel, & Leisure

Olympische Spiele 1936

Die Olympischen Sommerspiele 1936 finden vom 1. bis 16. August 1936 in Berlin statt°. 3.961 Athleten aus 49 Nationen nehmen an den Spielen teil° – ein neuer Rekord. Der bekannteste° Sportler dieser Spiele ist der amerikanische Leichtathlet Jesse Owens. Er gewinnt vier Goldmedaillen. Der erfolgreichste° deutsche Athlet ist der Kunstturner° Konrad Frey mit drei Goldmedaillen, einer Silbermedaille und zwei Bronzemedaillen. Die Nationalsozialisten missbrauchen° die Spiele als Propaganda.

Architektur
AP* Theme: Beauty & Aesthetics
Context: Architecture

Der Reichstag°

Zwischen 1884 und 1894 errichtet der Architekt Paul Wallot den Reichstag. Er ist das wichtigste° Gebäude der deutschen Politik: Bis 1918 trifft sich hier der Reichstag des Deutschen Kaiserreichs°, danach das Parlament der Weimarer Republik, und seit 1999 der Deutsche Bundestag. 1933 ist der legendäre Reichstagsbrand°. Heute besuchen Touristen oft die Glaskuppel. Sie ist 23,5 Meter hoch°, 40 Meter breit° und 800 Tonnen schwer°. Im Sommer 1995 verhüllen° die Künstler Christo und Jeanne-Claude den Reichstag komplett. 5 Millionen Besucher° kommen nach Berlin, um den Reichstag zu sehen.

Kultur
AP* Theme: Beauty & Aesthetics
Context: Cultural Perspectives

Karneval der Kulturen

Berlin ist eine internationale Stadt mit mehr als 500.000 Menschen aus 186 Ländern. Seit 1996 gibt es jedes Jahr ein Fest, um die Internationalität und Kulturenvielfalt° Berlins zu feiern: den Karneval der Kulturen. Es gibt einen großen Umzug° mit etwa 5.000 Teilnehmern und ein viertägiges Straßenfest mit mehr als 800 Künstlern – Musik, Tanz, Performance – aus über 70 Ländern. 2011 besuchen fast 1,5 Millionen Menschen das Event in Berlin-Kreuzberg. 750.000 sehen den Umzug. An den vier Tagen kann man viele kulinarische und handwerkliche° Sachen gcnießen°.

⌘ IM INTERNET

1. Suchen Sie Informationen über Marlene Dietrich. Wann beginnt ihre (*her*) Karriere? Suchen Sie die drei bekanntesten Filme.

2. Was ist die Museumsinsel? Suchen Sie Informationen über mindestens (*at least*) drei Museen der Museumsinsel.

3. Suchen Sie Beispiele für „Ostalgie" (*nostalgia for the East*).

Find out more at **vhlcentral.com**.

---

geteilt *divided* **beleuchtet** *illuminates* **ehemaligen** *former* **Stasi** *secret police* **Alltag** *everyday* **echten** *real* **Trabant** *car produced in East Germany* **Wohnzimmer** *living room* **zum Anfassen** *to touch* **finden... statt** *take place* **nehmen... teil** *participate* **bekannteste** *most well-known* **erfolgreichste** *most successful* **Kunstturner** *gymnast* **missbrauchen** *misuse* **Reichstag** *parliament building* **wichtigste** *most important* **des Deutschen Kaiserreichs** *of the German empire* **Reichstagsbrand** *Reichstag fire* **hoch** *high* **breit** *wide* **schwer** *heavy* **verhüllen** *cover with fabric* **Besucher** *visitors* **Kulturenvielfalt** *cultural diversity* **Umzug** *parade* **handwerkliche** *crafts* **genießen** *enjoy*

Was haben Sie gelernt? Complete the sentences.

1. Die Fläche Berlins ist _____892_____ Quadratkilometer.

2. Nach dem 2. Weltkrieg sind _(etwa) 600.000_ Wohnungen in Berlin zerstört.

3. Seit _____1989_____ ist Berlin nicht mehr geteilt.

4. Im _DDR Museum_ kann man ein DDR-Wohnzimmer sehen.

5. Der erfolgreichste deutsche Athlet bei den Olympischen Spielen 1936 ist _Konrad Frey_.

6. An den Olympischen Spielen 1936 nehmen 3.961 ___Athleten___ teil.

7. Paul Wallot errichtet den Reichstag zwischen ___1884___ und 1894.

8. Im Sommer 1995 kommen 5 Millionen ___Besucher___ nach Berlin, um den Reichstag zu sehen.

9. Der Karneval der Kulturen dauert (*lasts*) ___vier___ Tage.

10. Besucher sehen Künstler – Musiker, Tänzer etc. – aus über ___70___ Ländern beim Karneval der Kulturen.

 Practice more at **vhlcentral.com**.

Lesen Audio: Reading

Vor dem Lesen

AP* Theme: Contemporary Life
Context: Youth Culture

Strategien

Predicting content through formats

Recognizing the format of a text can help you to predict its content. For example, invitations, greeting cards, and classified ads follow easily identifiable formats, which usually give you a general idea of the information they contain. Look at the text below and identify it based on its format.

Uhrzeit	Montag	Dienstag	Mittwoch	Donnerstag	Freitag
7.55	Deutsch	Französisch	Biologie	Religion	Mathe
8.40	Englisch	Musik	Geschichte	Physik	Mathe
9.40	Sport	Geschichte	Mathe	Französisch	Englisch
10.25	Sport	Mathe	Englisch	Französisch	Chemie
11.25	Religion	Physik	Erdkunde	Erdkunde	Musik
12.10	Sozialkunde	Chemie	Deutsch	Deutsch	Bio

If you guessed that this is a page from a student's weekly planner, you are correct. You can now infer that it contains information about a student's weekly schedule, including days, times, classes, and activities.

Texte verstehen

Briefly look at the document. What is its format? What kind of information is given? How is it organized? What are the visual components? What types of documents usually contain these elements?

Verwandte Wörter

You have already learned that you can use cognates, as well as format, to help you predict the content of a document. With a classmate, make a list of all the cognates you find in the reading selection. Based on these cognates and the format of the document, can you guess what this document is and what it is for?

Karlswald-Universität
Studienkolleg Mittelhessen

4 Stunden pro Tag (Montag–Freitag)
2 Tutorien pro Woche

Kurse

- Grundstufe: Anfänger°
- Stufe 1: Einführung° I
- Stufe 2: Einführung II
- Stufe 3: fortgeschritten° I
- Stufe 4: fortgeschritten II
- Stufe 5/6: Vorbereitung° auf die DSH-Prüfung

Kosten

- Einstufungstest: 50 Euro
- Stufe 1, 2, 3 und 4: 410 Euro pro Kurs
- Stufe 5/6: 620 Euro

Unterbringung°

- In Studentenwohnheimen
- In Privatwohnungen

Studienkolleg Mittelhessen
Friedrichstraße 3 | D-35032 Marburg

ausländische *foreign* **die... wollen** *who want* **Anfänger** *beginner* **Einführung** *introduction*
fortgeschritten *advanced* **Vorbereitung** *preparation* **Unterbringung** *accommodations*

Die Deutschkurse an der Karlswald-Universität:
Deutschtraining für ausländische° Studenten, die in Karlswald studieren wollen°.

Stufe 1–4 vom   3. Januar bis 14. Februar
Stufe 5/6 vom   3. Januar bis 22. März

Große Auswahl° zusätzlicher Aktivitäten:

- Tagesausflüge° zu Städten der Region
  (Frankfurt, Eisenach, Heidelberg)
- Besuche von Sehenswürdigkeiten°
  (Elisabethkirche, Marburger Schloss)
- Besuche von Kulturveranstaltungen°
  (Theaterproduktionen, Konzerte)
- Sport und andere Aktivitäten

Suggestion Encourage students to record unfamiliar words and phrases that they learn from this reading in their personalized dictionaries.

**Intensives Training in Hörverständnis°,
Leseverständnis und Textproduktion.**

Tel.: (06421) 28 23 651 - Fax.: (06421) 28 23 652
www.uni-karlswald.de/studienkolleg

Auswahl *selection* **Tagesausflüge** *day trips* **Sehenswürdigkeiten** *places of interest*
Kulturveranstaltungen *cultural events* **Hörverständnis** *listening comprehension*

Nach dem Lesen

Antworten Sie Select the option that best completes the statement.

1. Das ist eine Broschüre für...
   a. ein deutsches Gymnasium.
   b. ein Institut für Deutschkurse.
   c. Studenten, die Englisch lernen wollen.

2. Studenten, die kein Deutsch sprechen, nehmen den Kurs...
   a. Grundstufe.   b. Stufe 3.   c. Stufe 5/6.

3. Jeden (*Every*) Tag haben Studenten in einem Kurs...
   a. 4 Stunden Deutschunterricht.
   b. 4 Stunden Tutorien.
   c. 2 Stunden Deutschunterricht.

4. Der Test am Ende der Stufe 5/6...
   a. ist intensives Training.
   b. hat kein Hörverständnis.
   c. heißt DSH-Prüfung.

5. Studenten wohnen...
   a. bei deutschen Familien.
   b. im Studentenwohnheim.
   c. in Frankfurt.

6. An Wochenenden besuchen Studenten...
   a. Studentenheime und Privatwohnungen.
   b. Frankfurt und andere Städte.
   c. die Universität.

7. Kurse kosten...
   a. 50 Euro.
   b. 1.030 Euro.
   c. 410 oder 620 Euro.

Suggestion Go over the answers with the whole class or have students check their answers in pairs.

8. Die Kurse der Stufe 1, 2, 3 und 4 dauern...
   a. 4 Wochen.   b. 6 Wochen.   c. 11 Wochen.

Richtig oder falsch? Mark the appropriate box.

	richtig	falsch
1. Das Studienkolleg Mittelhessen ist für deutsche Studenten.	☐	☑
2. Die Deutschkurse sind 5 Stunden jeden Tag.	☐	☑
3. Es gibt Tagesausflüge nach Frankfurt, Eisenach und Heidelberg.	☑	☐
4. Das Studienkolleg ist in der Friedrichstraße 3, D-35032 Marburg.	☑	☐

Hören

Strategien

Listening for cognates

You already know that cognates are words that have similar spellings and meanings in two or more languages, like *telephone* and **Telefon** or *activity* and **Aktivität**. Listen for cognates to improve your comprehension of spoken German.

 To help you practice this strategy, listen to these statements. Write down all the cognates you hear.

Vorbereitung

Based on the photograph, who do you think Julian and Anni are? Where are they? Do they know each other well? Where are they going this morning? What are they talking about?

Zuhören

Listen to the conversation and list any cognates you hear. Listen again and complete the highlighted portions of Julian's schedule.

4. April   Montag

9.30	*Kaffee mit Jasmin in der Cafeteria*	14.30	
10.00	*Seminar zur englischen Literatur*	15.00	lernen mit David
10.30		15.30	
11.00		16.00	
11.30		16.30	
12.00	*Mittagessen mit Karl in der Mensa*	17.00	Fußball spielen
12.30		17.30	
13.00		18.00	
13.30		18.30	
14.00	Englischvorlesung	19.00	*Konzert im Kulturladen*

Verständnis

 Richtig oder falsch? Indicate whether each sentence is **richtig** or **falsch**. Correct any false statements.

1. Anni lernt morgens in der Bibliothek.
   Richtig.

2. Julian und Anni studieren Architektur.
   Falsch. Julian studiert englische Literatur und Anni studiert Architektur.

3. Um 9.30 Uhr trinkt Julian mit Jasmin Kaffee.
   Richtig.

4. Anni hat um 2 Uhr eine Vorlesung.
   Falsch. Julian hat um 2 Uhr eine Vorlesung.

5. Anni findet Architektur interessant.
   Richtig.

6. Anni und Julian haben langweilige Professoren.
   Richtig.

7. Julian und Anni gehen am Nachmittag Fußball spielen.
   Falsch. Julian geht am Nachmittag Fußball spielen.

8. Julian geht am Abend in ein Konzert.
   Richtig.

 Pläne In pairs, discuss your plans for this weekend, including where and when you will do each activity.

Suggestion To check answers for **Zuhören**, have students work in pairs and ask each other questions about Julian's schedule.

Partner Chat You can also assign this activity on the Supersite. Students work in pairs to record the activity online. The pair's recorded conversation will appear in your gradebook.

Schreiben

Strategien

Brainstorming

Brainstorming can help you generate ideas on a specific topic. Before you begin writing, you should spend 10–15 minutes brainstorming, jotting down any ideas about the topic that occur to you. Whenever possible, try to write down your ideas in German. Express your ideas in single words or phrases, and jot them down in any order. While brainstorming, do not worry about whether your ideas are good or bad. Selecting and organizing ideas should be the second stage of your writing. The more ideas you write down while you are brainstorming, the more options you will have to choose from later on, when you start to organize your ideas.

Hobbys...
laufen
campen gehen
Tennis spielen
kochen
tanzen
schreiben
schwimmen
Fahrrad fahren

Thema

 Eine persönliche Beschreibung

Write a description of yourself to post on a Web site in order to find a German-speaking e-pal. Your description should include:

- your name and where you are from.
- your birthday.
- the name of your school and where it is located.
- the courses you are currently taking and your opinion of each one.
- your hobbies and pastimes.
- any other information you would like to include.

Hallo!

Ich heiße Erik Schneider und ich komme aus Köln. Ich bin Schüler am Schiller-Gymnasium. Ich fahre Ski, spiele Tennis und fahre Fahrrad...

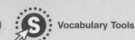 **Vocabulary Tools**

Lektion 2A

das Studium

der Abschluss, ⁼e / das Diplom, -e	*degree*
das Abschlusszeugnis, -se / das Diplom, -e	*diploma*
der Dozent, -en / die Dozentin, -nen	*college/university instructor*
das Fach, ⁼er	*subject*
das Seminar, -e	*seminar*
das Stipendium, -en	*scholarship*
die Veranstaltung, -en	*class; course*
die Vorlesung, -en	*lecture*
(die) Architektur	*architecture*
(die) Biologie	*biology*
(die) Chemie	*chemistry*
(die) Fremdsprache, -n	*foreign language*
(die) Geschichte	*history*
(die) Informatik	*computer science*
(die) Kunst, ⁼e	*art*
(die) Literatur	*literature*
(die) Mathematik	*math*
(die) Medizin	*medicine*
(die) Naturwissenschaft, -en	*science*
(die) Physik	*physics*
(die) Psychologie	*psychology*
(die) Wirtschaft	*business*
belegen	*to take (a class)*
gehen	*to go*
lernen	*to study; to learn*
studieren	*to study; to major in*

Sportarten

spielen	*to play*

der Stundenplan

der Montag, -e	*Monday*
der Dienstag, -e	*Tuesday*
der Mittwoch, -e	*Wednesday*
der Donnerstag, -e	*Thursday*
der Freitag, -e	*Friday*
der Samstag, -e	*Saturday*
der Sonntag, -e	*Sunday*
die Stunde, -n	*hour*
die Woche, -n	*week*
das Wochenende, -n	*weekend*
die Zeit, -en	*time*
morgens	*in the morning*
nachmittags	*in the afternoon*
abends	*in the evening*
montags	*on Mondays*
dienstags	*on Tuesdays*
mittwochs	*on Wednesdays*
donnerstags	*on Thursdays*
freitags	*on Fridays*
samstags	*on Saturdays*
sonntags	*on Sundays*

Orte

das Café, -s	*café*
der Hörsaal, Hörsäle	*lecture hall*
der Seminarraum, -räume	*(college/university) classroom*

zum Beschreiben

einfach	*easy*
interessant	*interesting*
langweilig	*boring*
nützlich	*useful*
nutzlos	*useless*
schwierig	*difficult*

Regular verbs *See pp. 56–57.*
Interrogative words *See p. 60.*
Telling time *See p. 62.*
Ordinal numbers and dates *See p. 63.*
gern/nicht gern *See p. 69.*

Lektion 2B

Sportarten

(der) Baseball	*baseball*
(der) Basketball	*basketball*
(der) (American) Football	*football*
(der) Fußball	*soccer*
(das) Golf	*golf*
(das) Hockey	*hockey*
(die) Leichtathletik	*track and field*
(das) Tennis	*tennis*
(der) Volleyball	*volleyball*
der Ball, ⁼e	*ball*
die Mannschaft, -en	*team*
das Schwimmbad, ⁼er	*swimming pool*
das Spiel, -e	*game*
der Spieler, - / die Spielerin, -nen	*player*
das Spielfeld, -er / der Platz, ⁼e	*field, court*
der Sport	*sports*
das Stadion, Stadien	*stadium*
Fahrrad fahren	*to ride a bicycle*
Ski fahren	*to ski*
gewinnen	*to win*
schwimmen	*to swim*
trainieren	*to practice*
verlieren	*to lose*

Orte

die Sporthalle, -n	*gym*

Freizeit

der Berg, -e	*mountain*
das Fahrrad, ⁼er	*bicycle*
die Freizeit	*free time*
die Freizeitaktivität, -en	*leisure activity*
das Hobby, -s	*hobby*
die Karte, -n	*card*
der Park, -s	*park*
das Schach	*chess*
der Strand, ⁼e	*beach*
der Wald, ⁼er	*forest*
angeln gehen	*to go fishing*
campen gehen	*to go camping*
essen gehen	*to eat out*
spazieren gehen	*to go for a walk*
klettern	*to (rock) climb*
kochen	*to cook*
(ein Pferd) reiten	*to ride (a horse)*
schreiben	*to write*
Spaß haben/machen	*to have fun / to be fun*
singen	*to sing*
tanzen	*to dance*
wandern	*to hike*

Ausdrücke

Sie spielen gern Schach. *They like to play chess.*
Sie verliert nicht gern. *She doesn't like to lose.*

Stem-changing verbs *See pp. 76–77.*
Common time expressions *See p. 80.*
Negative words *See pp. 82–83*

Familie und Freunde

Suggestion Ask students: Who are the people in the photo and what are they celebrating?

Teaching Tip Look for icons indicating activities that address the modes of communication. Follow this key:

→⚇←	Interpretive communication
←⚇→	Presentational communication
⚇↔⚇	Interpersonal communication

Communicative Goals

You will learn how to:

- talk about families
- talk about marital status
- describe people
- express ownership

Suggestion Point out to students that **die Eltern** has no singular form. Mention that nouns like **Eltern** and **Leute**, which exist only in the plural, have no grammatical gender in German.

Johanna Schmidts Familie

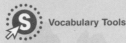 **Vocabulary Tools**

AP* Theme: Families & Communities
Context: Family Structure

Wortschatz

die Familie	*family*
das Baby, -s	*baby*
die Eltern	*parents*
das Geschwister, -	*sibling*
die Großeltern	*grandparents*
der Halbbruder, ⸚	*half brother*
die Halbschwester, -n	*half sister*
das Kind, -er	*child*
der Nachname, -n	*last name*
das Paar, -e	*couple*
der Schwager, ⸚	*brother-in-law*
die Schwägerin, -nen	*sister-in-law*
die Schwiegermutter, ⸚	*mother-in-law*
der Schwiegervater, ⸚	*father-in-law*
der Stiefbruder, ⸚	*stepbrother*
die Stiefmutter, ⸚	*stepmother*
die Stiefschwester, -n	*stepsister*
der Stiefsohn, ⸚e	*stepson*
die Stieftochter, ⸚	*stepdaughter*
der Stiefvater, ⸚	*stepfather*
der / die Verwandte, -n	*relative*
der Zwilling, -e	*twin*
die Haustiere	***pets***
der Fisch, -e	*fish*
der Hund, -e	*dog*
die Katze, -n	*cat*
der Vogel, ⸚	*bird*
der Familienstand	***marital status***
die Witwe, -n	*widow*
der Witwer, -	*widower*
geschieden	*divorced*
getrennt	*separated*
ledig	*single*
verheiratet	*married*
verlobt	*engaged*
zusammen	*together*
heiraten	*to marry*
zum Beschreiben	***to describe***
blaue/grüne/braune Augen	*blue/green/brown eyes*
blonde/braune/ schwarze Haare	*blond/brown/ black hair*
dunkel / hell	*dark / light*

Suggestion Point out to students that **Geschwister** is primarily used in the plural. Model this usage by asking individual students whether they have any siblings. Ex.: **Hast du noch Geschwister? Ja, ich habe eine Schwester und zwei Brüder.**

Point out that whereas *hair* in English is a collective singular noun, **die Haare** is a plural noun. Explain that **das Haar** refers to a single hair, or to hair in general.

Walter Gärtner

mein Großvater/Opa (*m.*)

Peter Schmidt   **Marianne Schmidt**

mein Vater (*m.*), Mariannes Mann (*m.*)   **meine Mutter (*f.*), Walter und Hannas Tochter (*f.*)**

Michaela Schmidt   **Daniel Schmidt**   **Johanna Schmidt**

meine Schwägerin   **mein Bruder (*m.*)**   **ich, Peter und Mariannes Tochter**

Jonas Schmidt   **Greta Schmidt**

mein Neffe (*m.*)   **meine Nichte (*f.*)**
Peter und Mariannes Enkelkinder

ACHTUNG

To say *my big/little brother/sister,* use **mein großer/kleiner Bruder** or **meine große/kleine Schwester**.

Ressourcen

v̂Text	WB pp. 33–34	LM p. 81	vhlcentral

Hanna Gärtner

meine Großmutter/Oma (*f.*)

Dieter Gärtner   **Renate Gärtner**

mein Onkel (*m.*),
Walter und Hannas
Sohn (*m.*)

meine Tante (*f.*),
Dieters Frau (*f.*)

Simon Gärtner   **Sophia Gärtner**   **Klara Gärtner**

mein Cousin (*m.*),
Walter und Hannas
Enkelsohn (*m.*)

meine Cousine (*f.*),
Simon und Klaras
Schwester (*f.*)

meine Cousine,
Simon und Sophias
Schwester,
Walter und Hannas
Enkeltochter (*f.*)

Zeus

Simon, Sophia und
Klaras Hund

Anwendung

1 Expansion Get students started by asking them questions about their own families. Ex.: **Haben Sie Geschwister?**

1 **Kombinieren** Match the people with the descriptions.

_g_ 1. Mariannes Bruder
_d_ 2. Daniels Frau
_a_ 3. Marianne und Peter
_c_ 4. Dieter und Renates Sohn
_h_ 5. Mariannes Vater
_f_ 6. Peter und Mariannes Sohn
_e_ 7. Daniels Tochter
_b_ 8. Dieters Frau

a. Johannas Eltern
b. Johannas Tante
c. Johannas Cousin
d. Johannas Schwägerin
e. Johannas Nichte
f. Johannas Bruder
g. Johannas Onkel
h. Johannas Opa

2 **Identifizieren** Write each person's family relationship to Dieter Gärtner.

BEISPIEL Hanna: _____die Mutter_____

1. Sophia: _____die Tochter_____
2. Marianne: _____die Schwester_____
3. Daniel: _____der Neffe_____
4. Peter: _____der Schwager_____
5. Simon: _____der Sohn_____
6. Johanna: _____die Nichte_____
7. Walter und Hanna: _____die Eltern_____
8. Renate: _____die Frau_____

3 **Kategorien** List at least four roles each person could have in a family.

Sample answers are provided.

BEISPIEL eine Frau, 40 Jahre alt
eine Mutter   _eine Tante_   _eine Cousine_   _eine Tochter_

1. ein Mann, 62 Jahre alt:

| ein Schwager | ein Großvater | ein Schwiegervater | ein Vater |

2. ein Kind, 3 Jahre alt:

| ein Sohn | ein Neffe | ein Enkelsohn | ein Bruder |

3. ein Mädchen, 15 Jahre alt:

| eine Cousine | eine Schwester | eine Tochter | eine Enkeltochter |

4. eine Frau, 50 Jahre alt:

| eine Oma | eine Tante | eine Schwägerin | eine Mutter |

4 **Hören Sie zu** Listen to Johanna's descriptions and indicate whether each statement is **richtig** or **falsch**, based on her family tree.

	richtig	falsch		richtig	falsch
1.	✓	☐	7.	☐	✓
2.	☐	✓	8.	☐	✓
3.	✓	☐	9.	✓	☐
4.	✓	☐	10.	☐	✓
5.	☐	✓	11.	☐	✓
6.	✓	☐	12.	✓	☐

 Practice more at **vhlcentral.com**.

Kommunikation

5 Beschreibungen Use words from the list to describe the images.

Compare your answers with a classmate's, and correct each other's work. <small>Sample answers are provided.</small>

| Enkelkinder | Großeltern | Neffe | Sohn | verheiratet | verlobt | Zwillinge |

▶ **BEISPIEL**

Das Paar ist verlobt.

5 Suggestion Give students cues to help them complete this activity. Ask them questions about the pictures. Ex.: **Wer sind die Leute? Wie alt ist das Kind?**

1.
Das Kind ist der Neffe.

2.
Die Babys sind Zwillinge.

3.
Der Mann und die Frau sind verheiratet.

4.
Die Mutter hat einen Sohn.

5.
Die Großmutter hat drei Enkelkinder.

6.
Die Großeltern begrüßen die Familie.

6 Brieffreunde Read Eva's letter to her penpal. Then, in pairs, take turns answering the questions.
<small>Sample answers are provided.</small>

Liebe Andrea,

hast du eine große Familie? Meine Familie ist nicht sehr groß. Ich habe eine große Schwester Nicole und einen kleinen Halbbruder Peter. Und wir haben einen Hund, Cäsar, und Miezi, unsere kleine Katze.

Nicole studiert Sportmedizin in Heidelberg. Peter ist fünf und geht in den Kindergarten.

Meine Familie ist sehr sportlich. Mein Stiefvater spielt Golf, meine Mutter und Nicole spielen Tennis, Peter spielt Fußball und ich mache Ballett.

Und wie ist deine Familie?

Liebe Grüße
deine Eva

1. Wie viele Personen wohnen mit Eva zusammen? <small>Drei Personen wohnen mit Eva zusammen: der Stiefvater, die Mutter, der Halbbruder.</small>
2. Hat sie auch Haustiere? <small>Ja, sie hat zwei Haustiere: einen Hund und eine Katze.</small>
3. Wie alt ist Peter? <small>Er ist fünf (Jahre alt).</small>
4. Was macht Evas Familie in der Freizeit? <small>Der Stiefvater spielt Golf, die Mutter und die Schwester spielen Tennis, der Halbbruder spielt Fußball und Eva macht Ballett.</small>
5. Wie groß ist Ihre (*your*) Familie? <small>Answers will vary.</small>

6 Virtual Chat You can also assign activity 6 on the Supersite. Students record individual responses that appear in your gradebook.

7 Arbeitsblatt Your instructor will give you a worksheet with statements about family relationships. Use the cues to ask your classmates about their families.

BEISPIEL Ich habe zwei Schwestern.

S1: Hast du zwei Schwestern?
S2: Ja, ich habe zwei Schwestern. (*You write his/her name.*)
OR
S2: Nein, ich habe keine Schwestern. (*You ask another classmate.*)

7 Suggestion Ask volunteers to share their results with the class.

8 Was machen sie gern? Use the vocabulary you learned in Kapitel 2 to talk with a classmate about what your family members enjoy doing.

8 Partner Chat You can also assign activity 8 on the Supersite. Students work in pairs to record the activity online. The pair's recorded conversation will appear in your gradebook.

BEISPIEL

S1: *Mein Bruder spielt gern Tennis. Was macht dein Bruder?*
S2: *Mein Bruder liest gern Bücher.*

6 Expansion Have students write their own responses to Eva's letter. You might provide them with real postcards which they have to "mail" back to you. Encourage volunteers to read their letters aloud to the class.

Aussprache und Rechtschreibung  Audio

Final consonants

The German consonants **b**, **d**, and **g** generally sound quite similar to their English counterparts.

Ball	**Bruder**	**Dezember**	**bringen**	**Golf**

However, when **b** appears at the end of a word or syllable, or before a **t**, it is pronounced like a **p**.

ab	**habt**	**gelb**	**Staub**	**liebt**

When **d** appears at the end of a word or syllable, it is pronounced like a **t**. The **-dt** letter combination is also pronounced **t**.

Geld	**Hund**	**Stadt**	**sind**	**Fahrrad**

As you learned in **2A**, when **g** appears at the end of a word or before a **t**, it is pronounced like a **k**. In standard German, **-ig** at the end of a word is pronounced like the German **ch**.

klug	**bringt**	**Tag**	**sagt**	**zwanzig**

Suggestion Remind students that the pronunciation of the final **-ig** sound has several regional variations. For more about the **ch** sound, see **Vol. 2, Lektion 2A**.

1 | **Aussprechen** Practice saying these words aloud.

1. Bank
2. sieben
3. Laub
4. lobt
5. danken
6. Boden
7. Abend
8. gehen
9. Junge
10. Berg
11. fragt
12. schwierig

2 | **Nachsprechen** Practice saying these sentences aloud.

1. Der Dieb klaut ein Fahrrad.
2. Der Besucher fragt Manfred ruhig um Rat.
3. Bernds Geschwister sind freundlich und großzügig.
4. Viele Diebe klauen viele Fahrräder.
5. Ingrids böser Bruder ist gierig und gemein.
6. Jörg sitzt im Zug und singt ein Lied.

Suggestion Have students look at the sample words and sentences on this page to identify cognates and words they already know. Tell students the meanings of any unfamiliar words or phrases.

3 | **Sprichwörter** Practice reading these sayings aloud.

Kindermund tut Wahrheit kund.[1]

Geld regiert die Welt.[2]

[1] Out of the mouths of babes. (lit. The mouths of children make known the truth.)

[2] Money rules the world.

Ressourcen

v̂Text   LM p. 82   vhlcentral

Ein Abend mit der Familie Video

Die Freunde essen bei Familie Yilmaz. Alle wissen (know), Torsten ist
Sabites Freund. Alle, nur einer nicht.

Vorbereitung Have students scan the
images on the pages before they watch
the video and try to guess what this
episode will be about.

ANKE Hallo! Willkommen, ich bin
Sabites Mutter.
GEORGE Freut mich sehr, Sie kennen zu lernen,
Frau Yilmaz. Ich bin George Bachman.

SABITE George, das ist meine jüngere
Schwester, Zeynep.
GEORGE Hallo, Zeynep, nett dich kennen
zu lernen.
SABITE Und das ist unser Vater.
GEORGE Herr Yilmaz, freut mich.

ANKE Das sind die Patatesli Sigara Böregi von
Faiks Großmutter.
MELINE Herr Yilmaz, Ihre Familie kommt aus
der Türkei?
FAIK Ja. Ich komme aus Ankara. Ich habe
dort Cousins und einen Onkel. Haben Sie
Geschwister?
MELINE Ich habe drei ältere Schwestern. Eine
ist verheiratet, eine ist getrennt, eine ist
verlobt. Ich habe auch eine Nichte, sie heißt
Ava und ist 12.

GEORGE Meine Eltern sind geschieden. Meine
Urgroßeltern kommen aus Heidelberg.
TORSTEN Mein Onkel lebt in Heidelberg. Er ist
Professor. Es ist eine schöne Stadt.

SABITE Hallo, Hans.
HANS Tut mir leid, dass ich zu spät komme.

HANS Hallo!
SABITE Hans, das sind meine Eltern, Anke
und Faik.
HANS Guten Abend, Herr Yilmaz. Guten
Abend, Frau Yilmaz. Für Sie.
ANKE Danke.
HANS Sehr erfreut.

1 **Richtig oder falsch?** Indicate whether each statement is **richtig**
or **falsch**.

1. Sabite hat einen jüngeren Bruder. Falsch.
2. Meline hat zwei ältere Schwestern. Falsch.
3. Melines Nichte heißt Ava. Richtig.
4. Faik kommt aus Ankara. Richtig.
5. Es gibt Sauerbraten bei Familie Yilmaz. Richtig.

6. Georges Eltern sind verheiratet. Falsch.
7. Torstens Onkel lebt in München. Falsch.
8. Georges Urgroßeltern kommen aus Berlin. Falsch.
9. Hans' Familie kommt aus Bayern. Richtig.
10. Max ist 18 und spielt Basketball. Falsch.

PERSONEN

 Anke

 Faik

 George

 Hans

 Meline

 Sabite

 Torsten

 Zeynep

HANS Bist du ihr Bruder?
TORSTEN Nein, Sabite ist meine Freundin. Ich bin Torsten. Nett dich kennen zu lernen.
HANS Freut mich.
MELINE Börek?
HANS Nein danke.

MELINE Frau Yilmaz, Ihr Sauerbraten ist köstlich.
ANKE Danke, Meline. Hans? Alles in Ordnung? Du isst nichts.
HANS Hmm? Ja, danke.

FAIK Hans, Ihre Familie kommt aus Bayern?
HANS Ja.
TORSTEN Ich habe eine Tante in München. Hast du Geschwister, Hans?
HANS Mein Bruder, Max, ist 18. Er ist sportlich und spielt gern Fußball.
MELINE Hat er eine Freundin?

SABITE Hans, alles in Ordnung?
MELINE Sabite!
SABITE Was?
MELINE Hans.
SABITE Was ist mit Hans? Oh. Ooooh.
ANKE Wir haben Strudel!

Nützliche Ausdrücke

- **Freut mich sehr, Sie kennen zu lernen.**
  Pleased to meet you.
- **Das ist meine jüngere Schwester.**
  This is my younger sister.
- **die Türkei**
  Turkey
- **Haben Sie Geschwister?**
  Do you have any siblings?
- **die Urgroßeltern**
  great-grandparents
- **Tut mir leid, dass ich zu spät komme.**
  Sorry for being late.
- **der Sauerbraten**
  marinated beef
- **Ihr Sauerbraten ist köstlich.**
  Your sauerbraten is delicious.
- **Er ist sportlich und spielt gern Fußball.**
  He's athletic and likes to play soccer.
- **Alles in Ordnung?**
  Everything OK?
- **einladen**
  to invite
- **das Abendessen**
  dinner

3A.1
- **Das ist unser Vater.**
  This is our father.

3A.2
- **Es ist eine schöne Stadt.**
  It's a beautiful city.

---

2 **Zum Besprechen** Draw your family tree. Include your parents, siblings, aunts, uncles, and grandparents. Then "introduce" your family to a classmate. Answers will vary.

BEISPIEL

S1: *Das ist meine Tante. Sie heißt Paula. Sie wohnt in New Jersey.*
S2: *Das ist mein Onkel. Er heißt...*

2 **Expansion** Have students present their partners' families to another pair.

3 **Erweiterung** Boreks are a popular Turkish snack with many varieties. In pairs, research another popular Turkish dish, and share your findings with the class. Answers will vary.

Ressourcen

v̂Text   VM   S
              p. 103   vhlcentral

IM FOKUS

AP* Theme: Families & Communities
Context: Relationships

Eine deutsche Familie Reading

Mit wem° die Deutschen leben (%)				
	Eltern	allein	Partner	allein mit Kind	sonstige°
18–24	63,5	15,9	15,8	1,4	3,4
25–29	19,8	25,2	48,6	3,1	3,3
30–34	6,8	20,1	66,9	4,5	1,7
35–44	3,3	14,9	74,1	6,3	1,4
45–54	1,3	13,6	78,8	5,0	1,4
55–64	0,3	16,9	79,4	2,2	1,3
65–74	0,1	25,0	70,8	2,1	2,1
75–79	0	41,8	52,0	2,2	3,9
80+	0	58,7	30,1	2,5	3,4

QUELLE: Bundesministerium

TANJA UND JENS SIND EIN deutsches Ehepaar mit zwei Kindern. Sie haben zwei Söhne, Finn und Lukas. Finn ist 11 Jahre alt und in der 5. Klasse. Lukas ist zwei Jahre älter als Finn und geht schon° in die 7. Klasse. Die Familie hat eine große Wohnung° und einen schönen Garten vor dem Haus. Jens arbeitet den ganzen Tag in einem Büro°. Tanja arbeitet als Krankenschwester°, aber sie ist nachmittags immer zu Hause, wenn Finn und Lukas um eins von der Schule nach Hause kommen. Abends spielen sie zusammen Fußball im Park oder fahren Fahrrad am Rhein.

In der Familie macht auch Jens Hausarbeit°, aber Tanja kocht und putzt° trotzdem mehr. Die Familie fährt einmal im Jahr zusammen in den Urlaub°.

Sind Jens und Tanja also eine „typisch" deutsche Familie? Das Leben in Deutschland ist vielfältiger geworden°. In der Wohnung links neben Jens und Tanja lebt eine Einwandererfamilie°, rechts von ihnen lebt ein allein erziehender° Vater mit seiner Tochter. Was ist also „typisch" für die deutsche Familie von heute? Vielleicht einfach Zusammenhalt° und Liebe.

schon *already* **Wohnung** *apartment* **Büro** *office* **Krankenschwester** *nurse* **Hausarbeit** *housework* **putzt** *cleans* **Urlaub** *vacation* **ist vielfältiger geworden** *has become more diverse* **Einwandererfamilie** *family of immigrants* **allein erziehender** *single parent* **Zusammenhalt** *sticking together* **Mit wem** *With whom* **sonstige** *miscellaneous*

Expansion Have students read the data in the chart aloud to practice saying numbers.

ÜBUNGEN

1 **Was fehlt?** Complete the statements.

1. Jens' Frau heißt _____Tanja_____.

2. Jens' _____Söhne_____ heißen Finn und Lukas.

3. Am Tag arbeitet _____Jens_____ im Büro.

4. Tanja _____arbeitet_____ als Krankenschwester.

5. Am Vormittag sind Finn und Lukas in der _____Schule_____.

6. Am Abend spielen Jens, Finn, Lukas und Tanja Fußball oder _____fahren Fahrrad_____ am Rhein.

7. Jens macht in der Familie auch _____Hausarbeit_____.

8. Die Familie fährt gemeinsam in den _____Urlaub_____.

9. In Deutschland leben die meisten (*most*) 18- bis 24-Jährigen mit ihren (*their*) _____Eltern_____.

10. Die meisten Deutschen, die älter als (*older than*) 80 Jahre sind, leben _____allein_____.

 Practice more at **vhlcentral.com**.

DEUTSCH IM ALLTAG

Die Familie

die Ehe	*marriage*
das Einzelkind	*only child*
die Hochzeit	*wedding*
die Mama	*mom*
der erste/zweite Mann	*first/second husband*
der Papa	*dad*
die Urgroßmutter	*great-grandmother*
der Urgroßvater	*great-grandfather*
der / die Verlobte	*fiancé(e)*
adoptieren	*to adopt*

DIE DEUTSCHSPRACHIGE WELT

Die Liebe
AP* Theme: Families & Communities
Context: Relationships

Ein Kuss° ist nicht nur° ein Kuss. In den meisten Teilen° Deutschlands sagt man „Kuss". Aber es gibt andere Möglichkeiten°, „Kuss" in der deutschsprachigen Welt zu sagen. **In der Schweiz** und **in Liechtenstein** sagt man „Müntschi". **In Österreich** und **in Bayern** ist ein Kuss ein „Bussi" oder ein „Busserl". **Auf Kölsch** (der Dialekt von Köln) ist das ein „Bütz".

Und wie sagt man „Ich liebe dich"? Ein paar° Varianten:
In Bayern und **in Österreich** sagt man „I mog di". **In der Schweiz** geht das so: „I liäbä di". Und **die Berliner** sagen „Ick liebe Dir".

Kuss *kiss* **nur** *only* **meisten Teilen** *most parts*
Möglichkeiten *possibilities* **Ein paar** *A couple of*

PORTRÄT

Angela Merkel
AP* Theme: Global Challenges
Context: Political Issues

Seit November 2005 hat Deutschland eine Bundeskanzlerin°: **Angela Merkel**. Viele Deutsche finden Merkel pragmatisch und solide, und im Magazin Forbes steht, sie ist eine der mächtigsten° Frauen der Welt. Die CDU°-Politikerin hat keine Kinder, aber sie hat einen wichtigen Unterstützer°, ihren Mann, Joachim Sauer. Sauer ist Professor für Chemie an der Humboldt-Universität in Berlin. Er hält sich am liebsten von den Medien fern°, aber wenn die mächtigsten Politiker der Welt zusammen essen, ist Sauer oft dabei. Und wer wäscht im Hause Sauer-Merkel die Wäsche°? Beide!

Bundeskanzlerin *female chancellor* **eine der mächtigsten** *one of the most powerful* **CDU** *Christian Democratic Union* **Unterstützer** *supporter* **hält sich am liebsten von den Medien fern** *prefers to stay away from the media* **wäscht... die Wäsche** *does the laundry*

🔗 IM INTERNET

Scheidung (*Divorce*): Eine Epidemie in den deutschsprachigen Ländern?

Find out more at **vhlcentral.com**.

---

2 **Richtig oder falsch?** Indicate whether each statement is **richtig** or **falsch**. Correct the false statements.

1. Der Dialekt, den man in Köln spricht, heißt „Bayerisch".
Falsch. Der Dialekt heißt Kölsch.

2. „I liäbä di" ist die schweizerische Art (*Swiss way*), „Ich liebe dich" zu sagen. Richtig.

3. Angela Merkel hat zwei Kinder.
Falsch. Angela Merkel hat keine Kinder.

4. Joachim Sauer ist mit Angela Merkel verheiratet. Richtig.

5. Joachim Sauer ist der deutsche Bundespräsident.
Falsch. Joachim Sauer ist Professor für Chemie.

3 **Sie sind dran** Use vocabulary from **Deutsch im Alltag** to write six sentences describing a famous American family. Then share the description with your classmates. Answers will vary.

3A.1

Possessive adjectives  Presentation

Startblock In both English and German, possessive adjectives indicate ownership or belonging.

Sabite ist **meine** Freundin.

Herr Yilmaz, **Ihre** Familie kommt aus der Türkei?

QUERVERWEIS

In **Kontext 3A**, you learned some possessive adjectives used with family vocabulary: **mein** Großvater, **meine** Mutter, **meine** Eltern.

- In **1A.1**, you learned about indefinite articles. Possessive adjectives are also referred to as **ein**-words since they take the same endings as the indefinite article **ein**. Each personal pronoun has a corresponding possessive adjective.

personal pronouns and possessive adjectives		
personal pronouns	**possessive adjectives**	
ich	mein	*my*
du	dein	*your (sing., inf.)*
er	sein	*his*
sie	ihr	*her*
es	sein	*its*
wir	unser	*our*
ihr	euer	*your (pl., inf.)*
Sie	Ihr	*your (sing./pl., form.)*
sie	ihr	*their*

Meine Schwester ist 16 Jahre alt.
My sister is 16 years old.

Wo ist **dein** Vater?
Where is your father?

- Possessive adjectives always precede the nouns they modify.

meine Mutter
my mother

deine Mutter
your mother

unsere Mutter
our mother

seine Mutter
his mother

Meine Schwester ist sehr sportlich.
My sister is very athletic.

- Like other **ein**-words, their endings change according to the gender, case, and number of the object possessed.

deine Mutter
your mother

dein Vater
your father

dein Baby
your baby

deine Eltern
your parents

Mein Großvater liebt **seine** Enkelkinder.
My grandfather loves his grandchildren.

- Like other **ein**-words, possessive adjectives have no added endings before singular masculine or neuter nouns in the nominative, or before singular neuter nouns in the accusative.

nominative and accusative of *ein*-words				
	masculine	**feminine**	**neuter**	**plural**
nominative	**ein** Vater **unser** Vater	**eine** Mutter **unsere** Mutter	**ein** Kind **unser** Kind	**keine** Brüder **unsere** Brüder
accusative	**einen** Vater **unseren** Vater	**eine** Mutter **unsere** Mutter	**ein** Kind **unser** Kind	**keine** Brüder **unsere** Brüder

Ihr Kind ist 3 Jahre alt.   Tobias liebt **seinen** Bruder.
Her child is 3 years old.   *Tobias loves **his** brother.*

- The formal possessive adjective **Ihr** corresponds to the formal personal pronoun **Sie**. The possessive adjective **ihr** can mean either *her* or *their*, depending on context.

Wo sind **Ihre** Eltern?   Rolf und Heike kochen für **ihre** Kinder.
*Where are **your** parents?*   *Rolf and Heike cook for **their** children.*

Christa kocht für **ihre** Enkelkinder.
*Christa cooks for **her** grandchildren.*

- The possessive adjective **euer** drops the second **e** when an ending is added. The possessive adjective **unser** may drop the **e** in the stem when an ending is added, but this form is rare.

euer Enkelsohn	**eure** Familie	**unser** Sohn	**uns(e)re** Tochter
your grandson	*your family*	*our son*	*our daughter*

Ressourcen

v̂**Text**

WB
pp. 35–36

LM
p. 83

vhlcentral

 **Jetzt sind Sie dran!**   Write the correct forms of the possessive adjectives.

Nominativ	**Akkusativ**	**Nominativ**	**Akkusativ**
mein	**mein**	**unser**	**unser**
1. *meine* Idee	5. meinen Bruder	9. unser Fahrrad	13. uns(e)re Verwandten
dein	**dein**	**euer**	**euer**
2. deine Eltern	6. deine Frage	10. eure Mannschaft	14. euren Sohn
sein	**sein**	**Ihr**	**Ihr**
3. sein Wörterbuch	7. seine Familie	11. Ihr Nachname	15. Ihre Hunde
ihr	**ihr**	**ihr**	**ihr**
4. ihr Familienstand	8. ihr Kind	12. ihre Hausaufgaben	16. ihr Problem

Anwendung

1 Was ist richtig? Select the appropriate form of the possessive adjective.

1. (Mein / Meine) Eltern essen gern Spaghetti.
2. (Unser / Unsere) Sohn spielt gut Fußball.
3. Markus und Sabine lieben (ihren / ihre) Eltern.
4. Andrea liebt (euren / euer) Hund.
5. Hat (dein / deinen) Bruder einen Sohn?
6. Sind (Ihr / Ihre) Großeltern hier?
7. Ich lese (mein / meine) Bücher nicht.
8. Mein Vater und (sein / seinen) Freund spielen Schach.

2 Was fehlt? Complete each sentence with the appropriate possessive adjective.

> **BEISPIEL** Treffen Sie _____Ihren_____ Mann im Restaurant?

1. Das Baby braucht ___seine___ Mutter.
2. Ali und Lara suchen ___ihren___ Hund.
3. Ich heiße Jan, und ___mein___ Nachname ist Bauer.
4. Sarah und ___ihre___ Schwester kochen gern zusammen.
5. Herr Schulz und ___seine___ Frau sind getrennt.
6. Siehst du ___deine___ Großeltern oft?
7. Wir lieben ___unsere___ Verwandten.
8. Kinder, wo sind ___eure___ Eltern?

3 Expansion Model using possessive adjectives with students' belongings. Ex.: **Ist das sein Kuli? Nein, das ist ihr Kuli.**

3 Schreiben Write a sentence about each item saying whose it is.

> **BEISPIEL**
> *Das sind meine Hefte.*

ich

1. du Das ist dein Computer.

2. er Das ist sein Fahrrad.

3. wir Das sind unsere Bleistifte.

4. sie Das ist ihr Rucksack.

5. Sie Das ist Ihr Buch.

6. ihr Das ist eure Tafel.

4 Antworten Sie Answer the questions with complete sentences. Answers will vary.

1. Wo wohnt Ihre Familie?
2. Wie heißt Ihre Mutter?
3. Wie ist ihr Nachname?
4. Wie alt ist Ihr Vater?
5. Welche Sportarten spielt Ihre Familie gern?
6. Spielen Ihre Großeltern Schach?
7. Wie heißt Ihr bester Freund / Ihre beste Freundin?
8. Welche Bücher lesen Ihre Freunde gern?

 Practice more at **vhlcentral.com**.

Kommunikation

5 **Familie und Freunde** With your partner, take turns asking and answering these questions. Answers will vary.

S1: *Hat deine Mutter Haustiere?*
S2: *Ja, meine Mutter hat zwei Haustiere. Ihre Katze heißt Muffin und ihr Hund heißt Sam. Wie ist dein Vater?*
S1: *Mein Vater ist Lehrer. Er ist vierzig Jahre alt und hat zwei Brüder.*

1. Hat deine Mutter Haustiere?
2. Wie ist dein Vater?
3. Wieviele Kinder haben deine Eltern?
4. Wo wohnt deine Familie?
5. Was machen deine Freunde am Samstag?
6. Was studiert dein bester Freund oder deine beste Freundin?

6 **Meine Familie** Use the cues to form questions. Then interview your classmates about their family members. Sample answers are provided.

BEISPIEL

S1: *Spricht deine Mutter Deutsch?*
S2: *Ja, meine Mutter spricht Deutsch.*
S3: *Nein, meine Mutter spricht kein Deutsch.*

1. Bruder / spielen / Fußball Spielt dein Bruder Fußball?
2. Vater / haben / ein Hund Hat dein Vater einen Hund?
3. Eltern / lesen / Bücher Lesen deine Eltern Bücher?
4. Großmutter / spielen / Tennis Spielt deine Großmutter Tennis?
5. Schwester / haben / grüne Augen Hat deine Schwester grüne Augen?
6. Onkel und Tante / fahren / Ski Fahren dein Onkel und deine Tante Ski?
7. Verwandte / schreiben / E-Mails Schreiben deine Verwandten E-Mails?
8. Familie / sein / groß Ist deine Familie groß?

7 **Ich sehe etwas** Tell the class about something of yours that you can see in the classroom. Then, repeat what the people before you said they saw. Answers will vary.

BEISPIEL

S1: *Ich sehe meinen Fußball.*
S2: *Ich sehe mein Buch und Stefan sieht seinen Fußball.*
S3: *Ich sehe meine Fotos, Maria sieht ihr Buch und Stefan sieht seinen Fußball.*

8 **Familienporträt** In small groups, take turns describing your family. Use possessive pronouns in the nominative and accusative case. After everyone has spoken, take turns describing your partners' families to the rest of the class. Answers will vary.

BEISPIEL

S1: *Das ist Inga. Ihre Mutter hat grüne Augen und braune Haare.*
S2: *Das ist Michael. Seine Mutter ist Lehrerin.*

5 **Expansion** After pairs have shared their answers, ask them to repeat what has been said, using the appropriate possessive adjective.
Ex.: **S1: Meine Mutter hat braune Augen. S2: Seine/Ihre Mutter hat braune Augen.**

5 **Virtual Chat** You can also assign activity 5 on the Supersite. Students record individual responses that appear in your gradebook.

6 **Expansion** If students answer a question negatively, encourage them to mention a different family member for whom the statement is true.
Ex.: **Spricht deine Mutter Deutsch? Nein, meine Mutter spricht kein Deutsch. Aber mein Vater spricht Deutsch.**

3A.2

Descriptive adjectives and adjective agreement

 Presentation

Startblock Adjectives can describe people, places, or things. Here are some adjectives commonly used to describe people and their physical attributes.

QUERVERWEIS

In **2A Kontext**, you learned a few adjectives to describe school subjects. In **3A Kontext**, you learned some additional adjectives to describe eye color, hair color, and marital status.

physical description			
alt	*old*	hübsch	*pretty*
blond	*blond*	jung	*young*
braunhaarig	*brown-haired*	klein	*small; short (stature)*
dick	*fat; thick*	kurz	*short (hair)*
dunkelhaarig	*dark-haired*	lang	*long (hair)*
dünn	*thin*	lockig	*curly*
glatt	*straight (hair)*	rothaarig	*red-headed*
groß	*big; tall*	schlank	*slim*
großartig	*terrific*	schön	*pretty; beautiful*
gut aussehend	*handsome*	schwarzhaarig	*black-haired*
hässlich	*ugly*	sportlich	*athletic*

- Use an adjective with no added endings after the verbs **sein**, **werden**, and **bleiben** (*to remain*).

Mein Bruder ist **klein**.
*My brother is **short**.*

Seine Mutter bleibt **sportlich**.
*His mother stays **in shape**.*

Deine Schwester wird **groß**.
*Your sister is getting **tall**.*

- When you use an adjective before a noun, you need to include an adjective ending.

Meine **großen** Schwestern spielen Fußball.
*My **big** sisters play soccer.*

Das ist eine **schöne** Katze.
*That's a **pretty** cat.*

Suggestion Tell students that **der**-words include the definite articles, **dieser** (*this*), **mancher** (*some*), **jeder** (*each*), and **solcher** (*such*), while **ein**-words include the indefinite articles, **kein**, and possessive adjectives.

For more about **der**-words, see **Vol. 2, 4B.2**.

- Adjective endings depend on the case, number, and gender of the noun they modify, and whether they are preceded by a **der**-word, an **ein**-word, or neither.

Sie lieben ihren **jungen** Sohn.
*They love their **young** son.*

Das **kleine** Baby hat **blaue** Augen.
*The **little** baby has **blue** eyes.*

- Adjectives after a **der**-word have these endings.

after *der*-words				
	masculine	**feminine**	**neuter**	**plural**
nominative	der **große** Bruder	die **blonde** Schwester	das **junge** Kind	die **alten** Großeltern
accusative	den **großen** Bruder	die **blonde** Schwester	das **junge** Kind	die **alten** Großeltern

Der **alte** Mann dort ist mein Opa.
*The **old** man over there is my grandpa.*

Die **große** Frau ist meine Tante.
*The **tall** woman is my aunt.*

Ich liebe die **schönen** Häuser in dieser Straße.
*I love the **pretty** houses on this street.*

Irene sucht ihren **kleinen** Cousin.
*Irene is looking for her **little** cousin.*

- Adjectives preceded by an **ein**-word have these endings.

after *ein*-words				
	masculine	**feminine**	**neuter**	**plural**
nominative	ein **großer** Bruder	eine **blonde** Schwester	ein **junges** Kind	meine **alten** Großeltern
accusative	einen **großen** Bruder	eine **blonde** Schwester	ein **junges** Kind	meine **alten** Großeltern

Mein **großer** Bruder ist ein **guter** Golfspieler.
*My **big** brother is a **good** golf player.*

Herr Wirth hat eine **sportliche** Tochter.
*Mr. Wirth has an **athletic** daughter.*

Ist deine **kleine** Schwester hier?
*Is your **little** sister here?*

Seine Großmutter hat einen **schönen** Vogel.
*His grandmother has a **beautiful** bird.*

- Unpreceded adjectives have these endings.

unpreceded				
	masculine	**feminine**	**neuter**	**plural**
nominative	**roter** Wein	**dicke** Milch	**altes** Brot	**große** Fische
accusative	**roten** Wein	**dicke** Milch	**altes** Brot	**große** Fische

Kleine Kinder brauchen **gute** Eltern.
***Small** children need **good** parents.*

Mein Vater hat **braune** Augen.
*My father has **brown** eyes.*

Altes Brot schmeckt nicht so gut.
***Old** bread doesn't taste so good.*

Unsere Geschwister haben **lockige** Haare.
*Our siblings have **curly** hair.*

- If multiple adjectives precede the same noun, they all take the same ending.

Ist das **kleine**, **rothaarige** Mädchen deine Schwester?
*Is the **little**, **red-headed** girl your sister?*

Sie hat einen **großen**, **gut aussehenden** Bruder.
*She has a **tall**, **good-looking** brother.*

- Use **sehr** before an adjective to mean *very*. The adverb **sehr** does not take any additional endings.

Ihre Haare sind **sehr** lang.
*Her hair is **very** long.*

Ich lese ein **sehr** gutes Buch.
*I'm reading a **very** good book.*

ACHTUNG

Some adjectives ending in -**el**, such as **dunkel**, drop the **e** in the stem when an ending is added.

Das ist ein dunkles Foto.
That's a dark photo.

Suggestion Point out that most endings for preceded adjectives are either -**e** or -**en**, and that the only other possible endings are -**er**, -**es**, and -**em**.

QUERVERWEIS

You learned the adverb **sehr** in **1A Kontext**, in the expression **sehr gut**. You will learn more about adverbs in **4A.1**.

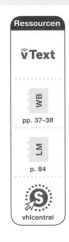

Ressourcen

v̂ Text

WB
pp. 37–38

LM
p. 84

vhlcentral

Jetzt sind Sie dran!   Write the nominative or accusative form of the adjectives.

Nominativ

1. der ___schlanke___ (schlank) Vater
2. ein ___verheirateter___ (verheiratet) Mann
3. die ___große___ (groß) Familie
4. eine ___alte___ (alt) Schwägerin
5. das ___verlobte___ (verlobt) Paar
6. die ___sportlichen___ (sportlich) Enkelkinder

Akkusativ

7. einen ___jungen___ (jung) Vater
8. die ___ledigen___ (ledig) Verwandten
9. einen ___dünnen___ (dünn) Hund
10. ein ___hübsches___ (hübsch) Mädchen
11. den ___kleinen___ (klein) Sohn
12. das ___blonde___ (blond) Kind

Anwendung

1 **Kombinieren** Match each adjective with its opposite.

<u>d</u> 1. hässlich   a. jung
<u>f</u> 2. kurz   b. dick
<u>e</u> 3. blond   c. klein
<u>a</u> 4. alt   d. schön
<u>c</u> 5. groß   e. schwarzhaarig
<u>b</u> 6. dünn   f. lang
<u>g</u> 7. lockig   g. glatt

2 **Was fehlt?** Complete the sentences.

1. Ich habe einen _____großen_____ (groß) Bruder.
2. Mein _____großer_____ (groß) Bruder spielt Fußball.
3. Er hat einen _____kleinen_____ (klein) Hund.
4. Der _____kleine_____ (klein) Hund hat sehr _____kurze_____ Haare.
5. Seine _____kurzen_____ (kurz) Haare sind auch sehr _____dünn_____ (dünn).
6. Hast du auch so einen _____kleinen_____ (klein), _____schönen_____ (schön) Hund?

3 **Was ist richtig?** Select the adjective that best completes each sentence.

BEISPIEL   Martin ist sehr nett und freundlich.
Er ist ein _____großartiger_____ (hässlicher, sportlicher, großartiger) Junge.

1. Sein Vater fährt viel Fahrrad und Ski. Er ist ein sehr _____sportlicher_____ (sportlicher, alter, blonder) Mann.
2. Deine Schwester hat schöne Haare. Sie ist ein _____hübsches_____ (großes, hässliches, hübsches) Mädchen.
3. Meine Mutter hat keine lockigen Haare. Sie hat _____glatte_____ (kleine, lange, glatte) Haare.
4. Meine Eltern sind nicht mehr zusammen. Ich habe _____geschiedene_____ (verheiratete, kurze, geschiedene) Eltern.
5. Ihre Enkeltochter ist 2 Jahre alt. Sie ist ein _____junges_____ (junges, hässliches, dickes) Kind.
6. Die Großeltern sind 80 Jahre alt. Die _____alten_____ (hübschen, alten, kleinen) Großeltern spielen Schach am Wochenende.

4 **Schreiben** Replace the underlined words with the words in parentheses and make any necessary changes.

BEISPIEL   <u>Das</u> kleine Mädchen ist sehr sportlich. (die)
Die kleinen Mädchen sind sehr sportlich.

1. <u>Der</u> rothaarige Sohn spielt Fußball. (mein)   Mein rothaariger Sohn spielt Fußball.
2. Ihr Großvater liest <u>das</u> lange Buch. (ein)   Ihr Großvater liest ein langes Buch.
3. Ich belege <u>einen</u> schwierigen Kurs. (den)   Ich belege den schwierigen Kurs.
4. <u>Der</u> kurze, dünne Junge ist nicht sehr sportlich. (die)   Die kurzen, dünnen Jungen sind nicht sehr sportlich.
5. Siehst du <u>die</u> kleinen Kinder? (das)   Siehst du das kleine Kind?

S Practice more at **vhlcentral.com**.

Kommunikation

5 Die Familie Müller In pairs, take turns describing the members of the Müller family. Answers will vary.

BEISPIEL

Moritz ist alt und klein.

Michael
Petra
Inez
Rex
Moritz
Alexander

6 Ein guter Freund Interview a classmate to learn about one of his/her friends. Use the questions below and add three more of your own. Answers will vary.

BEISPIEL

S1: Hat deine beste Freundin lange Haare?
S2: Nein, sie hat kurze Haare.

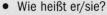

- Wie heißt er/sie?
- Wie alt ist er/sie?
- Ist er/sie groß oder klein?
- Hat er/sie blaue Augen?
- Ist er/sie dunkelhaarig?
- Ist er/sie sportlich?
- Ist er ein guter Schüler? / Ist sie eine gute Schülerin?

7 Raten Sie Choose a famous person. In small groups, take turns asking yes-or-no questions to determine the identity of each person. Answers will vary.

BEISPIEL

S1: Ist sie eine Frau?
S2: Ja.
S3: Hat sie blaue Augen?
S2: Nein.

8 Beschreiben Pick one of your family members and describe him or her to your partner. Take notes on your partner's description, and be prepared to describe his or her family member to the class. Answers will vary.

BEISPIEL

Mein Onkel ist ein großer Mann. Er hat kurze schwarze Haare...

- Wie alt ist er/sie?
- Wie ist sein/ihr Familienstand?
- Hat er/sie Kinder?
- Macht er/sie Sport?
- Hat er/sie Haustiere?
- Woher kommt er/sie?

5 Partner Chat You can also assign activity 5 on the Supersite. Students work in pairs to record the activity online. The pair's recorded conversation will appear in your gradebook.

6 Expansions
- Have students bring in photos of their family or friends. Ask students to describe the people in the photos to classmates.
  Ex.: **Das ist mein sportlicher Vater und hier ist meine hübsche Mutter.**
- Have students describe their partners' friends to the class.

6 Partner Chat You can also assign activity 6 on the Supersite. Students work in pairs to record the activity online. The pair's recorded conversation will appear in your gradebook.

8 Suggestion Tell students they can describe an actual family member or invent a fictional person.

Wiederholung

1 Wer ist wer?
In pairs, take turns choosing a person from the list and giving clues to help your partner guess which person you've chosen. Answers will vary. **1 Partner Chat** You can also assign activity 1 on the Supersite. Students work in pairs to record the activity online. The pair's recorded conversation will appear in your gradebook.

BEISPIEL

S1: Mein Vater ist ihr Mann. Meine Schwester ist ihre Tochter. Wer ist sie?
S2: Sie ist deine Mutter.

Bruder	Schwester
Cousin	Schwiegermutter
Enkeltochter	Sohn
Großvater	Tante
Schwager	Vater

2 Saras Familie
In pairs, say what each person in Sara's family is like and what he or she likes to do. Use vocabulary from **Kontext 2B**. Answers will vary. **2 Virtual Chat** You can also assign activity 2 on the Supersite. Students record individual responses that appear in your gradebook.

BEISPIEL

S1: Wie ist Saras Bruder?
S2: Ihr Bruder ist groß. Er spielt gern Tennis.

Bruder

1. Cousin

2. Neffe

3. Tante

4. Onkel

5. Großvater

6. Schwägerin

3 Arbeitsblatt
Your instructor will give you a worksheet with instructions to play Family Bingo. Get a different name for each square of the grid, then share your findings with the class. Answers will vary.

BEISPIEL

S1: Paula, hast du einen großen Bruder?
S2: Ja, mein Bruder Stefan ist sehr groß.
S1: Paula hat einen großen Bruder.

4 Verschiedene Menschen
In small groups, take turns picking someone in the illustration and describing him/her. The next person repeats the description and adds to it. Keep going around the group, trying to add as many details as possible. Answers will vary.

BEISPIEL

S1: Die Frau heißt Fatima. Sie ist hübsch.
S2: Die Frau heißt Fatima. Sie ist hübsch und liest gern.
S3: Die Frau heißt Fatima. Sie ist hübsch und liest gern. Morgen geht sie spazieren.

Daniel Fatima Annika

Mert und Lara

Yusuf und Tobias

Jana und Alexander

Emil und Eva

5 Diskutieren und kombinieren
Your instructor will give you and your partner each a picture of a family. Ask questions to find the six differences between the two pictures. Answers will vary.

BEISPIEL

S1: Ist Renate blond?
S2: Nein. Renate ist nicht blond. Sie ist dunkelhaarig.

6 Stammbaum
Create an illustrated family tree, and share it with a classmate. Tell your partner about each of your family members, including their names, how they are related to you, what they are like, and what they like or don't like to do. Answers will vary.

BEISPIEL

S1: Das ist meine Schwester. Sie heißt Steffi. Sie ist sehr sportlich.
S2: Fährt Steffi gern Fahrrad?

AP* Theme: Contemporary Life
Context: Health & Well-Being

Bauer Joghurt

The Bauer creamery was founded in 1887 in Wasserburg am Inn, Bavaria. Today, the company is managed by the fifth generation of the Bauer family. Known especially for their yogurt, Bauer also produces a variety of cheeses and other dairy products. The company has a reputation for excellent quality, using milk from cows fed on non-genetically modified food, with no added preservatives or artificial flavors.

Papa, wer ist dieser Bauer°?

Die Bauers, Schatz. Das ist eine Familie aus Bayern°.

Die machen alle Joghurt. Vom Opa bis zum Enkel.

Bauer *farmer* **Bayern** *Bavaria*

Verständnis Answer the questions in German.

1. Who are the Bauers, according to the girl's father? eine Familie aus Bayern

2. Which members of the Bauer family does the father mention? den Opa, den Enkel / das Enkelkind

Diskussion In pairs, discuss the answers to these questions. Answers will vary.

1. Do you know of other companies like Bauer that are family-owned? Are family-owned companies more likely to produce quality products? Explain.

2. What is the message of this commercial? Do you think it effectively conveys that message? Explain.

Communicative Goals

You will learn how to:

- describe people
- express an attitude about an action
- give instructions

Wie sind sie? Vocabulary Tools

Wortschatz

persönliche Beschreibungen	personal descriptions
(un)angenehm	(un)pleasant
arm	poor; unfortunate
bescheiden	modest
egoistisch	selfish
ernst	serious
freundlich	friendly
gemein	mean
gierig	greedy
großzügig	generous
intellektuell	intellectual
intelligent	intelligent
langsam	slow
mutig	brave
naiv	naïve
nervös	nervous
nett	nice
neugierig	curious
reich	rich
schlecht	bad
schüchtern	shy
schwach	weak
stolz	proud
toll	great
lächeln	to smile
lachen	to laugh
weinen	to cry
Berufe	*professions*
der Architekt, -en / die Architektin, -nen	architect
der Geschäftsmann (*pl.* Geschäftsleute) / die Geschäftsfrau, -en	businessman / businesswoman
der Ingenieur, -e / die Ingenieurin, -nen	engineer
der Journalist, -en / die Journalistin, -nen	journalist
der Rechtsanwalt, ⁻e / die Rechtsanwältin, -nen	lawyer

Ressourcen

vText | WB pp. 39–40 | LM p. 85 | vhlcentral

Er ist stark.

der Kellner, - (die Kellnerin, -nen)

Er ist schnell.

Er ist fleißig.

Sie sind faul.

der Besitzer, - (die Besitzerin, -nen)

diskret

müde

eifersüchtig

Sie ist besorgt.

Er ist traurig.

ACHTUNG

Note that the plural of **der Geschäftsmann** is **die Geschäftsleute**; **die Leute** means *people*.

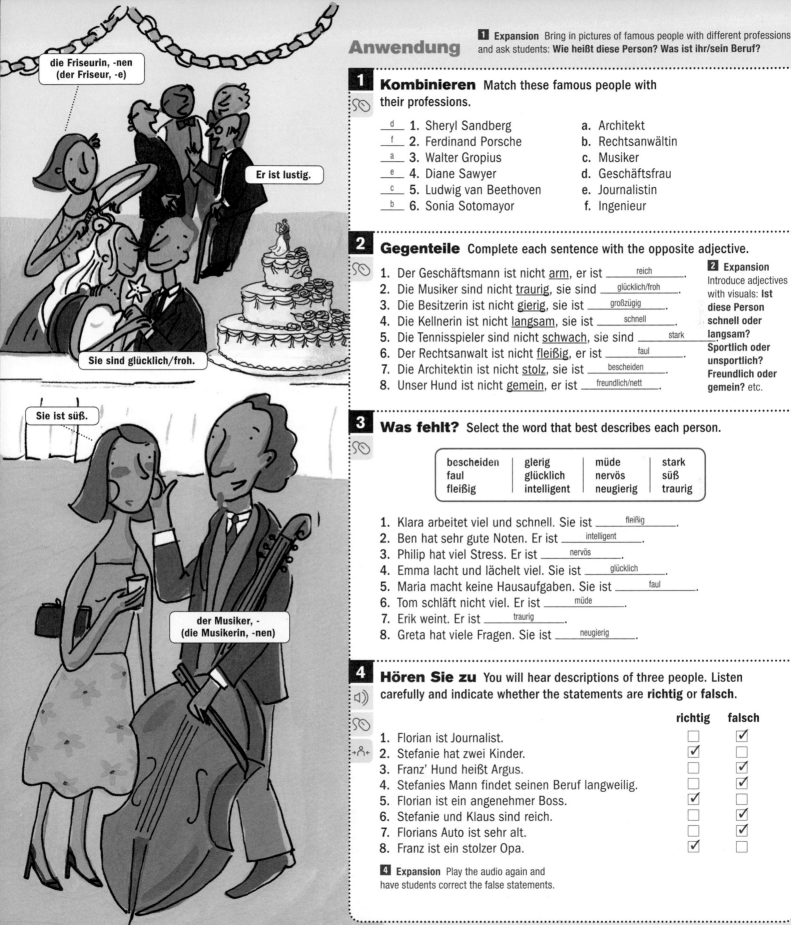

die Friseurin, -nen
(der Friseur, -e)

Er ist lustig.

Sie sind glücklich/froh.

Sie ist süß.

der Musiker, -
(die Musikerin, -nen)

Anwendung

1 Expansion Bring in pictures of famous people with different professions and ask students: **Wie heißt diese Person? Was ist ihr/sein Beruf?**

1 Kombinieren Match these famous people with their professions.

- _d_ 1. Sheryl Sandberg
- _f_ 2. Ferdinand Porsche
- _a_ 3. Walter Gropius
- _e_ 4. Diane Sawyer
- _c_ 5. Ludwig van Beethoven
- _b_ 6. Sonia Sotomayor

- a. Architekt
- b. Rechtsanwältin
- c. Musiker
- d. Geschäftsfrau
- e. Journalistin
- f. Ingenieur

2 Gegenteile Complete each sentence with the opposite adjective.

1. Der Geschäftsmann ist nicht <u>arm</u>, er ist _____reich_____.
2. Die Musiker sind nicht <u>traurig</u>, sie sind ___glücklich/froh___.
3. Die Besitzerin ist nicht <u>gierig</u>, sie ist ___großzügig___.
4. Die Kellnerin ist nicht <u>langsam</u>, sie ist ___schnell___.
5. Die Tennisspieler sind nicht <u>schwach</u>, sie sind ___stark___.
6. Der Rechtsanwalt ist nicht <u>fleißig</u>, er ist ___faul___.
7. Die Architektin ist nicht <u>stolz</u>, sie ist ___bescheiden___.
8. Unser Hund ist nicht <u>gemein</u>, er ist ___freundlich/nett___.

2 Expansion Introduce adjectives with visuals: **Ist diese Person schnell oder langsam? Sportlich oder unsportlich? Freundlich oder gemein?** etc.

3 Was fehlt? Select the word that best describes each person.

bescheiden	gierig	müde	stark
faul	glücklich	nervös	süß
fleißig	intelligent	neugierig	traurig

1. Klara arbeitet viel und schnell. Sie ist ___fleißig___.
2. Ben hat sehr gute Noten. Er ist ___intelligent___.
3. Philip hat viel Stress. Er ist ___nervös___.
4. Emma lacht und lächelt viel. Sie ist ___glücklich___.
5. Maria macht keine Hausaufgaben. Sie ist ___faul___.
6. Tom schläft nicht viel. Er ist ___müde___.
7. Erik weint. Er ist ___traurig___.
8. Greta hat viele Fragen. Sie ist ___neugierig___.

4 Hören Sie zu You will hear descriptions of three people. Listen carefully and indicate whether the statements are **richtig** or **falsch**.

	richtig	falsch
1. Florian ist Journalist.	☐	☑
2. Stefanie hat zwei Kinder.	☑	☐
3. Franz' Hund heißt Argus.	☐	☑
4. Stefanies Mann findet seinen Beruf langweilig.	☐	☑
5. Florian ist ein angenehmer Boss.	☑	☐
6. Stefanie und Klaus sind reich.	☐	☑
7. Florians Auto ist sehr alt.	☐	☑
8. Franz ist ein stolzer Opa.	☑	☐

4 Expansion Play the audio again and have students correct the false statements.

S Practice more at **vhlcentral.com**.

Kommunikation

7 Suggestion Have students brainstorm a list of adjectives to describe themselves and their ideal partner before they start composing their ads.

---

5 Berufe In pairs, take turns replying to the questions based on the images.

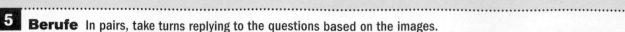

▶ **BEISPIEL**

S1: Ist Karl Musiker?
S2: Nein, er ist Kellner.

5 Virtual Chat You can also assign activity 5 on the Supersite. Students record individual responses that appear in your gradebook.

1. Ist Helga Ingenieurin?
Nein, sie ist Geschäftsfrau/Rechtsanwältin.

2. Ist Ulrich Architekt?
Nein, er ist Friseur.

3. Sind Markus, Jan und Tobias Rechtsanwälte?
Nein, sie sind Musiker.

4. Ist Birgit Kellnerin?
Nein, sie ist Journalistin.

5. Ist Stefan Friseur?
Nein, er ist Geschäftsmann.

6. Ist Claudia Musikerin?
Nein, sie ist Ingenieurin/Architektin.

---

6 Partnersuche Read Georg's personal ad and discuss with a partner whether Maria or Jessica would be a better match for him. Be ready to defend your opinion to the class. Answers will vary.

6 Partner Chat You can also assign activity 6 on the Supersite.

Georg, 32 Jahre

Hallo! Ich heiße Georg, ich bin 32 Jahre alt, 182 cm groß, schlank, dunkelhaarig und habe braune Augen. Ich bin ein netter Mann, optimistisch und intelligent. Ich habe viele Hobbys, spiele Fußball, Tennis und Handball, sehe gern Filme und koche auch gern und gut. Ich bin geschieden und habe eine kleine Tochter. Meine ideale Partnerin ist zwischen 26 und 32 Jahre alt, nicht zu klein (ca. 168 cm), blond, schlank, aktiv und sportlich. Sie muss gern essen und sie muss Kinder gern haben! Wenn du das bist, dann schicke mir eine E-Mail an nettergeorg@gvz.de.

6 Expansion Ask students to explain their choice of the ideal partner for Georg. Encourage them to use opposite adjectives. Ex.: **Jessica ist nicht groß, sie ist klein.**

Maria
23 Jahre
groß (182 cm)
lustig
schüchtern
aktiv

Jessica
28 Jahre
klein (165 cm)
sportlich
intellektuell
schlank

8 Suggestion As a class, brainstorm some of the questions partners will need to ask for this activity. Ex.: **Wo wohnst du? Was ist dein Beruf? Bist du verheiratet? Wie viele Kinder hast du?** Have pairs act out their conversations for the class.

---

7 Wunschpartner Now it's your turn to write a personal ad. Using Georg's ad as a model, describe yourself and your ideal girlfriend or boyfriend. Include details such as profession, age, physical characteristics, and personality. In groups, take turns reading the ads and guessing who wrote them.

---

8 Klassentreffen Imagine you are at the 10th reunion for your high-school class. With a partner, role-play a conversation between two old friends who haven't seen each other since graduation.

- Find out where your friend now lives and what his or her profession is.
- Ask about your friend's marital status, whether he or she has children, and, if so, what they are like.
- Ask your friend to describe his or her significant other.

---

9 Klatsch und Tratsch Heike is catching up with her cousin Lisa, who is a real **Klatschbase** (gossip). With a partner, write a conversation between Heike and Lisa in which Lisa gives her opinion of the guests at a recent family wedding. Answers will vary.

9 Expansion Hand out pictures of famous people to pairs or groups of students and ask them to write some gossip about each person.

BEISPIEL

S1: Wie ist Peters Frau?
S2: Sie ist hübsch und sehr schlank, aber eine unangenehme Person und ein bisschen gemein. Sie ist Journalistin, also der intellektuelle Typ.

Aussprache und Rechtschreibung  Audio

Consonant clusters

Some German consonant combinations are not common in English. In the clusters **gn**, **kn**, **pf**, and **ps**, both consonants are pronounced. Do not add a vowel sound between these consonants when you pronounce them.

| **Gnom** | **Knödel** | **Pferd** | **Napf** | **psychisch** |

The German **ng** is always pronounced like the English *ng* in *singer*, never like the consonant combination in *finger*, regardless of where it appears in a word.

| **Ring** | **fangen** | **jung** | **Prüfungen** | **entlang** |

Some German letters represent the sound of a consonant cluster. The letter **x** is pronounced like the consonant combination **ks**. The letter **z** and the consonant combinations **tz** and **ts** are pronounced like the *ts* in the English word *hats*. The letter combination **qu** is pronounced *kv*.

| **extra** | **Zahn** | **Qualität** | **sitzt** | **Äquator** |

1 **Aussprechen** Practice saying these words aloud.

1. Gnade
2. knicken
3. Pfeil
4. Topf
5. Pseudonym
6. lang
7. bringen
8. Examen
9. Zoo
10. Mozart
11. Quatsch
12. Aquarell

Suggestion Have students look at the sample words and sentences on this page to identify cognates and words they already know. Tell students the meanings of any unfamiliar words or phrases.

2 **Nachsprechen** Practice saying these sentences aloud.

1. Die Katze streckt sich und legt den Kopf in den Nacken.
2. Felix fängt eine Qualle aus dem Ozean.
3. Der Zoowärter zähmt ein quergestreiftes Zebra.
4. Herr Quast brät Knödel in der Pfanne.
5. Der Gefangene bittet Xerxes um Gnade.
6. Das Taxi fährt kreuz und quer durch die Schweiz.

3 **Sprichwörter** Practice reading these sayings aloud.

Pferde lassen sich zum Wasser bringen, aber nicht zum Trinken zwingen.[1]

Nachts sind alle Katzen grau.[2]

[1] You can lead a horse to water, but you can't make it drink.

[2] At night, all cats are grey.

Unsere Mitbewohner Video

George trifft Meline im Museum und Hans trifft Sabite am Brandenburger Tor.
Sie reden über ihre Mitbewohner. Oder reden sie über mehr?

Vorbereitung Before showing the video, ask students to brainstorm what adjectives they would use to describe each of the characters. Write these words on the board.

NATIONAL
communication
cultures
STANDARDS

GEORGE Hallo, Meline. Wer ist das?
MELINE Fritz Sommer. Langweilig. George, du sollst nicht immer alles so ernst nehmen.
GEORGE Du bist lustig.
MELINE Und du bist süß, mein kleiner amerikanischer Freund.

HANS Hallo, Sabite!
SABITE Hallo, Hans! Wie geht's? Oh, sei nicht traurig. Du bist nett und großzügig. Können wir Freunde sein?

MELINE Oh, armer Hans!
GEORGE Sei nicht gemein, Meline.
MELINE Bin ich nicht. Sabite ist künstlerisch, lebhaft und verrückt.

GEORGE Ist Sabite eine gute Mitbewohnerin?
MELINE Sabite ist eine liebenswürdige und bescheidene Person. Ihre Kunst ist hässlich und schlecht!

SABITE Ich bin so stolz auf dich, Hans. Du bist ein echter Freund. Danke, dass du mir hilfst.
HANS Keine Ursache.
SABITE Meline ist gemein.
HANS Meline ist unangenehm.

MELINE Hans ist intellektuell, aber naiv.
GEORGE Ihn als Mitbewohner zu haben, ist langweilig. Er liest und sieht fern bis um zwei Uhr früh. Ich habe morgens Uni.
MELINE Kann er nicht ohne Fernsehen lernen?
GEORGE Nein, das kann er nicht.

ÜBUNGEN

1 **Wer ist das?** Which character does each statement describe: George, Meline, Sabite, or Hans?

1. ___George___ ist besorgt um seine Noten.
2. ___Meline___ hat schöne Augen.
3. ___Sabite___ macht hässliche und schlechte Kunst.
4. Jungen finden ___Meline___ geheimnisvoll und faszinierend.
5. ___Hans___ ist nett und großzügig.

6. ___Hans___ ist ein echter Freund.
7. ___George___ ist ein netter Typ.
8. ___Sabite___ ist künstlerisch, lebhaft und verrückt.
9. ___George___ ist süß.
10. ___Hans___ ist intellektuell, aber naiv.

PERSONEN

George   Hans   Meline   Sabite

7

SABITE Ich möchte, dass sie einen neuen Freund hat.
HANS Bist du eifersüchtig?
SABITE Was?
HANS Sie ist lebhaft und hübsch. Sie hat sehr schöne Augen. Jungen finden sie geheimnisvoll und faszinierend.

8

SABITE Ist George ein guter Mitbewohner?
HANS Er ist ein netter Typ. Er ist besorgt um seine Noten. Ich sehe nachts fern und lese und er lernt bis zwei Uhr morgens.

9

SABITE Findest du sie hübsch?
HANS Wen?
SABITE Meline.
HANS Ich weiß nicht.

10

GEORGE Meline, Sabite meint es ernst mit Torsten. Du darfst nicht...
MELINE Ich finde nicht, dass sie gut zusammenpassen. Aber mach dir keine Sorgen. Ich kann sie nicht auseinanderbringen. Sie machen bald Schluss, auch ohne meine Hilfe.

Nützliche Ausdrücke

- **etwas ernst nehmen**
  to take something seriously
- **Du bist lustig.**
  You should talk. (lit. You're funny.)
- **Ihn als Mitbewohner zu haben, ist langweilig.**
  Having him as a roommate is boring.
- **Sei nicht traurig.**
  Don't be sad.
- **Danke, dass du mir hilfst.**
  Thanks for helping me.
- **Keine Ursache.**
  You're welcome.
- **Ich möchte, dass sie einen neuen Freund hat.**
  I want her to get a new boyfriend.
- **Jungen finden sie geheimnisvoll und faszinierend.**
  Boys find her mysterious and fascinating.
- **besorgt sein um**
  to be worried about
- **Du darfst nicht...**
  You mustn't...
- **Ich finde nicht, dass sie gut zusammenpassen.**
  I don't think they're a good match.
- **Schluss machen**
  to break up

3B.1
- **Ich kann sie nicht auseinanderbringen.**
  I can't break them up.

3B.2
- **Er ist besorgt um seine Noten.**
  He's worried about his grades.

3B.3
- **Mach dir keine Sorgen.**
  Don't worry.

---

2 **Schreiben** Write a brief description of a well-known person in your school or community, using as many descriptive adjectives as you can. Do not mention his/her name. Be prepared to read your description to the class, who will guess this person's identity. Answers will vary.

freundlich	intellektuell	schüchtern
glücklich	lustig	traurig
großzügig	mutig	...

3 **Vertiefung** Research a famous German person and present him/her to the class. Use adjectives to describe his/her physical appearance and personality. Be prepared to share your description with your classmates.
Answers will vary.

3 Suggestion You may wish to assign individuals for students to research, such as Diane Kruger, Hermann Hesse, Wilhelm Röntgen, Hugo Boss, etc.

You might also want students to use a visual aid for their presentation.

Ressourcen

vText   VM   p. 104   vhlcentral

Suggestion Point out to students that, as they have seen in the **Fotoroman**, German speakers also use **Freund/Freundin** to refer to a boyfriend or girlfriend. Encourage students to think about misunderstandings that might arise from the different ways that Americans and Germans use the word "friend."

IM FOKUS

Auf unsere Freunde!

 Reading

AP* Theme: Personal & Public Identities
Context: Alienation & Integration

> **TIPP**
>
> In German, many adjectives can be transformed into nouns.
>
> **bekannt → der / die Bekannte**
> *known*   *acquaintance*
>
> **besonders → (etwas) Besonderes**
> *special*   *something special*
>
> **gleich → das Gleiche**
> *same*   *the same one/the same thing*

IN DIESER° FACEBOOK-ZEIT HABEN wir alle viele „Freunde". Was ist also ein Kumpel°, mit dem Sie hin und wieder auf Partys gehen, und was ist ein echter° Freund? Deutsche sagen nicht so schnell „Freund" wie Amerikaner. In Deutschland ist es etwas Besonderes° ein „Freund" zu sein.

Wirklich gute Freunde hat man in Deutschland wahrscheinlich höchstens° vier oder fünf. Ein echter Freund zu sein bedeutet, dass° man sich sehr gut und vielleicht auch schon sehr lange kennt°. Die meisten Leute in Deutschland sagen, dass sie ihre Freunde schon aus der Schule oder aus der Kinderzeit kennen. Nur

weil° man einmal zusammen Kaffee getrunken hat°, ist man noch lange kein Freund.

In der Gruppe kennen sich alle mehr oder weniger gut. Trotzdem° nennen sich die Leute in einer Gruppe „Kumpel", nicht „Freunde". Die anderen Leute, die man kennt, nennt man meistens „Bekannte".

Es gibt also drei Gruppen von Menschen um eine Person: Die meisten Menschen sind Bekannte. Die größere Gruppe sind die Kumpel. Und nur eine sehr kleine Gruppe sind richtige Freunde. Aber mit diesen Freunden kann man alles teilen°. Also: Auf Freunde!

Auf unsere Freunde! *Here's to our friends!* **dieser** *this* **Kumpel** *buddy* **echter** *real* **etwas Besonderes** *something special* **wahrscheinlich höchstens** *probably at most* **bedeutet, dass** *means that* **sich... kennt** *know each other* **Nur weil** *Just because* **getrunken hat** *has drunk* **Trotzdem** *Nevertheless* **teilen** *share*

ÜBUNGEN

1 **Was fehlt?** Complete the statements.

1. In Deutschland sagt man nicht so schnell __Freund__ zu einer neuen Person.
2. Viele Deutsche kennen ihre Freunde aus der __Schule__ und aus der Kinderzeit.
3. Gute __Freunde__ nennt man in Deutschland nur vier oder fünf Personen.
4. Für __Amerikaner__ und für Deutsche hat das Wort „Freund" nicht die gleiche Bedeutung.

5. In __Deutschland__ ist ein Freund jemand, den (*whom*) man sehr gut kennt.
6. Einen echten Freund kennt man sehr gut und oft auch sehr __lange__.
7. Es gibt __drei__ Gruppen von Menschen um eine Person.
8. In einer __Gruppe__ sind alle gute Kumpel.
9. Die meisten Menschen, die man kennt, nennt man __Bekannte__.
10. Die Gruppe der Freunde ist eine sehr __kleine__ Gruppe.

DEUTSCH IM ALLTAG

Wie wir Menschen sind

aufrichtig	sincere
besserwisserisch	know-it-all (adj.)
eingebildet	arrogant
geduldig	patient
geizig	stingy
liebevoll	loving
locker	easy-going
oberflächlich	superficial
ruhig	calm
weise	wise
zuverlässig	reliable

DIE DEUTSCHSPRACHIGE WELT

Es wird geheiratet!°

Wie wünscht° man dem neuen Paar ein frohes Eheleben°? In **Bayern**, **Österreich** und **in der Schweiz** ist das **Brautstehlen°** eine lustige Tradition. Freunde stehlen die Braut und bringen sie von Gaststätte° zu Gaststätte. Der Bräutigam° muss sie finden... und alle Getränke bezahlen°! Die **Deutschen** und die **Österreicher** tragen den Ring meistens an der rechten° Hand. Aber **in der Schweiz** trägt man ihn an der linken° Hand. Die ist dem Herzen näher°.

Es wird geheiratet! *Someone's getting married!* **wünscht** *wishes* **Eheleben** *married life* **Brautstehlen** *stealing of the bride* **Gaststätte** *restaurant* **Bräutigam** *groom* **Getränke bezahlen** *pay for the drinks* **rechten** *right* **linken** *left* **dem Herzen näher** *closer to the heart* **AP* Theme:** Families & Communities **Context:** Family Structure

PORTRÄT

Tokio Hotel

AP* Theme: Beauty & Aesthetics
Context: Performing Arts

Die erfolgreiche° deutsche Band *Tokio Hotel* besteht° am Anfang aus den eineiigen° Zwillingen Bill und Tom Kaulitz. Schon als Kinder machen sie zusammen Musik. Als Duett treten sie unter dem Namen *Black Questionmark* auf°. Ihr Stiefvater ist auch Musiker und fördert° die Brüder. 2001 geben sie in ihrer Heimatstadt° Magdeburg ein Konzert. Dort treffen sie Gustav Schäfer und Georg Listing. Sie werden Freunde und treten zu viert unter dem Namen *Devilish* auf. 2005 nimmt die Universal Music Group die Band unter Vertrag°. Die vier nennen sich *Tokio Hotel* und sind schnell auf der ganzen Welt bekannt. Sie haben in Deutschland und Österreich vier Nummer-eins-Singles und verkaufen bis heute weltweit über 7 Millionen Alben°.

erfolgreich *successful* **besteht** *consists* **eineiigen** *identical* **treten...auf** *perform* **fördert** *supports* **Heimatstadt** *home town* **unter Vertrag** *under contract* **Alben** *albums*

🔗 IM INTERNET

Sind die Hochzeitsbräuche (*wedding traditions*) anders (*different*) in Deutschland als in den USA?

Find out more at **vhlcentral.com**.

3 Suggestion You may want to teach students the expression **ich glaube**.

---

2 **Richtig oder falsch?** Indicate whether each statement is **richtig** or **falsch**. Correct the false statements.

1. In Österreich ist es Tradition, den Bräutigam zu stehlen.
   Falsch. Es ist Tradition, die Braut zu stehlen.
2. In Deutschland trägt man den Ehering an der rechten Hand. Richtig.
3. *Tokio Hotel* ist eine erfolgreiche Band aus Österreich.
   Falsch. Die Band kommt aus Deutschland.
4. Bill und Tom Kaulitz sind Cousins. Falsch. Sie sind Brüder.
5. *Tokio Hotel* verkauft bis heute über 7 Millionen Alben. Richtig.

3 **Wie sind sie?** In pairs, describe each person in the photo on p. 120. How old do you think they are? What do you think their personalities are like? Are they friends or just classmates? Answers will vary.

Die deutschsprachige Welt Tell students that weddings in Germany typically have two parts: the legal ceremony (which is required) at the **Standesamt**, and the church wedding. Before the wedding day, friends and family may gather in front of the bride's home to break pottery, because "**Scherben bringen Glück**" (*shards bring luck*).

Ressourcen

vText vhlcentral

3B.1 **Modals** Presentation

Startblock In both English and German, modal verbs modify the meaning of another verb.

- Modals express an attitude towards an action, such as permission, obligation, ability, desire, or necessity. *May*, *can*, and *must* are examples of English modals.

Suggestion Explain to students that there are six modals in total. The modal **mögen** will be presented in **4A.2**.

modals	
dürfen	*to be allowed to, may*
können	*to be able to, can*
müssen	*to have to, must*
sollen	*to be supposed to*
wollen	*to want to*

- Except for **sollen**, all of the German modals are irregular in their present tense singular forms.

modals in the present tense					
	dürfen	**können**	**müssen**	**sollen**	**wollen**
ich	darf	kann	muss	soll	will
du	darfst	kannst	musst	sollst	willst
er/sie/es	darf	kann	muss	soll	will
wir	dürfen	können	müssen	sollen	wollen
ihr	dürft	könnt	müsst	sollt	wollt
Sie/sie	dürfen	können	müssen	sollen	wollen

Expansion Give students example sentences in English, with and without modals, to illustrate their use. Ex.: *He does his homework. He should do his homework. He must do his homework. He can do his homework. He wants to do his homework. He is allowed to do his homework.* Point out how each modal changes the meaning of the sentence.

- When you use a modal to modify the meaning of another verb, put the conjugated form of the modal in second position. Put the infinitive of the other verb at the end of the sentence.

Ich **muss** Französisch **lernen**.
*I **have to study** French.*

Ich **will** Französisch **lernen**.
*I **want to learn** French.*

- To form a yes-or-no question, move the modal verb to the beginning of the sentence, while the verb it modifies remains at the end.

    Willst du Wasser **trinken**?
    *Do you **want to drink** water?*

    Könnt ihr eurer Mutter **helfen**?
    *Can you **help** your mother?*

- **Dürfen** expresses permission.

    Mama, **darf** ich heute Nachmittag schwimmen gehen?
    *Mom, **may** I go swimming this afternoon?*

    Nein, Lina, du **darfst** heute nicht schwimmen gehen.
    *No, Lina, you **may** not go swimming today.*

- **Können** expresses ability.

    Peter **kann** Ski fahren.
    *Peter **can** ski.*

    Kannst du Fahrrad fahren?
    Can you ride a bicycle?

- **Müssen** expresses obligation.

    Jasmin und Moritz **müssen** viel lernen.
    *Jasmin and Moritz **have to** study a lot.*

    Muss Maria Spanisch lernen?
    *Does Maria **have to** learn Spanish?*

- **Sollen** conveys the expectation that a task be completed (*to be supposed to*). Note that, unlike the English *should* or *ought*, **sollen** implies an expectation that comes from someone other than the subject.

    Du **sollst** das Buch lesen.
    *You **are supposed to** read the book.*

    Soll ich nach Hause gehen?
    ***Should** I go home?*

- **Wollen** expresses desire.

    Sie **wollen** Musikerinnen werden.
    *They **want to** become musicians.*

    Willst du eine Katze haben?
    *Do you **want to** get a cat?*

Jetzt sind Sie dran! **Complete the sentences.**

1. Die Lehrerin __soll__ (sollen) langsam sprechen.
2. Ihr __sollt__ (sollen) eure Hausaufgaben nicht vergessen.
3. Was __sollen__ (sollen) wir heute machen?
4. Der Musiker __kann__ (können) Gitarre spielen.
5. Ich __kann__ (können) meinen Rucksack nicht finden.
6. __Kannst__ (Können) du nach Deutschland reisen?
7. Du __musst__ (müssen) ein Wörterbuch kaufen.
8. Ein Geschäftsmann __muss__ (müssen) sehr fleißig sein.
9. Wir __müssen__ (müssen) das Matheproblem an die Tafel schreiben.
10. Das Paar __darf__ (dürfen) heiraten.
11. Die Kinder __dürfen__ (dürfen) hier Fußball spielen.
12. Du __darfst__ (dürfen) nicht in das Klassenzimmer gehen.
13. Ich __will__ (wollen) Architektin werden.
14. Die Kinder __wollen__ (wollen) Fremdsprachen studieren.
15. __Wollt__ (Wollen) ihr die Fotos sehen?

Anwendung

1 Entscheiden Sie Select the correct form of the modal.

1. Ich (sollen / (soll)) Gitarre spielen.
2. Wir ((dürfen) / darf) keine Schokolade essen.
3. ((Willst) / Wollt) du in die Bibliothek gehen?
4. Ihr (musst / (müsst)) eure Großeltern begrüßen.
5. Annika ((kann) / können) ihre Cousine nicht finden.
6. Max und Nils (kann / (können)) samstags lange schlafen.

2 Was fehlt? Complete the sentences.

1. Die Kellner _____sollen_____ (sollen) das Essen bringen.
2. Du _____kannst_____ (können) Deutsch lernen.
3. Wir _____müssen_____ (müssen) einen Beruf finden.
4. Ihr _____dürft_____ (dürfen) einen Film sehen.
5. Ich _____will_____ (wollen) Journalist werden.

3 Schreiben Rewrite the sentences using the cues.

> **BEISPIEL** Antonia ist Musikerin. (wollen)
> *Antonia will Musikerin sein.*

1. Die Ingenieure bauen eine neue Maschine. (müssen) Die Ingenieure müssen eine neue Maschine bauen.
2. Der Journalist reist nach Deutschland. (dürfen) Der Journalist darf nach Deutschland reisen.
3. Die Geschäftsfrau und der Geschäftsmann sind nicht gierig. (sollen)
   Die Geschäftsfrau und der Geschäftsmann sollen nicht gierig sein.
4. Meine Tante und ich tanzen Tango. (können) Meine Tante und ich können Tango tanzen.
5. Ich werde Friseurin. (wollen) Ich will Friseurin werden.

4 Fragen Use the cues to form questions about the images.

4 Expansion Have students use these questions as the basis for a partner interview. Instead of using the subjects given, have them pose the questions to one another.
Ex.: **Darfst du schwimmen gehen? Ja, ich darf schwimmen gehen.**

> **BEISPIEL**
> ich / schwimmen
> gehen / dürfen
> *Darf ich schwimmen
> gehen?*

1. du / Ski fahren / können
Kannst du Ski fahren?

2. ich / jetzt lernen / sollen
Soll ich jetzt lernen?

3. Erika / Fußball spielen / wollen
Will Erika Fußball spielen?

4. wir / Musik hören / dürfen
Dürfen wir Musik hören?

5. Thomas / Musiker werden / wollen
Will Thomas Musiker werden?

6. ihr / viele Bücher lesen / müssen
Müsst ihr viele Bücher lesen?

 Practice more at **vhlcentral.com**.

Kommunikation

5 **Viele Wünsche** In pairs, take turns saying what each person wants to do. Then, imagine what they must or should do to achieve that goal.

Sample answers are provided.

BEISPIEL mein Bruder / nach Deutschland fahren

S1: *Mein Bruder will nach Deutschland fahren.*
S2: *Er soll Deutsch lernen.*

1. meine Freundin / Architektin werden Meine Freundin will Architektin werden.
2. ich / das Fußballspiel gewinnen Ich will das Fußballspiel gewinnen.
3. wir / einen Hund haben Wir wollen einen Hund haben.
4. mein Vater / ein neues Auto kaufen Mein Vater will ein neues Auto kaufen.
5. meine Schwester / gute Noten haben Meine Schwester will gute Noten haben.
6. mein Onkel / kurze Haare haben Mein Onkel will kurze Haare haben.

6 **Berufe** With a partner, offer advice to help these people get the jobs they want. Answers will vary.

BEISPIEL Mira und Maria / Ingenieurinnen

S1: *Mira und Maria wollen Ingenieurinnen werden.*
S2: *Sie sollen viel lernen.*

1. Emil und Hasan / Rechtsanwälte
2. David und Hanna / Musiker
3. Julia / Journalistin
4. Greta und Dilara / Geschäftsfrauen

7 **Einladungen** In small groups, take turns inviting each other to take part in these activities. If you turn down an invitation, explain what you want to do, should do, or must do instead, and suggest a different activity. Answers will vary.

BEISPIEL

S1: *Willst du Tennis spielen?*
S2: *Ich kann nicht. Ich muss Hausaufgaben machen. Aber wir können morgen spazieren gehen.*

1.

2.

3.

4.

5.

6.

3B.2 Prepositions with the accusative  Presentation

Startblock In **1B.1**, you learned the accusative endings for definite and indefinite articles. You also learned that the direct object in German always takes the accusative case. In addition, the objects of certain prepositions are always in the accusative case.

> Das Trinkgeld ist **für den Kellner**.
> *The tip is **for the waiter**.*

> Der Hund läuft **durch die Wälder**.
> *The dog is running **through the woods**.*

- Prepositions and prepositional phrases describe time, manner, and place, and answer the questions *when*, *how*, and *where*.

> **um** 8 Uhr
> *at 8 o'clock*

> **ohne** meinen Bruder
> *without my brother*

> **gegen** die Wand
> *against the wall*

- Here are some common accusative prepositions.

prepositions with the accusative							
bis	*until, to*	entlang	*along*	gegen	*against*	pro	*per*
durch	*through*	für	*for*	ohne	*without*	um	*around; at (time)*

> Der Besitzer kommt **durch die Tür**.
> *The owner is coming **through the door**.*

> Was hast du **gegen meinen Freund**?
> *What do you have **against my boyfriend**?*

- The prepositions **durch**, **für**, and **um**, when followed by the neuter definite article **das**, may be contracted to **durchs**, **fürs**, and **ums**. These contractions are frequently used in speech and are acceptable in writing.

> Das Spielzeug ist **fürs** Baby.
> *The toy is **for the** baby.*

> Die Kinder laufen **ums** Haus.
> *The kids are running **around** the house.*

- The accusative preposition **bis** is frequently used with time expressions. When **bis** comes before a proper noun, such as **Samstag** or **März**, no article is necessary.

> Ich bin **bis April** in Deutschland.
> *I'm in Germany **until April**.*

> Wir bleiben **bis nächsten Monat** in Köln.
> *We are staying in Cologne **until next month**.*

- **Pro** is also an accusative preposition. The object it precedes takes no article.

> Der Kellner verdient 300 Euro **pro Woche**.
> *The waiter earns 300 euros **per week**.*

> Das Auto fährt 230 Kilometer **pro Stunde**.
> *The car goes 230 kilometers **per hour**.*

- The accusative is also used with objects that precede **entlang**.

> Wir gehen **den Fluss entlang**.
> *We are going **down the river**.*

> Ich fahre **die Straße entlang**.
> *I'm driving **along the road**.*

Suggestion Help students remember the most common accusative prepositions with the mnemonic **DOGFU: durch, ohne, gegen, für, um** or by having them sing "**durch, für, gegen, ohne, um**" to the tune of "Raindrops keep falling on my head."

Ressourcen

v Text

WB
pp. 43–44

LM
p. 88

vhlcentral

Jetzt sind Sie dran! Select the preposition that best completes each sentence.

1. Die Frau geht (ohne / pro) ihren Mann einkaufen.
2. Der Hund läuft (durch / gegen) den Park.
3. Die Mutter braucht ein Spielzeug (um / für) ihre Tochter.
4. Was haben die Besitzer (gegen / bis) die Musik?
5. Die Kellnerin geht (durch / um) den Tisch.
6. Die Taxifahrt kostet 2 € (für / pro) Kilometer.
7. Ich gehe den Fluss (entlang / bis).
8. Die Journalisten arbeiten (gegen / bis) Mitternacht.

Anwendung und Kommunikation

1 **Was ist richtig?** Select the preposition that best completes each sentence.

| bis | entlang | für | gegen | ohne | um |

1. ___Um___ 8 Uhr muss ich arbeiten.
2. Der kleine Junge wirft den Ball ___gegen___ die Wand.
3. ___Ohne___ meine Schwester gehe ich nicht campen.
4. Das Auto fährt die Straße ___entlang___.
5. Sara kauft einen Kaffee ___für___ ihre Mutter.
6. Mein Onkel spielt ___bis___ 6 Uhr Fußball.

2 **Bilden Sie Sätze** Write eight sentences using items from each column. Pay attention to word order and accusative endings. Use each preposition once.

BEISPIEL Herr und Frau Becker / heute Abend eine Party geben / um / 8 Uhr
Heute Abend um 8 Uhr geben Herr und Frau Becker eine Party.

der Besitzer	angeln gehen	bis	Haustiere
du	beginnen	durch	Woche
ich	in Berlin bleiben	entlang	der Park
die Journalistin	50 Stunden arbeiten	für	19 Uhr
das Konzert	fahren	gegen	Samstag
Herr Bauer	laufen	ohne	die Straße
meine Schwester	lernen	pro	mein Bruder
wir	sein	um	die Prüfung

3 **Umfrage** In pairs, take turns asking and answering the questions. Answers will vary.

BEISPIEL

S1: *Um wie viel Uhr fährst du zur Uni?*
S2: *Ich fahre um 8 Uhr zur Uni.*

1. Um wie viel Uhr beginnt dein Unterricht?
2. Wie viele Stunden schläfst du pro Nacht?
3. Für wen kaufst du gern Blumen?
4. Ohne was kannst du nicht leben?
5. Gegen welche Mannschaften spielst du gern?

3 **Virtual Chat** You can also assign activity 3 on the Supersite. Students record individual responses that appear in your gradebook.

4 **Die Geburtstagsfeier** In small groups, write four sentences describing the illustration. Use at least four prepositions with the accusative.

Possible answers: Der Hund läuft durch das Spielfeld.
Die Äpfel sind für die Kinder. Die Jungen spielen ohne ihre Schwester. Die Eltern wollen um 12 Uhr essen.

 Practice more at **vhlcentral.com**.

3B.3   **The imperative**  Presentation

Startblock Imperatives are used to express commands, requests, suggestions, directions, and instructions.

Sei nicht traurig.

Mach dir keine Sorgen!

- The imperative forms are based on the present-tense conjugation patterns of **du**, **wir**, **ihr**, and **Sie**.

the *Imperativ* conjugation	
Indikativ	**Imperativ**
du kaufst	kauf(e)
ihr kauft	kauft
Sie kaufen	kaufen **Sie**
wir kaufen	kaufen **wir**

Mach deine Hausaufgaben!
Do your homework!

Backen wir einen Kuchen!
Let's bake a cake!

- To form an informal singular command, drop the **-st** from the present-tense **du** form of the verb. As in English, omit the subject pronoun with the second-person imperative.

Antworte auf die Frage!
Answer the question!

Schreib deinen Eltern eine E-Mail.
Write your parents an email.

- Verbs with an **a** to **ä** vowel change do not retain this change in the imperative. However, **e** to **ie** and **e** to **i** changes are retained in the imperative for **du**.

Fahr langsam!
Drive slowly!

Lies das Buch.
Read the book.

Nimm den Bleistift.
Take the pencil.

- The informal plural **ihr** command is identical to the present-tense form, without the pronoun.

Esst die Äpfel, Kinder!
Eat the apples, kids!

Lernt für die Prüfung.
Study for the exam.

- For formal commands, keep the subject **Sie** and invert the subject/verb word order of the present tense. Remember that the singular and plural forms are identical.

Probieren Sie den Kuchen!
Try the cake!

Warten Sie bitte hier.
Please wait here.

- The first person plural command is equivalent to the English *Let's...*. As with **Sie**, invert the subject/verb order of the present tense for **wir**.

Essen wir den Kuchen.
Let's eat the cake.

Gehen wir spazieren.
Let's go for a walk.

- In a negative command, **nicht** or **kein** follows the imperative form.

  Fahren Sie nicht so schnell!
  Don't drive so fast!

  Arbeite nicht so langsam!
  Don't work so slowly!

  Hör keine laute Musik!
  Don't listen to loud music!

  Macht kein Theater!
  Don't make a fuss!

QUERVERWEIS

See **2B.3** to review the use of **nicht** and **kein**.

- Use **bitte** to soften a command and make it polite. **Bitte** can be placed almost anywhere in a sentence, as long as it doesn't separate the verb from the subject pronoun **wir** or **Sie**.

  Öffnen Sie **bitte** Ihren Rucksack.
  *Open your backpack, **please**.*

  Geh nach Hause, **bitte**.
  *Go home, **please**.*

  Schlaft **bitte** nicht im Unterricht!
  Please don't sleep in class!

  Bitte nehmen Sie Platz.
  Please take a seat.

- The modals **können** and **wollen** are often used instead of the imperative for polite requests.

  Können Sie mir helfen?
  Can you help me?

  Wollen wir gehen?
  Shall we go?

- The verb **sein** has irregular imperative forms.

  Sei lieb!
  Be good! (sing., inf.)

  Seid diskret!
  Be discreet! (pl., inf.)

  Seien Sie mutig!
  Be brave! (form.)

  Seien wir realistisch!
  Let's be realistic!

- On signs or labels, and in recipes or printed instructions, infinitives are often used instead of imperatives. Here are some common commands and instructions found in everyday situations. Notice that in some cases, a command is conveyed by using an infinitive or the word **verboten** (*forbidden*), rather than the imperative.

common commands	
Drücken.	*Push.*
Ziehen.	*Pull.*
Bring mir...	*Bring me...*
Langsam fahren.	*Slow down.*
Warte.	*Wait.*
Sprechen Sie bitte langsamer.	*Please speak more slowly.*
Türen schließen.	*Keep doors closed.*
Rauchen verboten.	*No smoking.*
Betreten des Rasens verboten.	*Keep off the grass.*
Keine Zufahrt.	*Do not enter.*
Parkverbot.	*No parking.*

Ressourcen

v̂Text

WB
pp. 45–46

LM
p. 89

vhlcentral

Jetzt sind Sie dran! Select the correct imperative form to complete each sentence.

1. Herr Braun, (sprecht / (sprechen Sie)) bitte langsamer.
2. Schüler, (öffnen Sie / (öffnet)) eure Bücher auf Seite 34.
3. Philip, ((vergiss) / vergessen wir) deine Hausaufgaben nicht!
4. Kinder, ((seid) / sei) freundlich und nett!
5. Wir haben morgen eine Prüfung. ((Lernen wir) / Lernt) zusammen!
6. Nina, (fahrt / (fahr)) nicht so schnell!
7. Herr und Frau Schmidt, (warte / (warten Sie)) bitte einen Moment.
8. Wir haben Hunger. ((Essen wir) / Iss) den Strudel!

Anwendung

1 **Was fehlt?** Complete the sentences using the imperative.

 BEISPIEL Sebastian, _____Komm_____ (kommen)!

1. Herr Schneider, ___wiederholen Sie___ (wiederholen) bitte.
2. Marie und Lukas, _____esst_____ (essen) langsamer!
3. Felix, _____sei_____ (sein) nicht gemein!
4. Frau Fischer und Herr Wagner, ___nehmen Sie___ (nehmen) bitte eine Karte!
5. Paul und Else, _____macht_____ (machen) bitte kein Theater!
6. _____Sprechen_____ (sprechen) wir Deutsch!

2 **Bilden Sie Sätze** Write imperative commands for each person using the cues.

BEISPIEL Herr Braun: nicht so schnell fahren

Herr Braun, fahren Sie nicht so schnell!

1. Klara: Tennis mit Jan spielen   Klara, spiel Tennis mit Jan!
2. Wir: durch den Park gehen   Gehen wir durch den Park!
3. Max und Lara: den Text auf Seite 27 lesen   Max und Lara, lest/lesen Sie den Text auf Seite 27!
4. Herr Gärtner: heute bis 8 Uhr bleiben   Herr Gärtner, beiben Sie heute bis 8 Uhr!
5. Frau Weber: nicht nervös sein   Frau Weber, seien Sie nicht nervös!
6. Niklas: um 6 Uhr nach Hause kommen   Niklas, komm um 6 Uhr nach Hause!

3 **Schreiben** Tell these people not to do what they are doing.   Sample answers are provided.

BEISPIEL Lara ist eifersüchtig.

Sei nicht eifersüchtig, Lara!

3 Expansion Have students give additional affirmative commands for this activity. Ex.: **1. Seien Sie nicht gierig, Herr Becker! Seien Sie großzügig und nett!**

1. Herr Becker ist gierig.
Seien Sie nicht gierig, Herr Becker!
2. Tom und Jonas weinen.
Weint nicht, Tom und Jonas!
3. Lukas spielt schlechte Musik.
Spiel keine schlechte Musik, Lukas!
4. Frau Weber kauft hässliche Sachen.
Kaufen Sie keine hässlichen Sachen, Frau Weber!
5. Max und Lukas schreiben an die Wand.
Schreibt nicht an die Wand, Max und Lukas!
6. Wir bleiben hier.
Bleiben wir nicht hier!
7. Hanna telefoniert 4 Stunden pro Tag.
Hanna, telefonier nicht 4 Stunden pro Tag!
8. Otto und Emma essen den Kuchen.
Esst den Kuchen nicht, Otto und Emma!

4 **Konjugieren** Write a command for each image using the cues.   Sample answers are provided.

1. wir   Tanzen wir.

2. Nils   Nils, wirf den Ball!

3. Kinder / eure Bücher
Kinder, öffnet eure Bücher.

4. Frau Schulze / ein Glas Wasser
Frau Schulze, trinken Sie ein Glas Wasser.

5. wir   Gehen wir spazieren.

6. Greta / ein Bonbon
Greta, nimm ein Bonbon.

 Practice more at **vhlcentral.com**.

Kommunikation

5 **Befehle** In small groups, write eight sentences using **sollen**. Then, trade lists with another group and convert their sentences into commands. _{Answers will vary.}

> **BEISPIEL**
>
>
> **S1:** *Du sollst deine Hausaufgaben machen.*
> **S2:** *Mach deine Hausaufgaben.*

6 **Guter Rat** In pairs, use the imperative to give advice to each person or group. _{Answers will vary.}

> **BEISPIEL**   **deine Lehrerin**
>
>   *Sprechen Sie bitte langsamer.*

1. deine Mitschueler
2. deine beste Freundin oder dein bester Freund
3. deine Eltern oder deine Großeltern
4. dein Bruder oder deine Schwester
5. dein Schuldirektorin oder deine Schuldirektor
6. deine Katze oder dein Hund

7 **Ein paar Ratschläge** In pairs, list ten pieces of advice that you would give to a new German exchange student at your school. Use the affirmative and negative forms of the imperative. _{Answers will vary.}

> **BEISPIEL**
>
> **S1:** *Sei fleißig, aber nicht zu ernst!*
> **S2:** *Vergiss nicht deine Hausaufgaben!*

8 **Simon sagt** In groups of five, play Simon Says. One student gives commands using the **du, Sie, ihr**, and **wir** forms. The group members must perform or mime the activity, but only if the speaker says "**Simon sagt**". The first person to make a mistake becomes the new leader. _{Answers will vary.}

> **BEISPIEL**
>
> **S1:** *Simon sagt: „Tanzen wir!"*
> OR
> **S1:** *Laura und Michael, lauft um den Tisch!*

essen	laufen	schreiben
fahren	nehmen	sprechen
hören	öffnen	tanzen
fangen	sagen	weinen
lachen	schlafen	wiederholen

6 **Partner Chat** You can also assign activity 6 on the Supersite. Students work in pairs to record the activity online. The pair's recorded conversation will appear in your gradebook.

8 **Suggestion** If nobody makes a mistake, tell students to change leaders after three commands.

8 **Expansion** You may want to introduce students to the traditional German game **Kommando Pimperle**, similar to Simon Says.

Wiederholung

1 Etwas unternehmen

In pairs, make plans for what you will do today in each location. Use prepositions with the accusative. Answers will vary.

BEISPIEL

S1: Um 10 Uhr gehen wir in die Bibliothek.
S2: Ja, dort können wir gute Bücher für das Referat finden.

1 **Partner Chat** You can also assign activity 1 on the Supersite.

bis	gegen
durch	ohne
entlang	um
für	

1.

 2.

3.

 4.

2 Wollen und sollen

In small groups, take turns saying one thing that you want to do today, one thing you must do, one thing you can do, one thing you may do, and one thing you are supposed to do. Answers will vary.

BEISPIEL

S1: Ich will heute Abend in die Sporthalle gehen, aber ich muss Hausaufgaben machen.
S2: Ich soll für meinen Deutschkurs lernen, aber ich kann auch Tennis spielen.
S3: Ich kann nicht Tennis spielen. Ich muss...

3 Diskutieren und kombinieren

Your instructor will give you and a partner different worksheets with a list of occupations and profiles of several students. Take turns describing the students and matching their qualities to appropriate occupations. Answers will vary.

BEISPIEL

S1: Jana ist kreativ und gut in Mathe.
S2: Ah, dann ist Jana eine gute Architektin.

3 **Expansion** After partners have matched each student to the profession indicated, have them brainstorm alternative professions that would be compatible with the qualities listed.

4 Meine ideale Familie

Survey your classmates about their ideal family situation, and write down their answers. Then, in pairs, compare your results. Answers will vary.

BEISPIEL

S1: Wie ist deine ideale Familie?
S2: Meine ideale Familie ist sehr groß...

5 Arbeitsblatt

Your instructor will give you a worksheet with several activities listed. Survey your classmates to find someone who would like to do each of the activities with you. When someone says "yes", agree on a time and date. If someone says "no", they must give an excuse, explaining what they have to or are supposed to do instead. Answers will vary.

BEISPIEL

S1: Gehen wir morgen Abend ins Theater!
S2: Ich kann nicht. Ich muss für die Prüfung lernen.
S3: Ich komme gern. Gehen wir morgen um 7 Uhr!

6 Geschwister

In pairs, role-play a conversation between two siblings. The younger sibling asks to do things, and the older sibling tells him/her what to do and what not to do. Answers will vary.

BEISPIEL

S1: Darf ich Fußball spielen?
S2: Nein, das darfst du nicht! Iss dein Abendessen!

6 **Partner Chat** You can also assign activity 6 on the Supersite. Students work in pairs to record the activity online. The pair's recorded conversation will appear in your gradebook.

7 **Die Familie** With a partner, write a brief description of these five family members. Use the vocabulary you learned in **Lektionen 2A, 2B, 3A,** and **3B** to describe their interests, activities, physical characteristics, and personalities. Answers will vary.

BEISPIEL

Die Tochter heißt Mia. Sie ist zwölf Jahre alt. Sie hat blonde Haare und blaue Augen. Sie ist sehr aktiv und spielt gern Fußball.

7 Suggestion Encourage students to be creative in their descriptions, and to include information about how the characters are related to one another.

Die Familie

der Sohn der Vater der Cousin
die Tochter die Mutter

8 **Am Wochenende** In small groups, prepare a skit in which a group of friends makes plans for the weekend. Use vocabulary from **Kapitel 2.** Answers will vary.

BEISPIEL

S1: *Ich spiele gern Basketball! Können wir morgen Basketball spielen?*
S2: *Nein, bleiben wir hier! Wir müssen unsere Hausaufgaben machen!*
S3: *Ihr könnt hier bleiben, aber ich will...*

8 Suggestion Before dividing students into groups, have the class brainstorm a list of possible activities that could take place in the locations pictured.

Mein Wör|ter|buch

Add five words related to **die Familie** and **persönliche Beschreibungen** to your personalized dictionary.

klug

Übersetzung
clever, smart

Wortart
Adjektiv (Beschreibungswort)

Gebrauch
Der Mann ist klug. Ein kluger Mann spricht nicht zu viel.

Synonyme
intelligent, schlau

Antonyme
unintelligent, dumm

 **Vocabulary Tools**

Weiter geht's

Panorama

AP* Theme: Global Challenges
Context: Geography

Interactive Map

Die Vereinigten Staaten und Kanada

Anteil der Amerikaner mit deutschen Wurzeln: 15% (50 Millionen)

▶ **Kalifornien:** *5.517.470*
▶ **Pennsylvania:** *3.491.269*
▶ **Ohio:** *3.231.788*
▶ **Illinois:** *2.668.955*
▶ **Texas:** *2.542.996*
▶ **Wisconsin:** *2.455.980*

▶ **Michigan:** *2.271.091*
▶ **Florida:** *2.270.456*
▶ **New York:** *2.250.309*
▶ **Minnesota:** *1.949.346*
▶ **Indiana:** *1.629.766*
▶ **Missouri:** *1.576.813*

QUELLE: U.S. Census 2010

Anteil der Kanadier mit deutschen Wurzeln: 10% (3 Millionen)

▶ **Toronto:** *220.135*
▶ **Vancouver:** *187.410*
▶ **Winnipeg:**: *109.355*

▶ **Kitchener:** *93.325*
▶ **Montreal:** *83.850*

QUELLE: Canadian Census 2011

Die ersten deutschen Siedler in Kanada kommen zwischen 1750 und 1753 nach Nova Scotia. Die meisten von ihnen° sind Bauern und Kaufleute°. Zwischen 1919 und 1939 kommen fast 100.000 Deutsche nach Kanada. Auch von ihnen sind die meisten Bauern. Sie alle bringen ihre Familien mit und starten ein neues Leben in Nordamerika.

Berühmte Deutschamerikaner und Deutschkanadier

▶ **Levi Strauss,** *Unternehmer° (1829–1902)*
▶ **Frederick Louis Maytag I,** *Unternehmer (1857–1937)*
▶ **Dwight D. Eisenhower,** *Fünf-Sterne General und US-Präsident (1890–1969)*
▶ **Lou Gehrig,** *Baseballspieler (1903–1941)*
▶ **Henry Kissinger,** *Politiker (1923–)*
▶ **Almuth Lütkenhaus,** *Künstlerin° (1930–1996)*
▶ **Dany Heatley,** *Eishockeyspieler (1981–)*
▶ **Justin Bieber,** *Sänger° (1994–)*

Die meisten von ihnen *most of them* **Kaufleute** *tradespeople*
Unternehmer *entrepreneur* **Künstlerin** *artist* **Sänger** *singer*
verlässt *leaves* **Flöten** *flutes* **Immobilien** *real estate*
Fellhandel *fur trade* **reichste** *richest* **Vermögen** *fortune*

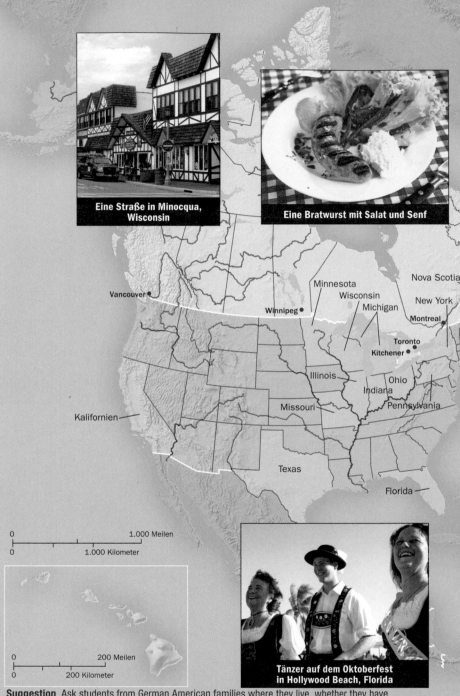

Eine Straße in Minocqua, Wisconsin

Eine Bratwurst mit Salat und Senf

Nova Scotia
Minnesota
Wisconsin
New York
Vancouver
Winnipeg
Michigan
Montreal
Toronto
Kitchener
Illinois
Ohio
Indiana
Missouri
Pennsylvania
Kalifornien
Texas
Florida

0 — 1.000 Meilen
0 — 1.000 Kilometer

0 — 200 Meilen
0 — 200 Kilometer

Tänzer auf dem Oktoberfest in Hollywood Beach, Florida

Suggestion Ask students from German American families where they live, whether they have any German traditions in their family, and whether they prepare any German dishes. This is a good opportunity to explore the richness of German American culture in the United States, and also to point out how some German customs have evolved.

Unglaublich, aber wahr!

1784 verlässt° **John Jacob Astor (1763–1848)** das Dorf Walldorf in Deutschland mit $25 und 7 Flöten° in Richtung USA. Durch Immobilien°- und Fellhandel° wird er reich und ist zur Zeit seines Todes der reichste° Mann Amerikas. Sein Vermögen° beträgt ungefähr $90 Millionen.

AP* Theme: Global Challenges
Context: Economic Issues

Menschen
Sandra Bullock

AP* Theme: Beauty & Aesthetics
Context: Performing Arts

Sandra Bullock wurde 1964 in Arlington, Virginia geboren°. Ihre Mutter ist Helga D. Meyer, eine deutsche Opernsängerin. Deshalb verbringt° Bullock, die neben Englisch fließend° Deutsch spricht, auch die ersten 12 Jahre ihres Lebens in der deutschen Stadt Fürth, bevor sie mit ihrer Familie in die USA zieht. Ihre erfolgreiche Karriere beinhaltet Filme wie *Gravity*, *Speed* und *Blind Side – Die große Chance*, für den sie einen Oscar als beste Hauptdarstellerin° erhält.

Feiern
German Fest

AP* Theme: Personal & Public Identities
Context: National Identity

Das German Fest in Milwaukee ist das größte „deutsche" Event Nordamerikas. Seit 1981 feiern die Menschen hier am letzten Juliwochenende Kultur deutschsprachiger° Länder und Regionen wie Österreich, Deutschland, Liechtenstein, Südtirol und der Schweiz. Besucher° tragen teilweise Dirndl und Lederhosen, hören traditionelle Blaskapellen° oder moderne Popmusik und bekommen Informationen über ihre deutsche Abstammung°. Im Jahr 2010 essen die Besucher unter anderem 20.000 Bratwürste, 9.000 Knödel°, 200 Spanferkel° und 15.000 Stück Strudel.

Geschichte
Deutsche in Texas

AP* Theme: Personal & Public Identities
Context: Alienation & Integration

1848 gibt es in Deutschland und vielen anderen europäischen Ländern (Frankreich, Dänemark, Österreich) Revolutionen und Aufstände° auf Grund von sozialen und wirtschaftlichen° Problemen. Nach der Mairevolution verlassen° viele Revolutionäre Deutschland und gehen in die USA. Sie leben in Städten wie zum Beispiel New Braunfels und Fredericksburg in Texas. Diesen deutschen Einfluss° kann man heute hier immer noch sehen. Unter anderem gibt es in Texas eine Form des Deutschen, die man Texas-Deutsch nennt.

Essen
Hamburger

AP* Theme: Contemporary Life
Context: Health & Well-Being

Der Hamburger – ein Sandwich aus einer Frikadelle° in einer Semmel° mit einem Salatblatt und einer Scheibe Tomate – hat etwas mit der Stadt Hamburg zu tun. Als deutsche Immigranten und Matrosen° Ende des 18. Jahrhunderts nach New York kommen, bekommen Sie hier „Steak im Hamburger Stil". Diese Steaks damals hatten mit heutigen Hamburgern außer dem Namen noch nicht viel zu tun. Erst mit der Erfindung des Fleischwolfs° im 19. Jahrhunderts werden aus Steaks im Hamburger Stil die heutigen Hamburger.

🔗 IM INTERNET

1. Welche anderen Gerichte (*dishes*) haben ihren Ursprung (*origin*) in deutschsprachigen Ländern?

2. Suchen Sie ein Rezept für ein deutsch-amerikanisches (oder österreichisch-amerikanisches) Gericht.

3. Suchen Sie Informationen über eine berühmte deutsch-amerikanische Person.

Find out more at **vhlcentral.com**.

---

wurde... geboren *was born*   **verbringt** *spends (time)*   **fließend** *fluent*   **Hauptdarstellerin** *lead actress*   **Aufstände** *uprisings*
wirtschaftlichen *economic*   **verlassen** *leave*   **Einfluss** *influence*   **Frikadelle** *meatball*   **Semmel** *bun*   **Matrosen** *sailors*
Erfindung des Fleischwolfs *invention of the meat grinder*   **deutschsprachiger** *German-speaking*   **Besucher** *Visitors*
Blaskapellen *brass bands*   **Abstammung** *descent*   **Knödel** *dumplings*   **Spanferkel** *suckling pigs*

🔗 Was haben Sie gelernt?   Complete the sentences.

1. Die meisten Amerikaner mit deutschen Wurzeln leben in <u>Kalifornien</u>.

2. Ungefähr <u>15 %</u> der amerikanischen Bevölkerung haben deutsche Wurzeln.

3. John Astor verlässt 1784 Deutschland mit <u>$25</u> und 7 Flöten.

4. Eine Schauspielerin, die fließend Deutsch spricht, ist <u>Sandra Bullock</u>.

5. Sandra Bullock wohnt in Fürth, bis sie <u>12 Jahre</u> alt ist.

6. Zwei deutsche Städte in Texas sind <u>New Braunfels</u> und Fredericksburg

7. Hamburger haben ihren Namen von der deutschen Stadt <u>Hamburg</u>.

8. Die Besucher essen jedes Jahr 200 Spanferkel und 20.000 Bratwürste auf dem <u>German Fest</u>.

9. Beim *German Fest* sehen <u>Besucher</u> viele Facetten deutschsprachiger Kultur.

Lesen

Audio: Reading

Vor dem Lesen

AP* **Theme:** Families & Communities
Context: Family Structure

Strategien

Predicting content from visuals

When you read in German, look for visual cues that can help you figure out the content and purpose of what you are reading. Photos and illustrations, for example, can give you a good idea of the main points of the reading. You may also encounter helpful visuals that summarize large amounts of data in a way that is easy to comprehend; these visuals include bar graphs, pie charts, flow charts, lists of percentages, and other diagrams.

Die beliebtesten° Haustiere

In Deutschland gibt es Haustiere in mehr als° 12 Millionen Haushalten.	
Katzen **16,5%** der Haushalte	
Hunde **13,8%** der Haushalte	
Kleintiere **5,9%** der Haushalte	
Vögel **5,7%** der Haushalte	
Aquarien° **5,7%** der Haushalte	

Auch in Österreich und der Schweiz sind Katzen und Hunde die beliebtesten Haustiere.

beliebtesten *most popular* **mehr als** *more than*
Aquarien *fish tanks*

 Texte verstehen Take a quick look at the visual elements of the article in order to generate a list of ideas about its content. Then compare your list with a classmate's. What elements did you both notice? What aspects did your partner notice that didn't catch your eye? Discuss and consolidate your ideas to produce a final list to share with the class.

Hunde und Katzen

Für viele Deutsche, Österreicher und Schweizer sind Haustiere sehr wichtig. Allerdings gibt es in diesen Ländern weit weniger vierbeinige° Freunde als in anderen europäischen Ländern. Zum Beispiel hat in Deutschland nur etwa jeder Vierte ein Haustier.

Welche Tiere findet man bei Deutschen, Österreichern und Schweizern am häufigsten°? Oft hört man, der Hund ist des Deutschen bester Freund. Statistiken zeigen° allerdings, dass nicht Hunde, sondern Katzen das Haustier Nummer 1 im deutschsprachigen Raum sind. Hunde stehen nur an Nummer 2.

vierbeinige *four-legged* **am häufigsten** *most frequently* **zeigen** *show*

Außerdem geht der allgemeine° Trend hin zu mehr° Katzen und weniger° Hunden. Andere beliebte Tiere sind Kleintiere wie Kaninchen° und Hamster. Vögel singen immer weniger in deutschsprachigen Haushalten°.

Haustiere sind oft ein wichtiger Teil° der Familie. Kinder lernen durch sie, soziale Kontakte zu pflegen°. Großstadtkinder, die mit einem Hund leben, haben später° oft weniger Probleme mit Kriminalität. Vor allem bei Singles sind Katzen beliebt, da sie alleine sein können, aber auch eine Art Partnerersatz sind.

Wer hat welches Haustier?

Status	Katzen	Hunde	Fische	Vögel
Ledig	23%	18%	7%	5%
Verheiratet	18%	18%	6%	5%
Frauen	17%	18%	7%	5%
Männer	17%	18%	6%	5%

allgemeine *general* **mehr** *more* **weniger** *fewer* **Kaninchen** *bunnies* **Haushalten** *households*
ein wichtiger Teil *an important part* **pflegen** *to cultivate* **später** *later*

Nach dem Lesen

Richtig oder falsch? Indicate whether each statement is **richtig** or **falsch**.
Expansion Have students correct the false statements.

	richtig	falsch
1. Fast jede Familie in Deutschland hat ein Haustier. Jeder Vierte in Deutschland hat ein Haustier.	☐	☑
2. Katzen sind das Haustier Nummer 1.	☑	☐
3. Der Trend in den nächsten Jahren geht zu mehr Hunden. Der Trend in den nächsten Jahren geht zu mehr Katzen.	☐	☑
4. Immer weniger Menschen haben Vögel.	☑	☐
5. Großstadtkinder mit Hunden haben mehr Probleme. Großstadtkinder mit Hunden haben weniger Probleme.	☐	☑
6. Viele Ledige haben Katzen als Haustiere.	☑	☐

Was ist richtig? Select the correct response according to the article.

1. Wie viel Prozent der Deutschen besitzen ein Haustier?
   a. 10%–20%   (b.) 20%–30%   c. 30%–40%

2. Welche Haustiere werden immer beliebter?
   (a.) Katzen   b. Vögel   c. Hunde

3. Welches Tier passt in die Kategorie Kleintiere?
   a. Katzen   b. Hunde   (c.) Hamster

4. Welches Haustier besitzen die meisten Deutschen?
   a. Hunde   b. Fische   (c.) Katzen

5. Welche Bevölkerungsgruppe hat die meisten Haustiere?
   a. Frauen   (b.) Ledige   c. Verheiratete

 Meine Haustiere With a partner, talk about the pets you or your family and friends have. Use the verb **haben** and possessive adjectives.

 BEISPIEL

S1: *Hast du eine Katze?*
S2: *Nein, ich habe einen Fisch, aber mein Onkel hat zwei Katzen…*

Partner Chat You can also assign this activity on the Supersite. Students work in pairs to record the activity online. The pair's recorded conversation will appear in your gradebook.

Hören

Strategien

Asking for repetition/Replaying the recording

Sometimes it is difficult to understand what people are saying, especially in a noisy environment. During a conversation, you can ask someone to repeat what they've said by saying **Wie bitte?** (*Excuse me?*) or **Entschuldigung?** In class, you can ask your instructor to repeat by saying **Wiederholen Sie, bitte.** (*Repeat, please.*)

 To help you practice this strategy, you will listen to a short conversation. Ask your instructor to repeat it or replay the recording, and then summarize what you heard.

Vorbereitung

Based on the photograph, where do you think Lena and Jasmin are? What do you think they are talking about?

Zuhören

 Now you are going to hear Lena and Jasmin's conversation. Write **M** next to adjectives that describe Jasmin's friend Maria. Write **T** next to adjectives that describe Lena's ex-boyfriend, Tobias. Some adjectives will not be used.

_M_ fleißig	___ langweilig
___ hübsch	_M_ intelligent
_T_ eifersüchtig	_T_ egoistisch
___ sportlich	___ langsam
_M_ großartig	_T_ verlobt
___ ernst	___ faul

Vor dem Hören Ask students questions about the two women in the picture to help them guess what they might be talking about. Brainstorm possible topics for the women's conversation and write them on the board. Ex.: **Über was sprechen Lena und Jasmin? Über die Arbeit? Über Familie? Über die Liebe?**

Verständnis

Wer ist das? Write the name of the person described by each statement.

1. ___Maria___ ist Jasmins neue Freundin.
2. ___Tobias___ ist egoistisch und eifersüchtig.
3. ___Jasmin___ lernt mit Maria für die Literaturprüfungen.
4. ___Lena___ ist allein glücklich.
5. ___Tobias___ ist mit Antonia verlobt.
6. ___Jasmin___ will mit Lena schwimmen gehen.

Richtig oder falsch Indicate whether each statement is **richtig** or **falsch**. Correct the false statements.

1. Lena studiert Literatur. Falsch. Jasmin studiert Literatur.
2. Tobias hilft Jasmin. Falsch. Maria hilft Jasmin.
3. Maria ist großartig. Richtig.
4. Lena ist ledig. Richtig.
5. Geschichte ist Jasmins Hobby. Richtig.
6. Tobias ist intelligent und fleißig. Falsch. Tobias ist egoistisch und eifersüchtig.

Schreiben

Strategien

Using idea maps

How do you organize ideas for a first draft? Often, the organization of ideas represents the most challenging part of the writing process. Idea maps are useful for organizing information. Here is an example of an idea map you could use when writing.

IDEA MAP

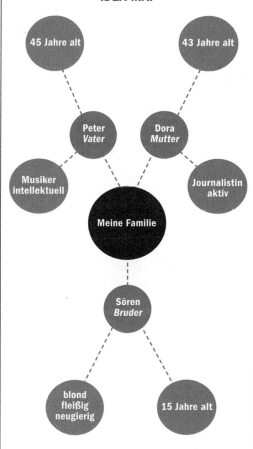

45 Jahre alt

43 Jahre alt

Peter
Vater

Dora
Mutter

Musiker
intellektuell

Journalistin
aktiv

Meine Familie

Sören
Bruder

blond
fleißig
neugierig

15 Jahre alt

Successful Language Learning Remind students to write their notes in German. Emphasize that they should not translate directly from English. Encourage them to use words and phrases they are familiar with and not rely too heavily on the dictionary.

Thema

 Briefe schreiben

A German friend you met online wants to know about your family. Using the verbs and grammar structures you learned in this unit, write a brief description of your family or an imaginary family, including:

- Names and relationships
- Physical characteristics
- Hobbies and interests

Suggestion Tell students that it may be helpful to write their idea maps on note cards, so that they can easily rearrange the ideas if necessary.

Here are some useful expressions for writing a letter or e-mail in German:

Salutations

Lieber Erik,	*Dear Erik,*
Liebe Anna,	*Dear Anna,*

Asking for a response

Ich hoffe, bald von dir zu hören.	*I hope to hear from you soon.*
Erzähl, was es Neues bei dir gibt!	*Let me know what's new with you!*

Closings

Bis bald!/Tschüss!	*So long!*
Mach's gut!	*All the best!*
Mit freundlichen Grüßen	*Yours sincerely*
Hochachtungsvoll	*Respectfully*

Suggestion Tell students that when the salutation ends with a comma, it is considered part of the first sentence of the letter, and the word that follows is not capitalized (unless it's a noun). Point out that an exclamation mark can be used instead of a comma, in which case the text that follows does start with a capitalized word.

Suggestion Point out the differences in formality in the closing expressions. For example, **Tschüss!** and **Mach's gut!** should only be used with friends and family, whereas **Mit freundlichen Grüßen** or **Hochachtungsvoll** are more formal.

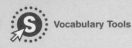 Vocabulary Tools

Lektion 3A

die Familie

das Baby, -s *baby*
der Bruder, ⸚ *brother*
der Cousin, -s *cousin (m.)*
die Cousine, -n *cousin (f.)*
die Eltern *parents*
das Enkelkind, -er *grandchild*
der Enkelsohn, ⸚e *grandson*
die Enkeltochter, ⸚ *granddaughter*
die Frau, -en *wife*
das Geschwister, - *sibling*
die Großeltern *grandparents*
die Großmutter, ⸚ *grandmother*
der Großvater, ⸚ *grandfather*
der Halbbruder, ⸚ *half brother*
die Halbschwester, -n *half sister*
das Kind, -er *child*
der Mann, ⸚er *husband*
die Mutter, ⸚ *mother*
der Nachname, -n *last name*
der Neffe, -n *nephew*
die Nichte, -n *niece*
die Oma, -s *grandma*
der Onkel, - *uncle*
der Opa, -s *grandpa*
das Paar, -e *couple*
der Schwager, ⸚ *brother-in-law*
die Schwägerin, -nen *sister-in-law*
die Schwester, -n *sister*
die Schwiegermutter, ⸚ *mother-in-law*
der Schwiegervater, ⸚ *father-in-law*
der Sohn, ⸚e *son*
der Stiefbruder, ⸚ *stepbrother*
die Stiefmutter, ⸚ *stepmother*
die Stiefschwester, -n *stepsister*
der Stiefsohn, ⸚e *stepson*
die Stieftochter, ⸚ *stepdaughter*
der Stiefvater, ⸚ *stepfather*
die Tante, -n *aunt*
die Tochter, ⸚ *daughter*
der Vater, ⸚ *father*
der / die Verwandte, -n *relative*
der Zwilling, -e *twin*

der Familienstand

die Witwe, -n *widow*
der Witwer, - *widower*
geschieden *divorced*
getrennt *separated*
ledig *single*
verheiratet *married*
verlobt *engaged*
zusammen *together*
heiraten *to marry*

die Haustiere

der Fisch, -e *fish*
der Hund, -e *dog*
die Katze, -n *cat*
der Vogel, ⸚ *bird*

zum Beschreiben

blaue / grüne / braune Augen
  blue / green / brown eyes
blonde / braune / schwarze Haare
  blond / brown / black hair
dunkel *dark*
hell *light*

Possessive adjectives *See p. 104.*
Descriptive adjectives *See p. 108.*

Lektion 3B

zum Beschreiben

(un)angenehm *(un)pleasant*
arm *poor; unfortunate*
bescheiden *modest*
besorgt *worried*
diskret *discreet*
egoistisch *selfish*
eifersüchtig *jealous*
ernst *serious*
faul *lazy*
fleißig *hard-working*
freundlich *friendly*
froh *happy*
gemein *mean*
gierig *greedy*
glücklich *happy*
großzügig *generous*
intellektuell *intellectual*
intelligent *intelligent*
langsam *slow*
lustig *funny*
müde *tired*
mutig *brave*
naiv *naïve*
nervös *nervous*
nett *nice*
neugierig *curious*
reich *rich*
schlecht *bad*
schnell *fast*
schüchtern *shy*
schwach *weak*
stark *strong*
stolz *proud*
süß *sweet; cute*
toll *great*
traurig *sad*
lächeln *to smile*
lachen *to laugh*
weinen *to cry*

Berufe

der Architekt, -en / die Architektin, -nen
  architect
der Besitzer, - / die Besitzerin, -nen
  owner
der Friseur, -e / die Friseurin, -nen
  hairdresser
der Geschäftsmann (*pl.* Geschäftsleute)
  / die Geschäftsfrau, -en
  businessman / businesswoman
der Ingenieur, -e / die Ingenieurin, -nen
  engineer
der Journalist, -en / die Journalistin, -nen
  journalist
der Kellner, - / die Kellnerin, -nen
  waiter / waitress
der Musiker, - / die Musikerin, -nen
  musician
der Rechtsanwalt, ⸚e / die
  Rechtsanwältin, -nen *lawyer*

Modalverben

dürfen *to be allowed to, may*
können *to be able to, can*
müssen *to have to, must*
sollen *to be supposed to*
wollen *to want to*

Prepositions with the accusative
  See p. 126.
Common commands *See p. 129.*

LEKTION 4A

LEKTION 4B

WEITER GEHT'S

Suggestion Have students look at the photo and identify the people and items they see. Ask them what they think this unit will be about.

Teaching Tip Look for icons indicating activities that address the modes of communication. Follow this key:

→🯆←	**Interpretive communication**
←🯆→	**Presentational communication**
🯆↔🯆	**Interpersonal communication**

Communicative Goals

You will learn how to:

- talk about food
- talk about grocery shopping

Wortschatz

Geschäfte	stores
die Bäckerei, -en	bakery
die Eisdiele, -n	ice cream shop
das Feinkostgeschäft, -e	delicatessen
das Fischgeschäft, -e	fish store
die Konditorei, -en	pastry shop
das Lebensmittelgeschäft, -e	grocery store
der Markt, ⁻e	market
die Metzgerei, -en	butcher shop
der Supermarkt, ⁻e	supermarket
einkaufen gehen	to go shopping
verkaufen	to sell

Essen	food
das Brot, -e	bread
das Brötchen, -	roll
die Butter	butter
der Joghurt, -s	yogurt
der Käse, -	cheese
das Öl, -e	oil
das Olivenöl, -e	olive oil
die Pasta	pasta
der Reis	rice
das Rezept, -e	recipe
die Zutat, -en	ingredient

Suggestion Tell students that many German speakers treat **Paprika** as a masculine noun and that some also treat **Joghurt** as a feminine or neuter noun, especially in Austria and Switzerland.

Fleisch und Fisch	meat and fish
die Garnele, -n	shrimp
das Hähnchen, -	chicken
die Meeresfrüchte (pl.)	seafood
das Rindfleisch	beef
der Schinken, -	ham
das Schweinefleisch	pork
der Thunfisch	tuna
das Würstchen, -	sausage

Obst und Gemüse	fruits and vegetables
die Ananas, -	pineapple
die Artischocke, -n	artichoke
die Himbeere, -n	raspberry
die Melone, -n	melon
die Traube, -n	grape

Ressourcen

vText | WB pp. 47–48 | LM p. 90 | vhlcentral

Suggestion Tell students that some words have more than one accepted plural form. Ex.: **die Ananas/die Ananasse; die Paprika/die Paprikas**.

Lebensmittel

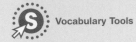 **Vocabulary Tools**

Suggestion Tell students that Germans typically buy fresh bread from a bakery, rather than the supermarket.

AP* Theme: Contemporary Life
Context: Health & Well-Being

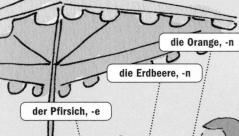

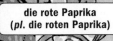

die Orange, -n

die Birne, -n

die Erdbeere, -n

der Pfirsich, -e

Obst

die Banane, -n

der Apfel, ⁻

die Karotte, -n

die Kartoffel, -n

Gemüse

die Zwiebel, -n

die rote Paprika (pl. die roten Paprika)

die Aubergine, -n

die grüne Bohne (pl. die grünen Bohnen)

der Pilz, -e

der Knoblauch

die Tomate, -n

ACHTUNG

Note that **der Salat** can refer to either *salad* or *lettuce*. A head of *lettuce* is **ein Salatkopf** (*m.*).

die Marmelade, -n

der Kuchen, -

die grüne Paprika
(*pl.* die grünen Paprika)

der Salat, -e

das Ei, -er

Anwendung

1 **Was passt zusammen?** Welche Wörter in Liste 1 passen zu (*match*) den Wörtern in Liste 2?

Liste 1		Liste 2
_d_	1. die Paprika	a. der Fisch
_b_	2. das Rindfleisch	b. das Fleisch
_c_	3. die Banane	c. das Obst
_a_	4. der Thunfisch	d. das Gemüse
_c_	5. die Orange	
_b_	6. das Würstchen	
_d_	7. der Salat	
_a_	8. die Garnele	

1 Expansion Go over the answers to this activity as a class. Ex.: **Die Paprika: Ist das Obst, Gemüse, Fleisch, Fisch? Und das Rindfleisch? Ist das eine Sorte Gemüse? Nein? Was ist das?**

2 **Lebensmittel** Schreiben Sie die Namen der Lebensmittel unter die Fotos.

 ▶ **BEISPIEL** *die Tomaten*

1. ___die Orangen___

2. ___die Garnelen___

3. ___das Brot___

4. ___der/die Käse___

5. ___die Würstchen___

3 **Was essen Sie gern?** Schreiben Sie die Namen der Lebensmittel, die (*that*) Sie gern, nicht so gern und nicht gern essen. Answers will vary.

gern	nicht so gern	nicht gern
1. _____	_____	_____
2. _____	_____	_____
3. _____	_____	_____

4 **Samstag ist Markttag** Hören Sie die Dialoge an und entscheiden Sie (*decide*), ob die Sätze (*sentences*) **richtig** oder **falsch** sind.

	richtig	falsch
1. Annika geht im Supermarkt einkaufen.	☐	☑
2. Sie kauft Garnelen und Thunfisch.	☐	☑
3. Thunfisch ist heute im Angebot (*on sale*).	☑	☐
4. Ein Kilo Garnelen kostet 8,30 €.	☑	☐
5. Am Obststand kauft Annika nur Äpfel und Bananen.	☐	☑
6. Annika macht einen Salat.	☑	☐

3 Expansion Survey the class to find out which foods are most popular. Ex.: **Wer isst gern Pizza? Heben Sie die Hand. Wer isst gern Brokkoli?**

 Practice more at **vhlcentral.com.**

Kommunikation

5 Was kann man hier kaufen? Welche drei Lebensmittel können Sie in den Geschäften kaufen? Vergleichen Sie (*Compare*) die Antworten mit einem Partner / einer Partnerin. Answers will vary.

▶ **BEISPIEL**

in der Eisdiele
das Eis
der Kaffee
die Cola

5 Virtual Chat You can also assign activity 5 on the Supersite.

5 Expansion Check students' answers by asking:
Was kauft man beim Bäcker? Was kauft man in der Metzgerei? Was kauft man auf dem Markt?

1. beim Bäcker

_____

_____

_____

> **TIPP**
>
> Auf Deutsch sagt man:
>
> Ich kaufe Brot **beim** Bäcker.
>
> Ich kaufe Fleisch **in der** Metzgerei.
>
> Ich kaufe Fisch **im** Fischgeschäft/ **im** Supermarkt.
>
> Ich kaufe Obst und Gemüse **auf dem** Markt.

2. in der Metzgerei

_____

_____

_____

3. auf dem Markt

_____

_____

_____

4. im Supermarkt

_____

_____

_____

5. im Fischgeschäft

_____

_____

_____

6 Kochen mit Freunden Sie und Ihre Freunde wollen am Abend zusammen kochen. Diskutieren Sie, was Sie alles brauchen und wer was kaufen soll (*who should buy what*). Answers will vary.

BEISPIEL

S1: *Wer bringt Obst und Gemüse?*
S2: *Ich bringe Salat. Thomas, bringst du das Obst?*
S3: *Ja, ich kann Trauben und Birnen bringen.*

7 Arbeitsblatt Sie sind Geschäftsbesitzer und Ihre Mitstudenten müssen erraten (*guess*), was man bei Ihnen kaufen kann und welches Geschäft Sie haben.

BEISPIEL

S1: *Verkaufen Sie Bananen?*
S2: *Nein.*
S3: *Verkaufen Sie Wurst?*
S2: *Ja.*
S1: *Haben Sie eine Metzgerei?*

8 Essen und trinken Fragen Sie Ihre Mitstudenten, was sie gern oder nicht gern essen und trinken. Finden Sie mindestens (*at least*) eine Person, die denselben Geschmack (*the same taste*) hat wie Sie. Answers will vary.

BEISPIEL

S1: *Ich esse gern Brot und Nutella am Morgen. Isst du auch Nutella?*
S2: *Nein, ich esse nicht gern Nutella.*
S3: *Ich esse gern Brot und Nutella. Und ich trinke morgens Kaffee. Du auch?*

Aussprache und Rechtschreibung  Audio

The German s, z, and c

The s sound in German is represented by **s**, **ss**, or **ß**. At the end of a word, **s**, **ss**, and **ß** are pronounced like the s in the English word *yes*. Before a vowel, **s** is pronounced like the s in the English word *please*.

| **Reis** | **Professor** | **weiß** | **Supermarkt** | **Käse** |

Suggestion Tell students that people in Southern Germany, Austria, and Switzerland typically pronounce **s** like the s in *yes*, even before vowels.

The German **z** is pronounced like the ts in the English word *bats*, whether it appears at the beginning, middle, or end of a word. The combination **tz** is also pronounced ts. The ending **-tion** is always pronounced *-tsion*.

| **Pilze** | **Zwiebel** | **Platz** | **Besitzer** | **Kaution** |

Only in loan words does the letter **c** appear directly before a vowel. Before **e** or **i**, the letter **c** is usually pronounced ts. Before other vowels, it is usually pronounced like the c in *cat*. The letter combination **ck** is pronounced like the ck in the English word *packer*.

| **Cent** | **Celsius** | **Computer** | **backen** | **Bäckerei** |

1 **Aussprechen** Wiederholen Sie die Wörter, die Sie hören.

1. lassen
2. lasen
3. weißer
4. weiser
5. sinnlos
6. seitens
7. selbst
8. Zeile
9. Katzen
10. letztes
11. Campingplatz
12. Fleck

2 **Nachsprechen** Wiederholen Sie die Sätze, die Sie hören.

1. Der Musiker geht am Samstag zum Friseur.
2. Es geht uns sehr gut.
3. Die Zwillinge essen eine Pizza mit Pilzen, Zwiebeln und Tomaten.
4. Jetzt ist es Zeit in den Zoo zu gehen.
5. Der Clown sitzt im Café und spielt Computerspiele.
6. Ich esse nur eine Portion Eis.

2 Suggestion Tell students that tuna, eggs, shrimp, and corn are all common pizza toppings in Germany.

3 **Sprichwörter** Wiederholen Sie die Sprichwörter, die Sie hören.

Aus den Augen, aus dem Sinn.[1]

Gegensätze ziehen sich an.[2]

[1] Out of sight, out of mind.
[2] Opposites attract.

Ressourcen

vText | LM p. 91 | vhlcentral

Börek für alle Video

George und Hans treffen Meline und Sabite im Supermarkt. George hat eine
Idee: Er macht Börek für seine Freunde. Aber kann George kochen?

Vorbereitung Have students scan the images and
try to guess what the characters will buy. Have them
create a grocery shopping list for the boys and another
one for the girls.

GEORGE Was möchtest du heute essen?
HANS Hmmm. Ich esse gerne Fleisch.
Rindfleisch, Schweinefleisch und Wurst...
GEORGE Los! Auf zur Fleischtheke!
HANS Ja!

SABITE Ich esse gern Tofu mit Pilzen
und Erdbeeren.
HANS Erdbeeren und was?
SABITE Pilze. Mit Tofu.

MELINE Müssen wir mit Hans und
George essen?
SABITE Ach, Meline, sei nett.

GEORGE Sabite, welche Zutaten kommen
in die Börek von deiner Mutter? Wir können
sie kochen.
SABITE Hmm. Lass mich überlegen. Kartoffeln,
Blätterteig, Zwiebeln. Kartoffeln kochen,
Zwiebeln braten, Teig aufrollen. Backen.

HANS Muss Meline mit uns essen? Sie ist
extrem unangenehm. Ich finde, das ist
eine ausgesprochen schlechte Idee.
GEORGE Meline ist lustig. Du magst
sie bestimmt.
HANS Das glaube ich kaum.
GEORGE Sie mag dich bestimmt.

GEORGE Ich mache heute Abend Börek!
SABITE Wir bringen Käse und Brot mit. Wann
sollen wir kommen?
GEORGE Kommt um halb sieben vorbei.
SABITE Perfekt.
MELINE Was ist perfekt?

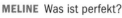

1 **Was fehlt?** Ergänzen Sie die Sätze mit den richtigen Informationen.

1. Hans isst gern Schweinefleisch und (Rindfleisch / Tofu).
2. Sabite isst gern Tofu mit Pilzen und (Wurst / Erdbeeren).
3. In die Börek von Frau Yilmaz kommen (Pilze / Zwiebeln).
4. Man muss die Zwiebeln (waschen / braten).
5. Meline und Sabite sollen um (zehn nach sieben / halb sieben)
bei Hans und George sein.

6. Sie bringen (Käse und Brot / Käse und Wurst) mit.
7. Hans findet die Idee ausgesprochen (schlecht / gut).
8. In Georges Börek ist kein (Blätterteig / Schafskäse).
9. Sabite ruft morgen (ihre Mutter / ihre Oma) an.
10. Hans und George haben noch (Milch und Äpfel / Joghurt
und Bananen).

PERSONEN

 George Hans Meline Sabite

1

GEORGE Tada! Prost!
HANS Prost!

8

SABITE George! Was...
GEORGE Ich weiß es nicht!

9

SABITE Wo ist der Schafskäse? Er gibt ihnen
erst noch den Geschmack.
GEORGE Schafskäse? Wieso...
SABITE Oh, nein. Oh, George, es tut mir
leid! Ich rufe morgen meine Mutter an und
schreibe es dann auf.

10

GEORGE Es ist schon okay. Der Butterkäse und
das Brot liegen dort.
MELINE Ich brate Eier und Kartoffeln.
HANS Gute Idee. Wir haben hier oben noch
Joghurt und Bananen.
SABITE Hier stehen noch Butter und
Marmelade für das Brot!

Nützliche Ausdrücke

- **die Wurst**
  cold cuts
- **Los! Auf zur Fleischtheke!**
  Let's go! To the butcher's counter!
- **der Blätterteig**
  phyllo dough
- **aufrollen**
  roll up
- **Kommt um halb sieben vorbei!**
  Come over at half past six!
- **Brauchen wir noch etwas?**
  Do we need anything else?
- **Ich finde, das ist eine ausgesprochen
  schlechte Idee.**
  I think it's an extremely bad idea.
- **Das glaube ich kaum.**
  I hardly think so.
- **Ich weiß es nicht!**
  I don't know!
- **der Schafskäse**
  Feta cheese

4A.1
- **Ich mache heute Abend Börek!**
  I'm making boreks tonight!

4A.2
- **Du magst sie bestimmt.**
  You really will like her.

4A.3
- **Ich rufe morgen meine Mutter an und
  schreibe es dann auf.**
  *I'll call my mother tomorrow, and I'll
  write it down.*

Suggestion Explain to students that **Wurst** can
refer to either sausage or cold cuts.

2 **Zum Besprechen** Sie und ein Freund möchten heute Abend eine
Party geben. Spielen Sie mit einem Partner einen Dialog. Welches
Essen wollen Sie servieren? Welche Zutaten brauchen Sie? Müssen
Sie einkaufen gehen? Wie kochen Sie das Essen? Answers will vary.

2 **Partner Chat** You can also assign activity 2 on the Supersite.

2 **Expansion** Have students work in groups to talk about German food.
Have they ever tried German food? What dishes have they heard of? Are
there any German stores or restaurants in your area? Invite students from
German-American families to share family recipes with the class.

3 **Vertiefung** Suchen Sie bekannte Lebensmittelhersteller (*food brands*)
in Deutschland, wie Knorr, Maggi oder Haribo. Finden Sie drei bekannte
Produkte. Präsentieren Sie der Klasse Ihre Resultate. Answers will vary.

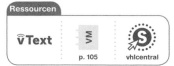

Ressourcen

vText | VM p. 105 | vhlcentral

IM FOKUS

Suggestion Before reading, ask students about their own shopping habits: **Wo kaufen Sie Ihr Essen? Hat Ihre Stadt einen „Farmer's Market"? Was kann man da kaufen?**

AP* Theme: Families & Communities
Context: Urban, Suburban, & Rural Life

Der Wiener Naschmarkt Reading

IN DEUTSCHLAND, ÖSTERREICH und der Schweiz hat fast jede Stadt° einen Marktplatz°. Er ist normalerweise im Zentrum der Stadt.

Große Städte haben oft mehr als einen Marktplatz. Berühmte° Marktplätze sind der Viktualienmarkt in München, der Alexanderplatz in Berlin, der Helvetiaplatz in Zürich und der Naschmarkt in Wien.

Der Naschmarkt ist einer der 26 Märkte in Wien. Er existiert seit über° 80 Jahren und liegt° sehr zentral. Viele Stände° auf dem Naschmarkt sind von Montag bis Samstag zwischen° 9 und 21 Uhr offen. Vor allem° samstagmorgens bei gutem Wetter° findet man alte und junge Menschen an den Ständen. Die Atmosphäre ist lebendig°: Menschen unterhalten sich° und Kunden handeln mit den Verkäufern°.

Märkte wie der Wiener Naschmarkt haben auch viele verschiedene° Waren: Es gibt Käse, Fleisch, Wurst, Obst und Gemüse. Natürlich gibt es auch Milchprodukte wie Käse und Joghurt. Außerdem° kann man Blumen oder Seife° kaufen. Der Markt ist auch sehr international mit italienischen, griechischen, türkischen und asiatischen Ständen.

Stände am Naschmarkt	
Lebensmittel	31
Gastronomie°	27
Obst und Gemüse	20
Fleischwaren	9
Backwaren°	8
Fisch	5
Blumen	2
Milchprodukte	2
Wein	1
Bier	1
Sonstiges°	1
QUELLE: Edition moKKa	

fast jede Stadt *almost every city* **Marktplatz** *market square* **Berühmte** *Famous* **existiert seit über** *has existed for more than* **liegt** *is located* **Stände** *stands* **zwischen** *between* **Vor allem** *Especially* **bei gutem Wetter** *when the weather is nice* **lebendig** *lively* **unterhalten sich** *chat* **Kunden handeln mit den Verkäufern** *buyers negotiate with the vendors* **verschiedene** *different* **Außerdem** *In addition* **Seife** *soap* **Gastronomie** *prepared foods* **Backwaren** *baked goods* **Sonstiges** *Other*

ÜBUNGEN

1 **Der Wiener Naschmarkt** Ergänzen Sie die Sätze.

1. Jede Stadt in Deutschland, __Österreich__ und der Schweiz hat einen Marktplatz.
2. Der Marktplatz ist normalerweise im __Zentrum__ der Stadt.
3. Ein berühmter Marktplatz in Berlin heißt __Alexanderplatz__.
4. In Wien gibt es __26__ Märkte.
5. Der Naschmarkt existiert seit über __80__ Jahren.
6. Viele Stände sind zwischen 9 und __21__ Uhr offen.
7. Die Atmosphäre auf dem Naschmarkt ist __lebendig__.
8. Der Naschmarkt ist sehr international mit italienischen, griechischen, __türkischen__ und asiatischen Waren.
9. An fünf Ständen kann man __Fisch__ kaufen.
10. Auf dem Naschmarkt gibt es __20__ Obst- und Gemüsestände.

 Practice more at **vhlcentral.com**.

DEUTSCH IM ALLTAG

Auf dem Markt

Ich hätte gern...	I would like...
ein Dutzend Eier	a dozen eggs
ein Pfund Kartoffeln	a pound of potatoes
100 Gramm Käse	100 grams of cheese
Das macht 3,80 €.	That's € 3.80.
Sonst noch etwas?	Anything else?
Was wünschen Sie?	What would you like?
Wie viel kostet das?	How much is that?

DIE DEUTSCHSPRACHIGE WELT

Das ist eine Tomate, oder?

Deutsche und Österreicher sprechen Deutsch, aber es gibt verschiedene Vokabeln. Deutsche sagen „Tomate". Was sagen Österreicher? Hier ist eine kurze Liste mit Essensvokabeln: **AP* Theme:** Global Challenges **Context:** Communication

In Deutschland	In Österreich
die Aprikose°	die Marille
grüne Bohnen	Fisolen
das Brötchen	die Semmel
das Hackfleisch°	das Faschierte
die Kartoffel	der Erdapfel
der Meerrettich°	der Kren
der Quark°	der Topfen
die Sahne°	der Obers
die Tomate	der Paradeiser

Aprikose apricot **Hackfleisch** ground meat **Meerrettich** horseradish **Quark** curd cheese **Sahne** cream

PORTRÄT

Wolfgang Puck
AP* Theme: Contemporary Life
Context: Entertainment, Travel, & Leisure

Wolfgang Puck ist ein österreichischer Koch°. Er lebt und arbeitet in den USA, hat aber auch Restaurants in Toronto, Dubai, London, Singapur und Tokio. Er ist sehr erfolgreich°: Der Umsatz° seiner Firmen ist mehr als 300 Millionen Dollar pro Jahr. In den USA hat er mehr als 70 Restaurants: Bistros, Cafés und Gourmetrestaurants. Ein sehr berühmtes und sehr teures° Restaurant ist das Spago in Beverly Hills. Das Essen in seinen Restaurants ist nicht nur amerikanisch. In fast jedem Restaurant kann man neben amerikanischen Burgern auch Wiener Schnitzel° und Kärntner Kasnudeln° bestellen.

Koch chef **erfolgreich** successful **Umsatz** total revenue **teures** expensive
Wiener Schnitzel Viennese schnitzel **Kärntner Kasnudeln** South Austrian cheese noodles

 ### 🔗 IM INTERNET

Wie viele Christkindlmärkte gibt es in Österreich? Wo sind sie? Welche Christkindlmärkte sind sehr berühmt?

Find out more at **vhlcentral.com**.

---

2 **Richtig oder falsch?** Korrigieren Sie die falschen Aussagen.

1. Das Brötchen heißt Semmel in Österreich. Richtig.

2. Eine Tomate heißt Marille in Österreich. Falsch. Sie heißt ein Paradeiser.

3. Wolfgang Puck ist ein deutscher Koch. Falsch. Er ist ein österreicher Koch.

4. Wolfgang Puck hat Restaurants nur in den USA. Falsch. Er hat Restaurants auch in Toronto, Dubai, London, Singapur und Tokio.

5. In fast jedem Restaurant von Wolfgang Puck kann man Wiener Schnitzel bestellen. Richtig.

3 **Auf dem Naschmarkt** Spielen Sie ein Gespräch zwischen einem Kunden (*customer*) und einem Verkäufer auf dem Naschmarkt. Integrieren Sie die folgenden Informationen: Grüße, zwei Produkte, Preise, Bezahlung (*payment*), Abschiede. Answers will vary.

BEISPIEL

3 **Suggestion** Encourage students to use phrases from the **Deutsch im Alltag** box in their role-plays.

S1: *Guten Tag.*
S2: *Grüß Gott. Kann ich Ihnen helfen?*
S1: *Ja. Ich hätte gerne...*

3 **Partner Chat** You can also assign activity 3 on the Supersite.

Ressourcen

 vText

 vhlcentral

4A.1

Adverbs  Presentation

Suggestion Teach students the mnemonic device "TMP" to help them remember that adverbs of <u>T</u>ime come before adverbs of <u>M</u>anner, which come before adverbs of <u>P</u>lace.

Suggestion On the board, write the sentence: **Ein Student fährt heute Nachmittag zu schnell zum Supermarkt.** Have students underline the adverbial phrases and identify which one describes time, which describes manner, and which describes place.

Startblock In German, as in English, adverbs are words or phrases that modify a verb, an adjective, or another adverb. Adverbs describe *when*, *how*, or *where* an action takes place.

Ich gehe **wirklich gern** einkaufen.

Ich mache **heute Abend** Börek!

- An adverb usually comes immediately before the adjective or adverb it modifies. Adverbs that frequently modify adjectives or other adverbs include **fast** (*almost*), **noch** (*yet; still; in addition*), **nur** (*only*), **schon** (*already*), **sehr, so** (*so*), **wirklich** (*really*), **ziemlich** (*quite*), and **zu** (*too*).

  Der Kuchen ist **fast** fertig.
  *The cake is **almost** ready.*

  Du isst **viel zu** schnell.
  *You eat **much too** quickly.*

- When an adverb modifies a verb, it generally comes immediately after the verb it modifies. Adverbs of time or place can also come directly before the verb.

  Ich esse **täglich** Gemüse.
  *I eat vegetables **every day**.*

  Morgens trinken wir **immer** Kaffee.
  *We **always** drink coffee **in the morning**.*

- Here are some common adverbs of time, manner, and place.

adverbs					
Wann?		**Wie?**		**Wo?**	
immer	*always*	allein	*alone*	da/dort	*there*
jetzt	*now*	bestimmt	*definitely*	drüben	*over there*
nie	*never*	leider	*unfortunately*	hier	*here*
oft	*often*	vielleicht	*maybe*	überall	*everywhere*
selten	*rarely*	zusammen	*together*	woanders	*somewhere else*
täglich	*daily*				

- Adverbs of time indicate *when* or *how frequently* an event occurs and answer the questions **wann?** and **wie oft?** (*how often?*).

  Wir gehen **morgen** einkaufen.
  *We're going shopping **tomorrow**.*

  Ich esse **selten** Kuchen.
  *I **rarely** eat cake.*

- If there is more than one time expression in a sentence, general time references are placed before adverbs of specific time.

  Die Bäckerei öffnet **am Sonntag um 9 Uhr**.
  *The bakery opens at **9 o'clock on Sunday**.*

  Samstag morgens um 11 Uhr frühstücke ich mit meinem Vater.
  *I have breakfast with my father **every Saturday morning at 11 o'clock**.*

- Adverbs of manner indicate *how* an action is done. They answer the question **wie?**

Ich mache das **allein**.	Du spielst **wirklich gut** Tennis.
*I'm doing this **by myself**.*	*You play tennis **really well**.*

- Adverbs of place describe locations or directions and answer the questions **wo?**, **wohin?**, and **woher?**

Woher kommst du?	Ich komme **aus Deutschland**.
*Where are you **from**?*	*I'm **from Germany**.*
Wohin geht ihr?	Wir gehen **in die Eisdiele**.
Where are you going?	*We're going **to the ice cream shop***.

- When there is more than one adverbial expression in a sentence, adverbs of time come first, followed by adverbs of manner, then adverbs of place.

Papa kauft **heute in der Konditorei** eine Geburtstagstorte.	Wir fahren **zusammen zum Supermarkt**.
*Dad is getting a birthday cake **today at the pastry shop**.*	*We're going **to the supermarket together***.
Heute Abend esse ich **vielleicht im Restaurant**.	Sie essen **morgen Abend bestimmt woanders**.
*Maybe I'll eat **at a restaurant tonight**.*	*They are **definitely** eating **somewhere else tomorrow night***.

- In **2B.3** you learned how to negate sentences with **nicht**. In sentences with adverbial expressions, **nicht** usually *precedes* general expressions of time, manner, and place, but *follows* adverbs of specific time.

Wir kaufen **nicht oft** Fleisch im Supermarkt.	Ich will **am Montag nicht** in die Schule gehen.
*We **don't often** buy meat at the supermarket.*	*I **don't** want to go to school **on Monday**.*
Die Gäste sind **noch nicht hier**.	Wir können **nicht mehr hier** warten.
*The guests **aren't here yet**.*	*We **can't** wait **here anymore***.

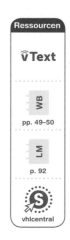

Ressourcen

v̂Text

WB
pp. 49–50

LM
p. 92

S
vhlcentral

Suggestion Point out to students that adverbs can make their speech and writing more informative and expressive. Give them a sample sentence, such as **Anna geht spazieren**. Ask them to make it more vivid by adding adverbs that describe where, how, and when the action takes place.

Jetzt sind Sie dran!   Geben Sie an (*Indicate*), ob die Adverbien die Zeit, die Art und Weise (*manner*) oder den Ort beschreiben.

1. Wir kochen heute Abend <u>zusammen</u>. <u>Art und Weise</u>
2. Marina ist <u>immer</u> besorgt. <u>Zeit</u>
3. Die Eltern trinken <u>gern</u> Rotwein. <u>Art und Weise</u>
4. Das Lebensmittelgeschäft ist <u>dort drüben</u>. <u>Ort</u>
5. Meine Schwester isst <u>nie</u> Obst und Gemüse. <u>Zeit</u>
6. Ihr trinkt <u>selten</u> Kaffee. <u>Zeit</u>

7. Du machst deine Hausaufgaben <u>allein</u>. <u>Art und Weise</u>
8. Ich fahre <u>schnell</u> zur Universität. <u>Art und Weise</u>
9. Petra hat <u>jetzt</u> keine Zeit. <u>Zeit</u>
10. Ich esse <u>oft</u> Käse und Brot. <u>Zeit</u>
11. Kann man Auberginen <u>überall</u> kaufen? <u>Ort</u>
12. Wir bleiben <u>hier</u> in Berlin. <u>Ort</u>

Anwendung

1 **Was ist richtig?** Wählen Sie (*Choose*) das adverbiale Element, das am besten passt.

BEISPIEL Ich gehe (die ganze Nacht / im Restaurant / morgens) in den Unterricht.

1. Yusuf macht (in der Bibliothek / im Fitnessstudio / in der Bäckerei) Hausaufgaben.
2. Wir möchten später (selten / beim Bäcker / im Park) ein Picknick machen.
3. Efe geht (im Hörsaal / im Supermarkt / im Café) einkaufen.
4. Das Restaurant ist (oft / überall / zusammen) voll (*crowded*).
5. Das Rezept ist (jetzt / fast / wirklich) einfach.
6. Thomas isst (dort / selten / allein) Fleisch.
7. Der Kuchen ist (abends / am Wochenende / sehr) gut.
8. Zum Mittagessen gehen wir (leider / in die Mensa / überall).

2 **Auf dem Campus** Setzen Sie das Adverb an die richtige Stelle.

BEISPIEL Wir essen um 6 Uhr. (immer)
Wir essen immer um 6 Uhr.

1. David vergisst immer seine Hausaufgaben. (fast)
   David vergisst fast immer seine Hausaufgaben.

2. Ich gehe im Supermarkt einkaufen. (oft)
   Ich gehe oft im Supermarkt einkaufen.

3. Paula geht nachmittags spazieren. (auf dem Campus)
   Paula geht nachmittags auf dem Campus spazieren.

4. Die Studenten essen in der Mensa. (nicht gern)
   Die Studenten essen nicht gern in der Mensa.

5. Ihr lernt in der Bibliothek. (abends)
   Ihr lernt abends in der Bibliothek.

6. Du gehst freitags tanzen. (im Club)
   Du gehst freitags im Club tanzen.

7. Die Professorin korrigiert die Prüfungen. (am Sonntag)
   Die Professorin korrigiert am Sonntag die Prüfungen./Die Professorin korrigiert die Prüfungen am Sonntag.

8. Julius fährt nach Berlin. (am Wochenende)
   Julius fährt am Wochenende nach Berlin.

3 Suggestion Remind students that they do not need to use words from each column in every sentence. Create one sentence together as a class, before having students work in groups.

3 **Was machen diese Leute?** Bilden Sie Sätze mit zwei Adverbien. Setzen Sie die Wörter in die richtige Reihenfolge (*order*). Answers will vary.

Subjekt	Objekt	Verb	Adverbien	
ich	das Auto	backen	gern	selten
du	die Hausaufgaben	fahren	jetzt	im Sommer
mein Vater	den Hund	kaufen	nächstes Jahr	überall
wir	einen Kuchen	machen	nie	um 9 Uhr
du und Dieter	einen Obstsalat	wandern	oft	am Wochenende
meine Freunde	einen Snack	waschen	schnell	zusammen

S Practice more at **vhlcentral.com.**

Kommunikation

4 **Wie und warum?** Was machen die Personen, wie machen Sie das und warum?
Erfinden Sie (*Make up*) ein kurzes Szenario. Benutzen Sie (*Use*) jedes der folgenden
Adverbien nur einmal (*once*): allein, langsam, oft, selten, vielleicht, zusammen. Sample answers are provided.

▶ **BEISPIEL**

S1: Wie geht er?
S2: Er geht schnell. Wohin geht er?
S3: Er geht vielleicht in den Park.

1. Sie lernen zusammen.

2. Er liest allein.
3. Er kocht vielleicht Reis.
4. Sie fährt langsam.
5. Sie fährt oft Fahrrad.

5 **Partnergespräch** Stellen Sie Ihrem Partner / Ihrer Partnerin Fragen. Answers will vary.

BEISPIEL

S1: Wie oft kochst du?
S2: Ich koche sehr oft. / Ich koche selten.

1. Wann lernst du?
2. Wann sind deine Kurse?
3. Wie oft gehst du in die Mensa?
4. Wann machst du deine Mittagspause?
5. Wie oft gehst du tanzen?
6. Wie oft fährst du zu den Großeltern?

6 **Meine Mitstudenten** Finden Sie für jede Aktivität eine Person aus
Ihrer Klasse.

BEISPIEL

S1: Isst du oft Fisch?
S2: Nein, ich esse nicht oft Fisch.
S3: Und du?

oft / Fisch essen
gut / Gitarre spielen
täglich / in der Sporthalle trainieren
selten / Gemüse essen
gern / am Wochenende tanzen gehen
oft / Schokomilch trinken
nie / samstags im Haus bleiben
immer / Eier zum Frühstück essen
gut / kochen können

5 **Virtual Chat** You can
also assign activity 5 on
the Supersite.

6 **Suggestion** Before
students begin the activity,
make sure they know how to
form the questions properly.
Emphasize that they must
answer using complete
sentences. During the activity,
circulate around the room and
interact with students, asking
them questions and keeping
them on task.

4A.2

The modal *mögen*  Presentation

Startblock In **2B Kontext**, you learned to express likes and dislikes using **gern** and **nicht gern**. Another way of expressing liking is with the modal **mögen**.

Ressourcen

v̂Text

WB
pp. 51–52

LM
p. 93

S
vhlcentral

- Like all the modal verbs, **mögen** is irregular in the singular.

Suggestion Point out that, as with other modals, the er/sie/es form of **mögen** is identical to its ich form.

mögen (*to like*)			
ich mag	*I like*	wir mögen	*we like*
du magst	*you like*	ihr mögt	*you like*
er/sie/es mag	*he/she/it likes*	Sie/sie mögen	*you/they like*

- While most modals modify another verb, **mögen** almost always modifies a noun.

  Mögt ihr diesen Joghurt?
  *Do you **like** this yogurt?*

  Nein, diesen Joghurt **mögen** wir **nicht**.
  *No, we **don't like** that yogurt.*

- Depending on context, you can use either **nicht** or **kein** to negate a statement with **mögen**.

  Ich **mag keine** grünen Paprika.
  *I **don't like** green peppers.*

  Magst du rote Paprika?
  *Do you **like** red peppers?*

  Nein, rote Paprika **mag** ich auch **nicht**.
  *No, I **don't like** red peppers either.*

- **Möchten** is the subjunctive form of **mögen**. Use **möchten** for polite requests and to say what you *would like* to have or do. **Möchten** may be followed by either a verb or a noun.

möchten			
ich möchte	*I would like*	wir möchten	*we would like*
du möchtest	*you would like*	ihr möchtet	*you would like*
er/sie/es möchte	*he/she/it would like*	Sie/sie möchten	*you/they would like*

  Wir **möchten** Fußball spielen.
  *We **would like** to play soccer.*

  Möchten Sie Kaffee oder Tee?
  ***Would** you **like** coffee or tea?*

ACHTUNG

While **gern** is always used with a verb, **mögen** is typically used with a noun:
Wir mögen Erdbeeren.
But: **Wir essen gern Erdbeeren.**

Ich mag keinen Tee.
But: **Ich trinke nicht gern Tee.**

Since **gern** is an adverb, it can also be used in combination with **mögen**, for emphasis:

Was magst du gern?
Das mag ich nicht so gern.

QUERVERWEIS

See **3B.1** to review the other modal verbs: **dürfen**, **können**, **müssen**, **sollen**, and **wollen**.

See **2B.3** to review negation.

Students will learn more about subjunctive forms in **Vol. 3, 1B.1**.

Suggestion Explain to students that "**Ich mag keine grünen Paprika.**", "**Grüne Paprika mag ich nicht.**", and "**Ich mag grüne Paprika nicht gern.**" all convey the same idea, but with slightly different emphasis.

Jetzt sind Sie dran! **Ergänzen Sie die Lücken mit den richtigen Formen der Modalverben mögen oder möchten.**

1. Die Kinder __mögen__ (mögen) Schokolade.
2. Ich __mag__ (mögen) keinen Fußball.
3. Julia __möchte__ (möchten) in die Konditorei gehen.
4. __Möchtest__ (Möchten) du Pasta oder Reis?
5. Anne __mag__ (mögen) russische Literatur.
6. __Möchten__ (Möchten) Sie einen Tisch am Fenster?
7. Ihr __möchtet__ (möchten) zur Bäckerei gehen.
8. __Magst__ (Mögen) du Meeresfrüchte nicht?
9. Ich __möchte__ (möchten) kein Fleisch essen.
10. Unsere Katzen __mögen__ (mögen) unseren Hund nicht.
11. __Mögt__ (Mögen) ihr Garnelen?
12. Wir __möchten__ (möchten) Pasta.

Anwendung und Kommunikation

1 **Wer mag was?** Schreiben Sie die Sätze um. Benutzen Sie **mögen** anstatt **essen** oder **trinken gern.** Some answers may vary.

> **BEISPIEL** Ich esse nicht gern Garnelen.
> *Ich mag keine Garnelen. / Ich mag Garnelen nicht.*

1. Meine Schwester isst gern Schokolade. Meine Schwester mag Schokolade.
2. Meine Eltern essen gern Bananen zum Frühstück. Meine Eltern mögen Bananen zum Frühstück.
3. Ich esse nicht gern Auberginen. Ich mag Auberginen nicht./Ich mag keine Auberginen.
4. Mein Mann und ich essen gern Pizza. Mein Mann und ich mögen Pizza.
5. Esst ihr gern Würstchen? Mögt ihr Würstchen?
6. Trinkst du nicht gern Kaffee? Magst du keine Kaffee?/Magst du Kaffee nicht?

2 **Pläne** Ergänzen Sie die Sätze mit der richtigen Form von **möchten** und mit Wörtern aus der Liste.

2 **Expansion** Have students write 5 sentences about what *they* would like to do this weekend, using **möchten**.

am Wochenende Fußball spielen	schlafen
im Biergarten essen	tanzen
heiraten	Tennis spielen

> **BEISPIEL**
> Ben und Simon
> *möchten am Wochenende Fußball spielen.*

1. Elias und Emma möchten heiraten .

2. Paula, du möchtest schlafen .

3. Professor Klein möchte Tennis spielen .

4. Alex und du, ihr möchtet tanzen .

5. Marie und ich, wir möchten im Biergarten essen .

3 **Was magst du?** Fragen Sie Ihren Partner / Ihre Partnerin, was er/sie (nicht) mag. Fragen Sie auch nach den anderen Personen in seiner/ihrer Familie. Answers will vary.

3 **Partner Chat** You can also assign activity 3 on the Supersite. Students work in pairs to record the activity online. The pair's recorded conversation will appear in your gradebook.

> **BEISPIEL**
> **S1:** *Magst du Thunfisch?*
> **S2:** *Nein, aber ich mag Käse.*
> **S1:** *Und dein Bruder? Mag er Thunfisch?*
> **S2:** *Nein, aber er mag Würstchen.*

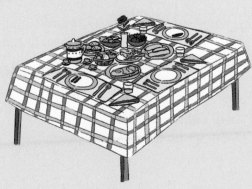

3 **Suggestion** You may want to teach students the words **igitt** and **lecker** for use in this activity.

 Practice more at **vhlcentral.com**.

4A.3   **Separable and inseparable prefix verbs**    Presentation

Startblock In German, many verbs have a prefix in their infinitive form.

Ich gehe wirklich gern **einkaufen**.

Lass mich **überlegen**.

- A verb with a prefix has the same conjugations as its base form, but the added prefix changes the meaning.

  Sucht ihr eure Eltern?
  *Are you **looking for** your parents?*

  Besucht ihr eure Verwandten?
  *Do you **visit** your relatives?*

- Some prefixes are always attached to the verb and others can be separated from it.

  Jakob **verkauft** sein Fahrrad.
  *Jakob **is selling** his bike.*

  Ich **kaufe** im Supermarkt **ein**.
  *I **shop** at the supermarket.*

- Here are some of the most common separable and inseparable prefix verbs.

verbs with separable prefixes	
anfangen	*to begin*
ankommen	*to arrive*
anrufen	*to call*
aufstehen	*to get up*
ausgehen	*to go out*
einkaufen	*to shop*
einschlafen	*to fall asleep*
mitbringen	*to bring along*
mitkommen	*to come along*
vorbereiten	*to prepare*
vorstellen	*to introduce*
zuschauen	*to watch*
zurückkommen	*to come back*

verbs with inseparable prefixes	
beantworten	*to answer*
besprechen	*to discuss*
bestellen	*to order*
besuchen	*to visit*
bezahlen	*to pay (for)*
erklären	*to explain*
verkaufen	*to sell*
verbringen	*to spend (time)*
überlegen	*to think over*
wiederholen	*to repeat*

- Separable prefixes are generally prepositions (**an, aus, mit**) or other parts of speech that carry meaning and can stand alone. In contrast, most inseparable prefixes (**be-, er-, ver-**) have no independent meaning and never stand alone.

  Heute Abend **gehen** wir zusammen **aus**.
  Tonight we're going out together.

  Ich **bestelle** die Pasta mit Garnelen.
  I'm ordering the pasta with shrimp.

  Stefan **steht** jeden Morgen um 6 Uhr **auf**.
  Stefan gets up at 6 o'clock every morning.

  Ihr **verkauft** euer Auto?
  You're selling your car?

Suggestion Tell students that separable prefix verbs are the "drama queens" of the grammar world. They like to "break up" and "get back together". They break off from the main verb and move to the end of the clause in the indicative and the imperative, but get back together when used with modals.

QUERVERWEIS

See **2B.1** to review the present tense of irregular verbs like **fangen** and **schlafen**.

You might want tell the students that the verb **vorstellen** is often used reflexively. Students will learn more about reflexive verbs in **Vol. 3, 1A.1** and **1A.2**.

Suggestion Give students the name of a celebrity and ask them to write sentences about what this celebrity does on a typical Saturday, using 5-6 separable or inseparable prefix verbs. Create the first sentence as a class.

ACHTUNG

When speaking, place the stress on the prefix of a separable prefix verb: **anrufen**, **einschlafen**. The prefix of an inseparable prefix verb is never stressed: **verkaufen**, **wiederholen**.

- When using a separable prefix verb in the present tense or the imperative, move the prefix to the end of the sentence or clause.

Wir **kaufen** auf dem Markt **ein**.
We're shopping at the market.

Bitte **stellen** Sie die Frau **vor**.
Please introduce the woman.

Kommst du **zurück**?
Are you coming back?

Ruf deine Eltern **an**!
Call your parents!

Wir **bringen** Käse und Brot **mit**.

Wir **laden** Meline und Sabite zu uns zu Börek **ein**?

- To make the sentence negative, add **nicht** immediately before the separable prefix.

Ich komme **nicht** zurück.
I'm not coming back.

Ruf deine Eltern **nicht** an!
Don't call your parents!

- When using a modal with a separable prefix verb, move the infinitive of the separable prefix verb to the end of the sentence.

Die Mädchen **möchten** morgen Abend **ausgehen**.
The girls want to go out tomorrow night.

Ich **muss** mit meinen Hausaufgaben **anfangen**.
I need to start my homework.

- The prefix of an inseparable prefix verb always remains attached to the beginning of the verb.

Ich **bezahle** die Lebensmittel.
I'll pay for the groceries.

Wiederholen Sie den Satz.
Repeat the sentence.

 **Jetzt sind Sie dran!**   **Schreiben Sie die richtige Form des Verbs in Klammern.**

1. Ich ___wiederhole___ den Satz. (wiederholen)
2. Wir ___rufen___ unsere Freunde ___an___. (anrufen)
3. Erwin und Marta ___verkaufen___ ihr Haus. (verkaufen)
4. Du musst heute Abend noch ___einkaufen___. (einkaufen)
5. Der Student ___stellt___ seine Eltern ___vor___. (vorstellen)

6. ___Gehen___ wir am Wochenende ___aus___? (ausgehen)
7. Papa ___bestellt___ gern Meeresfrüchte. (bestellen)
8. Ich ___verbringe___ eine Woche in Zürich. (verbringen)
9. Kannst du Brot ___mitbringen___? (mitbringen)
10. Wir ___besuchen___ unsere Verwandten in Salzburg. (besuchen)

Anwendung

1 **Befehle** Geben Sie Befehle (*commands*) in der **Sie**-Form.

BEISPIEL

aufstehen
Stehen Sie auf.

1. anrufen   Rufen Sie an.
2. einkaufen   Kaufen Sie ein.
3. bezahlen   Bezahlen Sie.
4. zuschauen   Schauen Sie zu.
5. nicht mitkommen   Kommen Sie nicht mit.

6. überlegen   Überlegen Sie.
7. anfangen   Fangen Sie an.
8. nicht einschlafen   Schlafen Sie nicht ein.
9. zurückkommen   Kommen Sie zurück.
10. nicht ausgehen   Gehen Sie nicht aus.

2 **Fragen** Formulieren Sie die Fragen um und benutzen Sie (*use*) dabei die angegebenen (*indicated*) Modalverben.

BEISPIEL

Kommst du mit? (können)
Kannst du mitkommen?

1. Gehst du aus? (wollen)   Willst du ausgehen?
2. Kaufen wir ein? (sollen)   Sollen wir einkaufen?
3. Kommt Lisa mit? (müssen)   Muss Lisa mitkommen?

4. Fangt ihr an? (möchten)   Möchtet ihr anfangen?
5. Schläfst du ein? (dürfen)   Darfst du einschlafen?
6. Schaut Nils zu? (können)   Kann Nils zuschauen?

3 **Was machen sie?** Schreiben Sie zu jedem (*each*) Foto einen Satz und benutzen Sie Präfixverben.

> Freunde anrufen
> heute Abend ausgehen
> die Bücher bezahlen
> einkaufen
>
> einschlafen
> die Grammatik erklären
> euren Hund mitbringen

▶ **BEISPIEL**

Herr Schröder
Herr Schröder erklärt die Grammatik.

ich
1. Ich schlafe ein.

Jana und Lina
2. Jana und Lina rufen Freunde an.

Emma und ihre Freunde
3. Emma und ihre Freunde gehen heute Abend aus.

Stefanie
4. Stefanie bezahlt die Bücher.

Frau Neumann und ihre Tochter
5. Frau Neumann und ihre Tochter kaufen ein.

ihr
6. Ihr bringt euren Hund mit.

Kommunikation

4 **Mein Tag** Füllen Sie einen Terminkalender mit Ihren Informationen aus und diskutieren Sie dann mit Ihrem Partner / Ihrer Partnerin, was **Sie täglich so machen.** Answers will vary.

4 Partner Chat You can also assign activity 4 on the Supersite. Students work in pairs to record the activity online. The pair's recorded conversation will appear in your gradebook.

BEISPIEL

S1: Ich stehe um 8 Uhr auf. Und du?
S2: Ich stehe um 8.30 Uhr auf. Meine erste Vorlesung fängt um 10 Uhr an. Und deine?

8.00 _Ich stehe auf._
9.00 _____
10.00 _____
11.00 _____
12.00 _____
13.00 _____
14.00 _____
15.00 _____

5 **Wer ist das?** Wählen Sie eine Person und schreiben Sie zwei Dinge auf, die diese (*this*) Person macht. Ihre Mitstudenten müssen raten (*guess*), wer es ist. Answers will vary.

BEISPIEL

S1: Sie kommt um 8 Uhr zur Uni.
Sie erklärt die Hausaufgaben und beantwortet unsere Fragen.
S2: Ist es die Professorin?

anfangen	ausgehen	besuchen	erklären	verbringen
ankommen	beantworten	bezahlen	mitbringen	vorbereiten
anrufen	besprechen	einkaufen	mitkommen	zurückkommen

6 **Ein Picknick machen** Sie und Ihre Freunde planen ein Picknick. Diskutieren Sie, wer was kauft, wer was mitbringt und was Sie alles machen müssen. Answers will vary.

BEISPIEL

S1: Sollen wir viele Freunde anrufen?
S2: Ja, und wir müssen auch viel Essen mitbringen.
S3: Ich bringe Wurst und Käse mit!

Wiederholung

1 Was magst du? Fragen Sie einen Partner / eine Partnerin, was er/sie mag oder nicht mag. Answers will vary.

1 **Partner Chat** You can also assign activity 1 on the Supersite.

BEISPIEL

S1: *Magst du Hähnchen mit Reis?*
S2: *Ja, ich mag Hähnchen mit Reis. Und du?*
S1: *Nein, ich mag Hähnchen mit Reis nicht. Magst du…?*

Würstchen mit Brot	Schweinefleisch mit Kartoffeln
Thunfisch mit Zwiebeln	Auberginen mit Tomaten
Pasta mit Pilzen	Schinken mit Brot
Hähnchen mit Reis	Pasta mit Käse
Garnelen mit Tomaten	Rindfleisch mit Salat

2 Das Wochenende Sagen Sie, was die Personen am Wochenende machen möchten. Wechseln Sie sich (*Take turns*) mit einem Partner / einer Partnerin ab. Answers will vary.

Klara

BEISPIEL

S1: *Was möchte Klara am Wochenende machen?*
S2: *Klara möchte am Wochenende gern lesen.*

2 **Virtual Chat** You can also assign activity 2 on the Supersite.

1. Petra und Klaus

2. Paul, Manfred, Andrea und Monika

3. Inge

4. Robert

3 Arbeitsblatt Fragen Sie Ihre Mitstudenten, wie oft, wie und wo sie diese Lebensmittel essen. Answers will vary.

BEISPIEL

S1: *Wie oft isst du Eier in der Mensa?*
S2: *Ich esse selten Eier in der Mensa.*

4 Was machen sie? Ein Student / Eine Studentin spielt eine Situation. Die anderen Studenten raten (*guess*) die Situation. Benutzen Sie vollständige (*complete*) Sätze. Answers will vary.

BEISPIEL

S1: *Fährst du Fahrrad?*
S2: *Nein.*
S1: *Reitest du ein Pferd?*
S2: *Ja.*

aufstehen	im Restaurant	einschlafen
ausgehen	bestellen	Fahrrad fahren
einen Kuchen	einen Freund	ein Pferd reiten
backen	besuchen	Volleyball spielen

5 Diskutieren und kombinieren Sie bekommen eine Tabelle von Ihrem Professor / Ihrer Professorin. Fragen Sie einen Partner / eine Partnerin, wann die Personen die Aktivitäten machen.

BEISPIEL

S1: *Wann geht Alex Lebensmittel einkaufen?*
S2: *Alex geht am Samstag Lebensmittel einkaufen.*

6 Der Wochenplan Entscheiden Sie (*Decide*), was Sie diese Woche machen wollen. Suchen Sie andere Studenten in der Gruppe, die das Gleiche planen und finden Sie eine gemeinsame Zeit, wann sie das machen können. Answers will vary.

BEISPIEL

S1: *Willst du diese Woche einkaufen gehen?*
S2: *Ja, ich will diese Woche einkaufen gehen.*
S1: *Können wir zusammen einkaufen gehen?*
S2: *Ja, gern.*
S1: *Hast du am Mittwoch Zeit?*
S2: *Nein, am Mittwoch habe ich keine Zeit. Hast du am Donnerstag Zeit?*
S1: *Ja, am Donnerstag habe ich Zeit. Um wie viel Uhr…*

Video

AP* Theme: Global Challenges
Context: Communication

Yello Strom

Die Firma Yello Strom ist eine deutsche Stromfirma°. In Deutschland können Kunden° zwischen verschiedenen° Stromfirmen wählen. Kundenservice° ist deshalb aber auch ein wichtiger Aspekt, um neue Kunden zu gewinnen. Yello Strom ist eine kreative Firma mit neuen Ideen. Kundenservice ist sehr wichtig für diese Firma. In diesem Werbeclip zeigt° die Firma, dass Kunden bei Yello Strom nur mit echten Menschen reden!

Auf dem Wochenmarkt°

„Sie haben drei gelbe° Bananen gewählt°."

„Guter Service geht anders°."

- -

Stromfirma *electric company* **Kunden** *customers* **verschiedenen** *different* **Kundenservice** *customer service* **zeigt** *shows* **Wochenmarkt** *farmer's market* **gelbe** *yellow* **gewählt** *selected* **anders** *differently*

 Verständnis Beantworten Sie die Fragen mit den Informationen aus dem Video.

1. Was möchte die Frau auf dem Markt?
   Sie möchte drei ____Äpfel____.

2. Was versteht der Verkäufer?
   Er versteht drei __(gelbe) Bananen__.

 Diskussion Diskutieren Sie die folgenden Fragen mit einem Partner / einer Partnerin. Answers will vary.

1. Wie finden Sie Telefonmenüs? Funktionieren sie gut? Sind sie praktisch oder frustrierend?

2. Wie findest du die Werbung (*commercial*)? Ist die Situation lustig oder nicht so lustig?

Kontext

Communicative Goals

You will learn how to:

- talk about food and meals
- describe flavors

Im Restaurant

Vocabulary Tools

AP* Theme: Contemporary Life
Context: Entertainment, Travel, & Leisure

Wortschatz	
im Restaurant	*at the restaurant*
die Beilage, -n	*side dish*
das Besteck	*silverware*
die Flasche, -n	*bottle*
der erste/zweite Gang	*first/second course*
das Gericht, -e	*dish*
die Hauptspeise, -n	*main course*
der Nachtisch, -e	*dessert*
die Rechnung, -en	*check*
die Tasse, -n	*cup*
das Trinkgeld	*tip*
die Vorspeise, -n	*appetizer*
Mahlzeiten	*meals*
das Abendessen	*dinner*
das Frühstück	*breakfast*
das Mittagessen	*lunch*
der Snack, -s	*snack*
Getränke	*drinks*
das Bier	*beer*
der Kaffee	*coffee*
die Milch	*milk*
das Mineralwasser	*sparkling water*
der Saft, ̈e	*juice*
der Tee	*tea*
das stille Wasser	*still water*
der Wein	*wine*
Essen beschreiben	*talking about food*
der Geschmack, ̈e	*flavor; taste*
fade	*bland*
lecker	*delicious*
leicht	*light*
salzig	*salty*
scharf	*spicy*
schwer	*rich, heavy*
süß	*sweet*
Ausdrücke	*expressions*
Ich hätte gern(e)...	*I would like...*
auf Diät sein	*to be on a diet*
hausgemacht	*homemade*

Explain that **ein Gericht** refers to a particular food item whereas **ein Teller** is the plate on which it is served.

Suggestion Point out the compound words **Hauptspeise**, **Vorspeise**, and **Speisekarte**. Ask students for a synonym for **Speise**.

Suggestion Point out that the word **Snack** has come into German from English. Tell students that Germans also use the word **die Zwischenmahlzeit**, while Austrians often say **die Jause**.

Suggestion Point out that the noun **Geschmack** comes from the verb **schmecken**.

der Koch, ̈e
(die Köchin, -nen *f.*)

Die Suppe schmeckt gut.
(schmecken)

der Kellner, -
(die Kellnerin, -nen *f.*)

die Gabel, -n

die Speisekarte, -n

Speisekarte

die Serviette, -n

der Teller, -

das Messer, -

die Tischdecke, -n

Sie bestellen.
(bestellen)

das Salz

das Glas, ¨er

der Pfeffer

der Esslöffel, -

der Teelöffel, -

Speisekarte

Suggestion Tell students that a soup spoon may also be referred to as **der Suppenlöffel**.

Anwendung

1 Expansion Have each pair come up with their own set of four words, and have the class guess which is the "odd word out".

1 Was passt nicht? Welches Wort passt nicht zu den anderen?

1. a. die Gabel
   b. das Messer
   c. (die Serviette)
   d. der Löffel

2. a. die Milch
   b. der Saft
   c. der Kaffee
   d. (das Salz)

3. a. (die Speisekarte)
   b. die Flasche
   c. die Tasse
   d. das Glas

4. a. salzig
   b. (stolz)
   c. scharf
   d. süß

5. a. die Kellnerin
   b. die Köchin
   c. (der Saft)
   d. der Koch

6. a. das Mittagessen
   b. (die Beilage)
   c. das Abendessen
   d. das Frühstück

2 Wie schmeckt's? Beschreiben Sie (Describe) den Geschmack der Lebensmittel. Sample answers are provided.

▶ **BEISPIEL** Die Bratwurst ist
scharf.

1. Der Saft ist
   süß.

2. Die Suppe ist
   schwer.

3. Der Salat ist
   leicht.

4. Der Käse ist
   salzig.

5. Das Brot ist
   fade.

6. Der Kuchen ist
   lecker.

3 Was bestellen wir? Hören Sie den Dialog an und markieren Sie, was Tom, Klara und Murat bestellen.

Essen	Tom	Klara	Murat
1. Steak	✓	☐	☐
2. Cola	☐	☐	✓
3. Meeresfrüchtesalat	☐	✓	☐
4. stilles Wasser	✓	☐	☐
5. gemischter Salat	✓	☐	☐
6. Brot	☐	✓	☐
7. Mineralwasser	☐	✓	☐
8. Rindfleisch	☐	☐	✓

3 Expansion Ask students questions to check their answers. Encourage them to respond with complete sentences. Ex.: **Wer bestellt das Steak? Was trinkt Murat? Wer möchte den Meeresfrüchtesalat?**

Kommunikation

4 **Verschiedene Mahlzeiten** Fragen Sie Ihren Partner / Ihre Partnerin, welche Mahlzeiten auf den Fotos zu sehen sind. Wechseln Sie sich ab (*Take turns*). Sample answers are provided.

4 **Virtual Chat** You can also assign activity 4 on the Supersite.

▶ **BEISPIEL**

das Frühstück
S1: Ist das das Frühstück?
S2: Nein, das ist das Abendessen.

1. die Vorspeise
Ist das die Vorspeise?
Nein, das ist der Nachtisch.

2. die Hauptspeise
Ist das die Hauptspeise?
Nein, das ist ein Getränk.

3. der Nachtisch
Ist das der Nachtisch?
Nein, das ist das Mittagessen.

4. das Abendessen
Ist das das Abendessen?
Nein, das ist das Frühstück.

5. ein Snack
Ist das ein Snack?
Nein, das ist das Abendessen.

6. das Mittagessen
Ist das das Mittagessen?
Nein, das ist ein Snack.

5 **Wo möchten wir heute Abend essen?** Sie möchten heute Abend ins Restaurant essen gehen. Lesen Sie die Speisekarte und überlegen Sie, was Sie zu jedem (*for each*) Gang bestellen wollen. Answers will vary.

Suggestion Explain to students that **Nachspeise** and **Dessert** are synonyms for **Nachtisch** commonly used on restaurant menus.

BEISPIEL

S1: Ich möchte gern den Tomatensalat mit Mozzarella als ersten Gang.
S2: Ich auch! Und als zweiten Gang bestelle ich das Hähnchen mit Reis.
S3: Wollt ihr auch Getränke bestellen?

7 **Expansion** Have students work in groups to create a commercial for their "ideal restaurant" and present it to the class. You may want to provide prompts. Ex.: **Unser Restaurant ist/hat… Das Essen ist… Wir servieren… In unserem Restaurant kann man… Die Atmosphäre ist… Die Kellner sind…**

Speisekarte

Vorspeisen
Tagessuppe
Chef-Salat mit Schinken, Käse und Ei
Bauern-Salat mit Schafskäse, Zwiebeln und Oliven
Tomatensalat mit Mozzarella

Beilagen
Kartoffelsalat
Karottensalat
Grüner Salat
Kartoffelpuffer
Sauerkraut

Nachspeisen
Apfelkuchen
Bananen mit Schokolade
hausgemachter Joghurt mit Himbeermarmelade
Obstsalat

Hauptspeisen
Würstchen mit Brötchen
Thunfisch mit Salat
Hähnchen mit Reis
Rindfleisch mit Pommes frites
Schweinefleisch mit Kartoffeln
Pasta mit Garnelen
Pasta mit Käse

Getränke
stillesWasser
Mineralwasser
Orangensaft
Milch
Kaffee
Tee

6 **Stress im Restaurant!** Sie sind im Restaurant und der Kellner bringt Ihr Essen. Aber auf dem Tisch gibt es kein Besteck, kein Brot, keine Getränke, kein Salz und so weiter. Sagen Sie dem Kellner, was er noch alles bringen soll. Answers will vary.

BEISPIEL

S1: Kann ich bitte auch Gabel und Messer haben?
S2: Und bitte zwei Glas Wasser!
S3: Natürlich. Möchten sie noch etwas (*anything else*)?

7 **Diskutieren und kombinieren** Wie sind die Restaurants „Zum Grünen Baum" und „Zur Stadtmauer"? Fragen Sie Ihren Partner / Ihre Partnerin, und ergänzen Sie die fehlenden (*missing*) Informationen.

BEISPIEL

S1: Was für ein Restaurant ist „Zur Stadtmauer"?
S2: Es ist ein vegetarisches Bistro. Und was für ein Restaurant ist „Zum Grünen Baum"?
S1: Dort gibt es traditionelle deutsche Gerichte. Welche Vorspeisen gibt es im Bistro?

Aussprache und Rechtschreibung

 Audio

The German *s* in combination with other letters

The letter combination **sch** is pronounced like the *sh* in the English word *fish*.

Fisch	**Schinken**	**Geschäft**	**Fleisch**	**Schule**

When an **s** appears at the beginning of a word in front of the letter **p** or **t**, it is also pronounced like the *sh* in *fish*. A prefix added to the word will not change the pronunciation of the **s**. However, if the **sp** or **st** letter combination occurs in the middle or at the end of a word, the **s** is pronounced like the *s* in the English word *restore*.

Speise	**stoppen**	**versprechen**	**Aspirin**	**Fenster**

In a few words borrowed from other languages, **sh** and **ch** are also pronounced like the *sh* in *fish*.

Chauffeur	**Cashewnuss**	**Shampoo**	**Champignon**	**charmant**

At the beginning of a word, the letter combination **tsch** is pronounced like the *ch* in *chat*. In the middle or at the end of a word, **tsch** is pronounced like the *tch* in *catch*.

tschüss	**Tschad**	**Tschechien**	**Rutsch**	**Klatschbase**

1 **Aussprechen** Wiederholen Sie die Wörter, die Sie hören.

1. Schaft	3. Sport	5. aufstehen	7. Aspekt	9. platschen
2. waschen	4. Strudel	6. Kasten	8. Putsch	10. Kutscher

2 **Nachsprechen** Wiederholen Sie die Sätze, die Sie hören.

1. Im Lebensmittelgeschäft kaufst du Schinken und Fisch.
2. In der Schule schwimmen alle Schüler im Schwimmbad.
3. Studenten spielen gern Videospiele.
4. Auf der Speisekarte steht Käsespätzle.
5. Der Tscheche sagt nicht mal tschüss.
6. Ich wünsche dir einen guten Rutsch ins neue Jahr!

2 **Suggestion** Point out that **Einen guten Rutsch ins neue Jahr!** is a common New Year's greeting in German.

2 **Expansion** Item 2 is a tongue twister. Have students take turns trying to say it as quickly as possible. You may also want to teach students the tongue twister **Fischers Fritz fischt frische Fische.**

3 **Sprichwörter** Wiederholen Sie die Sprichwörter, die Sie hören.

Reden ist Silber; Schweigen ist Gold.[2]

Besser spät als nie.[1]

[1] Better late than never.
[2] Talk is silver; silence is golden.

Fotoroman

Die Rechnung, bitte! Video

Vorbereitung Have students scan the script to find words and expressions related to food.

Torsten und Sabite sind bei einem romantischen Abendessen in einem schönen Restaurant. Aber es bleibt nicht so romantisch...

KELLNER Wir bieten eine leckere hausgemachte Pilzsuppe an. Nicht zu schwer.
SABITE Davon nehme ich einen Teller, bitte. Und als zweiten Gang nehme ich die Rindsrouladen.
KELLNER Sehr gerne. Und für Sie, mein Herr?
TORSTEN Als Vorspeise nehme ich den Salat und als Hauptspeise das Wiener Schnitzel, mit Salzkartoffeln, bitte.
KELLNER Ausgezeichnet.

SABITE Sie haben sehr gutes Essen in diesem Restaurant.
TORSTEN Ja. Meine ältere Schwester empfiehlt es guten Freunden wärmstens.

KELLNER Möchten Sie gerne noch einen Nachtisch?
MELINE Ach, ich muss auf meine Figur achten!
KELLNER Oh, nein, Sie sind doch extrem...
LORENZO Wir nehmen ein Stück Schwarzwälder Kirschtorte. Zwei Gabeln.
MELINE Und zwei Kaffee bitte.

SABITE Hallo!
MELINE Sabite! Hallo! Sabite, das ist Lorenzo. Lorenzo, das ist meine Mitbewohnerin, Sabite.
LORENZO Ciao.

LORENZO Ich komme aus Milano.
MELINE Lorenzo ist geschäftlich in Berlin. Er arbeitet im Bereich internationale Finanzen.
LORENZO Bist du auch Studentin?
SABITE Ja, ich studiere Kunst.

SABITE Ich liebe die Kunst von Kandinsky und Klee. Aber Italien hat die Meister... Michelangelo... Da Vinci...
LORENZO Ja. Du musst sie mal aus der Nähe sehen.
SABITE Ich hoffe, sie eines Tages sehen zu können. Mein Vater kommt aus der Türkei. Ich möchte dort gern ein Semester lang studieren.

ÜBUNGEN

1 **Richtig oder falsch?** Entscheiden Sie, ob die folgenden Sätze **richtig** oder **falsch** sind.

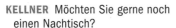

1. Sabite nimmt die Pilzsuppe und die Roulade. Richtig.
2. Torsten bestellt ein Schnitzel mit Salzkartoffeln. Richtig.
3. Torstens Schwester empfiehlt ihren Freunden das Restaurant. Richtig.
4. Meline und Lorenzo bestellen zwei Stück Schwarzwälder Kirschtorte. Falsch.
5. Lorenzo kommt aus Italien. Richtig.

6. Er studiert Kunst. Falsch.
7. Sabite mag die Kunst von Klee und Picasso. Falsch.
8. Sie möchte ein Jahr in der Türkei studieren. Falsch.
9. Sie möchte Istanbul kennen lernen. Richtig.
10. Sabite findet Torsten egoistisch. Richtig.

1 **Expansion** Have students correct the false sentences.

PERSONEN

 Torsten   **Sabite**   **Meline**   **Lorenzo**   **Kellner**

7

SABITE Torsten, ist alles in Ordnung?
TORSTEN Türkei? Du möchtest in der Türkei studieren?
SABITE Ich möchte Istanbul kennen lernen.

8

SABITE Hör auf. Noch studiert niemand in der Türkei. Entschuldige bitte.
TORSTEN Sabite!

9

SABITE Torsten ist... ist... ist so egoistisch!

10

TORSTEN Frauen. Und du bist also nicht Lukas?
LORENZO Die Rechnung, bitte!

Nützliche Ausdrücke

- **anbieten**
  to offer

- **Davon nehme ich einen Teller, bitte.**
  I would like a bowl of that, please.

- **die Rindsroulade**
  beef roulade

- **die Salzkartoffeln**
  boiled potatoes

- **Ich muss auf meine Figur achten.**
  I have to watch my weight.

- **die Schwarzwälder Kirschtorte**
  Black Forest cake

- **Er ist geschäftlich in Berlin.**
  He's in Berlin on business.

- **Er arbeitet im Bereich internationale Finanzen.**
  He works in international finance.

- **Ich hoffe, sie eines Tages sehen zu können.**
  I hope to see them someday.

- **ein Semester lang**
  for one semester

- **Hör auf!**
  Cut it out!

- **Noch studiert niemand in der Türkei.**
  No one's studying in Turkey just yet.

4B.1
- **Meine ältere Schwester empfiehlt es guten Freunden wärmstens.**
  My older sister highly recommends it to her close friends.

4B.2
- **Du musst sie mal aus der Nähe sehen.**
  You should see them up close.

---

2 **Zum Besprechen** Wählen Sie zu dritt ein Gericht aus Deutschland, Österreich oder der Schweiz und machen Sie eine Liste mit Zutaten. Präsentieren Sie der Klasse dann die Liste. Ihre Kommilitonen müssen das Gericht erraten (*guess*). Answers will vary.

2 **Expansion** Name some well-known German, Austrian or Swiss dishes (**Kaiserschmarrn, Sauerbraten, Knödel,** etc.), and ask students to find the main ingredients. Write any new words on the board.

3 **Vertiefung** In den USA ist Wiener Schnitzel vielleicht das berühmteste (*most famous*) Gericht aus den deutschsprachigen Ländern. Wissen Sie, woher es kommt? Kennen Sie andere Gerichte, die den Namen von Städten haben? Sample answers: Wiener Schnitzel: Wien (*Vienna*); Frankfurter (Würstchen), Hamburger, Nürnberger (Bratwürstchen), Berliner (*jelly doughnut*), Kassler (*smoked pork chop*)

IM FOKUS

Wiener Kaffeehäuser Reading

AP* Theme: Contemporary Life
Context: Entertainment, Travel, & Leisure

connections
cultures

KAFFEEHÄUSER IN ÖSTERREICH HABEN eine lange Tradition. Kaffeehäuser gibt es seit dem 18. Jahrhundert. In Wien findet man heute mindestens° 1.100 Kaffeehäuser. Typischerweise serviert ein Kellner einen Kaffee auf einem silbernen Tablett° mit einem Löffel, einem Glas Wasser und einem Keks. In den Kaffeehäusern trinkt man aber auch andere Getränke wie Kakao, Wasser und Wein. Zum Kaffee isst man oft Apfelstrudel, Gugelhupf° oder Sachertorte°. Oft besuchen Gäste° ein Kaffeehaus, bestellen einen Kaffee und bleiben viele Stunden. Hier diskutieren Gäste auch über Politik, Sport und andere Themen.

Wiener Kaffeehäuser haben spezielle Vokabeln: Sahne° heißt Obers. Ein kleiner oder großer Brauner ist ein Kaffee serviert mit Obers in einer kleinen Schale°. Eine Melange ist halb° Kaffee und halb geschäumte° Milch. Ein Kapuziner ist ein kleiner Mokka (ein Schwarzer oder Espresso pur) mit wenig Milch.

Es gibt auch andere Cafés in Wien. In einer Espresso-Bar trinkt man vor allem° Espresso und Cappuccino wie in Italien. In Stehcafés trinken Gäste Kaffee sehr schnell oder nehmen den Kaffee mit. Café-Konditoreien sind nicht nur Cafés. In der Konditorei kaufen Kunden hausgemachte Kuchen und Süßigkeiten°. Die neueste Version eines Cafés ist der amerikanische Import Starbucks. Hier findet man vor allem jüngere Österreicher.

Typische Cafépreise	
Kleiner Schwarzer	2,80 €
Kleiner Brauner	2,90 €
Melange	3,90 €
Großer Schwarzer	4,20 €
Großer Brauner	4,30 €
Einspänner	4,90 €
Kapuziner	4,90 €
Pharisäer	6,60 €

QUELLE: Café Korb in Wien

mindestens at least **Tablett** tray **Gugelhupf** Bundt cake **Sachertorte** chocolate torte **Gäste** guests **Sahne** cream **Schale** dish **halb** half **geschäumte** foamed **vor allem** above all **Süßigkeiten** sweets

ÜBUNGEN

1 **Wiener Kaffeehäuser** Ergänzen Sie die Sätze.

1. Wiener Kaffeehäuser haben eine __lange__ Tradition.

2. In Wien findet man mehr als __1.100__ Kaffeehäuser.

3. Auf einem Tablett serviert der Kellner den Kaffee, einen Löffel, ein __Glas Wasser__ und einen Keks.

4. Gäste bleiben oft __viele__ Stunden.

5. Neben Kaffee kann man auch __Kakao__, Wasser oder Wein trinken.

6. Typisches Essen in Kaffeehäusern sind __Apfelstrudel__, Gugelhupf und Sachertorte.

7. Ein Melange ist halb Kaffee und halb __(geschäumte) Milch__.

8. In Wien gibt es auch Espresso-Bars, __Stehcafés__ und Café-Konditoreien.

9. In einer Espresso-Bar trinken Gäste Kaffee wie in __Italien__.

10. Ein Kapuziner im Café Korb kostet __4,90 €__.

DEUTSCH IM ALLTAG

Am Tisch

Die Rechnung, bitte!	*Check, please!*
Die Speisekarte, bitte!	*The menu, please!*
Guten Appetit!	*Enjoy your meal!*
Noch einen Wunsch?	*Anything else?*
Herr Ober!	*Waiter!*
Prost!	*Cheers!*
Zum Wohl!	*Cheers!*

DIE DEUTSCHSPRACHIGE WELT

Ausländische Spezialitäten

In Deutschland besteht die Bevölkerung° ungefähr zu 8% aus° Ausländern°, in der Schweiz sind es fast 23%. Die Ausländer kommen aus vielen Ländern wie Italien, Griechenland°, der Türkei, Nordafrika und dem ehemaligen° Jugoslawien. Deshalb° ist die Restaurantszene in Deutschland, Österreich und der Schweiz auch sehr international. In jeder° Stadt gibt es Restaurants mit italienischen, griechischen und verschiedenen° asiatischen Speisen. Vor allem in Großstädten ist die Auswahl° sehr groß. Die populärsten Restaurants sind definitiv italienisch, aber man findet auch sehr viele asiatische Restaurants.

AP* Theme: Families & Communities
Context: Diversity
Bevölkerung *population* **besteht... aus** *consists of* **Ausländern** *foreigners* **Griechenland** *Greece* **ehemaligen** *former* **Deshalb** *Therefore* **jeder** *every* **verschiedenen** *various* **Auswahl** *selection*

PORTRÄT

Figlmüller
AP* Theme: Contemporary Life
Context: Social Customs & Values

Das Figlmüller ist ein sehr altes Restaurant in Wien. Es ist „die Heimat° des Schnitzels", ein Paradies für Schnitzelfans. Man findet das Restaurant in der Wollzeile im Zentrum Wiens. Das Restaurant existiert seit über 100 Jahren und ist berühmt° für seine Schnitzel, ein Stück Schweinefleisch mit Semmelbröselhülle°. Die Schnitzel sind ziemlich groß, dünn und sehr knusprig°. Dazu gibt es österreichische Weine. Bier und Kaffee gibt es hier nicht. Auch Süßspeisen finden Gäste nicht auf der Speisekarte. Aber Schnitzel sind hier sehr wichtig. Alle Ober servieren die Schnitzel in einem schwarzen Smoking°!

Heimat *home* **berühmt** *famous* **Semmelbröselhülle** *bread crumb crust* **knusprig** *crisp* **Smoking** *tuxedo*

🔗 IM INTERNET

Suchen Sie Informationen über die Mensa an der Universität Wien. Was können Studenten essen? Was können Studenten trinken? Wie viel kostet das Essen?

Find out more at **vhlcentral.com**.

3 Expansion After each group creates a menu, have them act out a short restaurant role-play using phrases from the **Deutsch im Alltag** box. Have students request the menu, order their food, and finally pay for it.

---

2 **Richtig oder falsch?** Korrigieren Sie die falschen Aussagen.

1. In deutschsprachigen Ländern gibt es viele internationale Restaurants.
   Richtig.
2. Die beliebtesten internationalen Restaurants sind italienisch. Richtig.
3. Das Restaurant Figlmüller ist ein sehr altes Restaurant in Wien. Richtig.
4. Das Restaurant Figlmüller hat eine Spezialität: Apfelstrudel.
   Falsch. Die Spezialität ist Schnitzel.
5. Fast 23% der Bevölkerung in Deutschland sind Ausländer.
   Falsch. Fast 23% der Bevölkerung in der Schweiz sind Ausländer.

3 **Eine Speisekarte** Schreiben Sie eine Speisekarte für ein Restaurant in Deutschland, Österreich oder der Schweiz. Geben Sie die Preise für die Speisen und die Getränke an.

BEISPIEL Restaurant „Zur Post"

Hauptspeisen		Nachtische	
Schweinebraten	6,90 €	Obstsalat	3,10 €
Pizza Marinara	5,50 €	Tiramisu	3,50 €

Ressourcen

 vText

 vhlcentral

QUERVERWEIS

See **1A.3** and **1B.1** to review the use of the nominative and accusative case.

comparisons · **4B.1**

The dative **Presentation**

Suggestion Remind students that the subject is "who does it", the direct object is "what gets 'verbed'", and the indirect object is "for whom or to whom".

Suggestion Provide the class with sentences in both German and English, and have students identify the subject, direct object, and indirect object. Point out the semantic difference between sentences such as: **Ich bringe den Kindern die Schokolade**, and **Ich bringe der Schokolade die Kinder**, or **Der Hund beißt den Mann**, and **Den Hund beißt der Mann**.

Startblock In **1B.1**, you learned that the direct object of a verb is always in the accusative case. When a verb has an indirect object, it is always in the dative case.

- An object in the dative case indicates *to whom* or *for whom* an action is performed.

  Ich bringe **dem Lehrer** einen Apfel.
  *I'm bringing **the teacher** an apple.*

  Zeig **der Lehrerin** deine Arbeit.
  *Show your work **to the teacher**.*

- Verbs that are frequently used with a dative object include **zeigen** (*to show*), **geben**, **bringen**, **empfehlen**, and **gehören** (*to belong to*). Note that the verbs **helfen** and **danken** also take a dative object, even though their English equivalents normally take a direct object.

  Wir helfen **den Kindern**.
  *We're helping (giving help to) **the kids**.*

  Sie dankt **dem Kellner**.
  *She's thanking (giving thanks to) **the waiter**.*

- The forms of the definite and indefinite articles that accompany dative nouns differ from the forms in the nominative or accusative case.

Students will learn more about verbs that take dative objects in **Vol. 2, 1A.3**.

Suggestion To help students memorize the definite articles, teach them the nonsense words "rese, nese, mrmn". These words are derived from the last letter of each article, moving from left to right across the table.

Suggestion To help students memorize the indefinite articles, teach them the nonsense phrase "blank-e blank-e, en-e, blank-e, mrmn (Blankie, blankie, any blankie, Merman?)", also derived from the endings placed on the article, moving from left to right across the table.

definite articles				
	masculine	**feminine**	**neuter**	**plural**
nominative	der Kellner	die Kellnerin	das Kind	die Kinder
accusative	den Kellner	die Kellnerin	das Kind	die Kinder
dative	dem Kellner	der Kellnerin	dem Kind	den Kindern

indefinite articles				
	masculine	**feminine**	**neuter**	**plural**
nominative	ein Kellner	eine Kellnerin	ein Kind	keine Kinder
accusative	einen Kellner	eine Kellnerin	ein Kind	keine Kinder
dative	einem Kellner	einer Kellnerin	einem Kind	keinen Kindern

Der Kellner bringt **der Frau** einen Salat.
*The waiter is bringing **the woman** a salad.*

Ich empfehle **einem Freund** das Restaurant.
*I'm recommending the restaurant **to a friend**.*

- The endings for possessive adjectives are the same as the endings for the indefinite articles.

QUERVERWEIS

See **3A.1** to review the use of possessive adjectives.

possessive adjectives				
	masculine	**feminine**	**neuter**	**plural**
nominative	mein Koch	meine Köchin	mein Kind	meine Kinder
accusative	meinen Koch	meine Köchin	mein Kind	meine Kinder
dative	meinem Koch	meiner Köchin	meinem Kind	meinen Kindern

Der Kellner bringt **meiner Frau** einen Salat.
*The waiter is bringing **my wife** a salad.*

Wir empfehlen unseren **Freunden** das Restaurant.
*We recommend the restaurant **to our friends**.*

- When using plural nouns in the dative case, add **-n** to any noun whose plural form does not already end in **-n** or **-s**.

nominative plural	dative plural
die Teller	den Tellern
die Esslöffel	den Esslöffeln
die Kaffees	den Kaffees
die Rechnungen	den Rechnungen

- A small number of singular masculine nouns also add the ending **-n** or **-en** in the accusative and dative cases. The **n**-nouns you have learned so far are: **der Architekt**, **der Journalist**, **der Junge**, **der Neffe**, and **der Student**.

Nils backt **seinem Neffen** einen Apfelkuchen.
*Nils is baking an apple pie **for his nephew**.*

Ich schreibe **dem Journalisten** eine E-Mail.
*I'm writing an e-mail **to the journalist**.*

- In the dative case, an adjective preceded by an **ein**-word or a **der**-word always ends in **-en**.

Anna kauft **dem kleinen** Jungen ein Eis.
*Anna is buying an ice cream for **the little** boy.*

Ich gebe **meiner kleinen** Schwester eine Banane.
*I'm giving **my little** sister a banana.*

- Adjectives in the dative that are not preceded by an article have endings similar to the definite article endings.

unpreceded adjective endings				
	masculine	**feminine**	**neuter**	**plural**
nominative	süßer Kuchen	süße Melone	süßes Getränk	süße Äpfel
accusative	süßen Kuchen	süße Melone	süßes Getränk	süße Äpfel
dative	süßem Kuchen	süßer Melone	süßem Getränk	süßen Äpfeln

Ich biete **guten** Freunde**n** immer gutes Essen an.
*I always serve good food to **good** friends.*

Die Lehrerin hilft **neuen** Studenten gern.
*The teacher likes to help **new** students.*

- Use the dative question word **wem** to ask *to whom?*

nominative	accusative	dative
wer?	**wen?**	**wem?**

Wem gibst du das Geschenk?
To whom are you giving the present?

Ich gebe **meiner Mutter** das Geschenk.
*I'm giving the present **to my mother**.*

Wem gehört diese Tasse?
*Who does this cup belong **to**?*

Sie gehört **meinem Opa**.
*It belongs to **my grandpa**.*

Suggestion Students often forget to add **-n** in the dative plural. Write sentences on the board in which the **n** is missing, and ask students to find the mistakes. Ex.: **Der Koch kocht den** <u>Kinder</u> **eine leckere Suppe. Die Kinder bringen ihren** <u>Freunde</u> **viele Geschenke.**

QUERVERWEIS

See **3A.2** to review adjective agreement in the nominative and accusative case.

See **2A.2** to review question words.

You might want to tell the students that they will learn more about **n**-nouns in **Vol. 2, 4B.1**.

ACHTUNG

In sentences with both direct and indirect objects, the dative object comes before the accusative object.

Suggestion Point out to students that these endings are similar to the endings of the definite articles, and also follow the "rese, nese, mrmn" pattern.

Ressourcen

v̂Text

WB
pp. 57–58

LM
p. 97

vhlcentral

Jetzt sind Sie dran!   **Wählen Sie den richtigen Artikel.**

1. Mama dankt (der / **dem**) Kellner.
2. Ich gebe (dem / **der**) Lehrerin die Hausaufgaben.
3. Moritz gibt (**seiner** / seinem) Mutter ein Parfüm.
4. Die Lehrerin hilft (**ihren** / ihrem) Schüler mit der Grammatik.
5. Die Großmutter backt (**ihrem** / ihrer) Enkelkind einen Kuchen.
6. Ich schreibe (**dem** / der) Besitzer eine E-Mail.

Anwendung

1 **Was fehlt?** Ergänzen Sie die Sätze mit den richtigen Substantivformen im Dativ.

BEISPIEL deine Freundin: Kaufst du _deiner Freundin_ einen MP3-Player?

1. meine Partnerin: Ich zeige ___meiner Partnerin___ die Hausaufgaben.
2. ihr Mann: Sie gibt ___ihrem Mann___ einen Kuss.
3. die Freunde: Er macht ___den Freunden___ ein leckeres Essen.
4. unser Opa: Ich schreibe ___unserem Opa___ eine lange E-Mail.
5. die alte Frau: Er bringt ___der alten Frau___ ein Mineralwasser.
6. die Kellnerin: Der Koch gibt ___der Kellnerin___ eine Tasse Tee.

2 **Pluralformen** Geben Sie die richtigen Pluralformen im Dativ an.

1. dem alten Hund: den alten Hunden
2. seiner lieben Tante: seinen lieben Tanten
3. der netten Katze: den netten Katzen
4. einem neugierigen Journalisten: neugierigen Journalisten
5. dem kleinen Mädchen: den kleinen Mädchen
6. keiner stolzen Frau: keinen stolzen Frauen
7. dem mutigen Kind: den mutigen Kindern
8. ihrem großen Neffen: ihren großen Neffen
9. meinem faulen Bruder: meinen faulen Brüdern

3 **Dativobjekte** Ergänzen Sie die Sätze mit der richtigen Form im Dativ.

1. Die Kellnerin empfiehlt ___meinen Brüdern___ (meine Brüder) die Vorspeise.
2. ___Wem___ (Wer) bringst du die Flasche Apfelsaft?
3. Ich gebe ___der Kellnerin___ (die Kellnerin) ein Trinkgeld.
4. Der gute Student hilft ___schlechten Studenten___ (schlechte Studenten) oft.
5. Du gibst ___einem schönen Mädchen___ (ein schönes Mädchen) rote Rosen.
6. ___Wem___ (Wer) soll ich das Besteck geben?
7. Kannst du ___meiner Mutter___ (meine Mutter) einen Nachtisch empfehlen?
8. Ich zeige ___meinem Freund___ (mein Freund) die Rechnung.
9. Die Kinder helfen ___ihren Eltern___ (ihre Eltern) gern.
10. Der Junge gibt ___den alten Hunden___ (die alten Hunde) Würstchen.

4 **Nettigkeiten** Bilden Sie Sätze. Sample answers are provided.

BEISPIEL sie / der Kellner / ein Trinkgeld / geben
Sie geben dem Kellner ein Trinkgeld.

1. die Frau / ihre Mutter / ein Kuchen / geben Die Frau gibt ihrer Mutter einen Kuchen.
2. ich / der Hund / sein Essen / vorbereiten Ich bereite dem Hund sein Essen vor.
3. der Schüler / die Lehrerin / eine Postkarte / schreiben Der Schüler schreibt der Lehrerin eine Postkarte.
4. er / seine Tochter / eine Vorspeise / bestellen Er bestellt seiner Tochter eine Vorspeise.
5. die Köchin / das Kind / ein Brötchen / geben Die Köchin gibt dem Kind ein Brötchen.
6. meine Frau / die Oma / eine Beilage / mitbringen Meine Frau bringt der Oma eine Beilage mit.

S Practice more at **vhlcentral.com**.

Kommunikation

5 **Was für ein Chaos!** Ihr Haus ist ein totales Chaos. Fragen Sie Ihren Partner / Ihre Partnerin, wem die Sachen gehören, die im Haus herumliegen. Answers will vary.

▶ **BEISPIEL**

S1: Wem gehört der Pullover?
S2: Er gehört meiner Schwester.

meine Eltern	die Köchin
eine Freundin	meine Schwester
der Kellner	ein Student

1.

2.

3.

4.

5.

6.

6 **Geschenke** Sehen Sie die Speisekarte auf Seite 164 an und erzählen Sie Ihrem Partner / Ihrer Partnerin, welche Gerichte Sie Ihrer Familie und Ihren Freunden empfehlen. Answers will vary.

BEISPIEL meine Tante

S1: Ich empfehle meiner Tante den Chef-Salat. Was empfiehlst du deiner Oma?
S2: Ich empfehle meiner Oma einen kleinen Tomatensalat mit Mozzarella!

1. Mutter/Vater
2. Großeltern
3. Lehrer/Lehrerin
4. Cousin/Cousine

5. Onkel/Tante
6. bester Freund/beste Freundin
7. Bruder/Schwester
8. Kommilitonen

7 **Wem tust du einen Gefallen?** Beantworten Sie die Fragen von Ihrem Partner / Ihrer Partnerin. Answers will vary.

BEISPIEL

S1: Wem zeigst du dein Zeugnis?
S2: Ich zeige meinen Eltern mein Zeugnis. Und du?

1. Wem schreibst du Postkarten im Sommer?
2. Wem kochst du ein Essen?
3. Wem kaufst du ein Buch?

4. Wem hilfst du bei den Hausaufgaben?
5. Wem stellst du deine Eltern vor?
6. Wem backst du einen Kuchen?

5 **Virtual Chat** You can also assign activity 5 on the Supersite.

6 **Suggestions**
• Even if students have been working well with the accusative and dative in isolation, they often have difficulty when they must use both cases in the same sentence. It may be helpful to have charts on the board, and to emphasize that the person who receives the recommendation will be in the dative, while the recommended dish will be in the accusative.

• Give students a few minutes to look at the menu on p. 164 and decide on their recommendations before they begin working with partners. Emphasize that they will be working with *both* the accusative and the dative. Ask a student volunteer to put an example on the board.

6 **Partner Chat** You can also assign activity 6 on the Supersite. Students work in pairs to record the activity online. The pair's recorded conversation will appear in your gradebook.

7 **Virtual Chat** You can also assign activity 7 on the Supersite. Students record individual responses that appear in your gradebook.

4B.2

Prepositions with the dative  Presentation

Startblock Certain prepositions are always followed by an object in the dative case.

QUERVERWEIS

See **3B.2** to review prepositions that take an object in the accusative case.

ACHTUNG

The prepositions **nach** and **zu** are also used in the set expressions **nach Hause** (*home*) and **zu Hause** (*at home*). **Ich gehe jetzt nach Hause. Er bleibt immer zu Hause.**

Suggestion Emphasize that the phrases **zu Hause** and **nach Hause** are idiomatic and should be memorized as "sound bites".

Mein Vater kommt **aus der Türkei**.

Ich glaube, es ist alles okay **mit den beiden**.

- Most dative prepositional phrases provide information about time and location.

<table>
<tr><td colspan="4" align="center">prepositions with the dative</td></tr>
<tr><td>aus</td><td>from</td><td>nach</td><td>after; to</td></tr>
<tr><td>außer</td><td>except for</td><td>seit</td><td>since; for</td></tr>
<tr><td>bei</td><td>at; near; with</td><td>von</td><td>from</td></tr>
<tr><td>mit</td><td>with</td><td>zu</td><td>to; for; at</td></tr>
</table>

Willst du **bei meinen Eltern** essen?
*Do you want to eat **at my parents' house**?*

Zum Geburtstag bekomme ich Geschenke.
*I get presents **on my birthday**.*

- Use **nach** before the names of countries or cities. Use **zu** with people, businesses, or other locations.

Wir fliegen morgen **nach Berlin**.
*We're flying **to Berlin** tomorrow.*

Gehst du **zur Bäckerei**?
*Are you going **to the bakery**?*

- The preposition **seit** is used with time expressions to indicate *since when* or *for how long* something has been taking place.

Seit wann wohnst du in Berlin?
Since when have you been living in Berlin?

Ich wohne **seit einem Jahr** in Berlin.
*I've been living in Berlin **for one year**.*

- The prepositions **bei**, **von**, and **zu** can combine with the definite article **dem** to form contractions. The preposition **zu** also forms a contraction with the definite article **der**.

bei + dem = **beim**
von + dem = **vom**

zu + dem = **zum**
zu + der = **zur**

Wir kaufen oft **beim** Supermarkt ein.
*We often shop **at the** supermarket.*

Ich esse immer Eier **zum** Frühstück.
*I always have eggs **for** breakfast.*

Ressourcen

v̂Text

WB
pp. 59–60

LM
p. 98

S
vhlcentral

 **Jetzt sind Sie dran!** **Wählen Sie die passenden Präpositionen.**

1. Der beste Tisch ist (aus dem / beim) Fenster.
2. Wann fährst du (zum / mit dem) Supermarkt?
3. (Vom / Außer dem) Supermarkt gibt es hier keine Geschäfte.
4. Deine Familie kommt (mit / aus) den USA.
5. (Seit / Außer) zwei Jahren lerne ich Spanisch.
6. Ninas Freund fährt (nach der / zur) Universität.
7. Ich wohne (zu / bei) meinen Eltern.
8. Wir essen Pizza (mit / bei) Besteck.

Anwendung und Kommunikation

1 Was ist richtig? Wählen Sie die passenden Präpositionen.

BEISPIEL Wir wohnen (seit)/ um) fünf Jahren hier.

1. Daniel kommt (mit/(aus)) Hamburg.
2. Er studiert (bei/(seit)) sechs Semestern an der Uni Heidelberg.
3. Er wohnt ((mit)/ von) drei Freunden zusammen.
4. Alle drei Monate fährt er ((nach)/ zu) Hause zu seinen Eltern.
5. Seine Mutter ist immer extrem glücklich, wenn ihr Sohn (nach/(zu)) Hause ist.
6. Am Wochenende spielt er (aus/(mit)) seinem Vater Tennis.
7. ((Außer)/ Aus) seinen Eltern besucht er auch seine Großeltern.
8. Daniel hat nächste Woche Geburtstag und er bekommt (nach/(von)) seinem Opa ein neues Auto.

2 Wer ist das? Setzen Sie die fehlenden Dativpräpositionen ein.

Christoph Waltz kommt (1) ___aus___ Österreich. Seine Großmutter arbeitet als junge Frau als Schauspielerin (*actress*) (2) ___bei___ einem Theater und (3) ___von___ dieser Großmutter hat er sein Talent. Waltz ist (4) ___seit___ vielen Jahren als ein großartiger Schauspieler berühmt. Für seine Rollen in den Filmen *Inglourious Basterds* und *Django Unchained* gewinnt er zwei Oscars. Beide Filme sind (5) ___von___ Quentin Tarantino. Waltz wohnt (6) ___mit___ seiner Frau in Hollywood, London und Berlin.

3 Seit wann? Seit wann macht Ihr Partner / Ihre Partnerin die folgenden Aktivitäten? Answers will vary.

BEISPIEL heute Vorlesungen haben

S1: *Seit wann hast du heute Vorlesungen?*
S2: *Ich habe seit 10 Uhr Vorlesung. Und du?*

1. hier studieren
2. Deutsch lernen
3. Kaffee trinken
4. einen Computer haben
5. ein Handy haben
6. Auto fahren

4 Fotoalbum Sehen Sie die Fotos an und beantworten Sie die Fragen von Ihrem Partner / Ihrer Partnerin. Answers will vary.

▶ **BEISPIEL**

S1: *Woher kommt Eriks Opa?*
S2: *Er kommt aus der Schweiz.*

1. Mit wem spricht Anna?
2. Wohin reisen Lena und Jasmin?
3. Wohin geht Annika?
4. Seit wann arbeitet Felix im Restaurant?

 Practice more at **vhlcentral.com**.

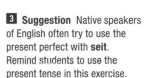

3 Suggestion Native speakers of English often try to use the present perfect with **seit**. Remind students to use the present tense in this exercise.

3 Partner Chat You can also assign activity 3 on the Supersite. Students work in pairs to record the activity online. The pair's recorded conversation will appear in your gradebook.

4 Suggestion Have students take turns asking and answering the questions. Make sure they understand that they should base their answers on the pictures, but that there is no single correct answer for each question, and they are welcome to respond imaginatively.

4 Virtual Chat You can also assign activity 4 on the Supersite. Students record individual responses that appear in your gradebook.

Wiederholung

National communication STANDARDS

1 Ankes Familie
Ankes Familie ist in einem Restaurant. Was bringt der Kellner den Familienmitgliedern (*family members*) zu trinken? Answers will vary.

1 Virtual Chat You can also assign activity 1 on the Supersite.

BEISPIEL die Schwester

S1: *Was bringt der Kellner Ankes Schwester?*
S2: *Er bringt ihrer Schwester ein Glas Milch.*

der Kaffee	das Mineralwasser	das stille Wasser
die Milch	der Orangensaft	der Tee

1. der Onkel
2. die Eltern
3. der Bruder
4. die Oma
5. die Tante
6. der Opa

2 Der Koch
Fragen Sie den Koch, was er den Personen zum Essen macht. Wechseln Sie sich ab. Sample answers are provided.

2 Partner Chat You can also assign activity 2 on the Supersite.

BEISPIEL

S1: *Herr Müller, was machen Sie dem Musiker zum Frühstück?*
S2: *Ich mache dem Musiker ein Schinkenbrot.*

der Musiker / das Frühstück

1. die Journalistin / das Abendessen
Herr Müller, was machen Sie der Journalistin zum Abendessen? Ich mache der Journalistin eine Suppe.

2. die Architektin / das Mittagessen
Herr Müller, was machen Sie der Architektin zum Mittagessen? Ich mache der Architektin Rindfleisch.

3. die Friseurin / das Mittagessen
Herr Müller, was machen Sie der Friseurin zum Mittagessen? Ich mache der Friseurin einen kleinen Salat.

4. der Geschäftsmann / das Abendessen
Herr Müller, was machen Sie dem Geschäftsmann zum Abendessen? Ich mache dem Geschäftsmann Fisch mit Garnelen.

5. die Dozentin / das Abendessen
Herr Müller, was machen Sie der Dozentin zum Abendessen? Ich mache der Dozentin Hähnchen mit Kartoffeln.

6. der Ingenieur / das Mittagessen
Herr Müller, was machen Sie dem Ingenieur zum Mittagessen? Ich mache dem Ingenieur Pasta.

3 Wie schmeckt's?
Sagen Sie einem Partner / einer Partnerin, was die Personen essen und wie sie es finden. Answers will vary.

BEISPIEL

S1: *Wie findet die Frau die Erdbeeren?*
S2: *Sie sind der Frau zu süß.*

3 Partner Chat You can also assign activity 3 on the Supersite.

fade	lecker	leicht	salzig	scharf	süß

1. der Mann
2. die Frau
3. das Mädchen

4. die Studenten
5. der Junge
6. die Kinder

4 Diskutieren und kombinieren
Sie sind Kellner / Kellnerin im Restaurant. Was sollen Sie den Gästen bringen? Fragen Sie Ihren Partner / Ihre Partnerin. Answers will vary.

BEISPIEL

S1: *Was braucht der junge Mann?*
S2: *Bring dem jungen Mann eine Serviette.*
S1: *Was braucht die alte Frau?*
S2: *Bring der alten Frau eine Gabel.*

4 Suggestion Briefly review vocabulary, to make sure students recall the names and genders of all the items pictured before beginning this activity.

5 Arbeitsblatt
Sie bekommen von Ihrem Professor / Ihrer Professorin eine Liste mit diversen Aktivitäten. Suchen Sie Kommilitonen, die diese Aktivitäten machen. Answers will vary.

BEISPIEL

S1: *Isst du täglich Eier zum Frühstück?*
S2: *Ja, ich esse täglich Eier zum Frühstück.*
OR
S1: *Wohnst du bei deinen Eltern?*
S2: *Nein, ich wohne nicht bei meinen Eltern.*

6 Wie lange? Finden Sie vier Dinge heraus, die Ihr Partner / Ihre Partnerin gern macht. Fragen Sie ihn/sie, seit wann er/sie das schon macht.

BEISPIEL

S1: *Was spielst du gern?*
S2: *Ich spiele gern Tennis.*
S1: *Seit wann spielst du Tennis?*
S2: *Seit drei Jahren.*

6 **Partner Chat** You can also assign activity 6 on the Supersite. Students work in pairs to record the activity online. The pair's recorded conversation will appear in your gradebook.

7 Interview Führen Sie ein Interview mit einem Partner / einer Partnerin. Wenn eine Person fertig ist, tauschen Sie (*exchange*) Rollen. Answers will vary.

7 **Virtual Chat** You can also assign activity 7 on the Supersite.

BEISPIEL

S1: *Bei wem wohnst du im Sommer?*
S2: *Ich wohne bei meinem Bruder.*

1. Woher kommst du?
2. Seit wann studierst du an der Uni?
3. Gehst du gern zum Supermarkt einkaufen?
4. Mit wem telefonierst du gern?
5. Bei wem wohnst du im Sommer?
6. Wohin möchtest du reisen?

8 Poetische Präpositionen Schreiben Sie mit einem Partner / einer Partnerin ein Gedicht aus fünf Sätzen. Außer der letzten Zeile (*line*) soll jede Zeile mit einer Dativ- oder Akkusativpräposition beginnen.

BEISPIEL

Mit dem Ball spiele ich.
Bei dem Metzger kaufen wir ein.
Durch die Stadt läuft die Mutter.
Außer Anton isst die Familie.
Der Hund schläft ein.

Mein Wör|ter|buch

Schreiben Sie noch fünf weitere Wörter in Ihr persönliches Wörterbuch zu den Themen **Lebensmittel** und **im Restaurant**.

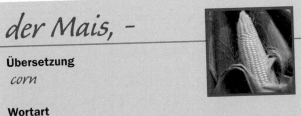

der Mais, -

Übersetzung
corn

Wortart
ein Substantiv

Gebrauch
Aus Mais kann man Popcorn machen.

Synonyme
—

Antonyme
—

 **Vocabulary Tools**

Panorama

AP* Theme: Global Challenges
Context: Geography
Interactive Map

Österreich

connections
cultures
NATIONAL
STANDARDS

Österreich in Zahlen

Suggestion Point out that Austria is slightly smaller than the state of Maine.

▶ **Fläche°:** *83.855 km² (Quadratkilometer) (60% der Fläche sind gebirgig°)*

▶ **Bevölkerung:** *8,2 Millionen Menschen*

▶ **9 Bundesländer°:** *Burgenland, Kärnten, Niederösterreich, Oberösterreich, Salzburg, Steiermark, Tirol, Vorarlberg, Wien*

▶ **Städte:** *Wien (1,7 Mio. Einwohner), Graz (264.000), Linz (190.000), Salzburg (148.000) und Innsbruck (121.000)*

▶ **Berge:** *der Großglockner (3.797 m), die Wildspitze (3.774 m)*

▶ **Flüsse°:** *die Donau, der Inn*

▶ **Währung°:** *der Euro (€) (seit 2002)*

▶ **Wichtige Industriezweige°:** *Banken, Tourismus*

▶ **Touristenattraktionen:** *Bergsport, Salzburger Festspiele°, Spanische Hofreitschule°, Wintertourismus*

Touristen können in Städten wie Wien und Salzburg viel Kultur genießen° oder in den Alpen Berg- und Wintersport betreiben. Für Firmen ist Österreich interessant, weil die Unternehmenssteuer° sehr niedrig° ist.

QUELLE: Österreichische Botschaft, Washington

Berühmte Österreicher

▶ **Maria Theresia,** *Kaiserin° (1717–1780)*

▶ **Wolfgang Amadeus Mozart,** *Komponist (1756–1791)*

▶ **Sigmund Freud,** *Neurologe (1856–1939)*

▶ **Gustav Klimt,** *Künstler° (1862–1918)*

▶ **Lise Meitner,** *Physikerin (1878–1968)*

▶ **Friedensreich Hundertwasser,** *Architekt (1928–2000)*

▶ **Elfriede Jelinek,** *Autorin (1946–)*

▶ **Falco,** *Musiker (1957–1998)*

Suggestion With books closed, tell students: **Wir sprechen sehr oft von Deutschland. Wie heißen die anderen Länder, in denen man Deutsch spricht?** After they answer, ask students what they already know about Austria: rivers, capital, size, money, famous Austrians, dialect, etc. Then have them open their books to the **Panorama** section and review the statistics. Ask comprehension questions: **Wie groß ist Österreich? Wie viele Menschen leben in Österreich?**

Fläche *surface area* gebirgig *mountainous* Bundesländer *states*
Flüsse *rivers* Währung *currency* Wichtige Industriezweige *Important industries* Festspiele *festivals* Hofreitschule *Riding School*
genießen *enjoy* Unternehmenssteuer *business tax* niedrig *low*
Kaiserin *empress* Künstler *artist* Pfefferminzbonbons *peppermint candies*
Geschmacksrichtung *flavor* jedem *every* Lakritz *licorice* Köpfe *heads*
Spendern *dispensers*

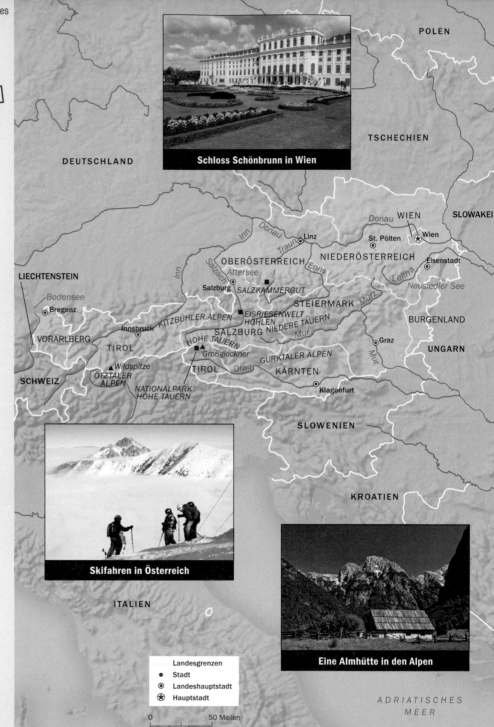

Schloss Schönbrunn in Wien

Skifahren in Österreich

Eine Almhütte in den Alpen

Unglaublich, aber wahr!

Der Österreicher Eduard Haas III. fängt 1927 an, Pfefferminzbonbons° mit dem Namen PEZ zu verkaufen. Der Name PEZ kommt von der ersten Geschmacksrichtung°, PfeffErminZ. PEZ gibt es heute mit jedem° Geschmack, sogar Chlorophyll und Lakritz°! Seit 1952 gibt es lustige Köpfe° auf den Spendern° wie Mickey Mouse und Donald Duck.
AP* Theme: Contemporary Life
Context: Youth Culture

Suggestion Tell students that Hundertwasser believed building more humane living spaces was the key to creating a healthier society.

Politik
AP* Theme: Global Challenges
Context: Political Issues

Internationale Institutionen in Wien

Politisch ist Österreich ein neutrales Land. Es ist Mitglied° in der Europäischen Union, aber nicht in der NATO. Seit 1980 ist Wien einer von vier Hauptsitzen° der Vereinten Nationen°. Die anderen Hauptsitze sind New York, Genf und Nairobi. Andere internationale Organisationen in Wien sind die IAEA (Internationale Organisation für Atomenergie) und die OPEC.

Sport
AP* Theme: Contemporary Life
Context: Entertainment, Travel, & Leisure

Olympische Spiele

Olympische Spiele und Österreich bedeuten vor allem° Olympische Winterspiele und alpiner Skisport. 1964 und 1976 treffen sich° Sportler aus aller Welt zu den Olympischen Winterspielen in Innsbruck. Erfolgreiche° österreichische Olympioniken° sind Felix Gottwald (nordischer Kombinierer°) mit drei Gold-, einer Silber- und drei Bronzemedaillen. Der Skispringer° Thomas Morgenstern und der Skifahrer Toni Sailer gewinnen jeweils° drei Goldmedaillen. In alpinen Skidisziplinen gewinnen Österreicher mehr Medaillen als jedes andere Land der Welt (34 Gold-, 39 Silber- und 41 Bronzemedaillen).

Musik
AP* Theme: Beauty & Aesthetics
Context: Performing Arts

Familie von Trapp in Amerika

Viele kennen° die Familie von Trapp aus dem Film *The Sound of Music*. Aber was passiert° mit der Familie nach der Emigration? 1939 emigriert die Familie mit nur vier Dollar in der Tasche° nach Amerika. Die von Trapps machen als „Trapp Family Singers" Karriere und kaufen 1942 eine Farm in Stowe, Vermont. Auch heute kann man die Farm als Gasthaus° besuchen — und man kann mit den von Trapps Weihnachten° feiern.

Suggestion Tell students that most Austrians aren't familiar with *The Sound of Music*, unless they are from Salzburg, where much of the movie was filmed.

Architektur
AP* Theme: Beauty & Aesthetics
Context: Architecture

Friedensreich Hundertwasser

Hundertwasser ist ein kontroverser österreichischer Architekt und Künstler. Er beginnt in den 50er Jahren in Österreich als Künstler mit revolutionären Ideen. Die Beziehung° zwischen Mensch und Natur ist ein zentrales Thema in seiner Kunst. Heute kann man seine Häuser in der ganzen Welt finden: in Magdeburg und Essen (Deutschland), in Napa Valley (USA), in Tel Aviv (Israel) und in Kawakawa (Neuseeland). Das Hundertwasserhaus in Wien ist ein Touristenmagnet und auch die Fassade der Müllverbrennungsanlage° Spittelau ist sehr berühmt.

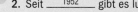 **IM INTERNET**

1. Wer sind die besten österreichischen Frauen bei Olympischen Spielen?

2. Was bedeuten dem Architekten Hundertwasser die Ideen Fensterrecht, Baummieter und Spiralhaus?

Find out more at **vhlcentral.com**.

Mitglied *member* **Hauptsitzen** *head offices* **Vereinten Nationen** *United Nations* **vor allem** *especially* **treffen sich** *meet* **Erfolgreiche** *Successful* **Olympioniken** *Olympic champions* **nordischer Kombinierer** *Nordic combined skier* **Skispringer** *ski jumper* **jeweils** *each* **kennen** *know* **passiert** *happens* **Tasche** *pocket* **Gasthaus** *inn* **Weihnachten** *Christmas* **Beziehung** *relationship* **Müllverbrennungsanlage** *waste incineration plant*

Expansion For homework, have each student print a picture of a Hundertwasser building or painting and bring it to class. Have students share their pictures in small groups, describe what they see, and tell whether or not they like his style.

 Was haben Sie gelernt? Ergänzen Sie die Sätze.

1. Der Name ___PEZ___ kommt von Pfefferminz.

2. Seit ___1952___ gibt es lustige Köpfe auf den PEZ-Spendern.

3. Offiziell ist Österreich ein ___neutrales___ Land.

4. Wien ist seit ___1980___ einer von vier Hauptsitzen der Vereinten Nationen.

5. 1939 emigriert die Familie ___von Trapp___ nach Amerika.

6. Die Familie von Trapp kauft 1942 eine Farm in ___Stowe___ in Vermont.

7. 1964 und ___1976___ sind die Olympischen Winterspiele in Innsbruck.

8. In alpinen Skidisziplinen gewinnen die Österreicher ___mehr___ Medaillen als jedes andere Land.

9. Hundertwasser ist ein kontroverser österreichischer ___Architekt___ und Künstler.

10. Hundertwassers Häuser kann man in Österreich, Deutschland, den USA, Israel und ___Neuseeland___ finden.

 Practice more at **vhlcentral.com**.

Lesen Audio: Reading

Vor dem Lesen
AP* Theme: Families & Communities
Context: Urban, Suburban, & Rural Life

Strategien

Scanning

Scanning involves glancing over a document in search of specific information. For example, you can scan a document to identify its format, to find cognates, to locate visual clues about the document's content, or to find specific facts. Scanning allows you to learn a great deal about a text without having to read it word for word.

Textart Was für ein Text ist das? Erklären Sie Ihre Antwort einem Partner / einer Partnerin.

eine E-Mail	**ein Blog**
eine Broschüre	ein Memo
eine Einkaufsliste	ein Artikel

Auf einen Blick Sehen Sie sich mit einem Partner / einer Partnerin den Text an.

A. Schreiben Sie drei Aktivitäten auf, die Sie im Text finden. Sample answers are provided.

schlafen
Inlineskates fahren
klettern

B. Welche Lehnwörter (*loan words*) und Kognate können Sie im Text finden? Diskutieren Sie Ihre Antworten. Sample answers are provided.

Sofas	Musik
Konzerthalle	Brunch
Jamsession	Inlineskates

http://www.die-ersten-monate-in-graz.com

Die ersten Monate in Graz

über mich	Hauptseite	Fotos	Kontakt

Besuch!
12. Oktober

Das Kunsthaus

Am Freitag besuchen mich meine Freunde Lukas, Jan und Paul für ein Wochenende in Graz. Super! Vier Jahre lang haben wir zusammen in Wien studiert. Jetzt sehen wir uns nur selten. Jan wohnt in Linz, Lukas arbeitet in Wien und Paul studiert immer noch. Alle können bei mir übernachten. Ich habe ein Gästezimmer° und zwei Sofas im Wohnzimmer°. Das funktioniert prima! Schlafen werden wir an diesem Wochenende ohnehin° nicht! Am Freitag geht's erstmal in die Hopfenlaube, eine tolle Konzerthalle, für eine Jamsession. Da ist die Musik immer toll und wir können über die guten alten Zeiten reden. Am Samstag geht's dann ins Café Schwalbennest frühstücken. Nach der langen Nacht ist ein guter Brunch extrem wichtig°. Das Café ist ganz in der Nähe° meiner Wohnung°. Anschließend° gehen wir bei schönem Wetter° eine Runde im Volksgarten Inlineskates fahren. Der Volksgarten ist total

Gästezimmer *guest bedroom* **Wohnzimmer** *living room* **ohnehin** *anyhow*
wichtig *important* **in der Nähe** *near to* **Wohnung** *apartment*
Anschließend *Afterwards* **bei schönem Wetter** *in nice weather*

Suche

schön und sehr zentral gelegen°. Später können wir auch noch die Treppen° zum Grazer Schlossberg hochklettern°. Vom Uhrturm kann man die ganze Stadt super sehen inklusive der wunderschönen Innenstadt. Und was machen wir bei Regen°? Dann können wir das Kunsthaus Graz besuchen. Dort gibt es immer moderne Ausstellungen°. Ich freue mich schon auf° das Wochenende und auf meine alten Freunde.

Archiv

▶ Prüfungsstress ☹
▶ Glücklich!
▶ Die Uni
▶ Es ist schon wieder° Montag...
▶ September
▶ August
▶ Juli
▶ Juni
▶ Mai
▶ April
▶ März

Der Uhrturm

zentral gelegen *centrally located* **Treppen** *stairs* **hochklettern** *to climb up* **Regen** *rain* **Ausstellungen** *exhibits* **freue mich...auf** *look forward to* **schon wieder** *once again*

Nach dem Lesen

 Das richtige Wort Ergänzen Sie die Aussagen mit den richtigen Informationen.

1. Am Freitag besuchen drei Freunde die Stadt ____Graz____ für ein Wochenende.

2. Am ____Freitag____ gehen die Freunde in die Hopfenlaube.

3. Am Samstag essen die Freunde __Frühstück/Brunch__ im Café Schwalbennest.

4. Anschließend gehen sie Inlineskates fahren im ____Volksgarten____.

5. Später können sie die ____Treppen____ zum Grazer Schlossberg hochklettern.

6. Bei Regen besuchen sie __das Kunsthaus Graz__.

 Informationen Schreiben Sie die richtigen Antworten. Schreiben Sie ganze Sätze.
Sample answers are provided.

BEISPIEL Wo wohnt Lukas?

Lukas wohnt in Wien.

1. Wer besucht Graz am Wochenende?
   Lukas, Jan und Paul besuchen Graz.

2. Warum wollen die Freunde in die Hopfenlaube gehen?
   Die Musik da ist toll.

3. Wann frühstücken die Freunde im Café Schwalbennest?
   Sie frühstücken dort am Samstag.

4. Was machen die Freunde im Volksgarten?
   Die Freunde fahren im Volksgarten Inlineskates.

5. Was kann man vom Uhrturm sehen?
   Man kann die ganze Stadt super sehen.

6. Was kann man im Kunsthaus Graz sehen?
   Im Kunsthaus Graz kann man moderne Ausstellungen sehen.

Ihre Heimatstadt Stellen Sie einem Partner / einer Partnerin Fragen: Was kann oder soll man in Ihrer Heimatstadt (*hometown*) machen?

BEISPIEL

S1: *Was muss man in deiner Heimatstadt sehen?*
S2: *In meiner Heimatstadt muss man das Kunstmuseum sehen.*
S1: *Wo kann man gut essen?*

Suggestion Give students a minute to prepare their lists of sights, and provide them with vocabulary as needed.

Partner Chat You can also assign this activity on the Supersite. Students work in pairs to record the activity online. The pair's recorded conversation will appear in your gradebook.

Hören

NATIONAL communication cultures STANDARDS

Strategien

Listening for the gist

When you listen to a conversation in German, try to figure out the main ideas that are being expressed, rather than trying to catch every word. Listening for the gist can help you follow what someone is saying, even if you can't hear or understand some of the words.

🔊 To help you practice this strategy, you will listen to three sentences. Jot down a brief summary of what you hear.

Vorbereitung

Schauen Sie sich das Foto an. Wer ist auf dem Foto? Wo sind sie? Was machen sie?

 ## Zuhören

Hören Sie sich den Podcast mit Andrea und der Reporterin an. Lesen Sie dann die Liste. Hören Sie sich den Podcast ein zweites Mal an und markieren Sie die Zutaten, die Sie hören.

Pilze	Nudeln
Kartoffel	Zwiebeln
Butter	Salz
Milch	Pfirsiche
Tomaten	Paprika
Schinken	Pfeffer
Knoblauch	Eier

Verständnis

Eine Zusammenfassung Ergänzen Sie die Zusammenfassung (*summary*) von dem Podcast mit Wörtern von der Liste.

den Schinken	die Nudeln	eine Reporterin
findet	frische Pilze	salzig
lecker	einen Podcast	schmeckt
Pfeffer	probieren	Zwiebeln

1. Wir hören ___einen Podcast___ mit der Köchin Andrèa.
2. In der Küche sind Andrea und ___eine Reporterin___.
3. Im Moment kann man auf dem Markt ___frische Pilze___ kaufen.
4. Heute kocht Andrea Nudeln mit Pfifferlingen (*chanterelles*). Sie sind sehr ___lecker___.
5. Die Pfifferlinge passen gut zum Schinken – er ist ziemlich ___salzig___.
6. Man braucht auch Vollmilch, Butter und ___Zwiebeln___.
7. Erst kocht Andrea ___die Nudeln___.
8. Dann brät sie ___den Schinken___ mit Butter.
9. Am Ende kommen noch Salz und ___Pfeffer___ dazu.
10. Die Reporterin ___findet___ das Gericht lecker!

Und Sie? Bereiten Sie mit einem Partner / einer Partnerin ein Rezept für eine Pizza vor. Welche Zutaten sollen auf die Pizza?

BEISPIEL

S1: *Was soll alles auf die Pizza?*
S2: *Pilze, Zwiebeln, Tomaten…*

Schreiben

Strategien

Adding details

How can you make your writing more informative or more interesting? You can add details by answering the "W" questions: Who? What? When? Where? Why? The answers to these questions will provide useful information that can be incorporated into your writing. Here are some useful question words that you have already learned.

Wer?	Wo?
Was?	Warum?
Wann?	Wie?

Compare these two statements.

„Ich muss einkaufen gehen."

„Nach der Schule muss ich Eier kaufen. Mit den Eiern kann ich eine leckere Omelette kochen."

While both statements give the same basic information (the writer needs to go shopping), the details provided in the second statement are much more informative.

Suggestion Remind students that adverbs, like the ones they learned in **4A.2**, can make their speech and writing more informative and expressive.

Thema

Grüße nach Salzburg

Sie entschließen sich (*decide*), ein Jahr in Österreich zu verbringen und bei einer Familie zu leben. Schreiben Sie eine Karte an Ihre Gastfamilie (*host family*). Sagen Sie der Familie, was Sie gern sehen wollen und was Sie machen wollen. Schreiben Sie fünf Sätze. Nennen Sie (*Give*) Details. Beantworten Sie dabei Fragen mit **wer?**, **was?**, **wo?**, **wie?** und **wann?**

Liebe Gastfamilie, bald komme ich nach Salzburg. Dann können wir zusammen den Uhrturm besuchen...

Expansion Before students start writing, have them come up with an ending to the sample sentence that answers each of the questions **was?**, **wo?**, **wer?**, **wie?**, and **wann?** Write the sentence on the board, underline the answers to each question, and label them with the appropriate interrogative term.

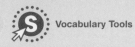 Vocabulary Tools

Lektion 4A

Obst und Gemüse

die Ananas, - *pineapple*
der Apfel, ⸚ *apple*
die Artischocke, -n *artichoke*
die Aubergine, -n *eggplant*
die Banane, -n *banana*
die Birne, -n *pear*
die grüne Bohne (*pl.* die grünen
   Bohnen) *green bean*
die Erdbeere, -n *strawberry*
die Himbeere, -n *raspberry*
die Karotte, -n *carrot*
die Kartoffel, -n *potato*
der Knoblauch *garlic*
die Melone, -n *melon*
die Orange, -n *orange*
die grüne Paprika (*pl.* die grünen
   Paprika) *green pepper*
die rote Paprika (*pl.* die roten
   Paprika) *red pepper*
der Pfirsich, -e *peach*
der Pilz, -e *mushroom*
der Salat, -e *lettuce; salad*
die Tomate, -n *tomato*
die Traube, -n *grape*
die Zwiebel, -n *onion*

Geschäfte

die Bäckerei, -en *bakery*
die Eisdiele, -n *ice cream shop*
das Feinkostgeschäft, -e *delicatessen*
das Fischgeschäft, -e *fish store*
die Konditorei, -en *pastry shop*
das Lebensmittelgeschäft, -e
   grocery store
der Markt, ⸚e *market*
die Metzgerei, -en *butcher shop*
der Supermarkt, ⸚e *supermarket*
einkaufen gehen *to go shopping*
verkaufen *to sell*

Essen

das Brot, -e *bread*
das Brötchen, - *roll*
die Butter *butter*
das Ei, -er *egg*
der Joghurt, -s *yogurt*
der Käse, - *cheese*
der Kuchen, - *cake; pie*
die Marmelade, -n *jam*
das Öl, -e *oil*
das Olivenöl, -e *olive oil*
die Pasta *pasta*
der Reis *rice*
das Rezept, -e *recipe*
die Zutat, -en *ingredient*

Fleisch und Fisch

die Garnele, -n *shrimp*
das Hähnchen, - *chicken*
die Meeresfrüchte (*pl.*) *seafood*
das Rindfleisch *beef*
der Schinken, - *ham*
das Schweinefleisch *pork*
der Thunfisch *tuna*
das Würstchen, - *sausage*

Ausdrücke

mögen *to like*

im Restaurant

der Pfeffer *pepper*
bestellen *to order*

- - - - - - - - - - - - - - - - - - - -

Adverbs *See p. 150.*
Separable and inseparable prefix
   verbs *See p. 156.*

Lektion 4B

im Restaurant

die Beilage, -n *side dish*
das Besteck *silverware*
der Esslöffel, - *soup spoon*
die Flasche, -n *bottle*
die Gabel, -n *fork*
der erste/zweite Gang, ⸚ *first/second
   course*
das Glas, ⸚er *glass*
das Gericht, -e *dish*
die Hauptspeise, -n *main course*
der Kellner, - / die Kellnerin,
   -nen *waiter / waitress*
der Koch, ⸚e / die Köchin, -nen *cook*
das Messer, - *knife*
der Nachtisch, -e *dessert*
die Rechnung, -en *check*
das Salz *salt*
die Serviette, -n *napkin*
die Speisekarte, -n *menu*
die Suppe, -n *soup*
die Tasse, -n *cup*
der Teelöffel, - *teaspoon*
der Teller, - *plate*
die Tischdecke, -n *tablecloth*
das Trinkgeld *tip*
die Vorspeise, -n *appetizer*
schmecken *to taste*

Mahlzeiten

das Abendessen *dinner*
das Frühstück *breakfast*
das Mittagessen *lunch*
der Snack, -s *snack*

Getränke

das Bier *beer*
der Kaffee *coffee*
die Milch *milk*
das Mineralwasser *sparkling water*
der Saft, ⸚e *juice*
der Tee *tea*
das stille Wasser *still water*
der Wein *wine*

Essen beschreiben

der Geschmack, ⸚e *flavor; taste*
fade *bland*
lecker *delicious*
leicht *light*
salzig *salty*
scharf *spicy*
schwer *rich, heavy*
süß *sweet*

Ausdrücke

Ich hätte gern(e)... / Ich möchte
   I would like...
auf Diät sein *to be on a diet*
hausgemacht *homemade*

- - - - - - - - - - - - - - - - - - - -

Dative articles and possessive
   adjectives *See pp. 170–171.*
Dative prepositions *See p. 174.*

Ressourcen
v̂ Text | vhlcentral

die Welt

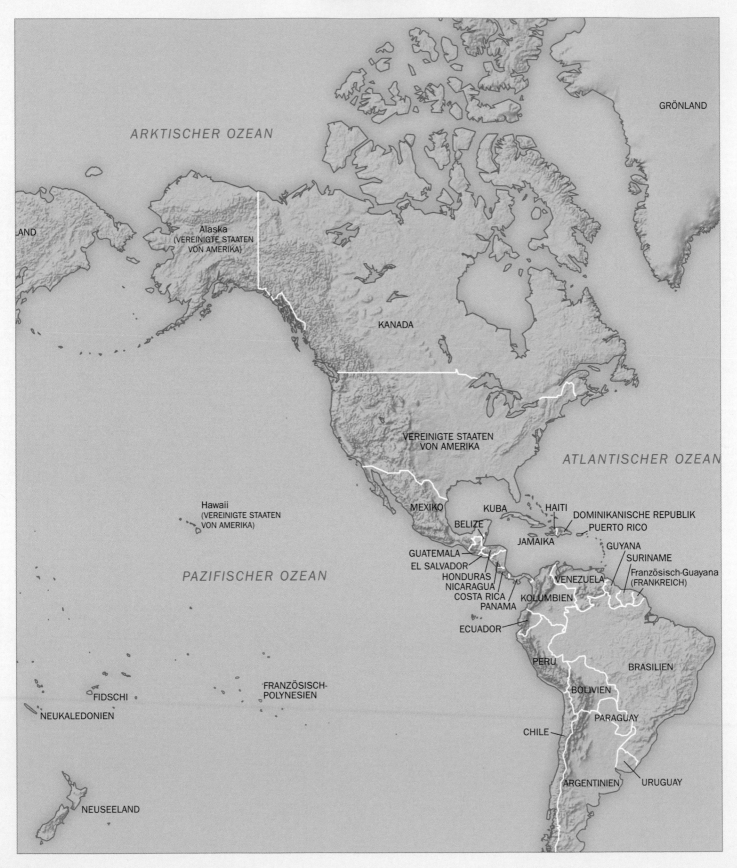

GRÖNLAND

ARKTISCHER OZEAN

...LAND

Alaska
(VEREINIGTE STAATEN
VON AMERIKA)

KANADA

VEREINIGTE STAATEN
VON AMERIKA

ATLANTISCHER OZEAN

Hawaii
(VEREINIGTE STAATEN
VON AMERIKA)

MEXIKO

KUBA

HAITI

DOMINIKANISCHE REPUBLIK
PUERTO RICO

BELIZE

JAMAIKA

GUATEMALA
EL SALVADOR
HONDURAS
NICARAGUA
COSTA RICA
PANAMA

GUYANA
SURINAME
Französisch-Guayana
(FRANKREICH)

VENEZUELA

KOLUMBIEN

PAZIFISCHER OZEAN

ECUADOR

PERU

BRASILIEN

FRANZÖSISCH-
POLYNESIEN

FIDSCHI

BOLIVIEN

NEUKALEDONIEN

PARAGUAY

CHILE

ARGENTINIEN

URUGUAY

NEUSEELAND

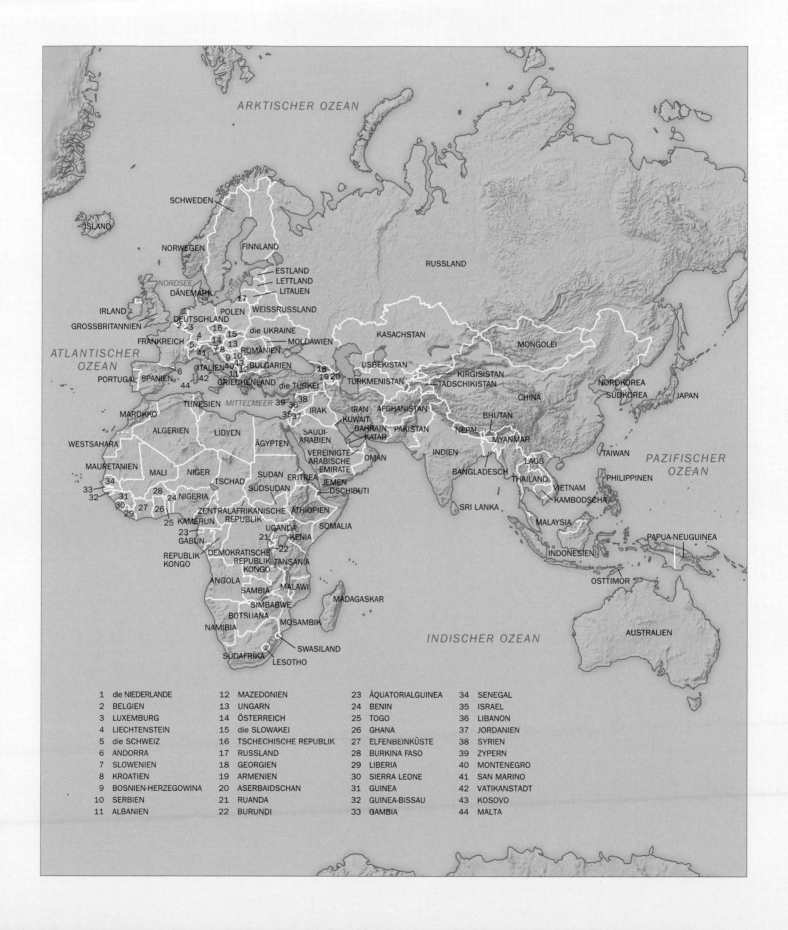

ARKTISCHER OZEAN

SCHWEDEN

ISLAND

NORWEGEN   FINNLAND

RUSSLAND

NORDSEE   ESTLAND
DÄNEMARK   LETTLAND
                    LITAUEN

IRLAND   1   POLEN   WEISSRUSSLAND   KASACHSTAN   MONGOLEI

GROSSBRITANNIEN   DEUTSCHLAND
                                    die UKRAINE
FRANKREICH   MOLDAWIEN
                    RUMÄNIEN
ATLANTISCHER
OZEAN   USBEKISTAN   KIRGISISTAN
                                        TADSCHIKISTAN   NORDKOREA
BULGARIEN   TURKMENISTAN   CHINA   SÜDKOREA   JAPAN
PORTUGAL   SPANIEN   GRIECHENLAND   die TÜRKEI
                                ITALIEN

TUNESIEN   MITTELMEER   IRAK   IRAN   AFGHANISTAN
MAROKKO   BHUTAN
                        KUWAIT   PAKISTAN   NEPAL
WESTSAHARA   ALGERIEN   LIBYEN   ÄGYPTEN   SAUDI-   BAHRAIN
                                                ARABIEN   KATAR   MYANMAR
                                                                    TAIWAN   PAZIFISCHER
MAURETANIEN   MALI   NIGER   VEREINIGTE   INDIEN   OZEAN
                                TSCHAD   SUDAN   ARABISCHE   OMAN   BANGLADESCH   LAOS
                                                EMIRATE   JEMEN   THAILAND   PHILIPPINEN
                        NIGERIA   SÜDSUDAN   ERITREA   DSCHIBUTI   SRI LANKA   VIETNAM
                                                                                KAMBODSCHA
            ZENTRALAFRIKANISCHE   ÄTHIOPIEN
            REPUBLIK   KAMERUN   UGANDA   SOMALIA   MALAYSIA   PAPUA-NEUGUINEA
                        GABUN   KENIA
                                DEMOKRATISCHE   INDONESIEN
            REPUBLIK   REPUBLIK   TANSANIA   OSTTIMOR
            KONGO   KONGO
                        ANGOLA   MALAWI
                                SAMBIA   INDISCHER OZEAN   AUSTRALIEN
                                SIMBABWE
                        BOTSUANA   MOSAMBIK
            NAMIBIA
                                    MADAGASKAR
                                            SWASILAND
            SÜDAFRIKA   LESOTHO

1 die NIEDERLANDE	12 MAZEDONIEN	23 ÄQUATORIALGUINEA	34 SENEGAL
2 BELGIEN	13 UNGARN	24 BENIN	35 ISRAEL
3 LUXEMBURG	14 ÖSTERREICH	25 TOGO	36 LIBANON
4 LIECHTENSTEIN	15 die SLOWAKEI	26 GHANA	37 JORDANIEN
5 die SCHWEIZ	16 TSCHECHISCHE REPUBLIK	27 ELFENBEINKÜSTE	38 SYRIEN
6 ANDORRA	17 RUSSLAND	28 BURKINA FASO	39 ZYPERN
7 SLOWENIEN	18 GEORGIEN	29 LIBERIA	40 MONTENEGRO
8 KROATIEN	19 ARMENIEN	30 SIERRA LEONE	41 SAN MARINO
9 BOSNIEN-HERZEGOWINA	20 ASERBAIDSCHAN	31 GUINEA	42 VATIKANSTADT
10 SERBIEN	21 RUANDA	32 GUINEA-BISSAU	43 KOSOVO
11 ALBANIEN	22 BURUNDI	33 GAMBIA	44 MALTA

Europa

Länder, in denen Deutsch
eine Amtssprache ist

BARENTSSEE

ISLAND
Reykjavik

EUROPÄISCHES
NORDMEER

SCHWEDEN   FINNLAND

NORWEGEN
Helsinki

RUSSLAND

Oslo   Stockholm

Tallinn
ESTLAND

NORDSEE   DÄNEMARK   Riga   LETTLAND   Moskau

OSTSEE   LITAUEN
Kopenhagen   Vilnius

ÖSTERREICH
LIECHTENSTEIN
Vaduz
die SCHWEIZ

RUSSLAND
Minsk
WEISSRUSSLAND

Dublin   die
NIEDERLANDE   Berlin   Warschau   Kiew

IRLAND   GROSS-
BRITANNIEN   Amsterdam   POLEN   die UKRAINE

London   DEUTSCHLAND
Brüssel
LUXEMBURG   BELGIEN   Prag   die SLOWAKEI   MOLDAWIEN
Paris   Luxemburg   TSCHECHISCHE   Kischinau
REPUBLIK   Bratislava

LIECHTENSTEIN   Wien
ATLANTISCHER   ÖSTERREICH   Budapest   SCHWARZES
OZEAN   FRANKREICH   Bern   Vaduz   SLOWENIEN   UNGARN   RUMÄNIEN   MEER
die SCHWEIZ   Ljubljana   Zagreb   Bukarest
ITALIEN   KROATIEN   Belgrad
Monaco   BOSNIEN-   SERBIEN   KOSOVO
HERZEGOWINA   Pristina   BULGARIEN   Ankara
Andorra la Vella   SAN   Sarajevo   MONTENEGRO   Sofia
MARINO   Podgorica   Skopje   die TÜRKEI
PORTUGAL   MONACO   Rom   Tirana   MAZEDONIEN
ANDORRA   Korsika   VATIKANSTADT   ALBANIEN
Madrid   GRIECHENLAND
Lissabon   SPANIEN   Nicosia
Sardinien   Athen
Balearische   Sizilien   ZYPERN
Inseln   Kreta

Algier   MITTELMEER
Tunis   Valletta   MALTA
Rabat

MAROKKO   Tripolis   Kairo

ALGERIEN   TUNESIEN   LIBYEN   ÄGYPTEN

0   500 Meilen
0   500 Kilometer

Deutschland

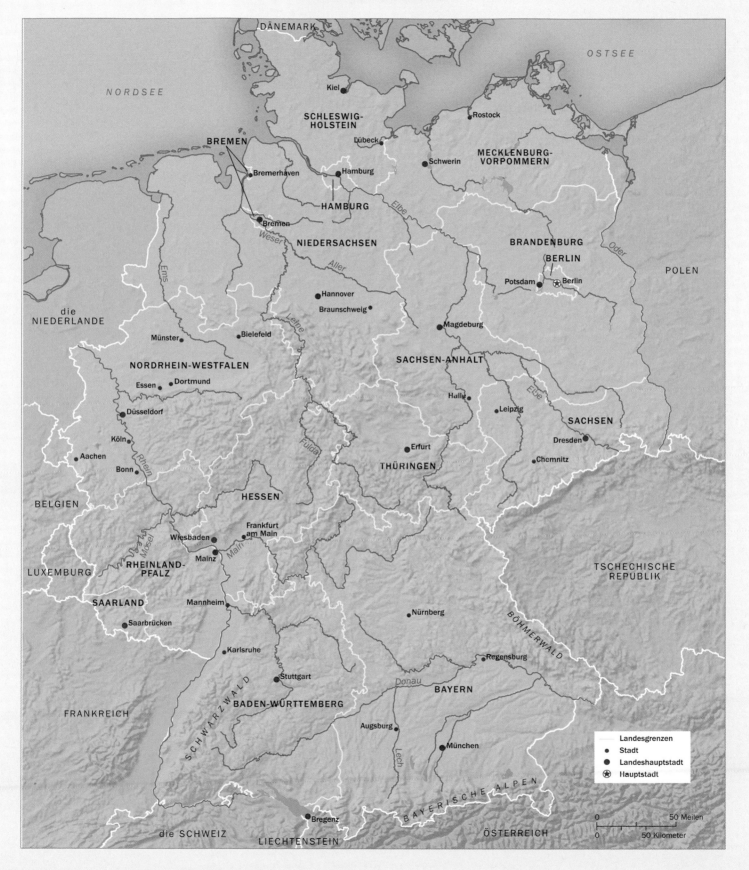

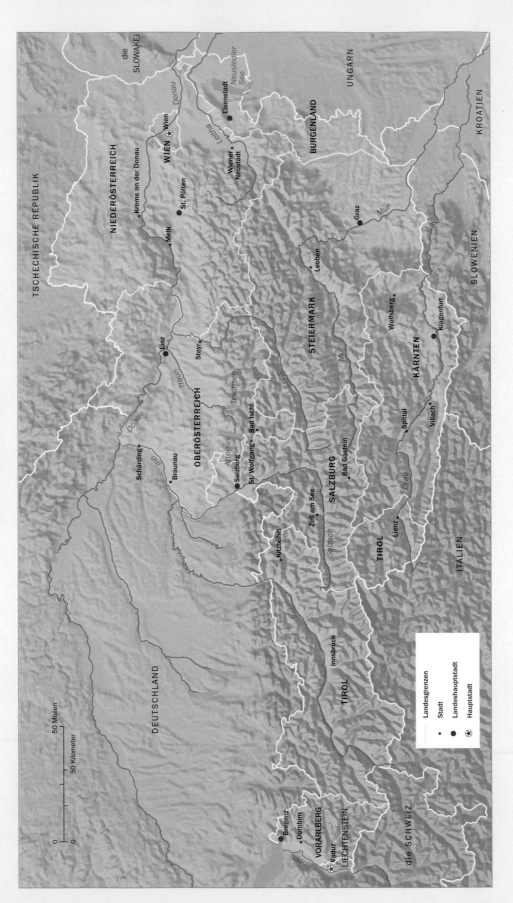

Österreich

Liechtenstein

die Schweiz

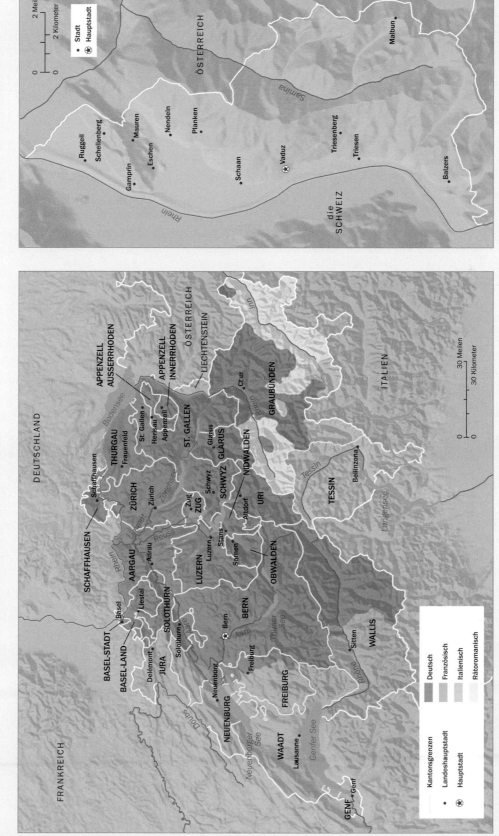

Declension of articles

definite articles				
	masculine	**feminine**	**neuter**	**plural**
nominative	der	die	das	die
accusative	den	die	das	die
dative	dem	der	dem	den
genitive	des	der	des	der

der-words				
	masculine	**feminine**	**neuter**	**plural**
nominative	dieser	diese	dieses	diese
accusative	diesen	diese	dieses	diese
dative	diesem	dieser	diesem	diesen
genitive	dieses	dieser	dieses	dieser

indefinite articles				
	masculine	**feminine**	**neuter**	**plural**
nominative	ein	eine	ein	-
accusative	einen	eine	ein	-
dative	einem	einer	einem	-
genitive	eines	einer	eines	-

ein-words				
	masculine	**feminine**	**neuter**	**plural**
nominative	mein	meine	mein	meine
accusative	meinen	meine	mein	meine
dative	meinem	meiner	meinem	meinen
genitive	meines	meiner	meines	meiner

Declension of nouns and adjectives

nouns and adjectives with *der*-words				
	masculine	**feminine**	**neuter**	**plural**
nominative	der gute Rat	die gute Landschaft	das gute Brot	die guten Freunde
accusative	den guten Rat	die gute Landschaft	das gute Brot	die guten Freunde
dative	dem guten Rat	der guten Landschaft	dem guten Brot	den guten Freunden
genitive	des guten Rates	der guten Landschaft	des guten Brotes	der guten Freunde

nouns and adjectives with *ein*-words				
	masculine	**feminine**	**neuter**	**plural**
nominative	ein guter Rat	eine gute Landschaft	ein gutes Brot	meine guten Freunde
accusative	einen guten Rat	eine gute Landschaft	ein gutes Brot	meine guten Freunde
dative	einem guten Rat	einer guten Landschaft	einem guten Brot	meinen guten Freunden
genitive	eines guten Rates	einer guten Landschaft	eines guten Brotes	meiner guten Freunde

unpreceded adjectives				
	masculine	**feminine**	**neuter**	**plural**
nominative	guter Rat	gute Landschaft	gutes Brot	gute Freunde
accusative	guten Rat	gute Landschaft	gutes Brot	gute Freunde
dative	gutem Rat	guter Landschaft	gutem Brot	guten Freunden
genitive	guten Rates	guter Landschaft	guten Brotes	guter Freunde

Declension of pronouns

personal pronouns										
nominative	ich	du	Sie	er	sie	es	wir	ihr	Sie	sie
accusative	mich	dich	Sie	ihn	sie	es	uns	euch	Sie	sie
accusative reflexive	mich	dich	sich	sich	sich	sich	uns	euch	sich	sich
dative	mir	dir	Ihnen	ihm	ihr	ihm	uns	euch	Ihnen	ihnen
dative reflexive	mir	dir	sich	sich	sich	sich	uns	euch	sich	sich

Glossary of Grammatical Terms

ADJECTIVE Words that describe people, places, or things. An attributive adjective comes before the noun it modifies and takes an ending that matches the gender and case of the noun. A predicate adjective comes after the verb **sein**, **werden**, or **bleiben** and describes the noun that is the subject of the sentence. Predicate adjectives take no additional endings.

Thomas hat eine sehr **gute** Stelle gefunden.
*Thomas found a really **good** job.*

Hast du mein **kleines** Adressbuch gesehen?
*Have you seen my **little** address book?*

Mein Bruder ist **klein**.
*My brother is **short**.*

Deine Schwester wird **groß**.
*Your sister is getting **tall**.*

Possessive adjectives Words that are placed before a noun to indicate ownership or belonging. Each personal pronoun has a corresponding possessive adjective. Possessive adjectives take the same endings as the indefinite article **ein**.

Meine Schwester ist hier.
***My** sister is here.*

Wo ist **dein** Vater?
*Where is **your** father?*

ADVERB Words or phrases that modify a verb, an adjective, or another adverb. Adverbs and adverbial phrases describe *when*, *how*, or *where* an action takes place.

Der Kuchen ist **fast** fertig.
*The cake is **almost** ready.*

Du isst **viel zu** schnell.
*You eat **much too** quickly.*

ARTICLE A word that precedes a noun and indicates its gender, number, and case.

Definite article Equivalent to *the* in English. Its form indicates the gender and case of the noun, and whether it is singular or plural.

der Tisch (*m. s.*)
the table
die Tische (*m. pl.*)
the tables
die Tür (*f. s.*)
the door

die Türen (*f. pl.*)
the doors
das Fenster (*n. s.*)
the window
die Fenster (*n. pl.*)
the windows

Indefinite article Corresponds to *a* or *an* in English. It precedes the noun and matches its gender and case. There is no plural indefinite article in German.

ein Tisch (*m.*)
a table
eine Tür (*f.*)
a door

ein Fenster (*n.*)
a window

CASE There are four cases in German. The case indicates the function of each noun in a sentence. The case of a noun determines the form of the definite or indefinite article that precedes the noun, the form of any adjectives that modify the noun, and the form of the pronoun that can replace the noun.

Nominativ (*nominative*): **Der Professor** ist alt.
The professor is old.

Akkusativ (*accusative*): Ich verstehe **den Professor**.
*I understand **the professor**.*

Dativ (*dative*): Der Assistent zeigt **dem Professor** den neuen Computer.
*The assistant is showing **the professor** the new computer.*

Genitiv (*genitive*): Das ist der Assistent **des Professors**.
*This is **the professor's** assistant.*

The nominative case The grammatical subject of a sentence is always in the nominative case. The nominative case is also used for nouns that follow a form of **sein**, **werden**, or **bleiben**. In German dictionaries, nouns, pronouns, and numbers are always listed in their nominative form.

Das ist **eine gute Idee**.
*That's **a good idea**.*

Die **Kinder** schlafen.
***The kids** are sleeping.*

The accusative case A noun that functions as a direct object is in the accusative case.

Der Lehrer hat **den Stift**.
*The teacher has **the pen**.*

Ich kaufe **einen Tisch**.
*I'm going to buy **a table**.*

Sie öffnet **die Tür**.
*She's opening **the door**.*

Ich habe **ein Problem**.
*I have **a problem**.*

The dative case An object in the dative case indicates to whom or for whom an action is performed.

Ich bringe **dem Lehrer** einen Apfel.
*I'm bringing **the teacher** an apple.*

Zeig **der Professorin** deine Arbeit.
*Show your work **to the professor**.*

The genitive case A noun in the genitive case modifies another noun. The genitive case indicates ownership or a close relationship between the genitive noun and the noun it modifies, which may be a subject or an object.

Thorsten hat die Rede **des Bundespräsidenten** heruntergeladen.
*Thorsten downloaded **the president's** speech.*

Das Mikrofon **der Professorin** funktioniert nicht.
***The professor's** microphone doesn't work.*

CLAUSE A group of words that contains both a conjugated verb and a subject, either expressed or implied.

Main (or independent) clause A clause that can stand alone as a complete sentence.

Ich bezahle immer bar, weil ich keine Kreditkarte habe.
I always pay cash, because I don't have a credit card.

Subordinate clause A subordinate clause explains how, when, why, or under what circumstances the action in the main clause occurs. The conjugated verb of a subordinate clause is placed at the end of that clause.

Ich lese die Zeitung, **wenn** ich Zeit **habe**.
*I read the newspaper **when** I **have** the time.*

COMPARATIVE The form of an adjective or adverb that compares two or more people or things.

Meine Geschwister sind alle **älter** als ich.
*My siblings are all **older** than I am.*

Die Fahrt dauert mit dem Auto **länger** als mit dem Zug.
*The trip takes **longer** by car than by train.*

CONJUNCTION A word used to connect words, clauses, or phrases.

Coordinating conjunctions Words that combine two related sentences, words, or phrases into a single sentence. There are five coordinating conjunctions in German: **aber** (*but*), **denn** (*because; since*), **oder** (*or*), **sondern** (*but, rather*), und (*and*). All other conjunctions are subordinating.

Ich möchte eine große Küche, **denn** ich koche gern.
*I want a big kitchen, **because** I like to cook.*

Lola braucht einen Schrank **oder** eine Kommode.
*Lola needs a closet **or** a dresser.*

Subordinating conjunctions Words used to combine a subordinate clause with a main clause.

Ich lese die Zeitung, **wenn** ich Zeit **habe**.
*I read the newspaper **when** I **have** the time.*

DEMONSTRATIVE Pronouns or adjectives that refer to something or someone that has already been mentioned, or that point out a specific person or thing.

Ist Greta online? –Ja, **die** schreibt eine E-Mail.
*Is Greta online? –Yes, **she's** writing an e-mail.*

Gefällt dir dieser Sessel? –Ja, **der** ist sehr bequem!
*Do you like that chair? –Yes, **it's** very comfortable!*

DER-WORDS Words that take the same endings as the forms of the definite article **der**. These include the demonstrative pronouns **dieser** (*this; that*), **jeder** (*each, every*), **jener** (*that*), **mancher** (*some*), and **solcher** (*such*), and the question word **welcher** (*which*).

Welcher Laptop gefällt dir am besten?
Which laptop do you like best?

Ich finde **diesen** Laptop am schönsten.
*I think **this** laptop is the nicest.*

DIRECT OBJECT A noun or pronoun that directly receives the action of the verb. Direct objects are in the accusative.

Kennst du **diesen Mann**?   Ich mache **eine Torte**.
*Do you know **that man**?*   *I'm making **a cake**.*

EIN-WORDS Words that take the same endings as the forms of the indefinite article **ein**. These include the negation **kein** and all of the possessive adjectives.

Hast du **einen** Hund?   Ich habe **keinen** Fußball.
*Do you have **a** dog?*   *I don't have **a** soccer ball.*

GENDER The grammatical categorization of nouns, pronouns, and adjectives as masculine, feminine, or neuter.

Masculine
articles: **der, ein**
pronouns: **er, der**
adjectives: **guter, schöner**

Feminine
articles: **die, eine**
pronouns: **sie, die**
adjectives: **gute, schöne**

Neuter
articles: **das, ein**
pronouns: **es, das**
adjectives: **gutes, schönes**

HELPING VERB *See VERB, Auxiliary verb.*

IMPERATIVE Imperatives are verb forms used to express commands, requests, suggestions, directions, or instructions.

Mach deine Hausaufgaben!   **Backen wir** einen Kuchen!
Do your homework!   *Let's bake a cake!*

INDIRECT OBJECT A noun or pronoun that receives the action of the verb indirectly. The indirect object is often a person to whom or for whom the action of the sentence is performed. Indirect objects are in the dative case.

Manfred hat **seinem Bruder** ein Buch geschenkt.
*Manfred gave **his brother** a book.*

INFINITIVE The basic, unconjugated form of a verb. Most German infinitives end in **-en**. A few end in **-ern** or **-eln**.

sehen, essen, lesen, wandern, sammeln
to see, to eat, to read, to hike, to collect

NOUN A word that refers to one or more people, animals, places, things, or ideas. Nouns in German may be masculine, feminine, or neuter, and are either singular or plural.

der **Junge**, die **Katze**, das **Café**
the boy, the cat, the café

Compound noun Two or more simple nouns can be combined to form a compound noun. The gender of a compound noun matches the gender of the last noun in the compound.

die Nacht + das Hemd = **das Nachthemd**
night + shirt = nightshirt

NUMBER A grammatical term that refers to the quantity of a noun. Nouns in German are either singular or plural. The plural form of a noun may have an added umlaut and/or an added ending. Adjectives, articles, and verbs also have different endings, depending on whether they are singular or plural.

Singular:
der **Mann**, die **Frau**, das **Kind**
the man, the woman, the child

Plural:
die **Männer**, die **Frauen**, die **Kinder**
the men, the women, the children

NUMBERS Words that represent quantities.

Cardinal numbers Numbers that indicate specific quantities. Cardinal numbers typically modify nouns, but do not add gender or case endings.

zwei Männer, **fünfzehn** Frauen, **sechzig** Kinder
two men, fifteen women, sixty children

Ordinal numbers Words that indicate the order of a noun in a series. Ordinal numbers add the same gender and case endings as adjectives.

der **erste** Mann, die **zweite** Frau, das **dritte** Kind
the first man, the second woman, the third child

PARTICIPLE A participle is formed from a verb but may be used as an adjective or adverb. Present participles are used primarily in written German. Past participles are used in compound tenses, including the **Perfekt** and the **Plusquamperfekt**.

Der **aufgehende** Mond war sehr schön.
The rising moon was beautiful.

Habt ihr schon **gegessen**?
Have you already eaten?

PREPOSITION A preposition links a noun or pronoun to other words in a sentence. Combined with a noun or pronoun, it forms a prepositional phrase, which can be used like an adverb to answer the question *when, how,* or *where.* In German, certain prepositions are always followed by a noun in the accusative case, while others are always followed by a noun in the dative case. A small number of prepositions are used with the genitive case.

ohne das Buch   **mit** dem Auto
without the book   *by car*

trotz des Regens
in spite of the rain

Two-way prepositions can be followed by either the dative or the accusative, depending on the situation. They are followed by the accusative when used with a verb that indicates movement toward a destination. With all other verbs, they are followed by the dative.

Stell deine Schuhe nicht **auf den Tisch**!
Don't put your shoes on the table!

Dein Schal liegt **auf dem Tisch**.
Your scarf is lying on the table.

PRONOUN A word that takes the place of a noun.

Subject pronouns Words used to replace a noun in the nominative case.

Maria ist nett.   **Der Junge** ist groß.
Maria is nice.   *The boy is tall.*

Sie ist nett.   **Er** ist groß.
She is nice.   *He is tall.*

Accusative pronouns Words used to replace a noun that functions as the direct object.

Wer hat **die Torte** gebacken?   Ich habe **sie** gebacken.
Who baked the cake?   *I baked it.*

Dative pronouns Words used to replace a noun that functions as the indirect object.

Musst du **deiner Oma** eine E-Mail schicken?
Do you need to send an e-mail to your grandma?

Nein, ich habe **ihr** schon geschrieben.
No, I already wrote to her.

Indefinite pronouns Words that refer to an unknown or nonspecific person or thing.

Jemand hat seinen Personalausweis vergessen.
Someone forgot his I.D. card.

Herr Klein will mit **niemandem** sprechen.
Mr. Klein doesn't want to speak with anyone.

Reflexive pronouns The pronouns used with reflexive verbs. When the subject of a reflexive verb is also its direct object, it takes an accusative reflexive pronoun. When the subject of a reflexive verb is not its direct object, it takes a dative reflexive pronoun.

Ich wasche **mich**.	Ich wasche **mir** das Gesicht.
I'm washing (myself).	*I'm washing my face.*

SUBJUNCTIVE A verb form (**der Konjunktiv II**) used to talk about hypothetical, unlikely or impossible conditions, to express wishes, and to make polite requests. German also has an additional subjunctive tense, der **Konjunktiv I**, used to report what someone else has said without indicating whether the information is true or false.

Ich **hätte** gern viel Geld.
I'd like to have a lot of money.

Wenn er sportlicher **wäre**, **würde** er häufiger trainieren.
If he were more athletic, he would exercise more.

SUPERLATIVE The form of an adjective or adverb used to indicate that a person or thing has more of a particular quality than anyone or anything else.

Welches ist **das größte** Tier der Welt?
What's the biggest animal in the world?

Wie komme ich **am besten** zur Tankstelle?
What's the best way to get to the gas station?

TENSE A set of verb forms that indicates if an action or state occurs in the past, present, or future.

Compound tense A tense made up of an auxiliary verb and a participle or infinitive.

Wir **haben** ihren Geburtstag **gefeiert**.
We celebrated her birthday.

VERB A word that expresses actions or states of being. German verbs are classified as *weak, mixed,* or *strong,* based on the way their past participles are formed.

weak: Ich **habe** eine Torte **gemacht**.	strong: Wir **haben** Kekse **gegessen**.
I made a cake.	*We ate cookies.*

mixed: Er **hat** eine CD **gebrannt**.
He burned a CD.

Auxiliary verb A conjugated verb used with the participle or infinitive of another verb. The auxiliary verbs **haben** and **sein** are used with past participles to form compound tenses including the **Perfekt** and **Plusquamperfekt**. **Werden** is used with an infinitive to form the future tense, and with a past participle to form a passive construction. Modals are also frequently used as auxiliary verbs.

Habt ihr den Tisch **gedeckt**?
Did you set the table?

Jasmin **war** noch nie nach Zürich **gefahren**.
Jasmin had never been to Zurich.

Wir **werden** uns in einer Woche wieder **treffen**.
We'll meet again in one week.

Es **wird** hier nur Deutsch **gesprochen**.
Only German is spoken here.

Modal verbs Verbs that modify the meaning of another verb. Modals express an attitude toward an action, such as permission, obligation, ability, desire, or necessity.

Ich **muss** Französisch **lernen**.	Ich **will** Französisch **lernen**.
I have to study French.	*I want to learn French.*

Principal parts German verbs are usually listed in dictionaries by their *principal parts* (**Stammformen**): the infinitive, the third-person singular present tense form (if the verb is irregular in the present), the third-person singular **Präteritum** form, and the past participle. Knowing the principal parts of a verb allows you to produce all of its conjugations in any tense.

geben (gibt)	gab	gegeben
to give (gives)	*gave*	*given*

Reflexive verbs Verbs that indicate an action you do to yourself or for yourself. The subject of a reflexive verb is also its object.

Ich **fühle mich** nicht **wohl**.	Wir **haben uns entspannt**.
I don't feel well.	*We've been relaxing.*

Reciprocal reflexive verbs Verbs that express an action done by two or more people or things to or for one another.

Wir rufen **uns** jeden Tag an.	**Meine Großeltern** lieben **sich** sehr.
We call each other every day.	*My grandparents love each other very much.*

Verb conjugation tables

Here are the infinitives of all verbs introduced as active vocabulary in **Mosaik**. Each verb is followed by a model verb that follows the same conjugation pattern. The number in parentheses indicates where in the verb tables, pages **A16–A25**, you can find the conjugated forms of the model verb. The word (*sein*) after a verb means that it is conjugated with **sein** in the **Perfekt** and **Plusquamperfekt**. For irregular reflexive verbs, the list may point to a non-reflexive model verb. A full conjugation of the simple forms of a reflexive verb is presented in Verb table 6 on page **A17**. Verbs followed by an asterisk (*) have a separable prefix.

abbiegen* (*sein*) like schieben (42)
abbrechen* like sprechen (47)
abfahren* (*sein*) like tragen (51)
abfliegen* (*sein*) like schieben (42)
abheben* like heben (29)
abschicken* like machen (3)
abstauben* like machen (3)
(sich) abtrocknen* like arbeiten (1)
adoptieren like probieren (4)
anbieten* like schieben (42)
anfangen* like fangen (23)
angeln like sammeln (5)
ankommen* (*sein*) like kommen (32)
anmachen* like machen (3)
anrufen* like rufen (40)
anschauen* like machen (3)
anstoßen* like stoßen (50)
antworten like arbeiten (1)
(sich) anziehen* like schieben (42)
arbeiten (1)
(sich) ärgern like fordern (26)
aufgehen* (*sein*) like gehen (28)
auflegen* like machen (3)
aufmachen* like machen (3)
aufnehmen* like nehmen (38)
aufräumen* like machen (3)
aufstehen* (*sein*) like stehen (48)
aufwachen* (*sein*) like machen (3)
ausfüllen like machen (3)
ausgehen like gehen (28)
ausmachen like machen (3)
(sich) ausruhen like sich freuen (6)
ausschalten* like arbeiten (1)
(sich) ausziehen* like schieben (42)
backen like mahlen (37)
(sich) baden like arbeiten (1)
bauen like machen (3)
beantworten like arbeiten (1)
bedeuten like arbeiten (1)
bedienen like machen (3)
(sich) beeilen like sich freuen (6)
beginnen like schwimmen (44)
behaupten like arbeiten (1)
bekommen like kommen (32)
belegen like machen (3)
benutzen like machen (3)
berichten like arbeiten (1)

beschreiben like bleiben (20)
besprechen like sprechen (47)
bestehen like stehen (48)
bestellen like machen (3)
besuchen like machen (3)
(sich) bewegen like heben (29)
(sich) bewerben like helfen (31)
bezahlen like machen (3)
bieten like schieben (42)
bleiben (*sein*) (20)
braten like schlafen (43)
brauchen like machen (3)
brechen like sprechen (47)
brennen like rennen (17)
bringen like denken (16)
buchen like machen (3)
büffeln like sammeln (5)
bügeln like sammeln (5)
bürsten like arbeiten (1)
danken like machen (3)
decken like machen (3)
denken like denken (16)
drücken like machen (3)
drucken like machen (3)
durchfallen* (*sein*) like fallen (22)
durchmachen* like machen (3)
dürfen (10)
(sich) duschen like sich freuen (6)
einkaufen* like machen (3)
einladen* like tragen (51)
einschlafen* (*sein*) like schlafen (43)
einzahlen* like machen (3)
empfehlen like stehlen (49)
entdecken like machen (3)
entfernen like machen (3)
entgegennehmen* like nehmen (38)
entlassen like fallen (22)
(sich) entschließen like fließen (25)
(sich) entschuldigen like machen (3)
(sich) entspannen like sich freuen (6)
entwerten like arbeiten (1)
entwickeln like sammeln (5)
erfinden like trinken (52)
erforschen like machen (3)
ergänzen like machen (3)
erhalten like fallen (22)
(sich) erinnern like fordern (26)

(sich) erkälten like arbeiten (1)
erkennen like rennen (17)
erklären like machen (3)
erzählen like machen (3)
essen (21)
fahren (*sein*) like tragen (51)
fallen (*sein*) (22)
fangen (23)
(sich) färben like machen (3)
faulenzen like machen (3)
fegen like machen (3)
feiern (2)
fernsehen* like geben (27)
finden like trinken (52)
fliegen (*sein*) like schieben (42)
folgen (*sein*) like machen (3)
(sich) fragen like machen (3)
(sich) freuen (6)
(sich) fühlen like sich freuen (6)
füllen like machen (3)
funktionieren like probieren (4)
geben (27)
gefallen like fallen (22)
gehen (*sein*) (28)
gehören like machen (3)
genießen like fließen (25)
gewinnen like schwimmen (44)
(sich) gewöhnen like sich freuen (6)
glauben like machen (3)
gratulieren like probieren (4)
grüßen like machen (3)
haben like haben (7)
handeln like sammeln (5)
hängen like machen (3)
heiraten like arbeiten (1)
heißen (30)
helfen (31)
heruntergehen* (*sein*) like gehen (28)
herunterladen* like tragen (51)
(sich) hinlegen* like machen (3)
(sich) hinsetzen* like machen (3)
hinterlassen like fallen (22)
hochgehen* (*sein*) like gehen (28)
hören like machen (3)
husten like arbeiten (1)
(sich) informieren like probieren (4)
(sich) interessieren like probieren (4)

joggen (*sein*) like machen (3)
(sich) kämmen like machen (3)
kaufen like machen (3)
kennen like rennen (17)
klettern (*sein*) like fordern (26)
klingeln like sammeln (5)
kochen like machen (3)
kommen (*sein*) (32)
können (11)
korrigieren like probieren (4)
kosten like arbeiten (1)
küssen like machen (3)
lächeln like sammeln (5)
lachen like machen (3)
laden like tragen (51)
landen (*sein*) like arbeiten (1)
lassen like fallen (22)
laufen (*sein*) (33)
leben like machen (3)
legen like machen (3)
leiten like arbeiten (1)
lernen like machen (3)
lesen (34)
lieben like machen (3)
liegen (35)
löschen like tragen (51)
lügen (36)
machen (3)
meinen like machen (3)
mieten like arbeiten (1)
mitbringen* like denken (16)
mitkommen* (*sein*) like kommen (32)
mitmachen* like machen (3)
mitnehmen* like nehmen (38)
mögen (12)
müssen (13)
nachmachen* like machen (3)
nehmen (38)
(sich) nennen like rennen (17)
niesen like machen (3)
öffnen like arbeiten (1)
packen like machen (3)
parken like machen (3)
passen like machen (3)
passieren (*sein*) like probieren (4)
probieren (4)
putzen like machen (3)

(sich) rasieren like probieren (4)
rauchen like machen (3)
recyceln like sammeln (5)
reden like arbeiten (1)
regnen like arbeiten (1)
reisen (*sein*) like machen (3)
reiten (*sein*) like pfeifen (39)
rennen (*sein*) (17)
reparieren like probieren (4)
retten like arbeiten (1)
sagen like machen (3)
schauen like machen (3)
scheitern (*sein*) like fordern (26)
schenken like machen (3)
schicken like machen (3)
schlafen (43)
schmecken like machen (3)
(sich) schminken like machen (3)
schneien like machen (3)
schreiben like bleiben (20)
schützen like machen (3)
schwänzen like machen (3)
schwimmen (*sein*) (44)
sehen like lesen (34)
sein (*sein*) (8)
(sich) setzen like machen (3)
singen like trinken (52)
sitzen (46)

sollen (14)
sortieren like probieren (4)
spazieren (*sein*) like probieren (4)
speichern like fordern (26)
spielen like machen (3)
sprechen (47)
springen (*sein*) like trinken (52)
spülen like machen (3)
starten (*sein*) like arbeiten (1)
staubsaugen like saugen (41)
stehen (48)
stehlen (49)
steigen (*sein*) like bleiben (20)
stellen like machen (3)
sterben (*sein*) like helfen (31)
(sich) streiten like pfeifen (39)
studieren like probieren (4)
suchen like machen (3)
surfen (*sein*) like machen (3)
tanken like machen (3)
tanzen like machen (3)
tragen (51)
träumen like machen (3)
(sich) treffen (*sein*) like sprechen (47)
treiben (*sein*) like bleiben (20)
(sich) trennen like sich freuen (6)
trinken (52)
tun (53)

üben like machen (3)
(sich) überlegen like machen (3)
übernachten like arbeiten (1)
überqueren like machen (3)
überraschen like machen (3)
umtauschen* like machen (3)
(sich) umziehen* (*sein*) like schieben (42)
untergehen* (*sein*) like gehen (28)
(sich) unterhalten* like fallen (22)
unterschreiben like bleiben (20)
(sich) verbessern like fordern (26)
verbringen like denken (16)
verdienen like machen (3)
vereinbaren like machen (3)
vergessen like essen (21)
verkaufen like machen (3)
verkünden like arbeiten (1)
(sich) verlaufen like laufen (33)
(sich) verletzen like machen (3)
(sich) verlieben like machen (3)
verlieren like schieben (42)
verschmutzen (*sein*) like machen (3)
(sich) verspäten like sich freuen (6)
(sich) verstauchen like machen (3)
verstehen like stehen (48)
versuchen like machen (3)
(sich) vorbereiten* like arbeiten (1)

vormachen* like machen (3)
vorschlagen* like tragen (51)
(sich) vorstellen* like machen (3)
wachsen (*sein*) like waschen (54)
wandern (*sein*) like fordern (26)
warten like arbeiten (1)
(sich) waschen (54)
wegräumen* like machen (3)
wegwerfen* like helfen (31)
weinen like machen (3)
werden (*sein*) (9)
wettmachen* like machen (3)
wiederholen like machen (3)
wiegen like schieben (42)
wischen like machen (3)
wissen (55)
wohnen like machen (3)
wollen (15)
(sich) wünschen like machen (3)
zeigen like machen (3)
ziehen (*sein*) like schieben (42)
zubereiten* like arbeiten (1)
zumachen* like machen (3)
(sich) zurechtfinden* like trinken (52)
zurückkommen* (*sein*) like kommen (32)
zuschauen* like machen (3)

Regular verbs: simple tenses

Infinitiv / Partizip I / Partizip II / Perfekt	INDIKATIV			KONJUNKTIV I	KONJUNKTIV II		IMPERATIV
	Präsens	Präteritum	Plusquamperfekt	Präsens	Präsens	Perfekt	
1 arbeiten	arbeite	arbeitete	hatte gearbeitet	arbeite	arbeitete	hätte gearbeitet	
(to work)	arbeitest	arbeitetest	hattest gearbeitet	arbeitest	arbeitetest	hättest gearbeitet	arbeite
	arbeitet	arbeitete	hatte gearbeitet	arbeite	arbeitete	hätte gearbeitet	
arbeitend	arbeiten	arbeiteten	hatten gearbeitet	arbeiten	arbeiteten	hätten gearbeitet	arbeiten wir
gearbeitet	arbeitet	arbeitetet	hattet gearbeitet	arbeitet	arbeitetet	hättet gearbeitet	arbeitet
gearbeitet haben	arbeiten	arbeiteten	hatten gearbeitet	arbeiten	arbeiteten	hätten gearbeitet	arbeiten Sie
2 feiern	feiere	feierte	hatte gefeiert	feiere	feierte	hätte gefeiert	
(to celebrate)	feierst	feiertest	hattest gefeiert	feierest	feiertest	hättest gefeiert	feiere
	feiert	feierte	hatte gefeiert	feiere	feierte	hätte gefeiert	
feiernd	feiern	feierten	hatten gefeiert	feiern	feierten	hätten gefeiert	feiern wir
gefeiert	feiert	feiertet	hattet gefeiert	feiert	feiertet	hättet gefeiert	feiert
gefeiert haben	feiern	feierten	hatten gefeiert	feiern	feierten	hätten gefeiert	feiern Sie
3 machen	mache	machte	hatte gemacht	mache	machte	hätte gemacht	
(to make; to do)	machst	machtest	hattest gemacht	machest	machtest	hättest gemacht	mache/mach
	macht	machte	hatte gemacht	mache	machte	hätte gemacht	
machend	machen	machten	hatten gemacht	machen	machten	hätten gemacht	machen wir
gemacht	macht	machtet	hattet gemacht	machet	machtet	hättet gemacht	macht
gemacht haben	machen	machten	hatten gemacht	machen	machten	hätten gemacht	machen Sie
4 probieren	probiere	probierte	hatte probiert	probiere	probierte	hätte probiert	
(to try)	probierst	probiertest	hattest probiert	probierest	probiertest	hättest probiert	probiere/probier
	probiert	probierte	hatte probiert	probiere	probierte	hätte probiert	
probierend	probieren	probierten	hatten probiert	probieren	probierten	hätten probiert	probieren wir
probiert	probiert	probiertet	hattet probiert	probieret	probiertet	hättet probiert	probiert
probiert haben	probieren	probierten	hatten probiert	probieren	probierten	hätten probiert	probieren Sie
5 sammeln	sammle	sammelte	hatte gesammelt	sammle	sammelte	hätte gesammelt	
(to collect)	sammelst	sammeltest	hattest gesammelt	sammlest	sammeltest	hättest gesammelt	sammle
	sammelt	sammelte	hatte gesammelt	sammle	sammelte	hätte gesammelt	
sammelnd	sammeln	sammelten	hatten gesammelt	sammlen	sammelten	hätten gesammelt	sammeln wir
gesammelt	sammelt	sammeltet	hattet gesammelt	sammlet	sammeltet	hättet gesammelt	sammelt
gesammelt haben	sammeln	sammelten	hatten gesammelt	sammlen	sammelten	hätten gesammelt	sammeln Sie

Reflexive verbs

Infinitiv Partizip I Partizip II Perfekt	INDIKATIV			KONJUNKTIV I	KONJUNKTIV II		IMPERATIV
	Präsens	Präteritum	Plusquamperfekt	Präsens	Präsens	Perfekt	
6 **sich freuen**	freue mich	freute mich	hatte mich gefreut	freue mich	freute mich	hätte mich gefreut	
(to be happy)	freust dich	freutest dich	hattest dich gefreut	freuest dich	freutest dich	hättest dich gefreut	freue/freu dich
	freut sich	freute sich	hatte sich gefreut	freue sich	freute sich	hätte sich gefreut	
sich freuend	freuen uns	freuten uns	hatten uns gefreut	freuen uns	freuten uns	hätten uns gefreut	freuen wir uns
sich gefreut	freut euch	freutet euch	hattet euch gefreut	freuet euch	freutet euch	hättet euch gefreut	freut euch
sich gefreut haben	freuen sich	freuten sich	hatten sich gefreut	freuen sich	freuten sich	hätten sich gefreut	freuen Sie sich

Auxiliary verbs

Infinitiv Partizip I Partizip II Perfekt	INDIKATIV			KONJUNKTIV I	KONJUNKTIV II		IMPERATIV
	Präsens	Präteritum	Plusquamperfekt	Präsens	Präsens	Perfekt	
7 **haben**	habe	hatte	hatte gehabt	habe	hötte	hatte gehabt	
(to have)	hast	hattest	hattest gehabt	habest	hättest	hättest gehabt	habe/hab
	hat	hatte	hatte gehabt	habe	hätte	hätte gehabt	
habend	haben	hatten	hatten gehabt	haben	hätten	hätten gehabt	haben wir
gehabt	habt	hattet	hattet gehabt	habet	hättet	hättet gehabt	habt
gehabt haben	haben	hatten	hatten gehabt	haben	hätten	hätten gehabt	haben Sie
8 **sein**	bin	war	war gewesen	sei	wäre	wäre gewesen	
(to be)	bist	warst	warst gewesen	seiest/seist	wärst/wärest	wärst/wärest gewesen	sei
	ist	war	war gewesen	sei	wäre	wäre gewesen	
seiend	sind	waren	waren gewesen	seien	wären	wären gewesen	seien wir
gewesen	seid	wart	wart gewesen	seiet	wärt/wäret	wärt/wäret gewesen	seid
gewesen sein	sind	waren	waren gewesen	seien	wären	wären gewesen	seien Sie
9 **werden**	werde	wurde	war geworden	werde	würde	wäre geworden	
(to become)	wirst	wurdest	warst geworden	werdest	würdest	wärst geworden	werde
	wird	wurde	war geworden	werde	würde	wäre geworden	
werdend	werden	wurden	waren geworden	werden	würden	wären geworden	werden wir
geworden	werdet	wurdet	wart geworden	werdet	würdet	wärt geworden	werdet
geworden sein	werden	wurden	waren geworden	werden	würden	wären geworden	werden Sie

Compound tenses

Hilfsverb	INDIKATIV		KONJUNKTIV I		KONJUNKTIV II	
	Perfekt	**Plusquamperfekt**	**Präsens**	**Perfekt**	**Präsens**	**Perfekt**
haben	habe	hatte	habe		hätte	
	hast gemacht	hattest gemacht	habest gemach		hättest gemach	
	hat gearbeitet	hatte gearbeitet	habe gearbeitet		hätte gearbeitet	
	haben studiert	hatten studiert	haben studiert		hätten studiert	
	habt gefeiert	hattet gefeiert	habet gefeiert		hättet gefeiert	
	haben gesammelt	hatten gesammelt	haben gesammelt		hätten gesammelt	
sein	bin gegangen	war gegangen	sei gegangen		wäre gegangen	
	bist gegangen	warst gegangen	seiest/seist gegangen		wärst/wärest gegangen	
	ist gegangen	war gegangen	sei gegangen		wäre gegangen	
	sind gegangen	waren gegangen	seien gegangen		wären gegangen	
	seid gegangen	wart gegangen	seiet gegangen		wärt/wäret gegangen	
	sind gegangen	waren gegangen	seien gegangen		wären gegangen	

	Futur I/II	**Futur I/II**	**Futur I/II**
werden	werde machen / gemacht haben	werde machen / gemacht haben	würde machen / gemacht haben
	wirst machen / gemacht haben	werdest machen / gemacht haben	würdest machen / gemacht haben
	wird machen / gemacht haben	werde machen / gemacht haben	würde machen / gemacht haben
	werden machen / gemacht haben	werden machen / gemacht haben	würden machen / gemacht haben
	werdet machen / gemacht haben	werdet machen / gemacht haben	würdet machen / gemacht haben
	werden machen / gemacht haben	werden machen / gemacht haben	würden machen / gemacht haben

Modal verbs

Infinitiv Partizip I Partizip II Perfekt	INDIKATIV			KONJUNKTIV I	KONJUNKTIV II		IMPERATIV
	Präsens	Präteritum	Plusquamperfekt	Präsens	Präsens	Perfekt	
10 dürfen *(to be permitted to)* dürfend gedurft/dürfen gedurft haben	darf darfst darf dürfen dürft dürfen	durfte durftest durfte durften durftet durften	hatte gedurft hattest gedurft hatte gedurft hatten gedurft hattet gedurft hatten gedurft	dürfe dürfest dürfe dürfen dürfet dürfen	dürfte dürftest dürfte dürften dürftet dürften	hätte gedurft hättest gedurft hätte gedurft hätten gedurft hättet gedurft hätten gedurft	*Modal verbs are not used in the imperative.*
11 können *(to be able to)* könnend gekonnt /können gekonnt haben	kann kannst kann können könnt können	konnte konntest konnte konnten konntet konnten	hatte gekonnt hattest gekonnt hatte gekonnt hatten gekonnt hattet gekonnt hatten gekonnt	könne könnest könne können könnet können	könnte könntest könnte könnten könntet könnten	hätte gekonnt hättest gekonnt hätte gekonnt hätten gekonnt hättet gekonnt hätten gekonnt	*Modal verbs are not used in the imperative.*
12 mögen *(to like)* mögend gemocht /mögen gemocht haben	mag magst mag mögen mögt mögen	mochte mochtest mochte mochten mochtet mochten	hatte gemocht hattest gemocht hatte gemocht hatten gemocht hattet gemocht hatten gemocht	möge mögest möge mögen möget mögen	möchte möchtest möchte möchten möchtet möchten	hätte gemocht hättest gemocht hätte gemocht hätten gemocht hättet gemocht hätten gemocht	*Modal verbs are not used in the imperative.*
13 müssen *(to have to)* müssend gemusst /müssen gemusst haben	muss musst muss müssen müsst müssen	musste musstest musste mussten musstet mussten	hatte gemusst hattest gemusst hatte gemusst hatten gemusst hattet gemusst hatten gemusst	müsse müssest müsse müssen müsset müssen	müsste müsstest müsste müssten müsstet müssten	hätte gemusst hättest gemusst hätte gemusst hätten gemusst hättet gemusst hätten gemusst	*Modal verbs are not used in the imperative.*
14 sollen *(to be supposed to)* sollend gesollt /sollen gesollt haben	soll sollst soll sollen sollt sollen	sollte solltest sollte sollten solltet sollten	hatte gesollt hattest gesollt hatte gesollt hatten gesollt hattet gesollt hatten gesollt	solle sollest solle sollen sollet sollen	sollte solltest sollte sollten solltet sollten	hätte gesollt hättest gesollt hätte gesollt hätten gesollt hättet gesollt hätten gesollt	*Modal verbs are not used in the imperative.*
15 wollen *(to want to)* wollend gewollt/wollen gewollt haben	will willst will wollen wollt wollen	wollte wolltest wollte wollten wolltet wollten	hatte gewollt hattest gewollt hatte gewollt hatten gewollt hattet gewollt hatten gewollt	wolle wollest wollev wollen wollet wollen	wollte wolltest wollte wollten wolltet wollten	hätte gewollt hättest gewollt hätte gewollt hätten gewollt hättet gewollt hätten gewollt	*Modal verbs are not used in the imperative.*

Mixed verbs

Infinitiv Partizip I Partizip II Perfekt	INDIKATIV			KONJUNKTIV I	KONJUNKTIV II		IMPERATIV
	Präsens	Präteritum	Plusquamperfekt	Präsens	Präsens	Perfekt	
16 denken	denke	dachte	hatte gedacht	denke	dächte	hätte gedacht	
(to think)	denkst	dachtest	hattest gedacht	denkest	dächtest	hättest gedacht	denke/denk
	denkt	dachte	hatte gedacht	denke	dächte	hätte gedacht	
denkend	denken	dachten	hatten gedacht	denken	dächten	hätten gedacht	denken wir
gedacht	denkt	dachtet	hattet gedacht	denket	dächtet	hättet gedacht	denkt
gedacht haben	denken	dachten	hatten gedacht	denken	dächten	hätten gedacht	denken Sie
17 rennen	renne	rannte	war gerannt	renne	rennte	wäre gerannt	
(to run)	rennst	ranntest	warst gerannt	rennest	renntest	wärest gerannt	renne/renn
	rennt	rannte	war gerannt	renne	rennte	wäre gerannt	
denkend	rennen	rannten	waren gerannt	rennen	rennten	wären gerannt	rennen wir
gerannt	rennt	ranntet	wart gerannt	rennet	renntet	wärt gerannt	rennt
gerannt sein	rennen	rannten	waren gerannt	rennen	rennten	wären gerannt	rennen Sie
18 senden	sende	sandte	hatte gesandt	sende	sendete	hätte gesandt	
(to send)	sendest	sandtest	hattest gesandt	sendest	sendetest	hättest gesandt	sende
	sendet	sandte	hatte gesandt	sende	sendete	hätte gesandt	
sendend	senden	sandten	hatten gesandt	senden	sendeten	hätten gesandt	senden wir
gesendet	sendet	sandtet	hattet gesandt	sendet	sendetet	hättet gesandt	sendet
gesendet haben	senden	sandten		senden	sendeten	hätten gesandt	senden Sie

Irregular verbs

Infinitiv Partizip I Partizip II Perfekt	INDIKATIV			KONJUNKTIV I	KONJUNKTIV II		IMPERATIV
	Präsens	Präteritum	Plusquamperfekt	Präsens	Präsens	Perfekt	
19 bitten	bitte	bat	hatte gebeten	bitte	bäte	hätte gebeten	
(to ask)	bittest	batest	hattest gebeten	bittest	bätest	hättest gebeten	bitte
	bittet	bat	hatte gebeten	bitte	bäte	hätte gebeten	
bittend	bitten	baten	hatten gebeten	bitten	bäten	hätten gebeten	bitten wir
gebeten	bittet	batet	hattet gebeten	bittet	bätet	hättet gebeten	bittet
gebeten haben	bitten	baten	hatten gebeten	bitten	bäten	hätten gebeten	bitten Sie
20 bleiben	bleibe	bliebe	war geblieben	bleibe	bliebe	wäre geblieben	
(to stay)	bleibst	bliebst	warst geblieben	bleibest	bliebest	wärest geblieben	bleibe/bleib
	bleibt	blieb	war geblieben	bleibe	bliebe	wäre geblieben	
bleibend	bleiben	blieben	waren geblieben	bleiben	blieben	wären geblieben	bleiben wir
geblieben	bleibt	bliebt	wart geblieben	bleibet	bliebet	wärt geblieben	bleibt
geblieben sein	bleiben	blieben	waren geblieben	bleiben	blieben	wären geblieben	bleiben Sie

Infinitiv Partizip I Partizip II Perfekt	INDIKATIV			KONJUNKTIV I	KONJUNKTIV II		IMPERATIV
	Präsens	Präteritum	Plusquamperfekt	Präsens	Präsens	Perfekt	
21 **essen**	esse	aß	hatte gegessen	esse	äße	hätte gegessen	
(to eat)	isst	aßest	hattest gegessen	essest	äßest	hättest gegessen	iss
	isst	aß	hatte gegessen	esse	äße	hätte gegessen	
essend	essen	aßen	hatten gegessen	essen	äßen	hätten gegessen	essen wir
gegessen	esst	aß	hattet gegessen	esset	äßet	hättet gegessen	esst
gegessen haben	essen	aßen	hatten gegessen	essen	äßen	hätten gegessen	essen Sie
22 **fallen**	falle	fiel	war gefallen	falle	fiele	wäre gefallen	
(to fall)	fällst	fielst	warst gefallen	fallest	fielest	wärest gefallen	falle/fall
	fällt	fiel	war gefallen	falle	fiele	wäre gefallen	
fallend	fallen	fielen	waren gefallen	fallen	fielen	wären gefallen	fallen wir
gefallen	fallt	fielt	wart gefallen	fallet	fielet	wäret gefallen	fallt
gefallen sein	fallen	fielen	waren gefallen	fallen	fielen	wären gefallen	fallen Sie
23 **fangen**	fange	fing	hatte gemacht	fange	finge	hätte gefangen	
(to catch)	fängst	fingst	hattest gemacht	fangest	fingest	hättest gefangen	fange/fang
	fängt	fing	hatte gemacht	fange	finge	hätte gefangen	
fangend	fangen	fingen	hatten gemacht	fangen	fingen	hätten gefangen	fangen wir
gefangen	fangt	fingt	hattet gemacht	fanget	finget	hättet gefangen	fangt
gefangen haben	fangen	fingen	hatten gemacht	fangen	fingen	hätten gefangen	fangen Sie
24 **flechten**	flechte	flocht	hatte geflochten	flechte	flöchte	hätte geflochten	
(to braid)	flichtst	flochtest	hattest geflochten	flechtest	flöchtest	hättest geflochten	flicht
	flicht	flocht	hatte geflochten	flechte	flöchte	hätte geflochten	
flechtend	flechten	flochten	hatten geflochten	flechten	flöchten	hätten geflochten	flechten wir
geflochten	flechtet	flochtet	hattet geflochten	flechtet	flöchtet	hättet geflochten	flechtet
geflochten haben	flechten	flochten	hatten geflochten	flechten	flöchten	hätten geflochten	flechten Sie
25 **fließen**	fließe	floss	war geflossen	fließe	flösse	wäre geflossen	
(to flow)	fließt	flossest/flosst	warst geflossen	fließest	flössest	wärest geflossen	fließe/fließ
	fließt	floss	war geflossen	fließe	flösse	wäre geflossen	
fließend	fließen	flossen	waren geflossen	fließen	flössen	wären geflossen	fließen wir
geflossen	fließt	flosst	wart geflossen	fließet	flösset	wärt geflossen	fließt
geflossen sein	fließen	flossen	waren geflossen	fließen	flössen	wären geflossen	fließen Sie
26 **fordern**	ford(e)re	forderte	hatte gefordert	fordere	forderte	hätte gefordert	
(to demand)	forderst	fordertest	hattest gefordert	forderest	fordertest	hättest gefordert	fordere/fordre
	fordert	forderte	hatte gefordert	fordere	forderte	hätte gefordert	
fordernd	fordern	forderten	hatten gefordert	forderen	forderten	hätten gefordert	fordern wir
gefordert	fordert	fordertet	hattet gefordert	forderet	fordertet	hättet gefordert	fordert
gefordert haben	fordern	forderten	hatten gefordert	forderen	forderten	hätten gefordert	fordern Sie
27 **geben**	gebe	gab	hatte gegeben	gebe	gäbe	hätte gegeben	
(to give)	gibst	gabst	hattest gegeben	gebest	gäbest	hättest gegeben	gib
	gibt	gab	hatte gegeben	gebe	gäbe	hätte gegeben	
gebend	geben	gaben	hatten gegeben	geben	gäben	hätten gegeben	geben wir
gegeben	gebt	gabt	hattet gegeben	gebet	gäbet	hättet gegeben	gebt
gegeben haben	geben	gaben	hatten gegeben	geben	gäben	hätten gegeben	geben Sie

Infinitiv / Partizip I / Partizip II / Perfekt	INDIKATIV			KONJUNKTIV I	KONJUNKTIV II		IMPERATIV
	Präsens	Präteritum	Plusquamperfekt	Präsens	Präsens	Perfekt	
28 gehen	gehe	ging	war gegangen	gehe	ginge	wäre gegangen	
(to go)	gehst	gingst	warst gegangen	gehest	gingest	wärest gegangen	gehe/geh
	geht	ging	war gegangen	gehe	ginge	wäre gegangen	
gehend	gehen	gingen	waren gegangen	gehen	gingen	wären gegangen	gehen wir
gegangen	geht	gingt	wart gegangen	gehet	ginget	wäret gegangen	geht
gegangen sein	gehen	gingen	waren gegangen	gehen	gingen	wären gegangen	gehen Sie
29 heben	hebe	hob	hatte gehoben	hebe	höbe	hätte gehoben	
(to lift)	hebst	hobst	hattest gehoben	hebest	höbest/höbst	hättest gehoben	hebe/heb
	hebt	hob	hatte gehoben	hebe	höbe	hätte gehoben	
hebend	heben	hoben	hatten gehoben	heben	höben	hätten gehoben	heben wir
gehoben	hebt	hobt	hattet gehoben	hebet	höbet/höbt	hättet gehoben	hebt
gehoben haben	heben	hoben	hatten gehoben	heben	höben	hätten gehoben	heben Sie
30 heißen	heiße	hieß	hatte geheißen	heiße	hieße	hätte geheißen	
(to be called)	heißt	hießest	hattest geheißen	heißest	hießest	hättest geheißen	heiß/heiße
	heißt	hieß	hatte geheißen	heiße	hieße	hätte geheißen	
heißend	heißen	hießen	hatten geheißen	heißen	hießen	hätten geheißen	heißen wir
geheißen	heißt	hießt	hattet geheißen	heißet	hießet	hättet geheißen	heißt
geheißen haben	heißen	hießen	hatten geheißen	heißen	hießen	hätten geheißen	heißen Sie
31 helfen	helfe	half	hatte geholfen	helfe	hälfe	hätte geholfen	
(to help)	hilfst	halfst	hattest geholfen	helfest	hälfest/hälfst	hättest geholfen	hilf
	hilft	half	hatte geholfen	helfe	hälfe	hätte geholfen	
helfend	helfen	halfen	hatten geholfen	helfen	hälfen	hätten geholfen	helfen wir
geholfen	helft	halft	hattet geholfen	helfet	hälfet/hälft	hättet geholfen	helft
geholfen haben	helfen	halfen	hatten geholfen	helfen	hälfen	hätten geholfen	helfen Sie
32 kommen	komme	kam	war gekommen	komme	käme	wäre gekommen	
(to come)	kommst	kamst	warst gekommen	kommest	kämest	wärest gekommen	komme/komm
	kommt	kam	war gekommen	komme	käme	wäre gekommen	
kommend	kommen	kamen	waren gekommen	kommen	kämen	wären gekommen	kommen wir
gekommen	kommt	kamt	wart gekommen	kommet	kämet	wäret gekommen	kommt
gekommen sein	kommen	kamen	waren gekommen	kommen	kämen	wären gekommen	kommen Sie
33 laufen	laufe	lief	war gelaufen	laufe	liefe	wäre gelaufen	
(to run)	läufst	liefst	warst gelaufen	laufest	liefest	wärest gelaufen	laufe/lauf
	läuft	lief	war gelaufen	laufe	liefe	wäre gelaufen	
laufend	laufen	liefen	waren gelaufen	laufen	liefen	wären gelaufen	laufen wir
gelaufen	lauft	lieft	wart gelaufen	laufet	liefet	wäret gelaufen	lauft
gelaufen sein	laufen	liefen	waren gelaufen	laufen	liefen	wären gelaufen	laufen Sie
34 lesen	lese	las	hatte gelesen	lese	läse	hätte gelesen	
(to read)	liest	la(se)st	hattest gelesen	lesest	läsest	hättest gelesen	lies
	liest	las	hatte gelesen	lese	läse	hätte gelesen	
lesend	lesen	lasen	hatten gelesen	lesen	läsen	hätten gelesen	les en wir
gelesen	lest	last	hattet gelesen	leset	läset	hättet gelesen	lest
gelesen haben	lesen	lasen	hatten gelesen	lesen	läsen	hätten gelesen	lesen Sie

Infinitiv Partizip I Partizip II Perfekt	INDIKATIV			KONJUNKTIV I	KONJUNKTIV II		IMPERATIV
	Präsens	**Präteritum**	**Plusquamperfekt**	**Präsens**	**Präsens**	**Perfekt**	
35 **liegen**	liege	lag	hatte gelegen	liege	läge	hätte gelegen	
(to lie; to be lying)	liegst	lagst	hattest gelegen	liegest	lägest	hättest gelegen	liege/lieg
	liegt	lag	hatte gelegen	liege	läge	hätte gelegen	
liegend	liegen	lagen	hatten gelegen	liegen	lägen	hätten gelegen	liegen wir
gelegen	liegt	lagt	hattet gelegen	lieget	läget	hättet gelegen	liegt
gelegen haben	liegen	lagen	hatten gelegen	liegen	lägen	hätten gelegen	liegen Sie
36 **lügen**	lüge	log	hatte gelogen	lüge	löge	hätte gelogen	
(to lie)	lügst	logst	hattest gelogen	lügest	lögest	hättest gelogen	lüge/lüg
	lügt	log	hatte gelogen	lüge	löge	hätte gelogen	
lügend	lügen	logen	hatten gelogen	lügen	lögen	hätten gelogen	lügen wir
gelogen	lügt	logt	hattet gelogen	lüget	löget	hättet gelogen	lügt
gelogen haben	lügen	logen	hatten gelogen	lügen	lögen	hätten gelogen	lügen Sie
37 **mahlen**	mahle	mahlte	hatte gemahlt/gemahlen	mahle	mahlte	hätte gemahlt/gemahlen	
(to grind)	mahlst	mahltest	hattest gemahlt/gemahlen	mahlest	mahltest	hättest gemahlt/gemahlen	mahle/mahl
mahlend	mahlt	mahlte	hatte gemahlt/gemahlen	mahle	mahlte	hätte gemahlt/gemahlen	
gemahlt/gemahlen	mahlen	mahlten	hatten gemahlt/gemahlen	mahlen	mahlten	hätten gemahlt/gemahlen	mahlen wir
gemahlt/gemahlen	mahlt	mahltet	hattet gemahlt/gemahlen	mahlet	mahltet	hättet gemahlt/gemahlen	mahlt
haben	mahlen	mahlten	hatten gemahlt/gemahlen	mahlen	mahlten	hätten gemahlt/gemahlen	mahlen Sie
38 **nehmen**	nehme	nahm	hatte genommen	nehme	nähme	hätte genommen	
(to take)	nimmst	nahmst	hattest genommen	nehmest	nähmest	hättest genommen	nimm
	nimmt	nahm	hatte genommen	nehme	nähme	hätte genommen	
nehmend	nehmen	nahmen	hatten genommen	nehmen	nähmen	hätten genommen	nehmen wir
genommen	nehmt	nahmt	hattet genommen	nehmet	nähmet	hättet genommen	nehmt
genommen haben	nehmen	nahmen	hatten genommen	nehmen	nähmen	hätten genommen	nehmen Sie
39 **pfeifen**	pfeife	pfiff	hatte gepfiffen	pfeife	pfiffe	hätte gepfiffen	
(to whistle)	pfeifst	pfiffst	hattest gepfiffen	pfeifest	pfiffest	hättest gepfiffen	pfeife/pfeif
	pfeift	pfiff	hatte gepfiffen	pfeife	pfiffe	hätte gepfiffen	
pfeifend	pfeifen	pfiffen	hatten gepfiffen	pfeifen	pfiffen	hätten gepfiffen	pfeifen wir
gepfiffen	pfeift	pfifft	hattet gepfiffen	pfeifet	pfiffet	hättet gepfiffen	pfeift
gepfiffen haben	pfeifen	pfiffen	hatten gepfiffen	pfeifen	pfiffen	hätten gepfiffen	pfeifen Sie
40 **rufen**	rufe	rief	hatte gerufen	rufe	riefe	hätte gerufen	
(to call)	rufst	riefst	hattest gerufen	rufest	riefest	hättest gerufen	rufe/ruf
	ruft	rief	hatte gerufen	rufe	riefe	hätte gerufen	
rufend	rufen	riefen	hatten gerufen	rufen	riefen	hätten gerufen	rufen wir
gerufen	ruft	rieft	hattet gerufen	rufet	riefet	hättet gerufen	ruft
gerufen haben	rufen	riefen	hatten gerufen	rufen	riefen	hätten gerufen	rufen Sie
41 **saugen**	sauge	saugte/sog	hatte gesaugt/gesogen	sauge	saugte/söge	hätte gesaugt/gesogen	
(to suck)	saugst	saugtest/sogst	hattest gesaugt/gesogen	saugest	saugtest/sögest	hättest gesaugt/gesogen	sauge/saug
saugend	saugt	saugte/sog	hatte gesaugt/gesogen	sauge	saugte/söge	hätte gesaugt/gesogen	
gesaugt/gesogen	saugen	saugten/sogen	hatten gesaugt/gesogen	saugen	saugten/sögen	hätten gesaugt/gesogen	saugen wir
gesaugt/gesogen	saugt	saugtet/sogt	hattet gesaugt/gesogen	sauget	saugtet/söget	hättet gesaugt/gesogen	saugt
haben	saugen	saugten/sogen	hatten gesaugt/gesogen	saugen	saugten/sögen	hätten gesaugt/gesogen	saugen Sie

Infinitiv / Partizip I / Partizip II / Perfekt	INDIKATIV			KONJUNKTIV I	KONJUNKTIV II		IMPERATIV
	Präsens	Präteritum	Plusquamperfekt	Präsens	Präsens	Perfekt	
42 schieben	schiebe	schob	hatte geschoben	schiebe	schöbe	hätte geschoben	
(to push)	schiebst	schobst	hattest geschoben	schiebest	schöbest	hättest geschoben	schiebe/schieb
	schiebt	schob	hatte geschoben	schiebe	schöbe	hätte geschoben	
schiebend	schieben	schoben	hatten geschoben	schieben	schöben	hätten geschoben	schieben wir
geschoben	schiebt	schobt	hattet geschoben	schiebet	schöbet	hättet geschoben	schiebt
geschoben haben	schieben	schoben	hatten geschoben	schieben	schöben	hätten geschoben	schieben Sie
43 schlafen	schlafe	schlief	hatte geschlafen	schlafe	schliefe	hätte geschlafen	
(to sleep)	schläfst	schliefst	hattest geschlafen	schlafest	schliefest	hättest geschlafen	schlafe/schlaf
	schläft	schlief	hatte geschlafen	schlafe	schliefe	hätte geschlafen	
schlafend	schlafen	schliefen	hatten geschlafen	schlafen	schliefen	hätten geschlafen	schlafen wir
geschlafen	schlaft	schlieft	hattet geschlafen	schlafet	schliefet	hättet geschlafen	schlaft
geschlafen haben	schlafen	schliefen	hatten geschlafen	schlafen	schliefen	hätten geschlafen	schlafen Sie
44 schwimmen	schwimme	schwamm	war geschwommen	schwimme	schwömme	wäre geschwommen	
(to swim)	schwimmst	schwammst	warst geschwommen	schwimmest	schwömmest	wärest geschwommen	schwimme/schwimm
	schwimmt	schwamm	war geschwommen	schwimme	schwömme	wäre geschwommen	
schwimmend	schwimmen	schwammen	waren geschwommen	schwimmen	schwömmen	wären geschwommen	schwimmen wir
geschwommen	schwimmt	schwammt	wart geschwommen	schwimmet	schwömmet	wäret geschwommen	schwimmt
geschwommen sein	schwimmen	schwammen	waren geschwommen	schwimmen	schwömmen	wären geschwommen	schwimmen Sie
45 schwören	schwöre	schwor	hatte geschworen	schwöre	schwüre	hätte geschworen	
(to swear)	schwörst	schworst	hattest geschworen	schwörest	schwürest/schwürst	hättest geschworen	schwöre/schwör
	schwört	schwor	hatte geschworen	schwöre	schwüre	hätte geschworen	
schwörend	schwören	schworen	hatten geschworen	schwören	schwüren	hätten geschworen	schwören wir
geschworen	schwört	schwort	hattet geschworen	schwöret	schwüret	hättet geschworen	schwört
geschworen haben	schwören	schworen	hatten geschworen	schwören	schwüren	hätten geschworen	schwören Sie
46 sitzen	sitze	saß	hatte gesessen	sitze	säße	hätte gesessen	
(to sit)	sitzt	saßest	hattest gesessen	sitzest	säßest	hättest gesessen	sitze/sitz
	sitzt	saß	hatte gesessen	sitze	säße	hätte gesessen	
sitzend	sitzen	saßen	hatten gesessen	sitzen	säßen	hätten gesessen	sitzen wir
gesessen	sitzt	saßet	hattet gesessen	sitzet	säßet	hättet gesessen	sitzt
gesessen haben	sitzen	saßen	hatten gesessen	sitzen	säßen	hätten gesessen	sitzen Sie
47 sprechen	spreche	sprach	hatte gesprochen	spreche	spräche	hätte gesprochen	
(to speak)	sprichst	sprachst	hattest gesprochen	sprechest	sprächest	hättest gesprochen	sprich
	spricht	sprach	hatte gesprochen	spreche	spräche	hätte gesprochen	
sprechend	sprechen	sprachen	hatten gesprochen	sprechen	sprächen	hätten gesprochen	sprechen wir
gesprochen	sprecht	spracht	hattet gesprochen	sprechet	sprächet	hättet gesprochen	sprecht
gesprochen haben	sprechen	sprachen	hatten gesprochen	sprechen	sprächen	hätten gesprochen	sprechen Sie
48 stehen	stehe	stand	hatte gestanden	stehe	stünde/stände	hätte gestanden	
(to stand)	stehst	standest/standst	hattest gestanden	stehest	stündest/ständest	hättest gestanden	stehe/steh
	steht	stand	hatte gestanden	stehe	stünde/stände	hätte gestanden	
stehend	stehen	standen	hatten gestanden	stehen	stünden/ständen	hätten gestanden	stehen wir
gestanden	steht	standet	hattet gestanden	stehet	stündet/ständet	hättet gestanden	steht
gestanden haben	stehen	standen	hatten gestanden	stehen	stünden/ständen	hätten gestanden	stehen Sie

Infinitiv / Partizip I / Partizip II / Perfekt	INDIKATIV			KONJUNKTIV I	KONJUNKTIV II		IMPERATIV
	Präsens	Präteritum	Plusquamperfekt	Präsens	Präsens	Perfekt	
49 stehlen	stehle	stahl	hatte gestohlen	stehle	stähle/stöhle	hätte gestohlen	
(to steal)	stiehlst	stahlst	hattest gestohlen	stehlest	stählest/stöhlest	hättest gestohlen	stiehl
	stiehlt	stahl	hatte gestohlen	stehle	stähle/stöhle	hätte gestohlen	
stehlend	stehlen	stahlen	hatten gestohlen	stehlen	stählen/stöhlen	hätten gestohlen	stehlen wir
gestohlen	stehlt	stahlt	hattet gestohlen	stehlet	stählet/stöhlet	hättet gestohlen	stehlt
gestohlen haben	stehlen	stahlen	hatten gestohlen	stehlen	stählen/stöhlen	hätten gestohlen	stehlen Sie
50 stoßen	stoße	stieß	hatte gestoßen	stoße	stieße	hätte gestoßen	
(to bump)	stößt	stießest/stießt	hattest gestoßen	stoßest	stießest	hättest gestoßen	stoße/stoß
	stößt	stieß	hatte gestoßen	stoße	stieße	hätte gestoßen	
stoßend	stoßen	stießen	hatten gestoßen	stoßen	stießen	hätten gestoßen	stoßen wir
gestoßen	stoßt	stießt	hattet gestoßen	stoßet	stießet	hättet gestoßen	stoßt
gestoßen haben	stoßen	stießen	hatten gestoßen	stoßen	stießen	hätten gestoßen	stoßen Sie
51 tragen	trage	trug	hatte getragen	trage	trüge	hätte getragen	
(to carry)	trägst	trugst	hattest getragen	tragest	trügest	hättest getragen	trage/trag
	trägt	trug	hatte getragen	trage	trüge	hätte getragen	
tragend	tragen	trugen	hatten getragen	tragen	trügen	hätten getragen	tragen wir
getragen	tragt	trugt	hattet getragen	traget	trüget	hättet getragen	tragt
getragen haben	tragen	trugen	hatten getragen	tragen	trügen	hätten getragen	tragen Sie
52 trinken	trinke	trank	hatte getrunken	trinke	tränke	hätte getrunken	
(to drink)	trinkst	trankst	hattest getrunken	trinkest	tränkest	hättest getrunken	trinke/trink
	trinkt	trank	hatte getrunken	trinke	tränke	hätte getrunken	
trinkend	trinken	tranken	hatten getrunken	trinken	tränken	hätten getrunken	trinken wir
getrunken	trinkt	trankt	hattet getrunken	trinket	tränket	hättet getrunken	trinkt
getrunken haben	trinken	tranken	hatten getrunken	trinken	tränken	hätten getrunken	trinken Sie
53 tun	tue	tat	hatte getan	tue	täte	hätte getan	
(to do)	tust	tatest	hattest getan	tuest	tätest	hättest getan	tue/tu
	tut	tat	hatte getan	tue	täte	hätte getan	
tuend	tun	taten	hatten getan	tuen	täten	hätten getan	tun wir
getan	tut	tatet	hattet getan	tuet	tätet	hättet getan	tut
getan haben	tun	taten	hatten getan	tuen	täten	hätten getan	tun Sie
54 waschen	wasche	wusch	hatte gewaschen	wasche	wüsche	hätte gewaschen	
(to wash)	wäschst	wuschest/wuschst	hattest gewaschen	waschest	wüschest/wüschst	hättest gewaschen	wasche/wasch
	wäscht	wusch	hatte gewaschen	wasche	wüsche	hätte gewaschen	
waschend	waschen	wuschen	hatten gewaschen	waschen	wüschen	hätten gewaschen	waschen wir
gewaschen	wascht	wuscht	hattet gewaschen	waschet	wüschet/wüscht	hättet gewaschen	wascht
gewaschen haben	waschen	wuschen	hatten gewaschen	waschen	wüschen	hätten gewaschen	waschen Sie
55 wissen	weiß	wusste	hatte gewusst	wisse	wüsste	hätte gewusst	
(to know)	weißt	wusstest	hattest gewusst	wissest	wüsstest	hättest gewusst	wisse
	weiß	wusste	hatte gewusst	wisse	wüsste	hätte gewusst	
wissend	wissen	wussten	hatten gewusst	wissen	wüssten	hätten gewusst	wissen wir
gewusst	wisst	wusstet	hattet gewusst	wisset	wüsstet	hättet gewusst	wisst
gewusst haben	wissen	wussten	hatten gewusst	wissen	wüssten	hätten gewusst	wissen Sie

Irregular verbs

The following is a list of the principal parts of all strong and mixed verbs that are introduced as active vocabulary in **Mosaik**, as well as other sample verbs. For the complete conjugations of these verbs, consult the verb list on pages **A14–A15** and the verb charts on pages **A16–A25**. The verbs listed here are base forms. See **Strukturen Volume 2, 2B.2** and **3A.1** to review **Perfekt** and **Präteritum** forms of separable and inseparable prefix verbs.

Infinitiv		Präteritum	Partizip II
backen	*to bake*	backte	gebacken
beginnen	*to begin*	begann	begonnen
bieten	*to bid, to offer*	bot	geboten
binden	*to tie, to bind*	band	gebunden
bitten	*to request*	bat	gebeten
bleiben	*to stay*	blieb	(ist) geblieben
braten (brät)	*to fry, to roast*	briet	gebraten
brechen (bricht)	*to break*	brach	gebrochen
brennen	*to burn*	brannte	gebrannt
bringen	*to bring*	brachte	gebracht
denken	*to think*	dachte	gedacht
dürfen (darf)	*to be allowed to*	durfte	gedurft
empfehlen (empfiehlt)	*to recommend*	empfahl	empfohlen
essen (isst)	*to eat*	aß	gegessen
fahren (fährt)	*to go, to drive*	fuhr	(ist) gefahren
fallen (fällt)	*to fall*	fiel	(ist) gefallen
fangen (fängt)	*to catch*	fing	gefangen
finden	*to find*	fand	gefunden
fliegen	*to fly*	flog	(ist) geflogen
fließen	*to flow, to pour*	floss	(ist) geflossen
frieren	*to freeze*	fror	(hat/ist) gefroren
geben (gibt)	*to give*	gab	gegeben
gehen	*to go, to walk*	ging	(ist) gegangen
gelten (gilt)	*to be valid*	galt	gegolten
genießen	*to enjoy*	genoss	genossen
geschehen (geschieht)	*to happen*	geschah	(ist) geschehen
gewinnen	*to win*	gewann	gewonnen
gleichen	*to resemble*	glich	geglichen
graben (gräbt)	*to dig*	grub	gegraben
haben (hat)	*to have*	hatte	gehabt
halten (hält)	*to hold, to keep*	hielt	gehalten
hängen	*to hang*	hing	gehangen
heben	*to raise, to lift*	hob	gehoben
heißen	*to be called, to mean*	hieß	geheißen
helfen (hilft)	*to help*	half	geholfen
kennen	*to know*	kannte	gekannt
klingen	*to sound, to ring*	klang	geklungen
kommen	*to come*	kam	(ist) gekommen
können (kann)	*to be able to, can*	konnte	gekonnt
laden (lädt)	*to load, to charge*	lud	geladen
lassen (lässt)	*to let, to allow*	ließ	gelassen
laufen (läuft)	*to run, to walk*	lief	(ist) gelaufen

Infinitiv		Präteritum	Partizip II
leiden	to suffer	litt	gelitten
leihen	to lend	lieh	geliehen
lesen (liest)	to read	las	gelesen
liegen	to lie, to rest	lag	gelegen
lügen	to lie, to tell lies	log	gelogen
meiden	to avoid	mied	gemieden
messen (misst)	to measure	maß	gemessen
mögen (mag)	to like	mochte	gemocht
müssen (muss)	to have, to must	musste	gemusst
nehmen (nimmt)	to take	nahm	genommen
nennen	to name, to call	nannte	genannt
preisen	to praise	pries	gepriesen
raten (rät)	to guess	riet	geraten
reiben	to rub, to grate	rieb	gerieben
riechen	to smell	roch	gerochen
rufen	to call, to shout	rief	gerufen
schaffen	to create	schuf	geschaffen
scheiden	to divorce	schied	geschieden
scheinen	to shine, to appear	schien	geschienen
schieben	to push, to shove	schob	geschoben
schießen	to shoot	schoss	geschossen
schlafen (schläft)	to sleep	schlief	geschlafen
schlagen (schlägt)	to beat, to hit	schlug	geschlagen
schließen	to close	schloss	geschlossen
schlingen	to loop, to gulp	schlang	geschlungen
schneiden	to cut	schnitt	geschnitten
schreiben	to write	schrieb	geschrieben
schwimmen	to swim	schwamm	(ist) geschwommen
sehen (sieht)	to see	sah	gesehen
sein (ist)	to be	war	(ist) gewesen
senden	to send	sandte/sendete	gesandt/gesendet
singen	to sing	sang	gesungen
sinken	to sink	sank	(ist) gesunken
sitzen	to sit	saß	gesessen
sollen (soll)	to be supposed to	sollte	gesollt
sprechen (spricht)	to speak	sprach	gesprochen
stehen	to stand	stand	gestanden
stehlen (stiehlt)	to steal	stahl	gestohlen
steigen	to climb, to rise	stieg	(ist) gestiegen
sterben (stirbt)	to die	starb	(ist) gestorben
stoßen	to push, to thrust	stieß	(hat/ist) gestoßen
streichen	to paint, to cancel	strich	gestrichen
streiten	to argue	stritt	gestritten
tragen (trägt)	to carry	trug	getragen
treffen (trifft)	to hit, to meet	traf	getroffen
treten (tritt)	to kick, to step	trat	(hat/ist) getreten
trinken	to drink	trank	getrunken
tun	to do	tat	getan
vergessen (vergisst)	to forget	vergaß	vergessen

Infinitiv		Präteritum	Partizip II
verlieren	*to lose*	verlor	verloren
wachsen (wächst)	*to grow*	wuchs	(ist) gewachsen
waschen (wäscht)	*to wash*	wusch	gewaschen
weisen	*to indicate, to show*	wies	gewiesen
wenden	*to turn, to flip*	wandte/wendete	gewandt/gewendet
werben (wirbt)	*to advertise*	warb	geworben
werden (wird)	*to become*	wurde	(ist) geworden
werfen (wirft)	*to throw*	warf	geworfen
winden	*to wind*	wand	gewunden
wissen (weiß)	*to know*	wusste	gewusst
wollen (will)	*to want*	wollte	gewollt
ziehen	*to pull, to draw, to move*	zog	(hat/ist) gezogen

Glossary

This glossary includes all active vocabulary introduced in **Mosaik**, as well as some additional words and expressions. The singular and plural endings listed for adjectival nouns are those that occur after a definite article. The numbers following each entry are as follows:

(2) **1A** = (**Mosaik** Volume) **Chapter, Lesson**

The entry would be in **Mosaik 2**, Chapter 1, Lesson A.

Abbreviations used in this glossary

acc.	accusative	*gen.*	genitive	*poss.*	possessive
adj.	adjective	*inf.*	informal	*prep.*	preposition
adv.	adverb	*interr.*	interrogative	*pron.*	pronoun
conj.	conjunction	*m.*	masculine noun	*sing.*	singular
dat.	dative	*n.*	neuter noun	*v.*	verb
f.	feminine noun	*nom.*	nominative		
form.	formal	*pl.*	plural		

Deutsch-Englisch

A

abbiegen *v.* to turn (2) **4A**
  rechts/links abbiegen *v.* to turn right/left (2) **4A**
abbrechen *v.* to cancel (2) **3B**
Abend, -e *m.* evening (1) **2B**
  abends *adv.* in the evening (1) **2A**
Abendessen, - *n.* dinner (1) **4B**
aber *conj.* but (1) **1B**
abfahren *v.* to leave (2) **4A**
Abfall, -̈e *m.* waste (3) **4B**
abfliegen *v.* to take off (2) **3B**
Abflug, -̈e *m.* departure (2) **3B**
abheben *v.* to withdraw (money) (3) **3A**
Absatz, -̈e *m.* paragraph (2) **1B**
abschicken *v.* to send (3) **3B**
Abschied, -e *m.* leave-taking; farewell (1) **1A**
Abschluss, -̈e *m.* degree (1) **2A**
  einen Abschluss machen *v.* to graduate (2) **1A**
Abschlusszeugnis, -se *n.* diploma (transcript) (1) **2A**
abstauben *v.* to dust (2) **2B**
sich abtrocknen *v.* to dry oneself off (3) **1A**
acht eight (1) **2A**
Achtung! Attention!
adoptieren *v.* to adopt (1) **3A**
Adresse, -n *f.* address (3) **2A**
Allee, -n *f.* avenue (3) **2B**
allein *adv.* alone; by oneself (1) **4A**
Allergie, -n *f.* allergy (3) **1B**
allergisch (gegen) *adj.* allergic (to) (3) **1B**
alles *pron.* everything (2) **3B**
  Alles klar? Everything OK? (1) **1A**
  alles Gute all the best (3) **2A**
  Alles Gute zum Geburtstag! Happy birthday! (2) **1A**
Alltagsroutine, -n *f.* daily routine (3) **1A**
  im Alltag in everyday life
als *conj.* as; when (2) **4A**
  als ob as if (3) **2A**
also *conj.* therefore; so (3) **1B**
alt *adj.* old (1) **3A**
Altkleider *pl.* second-hand clothing (3) **4B**
Altpapier *n.* used paper (3) **4B**
Amerika *n.* America (2) **2B**
amerikanisch *adj.* American (3) **2B**
Amerikaner, - / Amerikanerin, -nen *m./f.*
  American (3) **2B**
Ampel, -n *f.* traffic light (2) **2B**
an *prep.* at; on; by; in; to (2) **1B**, (3) **2B**
Ananas, - *f.* pineapple (1) **4A**
anbieten *v.* to offer (3) **4B**

anfangen *v.* to begin (1) **4A**
Angebot, -e *n.* offer
  im Angebot on sale (2) **1B**
angeln gehen *v.* to go fishing (1) **2B**
angenehm *adj.* pleasant (1) **3B**
  Angenehm. Nice to meet you. (1) **1A**
angesagt *adj.* trendy (2) **1B**
Angestellte, -n *m./f.* employee (3) **3A**
Angst, -̈e *f.* fear (2) **3A**
  Angst haben (vor) *v.* to be afraid (of) (2) **3A**
ankommen *v.* to arrive (1) **4A**
Ankunft, -̈e *f.* arrival (2) **3B**
Anlass, -̈e *m.* occasion (2) **1A**
  besondere Anlässe *m. pl.* special occasions (2) **1A**
anmachen *v.* to turn on (2) **4B**
Anruf, -e *m.* phone call (3) **3A**
  einen Anruf entgegennehmen *v.* to answer the phone (3) **3A**
anrufen *v.* to call (1) **4A**
  sich anrufen *v.* to call each other (3) **1A**
anschauen *v.* to watch, look at (2) **3A**
anspruchsvoll *adj.* demanding (3) **3B**
anstatt *prep.* instead of (2) **4B**
anstoßen *v.* to toast (2) **1A**
Antwort, -en *f.* answer
antworten (auf) *v.* to answer (1) **2A**
Anwendung *f.* application; usage
anziehen *v.* to put on (1) **1B**
  sich anziehen *v.* to get dressed (3) **1A**
Anzug, -̈e *m.* suit (2) **1B**
Apfel, -̈ *m.* apple (1) **1A**
Apotheke, -n *f.* pharmacy (3) **1B**
April *m.* April (1) **2A**, (2) **3A**
Arbeit, -en *f.* work (3) **3B**
  Arbeit finden *v.* to find a job (3) **3A**
arbeiten (an) *v.* to work (on) (1) **2A**, (2) **3A**
arbeitslos *adj.* unemployed (3) **2A**
Arbeitszimmer, - *n.* home office (2) **2A**
Architekt, -en / Architektin, -nen *m./f.*
  architect (1) **3B**
Architektur, -en *f.* architecture (1) **2A**
sich ärgern (über) *v.* to get angry (about) (3) **1A**
arm *adj.* poor; unfortunate (1) **3B**
Arm, -e *m.* arm (3) **1A**
Art, -en *f.* species; type (3) **4B**
Artischocke, -n *f.* artichoke (1) **4A**
Arzt, -̈e / Ärztin, -nen *m./f.* doctor (3) **1B**
  zum Arzt gehen *v.* to go to the doctor (3) **1B**
Assistent, -en / Assistentin, -nen *m./f.*
  assistant (3) **3A**
Aubergine, -n *f.* eggplant (1) **4A**
auch *adv.* also (1) **1A**

auf *prep.* on, onto, to (2) **1B**
  Auf Wiedersehen. Good-bye. (1) **1A**
aufgehen *v.* to rise (sun) (3) **4A**
auflegen *v.* to hang up (3) **3A**
aufmachen *v.* to open (2) **4B**
aufnehmen *v.* to record (2) **4B**
aufräumen *v.* to clean up (2) **2B**
aufregend *adj.* exciting (3) **4A**
aufrichtig *adj.* sincere (1) **3B**
aufstehen *v.* to get up (1) **4A**
aufwachen *v.* to wake up (3) **1A**
Auge, -n *n.* eye (1) **3A**; (3) **1A**
Augenbraue, -n *f.* eyebrow (3) **1A**
August *m.* August (1) **2A**, (2) **3A**
aus *prep.* from (1) **4A**
Ausbildung, -en *f.* education (3) **3A**
Ausdruck, -̈e *m.* expression
Ausfahrt, -en *f.* exit (2) **4A**
ausfüllen *v.* to fill out (3) **2A**
  ein Formular ausfüllen *v.* to fill out a form (3) **2A**
Ausgang, -̈e *m.* exit (2) **3B**
ausgefallen *adj.* offbeat (2) **1B**
ausgehen *v.* to go out (1) **4A**
Ausland *n.* abroad (2) **3B**
ausmachen *v.* to turn off (2) **4B**
sich ausruhen *v.* to rest (3) **1A**
ausschalten *v.* turn out, turn off (3) **4B**
Aussehen *n.* look (style) (2) **1B**
außer *prep.* except (for) (1) **4B**
außerhalb *prep.* outside of (2) **4B**
Aussprache *f.* pronunciation
Aussterben *n.* extinction (3) **4B**
sich ausziehen *v.* to get undressed (3) **1A**
Auto, -s *n.* car (1) **1A**, (2) **4A**
Autobahn, -en *f.* highway (2) **4A**

B

Baby, -s *n.* baby (1) **3A**
Bäckerei, -en *f.* bakery (1) **4A**
Badeanzug, -̈e *m.* bathing suit (2) **1B**
Bademantel, -̈ *m.* bathrobe (3) **1A**
sich baden *v.* to bathe, take a bath (3) **1A**
Badewanne, -n *f.* bathtub (2) **2A**
Badezimmer, - *n.* bathroom (2) **2A**, (3) **1A**
Bahnsteig, -e *m.* track; platform (2) **4A**
bald *adv.* soon
  Bis bald. See you soon. (1) **1A**
Balkon, -e/-s *m.* balcony (2) **2A**
Ball, -̈e *m.* ball (1) **2B**
Ballon, -e/-s *m.* balloon (2) **1A**
Banane, -n *f.* banana (1) **4A**

Bank, ⁻e *f.* bench (3) **2B**
Bank, -en *f.* bank (3) **2A**
   auf der Bank *f.* at the bank (3) **2B**
Bankangestellte, -n *m./f.* bank employee (3) **3B**
bar *adj.* cash (3) **2A**
   bar bezahlen *v.* to pay in cash (3) **2A**
Bargeld *n.* cash (3) **2A**
Bart, ⁻e *m.* beard (3) **1A**
Baseball *m.* baseball (1) **2B**
Basketball *m.* basketball (1) **2B**
Bauch, ⁻e *m.* belly (3) **1A**
Bauchschmerzen *m. pl.* stomachache (3) **1B**
bauen *v.* to build (1) **2A**
Bauer, -n / **Bäuerin,** -nen *m./f.* farmer (3) **3B**
Bauernhof, ⁻e *m.* farm (3) **4A**
Baum, ⁻e *m.* tree (3) **4A**
Baumwolle *f.* cotton (2) **1B**
Baustelle, -n *f.* construction zone (2) **4A**
beantworten *v.* to answer (1) **4B**
bedeuten *v.* to mean (1) **2A**
bedeutend *adj.* important (3) **4A**
bedienen *v.* to operate, use (2) **4B**
sich beeilen *v.* to hurry (3) **1A**
Beförderung, -en *f.* promotion (3) **3B**
beginnen *v.* to begin (2) **2A**
Begrüßung, -en *f.* greeting (1) **1A**
behaupten *v.* to claim (3) **4B**
bei *prep.* at; near; with (1) **4A**
Beilage, -n *f.* side dish (1) **4B**
Bein, -e *n.* leg (3) **1A**
Beitrag ⁻e *m.* contribution (3) **4B**
bekannt *adj.* well-known (3) **2A**
bekommen *v.* to get, to receive (2) **1A**
belegen *v.* to take (a class) (1) **2A**
benutzen *v.* to use (2) **4A**
Benutzername, -n *m.* screen name (2) **4B**
Benzin, -e *n.* gasoline (2) **4A**
Berg -e *m.* mountain (1) **2B**, (3) **4A**
berichten *v.* to report (3) **4B**
Beruf, -e *m.* profession; job (1) **3B**, (3) **3A**
Berufsausbildung, -en *f.* professional
   training (3) **3A**
bescheiden *adj.* modest (1) **3B**
beschreiben *v.* to describe (1) **2A**
Beschreibung, -en *f.* description (1) **3B**
Besen, - *m.* broom (2) **2B**
Besitzer, - / **Besitzerin,** -nen *m./f.* owner (1) **3B**
besonderes *adj.* special (3) **2A**
   nichts Besonderes *adj.* nothing special (3) **2A**
besorgt *adj.* worried (1) **3B**
Besorgung, -en *f.* errand (3) **2A**
   Besorgungen machen *v.* to run errands (3) **2A**
besprechen *v.* to discuss (2) **3A**
Besprechung, -en *f.* meeting (3) **3A**
besser *adj.* better (2) **4A**
Besserwisser, - / **Besserwisserin,** -nen *m./f.* know-
   it-all (1) **2A**
beste *adj.* best (2) **4A**
Besteck *n.* silverware (1) **4B**
bestehen *v.* to pass (a test) (1) **1B**
bestellen *v.* to order (1) **4A**
bestimmt *adv.* definitely (1) **4A**

besuchen *v.* to visit (1) **4A**
Bett, -en *n.* bed (2) **2A**
   das Bett machen *v.* to make the bed (2) **2B**
   ins Bett gehen *v.* to go bed (3) **1A**
Bettdecke, - n *f.* duvet (2) **2B**
bevor *conj.* before (2) **4A**
sich bewegen *v.* to move (around)
sich bewerben *v.* to apply (3) **3A**
Bewerber, - / **die Bewerberin,** -nen *m./f.*
   applicant (3) **3A**
Bewertung, -en *f.* rating (2) **3B**
bezahlen *v.* to pay (for) (1) **4A**
Bibliothek, -en *f.* library (1) **1B**
Bier, -e *n.* beer (1) **4B**
bieten *v.* to offer (3) **1B**
Bild, -er *n.* picture (2) **2A**
Bildschirm, -e *m.* screen (2) **4B**
Bioladen, ⁻ *m.* health-food store (3) **1B**
Biologie *f.* biology (1) **2A**
biologisch *adj.* organic (3) **4B**
Birne, -n *f.* pear (1) **4A**
bis *prep.* until (1) **3B**
   Bis bald. See you soon. (1) **1A**
   Bis dann. See you later. (1) **1A**
   Bis gleich. See you soon. (1) **1A**
   Bis morgen. See you tomorrow. (1) **1A**
   Bis später. See you later. (1) **1A**
   bis zu *prep.* up to; until (3) **2B**
Bitte. Please.; You're welcome. (1) **1A**
Blatt, ⁻er *n.* leaf (3) **4A**
blau *adj.* blue (1) **3A**
   blaue Fleck, -e *m.* bruise (3) **B1**
bleiben *v.* to stay (2) **1B**
   Bleiben Sie bitte am Apparat. *v.* Please
   hold. (3) **3A**
Bleistift, -e *m.* pencil (1) **1B**
Blitz, -e *m.* lightning (2) **3A**
blond *adj.* blond (1) **3A**
   blonde Haare *n. pl.* blond hair (1) **3A**
Blume, -n *f.* flower (1) **1A**
Blumengeschäft, -e *n.* flower shop (3) **2A**
Bluse, -n *f.* blouse (2) **1B**
Blutdruck *m.* blood pressure (3) **1B**
Boden, ⁻ *m.* floor; ground (2) **2A**
Bohne, -n *f.* bean (1) **4A**
   grüne Bohne *f.* green bean (1) **4A**
Boot, -e *n.* boat (2) **4A**
Bordkarte, -n *f.* boarding pass (2) **3B**
braten *v.* to fry (1) **2B**
brauchen *v.* to need (1) **2A**
braun *adj.* brown (2) **1B**
braunhaarig *adj.* brown-haired, brunette (1) **3A**
brechen *v.* to break (1) **2B**
   sich (den Arm / das Bein) brechen *v.* to break
   (an arm / a leg) (3) **1B**
Bremse, -n *f.* brake (2) **4A**
brennen *v.* to burn (2) **1A**
Brief, -e *m.* letter (3) **2A**
   einen Brief abschicken *v.* to mail a letter (3) **2A**
Briefkasten, ⁻ *m.* mailbox (3) **2A**
Briefmarke, -n *f.* stamp (3) **2A**
Briefträger, - / **Briefträgerin,** -nen *m./f.* mail
   carrier (3) **2A**

Briefumschlag, ⁻e *m.* envelope (3) **2A**
Brille, -n *f.* glasses (2) **1B**
bringen *v.* to bring (1) **2A**
Brot, -e *n.* bread (1) **4A**
Brötchen, - *n.* roll (1) **4A**
Brücke, -n *f.* bridge (3) **2B**
Bruder, ⁻ *m.* brother (1) **1A**
Brunnen, - *m.* fountain (3) **2B**
Buch, ⁻er *n.* book (1) **1A**
buchen *v.* to make a (hotel) reservation (2) **3B**
Bücherregal, -e *n.* bookshelf (2) **2A**
Buchhalter, - / **Buchhalterin,** -nen *m./f.*
   accountant (3) **3B**
büffeln *v.* to cram (for a test) (1) **2A**
Bügelbrett, -er *n.* ironing board (2) **2B**
Bügeleisen, - *n.* iron (2) **2B**
bügeln *v.* to iron (2) **2B**
Bundespräsident, -en / **Bundespräsidentin,**
   -nen *m./f.* (federal) president (2) **4B**
bunt *adj.* colorful (3) **2A**
Bürgermeister, - / **Bürgermeisterin,** -nen *m./f.*
   mayor (3) **2B**
Bürgersteig, -e *m.* sidewalk (3) **2B**
Büro, -s *n.* office (3) **3B**
Büroklammer, -n *f.* paperclip (3) **3A**
Büromaterial *n.* office supplies (3) **3A**
Bürste, -n *f.* brush (3) **1A**
bürsten *v.* to brush
   sich die Haare bürsten *v.* to brush one's hair (3) **1A**
Bus, -se *m.* bus (2) **4A**
Busch, ⁻e *m.* bush (3) **4A**
Bushaltestelle, -n *f.* bus stop (2) **4A**
Businessklasse *f.* business class (2) **3B**
Bußgeld, -er *n.* fine (monetary) (2) **4A**
Butter *f.* butter (1) **4A**

C

Café, -s *n.* café (1) **2A**
Camping *n.* camping (1) **2B**
CD, -s *f.* compact disc, CD (2) **4B**
Chef, -s / **Chefin,** -nen *m./f.* boss (3) **3B**
Chemie *f.* chemistry (1) **2A**
China *n.* China (3) **2B**
Chinese, -n / **Chinesin,** -nen *m./f.* Chinese
   (person) (3) **2B**
Chinesisch *n.* Chinese (language) (3) **2B**
Computer, - *m.* computer (1) **1B**
Cousin, -s / **Cousine,** -n *m./f.* cousin (1) **3A**

D

da there (1) **1A**
   Da ist/sind… There is/are… (1) **1A**
Dachboden, ⁻ *m.* attic (2) **2A**
dafür *adv.* for it (2) **2A**
daher *adv.* from there (2) **2A**
dahin *adv.* there (2) **2A**
damit *conj.* so that (3) **2A**
danach *conj.* then, after that (3) **1B**
danken *v.* to thank (1) **2A**
   Danke. Thank you. (1) **1A**
dann *adv.* then (2) **3B**
daran *adv.* on it (2) **2A**

darauf *adv.* on it (2) **2A**
darin *adv.* in it (2) **2A**
das *n.* the; this/that (1) **1A**
dass *conj.* that (3) **2A**
Datei, - en *f.* file (2) **4B**
Datum (*pl.* Daten) *n.* date (2) **3A**
davon *adv.* of it (2) **2A**
davor *adv.* before it (2) **2A**
Decke, -n *f.* blanket (2) **2B**
decken *v.* to cover (2) **2B**
  den Tisch decken *v.* to set the table (2) **2B**
denken *v.* to think (2) **1A**
  denken an *v.* to think about (2) **3A**
denn *conj.* for; because (2) **2A**
der *m.* the (1) **1A**
deshalb *conj.* therefore; so (3) **1B**
deswegen *conj.* that's why; therefore (3) **1B**
deutsch *adj.* German (3) **2B**
Deutsch *n.* German (language) (3) **2B**
Deutsche *m./f.* German (man/woman) (3) **2B**
Deutschland *n.* Germany (1) **4A**
deutschsprachig *adj.* German-speaking
Dezember *m.* December (1) **2A**, (2) **3A**
Diät, -en *f.* diet (1) **4B**
  auf Diät sein *v.* to be on a diet (1) **4B**
dick *adj.* fat (1) **3A**
die *f./pl.* the (1) **1A**
Dienstag, -e *m.* Tuesday (1) **2A**
  dienstags *adv.* on Tuesdays (1) **2A**
dieser/diese/dieses *m./f./n.* this; these (2) **4B**
diesmal *adv.* this time (2) **3B**
Digitalkamera, -s *f.* digital camera (2) **4B**
Ding, -e *n.* thing
Diplom, -e *n.* diploma (degree) (1) **2A**
diskret *adj.* discreet (1) **3B**
doch *adv.* yes (contradicting a negative statement or question) (1) **2B**
Dokument, -e *n.* document (2) **4B**
Donner, - *m.* thunder (2) **3A**
Donnerstag, -e *n.* Thursday (1) **2A**
  donnerstags *adv.* on Thursdays (1) **2A**
dort *adv.* there (1) **1A**
Dozent, -en / Dozentin, -nen *m./f.* college instructor (1) **2A**
draußen *prep.* outside; *adv.* out (2) **3A**
  Es ist schön draußen. It's nice out. (2) **3A**
dreckig *adj.* filthy (2) **2B**
drei three (1) **2A**
dritte *adj.* third (1) **2A**
Drogerie, -n *f.* drugstore (3) **2A**
drüben *adv.* over there (1) **4A**
drücken *v.* to push (1) **3B**; to print (2) **4B**
Drucker, - *m.* printer (2) **4B**
du *pron.* (*sing. inf.*) you (1) **1A**
dumm *adj.* dumb (2) **4A**
dunkel *adj.* dark (1) **3A**
dunkelhaarig *adj.* dark-haired (1) **3A**
dünn *adj.* thin (1) **3A**
durch *prep.* through (1) **3B**
durchfallen *v.* to flunk; to fail (1) **1B**
durchmachen *v.* to experience (2) **4B**
dürfen *v.* to be allowed to; may (1) **3B**
(sich) duschen *v.* to take a shower (3) **1A**

Dutzend, -e *n.* dozen (1) **4A**
DVD, -s *f.* DVD (2) **4B**
DVD-Player, - *m.* DVD-player (2) **4B**

E

Ecke, -n *f.* corner (3) **2B**
egoistisch *adj.* selfish (1) **3B**
Ehe, -n *f.* marriage (2) **1A**
Ehefrau, -en *f.* wife (1) **3A**
Ehemann, ⁻er *m.* husband (1) **3A**
Ei, -er *n.* egg (1) **4A**
Eichhörnchen, - *n.* squirrel (3) **4A**
eifersüchtig *adj.* jealous (1) **3B**
ein/eine *m./f./n.* a (1) **1A**
Einbahnstraße, -n *f.* one-way street (2) **4A**
einfach *adj.* easy (1) **2A**
einfarbig *adj.* solid colored (2) **1B**
eingebildet *adj.* arrogant (1) **3B**
einkaufen *v.* to shop (1) **4A**
  einkaufen gehen *v.* to go shopping (1) **4A**
Einkaufen *n.* shopping (2) **1B**
Einkaufszentrum, (*pl.* Einkaufszentren) *n.* mall; shopping center (3) **2B**
Einkommensgruppe, -n *f.* income bracket (2) **2B**
einladen *v.* to invite (2) **1A**
einmal *adv.* once (2) **3B**
eins one (1) **2A**
einschlafen *v.* to go to sleep (1) **4A**
einzahlen *v.* to deposit (money) (3) **2A**
Einzelkind, -er *n.* only child (1) **3A**
Eis *n.* ice cream (2) **1A**
Eisdiele, -n *f.* ice cream shop (1) **4A**
Eishockey *n.* ice hockey (1) **2B**
Eiswürfel, - *m.* ice cube (2) **1A**
elegant *adj.* elegant (2) **1B**
Elektriker, - / Elektrikerin, -nen *m./f.* electrician (3) **3B**
elf eleven (1) **2A**
Ell(en)bogen, - *m.* elbow (3) **1A**
Eltern *pl.* parents (1) **3A**
E-Mail, -s *f.* e-mail (2) **4B**
empfehlen *v.* to recommend (1) **2B**
Empfehlungsschreiben, - *n.* letter of recommendation (3) **3A**
endlich *adv.* finally (3) **1B**
Energie, -n *f.* energy (3) **4B**
energiesparend *adj.* energy-efficient (2) **2B**
eng *adj.* tight (2) **1B**
England *n.* England (3) **2B**
Engländer, - / Engländerin, -nen *m./f.* English (person) (3) **2B**
Englisch *n.* English (language) (3) **2B**
Enkelkind, -er *n.* grandchild (1) **3A**
Enkelsohn, ⁻e *m.* grandson (1) **3A**
Enkeltochter, ⁻ *f.* granddaughter (1) **3A**
entdecken *v.* to discover (2) **2B**
entfernen *v.* to remove (2) **2B**
entlang *prep.* along, down (1) **3B**
entlassen *v.* to fire; to lay off (3) **3B**
sich entschließen *v.* to decide (1) **4B**
(sich) entschuldigen *v.* to apologize; to excuse
  Entschuldigen Sie. Excuse me. (*form.*) (1) **1A**

Entschuldigung. Excuse me. (1) **1A**
sich entspannen *v.* to relax (3) **1A**
entwerten *v.* to validate (2) **4A**
  eine Fahrkarte entwerten *v.* to validate a ticket (2) **4A**
entwickeln *v.* to develop (3) **4B**
er *pron.* he (1) **1A**
Erdbeben, - *n.* earthquake (3) **4A**
Erdbeere, -n *f.* strawberry (1) **4A**
Erde, -n *f.* earth (3) **4B**
Erderwärmung *f.* global warming (3) **4B**
Erdgeschoss, -e *n.* ground floor (2) **2A**
Erfahrung, -en *f.* experience (3) **3A**
erfinden *v.* to invent (2) **3A**
Erfolg, -e *m.* success (3) **3B**
erforschen *v.* to explore (3) **4A**
ergänzen *v.* complete
Ergebnis, -se *n.* result; score (1) **1B**
erhalten *v.* to preserve (3) **4B**
sich erinnern (an) *v.* to remember (3) **1A**
sich erkälten *v.* to catch a cold (3) **1A**
Erkältung, -en *f.* cold (3) **1B**
erkennen *v.* to recognize (2) **3A**
erklären *v.* to explain (1) **4A**
erneuerbare Energie, -n *f.* renewable energy (3) **4B**
ernst *adj.* serious (1) **3B**
erster/erste/erstes *adj.* first (1) **2A**
erwachsen *adj.* grown-up (3) **2A**
erzählen *v.* to tell (2) **3A**
  erzählen von *v.* to talk about (2) **3A**
es *pron.* it (1) **1A**
  Es geht. (I'm) so-so. (1) **1A**
  Es gibt... There is/are... (1) **2B**
Essen, - *n.* food (1) **4A**
essen *v.* to eat (1) **2B**
  essen gehen *v.* to eat out (1) **2B**
Esslöffel, - *m.* soup spoon (1) **4B**
Esszimmer, - *n.* dining room (2) **2A**
etwas *pron.* something (2) **3B**
  etwas anderes something else (3) **2A**
euer (*pl. inf.*) *poss. adj.* your (1) **3A**

F

Fabrik, -en *f.* factory (3) **4B**
Fabrikarbeiter, - / Fabrikarbeiterin, -nen *m./f.* factory worker (3) **3B**
Fach, ⁻er *n.* subject (1) **2A**
fade *adj.* bland (1) **4B**
fahren *v.* to drive; to go (1) **2B**
  Auto fahren *v.* to drive a car (2) **4A**
  Fahrrad fahren *v.* to ride a bicycle (1) **2B**
  geradeaus fahren *v.* to go straight ahead (2) **4A**
Fahrer, - / Fahrerin, -nen *m./f.* driver (2) **4A**
Fahrgemeinschaft, -en *f.* carpool (3) **4B**
Fahrkarte, -n *f.* ticket (2) **4A**
  eine Fahrkarte entwerten *v.* to validate a ticket (2) **4A**
Fahrkartenschalter, - *m.* ticket office (2) **4A**
Fahrplan, ⁻e *m.* schedule (2) **4A**
Fahrrad, ⁻er *n.* bicycle (1) **2B**, (2) **4A**
Fahrstuhl, ⁻e *m.* elevator (2) **3B**
fallen *v.* to fall (1) **2B**

Familie, -n *f.* family (1) **3A**
Familienstand, ⁻e *m.* marital status (1) **3A**
Fan, -s *m.* fan (1) **2B**
fangen *v.* to catch (1) **2B**
fantastisch *adj.* fantastic (3) **2A**
Farbe, -n *f.* color (2) **1B**
färben *v.* to dye
  sich die Haare färben *v.* to dye one's hair (3) **1A**
fast *adv.* almost (1) **4A**
faul *adj.* lazy (1) **3B**
Februar *m.* February (1) **2A**, (2) **3A**
fegen *v.* to sweep (2) **2B**
feiern *v.* to celebrate (2) **1A**
Feiertag, -e *m.* holiday (2) **1A**
Feinkostgeschäft, -e *n.* delicatessen (1) **4A**
Feld, -er *n.* field (3) **4A**
Fenster, - *n.* window (1) **1A**
Ferien *pl.* vacation (2) **3A**
Fernbedienung, -en *f.* remote control (2) **4B**
fernsehen *v.* to watch television (2) **4B**
Fernsehen *n.* television (programming)
Fernseher, - *m.* television set (2) **4B**
fertig *adj.* ready; finished (3) **3B**
Fest, -e *n.* festival; celebration (2) **1A**
Festplatte, -n *f.* hard drive (2) **4B**
Feuerwehrmann, ⁻er / Feuerwehrfrau, -en
  (pl. Feuerwehrleute) *m./f.* firefighter (3) **3B**
Fieber, - *n.* fever (3) **1B**
  Fieber haben *v.* to have a fever (3) **1B**
finden *v.* to find (1) **2A**
Finger, - *m.* finger (3) **1A**
Firma (pl. die Firmen) *f.* firm; company (3) **3A**
Fisch, -e *m.* fish (1) **4A**, (3) **4A**
Fischgeschäft, -e *n.* fish store (1) **4A**
fit *adj.* in good shape (1) **2B**
Flasche, -n *f.* bottle (1) **4B**
Fleisch *n.* meat (1) **4A**
fleißig *adj.* hard-working (1) **3B**
fliegen *v.* to fly (2) **3B**
Flug, ⁻e *m.* flight (2) **3B**
Flughafen, ⁻ *m.* airport (2) **3B**
Flugticket, -s *n.* (plane) ticket (2) **3B**
Flugzeug, -e *n.* airplane (2) **3B**
Flur, -e *m.* hall (2) (1) **2A**
Fluss, ⁻e *m.* river (1) **3B**, (3) **4A**
folgen *v.* to follow (2) **1A**, (3) **2B**
Form, -en *f.* shape, form
  in guter/schlechter Form sein *v.* to be in/out of shape (3) **1B**
Formular, -e *n.* form (3) **2A**
  ein Formular ausfüllen *v.* to fill out a form (3) **2A**
Foto, -s *n.* photo, picture (1) **1B**
Frage, -n *f.* question (1) **1B**
fragen *v.* to ask (1) **2A**
  fragen nach *v.* to ask about (2) **3A**
  sich fragen *v.* to wonder, ask oneself (3) **1A**
Frankreich *n.* France (3) **2B**
Franzose, -n / Französin, -nen *m./f.* French (person) (3) **2B**
Französisch *n.* French (language) (3) **2B**
Frau, -en *f.* woman (1) **1A**; wife (1) **3A**
  Frau... Mrs./Ms.... (1) **1A**
Freitag, -e *m.* Friday (1) **2A**

freitags *adv.* on Fridays (1) **2A**
Freizeit, -en *f.* free time, leisure (1) **2B**
Freizeitaktivität, - en *f.* leisure activity (1) **2B**
Fremdsprache, -n *f.* foreign language (1) **2A**
sich freuen (über) *v.* to be happy (about) (3) **1A**
  Freut mich. Pleased to meet you. (1) **1A**
  sich freuen auf *v.* to look forward to (3) **1A**
Freund, -e / Freundin, -nen *m./f.* friend (1) **1A**
freundlich *adj.* friendly (1) **3B**
  Mit freundlichen Grüßen Yours sincerely (1) **3B**
Freundschaft, -en *f.* friendship (2) **1A**
Frischvermählte, -n *m./f.* newlywed (2) **1A**
Friseur, -e / Friseurin, -nen *m./f.* hairdresser (1) **3B**
froh *adj.* happy (1) **3B**
  Frohe Ostern! Happy Easter! (2) **1A**
  Frohe Weihnachten! Merry Christmas! (2) **1A**
früh *adj.* early; in the morning (1) **2B**
  morgen früh tomorrow morning (1) **2B**
Frühling, -e *m.* spring (1) **2B**, (2) **3A**
Frühstück, -e *n.* breakfast (1) **4B**
fühlen *v.* to feel (1) **2A**
  sich (wohl) fühlen *v.* to feel (well) (3) **1A**
füllen *v.* to fill
fünf five (1) **2A**
funktionieren *v.* to work, function (2) **4B**
für *prep.* for (1) **3B**
furchtbar *adj.* awful (2) **3A**
Fuß, ⁻e *m.* foot (3) **1A**
Fußball *m.* soccer (1) **2B**
Fußgänger, - / Fußgängerin, -nen *m./f.* pedestrian (3) **2B**

Gabel, -n *f.* fork (1) **4B**
Gang, ⁻e *m.* course (1) **4B**
  erster/zweiter Gang *m.* first/second course (1) **4B**
ganz *adj.* all, total (2) **3B**
ganztags *adj.* full-time (3) **3B**
Garage, -n *f.* garage (2) **1B**
Garnele, -n *f.* shrimp (1) **4A**
Gartenabfall, ⁻e *m.* yard waste (3) **4B**
Gärtner, - /Gärtnerin, -nen *m./f.* gardener (3) **3B**
Gast, ⁻e *m.* guest (2) **1A**
Gastfamilie, -n *f.* host family (1) **4B**
Gastgeber, - / Gastgeberin, -nen *m./f.* host/hostess (2) **1A**
Gebäck, -e *n.* pastries; baked goods (2) **1A**
Gebäude, - *n.* building (3) **2A**
geben *v.* to give (1) **2B**
  Es gibt... There is/are... (1) **2B**
Geburt, -en *f.* birth (2) **1A**
Geburtstag, -e *m.* birthday (2) **1A**
  Wann hast du Geburtstag? When is your birthday? (2) **3A**
geduldig *adj.* patient (1) **3B**
Gefahr, -en *f.* danger (3) **4B**
gefährdet *adj.* endangered; threatened (3) **4B**
gefallen *v.* to please (2) **1A**
Gefrierschrank, ⁻e *m.* freezer (2) **2B**
gegen *prep.* against (1) **3B**
gegenüber (von) *prep.* across (from) (3) **2B**
Gehalt, ⁻er *n.* salary (3) **3A**

hohes/niedriges Gehalt, ⁻er *n.* high/low salary (3) **3A**
Gehaltserhöhung, -en *f.* raise (3) **3B**
gehen *v.* to go (1) **2A**
  Es geht. (I'm) so-so. (1) **1A**
  Geht es dir/Ihnen gut? *v.* Are you all right? (inf./form.) (1) **1A**
  Wie geht es Ihnen? (form.) How are you? (1) **1A**
  Wie geht's (dir)? (inf.) How are you? (1) **1A**
gehören *v.* to belong to (1) **4B**
Geländewagen, - *m.* SUV (2) **4B**
gelb *adj.* yellow (2) **1B**
Geld, -er *n.* money (3) **2A**
  Geld abheben/einzahlen *v.* to withdraw/deposit money (3) **2A**
Geldautomat, -en *m.* ATM (3) **2A**
Geldschein, -e *m.* bill (money) (3) **2A**
gemein *adj.* mean (1) **3B**
Gemüse, - *n.* vegetables (1) **4A**
genau *adv.* exactly
  genauso wie just as (2) **4A**
genießen *v.* to enjoy
geöffnet *adj.* open (3) **2A**
Gepäck *n.* luggage (2) **3B**
geradeaus *adv.* straight ahead (2) **4A**
gern *adv.* with pleasure (1) **2B**
  gern (+verb) to like to (+verb) (1) **2B**
  ich hätte gern... I would like... (1) **4A**
  Gern geschehen. My pleasure.; You're welcome. (1) **1A**
Geschäft, -e *n.* business (3) **3A**; store (1) **4A**
Geschäftsführer, - / Geschäftsführerin, -nen *m./f.* manager (3) **3A**
Geschäftsmann, ⁻er / Geschäftsfrau, -en **(pl. Geschäftsleute)** *m./f.* businessman/businesswoman (1) **3B**
Geschenk, -e *n.* gift (2) **1A**
Geschichte, -n *f.* history (1) **2A**; story
geschieden *adj.* divorced (1) **3A**
Geschirr *n.* dishes (2) **2B**
  Geschirr spülen *v.* to do the dishes (2) **2B**
geschlossen *adj.* closed (3) **2A**
Geschmack, ⁻e *m.* flavor; taste (1) **4B**
Geschwister, - *n.* sibling (1) **3A**
Gesetz, -e *n.* law (3) **4B**
Gesicht, -er *n.* face (3) **1A**
gestern *adv.* yesterday (2) **1B**
gestreift *adj.* striped (2) **1B**
gesund *adj.* healthy (2) **4A**; (3) **1B**
  gesund werden *v.* to get better (3) **1B**
Gesundheit *f.* health (3) **1B**
geteilt durch divided by (1) **1B**
Getränk, -e *n.* beverage (1) **4B**
getrennt *adj.* separated (1) **3A**
gewaltfrei *adj.* nonviolent (3) **4B**
Gewerkschaft, -en *f.* labor union (3) **3B**
gewinnen *v.* to win (1) **2B**
Gewitter, - *n.* thunderstorm (2) **3A**
sich gewöhnen an *v.* to get used to (3) **1A**
gierig *adj.* greedy (1) **3B**
Giftmüll *m.* toxic waste (3) **4B**
Glas, ⁻er *n.* glass (1) **4B**
glatt *adj.* straight (1) **3A**
  glatte Haare *n. pl.* straight hair (1) **3A**

glauben *v.* to believe (2) **1A**
gleich *adj.* same
  ist gleich *v.* equals, is (1) **1B**
Glück *n.* happiness (2) **1A**
glücklich *adj.* happy (1) **3B**
Golf *n.* golf (1) **2B**
Grad *n.* degree (2) **3A**
  Es sind 18 Grad draußen. It's 18 degrees out. (2) **3A**
Gramm, -e *n.* gram (1) **4A**
Granit, -e *m.* granite (2) **2B**
Gras, ̈er *n.* grass (3) **4A**
gratulieren *v.* to congratulate (2) **1A**
grau *adj.* grey (2) **1B**
grausam *adj.* cruel
Grippe, -n *f.* flu (3) **1B**
groß *adj.* big; tall (1) **3A**
großartig *adj.* terrific (1) **3A**
Großeltern *pl.* grandparents (1) **1A**
Großmutter, ̈ *f.* grandmother (1) **3A**
Großvater, ̈ *m.* grandfather (1) **3A**
großzügig *adj.* generous (1) **3B**
grün *adj.* green (2) **1B**
  grüne Bohne (*pl.* die grünen Bohnen) *f.* green bean (1) **4A**
Gruß, ̈e *m.* greeting
  Mit freundlichen Grüßen Yours sincerely (1) **3B**
grüßen *v.* to greet (1) **2A**
günstig *adj.* cheap (2) **1B**
Gürtel, - *m.* belt (2) **1B**
gut *adj.* good; *adv.* well (1) **1A**
  gut aussehend *adj.* handsome (1) **3A**
  gut gekleidet *adj.* well dressed (2) **1B**
  Gute Besserung! Get well! (2) **1A**
  Guten Appetit! Enjoy your meal! (1) **4B**
  Guten Abend! Good evening. (1) **1A**
  Guten Morgen! Good morning. (1) **1A**
  Gute Nacht! Good night. (1) **1A**
  Guten Tag! Hello. (1) **1A**

H

Haar, -e *n.* hair (1) **3A**, (3) **1A**
Haartrockner, - *m.* hair dryer (3) **1A**
haben *v.* to have (1) **1B**
Hagel *m.* hail (2) **3A**
Hähnchen, - *n.* chicken (1) **4A**
halb half; half an hour before (1) **2A**
Halbbruder, ̈ *m.* half brother (1) **3A**
Halbschwester, -n *f.* half sister (1) **3A**
halbtags *adj.* part-time (3) **3B**
Hallo! Hello. (1) **1A**
Hals, ̈e *m.* neck (3) **1A**
  Hals- und Beinbruch! Break a leg! (2) **1A**
Halskette, -n *f.* necklace (2) **1B**
Hand, ̈e *f.* hand (3) **1A**
handeln *v.* to act
  handeln von *v.* to be about; have to do with (2) **3A**
Handgelenk, -e *n.* wrist (3) **1B**
Handgepäck *n.* carry-on luggage (2) **3B**
Handschuh, -e *m.* glove (2) **1B**
Handtasche, -n *f.* purse (2) **1B**
Handtuch, ̈er *n.* towel (3) **1A**
Handy, -s *n.* cell phone (2) **4B**

hängen *v.* to hang (2) **1B**
Hase, -n *m.* hare (3) **4A**
hässlich *adj.* ugly (1) **3A**
Hauptspeise, -n *f.* main course (1) **4B**
Hauptstraße, -n *f.* main road (3) **2B**
Haus, ̈er *n.* house (2) **2A**
  nach Hause *adv.* home (2) **1B**
  zu Hause *adv.* at home (1) **4A**
Hausarbeit *f.* housework (2) **2B**
  Hausarbeit machen *v.* to do housework (2) **2B**
Hausaufgabe, -n *f.* homework (1) **1B**
Hausfrau, -en / Hausmann, ̈er *f./m.* homemaker (3) **3B**
hausgemacht *adj.* homemade (1) **4B**
Hausmeister, - / Hausmeisterin, -nen *m./f.* caretaker; custodian (3) **3B**
Hausschuh, -e *m.* slipper (3) **1A**
Haustier, -e *n.* pet (1) **3A**
Heft, -e *n.* notebook (1) **1B**
Hefter, - *m.* stapler (3) **3A**
heiraten *v.* to marry (1) **3A**
heiß *adj.* hot (2) **3A**
heißen *v.* to be named (1) **2A**
  Ich heiße... My name is... (1) **1A**
helfen *v.* to help (1) **2B**
  helfen bei *v.* to help with (2) **3A**
hell *adj.* light (1) **3A**; bright (2) **1B**
Hemd, -en *n.* shirt (2) **1B**
herauf *adv.* up; upwards (2) **2A**
heraus *adv.* out (2) **2A**
Herbst, -e *m.* fall, autumn (1) **2B**, (2) **3A**
Herd, -e *m.* stove (2) **2B**
Herr Mr. (1) **1A**
herunter *adv.* down; downwards (2) **2A**
heruntergehen *v.* to go down (3) **2B**
  die Treppe heruntergehen *v.* to go downstairs (3) **2B**
herunterladen *v.* to download (2) **4B**
Herz, -en *n.* heart
  Herzlichen Glückwunsch! Congratulations! (2) **1A**
heute *adv.* today (1) **2B**
  Heute ist der... Today is the... (1) **2A**
  Welcher Tag ist heute? What day is it today? (2) **3A**
  Der Wievielte ist heute? What is the date today? (1) **2A**
hier *adv.* here (1) **1A**
  Hier ist/sind... Here is/are... (1) **1B**
Himmel *m.* sky (3) **4A**
hin und zurück there and back (2) **3B**
sich hinlegen *v.* to lie down (3) **1A**
sich hinsetzen *v.* to sit down (3) **1A**
hinter *prep.* behind (2) **1B**
hinterlassen *v.* to leave (behind)
  eine Nachricht hinterlassen *v.* to leave a message (3) **3A**
Hobby, -s *n.* hobby (1) **2B**
hoch *adj.* high (2) **4A**
hochgehen *v.* to go up, climb up (3) **2B**
  die Treppe hochgehen *v.* to go upstairs (3) **2B**
Hochwasser, - *n.* flood (3) **4B**
Hochzeit, -en *f.* wedding (2) **1A**
Hockey *n.* hockey (1) **2B**
Höflichkeit, -en *f.* courtesy; polite expression (1) **1A**
Holz, ̈er *n.* wood (2) **2B**

hören *v.* to hear; listen to (1) **2A**
Hörer, - *m.* receiver (3) **3A**
Hörsaal (*pl.* Hörsäle) *m.* lecture hall (1) **2A**
Hose, -n *f.* pants (2) **1B**
  kurze Hose *f.* shorts (1) **1B**
Hotel, -s *n.* hotel (2) **3B**
  Fünf-Sterne-Hotel *n* five-star hotel. (2) **3B**
Hotelgast, ̈e *m.* hotel guest (2) **3B**
hübsch *adj.* pretty (1) **3A**
Hund, -e *m.* dog (1) **3A**
Hundewetter *n.* terrible weather (2) **3A**
husten *v.* to cough (3) **1B**
Hut, ̈e *m.* hat (2) **1B**
Hybridauto, -s *n.* hybrid car (3) **4B**

I

ich *pron.* I (1) **1A**
Idee, -n *f.* idea (1) **1A**
Ihr (*form., sing/pl.*) *poss. adj.* your (1) **3A**
ihr (*inf., pl.*) *pron.* you (1) **1A**; *poss. adj.* her, their (1) **3A**
immer *adv.* always (1) **4A**
Immobilienmakler, - / Immobilienmaklerin, -nen *m./f.* real estate agent (3) **3B**
in *prep.* in (2) **1B**
Inder, - / Inderin, -nen *m./f.* Indian (person) (3) **2B**
Indien *n.* India (3) **2B**
indisch *adj.* Indian (3) **2B**
Informatik *f.* computer science (1) **2A**
sich informieren (über) *v.* to find out (about) (3) **1A**
Ingenieur, -e / Ingenieurin, -nen *m./f.* engineer (1) **3B**
Innenstadt, ̈e *f.* city center; downtown (3) **2B**
innerhalb *prep.* inside of, within (2) **4B**
Insel, -n *f.* island (3) **4A**
intellektuell *adj.* intellectual (1) **3B**
intelligent *adj.* intelligent (1) **3B**
interessant *adj.* interesting (1) **2A**
sich interessieren (für) *v.* to be interested (in) (3) **1A**
Internet *n.* Web (2) **4B**
  im Internet surfen *v.* to surf the Web (2) **4B**
Internetcafé, -s *n.* internet café (3) **2A**
Italien *n.* Italy (3) **2B**
Italiener, - / Italienerin, -nen *m./f.* Italian (person) (3) **2B**
Italienisch *n.* Italian (language) (3) **2B**

J

ja yes (1) **1A**
Jacke, -n *f.* jacket (2) **1B**
Jahr, -e *n.* year (2) **3A**
  Ein gutes neues Jahr! Happy New Year! (2) **1A**
  Ich bin... Jahre alt. I am... years old (1) **1B**
Jahrestag, -e *m.* anniversary (2) **1A**
Jahreszeit, -en *f.* season (2) **3A**
Januar *m.* January (1) **2A**, (2) **3A**
Japan *n.* Japan (3) **2B**
Japaner, - / Japanerin, -nen *m./f.* Japanese (person) (3) **2B**
Japanisch *n.* Japanese (language) (3) **2B**
Jeans *f.* jeans (2) **1B**
jeder/jede/jedes *adj.* any, every, each (2) **4B**

jemand *pron.* someone (2) **3B**
jetzt *adv.* now (1) **4A**
joggen *v.* to jog (1) **2B**
Joghurt, -s *m.* yogurt (1) **4A**
Journalist, -en / Journalistin, -nen *m./f.*
  journalist (1) **3B**
Jugendherberge, -n *f.* youth hostel (2) **3B**
jugendlich *adj.* young; youthful (3) **2A**
Juli *m.* July (1) **2A**, (2) **3A**
jung *adj.* young (1) **3A**
Junge, -n *m.* boy (1) **1A**
Juni *m.* June (1) **2A**, (2) **3A**
Juweliergeschäft, -e *n.* jewelry store (3) **2A**

K

Kaffee, -s *m.* coffee (1) **4B**
Kaffeemaschine, -n *f.* coffeemaker (2) **2B**
Kalender, - *m.* calendar (1) **1B**
kalt *adj.* cold (2) **3A**
sich (die Haare) kämmen *v.* to comb (one's hair)
  (3) **1A**
Kanada *n.* Canada (3) **2B**
Kanadier, - / Kanadierin, -nen *m./f.*
  Canadian (3) **2B**
Kandidat, -en *m.* candidate (3) **3A**
Kaninchen, - *n.* rabbit (3) **4A**
Karotte, -n *f.* carrot (1) **4A**
Karriere, -n *f.* career (3) **3B**
Karte, -n *f.* map (1) **1B**, *f.* card (1) **2B**; (2) **1A**
  eine Karte lesen *v.* to read a map (2) **3B**
  mit der Karte bezahlen *v.* to pay by (credit)
    card (3) **2A**
Kartoffel, -n *f.* potato (1) **4A**
Käse, - *m.* cheese (1) **4A**
Katze, -n *f.* cat (1) **3A**
kaufen *v.* to buy (1) **2A**
Kaufhaus, ̈er *n.* department store (3) **2B**
Kaution, -en *f.* security deposit (2) **2A**
kein *adj.* no (1) **2B**
  Keine Zufahrt. Do not enter. (1) **3B**
Keks, -e *m.* cookie (2) **1A**
Keller, - *m.* cellar (2) **2A**
Kellner, - / Kellnerin, -nen *m./f.* waiter/
  waitress (1) **3B**, (1) **4B**
kennen *v.* to know, be familiar with (2) **1B**
  sich kennen *v.* to know each other (3) **1A**
  (sich) kennen lernen *v.* to meet (one another)
    (1) **1A**
Keramik, -en *f.* ceramic (2) **2B**
Kernenergie *f.* nuclear energy (2) **1B**
Kernkraftwerk, -e *n.* nuclear power plant (3) **4B**
Kind, -er *n.* child (1) **1A**
Kino, -s *n.* movie theater (3) **2A**
Kiosk, -e *m.* newspaper kiosk (3) **2A**
Kirche, -n *f.* church (3) **2B**
Kissen, - *n.* pillow (2) **2B**
Klasse, -n *f.* class (1) **1B**
  erste/zweite Klasse, -n first/second class (2) **4A**
Klassenkamerad, -en / Klassenkameradin,
  -nen *m./f.* (K-12) classmate (1) **1B**
Klassenzimmer, - *n.* classroom (1) **1B**
klassisch *adj.* classical (3) **2A**
Kleid, -er *n.* dress (2) **1B**

Kleidergröße, -n *f.* clothing size (2) **1B**
Kleidung *f. pl.* clothes (2) **1B**
klein *adj.* small; short (stature) (1) **3A**
Kleingeld *n.* change (money) (3) **2A**
Klempner, - / Klempnerin, -nen *m./f.* plumber (3) **3B**
klettern *v.* to climb (mountain) (1) **2B**
klingeln *v.* to ring (2) **4B**
Klippe, -n *f.* cliff (3) **4A**
Knie, - *n.* knee (3) **1A**
Knoblauch, -e *m.* garlic (1) **4A**
Koch, ̈e / Köchin, -nen *m./f.* cook, chef (1) **4B**
kochen *v.* to cook (1) **2B**
Koffer, - *m.* suitcase (2) **3B**
Kofferraum, ̈e *m.* trunk (2) **4A**
Kombi, -s *m.* station wagon (2) **4B**
Komma, -s *n.* comma (1) **1B**
kommen *v.* to come (1) **2A**
Kommilitone, -n / Kommilitonin, -nen *m./f.*
  (university) classmate (1) **1B**
Kommode, -n *f.* dresser (2) **2A**
kompliziert *adj.* complicated (3) **2A**
Konditorei, -en *f.* pastry shop (1) **4A**
können *v.* to be able, can (1) **3B**
Konto (*pl.* Konten) *n.* bank account (3) **2A**
Konzert, -e *n.* concert (2) **1B**
Kopf, ̈e *m.* head (3) **1A**
Kopfhörer, - *m.* headphones (2) **4B**
Kopfschmerzen *m. pl.* headache (3) **1B**
Korea *n.* Korea (3) **2B**
der Koreaner, - / die Koreanerin, -nen *m./f.*
  Korean (person) (3) **2B**
Koreanisch *n.* Korean (language) (3) **2B**
Körper, - *m.* body (1) **1A**
korrigieren *v.* to correct (1) **2A**
Kosmetiksalon, -s *m.* beauty salon (3) **2A**
kosten *v.* to cost (1) **2A**
  Wie viel kostet das? *v.* How much is that? (1) **4A**
krank *adj.* sick (3) **1B**
  krank werden *v.* to get sick (3) **1B**
Krankenhaus, ̈er *n.* hospital (3) **1B**
Krankenpfleger, - / Krankenschwester, -n *m./f.*
  nurse (3) **1B**
Krankenwagen, - *m.* ambulance (3) **1B**
Krawatte, -n *f.* tie (2) **1B**
Kreuzfahrt, -en *f.* cruise (2) **3B**
Kreuzung, -en *f.* intersection (3) **2B**
Küche, -n *f.* kitchen (2) **2A**
Kuchen, - *m.* cake; pie (1) **4A**
Kuh, ̈e *f.* cow (3) **4A**
kühl *adj.* cool (2) **3A**
Kühlschrank, ̈e *m.* refrigerator (2) **2B**
Kuli, -s *m.* (ball-point) pen (1) **1B**
Kunde, -n / Kundin, -nen *m./f.* customer (2) **1B**
kündigen *v.* to resign (3) **3B**
Kunst, ̈e *f.* art (1) **2A**
Kunststoff, -e *m.* plastic (2) **2B**
kurz *adj.* short (1) **3A**
  kurze Haare *n. pl.* short hair (1) **3A**
  kurze Hose *f.* shorts (2) **1B**
kurzärmlig *adj.* short-sleeved (2) **1B**
Kurzfilm, -e *m.* short film
Kuss, ̈e *m.* kiss (2) **1A**
küssen *v.* to kiss (2) **1A**
  sich küssen *v.* to kiss (each other) (3) **1A**
Küste, -n *f.* coast (3) **4A**

L

lächeln *v.* to smile (1) **3B**
lachen *v.* to laugh (1) **3B**
Ladegerät, -e *n.* battery charger (2) **4B**
laden *v.* to charge; load (2) **4B**
Lage, -n *f.* location (2) **3B**
Laken, - *n.* sheet (2) **2B**
Lampe, -n *f.* lamp (2) **2A**
Land, ̈er *n.* country (2) **3B**
landen *v.* to land (2) **3B**
Landkarte, -n *f.* map (2) **3B**
Landschaft, -en *f.* landscape;
  countryside (3) **4A**
lang *adj.* long (1) **3A**
  lange Haare *n. pl.* long hair (1) **3A**
langärmlig *adj.* long-sleeved (2) **1B**
langsam *adj.* slow (1) **3B**
  Langsam fahren. Slow down. (1) **3B**
langweilig *adj.* boring (1) **2A**
Laptop, -s *m./n.* laptop (computer) (2) **4B**
lassen *v.* to let, allow (1) **2B**
laufen *v.* to run (1) **2B**
leben *v.* to live (1) **2A**
Lebenslauf, ̈e *m.* résumé; CV (3) **3A**
Lebensmittelgeschäft, -e *n.* grocery store (1) **4A**
lecker *adj.* delicious (1) **4B**
Leder, - *n.* leather (2) **1B**
ledig *adj.* single (1) **3A**
legen *v.* to lay (2) **1B**; *v.* to put; lay (3) **1A**
Lehrbuch, ̈er *n.* textbook (university) (1) **1B**
Lehrer, - / Lehrerin, -nen *m./f.* teacher (1) **1B**
leicht *adj.* light (1) **4B**; mild (3) **1B**
Leichtathletik *f.* track and field (1) **2B**
leider *adv.* unfortunately (1) **4A**
leiten *v.* to manage (3) **3B**
Lenkrad, ̈er *n.* steering wheel (2) **4A**
lernen *v.* to study; to learn (1) **2A**
lesen *v.* to read (1) **2B**
letzter/letzte/letztes *adj.* last (1) **2B**
Leute *pl.* people (1) **3B**
Licht, -er *n.* light (3) **4B**
Liebe, -n *f.* love (2) **1A**
  Lieber/Liebe *m./f.* Dear (1) **3B**
lieben *v.* to love (1) **2A**
  sich lieben *v.* to love each other (3) **1A**
lieber *adj.* rather (2) **4A**
liebevoll *adj.* loving (1) **3B**
Liebling, -e *m.* darling
  Lieblings- favorite (1) **4B**
liegen *v.* to lie; to be located (2) **1B**
lila *adj.* purple (2) **1B**
Linie, -n *f.* line
Lippe, -n *f.* lip (3) **1A**
Lippenstift, -e *m.* lipstick (3) **1A**
Literatur, -en *f.* literature (1) **2A**
LKW, -s *m.* truck (2) **4A**
LKW-Fahrer, - / LKW-Fahrerin, -nen *m./f.* truck
  driver (3) **3B**
lockig *adj.* curly (1) **3A**
  lockige Haare *n. pl.* curly hair (1) **3A**
Los! Start!; Go! (1) **2B**
löschen *v.* to delete (2) **4B**
Lösung, -en *f.* solution (3) **4B**

eine Lösung vorschlagen *v.* to propose a solution (3) **4B**
Luft, ⸚e *f.* air (3) **4A**
lügen *v.* to lie, tell a lie
Lust, ⸚e *f.* desire
  Lust haben *v.* to feel like (2) **3B**
lustig *adj.* funny (1) **3B**

M

machen *v.* to do; make (1) **2A**
  Mach's gut! *v.* All the best! (1) **3B**
Mädchen, - *n.* girl (1) **1A**
Mahlzeit, -en *f.* meal (1) **4B**
Mai *m.* May (1) **2A**, (2) **3A**
Mal, -e *n.* time
  das erste/letzte Mal the first/last time (2) **3B**
  zum ersten/letzten Mal for the first/last time (2) **3B**
mal times (1) **1B**
Mama, -s *f.* mom (1) **3A**
man *pron.* one (2) **3B**
mancher/manche/manches *adj.* some (2) **4B**
manchmal *adv.* sometimes (2) **3B**
Mann, ⸚er *m.* man (1) **1A**; *m.* husband (1) **3A**
Mannschaft, -en *f.* team (1) **2B**
Mantel, ⸚ *m.* coat (1) **1B**
Markt, ⸚e *m.* market (1) **4A**
Marmelade, -n *f.* jam (1) **4A**
Marmor *m.* marble (2) **2B**
März *m.* March (1) **2A**, (3) **3A**
Material, -ien *n.* material (2) **1B**
Mathematik *f.* mathematics (1) **2A**
Maus, ⸚e *f.* mouse (4) **4B**
Mechaniker, - / Mechanikerin, -nen *m./f.* mechanic (2) **4A**
Medikament, -e *n.* medicine (3) **1B**
Medizin *f.* medicine (1) **2A**
Meer, -e *n.* sea; ocean (1) **4A**
Meeresfrüchte *f. pl.* seafood (1) **4A**
mehr *adj.* more (2) **4A**
mein *poss. adj.* my (1) **3A**
meinen *v.* to mean; to believe; to maintain (1) **4B**
Meisterschaft, -en *f.* championship (1) **2B**
Melone, -n *f.* melon (1) **4A**
Mensa (*pl.* Mensen) *f.* cafeteria (college/university) (1) **1B**
Mensch, -en *m.* person
Messer, - *n.* knife (1) **4B**
Metzgerei, -en *f.* butcher shop (1) **4A**
Mexikaner, - / Mexikanerin, -nen *m./f.* Mexican (person) (3) **2B**
mexikanisch *adj.* Mexican (3) **2B**
Mexiko *n.* Mexico (3) **2B**
Miete, -n *f.* rent (2) **2A**
mieten *v.* to rent (2) **2A**
Mikrofon, -e *n.* microphone (2) **4B**
Mikrowelle, -n *f.* microwave (2) **2B**
Milch *f.* milk (1) **4B**
Minderheit, -en *f.* minority (3) **4B**
Mineralwasser *n.* sparkling water (1) **4B**
minus minus (1) **1B**
mir *pron.* myself, me (2) **3A**

Mir geht's (sehr) gut. *v.* I am (very) well. (1) **1A**
Mir geht's nicht (so) gut. *v.* I am not (so) well. (1) **1A**
mit with (1) **4B**
Mitbewohner, - / Mitbewohnerin, -nen *m./f.* roommate (1) **2A**
mitbringen *v.* to bring along (1) **4A**
mitkommen *v.* to come along (1) **4A**
mitmachen *v.* to participate (2) **4B**
mitnehmen *v.* to bring with (3) **2B**
  jemanden mitnehmen *v.* to give someone a ride (3) **2B**
Mittag, -e *m.* noon (1) **2A**
Mittagessen *n.* lunch (1) **4B**
Mitternacht *f.* midnight (1) **2A**
Mittwoch, -e *m.* Wednesday (1) **2A**
  mittwochs *adv.* on Wednesdays (1) **2A**
Möbel, - *n.* furniture (2) **2A**
Möbelstück, -e *n.* piece of furniture (2) **2A**
möbliert *adj.* furnished (2) **2A**
modern *adj.* modern (3) **2A**
modisch *adj.* fashionable (2) **1B**
mögen *v.* to like (1) **4B**
  Ich möchte… I would like… (1) **4B**
Monat, -e *m.* month (1) **2A**, (2) **3A**
Mond, -e *m.* moon (3) **4A**
Montag, -e *m.* Monday (1) **2A**
  montags *adv.* on Mondays (1) **2A**
Morgen, - *m.* morning (1) **2B**
  morgens *adv.* in the morning (1) **2A**
morgen *adv.* tomorrow (1) **2B**
  morgen früh tomorrow morning (1) **2B**
Motor, -en *m.* engine (2) **4A**
Motorhaube, -n *f.* hood (of car) (2) **4A**
MP3-Player, - *m.* mp3 player (2) **4B**
müde *adj.* tired (1) **3B**
Müll *m.* trash (2) **2B**; *m.* waste (3) **4B**
  den Müll rausbringen *v.* to take out the trash (2) **2B**
Müllwagen, - *m.* garbage truck (3) **4B**
Mund, ⸚er *m.* mouth (3) **1A**
Münze, -n *f.* coin (3) **2A**
Musiker, - / Musikerin, -nen *m./f.* musician (1) **3B**
müssen *v.* to have to; must (1) **3B**
mutig *adj.* brave (1) **3B**
Mutter, ⸚ *f.* mother (1) **1A**
Mütze, -n *f.* cap (2) **1B**

N

nach *prep.* after; to; according to (1) **4B**; *prep.* past (time) (1) **2A**
  nach rechts/links to the right/left (2) **2A**
nachdem *conj.* after (3) **2A**
nachmachen *v.* to imitate (2) **4B**
Nachmittag, -e *m.* afternoon (1) **2B**
  nachmittags *adv.* in the afternoon (1) **2A**
Nachname, -n *m.* last name (1) **3A**
Nachricht, -en *f.* message (3) **3A**
  eine Nachricht hinterlassen *v.* to leave a message (3) **3A**
nächster/nächste/nächstes *adj.* next (1) **2B**
Nacht, ⸚e *f.* night (1) **2B**
Nachtisch, -e *m.* dessert (1) **4B**
Nachttisch, -e *m.* night table (2) **2A**

nah(e) *adj.* near; nearby (3) **2B**
Nähe *f.* vicinity (3) **2B**
  in der Nähe von *f.* close to (3) **2B**
naiv *adj.* naïve (1) **3B**
Nase, -n *f.* nose (3) **1A**
  verstopfte Nase *f.* stuffy nose (3) **1A**
nass *adj.* wet (3) **4A**
Natur, *f.* nature (3) **4A**
Naturkatastrophe, -n *f.* natural disaster (3) **4A**
Naturwissenschaft, -en *f.* science (1) **2A**
Nebel, - *m.* fog; mist (2) **3A**
neben *prep.* next to (2) **1B**
Nebenkosten *pl.* additional charges (2) **2A**
Neffe, -n *m.* nephew (2) **4B**
nehmen *v.* to take (1) **2B**
nein no (1) **1A**
nennen *v.* to call (2) **1A**
nervös *adj.* nervous (1) **3B**
nett *adj.* nice (1) **3B**
neugierig *adj.* curious (1) **3B**
neun nine (1) **2A**
nicht *adv.* not (1) **2B**
  nicht schlecht not bad (1) **1A**
nichts *pron.* nothing (2) **3B**
nie *adv.* never (1) **4A**
niedrig *adj.* low (3) **3A**
niemals *adv.* never (2) **3B**
niemand *pron.* no one (2) **3B**
niesen *v.* to sneeze (3) **1B**
noch *adv.* yet; still; in addition (1) **4A**
normalerweise *adv.* usually (3) **1B**
Notaufnahme, -n *f.* emergency room (3) **1B**
Note, -n *f.* grade (on an assignment) (1) **1B**
Notfall, ⸚e *m.* emergency (3) **3B**
Notiz, -en *f.* note (1) **1B**
November *m.* November (1) **2A**, (2) **3A**
Nummernschild, -er *n.* license plate (2) **4A**
nur *adv.* only (1) **4A**
nützlich *adj.* useful (1) **2A**
nutzlos *adj.* useless (1) **2A**

O

ob *conj.* whether; if (3) **2A**
Obst *n.* fruit (1) **4A**
obwohl *conj.* even though (2) **2A**; *conj.* although (3) **2A**
oder *conj.* or (1) **1B**
Ofen, ⸚ *m.* oven (2) **2B**
öffentlich *adj.* public (2) **4A**
  öffentliche Verkehrsmittel *n.* public transportation (2) **4A**
öffnen *v.* to open (1) **2A**
oft *adv.* often (1) **4A**
ohne *prep.* without (1) **3B**
Ohr, -en *n.* ear (3) **1A**
Ökologie *f.* ecology (3) **4B**
ökologisch *adj.* ecological (3) **4B**
Oktober *m.* October (1) **2A**, (2) **3A**
Öl, -e *n.* oil (1) **4A**
Olivenöl, -e *n.* olive oil (1) **4A**
Oma, -s *f.* grandma (1) **3A**
online sein *v.* to be online (2) **4B**

Opa, -s *m.* grandpa (1) **3A**
orange *adj.* orange (2) **1B**
Orange, -n *f.* orange (1) **4A**
ordentlich *adj.* neat, tidy (2) **2B**
Ort, -e *m.* place (1) **1B**
Österreich *n.* Austria (3) **2B**
Österreicher, - / Österreicherin, -nen *m./f.*
  Austrian (person) (3) **2B**

P

Paar, -e *n.* couple (1) **3A**
packen *v.* to pack (2) **3B**
Paket, -e *n.* package (3) **2A**
Papa, -s *m.* dad (1) **3A**
Papier, -e *n.* paper
  Blatt Papier (*pl.* Blätter Papier) *n.* sheet of paper
  (1) **1B**
Papierkorb, ⁻e *m.* wastebasket (1) **1B**
Paprika, - *f.* pepper (1) **4A**
  grüne/rote Paprika *f.* green/red pepper (1) **4A**
Park, -s *m.* park (1) **1A**
parken *v.* to park (2) **4A**
  Parkverbot. No parking. (1) **3B**
Party, -s *f.* party (2) **1A**
  eine Party geben *v.* to throw a party (2) **1A**
Passagier, -e / Passagierin, -nen *m./f.*
  passenger (2) **3B**
passen *v.* to fit; to match (2) **1A**
passieren *v.* to happen (2) **1B**
Passkontrolle, -n *f.* passport control (2) **3B**
Passwort, ⁻er *n.* password (2) **4B**
Pasta *f.* pasta (1) **4A**
Patient, -en / Patientin, -nen *m./f.* patient (3) **1B**
Pause, -n *f.* break, recess (1) **1B**
Pension, -en *f.* guesthouse (2) **3B**
Person, -en *f.* person (1) **1A**
Personalausweis, -e *m.* ID card (2) **3B**
Personalchef, -s / die Personalchefin, -nen *m./f.*
  human resources manager (3) **3A**
persönlich *adj.* personal (1) **3B**
Pfanne, -n *f.* pan (2) **2B**
Pfeffer, - *m.* pepper (1) **4B**
Pferd, -e *n.* horse (1) **2B**
Pfirsich, -e *m.* peach (1) **4A**
Pflanze, -n *f.* plant (2) **2A**
Pfund, -e *n.* pound (1) **4A**
Physik *f.* physics (1) **2A**
Picknick, -s, *n.* picnic (3) **4A**
  ein Picknick machen *v.* to have a picnic (3) **4A**
Pilz, -e *m.* mushroom (1) **4A**
Pinnwand, ⁻e *f.* bulletin board (3) **3A**
Planet, -en *m.* planet (3) **4B**
  den Planeten retten *v.* to save the planet (3) **4B**
Platten, - *m.* flat tire (2) **4A**
  einen Platten haben *v.* to have a flat tire (2) **4A**
Platz, ⁻e *m.* court (1) **1A**
plus plus (1) **1B**
Politiker, - / Politikerin, -nen *m./f.* politician (3) **3B**
Polizeiwache, -n *f.* police station (3) **2A**
Polizist, -en / Polizistin, -nen *m./f.* police
  officer (2) **4A**
Post *f.* post office; mail (3) **2A**
  zur Post gehen *v.* to go to the post office (3) **2A**

Poster, - *n.* poster (1) **2A**
Postkarte, -n *f.* postcard (3) **2A**
Praktikum (*pl.* die Praktika) *n.* internship (3) **3A**
prima *adj.* great (1) **1A**
probieren *v.* to try (1) **3B**
  Probieren Sie mal! Give it a try!
Problem, -e *n.* problem (1) **1A**
Professor, -en / Professorin, -nen *m./f.*
  professor (1) **1B**
Programm, -e *n.* program (2) **4B**
Prost! Cheers! (1) **4B**
Prozent, -e *n.* percent (1) **1B**
Prüfung, -en *f.* exam, test (1) **1B**
Psychologe, -n / Psychologin, -nen *m./f.*
  psychologist (3) **3B**
Psychologie *f.* psychology (1) **2A**
Pullover, - *m.* sweater (2) **1B**
Punkt, -e *m.* period (1) **1B**
pünktlich *adj.* on time (2) **3B**
putzen *v.* to clean (2) **2B**
  sich die Zähne putzen *v.* to brush one's teeth (3) **1A**

Q

Querverweis, -e *m.* cross-reference

R

Radiergummi, -s *m.* eraser (1) **1B**
Rasen, - *m.* lawn, grass (1) **3B**
  Betreten des Rasens verboten. Keep off the
  grass. (1) **3B**
sich rasieren *v.* to shave (3) **1A**
Rasierer, - *m.* razor (3) **1A**
Rasierschaum, ⁻e *m.* shaving cream (3) **1A**
Rathaus, ⁻er *n.* town hall (3) **2A**
rauchen *v.* to smoke
  Rauchen verboten. No smoking. (1) **3B**
rausbringen *v.* to bring out (2) **2B**
  den Müll rausbringen *v.* to take out the trash (2) **2B**
realistisch *adj.* realistic (3) **2A**
Rechnung, -en *f.* check (1) **4B**
Rechtsanwalt, ⁻e / Rechtsanwältin, -nen *m./f.*
  lawyer (1) **3B**
Rechtschreibung *f.* spelling
recyceln *v.* to recycle (3) **4B**
reden *v.* to talk (2) **1A**
  reden über *v.* to talk about (2) **3A**
Referat, -e *n.* presentation (1) **2A**
Referenz, -en *f.* reference (3) **3A**
Regen *m.* rain (2) **3A**
Regenmantel, ⁻ *m.* raincoat (2) **3A**
Regenschirm, -e *m.* umbrella (2) **3A**
Regierung, -en *f.* government (3) **4B**
regnen *v.* to rain (1) **2A**, (2) **3A**
reich *adj.* rich (1) **3B**
Reis *m.* rice (1) **4A**
Reise, -n *f.* trip (2) **3B**
Reisebüro, -s *n.* travel agency (2) **3B**
reisen *v.* to travel (1) **2A**
Reisende, -n *m./f.* traveler (2) **3B**
Reiseziel, -e *n.* destination (2) **3B**
reiten *v.* to ride (1) **2B**

rennen *v.* to run (2) **1A**
Rente, -n *f.* pension
  in Rente gehen *v.* to retire (2) **1A**
Rentner, - / Rentnerin, -nen *m./f.* retiree (3) **3B**
reparieren *v.* to repair (2) **4A**
Restaurant, -s *n.* restaurant (1) **4B**
retten *v.* to save (3) **4B**
Rezept, -e *n.* recipe (1) **4A**; prescription (3) **1B**
Richter, - / Richterin, -nen *m./f.* judge (3) **3B**
Richtung, -en *f.* direction (3) **2B**
  in Richtung *f.* toward (3) **2B**
Rindfleisch *n.* beef (1) **4A**
Rock, ⁻e *m.* skirt (2) **1B**
rosa *adj.* pink (2) **1B**
rot *adj.* red (1) **3A**
rothaarig *adj.* red-haired (1) **3A**
Rücken, - *m.* back (3) **1A**
Rückenschmerzen *m. pl.* backache (3) **1B**
Rucksack, ⁻e *m.* backpack (1) **1B**
ruhig *adj.* calm (1) **3B**
Russe, -n / Russin, -nen *m./f.* Russian
  (person) (3) **2B**
Russisch *n.* Russian (language) (3) **2B**
Russland *n.* Russia (3) **2B**

S

Sache, -n *f.* thing (1) **1B**
Saft, ⁻e *m.* juice (1) **4B**
sagen *v.* to say (1) **2A**
Salat, -e *m.* lettuce; salad (1) **4A**
Salz, -e *n.* salt (1) **4B**
salzig *adj.* salty (1) **4B**
Samstag, -e *m.* Saturday (1) **2A**
  samstags *adv.* on Saturdays (1) **2A**
sauber *adj.* clean (2) **2B**
saurer Regen *m.* acid rain (3) **4B**
Saustall *n.* pigsty (2) **2B**
  Es ist ein Saustall! It's a pigsty! (2) **2B**
Schach *n.* chess (1) **2B**
Schaf, -e *n.* sheep (3) **4A**
Schaffner, - / Schaffnerin, -nen *m./f.* ticket
  collector (2) **4A**
Schal, -s *m.* scarf (2) **1B**
scharf *adj.* spicy (1) **4B**
schauen *v.* to look (2) **3A**
Scheibenwischer, - *m.* windshield wiper (2) **4A**
Scheinwerfer, - *m.* headlight (2) **4A**
scheitern *v.* to fail (3) **3B**
schenken *v.* to give (a gift) (2) **1A**
schicken *v.* to send (2) **4B**
Schiff, -e *n.* ship (2) **4A**
Schinken, - *m.* ham (1) **4A**
Schlafanzug, ⁻e *m.* pajamas (3) **1A**
schlafen *v.* to sleep (1) **2B**
Schlafzimmer, - *n.* bedroom (2) **2A**
Schlange, -n *f.* line (2) **3B**; *f.* snake (3) **4A**
  Schlange stehen *v.* to stand in line (2) **3B**
schlank *adj.* slim (1) **3A**
schlecht *adj.* bad (1) **3B**
  schlecht gekleidet *adj.* badly dressed (2) **1B**
schließlich *adv.* finally (2) **3B**
Schlüssel, - *m.* key (2) **3B**

schmecken *v.* to taste (1) **4B**

Schmerz, -en *m.* pain (3) **1B**

sich schminken *v.* to put on makeup (3) **1A**

schmutzig *adj.* dirty (2) **2B**

Schnee *m.* snow (2) **3A**

schneien *v.* to snow (2) **3A**

schnell *adj.* fast (1) **3B**

schon *adv.* already, yet (1) **4A**

schön *adj.* pretty; beautiful (1) **3A**

  Schön dich/Sie kennen zu lernen. Nice to meet you. (1) **1A**

  Schönen Tag noch! Have a nice day! (1) **1A**

  Es ist schön draußen. It's nice out. (2) **3A**

Schrank, ⸚e *m.* cabinet; closet (2) **2A**

schreiben *v.* to write (1) **2A**

  schreiben an *v.* to write to (2) **3A**

  sich schreiben *v.* to write one another (3) **1A**

Schreibtisch, -e *m.* desk (1) **1B**

Schreibwarengeschäft, -e *n.* paper-goods store (3) **2A**

Schublade, -n *f.* drawer (2) **2A**

schüchtern *adj.* shy (1) **3B**

Schuh, -e *m.* shoe (2) **1B**

Schulbuch, ⸚er *n.* textbook (K–12) (1) **1B**

Schule, -n *f.* school (1) **1B**

Schüler, - / Schülerin, -nen (K–12) *m./f.* student (1) **1B**

Schulleiter, - / Schulleiterin, -nen *m./f.* principal (1) **1B**

Schulter, -n *f.* shoulder (3) **1A**

Schüssel, -n *f.* bowl (1) **4B**

schützen *v.* to protect (3) **4B**

schwach *adj.* weak (1) **3B**

Schwager, ⸚ *m.* brother-in-law (1) **3A**

Schwägerin, -nen *f.* sister-in-law (1) **3A**

schwanger *adj.* pregnant (3) **1B**

schwänzen *v.* to cut class (1) **1B**

schwarz *adj.* black (2) **1B**

schwarzhaarig *adj.* black-haired (1) **3A**

Schweinefleisch *n.* pork (1) **4A**

Schweiz (die) *f.* Switzerland (2) **3A**

Schweizer, - / Schweizerin, -nen *m./f.* Swiss (person) (3) **2B**

schwer *adj.* rich, heavy (1) **4B**; *adj.* serious, difficult (3) **1B**

Schwester, -n *f.* sister (1) **1A**

Schwiegermutter, ⸚ *f.* mother-in-law (1) **3A**

Schwiegervater, ⸚ *m.* father-in-law (1) **3A**

schwierig *adj.* difficult (1) **2A**

Schwimmbad, ⸚er *n.* swimming pool (1) **2B**

schwimmen *v.* to swim (1) **2B**

schwindlig *adj.* dizzy (3) **1B**

sechs six (1) **2A**

See, -n *m.* lake (3) **4A**

sehen *v.* to see (2) **2B**

sehr *adv.* very (1) **3A**

Seide, -n *f.* silk (2) **1B**

Seife, -n *f.* soap (3) **1A**

sein *v.* to be (1) **1A**

  (gleich) sein *v.* to equal (1) **1B**

sein *poss. adj.* his, its (1) **3A**

seit since; for (1) **4B**

Sekt, -e *m.* champagne (2) **1A**

selten *adv.* rarely (1) **4A**

Seminar, -e *n.* seminar (1) **2A**

Seminarraum, -räume *m.* seminar room (1) **2A**

Sender, - *m.* channel (2) **4B**

September *m.* September (1) **2A**, (2) **3A**

Serviette, -n *f.* napkin (1) **4B**

Sessel, - *m.* armchair (2) **2A**

setzen *v.* to put, place (2) **1B**; *v.* to put, set (3) **1A**

Shampoo, -s *n.* shampoo (3) **1A**

sicher *adv.* probably (3) **2A**

Sicherheitsgurt, -e *m.* seatbelt (2) **4A**

sie *pron.* she/they (1) **1A**

Sie *pron.* (*form., sing./pl.*) you (1) **1A**

sieben seven (1) **2A**

Silvester *n.* New Year's Eve (2) **1A**

singen *v.* to sing (1) **2B**

sitzen *v.* to sit (2) **1B**

Ski fahren *v.* to ski (1) **2B**

Smartphone, -s *n.* smartphone (2) **4B**

SMS, - *f.* text message (2) **4B**

Snack, -s *m.* snack (1) **4B**

so *adv.* so (1) **4A**

Socke, -n *f.* sock (2) **1B**

Sofa, -s *n.* sofa; couch (2) **2A**

  Sofa surfen *v.* to couch surf (2) **3B**

Sohn, ⸚e *m.* son (1) **3A**

solcher/solche/solches *pron.* such (2) **4B**

sollen *v.* to be supposed to (1) **3B**

Sommer, - *m.* summer (1) **2B**, (2) **3A**

sondern *conj.* but rather; instead (2) **2A**

Sonne, -n *f.* sun (3) **4A**

Sonnenaufgang, ⸚e *m.* sunrise (3) **4A**

Sonnenbrand, ⸚e *m.* sunburn (3) **1B**

Sonnenbrille, -n *f.* sunglasses (2) **1B**

Sonnenenergie *f.* solar energy (3) **4B**

Sonnenuntergang, ⸚e *m.* sunset (3) **4A**

sonnig *adj.* sunny (2) **3A**

Sonntag, -e *m.* Sunday (1) **2A**

  sonntags *adv.* on Sundays (1) **2A**

Spanien *n.* Spain (3) **3B**

Spanier, - / Spanierin, -nen *m./f.* Spanish (person) (3) **2B**

Spanisch *n.* Spanish (language) (3) **2B**

spannend *adj.* exciting (3) **2A**

Spaß *m.* fun (1) **2B**

  Spaß haben/machen *v.* to have fun/to be fun (1) **2B**

  (keinen) Spaß haben *v.* to (not) have fun (2) **1A**

spät *adj.* late

  Wie spät ist es? What time is it? (1) **2A**

spazieren gehen *v.* to go for a walk (1) **2B**

Spaziergang, ⸚e *m.* walk

speichern *v.* to save (2) **4B**

Speisekarte, -n *f.* menu (1) **4B**

Spiegel, - *m.* mirror (2) **2A**

Spiel, -e *n.* match, game (1)c**2B**

spielen *v.* to play (1) **2A**

Spieler, - / Spielerin, -nen *m./f.* player (1) **2B**

Spielfeld, -er *n.* field (1) **2B**

Spielkonsole, -n *f.* game console (2) **4B**

Spitze! *adj.* great! (1) **1A**

Sport *m.* sports (1) **2B**

  Sport treiben *v.* to exercise (3) **1B**

Sportart, -en *f.* sport; type of sport (1) **2B**

Sporthalle, - n *f.* gym (1) **2A**

sportlich *adj.* athletic (1) **3A**

sprechen *v.* to speak (1) **2B**

  sprechen über *v.* to speak about (2) **3A**

Spritze, -n *f.* shot (3) **1B**

  eine Spritze geben *v.* to give a shot (3) **1B**

Spüle, -n *f.* (kitchen) sink (2) **2B**

spülen *v.* to rinse (2) **2B**

  Geschirr spülen *v.* to do the dishes (2) **2B**

  Spülmaschine, -n *f.* dishwasher (2) **2B**

Stadion (pl. Stadien) *n.* stadium (1) **2B**

Stadt, ⸚e *f.* city (2) **1B**; *f.* town (3) **2B**

Stadtplan, ⸚e *m.* city map (2) **3B**

Stahl *m.* steel (2) **2B**

stark *adj.* strong (1) **3B**

starten *v.* to start (2) **4B**

statt *conj.* instead of

Statue, -n *f.* statue (3) **2B**

staubsaugen *v.* to vacuum (2) **2B**

Staubsauger, - *m.* vacuum cleaner (2) **2B**

stehen *v.* to stand (2) **1B**

  Schlange stehen *v.* to stand in line (2) **3B**

stehlen *v.* to steal (1) **2B**

steif *adj.* stiff (3) **1B**

steigen *v.* to climb (2) **1B**

Stein, -e *m.* rock (3) **4A**

Stelle, -n *f.* place, position (3) **2A**; job (3) **3A**

  an deiner/Ihrer Stelle *f.* if I were you (3) **2A**

  eine Stelle suchen *v.* to look for a job (3) **3A**

stellen *v.* to put, place (2) **1B**

Stellenangebot, -e *n.* job opening (3) **3A**

sterben *v.* to die (2) **1B**

Stereoanlage, -n *f.* stereo system (2) **4B**

Stern -e *m.* star (3) **4A**

Stiefel, - *m.* boot (2) **1B**

Stiefmutter, ⸚ *f.* stepmother (1) **3A**

Stiefsohn, ⸚e *m.* stepson (1) **3A**

Stieftochter, ⸚ *f.* stepdaughter (1) **3A**

Stiefvater, ⸚ *m.* stepfather (1) **3A**

Stift, -e *m.* pen (1) **1B**

Stil, -e *m.* style (2) **1B**

still *adj.* still (1) **4B**

  stilles Wasser *n.* still water (1) **4B**

Stipendium, (pl. Stipendien) *n.* scholarship, grant (1) **2A**

Stock, ⸚e *m.* floor (2) **2A**

  erster/zweiter Stock first/second floor (2) **2A**

stolz *adj.* proud (1) **3B**

Stoppschild, -er *n.* stop sign (2) **4A**

Strand, ⸚e *m.* beach (1) **2B**

Straße, -n *f.* street (2) **4A**

sich streiten *v.* to argue (3) **1A**

Strom, ⸚e *m.* stream (3) **4A**

Student, -en / Studentin, -nen *m./f.* (college/university) student (1) **1A**

Studentenwohnheim, -e *n.* dormitory (1) **2A**

studieren *v.* to study; major in (1) **2A**

Studium (pl. Studien) *n.* studies (1) **2A**

Stuhl, ⸚e *m.* chair (1) **1A**

Stunde, -n *f.* lesson (1) **1B**; hour (1) **2A**

Stundenplan, ⸚e *m.* schedule (1) **2A**

Sturm, ⸚e *m.* storm (2) **3A**

suchen *v.* to look for (1) **2A**

  eine Stelle suchen *v.* to look for a job (3) **3A**

Supermarkt, ⸚e *m.* supermarket (1) **4A**
Suppe, -n *f.* soup (1) **4B**
surfen *v.* to surf (2) **4B**
  im Internet surfen *v.* to surf the Web (2) **4B**
süß *adj.* sweet, cute (1) **3B**, (1) **4B**
Süßigkeit, -en *f.* candy (2) **1A**
Sweatshirt, -s *n.* sweatshirt (2) **1B**
Symptom, -e *n.* symptom (3) **1B**

T

Tablet, -s *n.* tablet (2) **4B**
Tablette, -n *f.* pill (3) **1B**
Tafel, -n *f.* board, black board (1) **1B**
Tag, -e *m.* day (1) **1A**, (2) **3A**
  Welcher Tag ist heute? What day is it today? (2) **3A**
täglich *adv.* every day; daily (1) **4A**
Tal, ⸚er *n.* valley (3) **4A**
tanken *v.* to fill up (2) **4A**
Tankstelle, -n *f.* gas station (2) **4A**
Tante, -n *f.* aunt (1) **3A**
tanzen *v.* to dance (1) **2B**
Taschenrechner, - *m.* calculator (1) **1B**
Taschentuch, ⸚er *n.* tissue (3) **1B**
Tasse, -n *f.* cup (1) **4B**
Tastatur, -en *f.* keyboard (2) **4B**
Taxi, -s *n.* taxi (2) **4A**
Taxifahrer, - / Taxifahrerin, -nen *m./f.* taxi driver (3) **3B**
Technik *f.* technology (2) **4B**
  Technik bedienen *v.* to use technology (2) **4B**
Tee, -s *m.* tea (1) **4B**
Teelöffel, - *m.* teaspoon (1) **4B**
Telefon, -e *n.* telephone (2) **4B**
  am Telefon on the telephone (3) **3A**
Telefonnummer, -n *f.* telephone number (3) **3A**
Telefonzelle, -n *f.* phone booth (3) **2B**
Teller, - *m.* plate (1) **4B**
Tennis *n.* tennis (1) **2B**
Teppich, -e *m.* rug (2) **2A**
Termin, -e *m.* appointment (3) **3A**
  einen Termin vereinbaren *v.* to make an appointment (3) **3A**
teuer *adj.* expensive (2) **1B**
Thermometer, - *n.* thermometer (1) **1B**
Thunfisch, -e *m.* tuna (1) **4A**
Tier, -e *n.* animal (3) **4A**
Tierarzt, ⸚e / Tierärztin, -nen *m./f.* veterinarian (3) **3B**
Tisch, -e *m.* table, desk (1) **1B**
  den Tisch decken *v.* to set the table (2) **2B**
Tischdecke, -n *f.* tablecloth (1) **4B**
Toaster, - *m.* toaster (2) **2B**
Tochter, ⸚ *f.* daughter (1) **3A**
Toilette, -n *f.* toilet (2) **2A**
Tomate, -n *f.* tomato (1) **4A**
Topf, ⸚e *m.* pot (2) **2B**
Tor, -e *n.* goal (in soccer, etc.) (1) **2B**
Tornado, -s *m.* tornado (3) **4A**
Torte, -n *f.* cake (2) **1A**
Touristenklasse *f.* economy class (2) **3B**
tragen *v.* to carry; wear (1) **2B**
Trägerhemd, -en *n.* tank top (2) **1B**

trainieren *v.* to practice (sports) (1) **2B**
Traube, -n *f.* grape (1) **4A**
träumen *v.* to dream (2) **3A**
traurig *adj.* sad (1) **3B**
treffen *v.* to meet; to hit (1) **2B**
  sich treffen *v.* to meet (each other) (3) **1A**
treiben *v.* to float; to push
  Sport treiben *v.* to exercise (3) **1B**
Treibsand *m.* quicksand (3) **4A**
sich trennen *v.* to separate, split up (3) **1A**
Treppe, -n *f.* stairway (2) **2A**
trinken *v.* to drink (1) **3B**
Trinkgeld, -er *n.* tip (1) **4B**
trocken *adj.* dry (3) **4A**
trotz *prep.* despite, in spite of (2) **4B**
Tschüss. Bye. (1) **1A**
T-Shirt, -s *n.* T-shirt (2) **1B**
  tun *v.* to do (3) **1B**
  Es tut mir leid. I'm sorry. (1) **1A**
  weh tun *v.* to hurt (3) **1B**
Tür, -en *f.* door (1) **1B**
  Türen schließen. Keep doors closed. (1) **3B**
Türkei (die) *f.* Turkey (3) **2B**
Türke, -n / die Türkin, -nen *m./f.* Turkish (person) (3) **2B**
Türkisch *n.* Turkish (language) (3) **2B**
Turnschuhe *m. pl.* sneakers (2) **1B**

U

U-Bahn, -en *f.* subway (2) **4A**
übel *adj.* nauseous (3) **1B**
über *prep.* over, above (2) **1B**
übernachten *v.* to spend the night (2) **3B**
überall *adv.* everywhere (1) **4A**
Überbevölkerung *f.* overpopulation (3) **4B**
überlegen *v.* to think over (1) **4A**
übermorgen *adv.* the day after tomorrow (1) **2B**
überqueren *v.* to cross (3) **2B**
überraschen *v.* to surprise (2) **1A**
Überraschung, -en *f.* surprise (2) **1A**
überzeugend *adj.* persuasive (3) **1B**
Übung, -en *f.* practice, exercise
Uhr, -en *f.* clock (1) **1B**
  um... Uhr at... o'clock (1) **2A**
  Wie viel Uhr ist es? *v.* What time is it? (1) **2A**
um *prep.* around; at (time) (1) **3B**
  um... zu in order to (2) **3B**
Umleitung, -en *f.* detour (2) **4A**
umtauschen *v.* to exchange (2) **2B**
Umwelt, -en *f.* environment (3) **4B**
umweltfreundlich *adj.* environmentally friendly (3) **4B**
Umweltschutz *m.* environmentalism (3) **4B**
umziehen *v.* to move (2) **2A**, (3) **1A**
  sich umziehen *v.* to change clothes (3) **1A**
unangenehm *adj.* unpleasant (1) **3B**
und *conj.* and (1) **1B**
Unfall, ⸚e *m.* accident (2) **4A**
  einen Unfall haben *v.* to have an accident (2) **4A**
Universität, -en *f.* university; college (1) **1B**
unmöbliert *adj.* unfurnished (2) **2A**
unser *poss. adj.* our (1) **3A**

unter *prep.* under, below (2) **1B**
untergehen *v.* to set (sun) (3) **4A**
sich unterhalten *v.* to chat, have a conversation (1) **1A**
Unterkunft, ⸚e *f.* accommodations (2) **3B**
Unterricht, -e *m.* class, instruction (1) **1B**
unterschreiben *v.* to sign (3) **2A**
Unterwäsche *f.* underwear (2) **1B**
Urgroßmutter, ⸚ *f.* great grandmother (1) **3A**
Urgroßvater, ⸚ *m.* great grandfather (1) **3A**
Urlaub, -e *m.* vacation (2) **3B**
  Urlaub machen *v.* to go on vacation (2) **3B**
  Urlaub nehmen *v.* to take time off (3) **3B**
USA (die) *pl.* USA (3) **2B**

V

Vase, -n *f.* vase (2) **2A**
Vater, ⸚ *m.* father (1) **3A**
Veranstaltung, -en *f.* class; course (1) **2A**
Verb, -en *n.* verb (3) **1A**
verbessern *v.* to improve (3) **4B**
verbringen *v.* to spend (1) **4A**
verdienen *v.* to earn (3) **3B**
Vereinigten Staaten (die) *pl.* United States (3) **2B**
Vergangenheit, -en *f.* past (3) **4A**
vergessen *v.* to forget (1) **2B**
verheiratet *adj.* married (1) **3A**
verkaufen *v.* to sell (1) **4A**
Verkäufer, - / Verkäuferin, -nen *m./f.* salesperson (2) **1B**
Verkehr *m.* traffic (2) **4A**
Verkehrsmittel *n.* transportation (2) **4A**
  öffentliche Verkehrsmittel *n. pl.* public transportation (2) **4A**
verkünden *v.* to announce (3) **4B**
sich verlaufen *v.* to get lost (3) **2B**
sich verletzen *v.* to hurt oneself (3) **1B**
Verletzung, -en *f.* injury (3) **1B**
sich verlieben (in) *v.* to fall in love (with) (3) **1A**
verlieren *v.* to lose (1) **2B**
verlobt *adj.* engaged (1) **3A**
Verlobte, -n *m./f.* fiancé(e) (1) **3A**
verschmutzen *v.* to pollute (3) **4B**
Verschmutzung *f.* pollution (3) **4B**
sich verspäten *v.* to be late (3) **1A**
Verspätung, -en *f.* delay (2) **3B**
Verständnis, -se *n.* comprehension
sich (das Handgelenk / den Fuß) verstauchen *v.* to sprain (one's wrist/ankle) (3) **1B**
verstehen *v.* to understand (1) **2A**
verstopfte Nase *f.* stuffy nose (3) **1B**
versuchen *v.* to try (2) **3B**
Vertrag, ⸚e *m.* contract (3) **3A**
verwandt *adj.* related (3) **2A**
Verwandte, -n *m.* relative (1) **3A**
viel *adv.* much, a lot (of) (1) **4A**
  Viel Glück! Good luck! (2) **1A**
  Vielen Dank. Thank you very much. (1) **1A**
vielleicht *adv.* maybe (1) **4A**
vier four (1) **2A**
Viertel, - *n.* quarter (1) **2A**; neighborhood (3) **2B**
  Viertel nach/vor quarter past/to (1) **2A**

Visum (*pl.* **Visa**) *n.* visa (2) **3B**
Vogel, ⁻ *m.* bird (1) **3A**
voll *adj.* full (2) **3B**
  voll besetzt *adj.* fully occupied (2) **3B**
Volleyball *m.* volleyball (1) **2B**
von *prep.* from (1) **4B**
vor *prep.* in front of, before (2) **1B**; *prep.* to (1) **2A**
vorbei *adv.* over, past (2) **3A**
vorbereiten *v.* to prepare (1) **4A**
  sich vorbereiten (auf) *v.* to prepare oneself (for) (3) **1A**
  Vorbereitung, -en *f.* preparation
Vorhang, ⁻e *m.* curtain (2) **2A**
Vorlesung, -en *f.* lecture (1) **2A**
vormachen *v.* to fool (2) **4B**
Vormittag, -e *m.* midmorning (1) **2B**
vormittags *adv.* before noon (1) **2A**
Vorspeise, -n *f.* appetizer (1) **4B**
vorstellen *v.* to introduce (3) **1A**
  sich vorstellen *v.* to introduce oneself (3) **1A**
  sich (etwas) vorstellen *v.* to imagine (something) (3) **1A**
Vorstellungsgespräch, -e *n.* job interview (3) **3A**
Vortrag, ⁻e *m.* lecture (2) **2B**
Vulkan, -e *m.* volcano (3) **4A**

W

wachsen *v.* to grow (2) **1B**
während *prep.* during (2) **4B**
wahrscheinlich *adv.* probably (3) **2A**
Wald, ⁻er *m.* forest (1) **2B**, (3) **4A**
Wand, ⁻e *f.* wall (2) **1B**
wandern *v.* to hike (1) **2A**
wann *interr.* when (1) **2A**
  Wann hast du Geburtstag? When is your birthday? (1) **2B**
warm *adj.* warm (3) **2A**
warten *v.* to wait (for) (1) **2A**
  warten auf *v.* to wait for (2) **3A**
  in der Warteschleife sein *v.* to be on hold (3) **3B**
warum *interr.* why (1) **2A**
was *interr.* what (1) **2A**
  Was geht ab? What's up? (1) **1A**
  Was ist das? What is that? (1) **1B**
Wäsche *f.* laundry (2) **2B**
waschen *v.* to wash (1) **2B**
  sich waschen *v.* to wash (oneself) (3) **1A**
  Wäsche waschen *v.* to do laundry (2) **2B**
Wäschetrockner, - *m.* dryer (2) **2B**
Waschmaschine, -n *f.* washing machine (2) **2B**
Waschsalon, -s *m.* laundromat (3) **2A**
Wasser *n.* water (1) **4B**
Wasserfall, ⁻e *m.* waterfall (3) **4A**
Wasserkrug, ⁻e *m.* water pitcher (1) **4B**
Website, -s *f.* web site (2) **4B**
Weg, -e *m.* path (3) **4A**
wegen *prep.* because of (2) **4B**
wegräumen *v.* to put away (2) **2B**
wegwerfen *v.* to throw away (3) **4B**
weh tun *v.* to hurt (3) **1B**
Weihnachten, - *n.* Christmas (2) **1A**
weil *conj.* because (3) **2A**

Wein, -e *m.* wine (1) **4B**
weinen *v.* to cry (1) **3B**
weise *adj.* wise (1) **3B**
weiß *adj.* white (2) **1B**
weit *adj.* loose; big (2) **1B**; *adj.* far (3) **2B**
  weit von *adj.* far from (3) **2B**
  weiter geht's moving forward
welcher/welche/welches *interr.* which (1) **2A**
  Welcher Tag ist heute? What day is it today? (2) **3A**
Welt, -en *f.* world (3) **4B**
wem *interr.* whom (*dat.*) (1) **4B**
wen *interr.* whom (*acc.*) (1) **2A**
Wende, -n *f.* turning point (3) **4B**
wenig *adj.* little; not much (3) **2A**
wenn *conj.* when; whenever; if (3) **2A**
  wenn... dann if… then (3) **2A**
  wenn... nur if… only (3) **2A**
wer *interr.* who (1) **2A**
  Wer ist das? Who is it? (1) **1B**
  Wer spricht? Who's calling? (3) **3A**
werden *v.* to become (1) **2B**
werfen *v.* to throw (1) **2B**
Werkzeug, -e *n.* tool kit
wessen *interr.* whose (2) **4B**
Wetter *n.* weather (2) **3A**
  Wie ist das Wetter? What's the weather like? (2) **3A**
Wetterbericht, -e *m.* weather report (2) **3A**
wichtig *adj.* important (2) **3B**
wie *interr.* how (1) **2A**
  wie viel? *interr.* how much? (1) **1B**
  wie viele? *interr.* how many? (1) **1B**
  Wie alt bist du? How old are you? (1) **1B**
  Wie heißt du? (*inf.*) What's your name? (1) **1A**
wiederholen *v.* to repeat (1) **2A**
Wiederholung, -en *f.* repetition; revision
wiegen *v.* to weigh (2) **4B**
willkommen welcome (1) **1A**
  Herzlich willkommen! Welcome! (1) **1A**
Windenergie *f.* wind energy (3) **4B**
windig *adj.* windy (2) **3A**
Windschutzscheibe, -n *f.* windshield (2) **4A**
Winter, - *m.* winter (1) **2B**, (2) **3A**
wir *pron.* we (1) **1A**
wirklich *adv.* really (1) **4A**
Wirtschaft, -en *f.* business; economy (1) **2A**
wischen *v.* to wipe, mop (2) **2B**
wissen *v.* to know (information) (2) **1B**
Wissenschaftler, - / **Wissenschaftlerin, -nen** *m./f.* scientist (3) **3B**
Witwe, -n *f.* widow (1) **3A**
Witwer, - *m.* widower (1) **3A**
wo *interr.* where (1) **2A**
woanders *adv.* somewhere else (1) **4A**
Woche, -n *f.* week (1) **2A**
Wochenende, -n *n.* weekend (1) **2A**
woher *interr.* from where (1) **2A**; (2) **2A**
wohin *interr.* where to (1) **2A**
wohl *adv.* probably (3) **2A**
wohnen *v.* to live (somewhere) (1) **2A**
Wohnheim, -e *n.* dorm (2) **2A**
Wohnung, -en *f.* apartment (2) **2A**
Wohnzimmer, - *n.* living room (2) **2A**
Wolke, -n *f.* cloud (2) **3A**

wolkig *adj.* cloudy (2) **3A**
Wolle *f.* wool (2) **1B**
wollen *v.* to want (1) **3B**
Wörterbuch, ⁻er *n.* dictionary (1) **1B**
Wortschatz, ⁻e *m.* vocabulary
wünschen *v.* to wish (3) **1A**
  sich (etwas) wünschen *v.* to wish (for something) (3) **1A**
Würstchen, - *n.* (small) sausage (1) **4A**

Z

Zahn, ⁻e *m.* tooth (3) **1A**
  sich die Zähne putzen *m.* to brush one's teeth (3) **1A**
Zahnarzt, ⁻e / **Zahnärztin, -nen** *m./f.* dentist (3) **1B**
Zahnbürste, -n *f.* toothbrush (3) **1A**
Zahnpasta (*pl.* **Zahnpasten**) *f.* toothpaste (3) **1A**
Zahnschmerzen *m. pl.* toothache (3) **1B**
Zapping *n.* channel surfing
Zebrastreifen, - *m.* crosswalk (3) **2B**
Zeh, -en *m.* toe (3) **1A**
zehn ten (1) **2A**
zeigen *v.* to show (1) **4B**
Zeit, -en *f.* time (1) **2A**
Zeitschrift, -en *f.* magazine (3) **2A**
Zeitung, -en *f.* newspaper (2) **3B**, (3) **2A**
Zelt, -e *n.* tent (2) **3B**
Zeltplatz, ⁻e *m.* camping area (2) **3B**
Zeugnis, -se *n.* report card, grade report (1) **1B**
ziehen *v.* to pull (1) **3B**
ziemlich *adv.* quite (1) **4A**
  ziemlich gut pretty well (1) **1A**
Zimmer, - *n.* room (2) **1A**
  Zimmer frei vacancy (2) **2A**
Zimmerservice *m.* room service (2) **3B**
Zoll, ⁻e *m.* customs (2) **3B**
zu *adv.* too (1) **4A**; *prep.* to; for; at (1) **4B**
  bis zu *prep.* until (3) **2B**
  um... zu (in order) to (2) **3B**
  Zum Wohl! Cheers! (1) **4B**
zubereiten *v.* to prepare (2) **3A**
zuerst *adv.* first (2) **3B**
Zug, ⁻e *m.* train (2) **4A**
zumachen *v.* to close (2) **4B**
sich zurechtfinden *v.* to find one's way (3) **2B**
zurückkommen *v.* to come back (1) **4A**
zusammen *adv.* together (1) **3A**
zuschauen *v.* to watch (1) **4A**
Zutat, -en *m.* ingredient (1) **4A**
zuverlässig *adj.* reliable (3) **3B**
zwanzig twenty (1) **2A**
zwei two (1) **2A**
zweite *adj.* second (1) **2A**
Zwiebel, -n *f.* onion (1) **4A**
Zwilling, -e *m.* twin (1) **3A**
zwischen *prep.* between (2) **1B**
zwölf twelve (1) **2A**

Englisch-Deutsch

A

a ein/eine (1) **1A**

able: to be able to können *v.* (1) **3B**

about über *prep.* (2) **1B**
  to be about handeln von *v.* (2) **3A**

above über *prep.* (2) **1B**

abroad Ausland *n.* (2) **3B**

accident Unfall, ⸚e *m.* (2) **4A**
  to have an accident einen Unfall haben *v.* (2) **4A**

accommodation Unterkunft, ⸚e *f.* (2) **3B**

according to nach *prep.* (1) **4B**

accountant Buchhalter, - / Buchhalterin, -nen *m./f.* (3) **3B**

acid rain saurer Regen *m.* (3) **4B**

across (from) gegenüber (von) *prep.* (3) **2B**

address Adresse, -n *f.* (3) **2A**

adopt adoptieren *v.* (1) **3A**

afraid: to be afraid of Angst haben vor *v.* (2) **3A**

after nach *prep.* (1) **4B**; nachdem *conj.* (3) **2A**

afternoon Nachmittag, -e *m.* (1) **2B**
  in the afternoon nachmittags *adv.* (1) **2A**

against gegen *prep.* (1) **3B**

air Luft, ⸚e *f.* (3) **4A**

airplane Flugzeug, -e *n.* (2) **3B**

airport Flughafen, ⸚ *m.* (2) **3B**

all ganz *adj.* (2) **3B**; alle *pron.* (2) **3B**

allergic (to) allergisch (gegen) *adj.* (3) **1B**

allergy Allergie, -n *f.* (3) **1B**

allow lassen *v.* (1) **2B**
  to be allowed to dürfen *v.* (1) **3B**

almost fast *adv.* (1) **4A**

alone allein *adv.* (1) **4A**

along entlang *prep.* (1) **3B**

already schon (1) **4A**

alright: Are you alright? Alles klar? (1) **1A**

also auch *adv.* (1) **4A**

although obwohl *conj.* (3) **2A**

always immer *adv.* (1) **4A**

ambulance Krankenwagen, - *m.* (3) **1B**

America Amerika *n.* (3) **2B**

American amerikanisch *adj.* (3) **2B**; (person) Amerikaner, - / Amerikanerin, -nen *m./f.* (3) **2B**
  American football American Football *m.* (1) **2B**

and und *conj.* (1) **1B**

animal Tier, -e *n.* (3) **4A**

angry böse *adj.*
  to get angry (about) sich ärgern (über) *v.* (3) **1A**

anniversary Jahrestag, -e *m.* (2) **1A**

announce verkünden *v.* (3) **4B**

answer antworten *v.* (1) **2A**; beantworten *v.* (1) **4A**; Antwort, -en *f.*
  to answer the phone einen Anruf entgegennehmen *v.* (3) **3A**

anything: Anything else? Noch einen Wunsch? (1) **4B**; Sonst noch etwas? (1) **4A**

apartment Wohnung, -en *f.* (2) **2A**

appetizer Vorspeise, -n *f.* (1) **4B**

apple Apfel, ⸚ *m.* (1) **1A**

applicant Bewerber, - / Bewerberin, -nen *m./f.* (3) **3A**

apply sich bewerben *v.* (3) *3A*

appointment Termin, -e *m.* (3) **3A**

April April *m.* (1) **2A**

architect Architekt, -en / Architektin, -nen *m./f.* (1) **3B**

architecture Architektur, -en *f.* (1) **2A**

argue sich streiten *v.* (3) **1A**

arm Arm, -e *m.* (3) **1A**

armchair Sessel, - *m.* (2) **2A**

around um *prep.* (1) **3B**

arrival Ankunft, ⸚e *f.* (2) **3B**

arrive ankommen *v.* (1) **4A**

arrogant eingebildet *adj.* (1) **3B**

art Kunst, ⸚e *f.* (1) **2A**

artichoke Artischocke, -n *f.* (1) **4A**

as als *conj.* (2) **4A**
  as if als ob (3) **2A**

ask fragen *v.* (1) **2A**
  to ask about fragen nach *v.* (2) **3A**

assistant Assistent, -en / Assistentin, -nen *m./f.* (3) **3A**

at um *prep.* (1) **3B**; bei *prep.* (1) **4A**; an *prep.* (2) **1B**
  at...o'clock um...Uhr (1) **2A**

athletic sportlich *adj.* (1) **2B**

ATM Geldautomat, -en *m.* (3) **2A**

Attention! Achtung!

attic Dachboden, ⸚ *m.* (2) **2A**

August August *m.* (1) **2A**

aunt Tante, -n *f.* (1) **3A**

Austria Österreich *n.* (3) **2B**

Austrian österreichisch *adj.* (3) **2B**; (person) Österreicher, - / Österreicherin, -nen *m./f.* (3) **2B**

autumn Herbst, -e *m.* (1) **2B**

avenue Allee, -n *f.* (3) **2B**

awful furchtbar *adj.* (2) **3A**

B

baby Baby, -s *n.* (1) **3A**

back Rücken, - *m.* (3) **1A**

backache Rückenschmerzen *m. pl.* (3) **1B**

backpack Rucksack, ⸚e *m.* (1) **1B**

bad schlecht *adj.* (1) **3B**
  badly dressed schlecht gekleidet *adj.* (2) **1B**

baked goods Gebäck *n.* (2) **1A**

bakery Bäckerei, -en *f.* (1) **4A**

balcony Balkon, - e *m.* (2) **2A**

ball Ball, ⸚e *m.* (1) **2B**

balloon Ballon, -e *m.* (2) **1A**

ball-point pen Kuli, -s *m.* (1) **1B**

banana Banane, -n *f.* (1) **4A**

bank Bank, -en *f.* (3) **2A**
  at the bank auf der Bank *f.* (3) **2B**

bank account Konto (*pl.* Konten) *n.* (3) **2A**

bank employee Bankangestellte, -n *m./f.* (3) **3B**

baseball Baseball *m.* (1) **2B**

basketball Basketball *m.* (1) **2B**

bath: to take a bath sich baden *v.* (3) **1A**

bathing suit Badeanzug, ⸚e *m.* (2) **1B**

bathrobe Bademantel, ⸚ *m.* (3) **1A**

bathroom Badezimmer, - *n.* (3) **1A**

bathtub Badewanne, -n *f.* (2) **2A**

battery charger Ladegerät, -e *n.* (2) **4B**

be sein *v.* (1) **1A**
  Is/Are there... Ist/Sind hier...? *v.* (1) **1B**; Gibt es...? (1) **2B**

There is/are... Da ist/sind... *v.* (1) **1A**; Es gibt... (1) **2B**

beach Strand, ⸚e *m.* (1) **2B**

bean Bohne, -n *f.* (1) **4A**

beard Bart, ⸚e *m.* (3) **1A**

beautiful schön *adj.* (1) **3A**

beauty salon Kosmetiksalon, -s *m.* (3) **2A**

because denn *conj.* (2) **2A**; weil *conj.* (3) **2A**
  because of wegen *prep.* (2) **4B**

become werden *v.* (1) **2B**

bed Bett, -en *n.* (2) **2A**
  to go to bed ins Bett gehen *v.* (3) **1A**
  to make the bed das Bett machen *v.* (2) **2B**

bedroom Schlafzimmer, - *n.* (2) **2A**

beef Rindfleisch *n.* (1) **4A**

beer Bier, -e *n.* (1) **4B**

before vor *prep.* (2) **1B**; bevor *conj.* (2) **4A**
  before noon vormittags *adv.* (1) **2A**

begin anfangen *v.* (1) **4A**; beginnen *v.* (2) **4A**

behind hinter *prep.* (2) **1B**

believe glauben *v.* (2) **1A**; meinen *v.* (3) **4B**

belly Bauch, ⸚e *m.* (3) **1A**

belong gehören *v.* (1) **4B**

below unter *prep.* (2) **1B**

belt Gürtel, - *m.* (2) **1B**

bench Bank, ⸚e *f.* (3) **2B**

best beste/bester/bestes *adj.* (2) **4A**

All the best! Mach's gut! *v.* (1) **3B**; alles Gute (3) **2A**

better besser *adj.* (2) **4A**
  to get better gesund werden *v.* (3) **1B**

between zwischen *prep.* (2) **1B**

beverage Getränk, -e *n.* (1) **4B**

bicycle Fahrrad, ⸚er *n.* (1) **2B**

big groß, weit *adj.* (1) **3A**

bill (money) Geldschein, -e *m.* (3) **2A**

biology Biologie *f.* (1) **2A**

bird Vogel, ⸚ *m.* (3) **3A**

birth Geburt, -en *f.* (2) **1A**

birthday Geburtstag, -e *m.* (2) **1A**
  When is your birthday? Wann hast du Geburtstag? (1) **2B**

black schwarz *adj.* (2) **1B**
  black board Tafel, -n *f.* (1) **1B**
  black-haired schwarzhaarig *adj.* (1) **3A**

bland fade *adj.* (1) **4B**

blanket Decke, -n *f.* (2) **2B**

blond blond *adj.* (1) **3A**
  blond hair blonde Haare *n. pl.* (1) **3A**

blood pressure Blutdruck *m.* (3) **1B**

blouse Bluse, -n *f.* (2) **1B**

blue blau *adj.* (1) **3A**

board Tafel, -n *f.* (1) **1B**

boarding pass Bordkarte, -n *f.* (2) **3B**

boat Boot, -e *n.* (2) **4A**

body Körper, - *m.* (3) **1A**

book Buch, ⸚er *n.* (1) **1A**

bookshelf Bücherregal, -e *n.* (2) **2A**

boot Stiefel, - *m.* (2) **1B**

boring langweilig *adj.* (1) **2A**

boss Chef, -s / Chefin, -nen *m./f.* (3) **3B**

bottle Flasche, -n *f.* (1) **4B**

bowl Schüssel, -n *f.* (1) **4B**

boy Junge, -n *m.* (1) **1A**

brakes Bremse, -n *f.* (2) **4A**
brave mutig *adj.* (1) **3B**
bread Brot, -e *n.* (1) **4A**
break brechen *v.* (1) **2B**
  to break (an arm / a leg) sich (den Arm/Bein) brechen *v.* (3) **1B**
  Break a leg! Hals- und Beinbruch! (2) **1A**
breakfast Frühstück, -e *n.* (1) **4B**
bridge Brücke, -n *f.* (3) **2B**
bright hell *adj.* (2) **1B**
bring bringen *v.* (1) **2A**
  to bring along mitbringen *v.* (1) **4A**
  to bring out rausbringen (2) **2B**
  to bring with mitnehmen *v.* (3) **2B**
broom Besen, - *m.* (2) **2B**
brother Bruder, ⸚ *m.* (1) **1A**
brother-in-law Schwager, ⸚ *m.* (1) **3A**
brown braun *adj.* (2) **1B**
  brown-haired braunhaarig *adj.* (1) **3A**
bruise blauer Fleck, -e *m.* (3) **1B**
brush Bürste, -n *f.* (3) **1A**
  to brush one's hair sich die Haare bürsten *v.* (3) **1A**
  to brush one's teeth sich die Zähne putzen *v.* (3) **1A**
build bauen *v.* (1) **2A**
building Gebäude, - *n.* (3) **2A**
bulletin board Pinnwand, ⸚e *f.* (3) **3A**
burn brennen *v.* (2) **1A**
bus Bus, -se *m.* (2) **4A**
bus stop Bushaltestelle, -n *f.* (2) **4A**
bush Busch, ⸚e *m.* (3) **4A**
business Wirtschaft, -en *f.* (1) **2A**; Geschäft, -e *n.* (3) **4A**
  business class Businessklasse *f.* (2) **3B**
  businessman / businesswoman Geschäftsmann, ⸚er / Geschäftsfrau, -en *m./f.* (*pl.* Geschäftsleute) (1) **3B**
but aber *conj.* (1) **1B**
  but rather sondern *conj.* (2) **2A**
butcher shop Metzgerei, -en *f.* (1) **4A**
butter Butter *f.* (1) **4A**
buy kaufen *v.* (1) **2A**
by an *prep.* (2) **1B**; bei; von (1) **4B**
Bye! Tschüss! (1) **1A**

C

cabinet Schrank, ⸚e *m.* (2) **2A**
café Café, -s *n.* (1) **2A**
cafeteria Cafeteria, (*pl.* Cafeterien) *f.;* **(college/ university)** Mensa, Mensen *f.* (1) **1B**
cake Kuchen, - *m.* (1) **4A**; Torte, -n *f.* (2) **1A**
calculator Taschenrechner, - *m.* (1) **1B**
calendar Kalender, - *m.* (1) **1B**
call anrufen *v.* (1) **4A**; sich anrufen (3) **1A**; nennen *v.* (2) **1A**
  Who's calling? Wer spricht? (3) **3A**
calm ruhig *adj.* (1) **3B**
(to go) camping campen gehen *n.* (1) **2B**
camping area Zeltplatz, ⸚e *m.* (2) **3B**
can können *v.* (1) **3B**
Canada Kanada *n.* (3) **2B**
Canadian kanadisch *adj.* (3) **2B**; **(person)** Kanadier, - / Kanadierin, -nen *m./f.* (3) **2B**
cancel abbrechen, streichen *v.* (2) **3B**

candidate Kandidat, -en *m.* (3) **3A**
candy Süßigkeit, -en *f.* (2) **1A**
cap Mütze, -n *f.* (2) **1B**
car Auto, -s *n.* (1) **1A**
  to drive a car Auto fahren *v.* (2) **4A**
card Karte, -n *f.* (1) **2B**
career Karriere, -n *f.* (3) **3B**
caretaker Hausmeister, - / Hausmeisterin, -nen *m./f.* (3) **3B**
carpool Fahrgemeinschaft, -en *f.* (3) **4B**
carrot Karotte, -n *f.* (1) **4A**
carry tragen *v.* (1) **2B**
carry-on luggage Handgepäck *n.* (2) **3B**
cash bar *adj.* (3) **2A**; Bargeld *n.* (3) **2A**
  to pay in cash bar bezahlen *v.* (3) **2A**
cat Katze, -n *f.* (1) **3A**
catch fangen *v.* (1) **2B**
  to catch a cold sich erkälten *v.* (3) **1A**
celebrate feiern *v.* (2) **1A**
celebration Fest, -e *n.* (2) **1A**
cell phone Handy, -s *n.* (2) **4B**
cellar Keller, - *m.* (2) **2A**
ceramic Keramik, -en *f.* (2) **2B**
chair Stuhl, ⸚e *m.* (1) **1A**
champagne Sekt, -e *m.* (2) **1A**
championship Meisterschaft, -en *f.* (1) **2B**
change Kleingeld *n.* (3) **2A**
  to change clothes sich umziehen *v.* (3) **1A**
channel Sender, - *m.* (3) **4B**
  channel surfing Zapping *n.*
charge laden *v.* (3) **4B**
chat sich unterhalten *v.* (3) **1A**
cheap günstig *adj.* (2) **1B**
check Rechnung, -en *f.* (1) **4B**
Cheers! Prost! **4B**; Zum Wohl! (1) **4B**
cheese Käse, - *m.* (1) **4A**
chemistry Chemie *f.* (1) **2A**
chess Schach *n.* (1) **2B**
chicken Huhn, ⸚er *n.* (3) **4A**; **(food)** Hähnchen, - *n.* (1) **4A**
child Kind, -er *n.* (1) **1A**
China China *n.* (3) **2B**
Chinese (person) Chinese, -n / Chinesin, -nen *m./f.* (3) **2B**; **(language)** Chinesisch *n.* (3) **2B**
Christmas Weihnachten, - *n.* (2) **1A**
church Kirche, -n *f.* (3) **2B**
city Stadt, ⸚e *f.* (2) **1B**
  city center Innenstadt, ⸚e *f.* (3) **2B**
claim behaupten *v.* (3) **4B**
class Klasse, -n *f.* (1) **1B**; Unterricht *m.* (1) **1B**; Veranstaltung, -en *f.* (1) **2A**
  first/second class erste/zweite Klasse (2) **2A**
classical klassisch *adj.* (3) **2A**
classmate Kommilitone, -n / Kommilitonin, -nen; Klassenkamerad, -en / Klassenkameradin, -nen *m./f.* (1) **1B**
classroom Klassenzimmer, - *n.* (1) **1B**
clean sauber *adj.* (2) **2B**; putzen *v.* (2) **2B**
  to clean up aufräumen *v.* (2) **2B**
cliff Klippe, -n *f.* (3) **4A**
climb steigen *v.* (2) **1B**
  to climb (mountain) klettern *v.* (1) **2B**
  to climb (stairs) (die Treppe) hochgehen *v.* (3) **2B**
clock Uhr, -en *f.* (1) **1B**

  at... o'clock um... Uhr (1) **2A**
close zumachen *v.* (2) **2B**; nah *adj.* (3) **2B**
  close to in der Nähe von *prep.* (3) **2B**
closed geschlossen *adj.* (3) **2A**
closet Schrank, ⸚e *m.* (2) **2A**
clothes Kleidung *f.* (2) **1B**
cloud Wolke, -n *f.* (2) **3A**
cloudy wolkig *adj.* (2) **3A**
coast Küste, -n *f.* (3) **4A**
coat Mantel, ⸚ *m.* (2) **1B**
coffee Kaffee, -s *m.* (1) **4B**
coffeemaker Kaffeemaschine, -n *f.* (3) **3B**
coin Münze, -n *f.* (3) **2A**
  cold kalt *adj.* (2) **3A**; Erkältung, -en **f.** (3) **1B**
  to catch a cold sich erkälten *v.* (3) **1A**
college Universität, -en *f.* (1) **1B**
college instructor Dozent, -en / Dozentin, -nen *m./f.* (1) **2A**
color Farbe, -n *f.* (2) **1B**
  solid colored einfarbig *adj.* (2) **1B**
colorful bunt *adj.* (3) **2A**
comb Kamm, ⸚e *m.* (3) **1A**
  to comb (one's hair) sich (die Haare) kämmen *v.* (3) **1A**
come kommen *v.* (1) **2A**
  to come along mitkommen *v.* (1) **4A**
  to come back zurückkommen *v.* (1) **4A**
comma Komma, -s *f.* (1) **1B**
compact disc CD, -s *f.* (2) **4B**
company Firma (*pl.* die Firmen) *f.* (3) **3A**
complicated kompliziert *adj.* (3) **2A**
computer Computer, - *m.* (1) **1B**
computer science Informatik *f.* (1) **2A**
concert Konzert, -e *n.* (2) **1B**
congratulate gratulieren *v.* (2) **1A**
  Congratulations! Herzlichen Glückwunsch! (2) **1A**
construction zone Baustelle, -n *f.* (2) **4A**
contract Vertrag, ⸚e *m.* (3) **3A**
conversation: to have a conversation sich unterhalten *v.* (3) **1A**
cook kochen *v.* (1) **2B**; Koch, ⸚e / Köchin, -nen *m./f.* (1) **4B**
cookie Keks, -e *m.* (2) **1A**
cool kühl *adj.* (2) **3A**
corner Ecke, -n *f.* (3) **2B**
correct korrigieren *v.* (1) **2A**
cost kosten *v.* (1) **2A**
cotton Baumwolle *f.* (2) **1B**
couch Sofa, -s *n.* (2) **3B**
  to couch surf Sofa surfen *v.* (2) **3B**
cough husten *v.* (3) **1B**
country Land, ⸚er *n.* (2) **3B**
countryside Landschaft, -en *f.* (3) **4A**
couple Paar, -e *n.* (1) **3A**
courageous mutig *adj.*
course Veranstaltung, -en *f.* (2) **2B**; Gang, ⸚e *m.* (1) **4B**
  first/second course erster/zweiter Gang *m.* (1) **4B**
  main course Hauptspeise, -en *f.* (1) **4B**
court Platz, ⸚e *m.* (1) **1A**
cousin Cousin, -s / Cousine, -n *m./f.* (1) **3A**
cover decken *v.* (2) **2B**
cow Kuh, ⸚e *f.* (3) **4A**

cram (for a test) büffeln *v.* (1) **2A**
cross überqueren *v.* (3) **2B**
  to cross the street die Straße überqueren *v.* (3) **2B**
cross-reference Querverweis, -e *m.*
crosswalk Zebrastreifen, - *pl.* (3) **2B**
cruel grausam *adj.*; gemein *adj.* (1) **3B**
cruise Kreuzfahrt, -en *f.* (2) **3B**
cry weinen *v.* (1) **3B**
cup Tasse, -n *f.* (1) **4B**
curious neugierig *adj.* (1) **3B**
curly lockig *adj.* (1) **3A**
curtain Vorhang, ⁻e *m.* (2) **2A**
custodian Hausmeister, - / Hausmeisterin,
  -nen *m./f.* (3) **3B**
customer Kunde, -n /Kundin, -nen *m./f.* (2) **1B**
customs Zoll *m.* (2) **3B**
cut Schnitt, -e *m.* (2) **1B**
  to cut class schwänzen *v.* (1) **1B**
cute süß *adj.* (1) **3B**
CV Lebenslauf, ⁻e *m.* (3) **3A**

D

dad Papa, -s *m.* (1) **3A**
daily täglich *adv.* (1) **4A**
  daily routine Alltagsroutine *f.* (3) **1A**
dance tanzen *v.* (1) **2B**
danger Gefahr, -en *f.* (3) **4B**
dark dunkel *adj.* (1) **3A**
  dark-haired dunkelhaarig *adj.* (1) **3A**
darling Liebling, -e *m.*
date Datum (*pl.* Daten) *n.* (2) **3A**
  What is the date today? Der wievielte ist
  heute? (1) **2A**
daughter Tochter, ⁻ *f.* (1) **3A**
day Tag, -e *m.* (1) **1A**
  every day täglich *adv.* (1) **4A**
Dear Lieber/Liebe *m./f.* (1) **3B**
December Dezember *m.* (1) **2A**
decide sich entschließen *v.* (1) **4B**
definitely bestimmt *adv.* (1) **4A**
degree Abschluss, ⁻e *m.* (1) **2A**; Grad *n.* (2) **3A**
  It's 18 degrees out. Es sind 18 Grad
  draußen. (2) **3A**
delay Verspätung, -en *f.* (2) **3B**
delete löschen *v.* (2) **4B**
delicatessen Feinkostgeschäft, -e *n.* (1) **4A**
delicious lecker *adj.* (1) **4B**
demanding anspruchsvoll *adj.* (3) **3B**
dentist Zahnarzt, ⁻e / Zahnärztin, -nen *m./f.*
  (3) **1B**
department store Kaufhaus, ⁻er *n.* (3) **2B**
departure Abflug, ⁻e *m.* (2) **3B**
deposit (money) (Geld) einzahlen *v.* (3) **2A**
describe beschreiben *v.* (1) **2A**
description Beschreibung, -en *f.* (1) **3B**
desk Schreibtisch, -e *m.* (1) **1B**
despite trotz *prep.* (2) **4B**
dessert Nachtisch, -e, *m.* (1) **4B**
destination Reiseziel, -e *n.* (2) **3B**
detour Umleitung, -en *f.* (2) **4A**
develop entwickeln *v.* (3) **4B**
dictionary Wörterbuch, ⁻er *n.* (1) **1B**
die sterben *v.* (2) **1B**

diet Diät, -en *f.* (1) **4B**
  to be on a diet auf Diät sein *v.* (1) **4B**
difficult schwierig *adj.* (1) **2A**
digital camera Digitalkamera, -s *f.* (2) **4B**
dining room Esszimmer, - *n.* (2) **2A**
dinner Abendessen, - *n.* (1) **4B**
diploma Abschlusszeugnis, -se *n.* (1) **2A**; Diplom,
  -e *n.* (1) **2A**
direction Richtung, -en *f.* (3) **2B**
dirty schmutzig *adj.* (2) **2B**
discover entdecken *v.* (2) **2B**
discreet diskret *adj.* (1) **3B**
discuss besprechen *v.* (1) **4A**
dish Gericht, -e *n.* (1) **4B**
dishes Geschirr *n.* (2) **2B**
  to do the dishes Geschirr spülen (2) **2B**
dishwasher Spülmaschine, -n *f.* (2) **2B**
dislike nicht gern (+*verb*) (1) **3A**
divided by geteilt durch (1) **1B**
divorced geschieden *adj.* (1) **3A**
dizzy schwindlig *adj.* (3) **1B**
do machen *v.* (1) **2A**; tun *v.* (3) **1B**
  to do laundry Wäsche waschen *v.* (2) **2B**
  to do the dishes Geschirr spülen *v.* (2) **2B**
  to have to do with handeln von (2) **3A**
doctor Arzt, ⁻e / Ärztin, -nen *m./f.* (3) **1B**
  to go to the doctor zum Arzt gehen *v.* (3) **1B**
document Dokument, -e *n.* (2) **4B**
dog Hund, -e *m.* (1) **3A**
door Tür, -en *f.* (1) **1B**
dormitory (Studenten)wohnheim, -e *n.* (2) **2A**
down entlang *prep.* (1) **3B**; herunter *adv.* (2) **2A**
  to go down heruntergehen *v.* (3) **2B**
download herunterladen *v.* (2) **4B**
downtown Innenstadt, ⁻e *f.* (3) **2B**
dozen Dutzend, -e *n.* (1) **4A**
  a dozen eggs ein Dutzend Eier (1) **4A**
drawer Schublade, -n *f.* (2) **2A**
dream träumen *v.* (2) **3A**
dress Kleid, -er *n.* (2) **1B**
  to get dressed sich anziehen *v.* (3) **1A**
  to get undressed sich ausziehen *v.* (3) **1A**
dresser Kommode, -n *f.* (2) **2A**
drink trinken *v.* (1) **3B**
drive fahren *v.* (2) **4A**
  to drive a car Auto fahren *v.* (2) **4A**
driver Fahrer, - / Fahrerin, -nen *m./f.* (2) **4A**
drugstore Drogerie, -n *f.* (3) **2A**
dry trocken *adj.* (3) **4A**
  to dry oneself off sich abtrocknen *v.* (3) **1A**
dryer Wäschetrockner, - *m.* (2) **2B**
dumb dumm *adj.* (2) **4A**
during während *prep.* (2) **4B**
dust abstauben *v.* (2) **2B**
duvet Bettdecke, - n *f.* (2) **2B**
DVD DVD, -s *f.* (2) **4B**
DVD-player DVD-Player, - *m.* (2) **4B**
dye (one's hair) sich (die Haare) färben *v.* (3) **1A**

E

ear Ohr, -en *n.* (3) **1A**
early früh *adj.* (1) **2B**
earn verdienen *v.* (3) **3B**
earth Erde, -n *f.* (3) **4B**

earthquake Erdbeben, - *n.* (3) **4A**
easy einfach *adj.* (1) **2A**
eat essen *v.* (1) **2B**
  to eat out essen gehen *v.* (1) **2B**
ecological ökologisch *adj.* (3) **4B**
ecology Ökologie *f.* (3) **4B**
economy Wirtschaft, -en *f.* (1) **2A**
  economy class Touristenklasse *f.* (2) **3B**
education Ausbildung, -en *f.* (3) **3A**
egg Ei, -er *n.* (1) **4A**
eggplant Aubergine, -n *f.* (1) **4A**
eight acht (1) **2A**
elbow Ell(en)bogen, - *m.* (3) **1A**
electrician Elektriker, - / Elektrikerin,
  -nen *m./f.* (3) **3B**
elegant elegant *adj.* (2) **1B**
elevator Fahrstuhl, ⁻e *m.* (2) **3B**
eleven elf (1) **2A**
e-mail E-Mail, -s *f.* (2) **4B**
emergency Notfall, ⁻e *m.* (3) **3B**
emergency room Notaufnahme, -n *f.* (3) **1B**
employee Angestellte, -n *m./f.* (3) **3A**
endangered gefährdet *adj.* (3) **4B**
energy Energie, -n *f.* (3) **4B**
energy-efficient energiesparend *adj.* (2) **2B**
engaged verlobt *adj.* (1) **3A**
engine Motor, -en *m.* (2) **4A**
engineer Ingenieur, -e / Ingenieurin, -nen
  m./f. (1) **3B**
England England *n.* (3) **2B**
English (person) Engländer, - / Engländerin,
  -nen *m./f.* (3) **2B**; **(language)** Englisch *n.* (3) **2B**
enjoy genießen *v.*
  Enjoy your meal! Guten Appetit! (1) **4B**
envelope Briefumschlag, ⁻e *m.* (3) **2A**
environment Umwelt, -en *f.* (3) **4B**
  environmentally friendly umweltfreundlich
  adj. (2) **4B**
environmentalism Umweltschutz *m.* (3) **4B**
equal (gleich) sein *v.* (1) **1B**
eraser Radiergummi, -s *m.* (1) **1B**
errand Besorgung, -en *f.* (3) **2A**
  to run errands Besorgungen machen *v.* (3) **2A**
even though obwohl *conj.* (2) **2A**
evening Abend, -e *m.* (1) **2B**
  in the evening abends *adv.* (1) **2A**
every jeder/jede/jedes *adv.* (2) **4B**
everything alles *pron.* (2) **3B**
  Everything OK? Alles klar? (1) **1A**
everywhere überall *adv.* (1) **4A**
exam Prüfung, -en *f.* (1) **1B**
except (for) außer *prep.* (1) **4B**
exchange umtauschen *v.* (2) **2B**
exciting spannend *adj.* (3) **2A**; aufregend *adj.* (3) **4A**
Excuse me. Entschuldigung. (1) **1A**
exercise Sport treiben *v.* (3) **1B**
exit Ausgang, ⁻e *m.* (2) **1B**; Ausfahrt, -en *f.* (2) **4A**
expensive teuer *adj.* (2) **2B**
experience durchmachen *v.* (2) **4B**; Erfahrung,
  -en *f.* (3) **3A**
explain erklären *v.* (1) **4A**
explore erforschen *v.* (3) **4A**
expression Ausdruck, ⁻e *m.*

extinction Aussterben *n.* (3) **4B**
eye Auge, -n *n.* (1) **3A**
eyebrow Augenbraue, -n *f.* (3) **1A**

face Gesicht, -er *n.* (3) **1A**
factory Fabrik, -en *f.* (3) **4B**
factory worker Fabrikarbeiter, - / Fabrikarbeiterin, -nen *m./f.* (3) **3B**
fail durchfallen *v.* (1) **1B**; scheitern *v.* (3) **3B**
fall fallen *v.* (1) **2B**; (season) Herbst, -e *m.* (1) **2B**
  to fall in love (with) sich verlieben (in) *v.* (3) **1A**
familiar bekannt *adj.*
  to be familiar with kennen *v.* (2) **1B**
family Familie, -n *f.* (1) **3A**
fan Fan, -s *m.* (1) **2B**
fantastic fantastisch *adj.* (3) **2A**
far weit *adj.* (3) **2B**
  far from weit von *adj.* (3) **2B**
farm Bauernhof, ¨e *m.* (3) **4A**
farmer Bauer, -n / Bäuerin, -nen *m./f.* (3) **3B**
fashionable modisch *adj.* (2) **1B**
fast schnell *adj.* (1) **3B**
fat dick *adj.* (1) **3A**
father Vater, ¨ *m.* (1) **3A**
father-in-law Schwiegervater, ¨ *m.* (1) **3A**
favorite Lieblings- (1) **4B**
fear Angst, ¨e *f.* (2) **3A**
February Februar *m.* (1) **2A**
feel fühlen *v.* (1) **2A**; sich fühlen *v.* (3) **1A**
  to feel like Lust haben *v.* (2) **3B**
  to feel well sich wohl fühlen *v.* (3) **1A**
fever Fieber, - *n.* (3) **1B**
  to have a fever Fieber haben *v.* (3) **1B**
fiancé(e) Verlobte, -n *m./f.* (1) **3A**
field Spielfeld, -er *n.* (1) **2B**; Feld, -er *n.* (3) **4A**
file Datei, -en *f.* (2) **4B**
fill füllen *v.*
  to fill out ausfüllen *v.* (3) **2A**
  to fill up tanken *v.* (2) **4A**
filthy dreckig *adj.* (2) **2B**
finally schließlich *adv.* (2) **3B**
find finden *v.* (1) **2A**
  to find one's way sich zurechtfinden *v.* (3) **2B**
  to find out (about) sich informieren (über) *v.* (3) **1A**
fine (monetary) Bußgeld, -er *n.* (2) **4A**
  I'm fine. Mir geht's gut. (1) **1A**
finger Finger, - *m.* (3) **1A**
fire entlassen *v.* (3) **3B**; Feuer, - *n.*
firefighter Feuerwehrmann, ¨er / Feuerwehrfrau, -en (*pl.* Feuerwehrleute) *m./f.* (3) **3B**
firm Firma (*pl.* die Firmen) *f.* (3) **3A**
first erster/erste/erstes *adj.* (1) **2A**; zuerst *adv.* (2) **3B**
  first course erster Gang *m.* (1) **4B**
  first class erste Klasse *f.* (2) **4A**
fish Fisch, -e *m.* (1) **4A**
  to go fishing angeln gehen *v.* (1) **2B**
fish store Fischgeschäft, -e *n.* (1) **4A**
fit passen *v.* (2) **1A**; fit *adj.* (1) **2B**
five fünf (1) **2A**
flat tire Platten, - *m.* (2) **4A**

to have a flat tire einen Platten haben *v.* (2) **4A**
flavor Geschmack, ¨e *m.* (1) **4B**
flight Flug, ¨e *m.* (2) **3B**
flood Hochwasser, - *n.* (3) **4B**
floor Stock, ¨e *m.*; Boden, ¨ *m.* (2) **2A**
  first/second floor erster/zweiter Stock (2) **2A**
flower Blume, -n *f.* (1) **1A**
  flower shop Blumengeschäft, -e *n.* (3) **2A**
flu Grippe, -n *f.* (3) **1B**
flunk durchfallen *v.* (1) **1B**
fly fliegen *v.* (2) **3B**
fog Nebel, - *m.* (2) **3A**
follow folgen *v.* (2) **1A**
food Essen, - *n.* (1) **4A**
foot Fuß, ¨e *m.* (3) **1A**
football American Football *m.* (1) **2B**
for für *prep.* (1) **3B**; seit; zu *prep.* (1) **4B**
foreign language Fremdsprache, -n *f.* (1) **2A**
forest Wald, ¨er *m.* (1) **2B**
forget vergessen *v.* (1) **2B**
fork Gabel, -n *f.* (1) **4B**
form Formular, -e *n.* (3) **2A**
  to fill out a form ein Formular ausfüllen *v.* (3) **2A**
fountain Brunnen, - *m.* (3) **2B**
four vier (1) **2A**
France Frankreich *n.* (3) **2B**
French (person) Franzose, -n / Französin, -nen *m./f.* (3) **2B**; (language) Französisch *n.* (3) **2B**
free time Freizeit, -en *f.* (1) **2B**
freezer Gefrierschrank, ¨e *m.* (2) **2B**
Friday Freitag, -e *m.* (1) **2A**
  on Fridays freitags *adv.* (1) **2A**
friend Freund, -e / Freundin, -nen *m./f.* (1) **1A**
friendly freundlich *adj.* (1) **3B**
friendship Freundschaft, -en *f.* (2) **1A**
from aus *prep.* (1) **4A**; von *prep.* (1) **4B**
  where from woher *interr.* (1) **2A**
front: in front of vor *prep.* (2) **1B**
fruit Obst *n.* (1) **4A**
fry braten *v.* (1) **2B**
full voll *adj.* (2) **3B**
full-time ganztags *adj.* (3) **3B**
fully occupied voll besetzt *adj.* (2) **3B**
fun Spaß *m.* (1) **2B**
  to be fun Spaß machen *v.* (1) **2B**
  to (not) have fun (keinen) Spaß haben *v.* (2) **1A**
function funktionieren *v.* (2) **4B**
funny lustig *adj.* (3) **3B**
furnished möbliert *adj.* (2) **2A**
furniture Möbel, - *n.* (2) **2A**
  piece of furniture Möbelstück, -e *n.* (2) **2A**

game Spiel, -e *n.* (1) **2B**
game console Spielkonsole, -en *f.* (2) **4B**
garage Garage, -n *f.* (2) **1B**
garbage truck Müllwagen, - *m.* (3) **4B**
gardener Gärtner, - / Gärtnerin, -nen *m./f.* (3) **3B**
garlic Knoblauch *m.* (1) **4A**
gas Benzin, -e *n.* (2) **4A**
gas station Tankstelle, -n *f.* (2) **4A**

generous großzügig *adj.* (1) **3B**
German (person) Deutsche *m./f.* (3) **2B**; (language) Deutsch *n.* (3) **2B**
Germany Deutschland *n.* (1) **4A**
get bekommen *v.* (2) **1A**
  to get up aufstehen *v.* (1) **4A**
  to get sick/better krank/gesund werden *v.* (3) **1B**
gift Geschenk, -e *n.* (2) **1A**
girl Mädchen, - *n.* (1) **1A**
give geben *v.* (1) **2B**
  to give (a gift) schenken *v.* (2) **1A**
glass Glas, ¨er *n.* (1) **4B**
glasses Brille, -n *f.* (2) **1B**
global warming Erderwärmung *f.* (2) **4B**
glove Handschuh, -e *m.* (2) **1B**
go gehen *v.* (1) **2A**; fahren *v.* (1) **2B**
  to go out ausgehen *v.* (1) **4A**
  Go! Los! (1) **2B**
goal (in soccer) Tor, -e *n.* (1) **2B**
golf Golf *n.* (1) **2B**
good gut *adj.*; nett *adj.* (1) **1A**
  Good evening. Guten Abend! (1) **1A**
  Good morning. Guten Morgen! (1) **1A**
  Good night. Gute Nacht! (1) **1A**
  Good-bye. Auf Wiedersehen! (1) **1A**
  Good luck! Viel Glück! (2) **1A**
government Regierung, -en *f.* (3) **4B**
grade Note, -n *f.* (1) **1B**
grade report Zeugnis, -se *n.* (1) **1B**
graduate Abschluss machen, ¨e *v.* (2) **1A**
graduation Abschluss, ¨e *m.* (1) **1B**
gram Gramm, -e *n.* (1) **4A**
  100 grams of cheese 100 Gramm Käse (1) **4A**
granddaughter Enkeltochter, ¨ *f.* (1) **3A**
grandson Enkelsohn, ¨e *m.* (1) **3A**
grandchild Enkel, - *m.* (1) **3A**; Enkelkind, -er *n.* (1) **3A**
grandfather Großvater, ¨ *m.* (1) **3A**
grandma Oma, -s *f.* (1) **3A**
grandmother Großmutter, ¨ *f.* (1) **3A**
grandpa Opa, -s *m.* (1) **3A**
grandparents Großeltern *pl.* (1) **1A**
grape Traube, -n *f.* (1) **4A**
grass Gras, ¨er *n.* (3) **4A**
gray grau *adj.* (2) **1B**
great toll *adj.* (1) **3B**; prima *adj.*; spitze *adj.* (1) **1A**
great grandfather Urgroßvater, ¨ *m.* (1) **3A**
great grandmother Urgroßmutter, ¨ *f.* (1) **3A**
greedy gierig *adj.* (1) **3B**
green grün *adj.* (2) **1B**
green bean grüne Bohne (*pl.* die grünen Bohnen) *f.* (1) **4A**
greet grüßen *v.* (1) **2A**
greeting Begrüßung, -en *f.* (1) **1A**; Gruß, ¨e *m.* (1) **1A**
grocery store Lebensmittelgeschäft, -e *n.* (1) **4A**
ground floor Erdgeschoss, -e *n.* (2) **2A**
grow wachsen *v.* (2) **1B**
grown-up erwachsen *adj.* (3) **2A**
guest Gast, ¨e *m.* (2) **1A**
  hotel guest Hotelgast, ¨e *m.* (2) **3B**
guesthouse Pension, -en *f.* (2) **3B**
gym Sporthalle, -n *f.* (1) **2A**

H

hail Hagel *m.* (2) **3A**
hair Haar, -e *n.* (1) **3A**
hair dryer Haartrockner, - *m.* (3) **1A**
hairdresser Friseur, -e / Friseurin, -nen *m./f.* (1) **3B**
half halb *adj.* (1) **2A**
half brother Halbbruder, ⸚ *m.* (1) **3A**
half sister Halbschwester, -n *f.* (1) **3A**
hall Flur, -e *m.* (2) **2A**
ham Schinken, - *m.* (1) **4A**
hand Hand, ⸚e *f.* (3) **1A**
handsome gut aussehend *adj.* (1) **3A**
hang hängen *v.* (2) **1B**
  to hang up auflegen *v.* (3) **3A**
happen passieren *v.* (2) **1B**
happiness Glück *n.* (2) **1A**
happy glücklich *adj.* (1) **3B** froh *adj.* (1) (1) **3B**
  Happy birthday! Alles Gute zum Geburtstag! (2) **1A**
  Happy Easter! Frohe Ostern! (2) **1A**
  Happy New Year! Ein gutes neues Jahr! (2) **1A**
  to be happy (about) sich freuen (über) *v.* (3) **1A**
hard schwer *adj.* (3) **1B**
hard drive Festplatte, -en *f.* (2) **4B**
hard-working fleißig *adj.* (1) **3B**
hare Hase, -n *m.* (3) **4A**
hat Hut, ⸚e *m.* (2) **1B**
have haben *v.* (1) **1B**
  Have a nice day! Schönen Tag noch! (1) **1A**
  to have to müssen *v.* (1) **3B**
he er *pron.* (1) **1A**
head Kopf, ⸚e *m.* (3) **1A**
headache Kopfschmerzen *m. pl.* (3) **1B**
headlight Scheinwerfer, -e *m.* (2) **4A**
headphones Kopfhörer, - *m.* (2) **4B**
health Gesundheit *f.* (3) **1B**
health-food store Bioladen, ⸚ *m.* (3) **1B**
healthy gesund *adj.* (2) **4A**
hear hören *v.* (1) **2A**
heat stroke Hitzschlag, ⸚e *m.* (3) **1B**
heavy schwer *adj.* (1) **4B**
hello Guten Tag!; Hallo! (1) **1A**
help helfen *v.* (1) **2B**
  to help with helfen bei *v.* (3) **3A**
her ihr *poss. adj.* (1) **3A**
here hier *adv.* (1) **1A**
  Here is/are... Hier ist/sind... (1) **1B**
high hoch *adj.* (2) **4A**
highway Autobahn, -en *f.* (2) **4A**
hike wandern *v.* (1) **2A**
his sein *poss. adj.* (1) **3A**
history Geschichte, -en *f.* (1) **2A**
hit treffen *v.* (1) **2B**
hobby Hobby, -s *n.* (1) **2B**
hockey Hockey *n.* (1) **2B**
hold: to be on hold in der Warteschleife sein *v.* (3) **3B**
  Please hold. Bleiben Sie bitte am Apparat! (3) **3A**
holiday Feiertag, -e *m.* (2) **1A**
home Haus, ⸚er *adv.* (1) **1B**
  at home zu Hause *adv.* (1) **4A**
home office Arbeitszimmer, - *n.* (2) **2A**
homemade hausgemacht *adj.* (1) **4B**
homemaker Hausfrau, -en / Hausmann, ⸚er *f./m.* (3) **3B**
homework Hausaufgabe, -n *f.* (1) **1B**
hood Motorhaube, -en *f.* (2) **4A**
horse Pferd, -e *n.* (1) **2B**
hospital Krankenhaus, ⸚er *n.* (3) **1B**
host / hostess Gastgeber, - / Gastgeberin, -nen *m./f.* (2) **1A**
host family Gastfamilie, -n *f.* (1) **4B**
hot heiß *adj.* (2) **3A**
hotel Hotel, -s *n.* (2) **3B**
  five-star hotel Fünf-Sterne-Hotel *n.* (2) **3B**
hour Stunde,-n *f.* (1) **2A**
house Haus, ⸚er *n.* (2) **2A**
housework Hausarbeit *f.* (2) **2B**
  to do housework Hausarbeit machen *v.* (2) **2B**
how wie *interr.* (1) **2A**
  How are you? (form.) Wie geht es Ihnen? (1) **1A**
  How are you? (inf.) Wie geht's (dir)? (1) **1A**
  how many wie viele *interr.* (1) **1B**
  how much wie viel *interr.* (1) **1B**
human resources manager Personalchef, -s / die Personalchefin, -nen *m./f.* (3) **3A**
humble bescheiden *adj.*
hurry sich beeilen *v.* (3) **1A**
hurt weh tun *v.* (3) **1B**
  to hurt oneself sich verletzen *v.* (3) **1B**
husband Ehemann, ⸚er *m.* (1) **3A**
hybrid car Hybridauto, -s *n.* (3) **4B**

I

I ich *pron.* (1) **1A**
ice cream Eis *n.* (2) **1A**
ice cream shop Eisdiele, -n *f.* (1) **4A**
ice cube Eiswürfel, - *m.* (2) **1A**
ice hockey Eishockey *n.* (1) **2B**
ID card Personalausweis, -e *m.* (2) **3B**
idea Idee, -n *f.* (1) **1A**
if wenn *conj.;* ob *conj.* (3) **2A**
  as if als ob (3) **2A**
  if I were you an deiner/Ihrer Stelle *f.* (3) **2A**
  if... only wenn... nur (3) **2A**
  if... then wenn... dann (3) **2A**
imagine sich (etwas) vorstellen *v.* (3) **1A**
imitate nachmachen *v.* (2) **4B**
important wichtig *adj.* (2) **3B**; bedeutend *adj.* (3) **4A**
improve verbessern *v.* (3) **4B**
in in *prep.* (2) **1B**
  in the afternoon nachmittags *adv.* (1) **2A**
  in the evening abends *adv.* (1) **2A**
  in the morning morgens *adv.* (1) **2A**
  in spite of trotz *prep.* (2) **4B**
India Indien *n.* (3) **2B**
Indian indisch *adj.* (3) **2B**; **(person)** Inder, - / Inderin, -nen *m./f.* (3) **2B**
ingredient Zutat, -en *f.* (1) **4A**
injury Verletzung, -en *f.* (3) **1B**
inside (of) innerhalb *prep.* (2) **4B**
instead sondern *conj.* (2) **2A**
  instead of statt *prep.;* anstatt *prep.* (2) **4B**
intellectual intellektuell *adj.* (1) **3B**
intelligent intelligent *adj.* (1) **3B**
interested: to be interested (in) sich interessieren (für) *v.* (3) **1A**
interesting interessant *adj.* (1) **2A**

internet café Internetcafé, -s *n.* (3) **2A**
internship Praktikum (*pl.* die Praktika) *n.* (3) **3A**
intersection Kreuzung, -en *f.* (3) **2B**
introduce: to introduce (oneself) (sich) vorstellen *v.* (3) **1A**
invent erfinden *v.* (2) **3A**
invite einladen *v.* (2) **1A**
iron Bügeleisen, - *n.* (2) **2B**; bügeln *v.* (2) **2B**
ironing board Bügelbrett, -er *n.* (2) **2B**
island Insel, -n *f.* (3) **4A**
it es *pron.* (1) **1A**
Italian (person) Italiener, - / Italienerin, -nen *m./f.* (3) **2B**; **(language)** Italienisch *n.* (3) **2B**
Italy Italien *n.* (3) **2B**
its sein *poss. adj.* (1) **3A**

J

jacket Jacke, -n *f.* (2) **1B**
jam Marmelade, -n *f.* (1) **4A**
January Januar *m.* (1) **2A**
Japan Japan *n.* (3) **2B**
Japanese (person) Japaner, - / Japanerin, -nen *m./f.* (3) **2B**; **(language)** Japanisch *n.* (3) **2B**
jealous eifersüchtig *adj.* (1) **3B**
jeans Jeans, - *f.* (2) **1B**
jewelry store Juweliergeschäft, -e *n.* (2) **2A**
job Beruf, -e *m.* (3) **3B**; Stelle, -n *f.* (3) **3A**
  to find a job Arbeit finden *v.* (3) **3A**
job interview Vorstellungsgespräch, -e *n.* (3) **3A**
job opening Stellenangebot, -e *n.* (3) **3A**
jog joggen *v.* (1) **2B**
journalist Journalist, -en / Journalistin, -nen *m./f.* (3) **3B**
judge Richter, - / Richterin, -nen *m./f.* (3) **3B**
juice Saft, ⸚e *m.* (1) **4B**
July Juli *m.* (1) **2A**
June Juni *m.* (1) **2A**
just as genauso wie (2) **4A**

K

key Schlüssel, - *m.* (2) **3B**
keyboard Tastatur, -en *f.* (2) **4B**
kind nett *adj.*
kiosk Kiosk, -e *m.* (3) **2A**
kiss Kuss, ⸚e *m.* (2) **1A**; küssen *v.* (2) **1A**
  to kiss (each other) sich küssen *v.* (3) **1A**
kitchen Küche, -n *f.* (2) **2A**
knee Knie, - *n.* (3) **1A**
knife Messer, - *n.* (1) **4B**
know kennen *v.* (2) **1B**; wissen *v.* (2) **1B**
  to know each other sich kennen *v.* (3) **1A**
know-it-all Besserwisser, - / Besserwisserin, -nen *m./f.* (1) **2A**
Korea Korea *n.* (3) **2B**
Korean (person) Koreaner, - / Koreanerin, -nen *m./f.* (3) **2B**; **(language)** Koreanisch *n.* (3) **2B**

L

labor union Gewerkschaft, -en *f.* (3) **3B**
lake See, -n *m.* (3) **4A**
lamp Lampe, -n *f.* (2) **2A**

land landen *v.* (2) **3B**; Land, ⸚er *n.* (2) **3B**
landscape Landschaft, -en *f.* (3) **4A**
laptop (computer) Laptop, -s *m./n.* (2) **4B**
last letzter/letzte/letztes *adj.* (1) **2B**
last name Nachname, -n *m.* (1) **3A**
late spät *adj.* (1) **2A**
  to be late sich verspäten *v.* (3) **1A**
laugh lachen *v.* (1) **2A**
laundromat Waschsalon, -s *m.* (3) **4A**
laundry Wäsche *f.* (2) **2B**
  to do laundry Wäsche waschen *v.* (2) **2B**
law Gesetz, -e *n.* (3) **4B**
lawyer Rechtsanwalt, ⸚e / Rechtsanwältin,
  -nen *m./f.* (1) **3B**
lay legen *v.* (2) **1B**
lazy faul *adj.* (1) **3B**
leaf Blatt, ⸚er *n.* (3) **4A**
learn lernen *v.* (1) **2A**
leather Leder, - *n.* (2) **1B**
leave abfahren *v.* (2) **4A**
lecture Vorlesung, -en *f.* (1) **2A**; Vortrag, ⸚e *m.*
  (2) **2B**
lecture hall Hörsaal (*pl.* Hörsäle) *m.* (1) **2A**
leg Bein, -e *n.* (3) **1A**
leisure Freizeit *f.* (1) **2B**
lesson Stunde, -n *f.* (1) **1B**
let lassen *v.* (1) **2B**
letter Brief, -e *m.* (3) **2A**
  to mail a letter einen Brief abschicken *v.* (3) **2A**
  letter of recommendation
    Empfehlungsschreiben, - *n.* (3) **3A**
lettuce Salat, -e *m.* (1) **4A**
library Bibliothek, -en *f.* (1) **1B**
license plate Nummernschild, -er *n.* (2) **4A**
lie liegen *v.* (2) **1B**
  to lie down sich (hin)legen *v.* (3) **1A**
  to tell a lie lügen *v.*
light hell *adj.* (1) **3A**; leicht *adj.* (1) **4B**; Licht,
  -er *n.* (3) **4B**
lightning Blitz, -e *m.* (2) **3A**
like mögen *v.* **4B**; gern (+*verb*) *v.* (1) **2B**;
  gefallen *v.* (2) **1A**
  I would like... ich hätte gern... (1) **4A**; Ich
    möchte... (1) **4B**
line Schlange, -n *f.* (2) (1) **3B**; Linie, -n *f.*
  to stand in line Schlange stehen *v.* (2) **3B**
lip Lippe, -n *f.* (3) **1A**
lipstick Lippenstift, -e *m.* (3) **1A**
listen (to) hören *v.* (1) **2A**
literature Literatur, -en *f.* (1) **2A**
little klein *adj.* (1) **3A**; wenig *adj.* (3) **2A**
live wohnen *v.* (1) **2A**; leben *v.* (1) **2A**
living room Wohnzimmer, - *n.* (2) **2A**
load laden *v.* (2) **4B**
location Lage, -n *f.* (2) **3B**
long lang *adj.* (1) **3A**
  long-sleeved langärmlig *adj.* (2) **1B**
look schauen *v.* (2) **3A**
  to look at anschauen *v.* (2) **3A**
  to look for suchen *v.* (1) **2A**
  to look forward to sich freuen auf *v.* (3) **1A**
loose weit *adj.* (2) **1B**
lose verlieren *v.* (1) **2B**
  to get lost sich verlaufen *v.* (3) **2B**

love lieben *v.* (1) **2A**; Liebe *f.* (2) **1A**
  to fall in love (with) sich verlieben (in) *v.* (3) **1A**
  to love each other sich lieben *v.* (3) **1A**
loving liebevoll *adj.* (1) **3B**
low niedrig *adj.* (3) **3A**
luggage Gepäck *n.* (2) **3B**
lunch Mittagessen, - *n.* (1) **4B**

M

magazine Zeitschrift, -en *f.* (3) **2A**
mail Post *f.* (3) **2A**
  to mail a letter einen Brief abschicken *v.* (3) **2A**
mail carrier Briefträger, - / Briefträgerin,
  -nen *m.* (3) **2A**
mailbox Briefkasten, ⸚ *m.* (3) **2A**
main course Hauptspeise, -n *f.* (1) **4B**
main road Hauptstraße, -n *f.* (3) **2B**
major: to major in studieren *v.* (1) **2A**
make machen *v.* (1) **2A**
makeup: to put on makeup sich schminken *v.* (3) **1A**
mall Einkaufszentrum (*pl.* Einkaufszentren) *n.* (3) **2B**
man Mann, ⸚er *m.* (1) **1A**
manage leiten *v.* (3) **4B**
manager Geschäftsführer, - / die
  Geschäftsführerin, -nen *m./f.* (3) **3A**
map Karte, -n *f.* (1) **1B**; Landkarte, -n *f.* (2) **3B**
  city map Stadtplan, ⸚e *m.* (2) **3B**
  to read a map eine Karte lesen *v.* (2) **3B**
marble Marmor *m.* (2) **2B**
March März *m.* (1) **2A**
marital status Familienstand, ⸚e *m.* (1) **3A**
market Markt, ⸚e *m.* (1) **4A**
marriage Ehe, -n *f.* (2) **1A**
married verheiratet *adj.* (1) **3A**
marry heiraten *v.* (1) **3A**
match Spiel, -e *n.* (1) **2B**; passen *v.* (2) **1A**
material Material, -ien *n.* (2) **1B**
mathematics Mathematik *f.* (1) **2A**
May Mai *m.* (1) **2A**
may dürfen *v.* (1) **3B**
maybe vielleicht *adv.* (1) **4A**
mayor Bürgermeister, - / Bürgermeisterin,
  -nen *m./f.* (3) **2B**
meal Mahlzeit, -en *f.* (1) **4B**
mean bedeuten *v.* (1) **2A**; meinen *v.*
  (3) **4B**; gemein *adj.* (1) **3B**
meat Fleisch *n.* (1) **4A**
mechanic Mechaniker, - / Mechanikerin,
  -nen *m./f.* (2) **4A**
medicine Medizin *f.* (1) **2A**; Medikament, -e *n.* (3) **1B**
meet (sich) treffen *v.* (1) **2B**; **(for the first time)**
  (sich) kennen lernen *v.* (3) **1A**
  Pleased to meet you. Schön dich/Sie kennen zu
    lernen! (1) **1A**
meeting Besprechung, -en *f.* (3) **3A**
melon Melone, -n *f.* (1) **4A**
menu Speisekarte, -n *f.* (1) **4B**
Merry Christmas! Frohe Weihnachten! (2) **1A**
message Nachricht, -en *f.* (3) **3A**
Mexico Mexiko *n.* (3) **2B**
Mexican mexikanisch *adj.* (3) **2B**; **(person)**
  Mexikaner, - / Mexikanerin, -nen *m./f.* (3) **2B**
microphone Mikrofon, -e *n.* (2) **4B**

microwave Mikrowelle, -n *f.* (2) **2B**
midmorning Vormittag, -e *m.* (1) **2B**
midnight Mitternacht *f.* (1) **2A**
mild leicht *adj.* (3) **1B**
milk Milch *f.* (1) **4B**
minority Minderheit, -en *f.* (3) **4B**
minus minus (1) **1B**
mirror Spiegel, - *m.* (2) **2A**
mist Nebel, - *m.* (2) **3A**
modern modern *adj.* (3) **2A**
modest bescheiden *adj.* (1) **3B**
mom Mama, -s *f.* (1) **3A**
Monday Montag, -e *m.* (1) **2A**
  on Mondays montags *adv.* (1) **2A**
money Geld, -er *n.* (3) **2A**
month Monat, -e *m.* (1) **2A**
moon Mond, -e *m.* (3) **4A**
mop wischen *v.* (2) **2B**
more mehr *adj.* (2) **4A**
morning Morgen, - *m.* (1) **2B**
  in the morning vormittags (1) **2A**
  tomorrow morning morgen früh (1) **2B**
mother Mutter, ⸚ *f.* (1) **1A**
mother-in-law Schwiegermutter, ⸚ *f.* (1) **3A**
mountain Berg, -e *m.* (1) **2B**; (3) **4A**
mouse Maus, ⸚e *f.* (2) **4B**
mouth Mund, ⸚er *m.* (3) **1A**
move umziehen *v.* (2) **2A**; sich bewegen *v.*
movie Film, -e *m.*
movie theater Kino, -s *n.* (3) **2A**
mp3 player MP3-Player, - *m.* (2) **4B**
Mr. Herr (1) **1A**
Mrs. Frau (1) **1A**
Ms. Frau (1) **1A**
much viel *adv.* (1) **4A**
mushroom Pilz, -e *m.* (1) **4A**
musician Musiker, - / Musikerin, -nen *m./f.* (1) **3B**
must müssen *v.* (1) **3B**
my mein *poss. adj.* (1) **3A**
myself mich *pron.*; mir *pron.* (3) **1A**

N

naïve naiv *adj.* (1) **3B**
name Name, -n *m.* (1) **1A**
  to be named heißen *v.* (1) **2A**
  What's your name? Wie heißen Sie? (form.) /
    Wie heißt du? (inf.) *v.* (1) **1A**
napkin Serviette, -n *f.* (1) **4B**
natural disaster Naturkatastrophe, -n *f.* (3) **4A**
nature Natur, -en *f.* (3) **4A**
nauseous übel *adj.* (3) **1B**
near bei *prep.* (1) **4B**; nah *adj.* (3) **2B**
neat ordentlich *adj.* (2) **2B**
neck Hals, ⸚e *m.* (3) **1A**
necklace Halskette, -n *f.* (2) **1B**
need brauchen *v.* (1) **2A**
  to need to müssen *v.* (1) **3B**
neighborhood Viertel, - *n.* (3) **2B**
nephew Neffe, -n *m.* (2) **4B**
nervous nervös *adj.* (1) **3B**
never nie *adv.* **4A**; niemals *adv.* (2) **3 B**
New Year's Eve Silvester *n.* (2) **1A**

newlywed Frischvermählte, -n *m./f.* (2) **1A**
newspaper Zeitung, -en *f.* (2) **3B**
next nächster/nächste/nächstes *adj.* (1) **2B**
 next to neben *prep.* (2) **1B**
nice nett *adj.* (1) **3B**
 It's nice out. Es ist schön draußen. (2) **3A**
 Nice to meet you. Schön dich/Sie kennen zu lernen! (1) **1A**
 The weather is nice. Das Wetter ist gut. (2) **3A**
night Nacht, ⸚e *f.* (1) **2B**
 to spend the night übernachten *f.* (2) **3B**
night table Nachttisch, -e *m.* (2) **2A**
nine neun (1) **2A**
no nein (1) **1A**; kein *adj.* (1) **2B**
no one niemand *pron.* (2) **3B**
nonviolent gewaltfrei *adj.* (3) **4B**
noon Mittag, -e *m.* (1) **2A**
nose Nase, -n *f.* (3) **1A**
not nicht *adv.* (1) **2B**
 Do not enter. Keine Zufahrt. (1) **3B**
 not bad nicht schlecht (1) **1A**
 not much wenig *adj.* (3) **2A**
note Notiz, -en *f.* (1) **1B**
notebook Heft, -e *n.* (1) **1B**
nothing nichts *pron.* (2) **3B**
November November *m.* (1) **2A**
now jetzt *adv.* (1) **4A**
nuclear energy Kernenergie *f.* (3) **4B**
nuclear power plant Kernkraftwerk, -e *n.* (3) **4B**
nurse Krankenpfleger, - / Krankenschwester, -n *m./f.* (3) **1B**

ocean Meer, -e *n.* (3) **4A**
occasion Anlass, ⸚e *m.* (2) **1A**
 special occasions besondere Anlässe *m. pl.* (2) **1A**
October Oktober *m.* (1) **2A**
offer Angebot, -e *n.* (2) **1B**; bieten *v.* (3) **1B**; anbieten *v.* (3) **4B**
office Büro, -s *n.* (3) **3B**
office supplies Büromaterial, -ien *n.* (3) **3A**
often oft *adv.* (1) **4A**
oil Öl, -e *n.* (1) **4A**
old alt *adj.* (1) **3A**
 How old are you? Wie alt bist du? (1) **1B**
 I am... years old. Ich bin… Jahre alt. (1) **1B**
olive oil Olivenöl, -e *n.* (1) **4A**
on an *prep.*; auf *prep.* (2) **1B**
once einmal *adv.* (2) **3B**
one eins (1) **2A**; man *pron.* (2) **3B**
 by oneself allein *adv.* (1) **4A**
one-way street Einbahnstraße, -n *f.* (2) **4A**
onion Zwiebel, -n *f.* (1) **4A**
online: to be online online sein *v.* (2) **4B**
only nur *adv.* (1) **4A**
 only child Einzelkind, -er *n.* (1) **3A**
on-time pünktlich *adj.* (2) **3B**
onto auf *prep.* (2) **1B**
open öffnen *v.* (1) **2A**; aufmachen *v.* (2) **4B**; geöffnet *adj.* (3) **2A**
or oder *conj.* (1) **1B**
orange Orange, -n *f.* (1) **4A**; orange *adj.* (2) **1B**

order bestellen *v.* (1) **4A**
organic biologisch *adj.* (3) **4B**
our unser *poss. adj.* (1) **3A**
out draußen *adv.* (2) **3A**; heraus *adv.* (2) **2A**
 It's nice out. Es ist schön draußen. (2) **3A**
 to go out ausgehen *v.* (1) **4A**
 to bring out rausbringen (2) **2B**
outside draußen *prep.* (2) **3A**
 outside of außerhalb *prep.* (2) **4B**
oven Ofen, ⸚ *m.* (2) **2B**
over über *prep.* (2) **1B**; vorbei *adv.* (2) **3A**
 over there drüben *adv.* (1) **4A**
overpopulation Überbevölkerung *f.* (3) **4B**
owner Besitzer, - / Besitzerin, -nen *m./f.* (1) **3B**

pack packen *v.* (2) **3B**
package Paket, -e *n.* (3) **2A**
pain Schmerz, -en *m.* (3) **1B**
pajamas Schlafanzug, ⸚e *m.* (3) **1A**
pan Pfanne, -n *f.* (2) **2B**
pants Hose, -n *f.* (2) **1B**
paper Papier, -e *n.* (1) **1B**
 sheet of paper Blatt Papier (*pl.* Blätter) Papier *n.* (1) **1B**
paperclip Büroklammer, -n *f.* (3) **3A**
paper-goods store Schreibwarengeschäft, -e *n.* (3) **2A**
paragraph Absatz, ⸚e *m.* (2) **1B**
parents Eltern *pl.* (1) **3A**
park Park, -s *m.* (1) **1A**; parken *v.* (2) **4A**
 No parking. Parkverbot. (1) **3B**
participate mitmachen *v.* (2) **4B**
part-time halbtags *adj.* (3) **3B**
party Party, -s *f.* (2) **1A**
 to go to a party auf eine Party gehen *prep.* (3) **2B**
 to throw a party eine Party geben *v.* (2) **1A**
pass (a test) bestehen *v.* (1) **1B**
passenger Passagier, -e *m.* (2) **3B**
passport control Passkontrolle, -n *f.* (2) **3B**
password Passwort, ⸚er *n.* (2) **4B**
past Vergangenheit, -en *f.* (3) **4A**; nach *prep.* (1) **2A**
pasta Pasta *f.* (1) **4A**
pastries Gebäck *n.* (2) **1A**
pastry shop Konditorei, -en *f.* (1) **4A**
path Weg, -e *m.* (3) **4A**
patient geduldig *adj.* (1) **3B**; Patient, -en / Patientin, -nen *m./f.* (3) **1B**
pay (for) bezahlen *v.* (1) **4A**
 to pay by (credit) card mit der Karte bezahlen *v.* (3) **2A**
 to pay in cash bar bezahlen *v.* (3) **2A**
peach Pfirsich, -e *m.* (1) **4A**
pear Birne, -n *f.* (1) **4A**
pedestrian Fußgänger, - / Fußgängerin, -nen *m./f.* (3) **2B**
pen Kuli, -s *m.* (1) **1B**
pencil Bleistift, -e *m.* (1) **1B**
people Leute *pl.* (1) **3B**; Menschen *pl.*
pepper Paprika, - *f.* (1) **4A**; Pfeffer, - *m.* (1) **4B**
percent Prozent, -e *n.* (1) **1B**
period Punkt, -e *m.* (1) **1B**
person Person, -en *f.* (1) **1A**; Mensch, -en *m.*

personal persönlich *adj.* (1) **3B**
pet Haustier, -e *n.* (1) **3A**
pharmacy Apotheke, -n *f.* (3) **1B**
phone booth Telefonzelle, -n *f.* (3) **2B**
photo Foto, -s *n.* (1) **1B**
physics Physik *f.* (1) **2A**
picnic Picknick, -s *n.* (3) **4A**
 to have a picnic ein Picknick machen *v.* (3) **4A**
picture Foto, -s *n.* (1) **1B**; Bild, -er *n.* (2) **2A**
pie Kuchen, - *m.* (1) **4A**
pigsty Saustall, ⸚e *n.* (2) **2B**
 It's a pigsty! Es ist ein Saustall! (2) **2B**
pill Tablette, -n *f.* (3) **1B**
pillow Kissen, - *n.* (2) **1B**
pineapple Ananas, - *f.* (1) **4A**
pink rosa *adj.* (2) **1B**
place Ort, -e *m.* (1) **1B**; Lage, -n *f.* (2) **3B**; setzen *v.* (2) **2B**
 in your place an deiner/Ihrer Stelle *f.* (3) **2A**
plant Pflanze, -n *f.* (2) **2A**
plastic Kunststoff, -e *m.* (2) **2B**
plate Teller, - *m.* (1) **4B**
platform Bahnsteig, -e (2) **4A**
play spielen *v.* (1) **2A**
player Spieler, - / Spielerin, -nen *m./f.* (1) **2B**
pleasant angenehm *adj.* (1) **3B**
please bitte **1A**; gefallen *v.* (2) **1A**
 Pleased to meet you. Freut mich! (1) **1A**
plumber Klempner, - / Klempnerin, -nen *m./f.* (3) **3B**
plus plus (1) **1B**
police officer Polizist, -en / Polizistin, -nen *m./f.* (2) **4A**
police station Polizeiwache, -n *f.* (3) **2A**
politician Politiker, - / Politikerin, -nen *m./f.* (3) **3B**
pollute verschmutzen *v.* (3) **4B**
pollution Verschmutzung *f.* (3) **4B**
poor arm *adj.* (1) **3B**
pork Schweinefleisch *n.* (1) **4A**
position Stelle, -n *f.* (3) **3A**
post office Post, - *f.* (3) **2A**
 to go to the post office zur Post gehen *v.* (3) **2A**
postcard Postkarte, -n *f.* (3) **2A**
poster Poster, - *n.* (2) **2A**
pot Topf, ⸚e *m.* (2) **2B**
potato Kartoffel, -n *f.* (1) **4A**
pound Pfund, -e *n.* (1) **4A**
 a pound of potatoes ein Pfund Kartoffeln (1) **4A**
practice (sports) trainieren *v.* (1) **2B**; Übung, -en *f.*
pregnant schwanger *adj.* (3) **1B**
preparation Vorbereitung, -en *f.*
prepare vorbereiten *v.* (1) **4A**; zubereiten *v.* (2) **3A**
 to prepare oneself (for) sich vorbereiten (auf) *v.* (3) **1A**
prescription Rezept, -e *n.* (3) **1B**
presentation Referat, -e *n.* (1) **2A**
preserve erhalten *v.* (3) **4B**
president Präsident, - / Präsidentin, -nen *m./f.* (2) **4B**
 federal president Bundespräsident, - / Bundespräsidentin, -nen *m./f.* (2) **4B**
pretty hübsch *adj.* (1) **3A**
 pretty well ziemlich gut *adv.* (1) **1A**
principal Schulleiter, - *m.* / Schulleiterin, -nen *f.* (1) **1B**

print drucken *v.* (2) **4B**
printer Drucker, - *m.* (2) **4B**
probably wohl ; wahrscheinlich *adv.*(3) **2A**; sicher *adv.* (3) **2A**
problem Problem, -e *n.* (1) **1A**
profession Beruf, -e *m.* (1) **3B**
professional training Berufsausbildung, -en *f.* (3) **3A**
professor Professor, -en / Professorin, -nen *m./f.* (1) **1B**
program Programm, -e *m.* (2) **4B**
promotion Beförderung, -en *f.* (3) **3B**
pronunciation Aussprache *f.*
propose vorschlagen *v.* (3) **4B**
protect schützen *v.* (3) **4B**
proud stolz *adj.* (1) **3B**
psychologist Psychologe, -n / Psychologin, -nen *m./f.* (3) **3B**
psychology Psychologie *f.* (1) **2A**
public öffentlich *adj.* (2) **4A**
   public transportation öffentliche Verkehrsmittel *n. pl.* (2) **4A**
pull ziehen *v.* (1) **3B**
purple lila *adj.* (2) **1B**
purse Handtasche, -n *f.* (2) **1B**
push drücken *v.* (1) **3B**
put stellen *v.* (2) **1B**; legen *v.* (3) **1A**; setzen *v.* (3) **1A**
   to put away wegräumen *v.* (2) **2B**
   to put on anziehen *v.* (2) **1B**

Q

quarter Viertel, - *n.* (1) **2A**
   quarter past/to Viertel nach/vor (1) **2A**
question Frage, -n *f.* (1) **1B**
quicksand Treibsand *m.* (3) **4A**
quite ziemlich *adv.* (1) **4A**

R

rabbit Kaninchen, - *n.* (3) **4A**
rain Regen *m.* (2) **3A**; regnen *v.* (1) **2A**
raincoat Regenmantel, ¨ *m.* (2) **3A**
raise Gehaltserhöhung, -en *f.* (3) **3B**
rarely selten *adv.* (1) **4A**
rather lieber *adj.* (2) **4A**
rating Bewertung, -en *f.* (2) **3B**
razor Rasierer, - *m.* (3) **4A**
read lesen *v.* (1) **2B**
ready fertig *adj.* (3) **3B**
real estate agent Immobilienmakler, - / Immobilienmaklerin, -nen *m./f.* (3) **3B**
realistic realistisch *adj.* (3) **2A**
really wirklich *adv.* (1) **4A**
receive bekommen *v.* (2) **1A**
receiver Hörer, - *m.* (3) **3A**
recess Pause, -n *f.* (1) **1B**
recipe Rezept, -e *n.* (1) **4A**
recognize erkennen *v.* (2) **3A**
recommend empfehlen *v.* (1) **2B**
record aufnehmen *v.* (2) **4B**
recycle recyceln *v.* (3) **4B**
red rot *adj.* (1) **3A**
   red-haired rothaarig *adj.* (1) **3A**
reference Referenz, -en *f.* (3) **3A**

refrigerator Kühlschrank, ¨e *m.* (2) **2B**
related verwandt *adj.* (3) **2A**
relative Verwandte, -n *m.* (1) **3A**
relax sich entspannen *v.* (3) **1A**
reliable zuverlässig *adj.* (1) **3B**
remember sich erinnern (an) *v.* (3) **1A**
remote control Fernbedienung, -en *f.* (2) **4B**
remove entfernen *v.* (2) **2B**
renewable energy erneuerbare Energie, -en *f.* (3) **4B**
rent Miete, -n *f.* (2) **2A**; mieten *v.* (2) **2A**
repair reparieren *v.* (2) **4A**
repeat wiederholen *v.* (1) **2A**
repetition Wiederholung, -en *f.*
report berichten *v.* (3) **4B**
report card Zeugnis, -se *n.* (1) **1B**
reservation: to make a (hotel) reservation buchen *v.* (2) **3B**
resign kündigen *v.* (3) **3B**
rest sich ausruhen *v.* (3) **1A**
restaurant Restaurant, -s *n.* (1) **4B**
result Ergebnis, -se *n.* (1) **1B**
résumé Lebenslauf, ¨e *m.* (3) **3A**
retire in Rente gehen *v.* (2) **1A**
retiree Rentner, - / Rentnerin, -nen *m./f.* (3) **3B**
review Besprechung, -en *f.* (2) **4B**
rice Reis *m.* (1) **4A**
rich reich *adj.* (1) **3B**
ride fahren *v.* (1) **2B**; reiten *v.* (1) **2B**
   to give (someone) a ride (jemanden) mitnehmen *v.* (3) **2B**
   to ride a bicycle Fahrrad fahren *v.* (1) **2B**
ring klingeln *v.* (2) **4B**
rinse spülen *v.* (2) **2B**
rise (sun) aufgehen *v.* (3) **4A**
river Fluss, ¨e *m.* (1) **3B**
rock Stein, -e *m.* (3) **4A**
roll Brötchen, - *n.* (1) **4A**
room Zimmer, - *n.* (2) **1A**
room service Zimmerservice *m.* (2) **3B**
roommate Mitbewohner, - / Mitbewohnerin, -nen *m./f.* (1) **2A**
rug Teppich, -e *m.* (2) **2A**
run laufen *v.* (1) **2B**; rennen *v.* (2) **1A**
Russia Russland *n.* (3) **2B**
Russian (person) Russe, -n / Russin, -nen *m./f.* (3) **2B**; **(language)** Russisch *n.* (3) **2B**

S

sad traurig *adj.* (1) **3B**
salad Salat, -e *m.* (1) **4A**
salary Gehalt, ¨er *n.* (3) **3A**
   high/low salary hohes/niedriges Gehalt, ¨er *n.* (3) **3A**
sale Verkauf, ¨e *m.*
   on sale im Angebot (2) **1B**
salesperson Verkäufer, - / Verkäuferin, -nen *m./f.* (2) **1B**
salt Salz, -e *n.* (1) **4B**
salty salzig *adj.* (1) **4B**
same gleich *adj.*
Saturday Samstag, -e *m.* (1) **2A**
   on Saturdays samstags *adv.* (1) **2A**
sausage Würstchen, - *n.* (1) **4A**

save speichern *v.* (2) **4B**; retten *v.* (3) **4B**
   to save the planet den Planeten retten *v.* (3) **4B**
say sagen *v.* (1) **2A**
scarf Schal, -s *m.* (2) **1B**
schedule Stundenplan, ¨e *m.* (1) **2A**; Fahrplan, ¨e *m.* (2) **4A**
scholarship Stipendium (*pl.* Stipendien) *n.* (1) **2A**
school Schule, -n *f.* (1) **1B**
science Naturwissenschaft, -en *f.* (1) **2A**
scientist Wissenschaftler, - / Wissenschaftlerin, -nen *m./f.* (3) **3B**
score Ergebnis, -se *n.* (1) **1B**
screen Bildschirm, -e *m.* (2) **4B**
screen name Benutzername, -n *m.* (2) **4B**
sea Meer, -e *n.* (3) **4A**
seafood Meeresfrüchte *f. pl.* (1) **4A**
season Jahreszeit, -en *f.* (3) **3A**
seatbelt Sicherheitsgurt, -e *m.* (3) **4A**
second zweite *adj.* (1) **2A**
   second-hand clothing Altkleider *pl.* (3) **4B**
see sehen *v.* (1) **2B**
   See you later. Bis später! (1) **1A**
   See you soon. Bis gleich! / Bis bald. (1) **1A**
   See you tomorrow. Bis morgen! (1) **1A**
selfish egoistisch *adj.* (1) **3B**
sell verkaufen *v.* (1) **4A**
seminar Seminar, -e *n.* (1) **2A**
seminar room Seminarraum (*pl.* Seminarräume) *m.* (1) **2A**
send schicken *v.* (2) **4B**; abschicken *v.* (3) **3B**
separate (sich) trennen *v.* (3) **1A**
separated getrennt *adj.* (1) **3A**
September September *m.* (1) **2A**
serious ernst *adj.* (3) **3B**; schwer *adj.* (3) **1B**
set setzen *v.* (3) **1A**; **(sun)** untergehen *v.* (3) **4A**
   to set the table den Tisch decken *v.* (3) **4B**
seven sieben (1) **2A**
shampoo Shampoo, -s *n.* (3) **1A**
shape Form, -en *f.* (3) **1B**
   in good shape fit *adj.* (1) **2B**
   to be in/out of shape in guter/schlechter Form sein *v.* (3) **1B**
shave sich rasieren *v.* (3) **1A**
shaving cream Rasierschaum, ¨e *m.* (3) **1A**
she sie *pron.* (1) **1A**
sheep Schaf, -e *n.* (3) **4A**
sheet Laken, - *n.* (2) **2B**
   sheet of paper Blatt Papier (*pl.* Blätter) Papier *n.* (1) **1B**
ship Schiff, -e *n.* (2) **4A**
shirt Hemd, -en *n.* (2) **1B**
shoe Schuh, -e *m.* (2) **1B**
shop einkaufen *v.* (1) **4A**; Geschäft, -e *n.* (1) **4A**
   to go shopping einkaufen gehen *v.* (1) **4A**
shopping Einkaufen *n.* (2) **1B**
shopping center Einkaufszentrum, -(*pl.* Einkaufszentren) *n.* (3) **2B**
short kurz *adj.* (1) **3A**; **(stature)** klein *adj.* (1) **3A**
   short film Kurzfilm, -e *m.* (3) **2A**
   short-sleeved kurzärmlig *adj.* (2) **1B**
shorts kurze Hose, -n *f.* (2) **1B**
shot Spritze, -n *f.* (3) **1B**
   to give a shot eine Spritze geben *v.* (3) **1B**
shoulder Schulter, -n *f.* (3) **1A**

show zeigen *v.* (1) **4B**

shower: to take a shower (sich) duschen *v.* (3) **1A**

shrimp Garnele, -n *f.* (1) **4A**

shy schüchtern *adj.* (1) **3B**

sibling Geschwister, - *n.* (1) **3A**

sick krank *adj.* (3) **1B**

  to get sick krank werden *v.* (3) **1B**

side dish Beilage, -n *f.* (1) **4B**

sidewalk Bürgersteig, -e *m.* (3) **2B**

sign unterschreiben *v.* (3) **2A**; Schild, -er *n.*

silk Seide, -n *f.* (2) **1B**

silverware Besteck *n.* (1) **4B**

since seit (1) **4B**

sincere aufrichtig *adj.* (1) **3B**

  Yours sincerely Gruß, ⸚e (1) **3B**

sing singen *v.* (1) **2B**

single ledig *adj.* (1) **3A**

sink Spüle, -n *f.* (2) **2B**

sister Schwester, -n *f.* (1) **1A**

sister-in-law Schwägerin, -nen *f.* (1) **3A**

sit sitzen *v.* (2) **1B**

  to sit down sich (hin)setzen *v.* (3) **1A**

six sechs (1) **2A**

size Kleidergröße, -n *f.* (2) **1B**

ski Ski fahren *v.* (1) **2B**

skirt Rock, ⸚e *m.* (2) **1B**

sky Himmel *m.* (3) **4A**

sleep schlafen *v.* (1) **2B**

  to go to sleep einschlafen *v.* (1) **4A**

slim schlank *adj.* (1) **3A**

slipper Hausschuh, -e *m.* (3) **1A**

slow langsam *adj.* (1) **3B**

  Please speak more slowly. Sprechen Sie bitte langsamer! (1) **3B**

  Slow down. Langsam fahren. (1) **3B**

small klein *adj.* (1) **3A**

smartphone Smartphone, -s *n.* (2) **4B**

smile lächeln *v.* (2) **1A**

smoke rauchen *v.*

  No smoking. Rauchen verboten. (1) **3B**

snack Snack, -s *m.* (1) **4B**

snake Schlange, -n *f.* (3) **4A**

sneakers Turnschuhe *m. pl.* (2) **1B**

sneeze niesen *v.* (3) **1B**

snow Schnee *m.* (2) **3A**; schneien *v.* (2) **3A**

so so *adv.* (1) **4A**

  so far, so good so weit, so gut (1) **1A**

  so that damit *conj.* (3) **2A**

soap Seife, -n *f.* (3) **1A**

soccer Fußball *m.* (1) **2B**

sock Socke, -n *f.* (2) **1B**

sofa Sofa, -s *n.* (2) **2A**

soil verschmutzen *v.* (2) **2B**

solar energy Sonnenenergie *f.* (3) **4B**

solid colored einfarbig *adj.* (2) **1B**

solution Lösung, -en *f.* (3) **4B**

some mancher/manche/manches *pron.* (2) **4B**

someone jemand *pron.* (2) **3B**

something etwas *pron.* (2) **3B**

  something else etwas anderes *n.* (3) **2A**

sometimes manchmal *adv.* (2) **3B**

somewhere else woanders *adv.* (1) **4A**

son Sohn, ⸚e *m.* (1) **3A**

soon bald (1) **1A**

  See you soon. Bis bald.; Bis gleich. (1) **1A**

sorry: I'm sorry. Es tut mir leid. (1) **1A**

so-so (I'm so-so) Es geht. (1) **1A**

soup Suppe, -n *f.* (1) **4B**

soup spoon Esslöffel, - *m.* (1) **4B**

Spain Spanien *n.* (3) **2B**

Spanish (person) Spanier, - / Spanierin, -nen *m./f.* (3) **2B**; **(language)** Spanisch *n.* (3) **2B**

sparkling water Mineralwasser *n.* (1) **4B**

speak sprechen *v.* (1) **2B**

  to speak about sprechen über; reden über *v.* (2) **3A**

special besonderes *adj.* (3) **2A**

  nothing special nichts Besonderes *adj.* (3) **2A**

species Art, -en *f.* (3) **4B**

spelling Rechtschreibung *f.*

spend verbringen *v.* (1) **4A**

spicy scharf *adj.* (1) **4B**

split up sich trennen *v.* (3) **1A**

spoon Löffel, - *m.* (1) **4B**

sport Sport *m.* (1) **2B**; Sportart, -en *f.* (1) **2B**

sprain (one's wrist/ankle) sich (das Handgelenk / den Fuß) verstauchen *v.* (3) **1B**

spring Frühling, -e *m.* (1) **2B**

squirrel Eichhörnchen, - *n.* (3) **4A**

stadium Stadion (*pl.* Stadien) *n.* (1) **2B**

stairs Treppe, -n *f.* (2) **2A**

  to go up/down stairs die Treppe hochgehen/heruntergehen *v.* (3) **2B**

stamp Briefmarke, -n *f.* (3) **2A**

stand stehen *v.* (2) **1B**

  to stand in line Schlange stehen *v.* (2) **3B**

stapler Hefter, - *m.* (3) **3A**

star Stern, -e *m.* (3) **4A**

start starten *v.* (2) **4B**; anfangen *v.* (1) **4A**; beginnen *v.* (2) **2A**

station wagon Kombi, -s *m.* (2) **4B**

statue Statue, -n *f.* (3) **2B**

stay bleiben *v.* (2) **1B**

steal stehlen *v.* (1) **2B**

steering wheel Lenkrad, ⸚er *n.* (2) **4A**

stepbrother Halbbruder, ⸚ *m.* (1) **3A**

stepdaughter Stieftochter, ⸚ *f.* (1) **3A**

stepfather Stiefvater, -s⸚ *m.* (1) **3A**

stepmother Stiefmutter, ⸚ *f.* (1) **3A**

stepsister Halbschwester, -n *f.* (1) **3A**

stepson Stiefsohn, ⸚ *m.* (1) **3A**

stereo system Stereoanlage, -n *f.* (2) **4B**

still noch *adv.* (1) **4A**; still *adj.* (1) **4B**

  still water stilles Wasser *n.* (1) **4B**

stomachache Bauchschmerzen *m. pl.* (3) **1B**

stop sign Stoppschild, -er *n.* (2) **4A**

store Geschäft, -e *n.* (1) **4A**

storm Sturm, ⸚e *m.* (2) **3A**

stove Herd, -e *m.* (2) **2B**

straight glatt *adj.* (1) **3A**

  straight hair glatte Haare *n. pl.* (1) **3A**

  straight ahead geradeaus *adv.* (2) **4A**

strawberry Erdbeere, -n *f.* (1) **4A**

stream Strom, ⸚e *m.* (3) **4A**

street Straße, -n *f.* (2) **4A**

  to cross the street die Straße überqueren *v.* (3) **2B**

striped gestreift *adj.* (2) **1B**

strong stark *adj.* (1) **3B**

student Schüler, - / Schülerin, -nen *m./f.* (1) **1B**; **(college/university)** Student, -en / Studentin, -nen *m./f.* (1) **1A**

studies Studium (*pl.* Studien) *n.* (1) **2A**

study lernen *v.* (1) **2A**

stuffy nose verstopfte Nase *f.* (3) **1B**

style Stil, -e *m.* (2) **1B**

subject Fach, ⸚er *n.* (1) **2A**

subway U-Bahn, -en *f.* (2) **4A**

success Erfolg, -e *m.* (3) **3B**

such solcher/solche/solches *pron.* (2) **4B**

suit Anzug, ⸚e *m.* (2) **1B**

suitcase Koffer, - *m.* (2) **3B**

summer Sommer, - *m.* (1) **2B**

sun Sonne, -n *f.* (3) **4A**

sunburn Sonnenbrand, ⸚e *m.* (3) **1B**

Sunday Sonntag, -e *m.* (1) **2A**

  on Sundays sonntags *adv.* (1) **2A**

sunglasses Sonnenbrille, -n *f.* (2) **1B**

sunny sonnig *adj.* (2) **3A**

sunrise Sonnenaufgang, ⸚e *m.* (3) **4A**

sunset Sonnenuntergang, ⸚e *m.* (3) **4A**

supermarket Supermarkt, ⸚e *m.* (1) **4A**

supposed: to be supposed to sollen *v.* (1) **3B**

surf surfen *v.* (2) **4B**

  to surf the Web im Internet surfen *v.* (2) **4B**

surprise überraschen *v.* (2) **1A**; Überraschung, -en *f.* (2) **1A**

sweater Pullover, - *m.* (2) **1B**

sweatshirt Sweatshirt, -s *n.* (2) **1B**

sweep fegen *v.* (2) **2B**

sweet süß *adj.* (1) **3B**

swim schwimmen *v.* (1) **2B**

swimming pool Schwimmbad, ⸚er *n.* (1) **2B**

Switzerland die Schweiz *f.* (2) **3A**

Swiss schweizerisch, Schweizer *adj.* (3) **2B**; **(person)** Schweizer, - / Schweizerin, -nen *m./f.* (3) **2B**

symptom Symptom, -e *n.* (3) **1B**

T

table Tisch, -e *m.* (1) **1B**

  to set the table den Tisch decken (2) **2B**

tablecloth Tischdecke, -n *f.* (1) **4B**

tablet Tablet, -s *n.* (2) **4B**

take nehmen *v.* (1) **2B**

  to take (a class) belegen *v.* (1) **2A**

  to take out the trash den Müll rausbringen (2) **2B**

  to take a shower (sich) duschen *v.* (3) **1A**

  to take off abfliegen *v.* (2) **3B**

talk reden *v.* (2) **1A**

  to talk about erzählen von; sprechen/reden über *v.* (2) **3A**

tall groß *adj.* (1) **3A**

tank top Trägerhemd, -en *n.* (2) **1B**

taste schmecken *v.* (1) **4B**; Geschmack, ⸚e *m.* (1) **4B**

taxi Taxi, -s *n.* (2) **4A**

taxi driver Taxifahrer, - / Taxifahrerin, -nen *m./f.* (3) **3B**

tea Tee, -s *m.* (1) **4B**

teacher Lehrer, - / Lehrerin, -nen *m./f.* (1) **1B**

team Mannschaft, -en *f.* (1) **2B**

teaspoon Teelöffel, - m. (1) **4B**
technology Technik f. (2) **4B**
  to use technology Technik bedienen v. (2) **4B**
telephone Telefon, -e n. (2) **4B**
  on the telephone am Telefon (3) **3A**
telephone number Telefonnummer, -n f. (3) **3A**
television Fernsehen n.
  television (set) Fernseher -m. (2) **4B**
tell erzählen v. (2) **3A**
  to tell a story about erzählen von v. (2) **3A**
temperature Temperatur, -en f.
  What's the temperature? Wie warm/kalt ist
    es? (2) **3A**
tennis Tennis n. (1) **2B**
tent Zelt, -e n. (2) **3B**
ten zehn (1) **2A**
terrific großartig adj. (1) **3A**
test Prüfung, -en f. (1) **1B**
text message SMS, - f. (2) **4B**
textbook Lehrbuch, ̈er n.; Schulbuch, ̈er n. (1) **1B**
thank danken v. (1) **2A**
  Thank you. Danke! (1) **1A**
  Thank you very much. Vielen Dank! (1) **1A**
that das **1A**; dass conj. (3) **2A**
the das/der/die (1) **1A**
their ihr poss. adj. (1) **3A**
then dann adv. (2) **3B**
there da (1) **1A**
  Is/Are there...? Ist/Sind hier...? (1) **1B**;
    Gibt es...? (1) **2B**
  There is/are... Da ist/sind... (1) **1A**; Es
    gibt... (1) **2B**
  there and back hin und zurück (2) **3B**
  over there drüben adv. (1) **4A**
therefore also; deshalb conj. (3) **1B**
thermometer Thermometer, - n. (3) **1B**
these diese pron. (2) **4B**
  These are... Das sind... (1) **1A**
they sie pron. (1) **1A**
thick dick adj. (1) **3A**
thin dünn adj. (1) **3A**
thing Sache, -n f. (1) **1B**; Ding, -e n.
think denken v. (2) **1A**
  to think about denken an v. (2) **3A**
  to think over überlegen v. (1) **4A**
third dritter/dritte/drittes adj. (1) **2A**
this das **1A**; dieser/diese/dieses pron. (2) **4B**
  This is... Das ist... (1) **1A**
three drei (1) **2A**
through durch prep. (1) **3B**
throw werfen v. (1) **2B**
  to throw away wegwerfen v. (3) **4B**
thunder Donner, - m. (2) **3A**
thunderstorm Gewitter, - n. (2) **3A**
Thursday Donnerstag, -e m. (1) **2A**
  on Thursdays donnerstags adv. (1) **2A**
ticket Flugticket, -s n. (2) **3B**; Fahrkarte, -n f. (2) **4A**
ticket collector Schaffner, - / Schaffnerin,
  -nen m./f. (2) **4A**
ticket office Fahrkartenschalter, - m. (2) **4A**
tidy ordentlich adj. (2) **2B**
tie Krawatte, -n f. (2) **1B**
tight eng adj. (2) **1B**

time Zeit, -en f. (1) **2A**; Mal, -e n. (2) **3B**
  for the first/last time zum ersten/letzten
    Mal (2) **3B**
  the first/last time das erste/letzte Mal (2) **3B**
  this time diesmal adv. (2) **3B**
  What time is it? Wie spät ist es?; Wie viel Uhr
    ist es? (1) **2A**
times mal (1) **1B**
tip Trinkgeld, -er n. (1) **4B**
tired müde adj. (1) **3B**
tissue Taschentuch, ̈er n. (3) **1B**
to vor prep. (1) **2A**; nach; zu prep. (1) **4B**; auf,
  an prep. (2) **1B**
  (in order) to um...zu (2) **3B**
  to the right/left nach rechts/links (2) **2A**
toast anstoßen v. (2) **1A**
toaster Toaster, - m. (2) **2B**
today heute adv. (1) **2B**
  Today is... Heute ist der... (1) **2A**
  What day is it today? Welcher Tag ist heute? (2) **3A**
toe Zeh, -en m. (3) **1A**
together zusammen adv. (1) **3A**
toilet Toilette, -n f. (2) **2A**
tomato Tomate, -n f. (1) **4A**
tomorrow morgen adv. (1) **2B**
  the day after tomorrow übermorgen adv. (1) **2B**
  tomorrow morning morgen früh (1) **2B**
too zu adv. (1) **4A**; auch adv. (1) **1A**
tool kit Werkzeug, -e n.
tooth Zahn, ̈e m. (3) **1A**
toothache Zahnschmerzen m. pl. (3) **1B**
toothbrush Zahnbürste, -n f. (3) **1A**
toothpaste Zahnpasta (pl. Zahnpasten) f. (3) **1A**
tornado Tornado, -s m. (3) **4A**
toward in Richtung f. (2) **3B**
towel Handtuch, ̈er n. (3) **1A**
town Stadt, ̈e f. (3) **2B**
town hall Rathaus, ̈er n. (3) **2A**
toxic waste Giftmüll m. (3) **4B**
track Bahnsteig, -e m. (2) **4A**
track and field Leichtathletik f. (1) **2B**
traffic Verkehr m. (2) **4A**
traffic light Ampel, -n f. (3) **2B**
train Zug, ̈e m. (2) **4A**
transportation Verkehrsmittel, - n. (2) **4A**
  public transportation öffentliche
    Verkehrsmittel n. pl. (2) **4A**
trash Müll m. (2) **4A**
  to take out the trash den Müll rausbringen (2) **2B**
travel reisen v. (1) **2A**
travel agency Reisebüro, -s n. (3) **3B**
traveler Reisende, -n m./f. (2) **3B**
tree Baum, ̈e m. (3) **4A**
trendy angesagt adj. (2) **1B**
trip Reise, -n f. (2) **3B**
truck LKW, -s m. (2) **4A**
truck driver LKW-Fahrer, - / LKW-Fahrerin,
  -nen m./f. (3) **3B**
trunk Kofferraum, ̈e m. (2) **4A**
try probieren v. (1) **3B**; versuchen v. (2) **3B**
  Give it a try! Probieren Sie mal!
T-shirt T-Shirt, -s n. (2) **1B**
Tuesday Dienstag, -e m. (1) **2A**
  on Tuesdays dienstags adv. (1) **2A**

tuition fee Studiengebühr, -en f. (1) **2A**
tuna Thunfisch, -e m. (1) **4A**
Turkey die Türkei f. (3) **2B**
Turkish (person) Türke, -n / Türkin, -nen m./f.
  (3) **2B**; **Turkish (language)** Türkisch n. (3) **2B**
turn abbiegen v. (3) **2B**
  to turn right/left rechts/links abbiegen v. (2) **4A**
  to turn off ausmachen v. (2) **4B**; einschalten v.
    (3) **4B**
  to turn on anmachen v. (2) **4B**; auschalten v. (3) **4B**
turning point Wende, -n f. (3) **4B**
twelve zwölf (1) **2A**
twenty zwanzig (1) **2A**
twin Zwilling, -e m. (1) **3A**
two zwei (1) **2A**

U

ugly hässlich adj. (1) **3A**
umbrella Regenschirm, -e m. (2) **3A**
under unter prep. (2) **1B**
understand verstehen v. (1) **2A**
underwear Unterwäsche f. (2) **1B**
undressed: to get undressed sich ausziehen v. (3) **1A**
unemployed arbeitslos adj. (3) **2A**
unfortunate arm adj. (1) **3B**
unfortunately leider adv. (1) **4A**
unfurnished unmöbliert adj. (2) **2A**
university Universität, -en f. (1) **1B**
unpleasant unangenehm adj. (1) **3B**
until bis prep. (1) **3B**; bis zu prep. (3) **2B**
up herauf adv. (2) **2A**
  to get up aufstehen v. (1) **4A**
  to go up hochgehen v. (3) **2B**
USA die USA pl.; die Vereinigten Staaten pl. (3) **2B**
use benutzen v. (2) **4A**; bedienen v. (2) **4B**
  to get used to sich gewöhnen an v. (3) **1A**
useful nützlich adj. (1) **2A**
useless nutzlos adj. (1) **2A**

V

vacancy Zimmer frei f. (2) **2A**
vacation Ferien pl.; Urlaub, -e m. (2) **3B**
  to go on vacation Urlaub machen v. (2) **3B**
vacuum staubsaugen v. (2) **2B**
vacuum cleaner Staubsauger, - m. (2) **2B**
validate entwerten v. (2) **4A**
  to validate a ticket eine Fahrkarte
    entwerten v. (2) **4A**
valley Tal, ̈er n. (3) **4A**
vase Vase, -n f. (2) **2A**
vegetables Gemüse n. (1) **4A**
verb Verb, -en n. (3) **1A**
very sehr adv. (1) **3A**
  very well sehr gut (1) **1A**
veterinarian Tierarzt, ̈e / Tierärztin, -nen m./f.
  (3) **3B**
visa Visum (pl. Visa) n. (2) **3B**
visit besuchen v. (1) **4A**
vocabulary Wortschatz, ̈e m.
volcano Vulkan, -e m. (3) **4A**
volleyball Volleyball m. (1) **2B**

W

wait warten *v.* (1) **2A**
  to wait for warten auf *v.* (2) **3A**
waiter / waitress Kellner, - / Kellnerin,
  -nen *m./f.* (1) **3B**
  Waiter! Herr Ober! (1) **4B**
wake up aufwachen *v.* (3) **1A**
walk Spaziergang, ⸚e *m.*
  to go for a walk spazieren gehen *v.* (1) **2B**
wall Wand, ⸚e *f.* (2) **1B**
want wollen *v.* (1) **3B**
warm warm *adj.* (3) **2A**
wash waschen *v.* (1) **2B**
  to wash (oneself) sich waschen *v.* (3) **1A**
washing machine Waschmaschine, -n *f.* (2) **2B**
waste Müll *m.* (3) **4B**; Abfall, ⸚e *m.* (3) **4B**
wastebasket Papierkorb, ⸚e *m.* (1) **1B**
watch zuschauen *v.* (1) **4A**; anschauen *v.* (2) **3A**
  to watch television fernsehen *v.* (2) **4B**
water Wasser *n.*
  sparkling water Mineralwasser *n.* (1) **4B**
  still water stilles Wasser *n.* (1) **4B**
water pitcher Wasserkrug, ⸚e *m.* (1) **4B**
waterfall Wasserfall, ⸚e *m.* (3) **4A**
we wir *pron.* (1) **1A**
weak schwach *adj.* (1) **3B**
wear tragen *v.* (1) **2B**
weather Wetter *n.* (2) **3A**
  What's the weather like? Wie ist das Wetter? (2) **3A**
weather report Wetterbericht, -e *m.* (2) **3A**
Web Internet *n.* (2) **4B**
  to surf the Web im Internet surfen *v.* (2) **4B**
Web site Website, -s *f.* (2) **4B**
wedding Hochzeit, -en *f.* (2) **1A**
Wednesday Mittwoch, -e *m.* (1) **2A**
  on Wednesdays mittwochs *adv.* (1) **2A**
week Woche, -n *f.* (1) **2A**
weekend Wochenende, -n *n.* (1) **2A**
weigh wiegen *v.* (2) **4B**
welcome (herzlich) willkommen (1) **1A**
  You're welcome. Gern geschehen! (1) **1A**
well gut *adv.*
  I am (very) well. Mir geht's (sehr) gut. (1) **1A**
  I am not (so) well. Mir geht's nicht (so) gut. (1) **1A**
  Get well! Gute Besserung! (2) **1A**
well-dressed gut gekleidet *adj.* (2) **1B**
well-known bekannt *adj.* (3) **2A**
wet nass *adj.* (3) **4A**
what was *interr.* (1) **2A**
  What is that? Was ist das? (1) **1B**
  What's up? Was geht ab? (1) **1A**
when wann *interr.* (1) **2A**
whenever wenn *conj.* (3) **2A**
where wo *interr.* (1) **2A**
  where from woher *interr.* (1) **2A**
  where to wohin *interr.* (1) **2A**
whether ob *conj.* (3) **2A**
which welcher/welche/welches *interr.* (1) **2A**
white weiß *adj.* (2) **1B**
who wer *interr.* (1) **2A**
  Who is it? Wer ist das? (1) **1B**
whom wen *acc. interr.* (1) **2A**; wem *dat. interr.* (1) **4B**

whose wessen *interr.* (2) **4B**
why warum *interr.* (1) **2A**
widow Witwe, -n *f.* (1) **3A**
widower Witwer, - *m.* (1) **3A**
wife Ehefrau, -en *f.* (1) **3A**
win gewinnen *v.* (1) **2B**
wind energy Windenergie *f.* (3) **4B**
window Fenster, - *n.* (1) **1A**
windshield Windschutzscheibe, -n *f.* (2) **4A**
windshield wiper Scheibenwischer, - *m.* (2) **4A**
windy windig *adj.* (2) **3A**
wine Wein, -e *m.* (1) **4B**
winter Winter, - *m.* (1) **2B**
wipe wischen *v.* (2) **2B**
wise weise *adj.* (1) **3B**
wish wünschen *v.* (3) **1A**
  to wish (for something) sich (etwas)
    wünschen *v.* (3) **1A**
with mit (1) **4B**
withdraw (money) (Geld) abheben *v.* (3) **2A**
within innerhalb *prep.* (2) **4B**
without ohne *prep.* (1) **3B**
woman Frau, -en *f.* (1) **1A**
wonder sich fragen *v.* (3) **1A**
wood Holz *n.* (2) **2B**
wool Wolle *f.* (2) **1B**
work Arbeit, -en *f.* (3) **4B**; arbeiten *v.* (1) **2A**;
  funktionieren *v.* (2) **4B**
  at work auf der Arbeit (3) **3B**
  to work on arbeiten an *v.* (2) **3A**
world Welt, -en *f.* (3) **4B**
worried besorgt *adj.* (1) **3B**
write schreiben *v.* (1) **2A**
  to write to schreiben an *v.* (2) **3A**
  to write to one another sich schreiben *v.* (3) **1A**

Y

year Jahr, -e *n.* (2) **3A**
yellow gelb *adj.* (2) **1B**
yes ja **1A**; (**contradicting**) doch *adv.* (1) **2B**
yesterday gestern *adv.* (2) **1B**
yet noch *adv.* (1) **4A**
yogurt Joghurt, -s *m.* (1) **4A**
you du/ihr/Sie *pron.* (1) **1A**
young jung *adj.* (1) **3A**; jugendlich *adj.* (3) **2A**
your euer/Ihr *poss. adj.* (1) **3A**
youth hostel Jugendherberge, -n *f.* (2) **3B**

Index

Understanding the Index references

The numbers following each entry can be understood as follows:

(2A) **51** = (Chapter, Lesson) **page**

So, the entry above would be found in Chapter 2, Lesson A, page 51.

About the Authors

Christine Anton, a native of Germany, is Associate Professor of German and Director of the Language Resource Center at Berry College. She received her B.A. in English and German from the Universität Erlangen and her graduate degrees in Germanic Languages and Literatures from the University of North Carolina at Chapel Hill. She has published two books on German realism and German cultural memory of National Socialism, and a number of articles on 19th and 20th century German and Austrian literature, as well as on second language acquisition. Dr. Anton has received several awards for excellence in teaching and was honored by the American Association of Teachers of German with the Duden Award for her "outstanding efforts and achievement in the teaching of German." Dr. Anton previously taught at the State University of New York and the University of North Carolina, Chapel Hill.

Tobias Barske, a native of Bavaria, is an Associate Professor of German and Applied Linguistics at the University of Wisconsin-Stevens Point. He has a Ph.D. in German Applied Linguistics from the University of Illinois at Urbana-Champaign with emphases on language and social interaction as well as language pedagogy. He has also studied at the Universität Regensburg in Germany. Tobias has over 10 years of experience teaching undergraduate and graduate courses at the university level and has earned numerous awards for excellence in teaching.

Megan McKinstry has an M.A. in Germanics from the University of Washington. She is an Assistant Teaching Professor of German Studies and Co-Coordinator for Elementary German at the University of Missouri, where she received the University's "Purple Chalk" teaching award and an award for "Best Online Course." Ms. McKinstry has been teaching for over fifteen years.

Acknowledgments

On behalf of its authors and editors, Vista Higher Learning expresses its sincere appreciation to the teachers nationwide who reviewed materials from **Mosaik**. Their input and suggestions were vitally helpful in forming and shaping the program in its final, published form. Philippe Radelet from Benjamin Franklin High School, Baton Rouge, Louisiana provided a thorough accuracy check.

We also extend a special thank you to the contributing writers of **Mosaik** whose hard work was central to the publication.

Credits

Every effort has been made to trace the copyright holders of the works published herein. If proper copyright acknowledgment has not been made, please contact the publisher and we will correct the information in future printings.

Photography and Art Credits

All images © Vista Higher Learning unless otherwise noted. All Fotoroman photos provided by Xavier Roy.

Cover: Thorsten Frisch/500px.

Front Matter (SE): xiii: (l) Digital Vision/Getty Images; (r) Andres Rodriguez/Big Stock Photo; **xiv:** Johannes Simon/Getty Images; **xv:** (l) Konstantin Chagin/123RF; (r) Tyler Olson/Shutterstock; **xvi:** PH3/Patrick Hoffmann/WENN/Newscom.

Front Matter (TE): T11: Jean Glueck/Media Bakery; **T29:** Monkey Business Images/Bigstock; **T30:** Simmi Simons/iStockphoto; **T31:** Getty RF.

Chapter 1: Xavier Roy; 3: 36clicks/iStockphoto; **4:** Paula Diez; **8:** Laurence Mouton/Media Bakery; **9:** (l) Michaeljung/iStockphoto; (tr) Sashagala/Shutterstock; (br) Imac/Alamy; **13:** (tl) Anne Loubet; (tm) Igor Tarasov/Fotolia; (tr) Jack Hollingsworth/Corbis; (ml) Gualtiero Boffi/Shutterstock; (mml) Tupungato/Shutterstock; (mmr) Nicole Winchell; (mr) Tabitha Patrick/iStockphoto; (b) Eugenio Marongiu/Shutterstock; **15:** (tl) Lazar Mihai-Bogdan/Shutterstock; (tr) Vanessa Bertozzi; (ml) Nicole Winchell; (mm) Anne Loubet; (mr) Nicole Winchell; (bl) Gudrun Hommel; (bm) Nicole Winchell; (br) Paula Diez; **16:** Auremar/Fotolia; **20:** Richard Foreman/iStockphoto; **28:** Woodapple/Fotolia; **29:** (l) ChristArt/Fotolia; (tr) Arnd Wiegmann/RTR/Newscom; (br) Kyle Monk/Blend Images/Getty Images; **36:** (all) Nicole Winchell; **38:** Sarah2/Shutterstock; **39:** Monkey Business Images/Shutterstock **40:** (t) Shishic/iStockphoto; (m) PeterSVETphoto/Shutterstock; (b) Hollandse Hoogte/Redux; **41:** (tl),Vaclav Volrab/Shutterstock; (tr) Steve Raymer/Corbis; (m) CrazyD/iStockphoto; (b) Horst Galuschka/DPA/Corbis; **44:** Chris Schmidt/iStockphoto; **45:** StockLite/Shutterstock.

Chapter 2: 47: Xavier Roy; **50:** Chris Schmidt/iStockphoto; **54:** Sabine Lubenow/AGE Fotostock; **55:** (l) Heinz-Peter Bader/Reuters/Newscom; (tr) Ingolf Pompe/AGE Fotostock; (br) Laviana/Shutterstock; **56:** (l) Nicole Winchell; (r) Martin Bernetti; **58:** Nicole Winchell; **66:** (left col: t) IDP Manchester Airport Collection/Alamy; (left col: ml) Javier Larrea/AGE Fotostock; (left col: mm) Noam/Fotolia; (left col: mr) Martín Bernetti; (left col: bl) Ana Cabezas Martín; (left col: bm) Tetra Images/Alamy; (left col: br) Jacob Wackerhausen/iStockphoto; (right col) Martinap/Shutterstock; **74:** Roland Syba/Shutterstock; **75:** (tl) Imagebroker.net/SuperStock; (tr) Imago Sportfotodienst/Imago/Moritz Müller/Newscom; (m) Daniel Karmann/Picture-Alliance/DPA/AP Images; (b) Allan Grosskrueger/Shutterstock; **78:** (t) Nicole Winchell; (ml) Polka Dot Images/JupiterImages; (mm) Martín Bernetti; (mr) Robert Michael/Media Bakery; (bl) Losevsky Photo and Video/Shutterstock; (bm) Gudrun Hommel; (br) Nicole Winchell; **83:** Janne Hämäläinen/Shutterstock; **84:** Auremar/Shutterstock; **85:** (tl) Ilyashenko Oleksiy/Shutterstock; (tm) Martín Bernetti; (tr) Carlos Gaudier; (bl) Karens4/Big Stock Photo; (bml) Val Thoermer/Big Stock Photo; (bmr) Ben Blankenburg/Corbis; (br) Danny Warren/iStockphoto; **86:** (l) Neustockimages/iStockphoto; (r) JupiterImages; **87:** (tl) Martín Bernetti; (tm) Monkey Business/Fotolia; (tr) Katie Wade; (bl) Brand X Pictures/Fotosearch; (bml) Ana Cabezas Martín; (bmr) Anne Loubet; (br) Harry Neave/Fotolia; **88:** (tl) Gudrun Hommel; (tr) Noppasinw/Fotolia; (ml) Nicole Winchell; (mr) VVO/Shutterstock; (b) Bettmann/Corbis; **89:** (tl) Riccardo Sala/Alamy; (tr) Lexan/123RF; (m) Akg-images/Newscom; (b) Philip Lange/Shutterstock; **90–91:** Jorg Greuel/Getty Images; **92:** Jack Hollingsworth/Cardinal/Corbis; **93:** (t) Paylessimages/123RF; (b) Nadezda Verbenko/Shutterstock.

Chapter 3: 95: Xavier Roy; **102:** Westend61/Getty Images; **103:** (tl) John Dowland/Getty Images; (tr) Michael Gottschalk/AFP/Getty Images; (b) Wrangler/Shutterstock; **105:** George Olsson/iStockphoto; **106:** (tl) Martín Bernetti; (tm) Ray Levesque; (tr) Martín Bernetti; (bl) Martín Bernetti; (bml) David N. Madden/Shutterstock; (bmr) Martín Bernetti; (br) Prism68/Shutterstock; **112:** (t) Aspen Stock/AGE Fotostock; (ml) Martín Bernetti; (mm) Carlos Gaudier; (mr) Alexander Rochau/Fotolia; (bl) Imag'In Pyrénées/Fotolia; (bm) Pixtal/AGE Fotostock; (br) Raberry/Big Stock Photo; **116:** (top row: tl) José Blanco; (top row: tm) Michael Jung/iStockphoto; (top row: tr) Anne Loubet; (top row: bl) Rasmus Rasmussen/iStockphoto (top row: bml) Ana Cabezas Martín; (top row: bmr) Javier Larrea/AGE Fotostock; (top row: br) Martín Bernetti; (bottom row: l) Vanessa Nel/Shutterstock; (bottom row: r) Photoinjection/Shutterstock; **120:** OneInchPunch/Shutterstock; **121:** (l) Tatiana Lebedeva/Shutterstock; (r) David Fernandez/EPA/Newscom; (b) Sonya Etchison/Shutterstock; **123:** Anne Loubet; **125:** Minerva Studio /Shutterstock; **131:** Nicole Winchell; **132:** (left col: tl) Lichtmeister/Shutterstock; (left col: tr) Gudrun Hommel; (left col: bl) Martín Bernetti; (left col: br) Gudrun Hommel; (right col) Anne Loubet; **134:** (tl) Andre Jenny/Alamy; (tr) ShyMan/iStockphoto; (m) RosaIreneBetancourt 3/Alamy; (b) Frymire Archive/Alamy; **135:** (tl) Aspen Rock/